Living with Computers

FOURTH EDITION

THE DRYDEN PRESS

Harcourt Brace College Publishers
Fort Worth   Philadelphia   San Diego   New York   Orlando   Austin
San Antonio   Toronto   Montreal   London   Sydney   Tokyo

Living with Computers

FOURTH EDITION

Patrick G. McKeown

University of Georgia

Editor in Chief	Robert A. Pawlik
Acquisitions Editor	Richard J. Bonacci
Developmental Editor	Ruth E. Rominger
Project Editor	Sue A. Lister
Production Manager	Jacqui Parker
Book Designer/Cover Illustration	David A. Day
Photo/Permissions Editor	Greg Meadors

Address for Editorial Correspondence
The Dryden Press, 301 Commerce Street, Suite 3700, Fort Worth, TX 76102

Address for Orders
The Dryden Press, 6277 Sea Harbor Drive, Orlando, FL 32887
1-800-782-4479, or 1-800-433-0001 (in Florida)

ISBN: 0-03-096631-0

Library of Congress Catalog Card Number: 92-71698

Cover and block opener art by Gregory Arth Photographers, Hurst, TX

Many of the products designated in this book are trademarked. Their use has been respected through appropriate capitalization and spelling.

Credits appear on pages A-39–A-40, which constitute a continuation of the copyright page.

Printed in the United States of America

3 4 5 6 7 8 9 0 1   048   9 8 7 6 5 4 3 2

THE DRYDEN PRESS SERIES IN INFORMATION SYSTEMS

The HBJ College Outline Series

Living with Computers, Fourth Edition, remains true to the goals of its popular prior editions: to make students understand that they are surrounded by smart machines—that is, by machines that are controlled by computers—and that to be successful today they must be computer literate. Integral to these goals is the concept of the computer as a mind tool to be used to solve problems and to do work. *Living with Computers,* Fourth Edition, establishes the importance of students being able to use a computer and then helps them make the transition from being computer illiterate to being computer users. In the process, students will learn what the computer *can* and *cannot* do and *how* to use computers to solve problems and accomplish tasks. Students need not be experts on the inner workings of the computer to be competent users.

Integrated Approach

A key feature of *Living with Computers* is the integration of the information presented in the text with its array of supplements. The complete package includes the textbook, software, an *Instructor's Manual,* a *Study Guide,* a Pascal supplement, a testbook, a computerized testbank, teaching transparencies, *presentation software,* and a choice of lab manuals to accompany HBJ Bridge software, educational software, and commercial software. All these components are fully integrated. For example, if word processing is being discussed in the text, all elements of the package are integrated toward the presentation of this material. First, screen shots from various word processing packages are shown in the textbook to demonstrate word processing concepts. Second, there are transparencies, transparency masters, and presentation software showing important software screens. Third, there are tutorials in the lab manuals. Fourth, the *Instructor's Manual* suggests ways in which the instructor may use the software to teach the desired concepts and provides answers to the word processing questions and exercises in the textbook. The *Study Guide* summarizes the material for the student and provides further hands-on instruction on the use of word processing. The appendix to the *Instructor's Manual* contains additional assignments incorporating new basic skills pedagogy with the text material. And finally, the testbook provides questions to help the instructor prepare examinations on the material.

The Textbook

Living with Computers, Fourth Edition, and *Living with Computers with BASIC,* Fourth Edition, serve the needs of almost any introductory course in computers.

A flexible presentation allows a chapter sequence that will fit specific needs. This freedom of choice is made possible by the division of the book into blocks of chapters, each block covering an essential facet of computing. Block One, A Brief Introduction to Computers, covers computer literacy, and each chapter in that block also serves as a lead-in to a later, more detailed block of chapters on the same subject. Block One may be used in two ways: First, since it has introductory chapters on hardware, software, computer systems, and the societal implications of computers, it may be used as a self-contained introduction to computers. Second, as soon as any chapter in Block One is covered, the class may immediately cover the corresponding detailed block of material. Once in a detailed block, students can be taught the chapters within that block in almost any order.

Block Two, The Details of Hardware, which includes chapters on the CPU/internal memory, input/output, and secondary storage, may be covered anytime after Chapter 2 has been read. Block Three, Applications Software Packages, contains chapters on operating systems, word processing and graphics packages (including a new section on desktop publishing), spreadsheets and accounting packages, data base management packages, and telecommunications and networks. This block especially reflects the *Living with Computers* objectives in that it provides detailed discussions of nonprogrammer use of applications software to solve problems or accomplish tasks. Block Three may be studied anytime after Chapter 3 has been covered. Block Four, Information Systems, has four chapters that discuss in detail computer-based information systems, the systems analysis and design process, and program development. An overview of the most popular computer languages is also provided here. Block Four may be covered anytime after Chapter 4 has been read. Block Five, Human Aspects of Computer Use, has chapters dealing with computer crime and security problems and with issues of privacy and health. Computer careers and the future of computers are also covered. Block Five may be considered anytime after Chapter 5 has been read.

For instructors using *Living with Computers with BASIC,* the BASIC appendix is divided into three modules—Getting Started with BASIC, Control Structures and Subroutines, and Advanced Topics in BASIC. In addition, color is extensively used to set off programs and to improve the pedagogy. Users who do not wish to teach programming may easily skip this appendix, or avoid it entirely by choosing the alternative version, titled simply *Living with Computers,* Fourth Edition. Users who do wish to teach programming can move directly to this appendix after either Chapter 4, An Introduction to Information Systems, or Chapter 16, Program Development, depending on the depth of programming to be covered. "Try It Yourself" exercises are included in the BASIC sections to allow students to check their understanding more often, and there are programming exercises at the end of each module. Solutions to both types of exercises are in the *Instructor's Manual.*

Besides this flexible approach to the presentation of material, both versions of the Fourth Edition of *Living with Computers* offer the following special features.

Integration of the Personal Computer   Because of ever-increasing availability to students, the personal computer must play a large role in any introductory textbook on computers; to that end, the personal computer and personal computer software are integrated throughout the text. The block of chapters on appli-

A MODULAR INTRODUCTION TO COMPUTERS

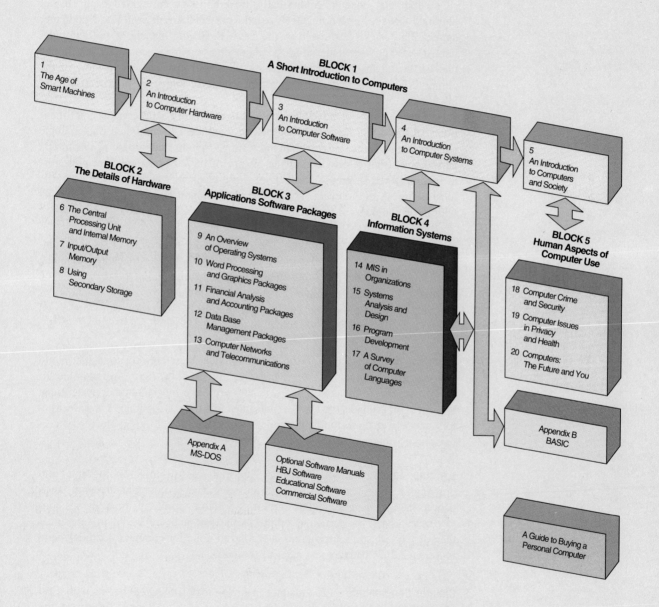

BLOCK 1
A Short Introduction to Computers

1 The Age of Smart Machines

2 An Introduction to Computer Hardware

3 An Introduction to Computer Software

4 An Introduction to Computer Systems

5 An Introduction to Computers and Society

BLOCK 2
The Details of Hardware

6 The Central Processing Unit and Internal Memory

7 Input/Output Memory

8 Using Secondary Storage

BLOCK 3
Applications Software Packages

9 An Overview of Operating Systems

10 Word Processing and Graphics Packages

11 Financial Analysis and Accounting Packages

12 Data Base Management Packages

13 Computer Networks and Telecommunications

BLOCK 4
Information Systems

14 MIS in Organizations

15 Systems Analysis and Design

16 Program Development

17 A Survey of Computer Languages

BLOCK 5
Human Aspects of Computer Use

18 Computer Crime and Security

19 Computer Issues in Privacy and Health

20 Computers: The Future and You

Appendix A
MS-DOS

Optional Software Manuals
HBJ Software
Educational Software
Commercial Software

Appendix B
BASIC

A Guide to Buying a Personal Computer

cations software is especially oriented toward the personal computer, because of the wide availability of applications software for personal computers. Yet care is taken to emphasize the continuing importance of the large computers for all users, and every chapter contains discussions of both the mainframe and personal computer aspects of the topic under consideration.

Boxed Inserts In *Living with Computers,* Fourth Edition, each chapter begins with a carefully selected up-to-date boxed insert that exemplifies the topic to be covered in that chapter. Additionally, boxed inserts throughout each chapter highlight insights into computer use and present current real-world computer applications. Views expressed in the news media by leaders of the computer industry also provide material for boxed inserts or margin quotations. It is hoped that the boxed inserts and margin quotations will give students a view of the computer industry that is by turns informative, amusing, provocative, and inspiring.

One category of boxed inserts—Bits of History—deserves special mention. All too often, historical material on computers is combined into a single chapter that students find less than interesting. To help students enjoy a historical perspective, brief discussions of the history of the chapter topics are presented in special boxed inserts at the ends of those chapters where such discussion is most pertinent and relevant. The *Instructor's Manual* contains an annotated list with page numbers for instructors who wish to cover them as a group.

Inclusion of a PC Buyer's Guide The special Guide to Buying a Personal Computer has been updated and may be read anytime after the first three chapters. The emphasis is on the *logic* behind the decision-making process involved in buying a personal computer, rather than on reviewing specific machines or software that may soon be outdated. The step-by-step procedure presented should help the student buyer make an appropriate, satisfying decision.

Other Essays In addition to the Buyer's Guide, there are three dazzling photo essays—on Manufacturing the Microchip, on Robotics and Artificial Intelligence, and on Computers at Work in the Arts. The binary number system and top-down program design are also presented this time as separate essays. Instructors may cover these topics in this additional depth, yet the length of the corresponding chapters is not expanded unnecessarily.

Exciting, Innovative Art Program Hundreds of full-color photographs and drawings highlight material under discussion. The photographs are both pertinent to the text material and as current as possible. Similarly, the drawings convey extra clarity to particular points in the text and are keyed to references therein. The illustration program is second to none for computer textbooks and is a tremendous pedagogical asset to the book.

Chapter Components Each chapter in *Living with Computers* begins with a set of Study Objectives and ends with a Review of Key Points—useful to the instructor in preparing lectures and helpful to the student in preparing for examinations. A list of Key Terms in each chapter gathers the large number of new words introduced. A Glossary at the end of the book defines each of these words and gives its chapter location. Finally, a set of Review Questions completes each chapter, reflecting the major points covered to help students assess their mastery of the chapter.

New to the Fourth Edition

The Fourth Edition has been updated in both its photo program and content. New photos illustrate the most recent software and hardware developments as well as new uses for computers. Boxes have been updated and new ones have been added throughout to demonstrate some of the many current uses of computers, from the Gulf War to finding missing children. Chapter content has been revised to include current topics such as multimedia, hypertext, virtual reality, touchscreens, and new Windows applications. Types of networks (LANS) are explored in further detail, new CASE software is discussed, the coverage of Object Oriented Programming has been expanded and new information on software piracy has been incorporated. Chapters on privacy and health issues and the future have been rewritten to include current concerns, as well as recent career information and predictions for the future. These and many more new topics make the Fourth Edition timely and relevant to students as they embark upon their computer literate futures.

Ancillary Components for the Instructor

The Fourth Edition of the *Living with Computers* package contains a complete set of ancillary components. This comprehensive instructional program offers everything needed to teach an introductory course on computers or information processing.

Instructor's Manual   For each chapter in the textbook, the *Instructor's Manual* (by Patrick G. McKeown) has a corresponding chapter composed of the following teaching aids: a teaching objective, a set of learning objectives, a chapter outline, an annotated list of the boxed inserts, a chapter review with suggested uses of transparencies and transparency masters, a list of teaching suggestions, an annotated list of suggested readings, answers to the review questions from the end of each chapter in the textbook, and a glossary of the key terms for the chapter. Of particular interest to many instructors will be the suggested readings, which list current, pertinent titles. These readings can be very helpful for preparing lectures or developing class projects. An exciting and substantial new appendix by Harvey Kaye has been added to the *Instructor's Manual* for this edition. Based on the current learning methodology of *Integrated Skills Reinforcement,* this appendix brings an added pedagogical component to the *Living with Computers* package. The extra exercises are specifically designed to reinforce students' basic reading, writing, listening, and speaking skills while improving their retention of the text material. The material has been class tested with remarkable results. Instructions on how to use the material are provided for use by the instructor. For the BASIC appendix in *Living with Computers with BASIC,* the *Instructor's Manual* contains solutions to the "Try It Yourself" and end-of-chapter exercises. The *Instructor's Manual* also includes abundant transparency masters.

Testbook   Thoroughly revised by Lorilee Sadler of Indiana University at Bloomington, the *Testbook* for the Fourth Edition contains over 2300 questions of different types. The *Testbook* covers all of the important concepts and terminology in the textbook and can be used to prepare quizzes or examinations. It is also available in a computerized version, in both IBM and Macintosh formats.

Transparencies   The *Living with Computers* package includes a boxed set of more than 100 full-color *Transparencies* to be used during lectures to demonstrate important concepts. There are also transparency masters in the *Instructor's Manual.*

Presentation Software   New to the Fourth Edition is a *Presentation Software* program by Randy Goldberg of Marist College. This multimedia program, which requires MS Windows 3.x, dramatically incorporates text, photographs, lecture outlines, and graphics to provide a powerful learning environment. It will serve as a valuable tool in the lecture hall and for self-study in the computer lab. Users of Asymetrix Toolbook will find this program a creative basis upon which to build and expand their multimedia presentation.

Video Tapes   An extensive library of video tapes is available free to adopters. Minimum purchase requirements apply. HBJ sales representatives have details about these tapes.

Ancillary Components for the Student

The integrated approach of *Living with Computers* is reflected in all support materials developed for students.

Computer Lab Manuals   Knowledge about computers is useful; however, it is the ability to actually use the computer to solve problems and accomplish tasks that is critical to becoming computer competent. To this end, we have made available to adopters of *Living with Computers* lab manuals for teaching three types of software: full-scale commercial software, educational versions of commercial software, and HBJ's own Bridge software. The tutorials in each manual are organized into skill-building sessions that include keystroke-by-keystroke instructions, *Try-It-Yourself* exercises, and end of session exercises. Lab manuals are available separately, or packaged with the text.

   Application Software Tutorials: A Computer Lab Manual Using WordPerfect 5.1, Lotus 1-2-3, dBASE III PLUS and dBASE IV introduces students to the most popular software packages. These class-tested tutorials will help students build proficiency in using the computer as a problem-solving tool.

   For those instructors who wish to provide inexpensive software for every student, a *Computer Lab Manual* is available packaged with educational versions of WordPerfect 4.2, dBASE III PLUS, and ALITE, an industry-standard spreadsheet.

Hands On: The HBJ Software lab manual introduces students to fundamental software concepts without requiring them to learn a great number of details. The manual and software effectively bridge the gap between intimidation and familiarity. Ideal for computer-aided instruction, this menu-driven program introduces students to the six most common categories of applications software.

HBJ: WRITE allows the user to create, edit, print, and save a document of up to 250 lines. HBJ: GRAPH allows the user to create, view, save, and print bar, pie, scatter, and line charts. HBJ: PLAN can handle up to 40 rows and 26 columns. The command and data entry formats conform with the industry-accepted modes. All arithmetic operations can be included in formulas and the resulting spreadsheet can be saved or printed as needed. HBJ: FILE can manage up to 100 records, each containing up to five fields. The records can be edited, sorted, searched, saved, and printed. HBJ: BUDGET enables the user to manage personal finances by setting up a budget, entering transactions, and reconciling checking accounts. HBJ: TALK is a unique program that simulates a telecommunications software package.

When packaged with the textbook, *Hands On: The HBJ Software* lab manual is provided to students for no additional charge. HBJ Bridge Software is provided free of charge as a master disk for duplication, or for a nominal charge packaged with the lab manual.

Programming   For instructors who wish to teach BASIC, programming tutorials are available in *Living with Computers with BASIC*. A Pascal supplement is available as well.

Written by Margaret Anderson of the University of Georgia, *Structured Programming Using Turbo Pascal*, Second Edition, presents a short course in the use of the ever popular Turbo Pascal language. It parallels the BASIC appendix in the Fourth Edition of *Living with Computers* in terms of material covered. In addition, wherever possible, the Pascal supplement uses the same examples and exercises as are used in the BASIC appendices.

Study Guide   Written by Robert D. Brown of the University of Georgia, the Fourth Edition of the *Study Guide* is organized to reflect the integrated approach of *Living with Computers*. Each chapter contains a thorough review, which summarizes key concepts and terms, and multiple-choice, true-false, matching, and short answer questions, complete with answers, which serve as an effective self-test.

The *Study Guide* also offers additional hints on BASIC programming and the use of productivity software, including several examples that clearly demonstrate an actual application of the software package.

Acknowledgments

Anyone familiar with the writing and production of a package such as this knows that it is very much the result of a team effort. For the Fourth Edition of *Living with Computers,* this team included many people who have either helped with writing the book or have worked on editorial and production aspects of its publication.

During the writing of all four editions of the textbook, I received help on numerous technical aspects of the computer from Andrew Seila of the College of Business Administration at the University of Georgia. Robert Sterns of the University of Georgia computer center also offered a wealth of historical knowledge. Robert A. Leitch of the University of South Carolina and Dennis Calbos of the Administrative Data Processing Department at the University of Georgia both greatly aided in the preparation of the systems chapters, while Robert Brown and Jennifer Teel worked very hard making sure the tutorials matched the software. I would also like to thank Charles R. McCain and Don Dershem of Mountain View College of the Dallas Community College District for their help. Charles provided many useful articles, and I benefitted greatly from my discussions with Don on the implementation of top-down design in BASIC. I am grateful for the help of each of these people. Other truly appreciated help came from Doug Hartley, University of Georgia, Athens; Colette Pirie, University of Georgia, Athens; and Cliff Ragsdale, Virginia Polytechnic Institute and State University.

As the text was being written, it was reviewed by a large number of people, including Coleman Barnett, Tarrant County Junior College Northeast; George A. Bohlen, University of Dayton; Kenlon H. Burcham, Wallace State College; Richard K. Cleek, University of Wisconsin Center—Washington County; Donald Dershem, Mountain View College of the Dallas Community College District; Richard A. Ernest, Sullivan Junior College; Ronald Flaxmeyer, University of Cincinnati; Y. H. Freedman, Mount Royal College; Robert S. Fritz, American River College; Peter Irwin, Richland College of the Dallas Community College District; Jan Karasz, Cameron University; Richard Lee Kerns, East Carolina University; Reinhard L. Knieriemen, Jr., Orange County Community College; Diane H. Krebs, Valparaiso University; Gary W. Martin, Solano Community College; Charles R. McCain, Mountain View College of the Dallas Community College District; Francisca O. Norales, Virginia State University; Debra A. Osz, Dret School; Guy Pollack, Mountain View College of the Dallas Community College District; Ajay Popat, University of Alabama, Birmingham; Nancy Schmitt-MacDonald, Barnes Business College; Al Schroeder, Richland College of the Dallas Community College District; Evan M. Thompson, California State University, Stanislaus; John Urquhart, Norfolk State University; and Louis Voit, McMurray College. I thank all of them for their careful reading of the manuscript and their thought-provoking comments. The final product reflects many of their ideas. Finally, I appreciate the work of Ashley McKeown and Ginger Brown on the *Instructor's Manual.*

During the editing and production of the book, a large number of people at Dryden/HBJ were involved and I want to name them all. I wish to express my thanks to Ruth Rominger and Sue Lister for coordinating and editing the project. Greg Meadors did an outstanding job of photo research, David A. Day executed a crisp new design and supervised the art program, Sheila Shutter handled our permissions work, and Jacqui Parker supervised the production process. As always, thanks to my editor, Richard Bonacci, for his ongoing efforts in publishing my texts.

Finally, no acknowledgments would be complete without mention of my wife, Carolyn McKeown, who has constantly supported me in the project, first by helping organize the work and then by reading material and offering suggestions. She was also the author of the innovative section on the health aspects of computer use. Without her support and that of my children, Ashley and Chris, I would not have been able to complete such a project.

Patrick G. McKeown

IN APPRECIATION

Key to the development of the materials for this Fourth Edition are those who, through all four editions, have class-tested, reviewed, responded to surveys, and assisted in innumerable ways. I owe them a great debt.

Scott Ahrens
Solano Community College

Margaret S. Anderson
University of Georgia, Athens

Carol Asplund
College of Lake County

Joe Dane Autry
Collin County Community College

Tim Baird
Harding University

Beth Barks
Southern Union State Junior College

Coleman Barnett
Tarrant County Junior College Northeast

Edward A. Berlin
Queensborough Community College

George A. Bohlen
University of Dayton

W. H. Bortels
University of Connecticut, Groton

Christopher R. Brown
Bemidji State University

Robert D. Brown
University of Georgia

Eileen Brownell
Junior College of Albany

Kenlon H. Burcham
Wallace State College

Dennis P. Calbos
University of Georgia

Nancy Lee Cameron
Corpus Christi State University

Richard Carney
Camden County Junior College

Walter Chesbro
Santa Rosa Junior College

Richard K. Cleek
University of Wisconsin Center—Washington County

William R. Cornette
Southwest Missouri State University

David W. Dalton
Florida State University

Christopher L. Danko
Solano Community College

Dean DeFino
Salisbury State College

Donald L. Dershem
Mountain View College of the Dallas Community College District

Branston A. DiBrell
Metropolitan State College

William C. Driskall
Southern Union State Junior College

Nora Duseault
Herkimer County Community College

Grant Eastman
Tulsa Junior College

Michael Ellerson
University of Georgia, Athens

Richard A. Ernest
Sullivan Junior College

Ronald Flaxmeyer
University of Cincinnati

Patricia Fouts
Virginia Polytechnic Institute

Y. H. Freedman
Mount Royal College

Theodore W. Frick
Indiana University

Robert S. Fritz
American River College

Jack Goebel
Montana College of Mineral Science and Technology

Thomas J. Hammell
University of Connecticut— East Lyme

Donald L. Henderson
Mankato State University

Russell Hollingsworth
Tarrant County Junior College Northeast

Peter L. Irwin
Richland College of the Dallas Community College District

Bill Jackson
Metropolitan State College

Jan Karasz
Cameron University

Richard Lee Kerns
East Carolina University

Bob King
Camden County Junior College

Reinhard L. Knieriemen, Jr.
Orange County Community College

M. C. Kolatis
County College of Morris

Diane H. Krebs
Valparaiso University

Catherine Leach
Henderson State University

Robert A. Leitch
University of South Carolina, Columbia

Stan Marder
Mesa College

Gary W. Martin
Solano Community College

Charles R. McCain
Mountain View College of the Dallas Community College District

James McCain
State University of New York at Brockport

Francisca O. Norales
Virginia State University

Edward J. O'Connell, Jr.
Syracuse University

Pam Ogaard
Bismarck State College

Debra A. Osz
Dret School

Sheilah Pantaleo
Allegany Community College

Jeanette Parker
Southern Union State Junior College

Michael A. Perl
Brookhaven College

Gerhard Plenert
California State University, Chico

Guy Pollack
Mountain View College of the Dallas Community College District

Ajay Popat
University of Alabama, Birmingham

Judy Preston
Brookhaven College

Bruce Purcell
Santa Rosa Junior College

Cliff Ragsdale
Virginia Polytechnic Institute and State University

David Ribeiro
Solano Community College

Tom Scharnberg
Tarrant County Junior College Northeast

Nancy Schmitt-MacDonald
Barnes Business College

Al Schroeder
Richland College of the Dallas Community College District

Gregory L. Scott
El Camino College

Mr. L. W. Simmerson
Solano Community College

Faye Simmons
State University of New York

Steve Spencer
University of Georgia

Uthai Tanlamai
California State University, Fresno

Richard Terry
Brigham Young University

Glenn N. Thomas
Kent State University

Evan M. Thompson
California State University, Stanislaus

Bill Todd
Williamsburg Technical College

John Urquhart
Norfolk State University

Louis Voit
McMurray College

Douglas R. Vogel
University of Arizona

Karen Weil-Yates
Hagerstown Junior College

To the memory of my father,
Maxwell B. McKeown, 1912–1984

CONTENTS

BLOCK THREE—Applications Software Packages   250

BLOCK FIVE—Human Aspects of Computer Use 574

APPENDIXES

Living with Computers

FOURTH EDITION

BLOCK ONE

A Brief Introduction to Computers

Block One of this textbook provides a brief overview of the use of computers in the world today. In so doing, it introduces the computer and some computer terminology. Block One also serves as a preview of the remaining sections of the book. After Chapter 1, each chapter in this block serves as a lead-in to a block of chapters that appears later in the book. Therefore, after reading this first block of chapters, you may read any other block without reading the intervening ones.

The remaining four blocks in this textbook elaborate on material covered in each of the next four chapters. Block Two, The Details of Hardware, continues the discussion of hardware begun in Chapter 2, while Block Three, Applications Software, continues the discussion of software begun in Chapter 3. Block Four, Information Systems, explores in more detail the initial discussion of information systems in Chapter 4. Block Five, Human Aspects of Computer Use, elaborates on the survey of that topic given in Chapter 5.

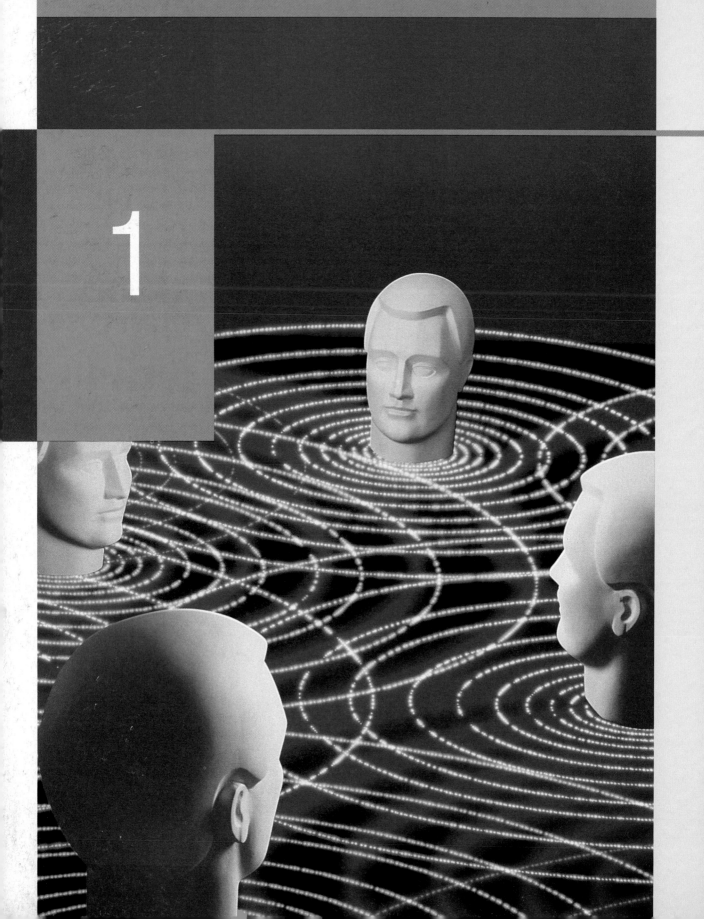

1

The Age of Smart Machines

This chapter provides an overview of the role of computers as smart machines and discusses the concept of the computer as a mind tool—that is, a device that can ease our mental labors while also enabling us to extend our creative abilities. The first section of the chapter describes the prevalence of smart machines in society today, discusses the importance of information to organizations, and relates smart machines to computers. Examples of tools that are being replaced by the computer are listed. Also, the advantages and limitations of the computer are discussed. The second section provides an overview of computer terminology and considers the importance of computer literacy in the world today. The third section discusses the types and sizes of computers. Some of the more important applications of the present-day computer are reviewed in the final section of the chapter. Reading this chapter should give you a good understanding of what a computer can and cannot do, as well as a sound beginning vocabulary of computer terminology.

STUDY OBJECTIVES

After reading this chapter, you should be able to

- point out various smart machines in the world around us and understand the importance of information;
- understand the concept of the computer as a mind tool;
- list various tools being replaced by the computer;
- discuss the difference between data and information;
- differentiate between computer hardware and software and discuss the importance of programming;
- understand the importance of computer literacy in the world today;
- identify the different types and sizes of computers;
- list applications of the computer in the world around us;
- understand the many uses of multimedia;
- recognize the many ways in which the computer affects our lives.

WILL YOU DRIVE A "SMART" CAR?

It is 1996, and you have just arrived at Hartsfield Airport in Atlanta for the Olympic Games. You hop into your "smart" rental car and punch your destination—the swimming venue—into a touchscreen mounted on the dashboard. With this information, an onboard computer, guided by a satellite and sensors in the road, uses a voice synthesizer to guide you to the swimming pool while bypassing the major expressway traffic jams that Atlanta is famous for. The system instructs you in your native language to "take a right at the next intersection. Now, exit at Martin Luther King Jr. Drive."

Does this idea sound like something out of *Star Trek?* Although it might, 25 automobiles with such systems have already actually been tested in Los Angeles. Orlando, currently, is testing 100 cars, and Chicago plans to test 4,000 cars in 1994. In the Los Angeles test, drivers received constantly updated information about accidents, congestion, and construction projects, and the computer suggested alternative routes. In the Orlando test, information on lodging, restaurants, and entertainment will also be available to drivers. In the Chicago test, the test vehicles will send information on traffic conditions back to the traffic center as well as receive it.

In all of these tests, so-called Intelligent Vehicle Highway Systems (IVHS) are being considered. In IVHS, traffic data are relayed from highway sensors by satellite to a central computer and then to in-car computers that display electronic maps. The computer navigates the driver through the least congested route using voice synthesizers or flashing arrows. Such a system is technically possible now, but whether it will be used for the 1996 Olympic Games will depend on the availability of federal funding.

Source: David Beasley, "Automatic Transmission," *The Atlanta Constitution,* May 20, 1991, pp. D1, D3.

"Smart" cars provide directions to drivers.

The "smart" car just discussed is not a vision of the future—it is in large-scale testing at several locations around the country. What differentiates this car from current vehicles is its widespread use of computers to handle guidance and communication tasks. It is an example of a **smart machine,** computer-based machines that can make decisions and provide information. These smart machines have become commonplace in the last few years, and, in fact, it is almost impossible to go through a single day without some contact with one. Examples of smart machines you may use include the following:

- programmable microwave ovens
- programmable videocassette recorders and compact disk players
- digital wristwatches
- checkout scanners
- touchtone, programmable telephones
- fax machines
- automatic teller machines (ATMs)
- personal computers and computer terminals in offices

Automatic teller machines provide both information and cash—any time of the day, any day of the week.

If you look around, you will, no doubt, find many other smart machines in addition to those listed. For example, "smart" weapons were credited with shortening the Gulf War of 1991 and reducing loss of life on both sides of the conflict. Undoubtedly, many more will appear in the near future.

Smart machines have become so widely used at work that business and industry would quickly come to a halt if smart machines suddenly quit working. The scope of **information technology,** as the use of smart machines is often referred to, grows daily as new machines are developed and placed on the market. For example, it is estimated that over 66 percent of all homes in the United States have a VCR and that over 350,000 ATMs are in use. In addition, in 1989, 70 percent of U.S. white-collar workers used a computer, whereas only 25 percent used them in 1983. It is safe to say that, during the last ten years, smart machines have dramatically changed the way we live and that we are, indeed, living in the age of smart machines!

What differentiates smart machines from their predecessors is that these machines not only carry out operations to reduce human labor, but also provide information about those operations. For example, while the obvious use of a checkout scanner is to speed the entry of prices, thereby allowing the customer to spend less time waiting in line, it also provides the store manager with information on sales and inventory levels. Similarly, an ATM can confirm our checking and savings balances, supply us with cash (if the balance is sufficient), accept deposits, and update our accounts for a bank hundreds of miles away.

The capability of smart machines to provide information as well as carry out a user's instructions has made our society increasingly dependent on them. John Naisbitt, a noted authority on the progress of Western society, predicted this outcome in *Megatrends* (1983), *Re-Inventing the Corporation* (1985, with Patricia Aburdene), and *Megatrends 2000* (1990). In these books, Naisbitt discusses the evolution of the United States from an agricultural society 100 years ago to an industrial society in the first two-thirds of this century to what he calls an **information society,** built on the transfer of information. He notes that in

> It is not too much to say that we are moving from an economy that rested on the motor car to an economy that rests on the computer.
>
> *John Naisbitt and Patricia Aburdene*
>
> *Re-Inventing the Corporation* (New York: Warner, 1985), p. 19.

1950, information professionals—teachers, programmers, analysts, clerks, bureaucrats, and accountants—accounted for only 17 percent of the American work force. In 1983, this number had risen to over 65 percent. A second study showed that between 1970 and 1990, *90 percent of all new jobs* were in the information and knowledge areas and predicted that by the year 2000, over 75 percent of all jobs will be in this area.[1]

In 1985, the information industry made up 3.3 percent of the gross national product (GNP). It has been predicted that the information industry will be the largest industry in the world by 1995, making up 6 percent of the GNP. Furthermore, the data processing and communications industry, which was a $300 million industry as recently as 1987, is predicted to account for $1 *trillion* during the 1990s.[2] Figure 1-1 shows how our economy will become more information based over the next few years.

As further evidence of the importance of the smart machine in the business world today, consider that presently all organizations, both public and private,

---

[1] Richard Crawford, *In the Era of Human Capital* (New York: Harper Business, 1991), p. 26.
[2] William R. Synnott, *The Information Weapon* (New York: John Wiley, 1987), p. 3.

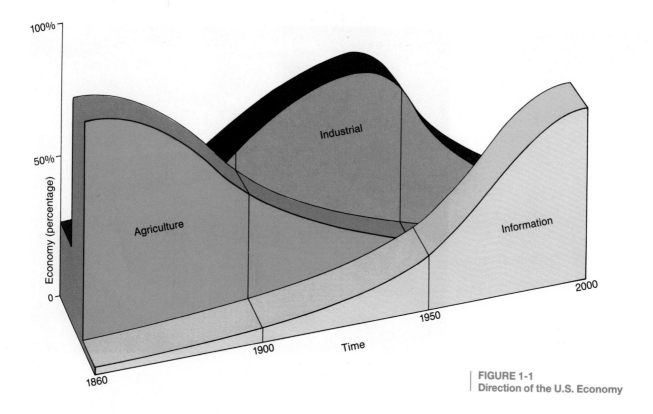

FIGURE 1-1
Direction of the U.S. Economy

profit and nonprofit, have some form of **information system (IS)** that enables an efficient management of information. An IS combines smart machines and human users to transform raw facts into a form that can be used to make decisions. In many situations, the smart machines are tied together to form a **network** that enables them to share information, leading to increased productivity. The most successful organizations are those that have learned to treat information as their most important asset, which they can use to gain a competitive advantage in the marketplace.

Computers and the Smart Machine

The feature common to all smart machines is their use of computer technology to supply "intelligence." A **computer** is *a machine that stores and manipulates symbols using instructions from a human user.* All computers are built around tiny pieces of silicon ($\frac{1}{16}$ to $\frac{1}{2}$ inch square) called **computer chips,** which utilize miniaturized electronic circuitry to carry out instructions from the user. When one of these computer chips is installed in a machine, such as a VCR or a fax machine, and is programmed to direct the machine's operations, the chip is referred to as a **microprocessor.**

We often encounter computers in the form of a terminal linked to a large centralized computer, or sitting on our desk in the form of a personal computer. Regardless of the form in which we find it, remember that the computer is a special type of tool—a very powerful **mind tool** that extends but does not replace the human mind. We have long used tools to ease our physical labors. In fact, the aim of the Industrial Revolution was to enhance production by using

A personal computer brings the power of computing to the desktop.

tools and machines to increase human physical productivity. Now the computer can do the same thing for our mental labors.

Some Tools Being Replaced by the Computer

Like the telephone, the computer has become indispensable to many professionals.

John Scully, president and CEO, Apple Computer

"Professionals and Their Computers," *Personal Computing,* October 1987, p. 228.

As examples of easing mental effort by using the computer, consider five tools commonly used in offices everywhere—the calculator, the typewriter, the file cabinet, the drafting table, and the telephone. All these tools are to some extent being replaced or enhanced by the computer; in the process, the human effort is reduced through the power of the computer.

Like a calculator, the computer can perform calculations. But the real power of the computer is its capability to allow the user to determine the effect of changes in the data or of changes in the assumptions underlying the calculations. Similarly, computers can be used to create and revise documents with far greater ease than the standard typewriter. Computers can actually be used to develop professional-typeset-quality documents ready for publication. While it will be a long time before all storage of information on paper is ended, computers can now store information much more efficiently than filing cabinets, and computers allow the user to retrieve needed items of information without searching through many file folders. Drafting tables are also rapidly being replaced by computers that enable the user to either draw freehand or combine figures from a figure library to create a complete drawing. Finally, fax machines have now made it possible not just to talk over the telephone but also to send text and drawings over telephone lines to distant points.

Advantages and Limitations of the Computer

Two features of the computer strongly contribute to the rapid replacement of many "paper and pencil" tools. These are *speed* and *accuracy.* A computer is limited only by the speed at which electrical signals can be transmitted. This enables even personal computers to execute millions of operations per second in processing raw facts called **data** into a usable form known as **information.** The computer's speed enables it to carry out a desired operation in a fraction of the time needed to do the same thing manually. In terms of accuracy, a computer will do *exactly* what it is instructed to do without error. This enables the computer to repeat the same operations as many times as necessary, without error.

Of course, the computer does have limitations. A computer does not have reasoning capabilities. Rather, it must use instructions from the user to process the data the user inputs. If either the instructions or the data entered are incorrect, the results from the computer will also be incorrect. The fact that a computer can generate erroneous results has led to use of the term **computer error.** However, this term is itself in error since the problem is not with the computer, but with the instructions or data given it by the human user. An acronym even exists to describe this process: GIGO—garbage in, garbage out! So when you receive an incorrect bill or are charged an incorrect amount by a computerized checkout system, remember it's not the computer that has caused the problem; it's the data or instructions input by a human user!

Since computers play such a large role in our lives, it is very useful to have at least a basic understanding of how they work and what they can and cannot do. In this section, we will look at what a computer can do, the parts of the computer, and some ideas on computer use.

As mentioned earlier, a computer processes data into information. Recall that data are the raw facts that are entered into the computer for processing and that information is data that have been processed into a form that is useful to the user. Data can be in the form of numbers, letters of the alphabet, or any other type of symbols. On the other hand, information is the arrangement of data into tables, graphs, and reports. Because of this terminology, the operations that the computer performs are sometimes referred to as **data processing.** Figure 1-2 shows the process of converting data into information.

Parts of the Computer

Processing data into information requires that the two primary elements of the computer—hardware and software—work together to accomplish the desired task. The computer's machinery is referred to as **hardware** and is made up of

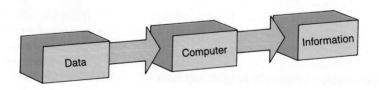

FIGURE 1-2
Conversion of Data into Information

FINDING MISSING KIDS WITH COMPUTERS

Losing a child is a great fear of every parent. If a child is kidnapped, time may be as great an enemy as the kidnapper, because a child's features change dramatically in only a few months or years. To help the parents and authorities searching for over 7,000 missing children in the United States, the National Center for Missing and Exploited Children (NCMEC) has developed a computer system that "ages" children electronically. This has helped authorities find children who have been missing for several years.

A computer software package called PhotoSketch uses all types of information about a missing child to create a current image of the child. This process uses videotapes, photos, information on identifying marks, and even photographs of parents and siblings to determine genetic effects on physical development. The software package integrates all information about the child into a composite photo that is then modified by simulating the basic structural changes that take place during aging.

Once the "aged" photo has been created, NCMEC disseminates it in various ways, including publishing flyers that reach 55 million households per week. This campaign generates as many as 4,000 to 5,000 leads for each child portrayed on a flyer. Many of these leads come in through the NCMEC hotline: 1-800-THE-LOST.

Sources: "National Center for Missing Children," *Government Technology*, February 1991, p. 17; and Patricia Keefe, "High Tech Helps Speed Location of Missing Children," *Computerworld*, October 21, 1991, p. 63.

NATIONAL CENTER FOR MISSING & EXPLOITED CHILDREN

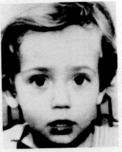

CHILD AT AGE 2 WHEN ABDUCTED

AGE-PROGRESSION AS 7 YR. OLD

RECOVERY PHOTOGRAPHS AGE 7

An "aging" computer program simulated the aging process in the photo of this child.

electronic devices and circuits. The human-provided logic and instructions to the computer are termed **software.** A common saying that helps to differentiate hardware from software is "If you bump into it, then it's hardware!"

A great deal has been written and said about the marvels of computer hardware, and hardly a week goes by without the introduction of a smaller, faster, or less expensive computer. However, hardware can do *nothing* without software to supply instructions. The software is made up of one or more lists of instructions called **programs.** The process by which programs are developed is called **programming.** Many smart machines in everyday use have instructions already built into a computer chip so that all the user needs to do is press a button. Computer instructions in this form, known as **firmware,** blur the line between hardware and software.

Over the past 20 years, computers have become faster and smaller while also becoming much less expensive. Had the automobile industry undergone the same transformation, a Rolls Royce might cost $2.50 and get over 100 miles to the gallon! A computer that cost over $4,000 a few years ago can now be purchased for less than $1,000. However, while hardware costs have been dropping, software costs have not changed very much. The reason for this dichotomy is that hardware can be mass produced on a factory assembly line, but each piece of software must be created anew by individuals or groups of programmers. Developing software is a creative task similar to writing a novel or painting a portrait; as a result, the cost of software remains high compared to the cost of hardware.

Programming often entails writing sophisticated programs required to handle very complex processing.

Computer Literacy—A Requirement for Living

Computer literacy is a growing social concern. But, what is computer literacy? It has been defined variously as the ability to write programs to solve problems, a detailed understanding of the machinery of the computer, or a knowledge of the many uses of the computer. However, we will define **computer literacy** as *an understanding of what a computer can and cannot do and an ability to make the computer do what the user desires.* This definition emphasizes using the computer as a mind tool to solve problems and accomplish tasks more efficiently.

The importance of computer literacy was once hotly debated, but now most people agree that all students should be exposed to computers at some time during their academic careers. Today, students must be prepared to function in a society in which computers and other smart machines are the rule rather than the exception. This view was well stated by Dr. John Kemeny, past president of Dartmouth College and co-inventor of BASIC (Beginner's All-purpose Symbolic Instruction Code), the most popular computer language for personal computers. According to Kemeny, "In the next three decades, intelligence will be built into most manufactured objects and those who lack even minimal computer literacy will have difficulty functioning in everyday life."[3]

It is important to remember that *it is not necessary to learn programming to be a computer user.* In the past this was not true; every user also had to be

---

[3]Richard A. Shaffler, "Courses in Computer Literacy Beginning to Draw Bad Marks," *The Wall Street Journal,* September 16, 1983, p. 37.

> **A computer illiterate can be two things: A person who doesn't know how to utilize a computer or software tool to perform his job; or a person who dramatically underutilizes the features of a software package or computer.**
>
> *Elliot Masie, president of the Association of Computer Training & Support (ACTS)*
>
> Quoted in "Defeating Computer Illiteracy," *Computerworld,* December 3, 1990, p. 116.

Engineers often become proficient end users as they take advantage of computer capabilities to help solve problems they encounter in their work.

a proficient programmer. Now an enormous amount of software available in retail outlets performs many standard tasks. **Computer packages** that contain commercial software include an explanation of the software as well as instructions for its use. Computer packages make the computer available to everyone, not just to those people who have learned to program.

Note that our definition of computer literacy does not assume either an understanding of the electronics that make up the computer's machinery or the ability to write programs. The definition *does* assume an understanding of a computer's uses and limitations and a knowledge of the software packages needed to accomplish a desired end. However, if the purpose for which you wish to use the computer requires a greater understanding of hardware or programming, then you must increase your knowledge to meet your needs.

Beyond computer literacy, two additional levels of knowledge have been defined. **Computer competence** means that an individual can use the computer to solve sophisticated problems in his or her field of expertise. The computer-competent person is comfortable using the computer and looks for better ways to use it for problem solving. Another term often used to describe the person who reaches this level of computer use is *end user.* **End users** are very involved in using existing software to its fullest extent to do their jobs more effectively. However, end users usually are not information-systems professionals or computer scientists, and they are usually not interested in developing applications for others to use. These tasks are normally handled by individuals who have achieved **computer mastery.** This term refers to information-systems professionals or computer scientists whose jobs center around computing and who have acquired the knowledge necessary for success in this field.

TYPES OF COMPUTERS

Now that we know what a computer is, we can consider the types of computers used in information systems today. In terms of size (the most common means of classification), computers fit broadly into three types—mainframes, minicomputers, and microcomputers, which are also called personal computers.

A **mainframe** is a very large, expensive computer (usually selling for well over $1 million) that requires a special support staff and a special physical environment (for example, air conditioning). Mainframes are usually housed in a computer center and are generally used in large business, government, or academic institutions where they support multiple users (usually more than 100 at one time) and can handle multiple processing tasks concurrently. This means that a mainframe can, for example, do a statistical analysis for one user, print a report for a second user, and process student grades concurrently.

Users access a mainframe on **computer terminals** that interface with the computer. These terminals are usually composed of a keyboard for entering data and instructions and a display screen for viewing the work and any resulting output. They usually do not have their own computing capabilities.

A subset of mainframes is **supercomputers,** or "monsters," which are the biggest and fastest computers in use today. These very large computers are used almost exclusively for research projects that require extremely high-speed processing and large storage capacities.

At the other extreme in terms of size are **personal computers (PCs),** which are small, one-user computers. These computers are relatively inexpensive

For us, a mainframe is the only platform we would trust to run nearly all our mission-critical applications.

Richard Lewis, Director of Information Systems at All-Phase Electric Supply Co.

Quoted in "Ten Reasons to Stand By Your Mainframe," *Computerworld,* November 18, 1991, p. 75.

(Left) Supercomputers like the one shown here are the fastest computers in use today. (Right) A mainframe computer can support multiple users and multiple computing activities.

A personal computer like this Macintosh can enhance the life of a handicapped person in many ways.

to purchase ($500 to $5,000) and do not require a special environment or special user knowledge. They fit on a desktop and are sometimes referred to as **desktop computers.** Such personal computers are commonly used by a single user to handle one task at a time. PCs are slower than mainframes and cannot store as much data.

Somewhere between a mainframe and a personal computer is the **minicomputer** (also called a *midrange* or *midsize* computer), which is used by organizations that need more processing power than is available with personal computers, but less than a mainframe offers. A minicomputer can support multiple users and may have some support staff, but not on the same level as a mainframe. Like mainframes, minicomputers can handle multiple users and multiple tasks concurrently through the use of terminals.

A special type of terminal is a **workstation,** a high-performance, single-user device that has characteristics of both a stand-alone PC and a terminal. Like PCs, workstations have built-in computing power. However, they are also connected to a minicomputer or a mainframe and to other workstations to take advantage of the increased computing power of the larger machine and to share information. Workstations also differ from PCs in that they can carry out multiple tasks concurrently. The NeXT computer, developed by Steven Jobs—cofounder of Apple Computers—is considered by many to be a workstation because of the capabilities it offers beyond those available on a PC. Hewlett-Packard and Sun are also well known for their workstations.

Table 1-1 compares the differences between the various computers just discussed. This table lists computers from the smallest—the PC—to the largest—the supercomputer—and compares cost, number of simultaneous users, and the number of tasks that can be carried out concurrently. It also arranges the computers in order of speed from slowest to fastest. The PC is shown to be able to accomplish one or multiple tasks because different sizes and types of PC have different capabilities.

Like a mainframe, a midrange computer can serve multiple users, but it does not usually require the extensive support that the larger computer does.

Currently the dividing line between personal computers and workstations is hazy as personal computers become more powerful and can support multiple tasks. For simplicity's sake, in the remainder of this text we will include workstations with personal computers since both computers have single-user capability. Similarly, we will include minicomputers and supercomputers whenever we refer to mainframes since each can accommodate multiple users.

From Monsters to Micros

Of the various categories of computers discussed above, the personal computer has received by far the most publicity over the last decade. This is due in part to the phenomenal growth in the use of personal computers since their introduction in 1975. This growth since 1985 is shown in Figure 1-3.

Given the prevalence of PCs in all phases of our lives—business and industry, home and hobby, science and technology, and education—it is surprising that the original IBM PC was introduced as recently as 1981 and the Apple Macintosh in 1984. In the few years since the introduction of these

> **The first decade of [personal] computers has rendered 100 million individuals into more productive analysts and writers.**
>
> *Andrew Grove, CEO of Intel Corporation*
>
> Quoted in "Intel Chief Focuses on Future of the PC," *PC Week,* November 11, 1991, p. S/22.

TABLE 1-1
Comparison of Different Sizes of Computers

Computer	Size	Cost	Number of Users	Number of Tasks
PC	Small	<$5,000	One	One/multiple
Minicomputer	Medium	<$100,000	Multiple	Multiple
Mainframe	Large	>$1,000,000	Multiple	Multiple
Supercomputer	Large	>$2,000,000	Multiple	Multiple

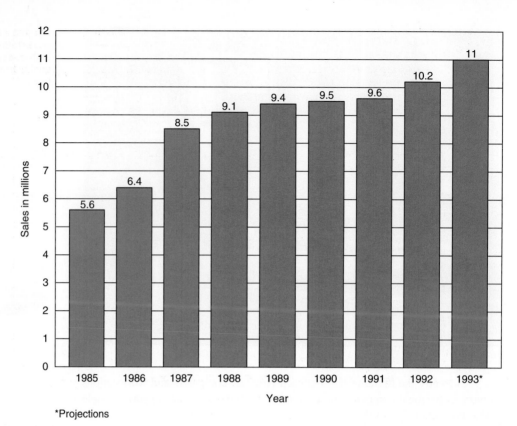

FIGURE 1-3
Personal Computer Sales

Source: International Data Corp.

ground-breaking machines, the PC has become commonplace in all facets of our lives. It is estimated that in 1991 about 25 million PCs were being used in U.S. businesses, 17 million homes had a PC, and 46 percent of U.S. children use a PC in school. Figure 1-4 shows 1990 sales of PCs in various fields.

The growth of personal computer use is mainly due to the large amount of software developed that allows the use of this mind tool without the need to learn programming. While larger computers also have software available, it is not always as accessible or easy to use. A second factor in the phenomenal growth of the personal computer is its instant access. To gain access to the larger computers, a user may have to wait until a terminal is available. An account number is usually required as well.

It is important to remember that while the personal computer is often publicized in the national media, it will never replace larger computers. In fact, the growth in use of personal computers has been matched by an equivalent growth in the use of mainframe computers—for several reasons. First is the demand by PC users for information stored on mainframes, since the larger machines offer storage capacity beyond that possible on personal computers. Second is the incredible computing speed available only on mainframes and supercomputers. One study showed that a supercomputer performed in 90 seconds the same operation that one of the faster personal computers required *20 hours* to perform.

As we shall see in later chapters, the difference between the two sizes of computers is really just that—a difference in size. The principles of operation are the same, and once you have become familiar with one, it is very easy to

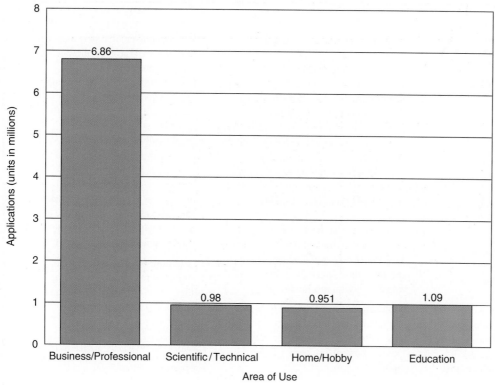

FIGURE 1-4
1990 Sales of PCs

Source: International Data Corp.

learn to use the other. In either case, the computer is a tool of the mind that can make our information processing labors much easier.

Classifying Computers by Logic and Purpose

In addition to classifying computers by size, we may also classify them by their type of logic and their purpose. In terms of type of logic used, a computer can be either a digital computer or an analog computer. A **digital computer** uses numbers and is therefore a *counting machine*. An **analog computer** uses physical relationships and is a *measuring machine*. Analog computers are often used to work with physical measurements. Today almost all computers are digital, so we will consider only this type of computer.

In terms of its purpose, a computer may be classified as a special-purpose computer or a general-purpose computer. A **special-purpose computer** is designed for only one purpose. The microprocessor chips installed in many of the smart machines discussed earlier are actually special-purpose computers that can carry out only a designated purpose. Similarly, the computers used for arcade games or for guiding the National Aeronautics and Space Administration's (NASA's) space shuttles are also examples of special-purpose computers that cannot be used for other purposes. A **general-purpose computer,** on the other hand, can be used for many applications. For example, the same general-purpose computer may be used to play games, to handle payroll computations, to use graphics to design buildings, or to solve complex mathematical problems. In this

> **I see PCs as the natural evolution for applications that never belonged on a huge machine that needs its own room to cool.**
>
> *James Cannavino, president,*
> *Entry Systems Division, IBM*
>
> Quoted in "IBM's Cannavino: Sign of the Times," *PC Week,* February 27, 1989, p. 13.

IT'S GOING TO BE A DIGITAL WORLD

Before the computer chip became widely available, we lived in an analog world. Our watches, telephones, televisions, music systems, and automobile speedometers were all analog machines that monitored conditions such as movement, temperature, and sound and converted them into a continuous analogous representation. However today, many of these same machines are being converted into digital machines that break the relationships into discrete units.

While analog machines can capture the subtle nature of the real world, they cannot make repeated copies of their output without marked signs of deterioration. On the other hand, digital output can be copied repeatedly with no loss of integrity. For example, it is possible to make repeated digital copies of copies of a CD, but copies of a copy of a record or audiotape quickly become useless.

Machines that have already been converted to a digital format include telephones, clocks and watches, and speedometers. Similarly, examples of the latest digital machines are:

- Interactive compact disks (CD-I), which include video images, as well as audio, and which can be played over a normal TV using a CD-I player;

- Portable players that play a $2\frac{1}{2}$-inch minidisk (MD) for 74 minutes with no skips due to jolts;

- Digital audiotape (DAT) that allows individuals to record music of the same quality as is currently available on CDs;

- 35mm still cameras that allow you to have your pictures placed on a CD with up to 100 photos per disk and a companion player that allows you to display the photos on your television;

- Musical keyboards that can be coupled with a PC or Nintendo Entertainment System.

In addition, other uses of digital technology may provide us with sources and forms of information that no one can yet imagine.

Sources: Alan Freedman, *The Computer Glossary,* 4th ed. (Point Pleasant, Pa.: The Computer Language Co., 1989), p. 17; and Edmond C. Baig, "Totally Digital," *U.S. News & World Report,* November 25, 1991, pp. 78, 81.

The Phillips Compact Disc Interactive player brings video, pictures and animation to the CD.

text, primary attention is given to the general-purpose digital computer, because it is the most commonly encountered type of computer.

LIVING WITH COMPUTERS

In view of the widespread use of microprocessors in smart machines such as VCRs, telephones, and microwave ovens and the dependence of business and industry on computers, it should be obvious that we are indeed "living with

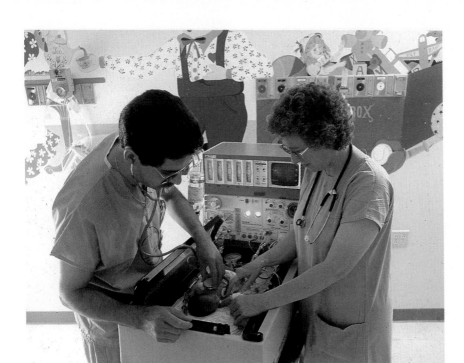

computers." Rarely does a day go by without a report in newspapers or magazines or on television of some new application of the computer. To show you some of the many seen and unseen impacts of the computer, computer applications in various areas of the world around us are summarized in this section. Other applications are discussed in detail in later chapters.

Applications in Business, Industry, and Government

You are undoubtably familiar with many business uses of computers that affect your life everyday—for example, computerized mailing lists and billings—but businesses also use the computer for many "behind-the-scenes" tasks. For example, many companies rely exclusively on the computer for monitoring inventory and ordering, receiving, and paying for goods. Data processing is also important in many companies for computing payrolls applying to many different pay scales and deductions. A not-so-hidden business use of the computer is the point-of-sale (POS) system that is used at retail checkout counters to speed the processing and automate inventory control. Airlines and national hotel chains depend on large mainframe computers to handle reservation systems. Very few offices today are without either a personal computer or a terminal hooked into a mainframe. The PC is often used for various clerical operations, such as word processing, while the terminal allows the office to link into the corporate information center.

On the financial side, banks have for some time been using a computerized check-handling system involving magnetic ink. Now, ATMs and bank-by-telephone services have made the computer even more important in banking. Financial institutions also make heavy use of computers to process and store many transactions each day. The use of computers for **electronic funds transfer**

Hotel reservation systems have multiple terminals tied into a mainframe to handle the many requests made each hour.

(EFT) means that many people can now transfer money and make purchases from the comfort of home. Another development involves the use of a computer chip in a card that allows the user to make purchases without checks or credit card verification.

Industries of all sizes and types are relying heavily on computers to manage large inventories necessary for manufacturing industries, to help design products and manufacturing processes, and to control machines that build the products. The management of inventories is critical—too much inventory is expensive and too little inventory can shut down the entire manufacturing or supply process. Two areas in which the computer has improved productivity are computer-aided design (CAD) and computer-aided manufacturing (CAM). In CAD, computers replace drafting machines, thereby speeding the design process; in CAM, microprocessors control various manufacturing processes, such as continuous-flow paper making.

Automated machines called **robots** are commonly used to reduce costs and defects while increasing safety in manufacturing tasks that are unsafe or boring. These robots are not the walking, talking variety seen in various science fiction movies, but are primarily microprocessor-controlled "arms" that can perform the same hot, dirty, or dangerous task—such as welding or painting automobile bodies—time after time without loss of concentration or reduction in efficiency.

Governments at the local, state, and national levels have found the computer to be an important tool in efficiently serving their citizenry. For example, computers were an integral part of many weapons used in the 1991 Gulf War. In fact, computers are a crucial element of most U.S. armed forces defense systems in use today. The Internal Revenue Service (IRS) uses computers to compare financial records of businesses and individuals to detect possible tax fraud. Recently, IRS agents have used laptop personal computers for their auditing duties. Similarly, the Bureau of the Census would not be able to complete the U.S. population count without the help of many mainframe computers.

(Top) Today, even sweaters are being designed on computer-aided design (CAD) systems. (Bottom) Robots on automobile assembly lines perform the repetitive, boring, or dangerous jobs.

PCs IN SMALLTOWN AMERICA

There is no doubt that PCs are now commonplace in large organizations, but only about one-half of small businesses are currently using a computer. In an innovative research program to determine consumer preferences for computer products, Apple Computer has given more than $300,000 in hardware and software to small businesses and public organizations in a small town in Oregon. The town, Jacksonville, was chosen because of its size—2,200 residents—and its proximity to Applegate Valley.

In this project, Apple sought two groups of people: those who had been too intimidated by or too busy to invest in PCs and those who had already used a PC. Thirty-one businesses, the elementary school, library, city government, chamber of commerce, and the police and fire departments were all given newer models of the Macintosh computer. Over half of those receiving a computer had never used one before. Apple also provided training and specialized software, and its representatives made regular visits to Jacksonville to monitor progress.

The results of this research project have been very positive, with most recipients reporting high satisfaction with the products and improved efficiency in their jobs. An average of 12 tasks that were previously accomplished by hand were computerized. For example,

- a jeweler uses his PC for word processing and bookkeeping and hopes to start designing jewelry on the computer;
- a tax service owner has automated his tax preparation process;
- a bed and breakfast owner has launched a reservation service and newspaper.

In addition, the experiment brought unexpected benefits to the town, including bringing together people, who did not know each other previously, to use computers. Apple plans to continue monitoring the Jacksonville experiment as well as repeating it in other countries.

Source: Jeff Bernard, "Ripe with Possibilities," *The Atlanta Constitution,* November 5, 1991, p. C-1.

There is high satisfaction with Apples in Jacksonville.

Other national agencies make widespread use of computers to process the ever-increasing backlog of paperwork or to carry out assigned duties. For example, the National Oceanic and Atmospheric Administration (NOAA) uses supercomputers to make long-range weather forecasts and uses PCs to compute the effect of acid rain on the environment. Also, the Environmental Protection Agency (EPA) uses computers to predict the effect of oil spills like the one that damaged the Persian Gulf in 1991.

Computers are used in the various state legislative bodies around the country to speed up the processing of legislative acts. National, state, and local law enforcement agencies use computers to fight crime in many ways. For example, a computer analysis of crime patterns in Seattle enabled the police department to assign more officers to critical areas and reduce the time needed to respond to emergency calls.

This satellite photo shows an oil spill in the Persian Gulf.

Medical, Educational, and Sports Applications

The advances brought about by the use of information technology are very visible in the fields of medicine and education. In the medical field, the computer is being used in every conceivable way to diagnose and treat all types of diseases and conditions. Probably the best known computerized diagnostic tool is the computerized axial tomography (CAT) scan, which allows the doctor to visualize a cross section of the body part through a series of X rays that are combined by the computer. Magnetic resonance imaging (MRI), a relatively new technique that is complementary to computerized axial tomography, relies on computer-visualized images of organs produced through the behavior of the nuclei of atoms in our bodies in a magnetic field. Treatment of diseases is being improved through the use of microprocessor-controlled smart machines that release just the right amount of a medicine into the bloodstream at just the right time.

Doctors may now be assisted in diagnosis and treatment by software packages called **expert systems (ESs).** Each package provides the physician with expert advice to formulate questions for patients and suggest treatment based on the answers. The computer has also been extremely useful in making handicapped individuals more independent and better able to live productive lives. For example, it is now possible for an individual with head injuries and speech loss to carry on a conversation using a personal computer equipped with a speech synthesizer, or for a quadriplegic to gain physical independence in a wheelchair controlled by a microprocessor. Blind people are finding that personal computers can be programmed to verbalize text on the screen, and deaf people are using computers to answer telephone calls by displaying a message on the screen.

In education, the computer is being used at all levels, from kindergarten to college. Colleges have been adding PCs to the mainframe and minicomputer they have used for years, and some institutions require incoming students to purchase a PC for class use.

At the elementary school level, the greatest current uses are in computer-aided instruction (CAI), in which the computer acts as a tutor to the student, and in computer-managed instruction (CMI), which frees teachers from many administrative chores that distract from their main purpose of classroom teaching. Many students find CAI a better way to learn since it is nonjudgmental and self-paced. The software determines the student's level of understanding by the

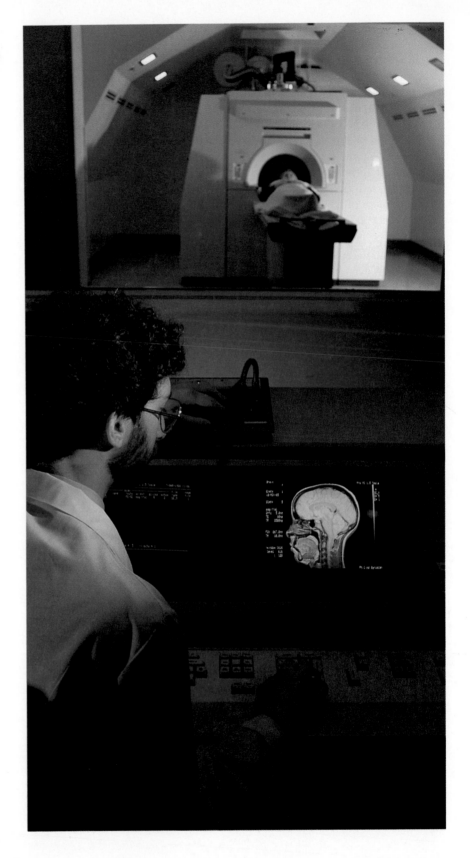

MRI measures the behavior of nuclei in our body in a magnetic field. Then a computer generates a clear image of the data—here, the inside of a patient's skull.

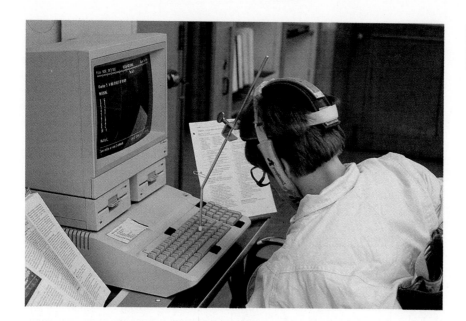

A pointer attached to headgear enables this handicapped student to press keys on the keyboard and do work.

number of correct responses to test questions and adjusts the pace of the lesson to match the level of response. Teachers find that newer software, with its high-quality graphics and animation, can hold the interest of even the easily distracted student far better than many standard teaching methods.

At the secondary school and college levels, personal computers are helping students learn to use software packages and computer programming. At the college level, mainframe computers are also used to teach programming. Further, computers can enhance learning in areas, such as biology or psychology, that are not normally associated with computers. In these courses, the student uses the computer to run simulated experiments to learn the techniques of scientific investigation.

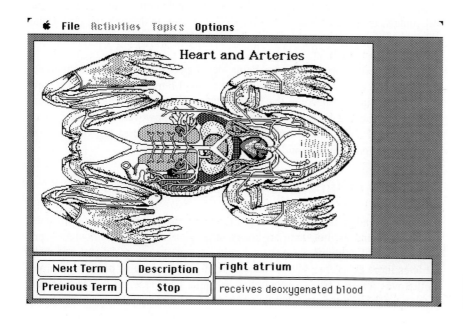

Educational computer software makes learning science concepts easier.

Retarded, learning disabled, and handicapped students have been taught successfully with the computer. For these special students, the computer is never tired and, when combined with appropriate software, can be a very interesting teacher.

In the area of sports, computers analyze large amounts of data to help coaches scout opponents and prospective players. The computer has also helped athletes by graphically breaking up their body movements for closer study to improve technique. Individuals and teams in various sports have improved their performance by using the computer to find weak points to improve upon and strong points to stress.

Multimedia

The PC revolutionized the computer industry only a decade ago, but it is already becoming more than just a tool for crunching numbers and processing words. It is being used increasingly in combination with audio and video equipment—such as VCRs, laser disks, CDs, and high-fidelity stereo—to produce interactive, full-motion videos, or what is referred to as **multimedia.** It is predicted that the market for multimedia will increase dramatically over the next few years. Recently, for example, a multimedia presentation is credited with helping Atlanta, Georgia, win the bid for the 1996 Summer Olympics.

Multimedia applications greatly enhance the learning process. In business, multimedia already is being used for sales demonstrations and training and is expected to become an important part of the over $4-billion worldwide market for presentations. In education, a multimedia system would have many uses: Geography lessons could include a mix of words, maps, video, and sound. A history film could be paused so the student could "call up" related history videos for viewing. A multimedia French language system has already been developed by Stanford University and Massachusetts Institute of Technology (MIT), in conjunction with Apple Computer, Inc. In this combination of PC, television, sound, and innovative software, a Macintosh computer is loaded with information about Paris, including color pictures, video clips, maps, street sights and sounds, and even a Parisian, who leads the viewer through the city. Using a mouse, a student can explore various popular locales, visit natives, and, along the way, learn French.

Multimedia applications are being developed for various other markets, including, and perhaps most especially, the home. Many industry leaders believe that multimedia may become the system that will make the PC as widespread as the television and VCR are today. Analysts agree, however, that such a development will probably not occur until multimedia systems cost less than $1,000, which may happen by the mid-1990s.

Applications in Our Personal Lives

We have already discussed the importance of the microprocessor in smart machines around us, but there are many other areas in which computers—primarily personal computers—can help us carry out various tasks and can make our lives more enjoyable. While the high level of home use of personal computers that was forecast five years ago has not quite been reached, a large segment of the population has found that they can do their primary jobs more efficiently,

MULTIMEDIA HELPS CONVICT CHILD ABUSERS

A pressing problem in courts all over the United States is obtaining convictions in child abuse cases. The accused assailants often go free because the young witnesses do not want to be in the same room as their abuser or are too traumatized to face them. To solve this problem, the Bexar County District Attorney's office in San Antonio, Texas, has turned to a multimedia system. The Multimedia Information Network Exchange (Minx) system incorporates full-motion and full-color video and voice and data transmission into two desktop workstations, one in the courtroom and one in the room with the youthful witness. The workstations, which look like ordinary television sets, are linked via television cable and computer control unit.

Since children usually feel no fear in talking to the TV look-alike in the "Teddy Bear Room," they can testify freely about their terrifying experiences without feeling the threatening physical presence of the defendant. Through a voice-activated system, the witness can see and hear what is going on in the courtroom while the judge and jury and the prosecuting and defense attorneys have access to the witness through monitors. Since this is a two-way system, it does not appear to violate the defendant's Sixth Amendment rights to confront the accuser, and videotapes of the proceedings are used for the appellate process. In the first five cases in which it was used, the Minx system had a 100-percent conviction rate.

Source: Carol Hilderbrand, "Multimedia Eases Testimony," *Computerworld,* July 1, 1991, p. 35.

Multimedia can include text, stills, animation, video and sound.

provide services to various clubs and organizations, or manage their hobbies better by using a personal computer. For example, if a sports booster club needs a mailing list of members, a personal computer and printer combined with appropriate software can do the job in a fraction of the time required of an individual using a typewriter. Or, if a bird watcher wants to catalog the birds observed by year and location, he or she may do this easily with a computer.

Computer and video games have been providing enjoyment for countless numbers of children of all ages for almost 30 years. Many of today's "computer old-timers" got their start by playing the Star Trek game on mainframe computers. The proliferation of personal computers has simply increased the game playing. In fact, one of the perennial best-selling PC software packages is Flight Simulator, which allows the player to fly a variety of aircraft to various airports across the country. This concept has been incorporated into the MBA program

Management Flight Simulator at MIT provides management students with a realistic application of decision making.

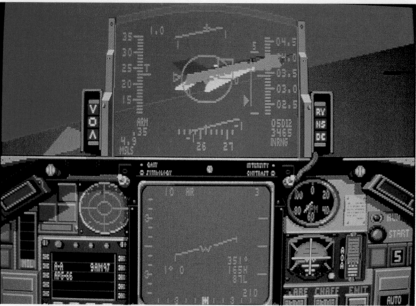

In computer games like the one shown here, players virtually have to learn to fly if they want to compete successfully!

HARBOUR TOWN
SUSAN   E
Hole: 18 Par: 4 Shots: 4
Ball to Pin: 40 FT.
Menu Setup Top Scores Drop

Skip Grid Profile

SWING P

● Address
● Draw
● Straight   Gimmie Rotate CLUB
● Fade   Lie
● Chip ● User1
● Putt ● User2   GREEN WIND

0   P

at MIT in a program called Management Flight Simulator, in which new students learn about managing an airline company. Logic games, including chess, popular board games such as Monopoly or Scrabble, and many adventure/detective games that require the player to make decisions in order to score points are also popular types of games for the PC. In addition, the extremely popular Nintendo game systems offer graphics that are much improved over those of the older game systems.

Computers are becoming a fact of life in other areas of recreation. For example, at EPCOT (Experimental Prototype Community of Tomorrow) in Walt

BITS OF HISTORY

Early Attempts at a Mind Tool

Humans have always tried to make the basic operations of writing and counting easier. The first successful counting device was the Chinese abacus, which is very fast in the hands of an experienced operator. After the Renaissance in Europe, individuals concentrated on building machines that could perform arithmetic operations. In 1614, John Napier of Scotland invented logarithms and the slide rule. In 1643, Blaise Pascal of France created a machine that could add and subtract. In 1673, Gottfried Wilhelm von Leibnitz of Germany developed a calculator that could multiply.

The first attempt at anything that approaches our definition of a computer occurred in 1820 when Englishman Charles Babbage built a machine to make arithmetic computations. His Difference Engine was a special-purpose device for calculating the values of polynomials of the form $x^2 + 3x + 20$ to an accuracy of six places. After this success, Babbage tried to develop a more sophisticated device—the **Analytical Engine**—which would be able to perform any type of arithmetic calculation. The crucial conceptual breakthrough in the Analytical Engine was that it would *store* the series of operations to be made. Babbage was aided by Lady Ada Lovelace, the daughter of English poet Lord Byron. Lovelace clearly described Babbage's ideas in written form, supplementing notes on his work with ideas of her own. Unfortunately, the technology of the time was not advanced enough for Babbage to build his machine, which used gears and wheels to carry out the necessary logic. A model that was built later from his plans worked as Babbage claimed it would.

Many of the ideas of Babbage and Lovelace were very advanced. In fact, if the technology had been available to build Babbage's Analytical Engine in 1840, the computer might have been developed 100 years earlier than it was. As an example of their farsighted ideas, consider this quote from Lady Lovelace. Her words may also be applied to modern computers:

The Analytical Engine has no pretension whatever to *originate* anything. It can do whatever *we know how to order it to perform*. It can *follow* analysis; but it has no way of *anticipating* any analytical relations or truths. Its province is to assist us in making *available* what we are already acquainted with.

For her tireless effort on this "grandfather" of the modern computer, Lady Lovelace has been honored by having a computer language named after her; the language is Ada.

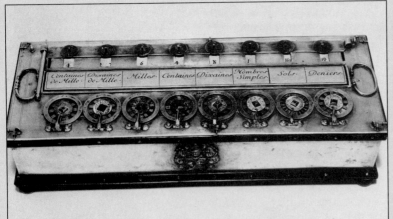

Pascal's adding machine, called the Pascaline, used wheels and gears to add and subtract numbers.

Babbage's Difference Engine was designed to compute mathematical tables.

Disney World near Orlando, Florida, computers run the entire show, including the fountains, the rides, the information service, and the animated figures in the shows. There is even a special presentation on the impact of computers at EPCOT. Similarly, the popular Andrew Lloyd Webber musical *Starlight Express* uses six separate computer systems to run the lights, sound system, and other elements of the scenery.

A LOOK AHEAD

The purpose of this textbook is to provide information and experience to enable you to function in a world rapidly becoming populated with smart machines. In the process you should become computer literate. The next four chapters in this introductory block cover hardware, software, information systems, and the effect of the computer on our society—the material necessary for the first half of our definition of computer literacy, that is, knowing what a computer can and cannot do. The remaining chapters of the textbook expand these five introductory chapters. If you combine this material with the software that accompanies this book or is provided by your instructor, you will become fully computer literate by learning how to make the computer do what you want done.

REVIEW OF KEY POINTS

1. The world is rapidly being populated with smart machines that not only carry out tasks, but also make decisions and provide information. Smart machines are, in reality, a type of computer based on the microprocessor computer chip.
2. Because the computer can help ease our mental labors, it is often referred to as a mind tool. Many of today's tools—including calculators, typewriters, file cabinets, drafting tables, and the telephone—are being replaced or enhanced by the computer.
3. A computer is a machine that stores and manipulates symbols quickly and accurately. The two parts of a computer are hardware and software. Hardware is the electronic part, and software is the set of instructions that directs the computer's activities.
4. The process of developing software is called programming, and the resulting software is made up of one or more programs. However, by using commercially available software packages, an individual may be able to use a computer without being a programmer.
5. Computer literacy is an understanding of what a computer can and cannot do and an ability to make the computer do what is desired.
6. Computers can be classified according to size as supercomputers, mainframes, minicomputers, workstations, and personal computers. The use of mainframe computers and personal computers is increasing simultaneously, and both are important tools in the information society.
7. Computers may also be classified by the type of logic they use or by the purpose for which they are designed.

8. The computer has applications in many fields and affects our lives in numerous ways.

9. Multimedia is the combination of the computer and various audio and video devices.

KEY TERMS

analog computer
Analytical Engine
computer
computer chip
computer competence
computer error
computer literacy
computer mastery
computer package
computer terminal
data
data processing
desktop computer
digital computer
electronic funds transfer (EFT)
end user
expert system (ES)
firmware
general-purpose computer
hardware

information
information society
information system
information technology
mainframe
microprocessor
mind tool
minicomputer
multimedia
network
personal computer (PC)
program
programming
robots
smart machines
software
special-purpose computer
supercomputer
terminal
workstation

REVIEW QUESTIONS

1. List those machines in your home that are "smart." Discuss other machines that could be improved if they were made "smart."
2. What differentiates smart machines from other types of machines? What element is at the heart of any smart machine?
3. Discuss why the computer is referred to as a "mind tool."
4. Why are information systems important to organizations?
5. List some examples of organizations that are heavily dependent on information as an asset.
6. What are the levels of computer use beyond computer literacy? What is an *end user*?

7. List three current or future situations for which you must become computer literate.
8. Why do we say that computer hardware is useless without software?
9. What are two important advantages of the computer?
10. Discuss why the term *computer error* is a misrepresentation.
11. Discuss the difference between data and information.
12. Explain the term *data processing*. What are the input and output for data processing? Give an example.
13. List the various classifications of computer in the categories of

size, logic, and purpose. In each category, which type is the most prevalent?

14. What are the important differences between a workstation and a personal computer?

15. Discuss three applications of computers that affect you on a daily basis. What is multimedia?

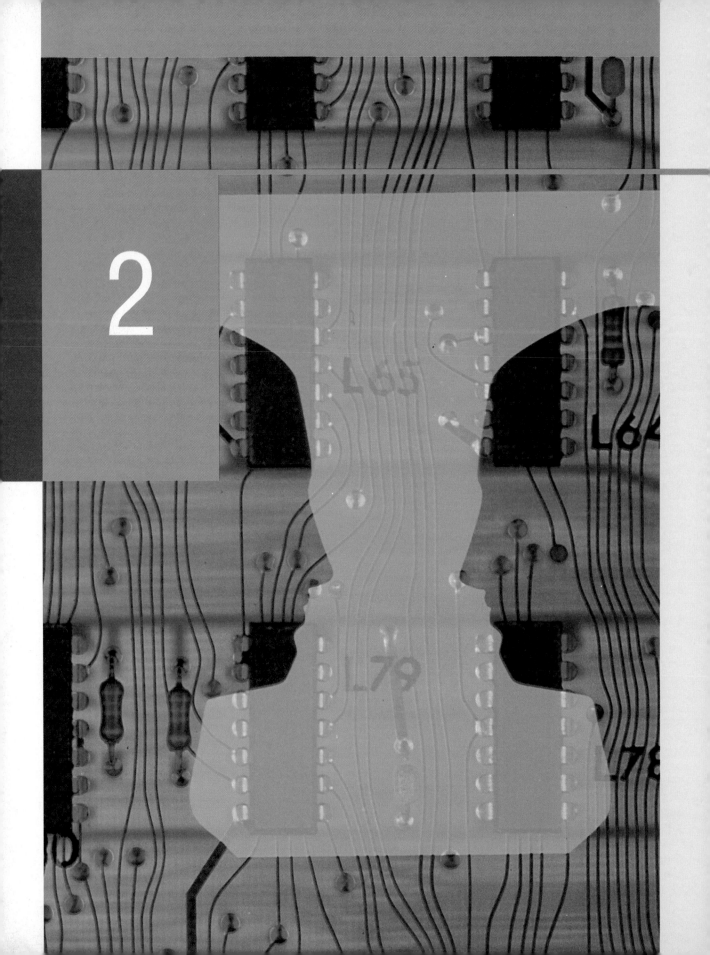

2

An Introduction to Computer Hardware

In Chapter 1 we said that the computer has two parts—hardware and software. Here in Chapter 2 we discuss the computer's hardware components. More details and specifics of hardware are addressed in Block Two, The Details of Hardware, for which this chapter serves as an introduction.

This chapter introduces the various hardware devices that make up a computer. Coverage of this topic includes a look at the components of a conceptual computer and how it works. We then discuss some hardware elements and how they combine to "build" a computer. We also will discuss briefly the manner in which a computer stores symbols.

STUDY OBJECTIVES

After reading this chapter, you should be able to

- understand conceptually how a computer works;
- recognize the four major hardware components of the computer;
- understand how these four components interact to manipulate and store symbols;
- describe the various units of a mainframe computer;
- put together a personal computer using examples of each of the elements;
- discuss how a computer stores symbols in the processing/internal memory unit;
- include in your vocabulary the most important computer hardware terminology.

MONITORING WEATHER AT PORTLAND GENERAL ELECTRIC

At Portland General Electric (PGE), an electric power utility company in Portland, Oregon, monitoring the weather and smokestack emissions is not just a sidelight, it's a requirement of doing business. Because PGE operates a nuclear power plant, the Nuclear Regulatory Commission (NRC) requires that weather conditions, which might affect the dispersal of routine low levels of radiation released from the plant, be monitored daily. This includes measuring wind speeds and directions and other atmospheric conditions. Similarly, to meet air quality and stack emission requirements of the Oregon state environmental office, PGE must monitor the emissions from its coal plant and two combustion turbine plants.

While keeping accurate environmental records can be expensive, PGE's failure to do so could result in regulatory fines. In 1986, when a PC system was installed, PGE used a monitoring system that involved collecting magnetic tapes from weather and emissions data loggers, mounting the tape on PGE's mainframe, and executing a program to produce the needed reports. This system involved a lag of several days between the collection of data and the meteorologist's being able to check it for possible malfunctions in the data recording device. Thus, any malfunctions would not be discovered for several days. The data logger was backed up by strip charts, but significant additional labor was required to convert the data to a usable form.

To speed up the processing of weather data, in 1989 PGE installed a local area network (LAN) composed of PCs that accept the data from an improved data logger/cassette recorder system. These PCs are used to check the data for reasonableness using a series of BASIC programs written by meteorologist Terry Worrell. After being processed by PCs on the LAN, the data are transferred to PGE's mainframe, where more accuracy checks are run before the data are included in reports that are sent to the NRC. The data are also transferred to a PC-based data base management program that generates reports for the state environmental office.

Source: Interview with Terry Worrell, meteorologist at PGE, November 6, 1991.

Data retrieval devices combined with a PC have enabled Portland Gas and Electric to monitor closely the environmental conditions around its power plant.

As defined in Chapter 1, computer **hardware** is the electronic part of the computer that stores and manipulates symbols under the direction of the computer software. In the preceding box, various types of computer hardware, including a personal computer and a mainframe, are used to monitor the weather at Portland General Electric.

Because the hardware's operations are electronic, the computer is both fast and accurate. The speed of many operations performed within the computer is limited only by the speed of electricity. These operations also obey physical laws that do not change from operation to operation and are therefore accurate. If you will recall, a computer mistake can almost always be traced to a human error, either in the design of the computer or in the software.

To understand how the computer hardware is combined to make a machine that stores and manipulates symbols, we first look at a **conceptual computer,** which can demonstrate the major functions of a computer without involving the operational details of the machine. The conceptual computer shown in Figure 2-1 has four major elements: input, processing/internal memory, secondary storage, and output. The figure also shows the flow of data into the computer and of processed information out of the computer.

A computer must be able to **input,** or receive, the data to be manipulated and the software instructions for manipulating those data. Input to a computer performs the same function as the input humans receive through sight, hearing, touch, taste, and smell. In the PGE example at the beginning of the chapter, input to the PC is from the weather data logger cassette tapes and input to the mainframe is from the PC.

Once the data and instructions are input, the computer must be able to store them internally and then process the data based on the instructions. This storage and processing, which occurs in the **processing/internal memory unit,** can involve many different types of operations, including arithmetic operations

> **I would not want to waste anyone's time by documenting the generality that computing has changed the world.**
>
> *William F. Buckley, Jr.,*
> *author and editor*
>
> ". . . Makes a Difference Where You Are," *Personal Computing,* October 1989, p. 23.

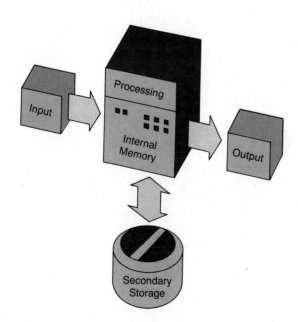

FIGURE 2-1
The Conceptual Computer

(addition, subtraction, and so on) on numbers, operations on letters of the alphabet, and operations that result in pictures (known as graphics). The processing/internal memory unit is comparable to the human brain, which also stores and operates on data. In the PGE example, the PC processes the weather data to check them for reasonableness and to prepare them for further processing by the mainframe.

Because the internal memory of a computer does not have an unlimited capacity, a storage area is needed outside of the computer to hold the data and information, which can be brought back into the internal memory as needed. This external storage unit is called **secondary storage.** Another reason for having secondary storage is that the computer's internal memory is erased when the power to the computer is turned off. Anything in internal memory that must be saved before the power is turned off should be transferred to secondary storage. The file cabinets we use to save large amounts of data and information are analogous to a computer's secondary storage.

Finally, because the processed information is of no use unless it is provided to the user, the computer has a process called **output.** We humans output the results of our brains' operations in the form of speech, writing, pictures, or body movements. In the PGE example, output from the PC is in an electronic form that is sent directly to the mainframe, where it is processed and output as printed reports.

ELEMENTS OF HARDWARE

We have looked at a conceptual computer and have discussed the parts of a computer in general terms. We have also seen how the input of data into the computer, the flow of data and information between the computer and secondary storage, and the output of information from the computer link the components of the conceptual computer together. Before we discuss further how a computer works, we should look at the four major parts of a real computer. After reading this section, you should have a clear idea of the main components of a computer.

Input

The many methods of input to a computer range from grocery checkout bar codes to easy-to-use voice input. Currently, the most popular form of input is the typewriterlike **keyboard,** which sends the appropriate electrical signal to the computer when the user presses a key. The symbol corresponding to this key is stored in the computer's internal memory and usually is shown simultaneously on the screen.

Other common forms of input include the joystick used for games and a device called a **mouse** that communicates with the computer when the user moves it over a flat surface and presses one or more buttons. **Touchscreens** that transmit a signal to the computer based on what part of the screen is touched are used in various situations, as are **light pens** that the user points at a portion of the screen to select it for further investigation. Touch screens provide information to visitors all over EPCOT Center at Walt Disney World in Florida. A visitor merely touches one of several colored areas on the screen to receive a message about a feature of EPCOT. The newest forms of input are **pen-based computing** and **voice recognition.** In the former case, the user writes on the screen; in the latter case, the user speaks to the computer.

(Top left) By touching the stylus to various points on the touchpad, the user can make changes to the map on the screen. (Top right) To select from the menu, the user simply points at a particular place on the screen. (Bottom) With a bar code reader, important price and inventory information can be input easily to the computer.

Processing/Internal Memory

To manipulate and store symbols, the computer must have a "brain" that can perform certain predetermined operations and "remember" information. This "brain" is the processing/internal memory unit of the computer and is made up of three parts: (1) the arithmetic–logic unit, where actual processing is carried out; (2) the control unit, which directs all of these operations; and (3) the internal, or main, memory. The control unit and the arithmetic–logic unit together form the **central processing unit (CPU)** of the computer.

All three units use the computer chips discussed in Chapter 1. Recall that a **chip** is a tiny piece of silicon that packs many thousands of electronic elements into a tiny area. These elements, called **transistors,** actually carry on the control and logic operations at over 1 million operations per second! A combination of transistors and circuits on a chip results in an **integrated circuit** that is the key to the power and speed of all computers today (it will be discussed in more detail in Chapter 6). Because the chip is so small, it must be attached to a carrier device with wire prongs. This plugs it into the main circuit board, which contains other chips for the CPU, the main memory, and the control of input, output, and secondary storage devices.

A CPU chip, or **microprocessor,** contains the control unit and the arithmetic–logic unit. The **control unit** manages the processing of data into information and the **arithmetic–logic unit (ALU)** handles the actual processing by performing arithmetic and logic operations on the data. Mainframe computers

A microchip is so small that it and its holder can easily pass through the eye of a needle.

This computer circuit board, consisting of many electronic devices soldered onto a printed circuit, can control various operations of the computer.

will have several CPU chips, but a personal computer will usually have only one. Having multiple CPU chips enables the mainframe to run faster and handle the large volume of processing for which it is responsible.

To help you understand what is going on in the CPU with the control and arithmetic–logic units, think of these units as two clerks working inside the computer: the head clerk (the control unit) and the working clerk (the arithmetic–logic unit). The head clerk's job is to tell the working clerk what calculations and comparisons to do based on instructions from the keyboard. The working clerk can only add, subtract, or compare two data items and must be told by the head clerk specifically what to do. Since the head clerk cannot do these calculations or comparisons and the working clerk cannot understand instructions from the keyboard, the two clerks must work together.

To store the data internally, the head clerk uses a blackboard (the internal memory). While the working clerk can communicate only with the head clerk, the head clerk can communicate with the user through a bulletin board (the screen) on which results are posted. The head clerk also stores data and information in file cabinets (the secondary storage).

To carry out a task, the head clerk receives instructions over the phone (the keyboard) and looks up the meaning of these instructions in a reference manual (the software). After interpreting the instructions, the head clerk retrieves needed data from the blackboard (the internal memory) and sends these data, and instructions as to what should be done with them, to the working clerk for action. After carrying out the instructions, the working clerk returns the result of this operation to the head clerk, who writes it on the blackboard. The head clerk may send results to the filing cabinets or retrieve additional data from there. The head clerk may also post results on the bulletin board or send them out to be printed.

Internal Memory

The third part of processing/internal memory is the **internal memory,** which also is made up of computer chips. Internal memory is divided into two major types—random-access memory and read-only memory. **Random-access memory (RAM)** is the section of memory that is available for storing the instructions to the computer and the symbols that are to be manipulated. It is the internal memory that is accessible to the user; it is called RAM because any area of the memory can be accessed with equal ease regardless of where a piece of information is located. A shortcoming of RAM is that it is **volatile**—the memory exists only while the computer is turned on or is connected to the mainframe. This volatility and the limited availability of internal memory require that secondary storage be used to save information before the computer is turned off or is disconnected from the mainframe.

Read-only memory (ROM) is the section of memory that is placed in the computer during the manufacturing process, and it is nonvolatile. This type of memory gives the CPU instructions during the startup or **booting process,** before the user has given the computer any instructions. When the computer is started up, ROM tells it to go to secondary storage to read instructions into RAM that allow the computer to process data into information. ROM is also useful in managing many of the computer's operations, such as providing the characters on the screen when a key is pressed or results are being displayed.

CPU speed and the typical amount of memory available have both increased by more than a factor of 10 since 1981, and the rate of improvement is likely to continue for another 10 years.

William Gates, founder and CEO, Microsoft Software

Quoted in "The Future of High-Performance Personal Systems," *MIPS Special Supplement*, February 1989, p. 8.

KEEPING THE TRAINS ROLLING WITH COMPUTERS

After running for many years on equipment designed in the first half of this century, the railroad industry is now beginning to use computers to dispatch and control trains. The industry's main objectives in using computers are to improve safety, cut maintenance costs, save fuel, and more efficiently use its 221,000 miles of track and 1.3 million freight cars. Currently, most railroads use a system of in-track sensors and radio transmitters to track the trains. This system has an accuracy of about 3 miles, which means that, for safety's sake, dispatchers have to give each train a 6-mile cushion. This causes trains to run more slowly than needed, wait at sidetracks for long periods, and, in general, run very inefficiently.

Consider the system being tested by Burlington Northern on 250 miles of its track. Custom-designed computer chips are installed on the test locomotives, which communicate with the air force's Global Position System (GPS) satellites to determine the exact location of a given train. The location of the locomotive is sent to a minicomputer used by the dispatchers.

The new system can determine the locomotive's location to within 150 feet, allowing Burlington Northern to operate its trains more frequently and get them to their destinations more quickly. During the test period, the company determined that installing the computer system in all its locomotives would have prevented *all* accidents that occurred on the railroad. Most such accidents were caused when trains exceeded normal speeds and ran through signals. Burlington Northern has decided to install the computer system in all its trains and expects a $1 billion payoff over a 15-year period.

Sources: Hal Straus, "Railroads Rolling into the Space Age," *The Atlanta Journal,* May 2, 1989, pp. D1–D2; and interview with Edward Butt of Burlington Northern, November 7, 1991.

The computer monitors shown here give the train dispatcher almost instantaneous control over the trains at this trackyard.

Secondary Storage

Because of the limited amount of internal storage and the volatility of RAM, some form of storage external to RAM is necessary to permanently store data and programs. This **secondary storage** usually comes in one of two forms of magnetic storage media—disk or tape. With either of these, stored information is accessed by internal memory when the control unit decides that this information is needed. Because the secondary storage unit must locate the information, read it from the disk or tape, and then transfer it to internal memory, secondary storage is a much slower form of memory than internal memory. However, this slow transfer of information is balanced by the virtually unlimited storage capacity.

Disk secondary storage uses a **computer disk** to store information as a form of **direct-access storage** in which information may be accessed in any order, regardless of the order in which the information was stored. A disk is a thin, recordlike piece of metal or plastic that is covered with an iron oxide whose magnetic direction can be arranged to represent symbols. This magnetic arrangement is accomplished by a device known as a **disk drive,** which spins the disk while reading and writing information onto it. This process of transferring information to and from the disk is accomplished by the **read/write head,** which, depending on the type of disk, rides either directly on or immediately above the disk. In a sense, a disk is like a CD that is "played" by the disk drive. However, there are two crucial differences between a computer disk and a CD. First, signals on the computer disk are recorded magnetically rather than by a laser beam burning pits into the surface of the compact disk. Second, the computer can record data on a disk in addition to playing it.

Mainframe computers have large **disk packs** made up of ten disks, each about the size of a record album. These disk packs usually remain in the disk drive except when a special need requires a transfer. Because these disk packs can hold so much information, many users can store data on a single disk pack. When a user connects to the mainframe, his or her user number tells the computer where to look on the disk pack for the user's data.

To store information, personal computers use both plastic disks, called **floppy disks,** and metal disks, called **hard disks.** Floppy disks, which are made of Mylar® and covered with an iron oxide, are easily moved, but they hold only a fraction of the data stored on a hard disk or a mainframe disk pack. For this reason, a user may need several floppies to store all needed data or information. Floppies come in two sizes, $5\frac{1}{4}$ inches and $3\frac{1}{2}$ inches in diameter; the size required depends on the type of disk drive being used. A hard disk is a scaled-down version of a mainframe disk pack. The hard disk rotates at a much faster speed than the floppy and stores a great deal more information.

The **optical** or **video disk,** the newest form of secondary storage, can hold *billions* of characters. Optical disks are similar to compact disks used for music except that they are larger and can hold more information. Currently, most optical disks, like audio CDs, are *read-only* storage devices, but more and more read and write optical disk systems are coming into use.

Magnetic tape that is used for secondary storage can be either reel-to-reel or cassette. Like a disk, tape is covered with iron oxide that is arranged magnetically to store symbols. A tape can easily store millions of characters. However, it is much slower than a disk for transferring information since the tape

Mainframe computers use tape for much of their secondary storage.

Because of the amount of data they can store and their smaller size, microfloppy disks ($3\frac{1}{2}$ inches in diameter) are becoming very popular for use on all types of personal computers.

OPTICAL DISK SYSTEM FINGERS CRIME SUSPECTS

In television detective stories, a fingerprint is always a crucial clue, since it enables the detective to determine the identity of the suspect. Unfortunately, finding a fingerprint does not always result in an identification in actual police work. For example, at the State of Georgia Crime Information Center, there are almost 10 million fingerprint cards to be checked when a suspect or "latent" print comes in. Obviously, it is almost impossible to check all these fingerprint cards manually, and as a result, many latent prints go unmatched. In one year, 40,000 latent prints from crime scenes were handled, but only 952 suspects were identified. As a result of this horrendous matching problem, latent prints can usually be used only to check against suspects in custody.

To match fingerprints more expediently, the state of Georgia implemented, in 1989, the Automated Fingerprint Identification System (AFIS). Fingerprint information is stored on an optical disk and when a latent print comes in for checking, its characteristics are entered into the computer and compared to fingerprints on the optical disks. In the first three years of use, AFIS identified 170 suspects from previously unsolved crimes—mostly burglaries. In one murder case, a latent print was entered into the system and, 22 minutes later, a match was found. This led to the arrest of a previously unconsidered suspect. "It was a cold hit," said a Georgia Bureau of Investigation spokesman. "We didn't even know he existed. We had no idea he was involved."

The AFIS program is now integrated with the Computer Crime History (CCH) to enable easy updating of information in the CCH based on fingerprint "hits." This allows authorities to compile a suspect's criminal history in a day rather than the previously required three weeks. AFIS is also configured to accept fingerprint cards created using a "live scan" process, which digitizes the print images rather than using the traditional ink printing method, once local law enforcement agencies install the necessary equipment to carry out this process.

Source: Elizabeth Coady, "New Computerized System Fingered Slaying Suspect," *The Atlanta Journal-Constitution,* February 17, 1989, p. 17-A, as updated by the author in 1991.

After the computer selects possible matches to the latent fingerprint, the matches are displayed on a computer monitor for further comparison by a human user.

must first be *mounted* on a **tape drive,** where a read/write head similar to that used on a disk drive transfers information to and from the tape. Another drawback of a tape system is that the information must be accessed in the *same* sequence in which it was stored on the tape. This type of access is termed **sequential access.**

Mainframe computers depend upon reel-to-reel tapes to store information not needed immediately, such as financial statistics, payroll records, student academic records, and so on, and to make backups of information from disk packs. A **backup** is a copy of the information on the disk; it can be used to restore information if an equipment problem causes the disk to fail. Personal computers use a form of **tape cartridge** to back up hard disks.

Output

The two most popular output devices are the printer and the video screen, or monitor. A **monitor** is required for almost any computer system for two reasons. First, the data or instructions being input from the keyboard or other input device are shown on the monitor. A blinking rectangle or underline called a **cursor** moves on the screen as the data or instructions are input. Second, the monitor is an almost instantaneous outlet for the result of the processing.

Several varieties of monitors are available, but the primary distinction is between **monochrome monitors** and **color monitors.** Monochrome or single-color monitors display light symbols on a darker background—as compared to color monitors, which can display many colors on the screen. The question of which monitor—monochrome or color—is better depends on the task to be completed and the budget of the user. This question will be addressed in more detail in Chapters 7 and 10.

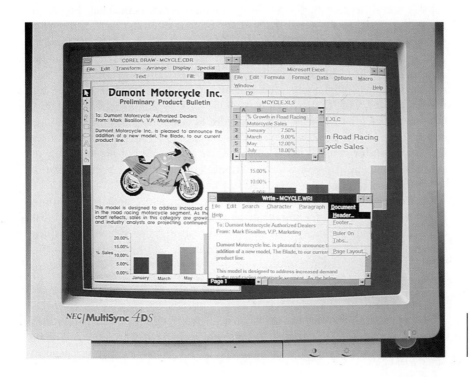

Color monitors are often a necessity—as, for example, when colorful graphics are needed to show the exact color of a product.

Often a user will view the results of processing on the monitor screen and then decide that **hard copy** is needed, in the form of a printed page. Such hard copy is useful because the output to the monitor is not permanent. For mainframe users, it is usually very easy to divert the output on the monitor to a page printer at a computer center. A **page printer** is a high-speed printer that can print an entire page in one motion. For personal computer users, a large number of printers are available today in varying speeds, qualities of print, and price ranges. The most commonly used printer for personal computers is the **dot matrix printer,** which creates symbols on the page by printing a matrix of dots. Other types of printers commonly used with PCs are ink jet printers and laser printers. The **ink-jet printer** sprays ink on the page to create letters and pictures. The **laser printer** is much like a copier except that instead of photocopying an existing document, it converts output from a computer into a printed form. A full discussion of printers is presented in Chapter 7.

We can also use secondary storage for input and output by outputting results to a disk or tape for storage or by reading data or instructions from disk or tape. Read-only secondary storage, such as cartridges or video disks, is also designed to be used as an input to the computer.

Terminals

A type of input/output device that is used for work with mainframes or with a computer network is the terminal. A **terminal** is made up of a keyboard and a monitor and is used primarily for input and output. It may or may not have its

DALLAS POLICE TAKE BYTE OUT OF CRIME

In police work, not knowing the adversary can lead to an officer's being wounded or even killed. However, in Dallas, Texas, officers on patrol now use computers in their cruisers to speed the identification process. Each patrol car is equipped with a mobile data terminal that is linked via radio to the city hall data center. Instead of calling the dispatcher to make inquiries about a car license tag or the identification of a suspect, officers simply type in the tag number and the information is relayed to the data center computer, which then returns the status of the automobile. Since the data terminals were installed, the number of license checks has doubled, and many officers agree that, by itself, this capability makes the system worthwhile.

Beyond making license checks easier, however, the mobile terminals can relay information on the status of the driver of a vehicle that has been stopped. Instead of having to read the information over the radio and wait for a response, the new system quickly provides information that can save lives. The terminal screen also acts as a link between an officer and the dispatcher as well as with other officers. In effect, it acts as electronic mail on the roads. For example, when an officer returns to the vehicle, he or she can check the screen for a list of calls to be answered, with high-priority calls being highlighted in a different color. In addition, the officer can trade information with other Dallas police personnel. In one case, it was possible to relay the tag number of a shooting suspect to the data center and have a patrol car waiting for the suspect when he returned home!

Source: Clinton Wilder, "City Cops Take Byte Out of Crime," *Computerworld,* October 29, 1990, p. 76.

> ## We work the crud out of it, that's for sure.
>
> *Dallas Police Officer*
> *David Vestal*
>
> Quoted in "City Cops Take Byte Out of Crime," *Computerworld,* October 29, 1990, p. 76.

The mobile computers installed in Dallas police squad cars give officers access to the police data center.

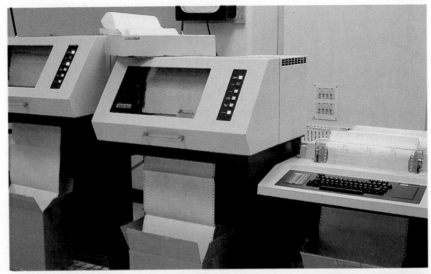

The personal computer printer sitting on top of the mainframe printer monitors the operation of the larger printer.

Employees use this mainframe printer to obtain a hard copy of the results shown on the terminal screen.

own CPU or secondary storage. When it does not have either of these, it is usually referred to as a **dumb terminal.** A PC can also be used as a terminal when it acts as an input/output device for a mainframe or network. Another name for a terminal is **VDT,** for **video display terminal.**

Input/Output Telecommunication

A device that facilitates both input and output is the **modem,** which sends and receives information between computers over telephone lines. The modem converts the electrical signals from RAM in the computer into the type of electrical signals that can travel over telephone lines. In other words, the digital output from the computer must be modulated into an analog form before it can be sent over a telephone line, and the analog input received over the telephone line must be demodulated into digital form before it can be used for input into the computer.

The term *modem* is used because the device MOdulates/DEModulates signals. With a modem, a computer terminal or a personal computer can be used to communicate with a mainframe or another personal computer. In either case, the modem acts as both an input device and an output device so the computer can send and receive information over the telephone lines. This is very useful

Terminals are often used to link multiple users to the mainframe computer.

A modem can link a PC to other PCs or to a mainframe computer.

for persons who wish to work at home, access a computerized information service to research some topic, or simply communicate with other computer users.

THE COMPLETE COMPUTER

Now that we have considered the four major components of computer hardware in detail, we can put together a basic computer system. By a **system** we mean all the items that will go together to produce a working whole. The mainframe computer system shown in Figure 2-2 includes multiple terminals (keyboard and monitor) for input and output, a CPU for processing/internal memory, a disk drive with disk pack and reel-to-reel tape for secondary storage, and a page printer for output.

A corresponding personal computer system is shown in Figure 2-3. As with the mainframe computer, a keyboard and a monitor are used for input and output. In addition, a mouse is shown as a source of input. The processor/internal memory unit includes both RAM and ROM, while secondary storage is made up of a floppy disk drive and a hard disk. For output, a portable printer is used in addition to the monitor. A modem is also included for communication with a mainframe or other personal computers.

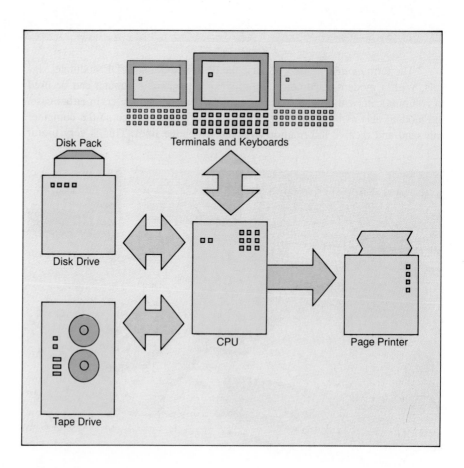

FIGURE 2-2
Mainframe Computer System

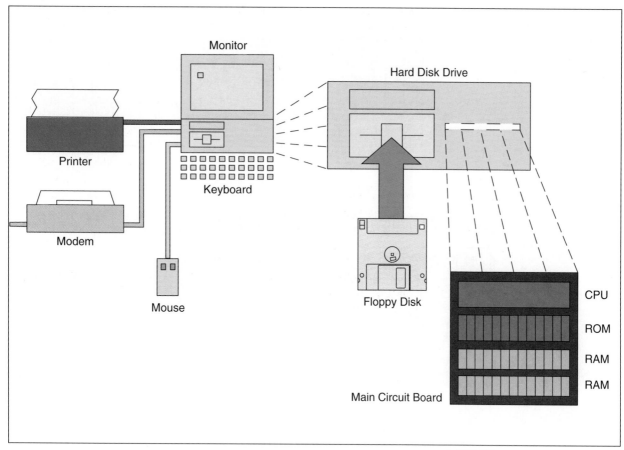

FIGURE 2-3
Personal Computer System

A Closer Look at PC Keyboards

The five main pieces of hardware for a personal computer are the keyboard, the system unit, the monitor, the disk drive, and the printer. Of these, the keyboard is an essential piece of hardware; it is also the most complicated to use. For these reasons, it is useful to look more closely at the two most widely used keyboards for personal computers that run the same software as the original IBM PC—the so-called **IBM compatible PCs.** These two keyboards are shown in Figure 2-4.

Figure 2-4a illustrates the older of the two keyboards. It was introduced for use with the original IBM PCs and PC ATs. Figure 2-4b illustrates the newer, enhanced keyboard that is standard with the IBM PS/2 personal computer. The operations are the same for each of these keyboards.

The first thing to note about these keyboards relative to the standard type-writer keyboard is their increased size. Instead of the approximately 50 keys on a typewriter keyboard, there are 84 keys on the AT-style keyboard and 101 keys on the PS/2 keyboard. These additional keys are for uses particular to the software being used; their purposes are discussed in Table 2-1. While not all these operations will be meaningful to you now, they will come to mean more as you begin to work with various types of software.

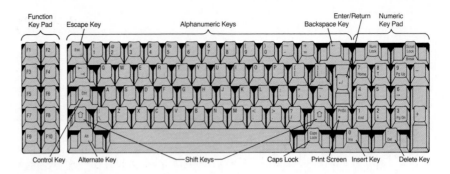

FIGURE 2-4a
Original IBM Compatible
Keyboard

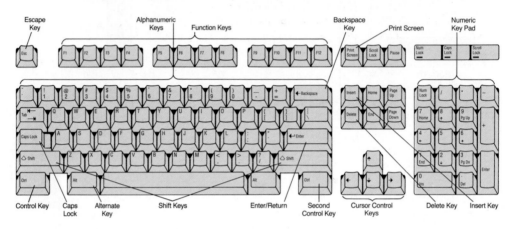

FIGURE 2-4b
Newer Enhanced IBM
Compatible Keyboard

TABLE 2-1
Keys on IBM Keyboards

Key	Name	Purpose
F1–F12	Function keys	Operation depends on package
0–9	Numeric keypad	Cursor control; if Num Lock key is pressed, same action as keys on calculator
↑,→,←,↓	Arrow keys	Cursor control
Esc	Escape key	Aborts the current operation
Tab	Tab key	Tabs the cursor to the next tab stop
Ctrl	Control key	Gives special operating commands when used with other keys
Shift	Shift key	Shifts to opposite case
Alt	Alt key	Gives another meaning to a key when pressed simultaneously with that key
Backspace	Backspace key	Deletes character to left of current position
Ins	Insert key	Switches between insert and replace modes in word processing
Del	Delete key	Deletes character under cursor
Enter	Enter key	Designates the end of a command or line of input
PrtSc	Print screen	Causes the screen contents to be printed when pressed simultaneously with the shift key
Caps Lock	Uppercase lock	Shifts the alphabetic keyboard to upper case until pressed again
Scroll Lock/Break		When combined with Ctrl key, aborts current operation

In the earlier discussion of the conceptual computer, we noted that the CPU handles the actual processing of data into information, following instructions input by the user. We also discussed the importance of the two types of internal memory and the use of secondary storage in the processing operation. To handle this processing and storage, computer chips contain microscopic transistorized switches that are either "on" or "off." Because of this system of processing and storing data, the base 2, or **binary**, **number system** is used for both processing and storage. Each transistorized switch corresponds to one **bit** (BInary digiT) of storage. This means that instead of the 10 digits, 26 letters (upper- and lower-case), and various punctuation marks used by humans for processing data into information, the computer represents these symbols with a group of switches, each with just these two conditions—"on" or "off," 1 or 0.

For storing the nonnumeric data, processed information, and instructions in the form of letters, punctuation marks, and special symbols, a standard representation involving groups of eight bits, called a **byte,** has been devised. Each pattern of eight bits represents a given symbol. Several patterns of bits have been suggested, but the two most commonly used codes are **EBCDIC** (pronounced "eb-suh-dick"), which is an acronym for Extended Binary Coded Decimal Interchange Code, and **ASCII** (pronounced "as-key"), which is an acronym for American Standard Code for Information Interchange. EBCDIC was developed by IBM for use on its mainframe computers, while ASCII has become the standard code for personal computers. For example, the letter A is coded as 01000001 in ASCII and as 11000001 in EBCDIC. Note that each of these groups of eight bits is either 1 or 0. Because each character can be represented by one byte in either ASCII or EBCDIC, the terms *byte* and *character* are commonly used interchangeably.

These codes are used for transmitting information between the keyboard and internal memory and between internal memory and the display screen as well as for storing information in internal memory and secondary storage. Figure 2-5 shows the letter A being transmitted from the keyboard into internal memory with the ASCII code, and Appendix C shows the ASCII codes for letters and symbols.

Storing Information

As discussed earlier, data, information, and instructions must be stored in both the internal memory and the secondary storage of a computer. In internal memory, both random-access memory and read-only memory use memory chips to

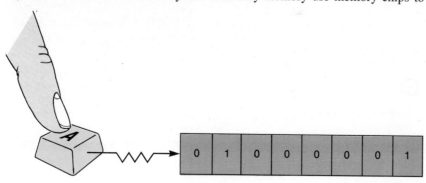

FIGURE 2-5
Transmittal of Letter A
from Keyboard

BITS OF HISTORY

50 Years of Development

The First Computer

For a machine as important as the computer, it is strange to think that the question of who built the first computer was settled in court. A 1973 lawsuit invalidated early patents on the computer, because the judge decided the wrong persons had received credit for developing the first computer.

The early history of the computer involves three individuals, or groups of individuals, and the machines they built. One pair of individuals were John V. Atanasoff of Iowa State University and his graduate assistant, Clifford Berry, who began work on an electronic computer before World War II and finished a working prototype in 1942. Although there was a great deal of interest in computers that could compute artillery tables during the war, the Atanasoff–Berry Computer, or ABC, did not receive much attention. Iowa State did not even attempt to patent the device, and neither man followed up on this early work. The ABC was eventually forgotten and only a few parts of the original machine remain.

Another important individual in the development of the computer is Howard Aiken. In 1944, Aiken completed the MARK I computer for IBM in cooperation with Harvard University. Even though the MARK I had 760,000 electrical parts connected by 500 miles of wiring, it was not completely electronic, because it used 3,000 electromechanical relays as switches. It was so big that an entire building on Harvard's campus was set aside for it.

The pair of individuals who usually receive the credit for developing a purely electronic computer are J. Presper Eckert, Jr., and John Mauchly. Eckert was working on a government project to build a fast computing device when he visited Atanasoff at Iowa State to learn about the ABC. After his meeting, Eckert and Mauchly built the ENIAC (Electrical Numerical Integrator And Calculator) for the war effort. Unfortunately, it was not finished until 1946, after the war. The ENIAC contained 18,000 vacuum tubes and 80,000 resistors and capacitors, weighed 30 tons, and occupied over 15,000 square feet. It was much faster than the MARK I, because it could multiply two numbers in 0.0003 second, compared with over 0.05 second for the MARK I. However, ENIAC used so much electricity that the lights in the section of Philadelphia in which it was located supposedly dimmed each time the computer ran. The ENIAC, which ran for nine years, is now on exhibit at the Smithsonian Institution.

An important advance over the ENIAC was the EDVAC (Electronic Discrete Variable Automatic Computer) developed by John von Neumann. The EDVAC utilized the concept of the stored program, which meant the computer did not have to be rewired for each job as the ENIAC did.

The 1973 court decision named the Atanasoff–Berry team as the builders of the first computer, rather than Eckert and Mauchly. Aiken is best known for getting IBM interested in computers, but the MARK I contributed little to

The Atanasoff–Berry computer was the first electronic computer built, but only a few parts of this computer exist today.

The MARK I computer was the first computer built by International Business Machines Corporation.

J. Presper Eckert, Jr., is shown with the ENIAC computer that he and John Mauchly jointly designed and built.

later developments of the computer. Von Neumann is remembered for adding the stored program concept to the computer.

Generations of Computers

The subsequent development of computers is usually described as occurring in generations. The first generation, which began with Eckert and Mauchly's ENIAC, is considered to span the period 1946–1959. This generation of computers is characterized by the use of vacuum tubes in the CPU and internal memory units, the first commercial computers, and many fundamental advances in computing. The first commercial computer was the UNIVAC 1 (UNIVersal Automatic Computer), which was sold to the Census Bureau in 1951.

In the second generation of computers, 1959–1964, the vacuum tube was replaced by the transistor. The transistor, a solid-state device, was the major breakthrough that allowed computers to have reasonable size and

UNIVAC 1, a first-generation computer and the first computer available commercially, was used to predict the outcome of the 1952 presidential election.

The IBM 360 series of mainframe computers was an extremely popular third-generation computer that played a large role in making IBM a dominant force in the computer industry.

The four generations of computers as exemplified by vacuum tubes, transistorized circuit boards, integrated circuits, and microprocessors.

power. A solid-state device is made of minerals so that it can be instructed to allow or not allow a flow of current. Because solid-state devices did not use the hot filament that was in vacuum tubes, the use of transistors reduced the computer's heat output and power requirement. Transistors also increased the reliability of the computer, because they did not burn out the way vacuum tubes did. This breakthrough in turn reduced the cost of owning and operating a computer. This period saw tremendous growth in the use of computers by government, business, and industry.

The introduction of the integrated circuit in 1965 was the beginning of the third generation of computers. With this technological advance, an entire circuit board containing transistors and connecting wires could be placed on a single chip. This development meant greater reliability and compactness combined with low cost and power requirements. During this period, IBM controlled the mainframe market with its 360 (later to be 370) series of computers. This series was so well

designed and built that its successors are still in heavy use today.

The fourth and current generation of computers began in 1971 with the introduction of the microprocessor—a central processing unit on a chip. This generation includes the introduction of supercomputers. These "monster computers" are in heavy demand for military and meteorological applications that require a high speed of operation. Another important advance of this generation has been the introduction of the personal computer, because the power of the computer has been made available to anybody who wishes to use one.

A possible "fifth generation" of computers has recently been discussed in the media. The Japanese government has a broad-ranging plan to leapfrog American superiority in hardware with a fifth-generation computer that will include parallel processors—several CPUs working in parallel to speed up execution time. No one knows how successful this particular plan will be, but we probably won't have to wait long to find out.

TABLE 2-2
Memory Relationships

1 bit	=	1 on/off switch
1 byte	=	8 bits
1 Kbyte	=	1,024 bytes
1 Mbyte	=	1,024 Kbytes (1,048,576 bytes)
1 Gbyte	=	1,024 Mbytes (1,073,741,824 bytes)

store data, information, and instructions in binary form. The amounts of RAM and ROM available in a particular computer are measured in **Kbytes** (kilobytes) where 1 Kbyte = 1,024 bytes or characters. The letter K stands for *kilo*, which is Greek for 1,000. Even though 1,024 (which is 2^{10}) does not exactly equal 1,000, the term *Kbyte* or simply the letter K has become a standard measure of storage capacity meaning roughly 1,000. For example, 64K of memory means $64 \times 1,024 = 65,535$ bytes of memory. The next measure of memory after a Kbyte is a **Mbyte** (megabyte), which is 1,024 Kbytes, or approximately 1 million (2^{20}) bytes, of storage. Finally, the largest commonly used measure of storage is the **Gbyte** (gigabyte), which is 1,024 Mbytes or approximately 1 *billion* (2^{30}) bytes of storage. Table 2-2 shows these memory relationships.

Early personal computers had less than 16K of RAM, but current machines can have over 16 Mbytes of RAM with 1 Mbyte being a common amount of memory. Mainframe computers usually have at least 64 Mbytes of internal memory available. Less ROM is needed because it is used for a special purpose that the computer designer knows in advance and because the amount varies from computer to computer. In a later chapter, we will discuss special chips that combine the characteristics of RAM and ROM.

Secondary storage is also measured in Kbytes, Mbytes, and Gbytes. Tape and disk storage on mainframe computers is measured in megabytes, and personal computer hard disks storing 40, 80, and over 100 Mbytes are common today. Personal computer floppy disks and microdisks hold from 360 Kbytes to 2.88 Mbytes. Optical disks can store gigabytes of data and information!

1. A conceptual computer is composed of input, output, processing/internal memory, and secondary storage units.

2. The input unit sends data and instructions to the computer; the keyboard is a common input device, with the mouse coming into more common use for personal computers.

3. The processing/internal memory unit performs the manipulation and storage of symbols within the computer.

4. The processing unit is usually referred to as the central processing unit (CPU). It is made up of the control unit and the arithmetic–logic unit (ALU).

5. Internal memory is made up of random-access memory (RAM) and read-only memory (ROM). RAM is accessible to the user for storage of data, programs, and processed information. ROM is built into the computer by the manufacturer and is needed to start up the computer and handle certain operations within the computer.

6. Both the CPU and internal memory are built onto silicon chips that can contain 1 million transistors to handle memory and processing operations.

7. Secondary storage is needed because RAM is both limited and volatile; tape and disk are common secondary storage devices. Mainframe computers use disk packs while personal computers use floppy and hard disks.

8. The output unit transmits the results from the computer to the user; the monitor and printer are common output devices.

9. Communication with another computer is accomplished with a modem that translates computer data into a form that can be transmitted over telephone lines.

10. The binary number system is used in computers because the computer uses on/off switches to handle processing and storage.

11. The EBCDIC or ASCII codes are systems for representing letters, digits, and symbols in eight bits each (a byte); one character corresponds to one byte. EBCDIC is used on IBM mainframes; ASCII is used on all personal computers.

12. Memory is measured in Kbytes (1,024 bytes), Mbytes (1,024 Kbytes), or Gbytes (1,024 Mbytes). Mainframes usually have at least 64 Mbytes of internal storage while personal computers commonly have at least 1 Mbyte of RAM.

13. Secondary storage for mainframes and hard disks for personal computers can store Mbytes of information. Floppy disks and microdisks hold from 360 Kbytes to 2.88 Mbytes.

KEY TERMS

arithmetic–logic unit (ALU)
ASCII (American Standard Code for
    Information Interchange)
backup
binary number system
bit
booting process
byte
cartridge
central processing unit (CPU)
chip
color monitor
computer disk
conceptual computer
control unit
cursor
direct-access storage
disk drive
disk pack
dot matrix printer
dumb terminal
EBCDIC (Extended Binary Coded
    Decimal Interchange Code)
floppy disks
Gbyte
hard copy
hard disk
hardware
IBM compatible PCs
ink-jet printer
input
integrated circuit
internal memory

Kbytes
keyboard
laser printer
light pen
magnetic tape
Mbyte
microprocessor
modem
monitor
monochrome monitor
mouse
optical disk
output
page printer
pen-based computing
printer
processing/internal memory unit
random-access memory (RAM)
read-only memory (ROM)
read/write head
secondary storage
sequential access
system
tape
tape cartridge
tape drive
terminal
touchscreen
transistor
video disk
video display terminal (VDT)
voice recognition
volatile

1. List the four main parts of the conceptual computer.
2. Which part of the computer is comparable to the human brain? to the use of file cabinets?
3. List four items commonly used to input data to a computer.
4. List the two main parts of the processing unit of the computer. What is this combination called?
5. Why are both units needed in the CPU?
6. Differentiate between RAM and ROM. Which is accessible to the user for storage of data, programs, and information?
7. Why is RAM considered to be a volatile form of internal memory? Why is ROM not volatile?
8. Which type of secondary storage device is a direct-access device? Which is a sequential-access secondary storage device?
9. What sizes of disks are available for personal computers? What are the sizes called?
10. List two commonly used output devices for a computer.
11. How are monitors differentiated?
12. Explain the meaning of the term *modem* in computer communications. What is the purpose of a modem?
13. Explain why computers use the binary number system.
14. What are the EBCDIC and ASCII representations of the letter *A*?
15. How much random-access memory is available on most personal computers? What amounts of storage are available for mainframe and personal computer secondary storage?

3

An Introduction to Computer Software

In this chapter, we will introduce the other half of the computer, that is, the software that directs the actions of the hardware. The discussion will cover the importance of software for the successful use of the computer; the three major types of software—systems software, utility software, and applications software; and some important terminology of software packages. (Chapter 9 provides a more complete discussion of systems and utility software.) Six important types of applications packages are introduced in this chapter: word processing, graphics, financial analysis, accounting, data base management, and telecommunications. In each case we will show examples of their use. (Chapters 10 through 13 provide more detailed discussions of these packages.) An introduction to integrated software and desktop publishing is also included in this section.

STUDY OBJECTIVES

After reading this chapter, you should be able to

- understand the importance of software in the successful use of a computer;
- discuss the three major types of software: systems, utility, and applications software;
- recognize the most important terminology of software packages;
- discuss types of user interfaces;
- discuss the difference between a menu-driven package and a command-driven package;
- explain the use of graphical user interfaces;
- list the six important types of applications software widely available for personal computers: word processing, graphics, financial analysis, accounting, data base management, and telecommunications;
- discuss the use of integrated packages and desktop publishing.

SOFTWARE DOWN ON THE FARM

In the world of agribusiness, the key to success is cutting costs. Because farmers have little or no control over the prices they will receive for their crops, their profit often depends on how little they spend on the production side. In the past, much of this cost-cutting depended on experience, guesswork, and just plain luck. However, today, many farmers are using computers to help them run their businesses. In fact, it has been estimated that almost half of all full-time farmers use a computer to help run the farm.

In managing a farm, computer software is used for a wide variety of tasks, ranging from basic accounting to making decisions about crops. One estimate put the number of software packages available to farmers at close to 2,000. Examples of the applications of computer software on the farm are

■ ranking milk cows according to volume of milk produced so that less productive cows can be culled, which may result in a significant reduction in feed costs;

■ assisting potato farmers in determining when to apply pesticides to their crops and when to irrigate their fields, depending on the temperature and humidity;

■ allowing farmers to draw their fields to scale, indicating crops, drainage problems, pest control problems, fertilizer applications, and other pertinent information, some of which can be obtained from satellite photos, about each field.

While the computer produces important information in the planning process, the farmer still must make the final decisions about when to plant, when to harvest, and when to buy and sell. For farmers who are used to paying over $100,000 for their equipment, the cost of a personal computer and the associated software is small potatoes compared to the savings it can produce.

Sources: "Computer Has Grown into a Useful Piece of Farm Equipment," *The Atlanta Journal,* August 21, 1989, p. B9; and interview with John Brunz, executive director of the Association of Agricultural Computing Companies, November 4, 1991.

Computers are becoming a crucial element in managing the modern farm.

Software has been described as the "driving force" of computers and the "wizard in the machine"; its importance to the use of computers cannot be minimized. Even though the hardware advances of the recent decade have been mind-boggling, the computer without software—without the instructions given it by the user or the manufacturer—would be nothing except a well-constructed combination of silicon chips and electronic circuitry. While there are only so many ways that chips and circuitry can be combined to build a computer, the number of different activities a computer can be instructed to perform by software is virtually limitless. The idea of a computer without software has been described as everything from a car without a driver to a camera without film. Any such analogy makes the point: Computer hardware *must* have software to direct it.

In 1990, worldwide sales of computer software were estimated to be over $80 billion, but it is expected that over $1 *trillion* of software will be sold annually by the year 2000. Because each software program must be created by one or more human programmers, not all software has decreased in price as hardware has. Programs that sold for around $500 when introduced in the mid-1980s still sell for that price or for even more.

Uses of software include just about every application imaginable—from playing games to running the family farm as discussed in the opening box. In this chapter, we will introduce the various types of software and the terminology involved in using software. Detailed discussions of the material introduced here are given in Block Three, Applications Software.

Programs and Programming

In Chapter 2, we discussed the idea that a computer manipulates and stores symbols by turning switches on and off. For the computer to know which switches should be on and which off, it must be given very specific instructions or rules. This set of instructions is called a **computer program.** The process of developing the set of instructions that will control the computer and direct it to per-

> **I believe the average businessperson thinks of software as the real power behind computer technology.**
>
> *Gari Grimm, president, WordStar International*
>
> Quoted in "View from the Top," *Personal Computing,* October 1989, p. 268.

> **The software people are the driving force in the computer market and are at the leading edge of computer development.**
>
> *John Imlay, chairman, Management Science America; past president, Association of Data Processing Service Organizations*
>
> From an interview with the author.

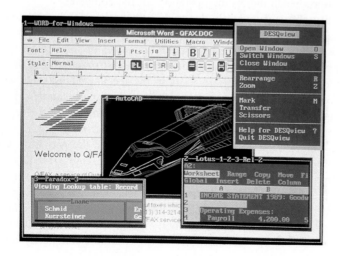

> **Without software, the computer— whether mainframe or personal— can do nothing.**

form a desired action is called **programming.** All software, whether built into the machine by the manufacturer, purchased by the user, or developed by the user, is the result of a person or a group of people creating the set of instructions for the computer.

Since the computer knows only what the program tells it, the program must tell it *everything* it needs to know about the process being executed or the problem being solved. This requires a step-by-step approach, developed by the programmer in such a way that no steps are assumed to be known by the computer. These steps are then converted into a program that is written in a **computer language.** There are many (well over 100) computer languages that can be used to communicate with a computer. Each computer language, like a human language, has its own vocabulary and grammatical rules, but most share a similar logical approach to communication with the computer. Commonly used languages are BASIC, COBOL, FORTRAN, Pascal, LOGO, and C. These and other languages will be discussed in Chapter 17.

Many would-be computer users think programming is the only role of a computer and do not purchase a computer because they do not want to have to learn to program. However, as we have discussed previously, the abundance of software available makes it unnecessary to learn programming to be a successful computer user.

TYPES OF SOFTWARE

An ever-growing number of software packages are available to the computer user. In fact, nobody can make even a reasonable estimate of the number of programs that are available. With this wide variety of software, beginning users can become confused about what they need to purchase. To unravel all of the talk about software packages, we must first categorize the types of software that are used in a computer. The three major categories are systems software, utility software, and applications software. Usually, all three of these software types are at work in the computer at the same time, each serving a different purpose.

The first of these, **systems software,** is extremely important because it controls the operations of the other two types of software as well as controlling the computer itself. The most important part of systems software is the **operating system,** which directs the operations of the computer.

Utility software controls day-to-day "housekeeping" operations. These include such operations as making copies of information, displaying a list of user information, and using different computer languages on a computer.

Applications software constitutes the greatest proportion of the software used on computers. This software performs the specialized tasks that we hear so much about, including calculating payrolls, guiding space shuttles, doing word processing or home budgeting, and playing games. The box at the beginning of the chapter describes the use of applications software in farming.

We can view these three types of software and the way they work concurrently in the computer as an "onion," shown in Figure 3-1. The outer layer of the onion is applications software, which is evident to the user since it is the software that actually performs the desired task. Underneath the applications software is the utility software, which is invisible to the user until a housekeeping chore—such as copying information—is required. Finally, at the core of our "onion" is the systems software, which is almost completely invisible to the user.

Information processing is driven by innovative applications software of a wide variety.

*David S. Samuels, president,
State of the Art Accounting
Software*

Quoted in "View from the Top,"
Personal Computing, October 1989,
p. 268.

FIGURE 3-1
The Onion View of Software

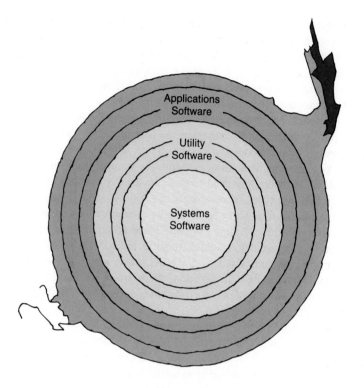

Systems Software

Systems software controls the operation of the computer and makes it possible for the other types of software to execute their tasks. The primary component of systems software is known as the operating system. The operating system manages the many tasks that are going on concurrently within a computer, such

Mainframe operating systems manage the allocation of computer time and resources to multiple users.

as handling the input and output operations and managing the transfer of information between internal memory and the secondary storage. On mainframes, the operating system manages the allocation of processing capability to each of the numerous persons who may be using the computer simultaneously. In this environment, the operating system must also handle all of the requests for different types of operations that come from each of the users.

On a personal computer, the operating system deals with only one user, so an important operation is managing the transfer of information between the internal memory and secondary storage. Since all PCs in use today have the capability of using magnetic disks as secondary storage, the term **disk operating system (DOS)** is commonly used to describe a PC's operating system. Several different brands and types of computers can use the same operating system, so it has been possible to achieve some degree of standardization among personal computers through the operating systems. Three commonly used **generic operating systems** that are not machine specific are MS-DOS (Microsoft DOS), OS/2 (Operating System/Two), and UNIX, all of which run on a variety of makes and models of PCs. In addition, there are several machine-specific or **proprietary operating systems** for machines such as the Apple II series and the Macintosh series of PCs.

These three generic PC operating systems are differentiated by the number of tasks and users they can control. **MS-DOS** is directed toward the use of a single machine to run a single piece of applications software. It is currently the most popular of the three operating systems, with millions of PCs using it. The capability of a personal computer to run MS-DOS software is usually considered

Personal computer operating systems are directed primarily at single-user computer systems.

the criterion for determining whether or not it is an **IBM compatible PC,** that is, a PC that runs software written for the original IBM PC or one of its successors, the IBM PC XT, PC AT, or PS/2 series of computers. Computers that are *not* IBM compatible include the Apple II and Apple Macintosh series.

OS/2 is a single-user, multitasking operating system that was jointly developed in 1987 by IBM and the country's largest PC software developer, Microsoft. With OS/2, a user can run multiple tasks concurrently. For example, the user can work with a word processing package and, at the same time, run a mathematical model that requires several hours to complete its calculations. Finally, **UNIX,** which was originally developed by AT&T for use on minicomputers, has been converted to run on PCs and can direct multiple machines running multiple tasks in a network.

Utility Software

Working on a computer—either a mainframe or a personal computer—requires that the user keep track of a library of information that is organized into files. **Files** are units of information (programs, documents, data, and so on) to which the user or software can assign a name. The systems, utility, and applications software all work with files. A common utility software command is to provide a list of the names of the files. Files are often modified, copied between disks or between disk and tape, or combined with language software to write and run programs. These and numerous other operations fall into the utility software category.

In many cases, the utility software is integrated with the system software in such a way that the user gives a single command and the combination of operating system and utility software carries it out. For example, Figure 3-2 shows the result of using the MS-DOS directory command (DIR), which lists

> **We're going to create the software that puts a computer on every desk and in every home.**
>
> *William Gates, founder and CEO, Microsoft Software*
>
> Quoted in Susan Lammers, *Programmers at Work* (Redmond, Wash.: Microsoft Press, 1986), p. 82.

```
A:\-> dir

Volume in drive A is MSWARE1-400
Directory of  A:\

RESUME           24751    1-20-90    1:04p
PRESNTED 390      5558    1-01-80    1:40a
RAGSDALE VPI      2827    1-22-90   10:05a
FLAATL   CHR      4119    1-01-80   11:49a
MISC              2842    2-27-90    6:03a
WORDPROC DOC      2268    4-17-90    4:20p
CHRISLTR 221      3050    2-21-90   12:50a
RESUME   290     26852    2-27-90    6:07a
SUMMARY  90       2955    1-01-80    8:10a
PUBS     390     10758    1-01-80    1:36a
DRAFT    DAT       528    3-02-90   12:29a
DATA1    DAT       528    3-02-90   10:35a
EXAM2    F88      3484   11-14-88    6:51a
PROJECTE INP       936    3-02-90    5:58a
PLAYER   DAT       230    3-07-90   12:08a
MS815             3286    2-18-88   12:08p
FIG3-13  PIX      2317    4-19-90   12:06p
    17 File(s)    256000 bytes free

A:\->
```

FIGURE 3-2
MS-DOS Directory Command

GETTING HELP WITH ALGEBRA

For many students entering the ninth grade, the prospect of studying algebra gives them chills. They have heard "horror" stories from older students about the difficulties they will face with such arcane topics as graphing, factoring equations, solving systems of equations, and formulating word problems. When students go into an algebra class, they see teachers writing strange symbols on the blackboard, and they find it is much more fun to send a note to a friend than it is to pay attention. As a result, many students fall behind and lose interest. Now, however, a new educational software system may take much of the fear out of learning algebra.

Learning Logic is a system developed by the National Science Center Foundation, a nonprofit group dedicated to improving mathematics education in the United States. It allows students to work on a progression of lessons at their own pace. When a student fails to solve a problem, Learning Logic explains why the answer was wrong and provides another similar problem to be solved. In a year-long study in one high school, the system dramatically improved test results in the Algebra I class. Prior to the introduction of Learning Logic, 35 percent of the ninth graders dropped the course. Subsequently, only 12 percent dropped the course. Similarly, only 23 percent of the students failed Algebra I, as compared to 44 percent the previous year.

> **This system is designed to teach a process that's understandable, to keep students in the pipeline, and let teachers be mentors, be tutors.**
>
> *Dr. Fred Davison, President, National Science Center Foundation*
>
> Quoted in McKay Jenkins, "Count on Computers to Solve the Problem," *The Atlanta Journal-Constitution*, August 21, 1991, p. G2.

the names of files on the user's disk. This is an operating system command that actually carries out a utility software operation. There also exists utility software, separate from the operating system, for working with files. Examples include PC Tools and the Norton Utilities.

Applications Software

By far the largest amount of software available to the computer user is in the area of applications software. The applications for which software has been writ-

The Learning Logic system runs on a UNIX-based system using a special type of workstation called an **x-terminal,** which uses high-resolution graphics to display subscripts and special symbols on the screen. When fully implemented, the Learning Logic system will be composed of three online systems—Calculator, Graphulator, and Formulator—that, respectively, allow the student to make complex calculations, graph as many as four equations on the screen, and enter equations for which various operations can be carried out. The Formulator allows the student to carry out factoring, expanding, line multiplication, line addition, and root finding. Initial experience suggests that this system will foster student exploration and problem-solving skills and allow the teacher to become a mentor to the students.

Source: McKay Jenkins, "Count on Computers to Solve the Problem," *The Atlanta Journal-Constitution,* August 21, 1991, p. G2.

Students at the National Science Center are using Learning Logic software to learn scientific concepts at their own pace.
From National Science Center Foundation.

ten cover the entire range of human activities. Applications software is available for a wide range of topics, such as religion, politics, astronomy, marriage counseling, contract bridge, horse racing, generation of lottery numbers, genealogy, finance, word processing, and ham radio. All the computer applications discussed in Chapter 1 are examples of the use of applications software. In fact, it would be safe to say that software exists (or will soon exist) for any topic you can think of.

Most applications software is available in the form of **software packages,** which include programs and a written description, called the **documentation,** of the program. The documentation will often include a **user's manual** that provides detailed instructions on using the package.

A problem with applications software is how to find the proper software for a given application. Mainframe computer centers usually have libraries that contain information on new software as well as offer classes on using software. Personal computer software is widely advertised in specialty magazines such as *Byte* and *PC/Computing* and is sold through retail outlets and by mail. Software packages are often reviewed in newspapers and magazines, and seminars and classes on using existing software are also available.

Software Package Terminology

The use of computer packages has spawned a new software terminology, which a new user needs to learn. One overused term in reference to computer packages and to computers in general is "user friendly." A **user-friendly** package is supposed to be easy to use. Unfortunately, many packages that are advertised as user friendly are really quite difficult to use because of their complexity. In some cases it is not possible for sophisticated business packages to be totally user friendly because they are designed to solve complicated problems. Successful use of these packages may actually require many hours of instruction.

Different software packages have different types of **user interface,** that is, different ways to enter data and commands. The three most common of these user interfaces are menu driven, command driven, and graphical. In a **menu-driven package,** a **menu** either gives the user a list of commands from which to choose or requests that data be entered, in a particular form. Two very common methods of menu selection are (1) to enter a letter or a number and (2) to move the highlighting to the desired selection. In many cases, the user will not only select from a menu, but will also be asked to enter a file name or specific data. For example, in an accounting package, a menu may request users to enter the amounts they wish to budget for various categories. Figure 3-3 shows the

(Left) Many computer magazines carry information on software as well as reviews of various packages. (Right) Software for personal computers is often sold in boxes that contain both a software disk and written instructions.

On a mainframe computer system, software programs and data are often stored on disk until a user requests them.

menu system from the WordPerfect word processing package, in which the user makes a selection simply by entering a number. Figure 3-4 shows the menu system for Lotus 1-2-3, in which the user can move the highlighting to make a selection or can enter the first letter of the desired option.

One widely used type of menu system is the **pull-down menu,** so called because making a selection from a menu results in the appearance of a submenu, from which a choice can be made. Figure 3-5 shows the use of a pull-down menu system on the Apple Macintosh.

At the opposite extreme from menu-driven packages are command-driven packages. A **command-driven package** does not provide a list of commands to choose from or request a specific type of data; instead, it simply waits for the user to enter the appropriate command or data. It may show a **prompt** to alert

```
Format

    1 - Line
            Hyphenation                  Line Spacing
            Justification                Margins Left/Right
            Line Height                  Tab Set
            Line Numbering               Widow/Orphan Protection

    2 - Page
            Center Page (top to bottom)  New Page Number
            Force Odd/Even Page          Page Numbering
            Headers and Footers          Paper Size/Type
            Margins Top/Bottom           Suppress

    3 - Document
            Display Pitch                Redline Method
            Initial Codes/Font           Summary

    4 - Other
            Advance                      Overstrike
            Conditional End of Page      Printer Functions
            Decimal Characters           Underline Spaces/Tabs
            Language

Selection: 0
```

FIGURE 3-3
Menu System in WordPerfect 5.1

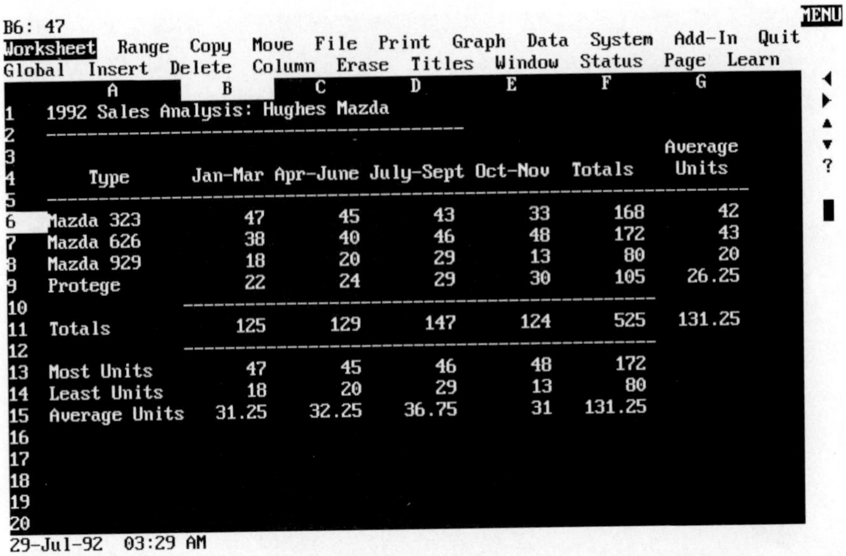

FIGURE 3-4
Menu System in Lotus 1-2-3

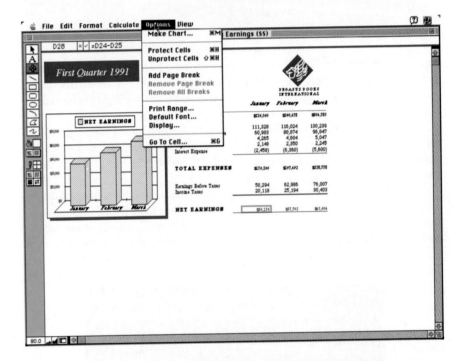

FIGURE 3-5
Pull-Down Menu Interface

the user that it is time to enter a command or data and to indicate where to enter it. Using a command-driven package requires that the user read the package documentation to learn the necessary commands, or take classes in using the package. Examples of command-driven packages are the MS-DOS operating system and the dBASE data base management software. In Figure 3-2, shown earlier, the DIR (directory) command was entered at the MS-DOS prompt (the > symbol).

The type of user interface that is currently gaining popularity is the **graphical user interface,** or **GUI.** In a GUI, **icons** (pictures) are used to represent the functions to be performed, and a mouse is used to position the cursor or pointer

over the desired function. Once you have positioned the cursor over an icon, you press a button on the mouse and the function is carried out. With a little practice, it is possible to make choices from the menu—enter commands—very quickly. The use of GUI was pioneered on the Apple Macintosh, but many packages for IBM compatible computers now use a GUI. In fact, one of the reasons the popular Windows operating environment was developed was to provide MS-DOS users with this type of interface. Figure 3-6 shows the use of a GUI on the Apple Macintosh, and Figure 3-7 shows its use in Windows 3.1.

There are advantages and disadvantages to all three types of interfaces, and what appears to be an advantage in one may be a disadvantage in another. For packages with a menu-driven interface or a GUI, the advantage is that the user does not have to learn a series of commands before using the package. The user has only to make a selection from a menu or choose the appropriate icon. However, once the user has learned the commands for the package, it can be bothersome to wait for the the next menu or set of icons before making a selection. For a novice user, a command-driven interface can be difficult to use because it is necessary to know both the proper commands and the appropriate spot on the screen to enter them. Of course, once the data format and list of

It's just a different world [Windows] and just a dramatically better way of using a PC.

Bill Gates, founder and CEO of Microsoft

Quoted in Russell Glitman, "Windows 3.0: The Realization of Bill Gates' Grand Plan," *PC Week,* May 22, 1990, p. S–15.

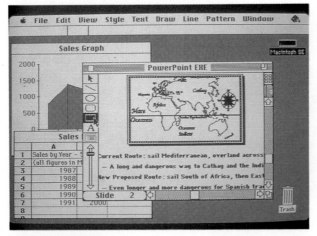

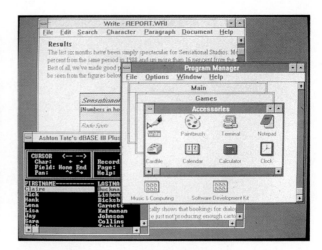

FIGURE 3-6 (left)
Graphical User Interface on
Apple Macintosh

FIGURE 3-7 (right)
Graphical User Interface in
Windows 3.1

commands are learned, data or commands can be quickly entered to a command-driven package.

Some packages allow users to begin with a menu-driven format and then move to a command-driven format as they become familiar with the package. For example, the package may have you enter the first letter of a command rather than moving the highlighting to the command, or may permit you to actually turn off the menu system. Lotus 1-2-3 is an example of the first type of package and dBASE is an example of the second.

APPLICATIONS SOFTWARE FOR THE PERSONAL COMPUTER

Currently, a great deal of business applications software is used on mainframe computers to handle the many large-scale processing tasks that businesses face. At the same time, personal computer applications software is becoming more and more important both in business and at home. While mainframe computers are used for large-scale data processing applications, applications software on a PC is often used to perform various types of analyses, handle record keeping, carry out text preparation, and so on. Because PC applications software allows individuals to increase their productivity, it is often referred to as **personal productivity software.** The six most widely used types of applications software for the PC are word processing, graphics, spreadsheets, accounting software, data base management, and telecommunications. Figure 3-8 shows the distribution of sales of PC software packages in 1991.

The discussion here briefly describes what each type of package can do for a user. (The packages are discussed in much more detail in Chapters 10–13.) Integrated software and desktop publishing are also introduced in this section.

Word Processing

The user was empowered by the [PC] technology rather than being alienated from it.

Mitch Kapor, founder of Lotus Development Corporation

Quoted in Richard March, "Explosive PC Decade Ends on Cautious Note," *PC Week,* January 1, 1990, p. 10.

One of the most useful functions of a personal computer is the ability to easily compose, edit, and print various types of documents with **word processing software.** While text entry, editing, and printing are important capabilities of word processing software, they are not the only ones. In fact, the software can do a

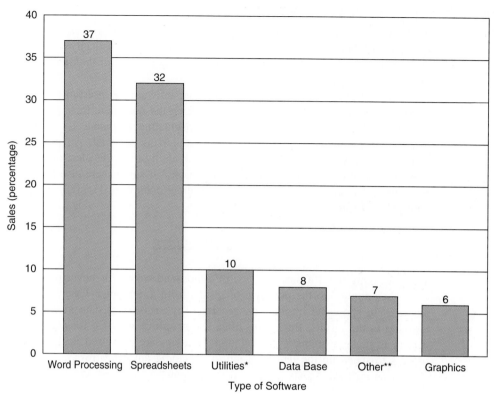

*Including telecommunications
**Including accounting software

FIGURE 3-8
1991 PC Software Market Share

Source: Computer Intelligence, La Jolla, CA.

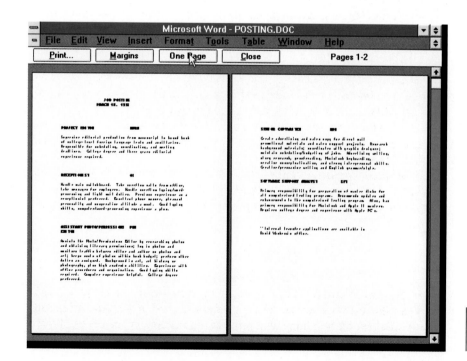

Microsoft Word, an extremely
popular word processing package,
allows the user to preview the
document before printing it.

great many more tasks. For example, it allows easy setting of margins, line spacing, and tabs to arrive at a desired page format. When the text is entered from the keyboard, lines will "wrap around" the margins by automatically continuing to the next line. All these free the user from having to monitor the margins and "return" the cursor at the appropriate time.

Other useful functions of word processing software are inserting, deleting, or striking over material on the screen; searching the document for a particular sequence of characters; centering material; paginating automatically; and, on most packages, underlining, boldfacing, or italicizing material. An important operation with word processing software is the ability to "cut" electronically a block of material from the document and "paste" it somewhere else either in the current document or in a completely different document. Figure 3-9 shows a document being created in WordPerfect 5.1.

Graphics Software

The old saying that "a picture is worth a thousand words" is never more true than when applied to the portrayal of results from a computer. Using a bar or pie chart to show the information generated by analysis of data gives added meaning to the results. Businesses often use **graphics** software for analysis of data or to make a dramatic presentation. Graphics are also used in the design process to speed up the laborious job of designing anything from a computer chip to an airliner. Artists are also using "paint packages" to create fantastic artwork on the computer.

For business analysis and presentation purposes, the most commonly used types of graphics are the line chart, which simply connects a series of points; the pie chart, which assigns a section of a round pie proportional to the quantity of data; the bar chart, which draws a series of either horizontal or vertical bars

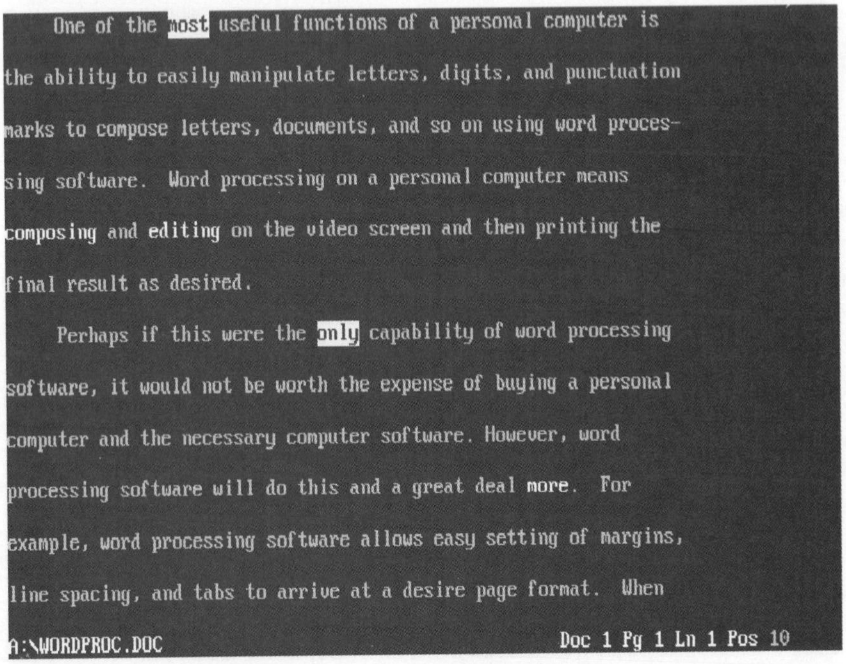

One of the most useful functions of a personal computer is the ability to easily manipulate letters, digits, and punctuation marks to compose letters, documents, and so on using word processing software. Word processing on a personal computer means composing and editing on the video screen and then printing the final result as desired.

Perhaps if this were the only capability of word processing software, it would not be worth the expense of buying a personal computer and the necessary computer software. However, word processing software will do this and a great deal more. For example, word processing software allows easy setting of margins, line spacing, and tabs to arrive at a desire page format. When

A:\WORDPROC.DOC   Doc 1 Pg 1 Ln 1 Pos 10

FIGURE 3-9
Document in WordPerfect 5.1

FIGURE 3-10
Presentation Graphics

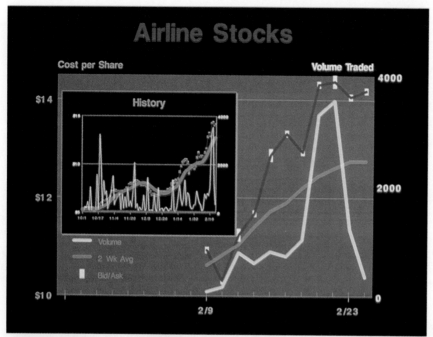

Paint packages can be used to develop beautiful, complex pictures on the computer screen.

GETTING HELP FROM YOUR PC IN GETTING THERE

Have you ever wanted to go across the state or across the nation but were unsure of the best route to follow? If you ask your friends which route to follow, you will probably get different answers, each of which is the "best," according to each friend. If you have faced this problem, then AUTOMAP, the PC-based software package, may answer your question.

AUTOMAP, which runs on both IBM compatible PCs and the Apple Macintosh, will provide an onscreen map showing the fastest, prettiest, or most convenient route between any two points in the United States. You can look at the entire United States or zoom in on a particular region to obtain more detail. The software will print the map and detailed driving instructions that list the roads you will be traveling, the exact distance you will travel on a particular road, where to turn, and which signs to look for. AUTOMAP contains information about 359,220 miles of roads and 51,921 places. It is programmed to find the best route for your requirements and to provide you with alternative routes, in case you decide to wander. Surveys show that AUTOMAP can reduce driving time and related costs for its users.

Source: Allison Sprout, "PC Road Atlas," *Fortune,* October 7, 1991, p. 116.

Automap software can help travelers find the fastest, prettiest, or most convenient route between two locations.

depicting the data; and the scatter diagram, which plots points on the X–Y scale. Figure 3-10 shows a presentation graph created with Harvard Graphics—a popular presentation graphics program.

Spreadsheets

Also known as **financial analysis software,** this use of the personal computer is built around a table of rows and columns called a **spreadsheet.** The user enters values and labels into **cells** at the intersection of the rows and columns. Various relationships between the values in the table are then defined using formulas that are also entered in cells. Whenever the user changes a value, the package uses the formulas to recompute all other values that depend on the changed value.

This sort of analysis allows the user to determine the effect of changing the values or assumptions in the spreadsheet. The capability of spreadsheet software to recalculate all values whenever a single value or assumption is changed is extremely important. A manager working with the budgetary or planning process can test many assumptions or scenarios by changing a few values or formulas and then letting the spreadsheet do the work. Most spreadsheets now also incorporate both graphics and data base management capabilities. Figure 3-11 shows a spreadsheet and corresponding graph created in Lotus 1-2-3.

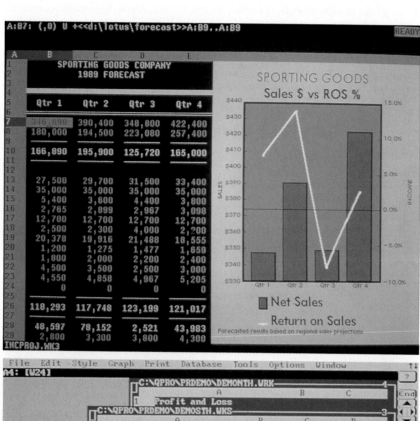

FIGURE 3-11
Lotus 1-2-3 Spreadsheet

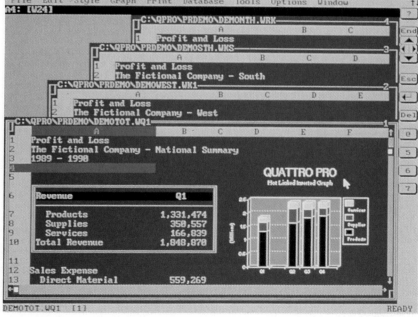

Quattro Pro from Borland is a competitor of Lotus 1-2-3.

Accounting Software

For businesses, **accounting software** is extremely important since the accounting function enables a business to keep up-to-date and accurate records of its financial position. Using the output from accounting software, a firm is better able to make both short-term and long-term plans. Accounting packages come in various levels of specialization, ranging from general packages to industry-specific packages and even firm-specific packages.

While it is unrealistic to think that a family needs full-scale accounting software, there are home budgeting software packages available that meet the needs of the average family. These packages allow a family to computerize its budget and to record cash inflows and outflows in a manner similar to business accounting packages. Figure 3-12 shows the use of a popular **personal budgeting package**—Managing Your Money.

Data Base Management Software

A common operation both at work and at home is that of storing information. This storage may be as simple as a 3- by 5-inch index card box of recipes or as complex as rows of filing cabinets containing personnel records. We may wish to rearrange the information or search for a particular element or group of elements that has specific attributes. With **data base management software,** a user can perform the same operations on a computer. In a sense, this type of package acts as an "electronic filing clerk." The term **data base** refers to *a collection of information that is arranged for easy manipulation and retrieval.*

The simplest data base management packages enable their users to create a single data base file that can be rearranged or searched as needed. More sophis-

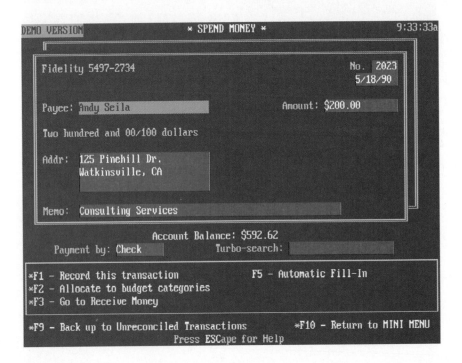

FIGURE 3-12
Personal Budgeting Package

ticated packages enable the user to work with multiple data base files to find and manage information. An important operation using data base management software is **sorting.** When a data base file is sorted, it is arranged according to characteristic, for example, in alphabetical order or in numerical order, depending on the user's need.

Another important operation in working with a data base is that of retrieving elements that match a given criterion. The user can also specify a second and even a third criterion, and the elements that match all of the criteria can then be output. Data base management packages are very important when an individual or a firm must manage large volumes of data in such a way that information needed to make a decision is easily found. Figure 3-13 shows a list of data base records from dBASE IV.

FIGURE 3-13
Data Base Records from
dBASE IV

| Records | Organize | Fields | Go To | Exit | | |

INVOICE	INV_DATE	DEALER_NUM	PRODUCT	SALES_REP	LOCATION	QUANTITY
3271	05/10/92	NY2509	SB2200	NY100	Erie	1
3272	05/12/92	VA3782	SB2800	VA200	Chesapeake	1
3273	05/12/92	MD8943	DS1800	MD250	Chesapeake	1
3274	05/13/92	NY1765	DS1800	NY100	Ontario	1
3275	05/17/92	VA3782	DS1800	VA200	Chesapeake	1
3276	05/18/92	PA2784	SB3000	PA100	Erie	1
3277	05/20/92	MD8943	SB2800	MD250	Chesapeake	1
3278	05/22/92	VA2556	SB2500	VA200	Chesapeake	1
3279	05/25/92	PA7843	SB2200	PA100	Erie	1
3280	05/26/92	MD3789	SB2700	MD250	Chesapeake	1

| Browse | C:\dbase\SALES | Rec 1/10 | File | |

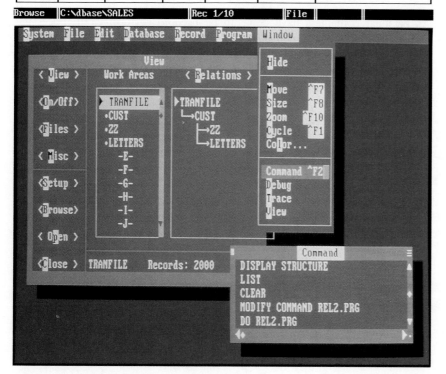

FoxPro is another popular data base management package for use on personal computers.

Telecommunications Software

In our discussion of computer hardware, we mentioned that the computer could be used for communication. Software and hardware are now available that allow us to use a personal computer for communication with other computers. The **telecommunications software** is combined with a modem to make the computer output and input compatible with telephone transmission signals. The combination of the communication package and the modem then allows the personal computer user to communicate with mainframe computers or with other personal computers. There are national networks that can be used via the communication package/modem combination to send electronic mail, post messages on an electronic bulletin board, or access national general-purpose or special-interest data bases. Figure 3-14 shows a list of telephone numbers that have been stored in a popular telecommunications package—Procomm Plus—for future calls.

Telecommunications links also allow both mainframes and personal computers to be linked in what are called **computer networks.** A computer network can be a **wide area network (WAN)** that connects computers over great distances or a **local area network (LAN)** that connects computers within the same geographic area. LANs have generated a great deal of interest because of the need for personal computer users to share information and peripherals. Another important consideration is the micro-to-mainframe link, which allows users of personal computers to communicate with mainframes to obtain information or to carry out processing projects that are too big for a personal computer. It has been said that the stand-alone computer (one that is not connected to other computers) will soon be a thing of the past.

Integrated Software

As personal computers have come to be used to perform word processing, graphic design, spreadsheet analysis, data base management, accounting, and telecommunications, users have needed the capability of moving back and forth between these and other types of packages. For example, a person using a word processing package to write a report may need to include in the document a table

FIGURE 3-14
(Left) Telephone Numbers Stored on Procomm Plus. (Right) Prodigy offers its subscribers many options, such as this market update service.

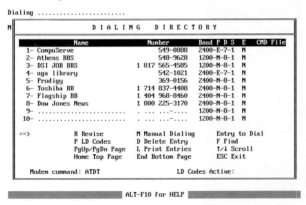

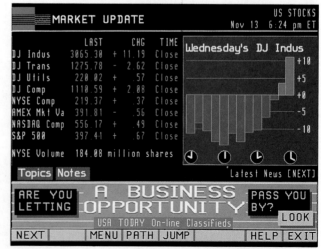

from a spreadsheet package or a bar chart from a graphics package. One way to handle this task is to cut the table or chart physically from the hard copy of the spreadsheet or graphics document and paste it into the hard copy of the word processing document. However, this can be very inconvenient and can result in a document with an unprofessional appearance.

What the user would like to do is electronically shift the table or chart from the spreadsheet or graphics package into the word processing document. This too can be a problem if the form in which a table or chart is saved is incompatible with the form the word processing package can accept. To provide an easy-to-use method for working simultaneously with multiple operations—that is, graphics, spreadsheets, word processing, and so on—integrated packages have been developed. An **integrated package** contains some or all of the most commonly used operations, with a specific procedure for shifting between operations. Popular integrated packages for personal computers include Lotus Works from Lotus, Framework from Ashton-Tate, and Microsoft Works. Because of their importance to users today and their close relationship to spreadsheets, integrated packages are discussed in Chapter 11 on financial analysis packages.

The use of multiple operations and the capability to transfer information between operations are often tied together through windows. A **window** is a section of the monitor screen that displays the current status of an operation. For example, an integrated package may use a window to display the status of a spreadsheet while a word processing document is being edited. Windows may also be used to display the current status of multiple operations that are using the same data. For example, an integrated package may use one window to display a spreadsheet and another window to display the graph associated with that spreadsheet. Windows are also used with some operating systems to show the output from different packages that are running concurrently on the computer and to show full-motion video on the screen. Figure 3-15 shows an example of the use of windows in an integrated package.

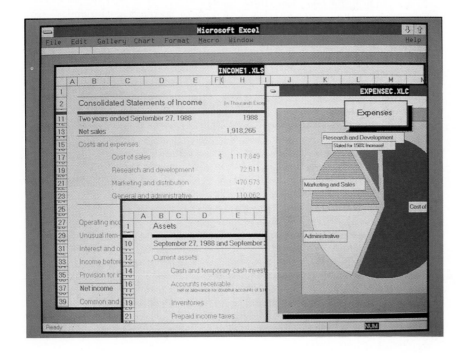

FIGURE 3-15
Uses of Windows

An **operating environment** is a type of software that is growing in use. It works with MS-DOS to provide one or more of the following features: a graphical interface, the capability to concurrently run multiple tasks, and the capability to use windows to see the output for programs that are running concurrently. The growing popularity of operating environments tends to reduce the need for integrated packages, since operating environments allow a user to switch between applications without leaving the package. Popular types of operating environment packages are Windows 3.1, Desqview, and GEOS. Operating environments will be discussed in detail in Chapter 9.

Desktop Publishing

One of the best examples of the power of personal computing lies in the area of desktop publishing. **Desktop publishing** combines word processing, graphics, and special page definition software to create documents that rival those available from professional typesetting houses. That is, a document created on a word processor is combined with graphics and then transformed into a form like that seen on the pages of this textbook. This involves such operations as the use of various sizes and types of fonts and typefaces, the use of proportional spacing to lead to a flush-right margin and an attractive text layout, and the combination of text and graphics on the page in a meaningful manner. Desktop publishing is covered in more detail as a part of Chapter 10 on word processing and graphics. Figure 3-16 shows a document being worked on with a popular desktop publishing package—Pagemaker from Aldus.

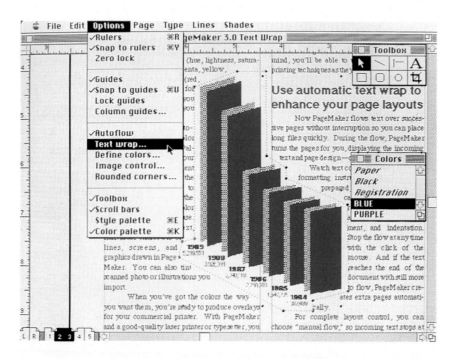

FIGURE 3-16
Document in Desktop Publishing Package

Buying Computer Software

While it is impossible to give a complete guide to buying all types of software in a paragraph or two, some general guidelines for would-be software users may be helpful. A more complete discussion and purchase guidelines for each type of software will be given in later chapters where the various types of software are discussed.

The most general guideline that can be given is the same one that you would apply to buying a car: Try it before you buy. First, determine the software that you think will fit your needs. Second, find a source of this type of software, such as a computer store. Then go to that store and try out the software on your type of computer. Be sure to allow enough time to try all of the functions of the software needed for your particular use. If the software fails to perform as advertised or the store does not want you to take the time to try out the software, go elsewhere. Remember, a piece of software that works fine on an Apple II will not work on an IBM PS/2, Compaq Deskpro, or even an Apple Macintosh. For this reason, it is crucial to match up your hardware and operating system with the prospective software before buying.

If you have not yet purchased a personal computer, select the software first, determine which computer runs the software, and then buy the two—hardware and software—as a package. This approach comes closest to ensuring that you will be happy with both.

When you are buying the software, you should be aware of two types of inexpensive utility and application software: freeware and shareware. **Freeware** is software that is distributed at a very low (often zero) cost by computer users' groups or by individuals. It is not copyrighted; therefore, it is in the **public domain** and may be copied legally. In fact, it is usually placed on electronic bulletin boards, so anyone with a modem and telecommunications software can transfer it to his or her computer. One shortcoming of freeware is that, usually, there is little or no support beyond that included with the software.

Whereas freeware is distributed without support, **shareware** is software for which support is available for a small fee (often from $25 to $89). Users who pay the fee are then registered and become eligible to receive new versions of the software as they become available, as well as continuous support for the product.

> **With the right match of user and software, positive results are almost assured.**
>
> *Fred Gibbons, chairman,*
> *Software Publishing Company*
>
> Quoted in "One Size of Software Doesn't Fit All," *Personal Computing,* October 1987, p. 232.

BITS OF HISTORY

A Software Time Line

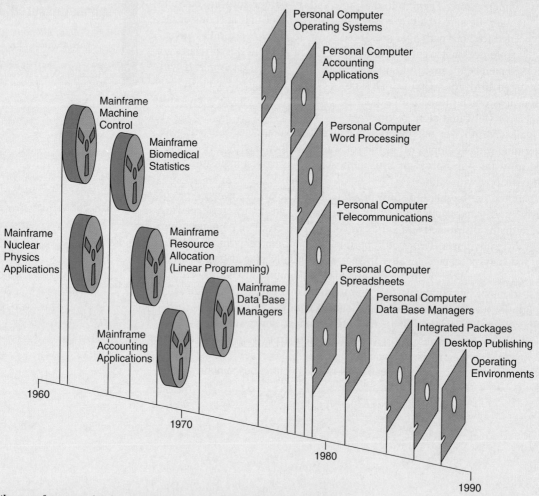

As in the case of computer hardware, software has moved—almost explosively since the late 1970s—from being the tool mainly of large research institutions to contributing immensely to the productivity of small businesses and interest groups and individual users.

1. The computer hardware must have software, in the form of computer programs, to control its actions. Software is the crucial element in the computer.

2. A software package is made up of one or more computer programs and some type of documentation. Software packages allow nonprogrammers to use the computer to achieve a desired objective.

3. Computer programs are written in one of many computer languages and provide the instructions that the computer must follow.

4. There are three types of software: systems, utility, and applications. Systems software manages the computer's operations; utility software handles housekeeping chores, including keeping track of a user's files; applications software performs the actual tasks as directed by the user.

5. The key part of the systems software is the operating system that manages the operations of all other parts of the computer. On a personal computer, this is usually referred to as a disk operating system, or DOS.

6. Applications software packages have become very popular.

7. Packages can also be menu driven or command driven depending on whether the user chooses from a menu or must already know the information to be entered.

8. Graphical user interfaces combined with a mouse have been found to be very easy to use.

9. The six most important types of business software packages for the personal computer are word processing, graphics, spreadsheets, accounting, data base management, and telecommunications.

10. Word processing software allows a user to compose, edit, and print documents from the computer keyboard. Graphics packages are useful in analyses of data, in presentations, and for creating art forms using the computer.

11. Financial analysis software creates budgets or forecasts from a table (also called a spreadsheet) of values, labels, and formulas. Accounting packages enable a business to monitor its financial well-being; personal budgeting packages do much of the same for the individual.

12. With a data base management package, a user can manipulate large files of data to find desired information.

13. Telecommunications software enables the computer to use a modem and telephone lines to link up with other computers.

14. Integrated software combines all of the applications software capabilities into one package. An operating environment allows MS-DOS–based machines to carry out multitasking.

15. Desktop publishing combines word processing, graphics, and page layout to publish documents of a professional standard.

KEY TERMS

accounting software
applications software
cells
command-driven package
computer language
computer network
computer package
computer program
data base
data base management software
desktop publishing
disk operating system (DOS)
documentation
files
financial analysis software
freeware
generic operating system
graphical user interface (GUI)
graphics software
IBM compatible PC
icons
integrated package
local area network (LAN)
menu
menu driven package

MS-DOS
operating environment
operating system
OS/2
personal budgeting software
personal productivity software
programming
prompt
proprietary operating system
pull-down menu
shareware
software
software package
sorting
spreadsheet
systems software
telecommunications software
UNIX
user friendly
user's manual
utility software
wide area network (WAN)
window
word processing software
x-terminal

1. Discuss the importance of software to the use of a computer.
2. Explain the role of programming in the preparation of computer software.
3. Name the three major categories of software that work concurrently in a computer. Discuss the purpose of each type of software.
4. What is a DOS? What role does it play in the use of the personal computer?
5. What type of software allows a user to keep track of a library of files? What is a common operation performed with a library of files?
6. Explain why the availability of software packages opens up the use of computers to many people.
7. What is the difference between a menu-driven package and a command-driven package? Discuss the advantages and disadvantages of each.
8. How is a mouse used in selecting commands? What is an icon? What is a pull-down menu?
9. List the six different business applications software packages discussed in the text. Which of these would you like to have available for your use? What would you use it for?
10. Discuss a situation in your home, school, club, fraternity, or sorority in which a financial analysis package (spreadsheet) would be useful to you.
11. Discuss a use for a data base management package. (Hint: Such packages can generate mailing lists by matching the names and a desired criterion.)
12. Discuss the use of a graphics package to analyze the data from a midterm examination.
13. Discuss how you might use a telecommunications software package.
14. Discuss how you might use an integrated package. How does an integrated package differ from an operating environment?
15. Discuss how you might use desktop publishing.

4

An Introduction to Information Systems

This chapter is an overview of information systems and their impact on organizations. We will define information systems, discuss them briefly, and then discuss each of the types of information systems that are used in organizations. The chapter next takes up the process known as systems analysis and design for assessing and solving problems within information systems. A seven-step procedure is outlined for systems analysis and design and an important type of problem that is addressed by systems analysis and design—software development—is discussed.

STUDY OBJECTIVES

After reading this chapter, you should be able to

- understand the importance of information systems to any organization;
- describe the various managerial levels in an organization;
- discuss various types of information systems and their relationship to managerial levels;
- understand the role of the office information system relative to the other types of information systems;
- describe the characteristics of an expert system and a strategic information system;
- understand the systems analysis and design process and the role of the systems analyst;
- list the seven steps in the systems life cycle and discuss the role each plays in the analysis and design of an information system;
- explain the relationship between software development and the process of systems analysis and design.

INFORMATION SYSTEMS AT WAL-MART

One of the reasons that Wal-Mart is the fastest-growing retailer in the United States is its emphasis on the use of information systems (IS) to support retail operations. Wal-Mart, which grew from 276 stores to over 1,400 by 1990, has always viewed information technology as a key part of its strategic thrust. As one industry analyst put it,

Wal-Mart stands out in the use of information technology because it was the first retailer to realize that IS was "integral to their success. They've been pursuing this for the last ten years." It is estimated that Wal-Mart has invested over $500 million in information technology over the last five years.

Wal-Mart has the industry's first private satellite network, which links almost 1,600 computers at stores, distribution centers, and central management in Arkansas. This satellite network gives Wal-Mart the capability to collect and distribute ordering and sales information quickly. It also allows for the constant flow of information between the operating, merchandising, and distributing functions. Wal-Mart also has information systems that monitor each store's daily sales and

inventory and send these data to Wal-Mart's 17 distribution centers around the country. This allows Wal-Mart to provide a "quick response" to sales trends without carrying large in-store inventories—the retail industry's equivalent to the use of just-in-time systems in the manufacturing industry.

In addition to these systems, online storage capacity is growing at the rate of 100 percent per year, and about 5,000 terminals are added each year, including point-of-sale devices, personal computers, and handheld radio units. There are also over 4,000 users of the company's office information system.

Source: Ellis Booker, "IS Trailblazing Puts Retailer on Top," *Computerworld*, February 12, 1990, pp. 69–70.

Wal-Mart's point-of-sale/IS system has helped to make it one of the nation's fastest-growing retail chains.

INFORMATION SYSTEMS IN ORGANIZATIONS

Recall from Chapter 1 that information systems are crucial to an organization's well-being because of the value of information. Multiple information systems are often required to facilitate the processing, storage, retrieval, and flow of information throughout the organization. This is clearly shown in the box that discusses the importance of information systems to the success of the retailing giant Wal-Mart. An **information system** may be defined as *a combination of support staff, hardware, and software that facilitates the processing, storage, retrieval, and flow of information to support decision making.* In this definition, information systems are more than just computer hardware and software; they also must include the all-important human support staff, and they must serve to support the managerial decision making that ultimately determines the future well-being of the organization.

At one time, information systems depended strictly on manual processing of raw data into information that managers used in making decisions. For the last 30 years, the computer has taken over more and more of this manual processing. Now the **computer-based information system (CBIS)** has become synonymous with the concept of the information system in general, and it would be virtually impossible for businesses to be competitive without computers. The term **data processing** has been closely tied to CBISs because of the need to process data into a meaningful form. However, data processing is only the purely mechanical function of processing raw data. For a CBIS to be truly useful to management, it must provide the information in a useful form, for example, as a report, as graphics, or as spreadsheet analysis. This requires a data base management system of the type discussed in Chapter 3 to store the processed data in a data base. Recall that a **data base** is a collection of information that is arranged for easy manipulation and retrieval. Once stored in the data base, the information can be retrieved as needed by the **data base management system (DBMS).** A conceptual CBIS is shown in Figure 4-1, which illustrates the relationship between raw data, information, the data base, and the DBMS.

Systems in General

An information system is one of many *systems* that simultaneously coexist within an organization. A **system** is *a group of elements (people, machines, cells, etc.) organized for the purpose of achieving a particular goal.* Within the organization, there may also be a management system, a manufacturing system, a distribution system, and so forth. However, because the information system provides information to all of these other systems, and because it relies on computers, we provide an in-depth discussion of it in this chapter. While the discussion of systems analysis and design later in the chapter is aimed at developing information systems, the process can be used in developing any type of system.

Most systems have some attributes in common, including input, processing, output, feedback, an environment, and a boundary. The **input, processing, and output** elements have much the same relationships in a system generally as they do in a computer. Data enter the system as input, which is processed in some way and then output as information. **Feedback** is a form of output that, when sent back to the input or processing function of the system for review, indicates to the system whether a change in operation is necessary. Feedback can come from within the system or from the environment. In a sense, feedback acts as a monitor to ensure that the system is meeting its goal.

Surrounding and interacting with the input, processing, output, and processing elements of the system are the environment and the boundary. The **environment** includes everything not in the system, and the **boundary** separates the system from the environment. Figure 4-2 shows the relationships among these elements.

As we said earlier, CBISs are extremely important to the efficient management of any organization. Various types of information systems have been

FIGURE 4-1
Conceptual View of CBIS

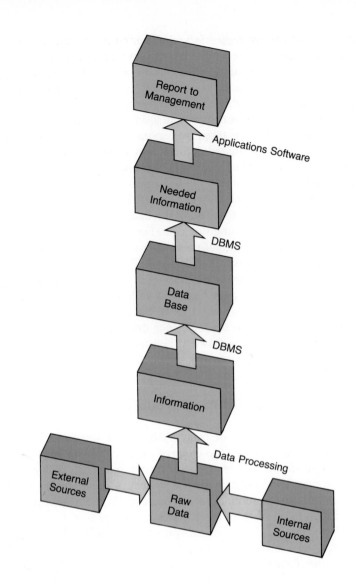

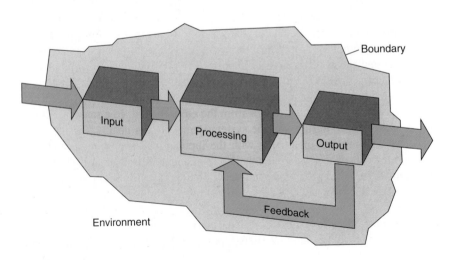

FIGURE 4-2
The Elements of a System

developed to meet the many needs of the decision makers for different types of information. These information systems may be classified according to the type of information they provide and the managerial level to which the information is provided. To help you understand how different types of information systems serve different managerial levels in the organization, we will first examine the managerial levels. Then we will discuss five different types of information systems—the transaction processing system, the management information system, the decision support system, the executive information system, and the office information system—and the ways in which they meet the information needs of the organization.

Managerial Levels

To understand the various types of information systems within an organization, we must look first at the various managerial levels in an organization. At the lowest, or *operational,* management level, the foremen and supervisors need detailed information on the day-to-day operation of the company's production process. These managers must make decisions about ordering parts, assigning jobs, checking shipments, and so on, and their decisions are made on the basis of rules and policies set at higher management levels. Because of the structure in the decisions at this level and because the decision maker can be given a list of rules to follow to make decisions, the decisions are said to be **programmable.**

At the next higher level in the organization are the middle-level managers, who need summary reports on the firm's operation to make **tactical decisions**

Operational managers like this factory supervisor often make programmed decisions based on the information they receive from various sources.

Middle-level managers often use decision support systems to help them make tactical decisions.

To make strategic decisions, top-level managers require the different types of information provided by an executive information system.

to implement the policy or **strategic decisions** made at the top level of the company. The decisions at these two upper levels are not as easily programmable as those at the lower level. The pyramid in Figure 4-3 demonstrates the relative number of people in the organization who make each type of decision.

From Figure 4-3 we can see that there is a broad base of day-to-day operational decision makers, fewer tactical decision makers, and only a few strategic decision makers. The flow of decision making is from the top down; each level depends on the level above for the policy to use in making its decisions. For the operational managers and some tactical managers, timely reports are very important to decision making. For the tactical and strategic managers, more long-term information about the financial health of the firm is needed. In addition, these managers must have the ability to make forecasts about the company's future. The various information systems in the organization must be designed to ensure that the appropriate information is available to each level of the managerial pyramid.

How Information Systems Support Management

There are five types of information systems that are commonly thought of as providing support for managerial decision making: the transaction processing system, the management information system, the decision support system, the executive information system, and the office information system. While some of these—notably the management information system—may be given a different name in some contexts, the function is generally the same, as we will describe shortly.

Figure 4-4 shows the three levels of management and their relationships to the various information systems. We see, at the bottom of the managerial pyramid, the **transaction processing system (TPS),** which supplies information to the operational manager about the many daily transactions that are the lifeblood of any organization. The TPS does this by performing the data processing function of converting raw data into a form that is stored in a data base and then accessed by the manager for the most up-to-date information. Once the information is in the data base, it is then possible to use a DBMS like those discussed

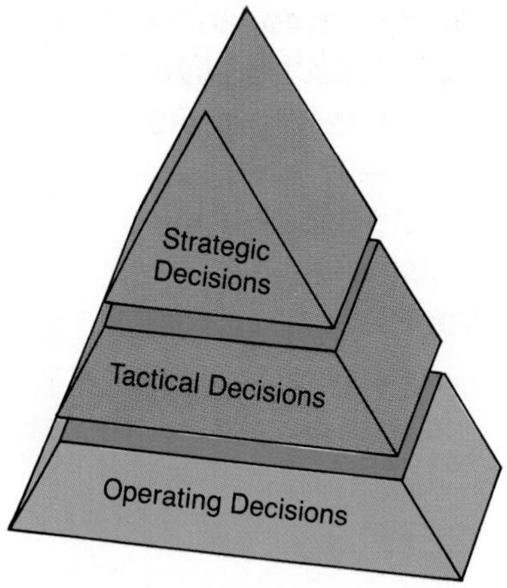

FIGURE 4-3
Levels of Management Decision Making

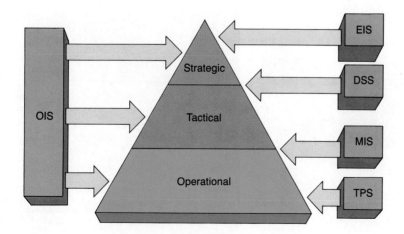

FIGURE 4-4
Relationship of Information Systems to Managerial Levels

in Chapter 3 on either a mainframe or a PC to retrieve the needed data. In addition to providing information directly to the operational managers, the data base is a source of information for the other types of information systems at the higher levels of management.

Transaction processing systems can be classified according to the manner in which the data are input, processed, and output; that is, the TPS can use batch, transactional, or real-time processing.

In a **batch processing system,** the data from multiple users or time periods are combined, input, and processed as a batch. Payroll systems are often batch systems. In **transactional processing,** each transaction is processed as it occurs. In a transactional processing system, the data are processed at the time of entry rather than being held for later processing. Grocery checkout systems are good examples of transactional processing systems. In **real-time processing,** the processing of the transaction can actually affect the transaction itself. Such processing may be necessary when several users are competing for the same resources, as with an airline reservation system.

At the level above the TPS in the managerial pyramid is the management information system. The **management information system (MIS)** is aimed at helping managers make decisions by providing them with reports that are timely and to the point. The MIS is very important to operational and lower-level tactical managers because they need the information from these reports to make their programmable decisions. While upper-level tactical and strategic managers also use the reports generated by the MIS, their decisions cannot be programmed and must depend on intuition and problem solving. For this reason, they use information from many other sources in addition to the MIS reports. An example of a report that would be provided by the MIS is one regarding the level of employee turnover in various departments. This report would be generated from attendance data provided by department managers and would aid the company personnel manager in making decisions about company personnel policies.

To further aid the upper levels of decision makers, a **decision support system (DSS)** combines data with mathematical models to provide alternative solutions to problems facing tactical and strategic managers. A DSS goes further than the MIS to help the decision maker with more complex problems. A DSS allows a decision maker to use mathematical models to determine the effect that different assumptions would have on the future of the company.

(Left) Modern batch systems can handle the huge volume of remittances that a large billing department must process. **(Center)** A transaction system such as this automated hotel checkout system processes data as they are entered. **(Right)** Airline reservation systems must use real-time transaction processing.

While both MIS and DSS help managers make decisions, there is a crucial difference between them that depends on the degree of structure in the decision. If a decision is highly structured—that is, if the decision can be made using set policies—then the reports that an MIS provides are sufficient to make the decision. For example, a decision on how many spare parts to keep on hand for production equipment can usually be made based on reports generated by an MIS. On the other hand, if the decision is unstructured and cannot be made using clearly defined policies, then a DSS must be used. For example, the decision on how to finance a company's debt might be based on forecasts on sales and future interest rates. This type of decision is very unstructured and must be made using the models supplied by a DSS.

At the top levels of management in many organizations, executives are just beginning to exploit the power of computers to provide them with the information needed to make decisions. In more and more cases, they are doing this through the use of an **executive information system (EIS).** An EIS differs from a DSS in that while the DSS uses models to find alternative solutions to problems, the EIS is a personalized means of presenting information to the top-level executive. Using an EIS, executives can monitor the daily operations of the organization using either a graphical or a report format to present the information. In many EISs a mouse or a touchscreen, rather than a keyboard, is used for input, allowing the executive to make selections quickly and easily by simply pointing to a picture. Also, the EIS depends on external data sources far more than either the MIS or the DSS since the top-level executive is often more interested in what is happening in national and global markets than are lower-level managers.

Note that in Figure 4-4, the **office information system (OIS)** is shown spanning the entire range of managerial levels, because the OIS provides a sup-

Managers frequently rely on decision support systems for help in solving complex problems.

High-quality graphics are often a part of an executive information system.

port structure throughout the organization. For managers at all levels it provides printed reports through word processing and copying operations. It also provides quick communications between managers through electronic mail. The OIS facilitates managerial access to external information sources through facsimile transmission and other telecommunications operations. In general, OIS is the glue that holds the entire information system together by providing the needed support operations.

Table 4-1 summarizes the input, processing, output, and level of use for the five information systems discussed in this section.

Using Information Systems

As an example of the interaction of the various types of information systems, consider a company that has handwritten raw data on each of its transactions for the past month. Management wishes to find out which customers are purchasing the largest dollar volume from the company and which salespeople are doing the most business. The current handwritten data, because they are in the form of individual transactions and do not contain totals, is not useful to the company. Before these data on transactions can be used to answer management's questions, they must first be processed into an electronic form. This processing is handled by the transaction processing system and stored on a data base using the DBMS.

At this point, however, there is still only a large number of transactions, though now in an electronic rather than a paper form. The next step is for the

TABLE 4-1
Summary of Types of Information Systems

Information System	Input	Processing	Output	Level of Use
Transaction processing system (TPS)	Raw data	Conversion to information	Information in data base	Operational
Management information system (MIS)	Summary data from data base	Generation of reports	Reports on organizational activities	Operational and tactical
Decision support system (DSS)	Specific data from data base	Mathematical analyses; forecasts	Alternative solutions to problems	Tactical and strategic
Executive information system (EIS)	Internal and external data	Graphical presentations	Answers to questions	Strategic
Office information system (OIS)	Information to be transcribed, transmitted, or stored	Word processing; electronic mail; disk storage and retrieval	Paper and electronic documents; mail	All levels

MIS to retrieve specific information to generate reports that will answer some of management's questions. In this case, the specific information is the total sales for each customer, arranged in descending order of dollar volume, and the total sales for each salesperson, once again arranged in descending order by dollar volume. With a word processor, the OIS can then produce a printed report that will be forwarded to operational management and, if needed, to higher-level management.

At the same time, as in the process shown in Figure 4-5, the DSS may query the data base for specific information that can be used with a mathematical model to generate sales forecasts. These forecasts will go to middle management for use in preparing the next year's budget. The EIS can also use the data base to create a graphical presentation that upper management can then use to make long-range plans about the sales force and about various products.

Other Types of Information Systems

Two types of information systems that are becoming increasingly important to companies of all sizes are expert systems and strategic information systems. An **expert system (ES)** combines the knowledge and rules of several experts on a given subject and stores this information in the computer. The computer thus becomes an "expert" on the subject by synthesizing the knowledge and rules to aid humans in decision making. ESs have been successfully used in searching for oil, making medical diagnoses, finding problems with large machinery, and giving advice on business decisions. They were originally designed to run on mainframes or large minicomputers. However, with the increasing speed and size of PCs, they are now being used on many smaller computers.

While the traditional use of information systems is to automate basic operations such as payroll and to support managerial decision making, some forward-thinking companies are beginning to use their information systems as strategic weapons in the constant battle for market share. A **strategic information system (SIS)** is typically used to support or develop a company's competitive strategy.

> **Strategic systems alone don't make a firm more competitive; they help people become more competitive.**
>
> *Dean Meyer and Mary Boone, authors of* The Information Edge
>
> Quoted in "The End of the Rainbow," *Information Week,* July 23, 1990, p. 60.

FIGURE 4-5
Example Uses of Types of
Information Systems

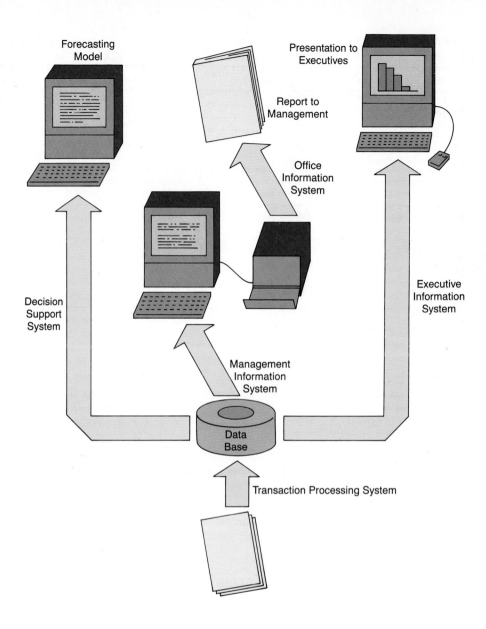

Examples of the ways that an SIS can be used include increasing product differentiation, creating or distributing an innovative product, and reducing costs to increase the company's market penetration. As discussed in the box at the beginning of this chapter, Wal-Mart uses SISs to turn information to its competitive advantage.

Chapter 14 will discuss other examples of the use of ESs and SISs and will present a more detailed discussion of the other information systems in an organization.

SYSTEMS ANALYSIS AND DESIGN

As defined, all information systems are a combination of humans, hardware, and software. For an information system to carry out its purpose—that is, for it to support managerial decision making—it must be correctly designed and then

```
        The research is now complete, and Your Wine Advisor is selecting.

The bottlings that Anthony Dias Blue feels are most appropriate for your
selection criteria will now be listed sequentially, beginning with the best
selection.

Please wait. It will take a little more time to select your wines.

White wines are being selected to go with Shellfish and no sauce.




Hacienda Wine Cellar Chenin Blanc 1984  Dry Chenin Blanc.  Clarksburg.
Average dryness, Light 3 stars. 0.85% residual sugar.  Soft, fruity,
balanced, clean, extremely charming. Probably priced at $5 to $10.
 This is a good choice with your selected main course and sauce.
Anthony Dias Blue considers this wine to be a very good value.
Do you want the next wine (if there is one)?
YES                      NO
```

There are innumerable, and perhaps unexpected, areas in which good advice would be appreciated. This expert system can tell you which wine would go well with a special meal you're planning.

programmed or purchased. This process is known as **systems analysis and design.** As the name implies, this process involves developing a system design to meet a new need or to solve a problem in an existing system. Unfortunately, the process is much more complex than this description. In fact, this process has spawned an entirely new occupation whose practitioners are known as systems analysts. The **systems analyst** carries out the problem-solving process to determine the cause of the current system's problem, suggests solutions to this problem, and then sees that one of these solutions is implemented. The new system may be one that must be programmed, or it may be a hardware or software system that can be purchased from an outside vendor. In the former case, the new system must be designed in such a way that the programmer can follow the design to create the software. In the latter case, the analyst must know enough about the various commercial systems to make a recommendation to management.

The Role of the Systems Analyst

In almost every systems analysis and design process, there are three groups of people to be considered: (1) the users of the system, (2) the information professionals or computer vendors who will actually implement the new system, and (3) the management who must oversee the transition from the old system to the new.

The complicating factor with these three groups is that each group views the problem in a different light. The users know they have a problem, but they don't know how to solve it. The information professionals or computer vendors can probably solve the problem, but they are not aware it exists and may not understand the terminology that the users use to describe the problem. Management may not know there is a problem or how to solve it but it does control the money needed to solve the problem. The individual who must work with all three groups to ensure that the problem is solved is the systems analyst. This person must understand the problem from the users' point of view, must under-

GEOGRAPHICAL INFORMATION SYSTEM MAY HELP DECIDE WHO RULES AMERICA IN THE 1990s

It [redistricting] was a very tedious, error-prone, and laborious exercise that no one enjoyed.

Robert K. Bratt, executive director of the Civil Rights Division of the U.S. Justice Department

Quoted in "GIS Eases Redistricting Worry," *Computerworld,* October 7, 1991, p. 65.

Shortly after the 1990 U.S. census was completed, the reapportionment battle began, and for the first time in the process, computers are playing a prominent role. Every ten years, the House of Representatives must be reapportioned to take into account the new Census Bureau population tabulation. Depending on population gains and losses, this means that some some states may lose seats while others may gain seats. After it is determined which states gain and which lose, the state legislatures begin the actual reapportionment process for the seats in their state by redrawing their House districts. This is an extremely important process, because the new makeup of a House district could cause a political party to lose a seat. (Creating districts that are favorable to one party or the other is known as "gerrymandering," after a governor of Massachusetts, named Gerry, who created an oddly shaped district in 1812 that ensured victory for his party.)

As recently as 1980, districts were created with little or no involvement of computers. However, both political parties made extensive use of computers in the 1990 reapportionment process, using a **geographical information system (GIS)** to integrate the official census map of the United States with the 1990 census count. The census map—TIGER for Topographically Integrated Geographic Encoding and Referencing system—divides the country into 9 million census blocks, for each of which a population count is known. The GIS can then be used to create many different districting plans. For example, the state of Georgia, which gained a seat as a result of the 1990 census, used workstations to create approximately 2,300 plans as compared to around 100 plans considered in 1980. So, if in 1992, you wonder how your House district came to be shaped as it is, a computer was probably involved in the process.

Source: Tom Baxter, "Computers Are Latest Weapons in Reapportionment Wars," *The Atlanta Journal-Constitution,* April 2, 1989, p. A-6, as updated by the author in 1991.

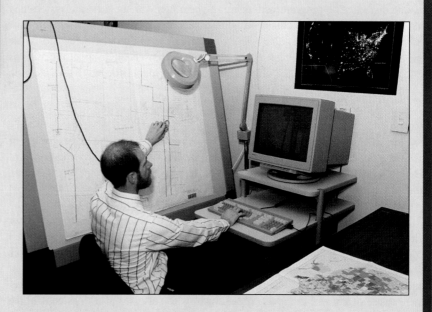

Census maps on computer.

stand the solution methodology of the information professionals, and must have a feel for the budgetary constraints of management. In a sense, the systems analyst must act as an intermediary between the users and the information professional or vendors while also being responsible to management. This relationship is shown in Figure 4-6.

The Systems Life Cycle

The process of systems analysis and design can be thought of as a sequence of seven steps, with each step depending upon the successful completion of the previous steps. These seven steps are also referred to as the **systems life cycle** since they describe the conception, birth, and growth of the system. Figure 4-7 shows the seven steps as they appear in the systems life cycle.

We begin the seven-step systems life cycle at problem definition, when management becomes aware that either an existing system is not working correctly or a new system is needed. The process of management becoming aware that a problem exists depends on many environmental and behavioral situations, some of which will be discussed in Chapter 15. For the time being, we will just assume that management is aware of a problem. As we move from problem definition through the feasibility study all of the way to the final implementation

A systems analyst must understand a client's needs before designing a system.

FIGURE 4-6
The Role of the Systems Analyst

Source: William S. Davies, *Systems Analysis
and Design,* © 1983 by Addison-Wesley
Publishing Co., Inc. Reprinted by permission
of Addison-Wesley Publishing Co., Inc.,
Reading, Mass.

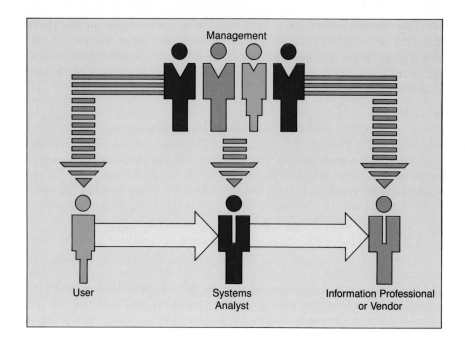

and maintenance steps, we are moving from a broad, logical understanding of the problem to a detailed solution of the problem. The process of moving from the broad and logical to the narrow and physical is termed a **top-down,** or **structured, approach** to systems analysis and design. One way to think of this is as the process of constructing a building. The process goes from an idea to a set of preliminary sketches to preliminary plans to blueprints to the actual construction process. In both the construction of a building and the process of systems analysis, the movement is from a logical concept to a physical system.

In the first three steps—problem definition, feasibility study, and analysis—the systems analyst gathers data, decides what problem is to be solved, determines if solving the problem is feasible, and generates alternative solutions to the problem—moving closer and closer to a detailed understanding of the required system.

In the next step—systems design—users and management select one of the alternative logical solutions, and the systems analyst develops a physical design to match this alternative. Next—in the acquisition/programming step— any hardware specified in the systems design step is acquired. A decision is also made as to whether to use a software package or develop special software. If the decision is to acquire a software package, it too is acquired at this stage. If, on the other hand, the decision is to develop special software, it is programmed in this step.

Any hardware and/or software acquired in the acquisition/programming design step is installed in the implementation step. If any software was programmed in the previous step, in this step it is also installed. In either case, a great deal of work must be carried out to install and test the new system and to convert the existing data to a form that can be input into the new system.

In the last step—maintenance—the solution is in place and the job is to iron out any day-to-day problems and keep the system running. During the maintenance stage, if so much maintenance work is necessary to keep the system

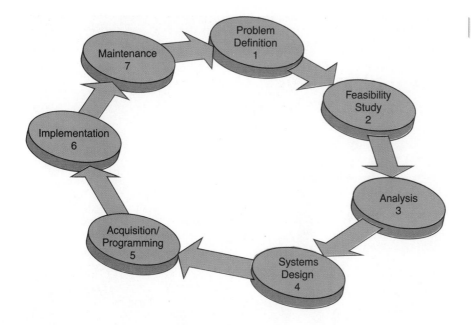

FIGURE 4-7
The Systems Life Cycle

running that it becomes obvious the current system is not adequate because of changing information requirements or business conditions or because of technological breakthroughs, we move back to the problem definition state and start the life cycle over again.

We will now consider the systems life cycle briefly. Chapter 15 will take up this topic in more detail.

Problem Definition

The systems analysis and design process begins with the determination that a problem exists in the current system. Complaints from users of a system may signal that a problem exists, management may find the current system too expensive even though it is working in an acceptable manner, or the output from the system may not match the system's objectives. Once an awareness of the problem exists, the problem definition stage begins.

The first step in problem definition is assigning a systems analyst to investigate the problem. The analyst meets with management and users to obtain a broad understanding of the problem. Based on these meetings, the analyst prepares a written declaration of his or her understanding of the user's objectives and the scope of the problem. When users and management, in the form of a steering committee, agree on the objectives and scope of the problem, the systems analyst moves to the next step.

Feasibility Study

Now the systems analyst can investigate the nature of the problem. A feasibility study is carried out to answer the following questions:

1. Is the problem worth solving?
2. Is a solution to the problem possible?

In the problem definition step of the systems life cycle, the systems analyst becomes very familiar with the client's problem.

If the answer to either question is no, then the systems analysis and design process is terminated.

In a feasibility study, the analyst does not attempt actually to find a solution to the problem. Instead, the objective is to come to an initial understanding of the problem and to decide whether or not it is feasible to proceed with a full-scale study of the problem.

An important result of this stage of the systems life cycle is the cost/benefit analysis that the systems analyst prepares. This analysis should take into account both monetary and nonmonetary costs and benefits of solving the problem. If this cost/benefit analysis shows that the costs will outweigh the potential benefits, the systems analyst will recommend that the project be scrapped. Using the analyst's report, the steering committee will decide whether or not to continue the process.

Analysis

After the feasibility study has shown that the problem is worth solving and that there is a good chance that an acceptable solution exists, the analysis stage of the process begins. In this stage, the analyst works closely with the user to develop a logical model of the system. A **model** is *a simplified version of reality* and as such does not attempt to capture every detail of the system. Instead, the model is useful for conceptualizing the way the system works and for determining what must be done to solve the problem. It is important at this stage for the analyst and the user to work together, since it is the user who knows what must be done and the analyst who can figure out how to do it.

The development of the logical model is made easier if the analyst uses a tool known as a **data flow diagram.** A data flow diagram is simply a pictorial representation of the flow of data into and out of the system. At this stage the data flow diagram can be fairly elementary since we are not seeking to capture the detail of the model. Figure 4-8 shows the symbols used in data flow diagrams, and Figure 4-9 shows a simple data flow diagram for a situation in which various types of data are accumulated and tabulated before being stored in an inventory file for use later in the processing operation.

At each step of the systems analysis and design process, beginning with the problem definition step, the systems analyst collects and analyzes data. In the initial step, very general data are collected from interviews and written descriptions of the system. Then, as the process continues, more and more detailed data are collected from interviews with people close to the day-to-day operation of the system, from operational reports, and from actual data that are flowing through the system. At this, the analysis step, the data flow diagram is used to understand the flow of these data through the system. Data collection is

FIGURE 4-8
Data Flow Diagram Symbols

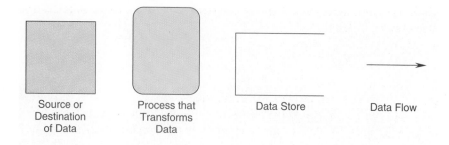

Source or Destination of Data

Process that Transforms Data

Data Store

Data Flow

not a one-time-only process but is an ongoing process in which the level of detail becomes greater at each step.

Once the analyst has developed a logical model of the system, he or she needs to develop a logical design that solves the problem defined earlier. This requires the analyst to use all of his or her experience, education, and creativity. Care must be taken to consider all factors, including the human and organizational ones. A logical solution will never be implemented if it runs counter to the objectives of the organization or if it requires people to act in a manner that they perceive as not being in their best interests.

Once the logical design has been developed, it must be validated against the problem definition to ensure that the design actually solves the problem. The analyst does this by discussing the logical design with the steering committee.

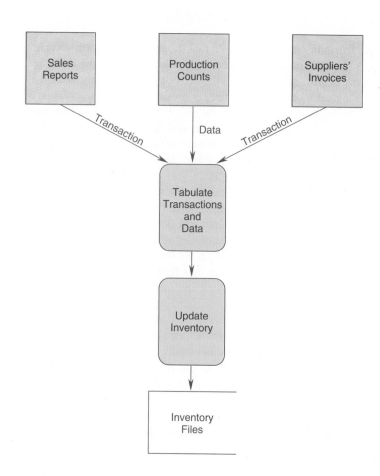

FIGURE 4-9
Data Flow Diagram

Once that group agrees to a design, the systems analyst can move on to the next step—systems design.

Systems Design

After the analysis step of the process, the analyst knows what must be done to solve the problem but has not yet worked out the best way to do it. The solution process requires that the systems analyst develop a number of plans for a new system and present each to the potential user for comments. It is at this stage that close contact between the analyst and the user is extremely important to ensure that the new system will solve the problems in the existing system without introducing any new ones. The process of developing a physical design to match the logical design developed in the analysis step requires that the analyst consider the problem from the output, input, and process points of view. That is, the analyst needs to determine what outputs are required from the information system being designed and what form these outputs should take, what inputs are going into the system and what form the data are in, and what process will be utilized to convert the specified inputs into the desired outputs. After considering the outputs, inputs, and process, the analyst develops alternative physical designs to give the steering committee a choice of ways to revise the system. A useful tool for describing the various alternatives to the committee is the **systems flowchart,** similar to the data flow diagram except that the emphasis is on the hardware devices involved in the design. Figure 4-10 shows the systems flowchart symbols, and Figure 4-11 shows one physical design corresponding to the data flow diagram shown in Figure 4-9.

Usually, the steering committee is given at least three alternatives. After considering these alternatives, the steering committee has a decision to make: It

In the systems design and acquisition/programming steps, the analyst develops a logical design and then a physical design of the final system.

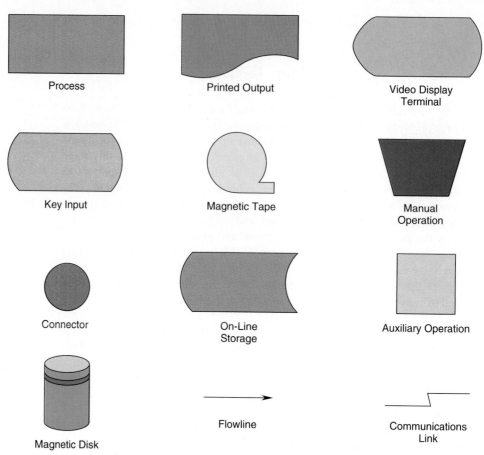

Process   Printed Output   Video Display Terminal

Key Input   Magnetic Tape   Manual Operation

Connector   On-Line Storage   Auxiliary Operation

Magnetic Disk   Flowline   Communications Link

FIGURE 4-10
Systems Flowchart Diagrams

can decide that the overall cost is too great for any further development, or it can decide to use one of the alternatives the analyst offers, or it can ask the analyst to develop yet another design that contains characteristics not included in any of the previous alternatives.

Acquisition/Programming

If the user–management steering committee selects one of the analyst's physical designs, then the process of acquisition/programming can begin, using the chosen alternative as the general strategy. This process should answer the question of specifically which hardware and software systems should be purchased or, if software programs are to be developed, what the design of the software should be. This process will include the specifications on the computer hardware and software that will be needed to implement the alternative chosen by the user. If the software can be purchased from a commercial vendor, then the specifications should give all of the information necessary to choose the package. On the other hand, if the software is going to be developed by programmers, the specifications should be detailed enough for the programmers to understand what is required of their programs. These specifications are analogous to an engineer's blueprints in that they should show the user what the finished product will look like and they should guide the actions of the programmers.

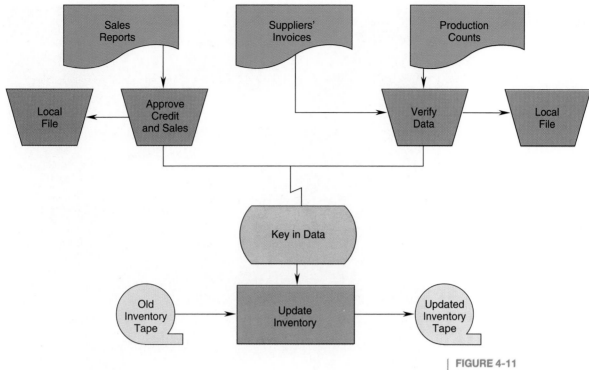

FIGURE 4-11
Systems Flowchart

If any hardware items or software packages are to be acquired, various vendors are given these detailed specifications and are asked to offer bids for the time and money involved in preparing the packages. Based on the resulting proposals, the hardware and software packages are purchased.

If software is to be developed, various tools are used to design the software to meet the specifications from the previous step, and the software is written.

Implementation

In this step, all of the detailed plans developed in the previous step are put into action, including actual installation of the previously purchased hardware and commercial software or installation of the programs that were written to make up the new software. Regardless of whether commercial software or specially developed software is used, this process involves testing the hardware and software in actual use situations, preparing documentation on the use of the new system, training personnel to use the new system, and evaluating the new system to determine whether or not it is performing satisfactorily. A commonly used approach to the implementation process is to have the old and new systems running side by side until it is clear that the new system is going to handle the required tasks. This is known as a **parallel conversion**—as compared to a **direct conversion,** in which the old system is discarded and the new system used immediately. Failure to test a new system adequately before doing away with the old one can have a profoundly negative effect on the organization if problems are found in the new system after the old system has been discarded.

Another problem in the implementation process for a new system involves resistance to change by the personnel of the organization. This problem can be avoided to a large extent if management sees to it that the personnel are involved

in all stages of the analysis, design, and implementation process and if a high priority is placed on training personnel on the new system.

If software has been specially written, testing is extremely important to ensure that the programs are error free and perform according to the user's needs. The systems analyst should be very involved in the development of test plans, the writing of operating and security procedures, and the formal testing of all components and procedures.

Once all systems have been installed and tested, the next step is to convert the data used in the old system to a form that can be input into the new information system. This can be time consuming, requiring careful validation of the data as they are moved to the new system. Only after the new system has been installed and tested, the personnel trained on the new system, the data converted to the new system, and the entire system validated as working correctly is the implementation step completed.

Maintenance

Any system, no matter how well designed, will need to be continually modified to handle changes in input, output, or logic requirements. This is done through maintenance, the ongoing process of keeping a system up to date by making necessary changes. While it may seem like a minor part of the analysis, design, and implementation process, maintenance of existing systems has been shown to take up about 70 percent of a professional programmer's work time.

The system must be maintained over time to ensure that it continues to perform as originally designed and implemented.

Maintenance consists of two important steps: determining what needs to be changed and then making the change. Determining what needs to be changed is very similar to the problem definition step in that it requires the systems analyst to study a situation and to pinpoint the problem. Once the problem is defined, changing the existing system is a small-scale version of the systems life cycle that can involve all the steps shown in Figure 4-7. This is why we show the life cycle as a continuing process.

The ease with which an existing system can be maintained depends a great deal on the system documentation, made up of the descriptions and instructions that come with the hardware and commercial software or the documentation for programmed software that was written during the programming step. Without this documentation, changing the system may be virtually impossible and the existing system may have to be junked in favor of an entirely new system—a potentially expensive process.

MORE ON THE PROCESS OF DEVELOPING SOFTWARE

While we have encouraged the use of purchased software packages to solve problems using computers, there will always exist those situations in which it will be necessary to develop software by writing computer programs. These are usually cases in which problems exist that are not general enough to be addressed by a commercial software company or the user finds that the software does not suit his or her needs.

In the acquisition/programming step of the systems analysis and design process, we noted that if some or all of the software is to be written rather than purchased commercially, the programs are written in this step of the process.

In general, the process of creating software moves from a step-by-step statement of the solution to the problem, called an **algorithm,** to a program flow-chart or to pseudocode. A **program flowchart,** a pictorial form of the logic needed to solve the problem, is similar to a systems flowchart except that it is directed at the more detailed logic of a computer program. **Pseudocode** is a structured form of English that allows the systems analyst to express the logic of the program in a form that the programmer easily understands. Once the logic of the program has been expressed as either a program flowchart or pseudocode, it is possible for a programmer who knows little about the original problem to write a computer program that will match the logic. This is where the systems analyst acts as an intermediary for the user and the programmer. In this case, the user understands the problem but does not know how to write a program to

All programs consist of a series of steps that must implement the logic needed to solve a stated problem or to carry out a given task.

solve it, and the programmer can write a program but does not know anything about the problem. The systems analyst has some knowledge of both sides.

The next step is for the programmer actually to write one or more programs that will give the computer the instructions it needs to solve the problem.

Programming Computers

To program a computer—that is, to give the computer a sequence of instructions—requires an ability to communicate with the computer. To understand how this communication can take place, we must realize that the computer does

SOFTWARE FROM J. P. MORGAN

Very few people would think of software development when they hear the name J. P. Morgan. Instead, they usually think of money. This is not surprising given that J. P. Morgan & Co. is the fifth largest bank in the United States and is possibly the most widely respected financial institution in the country. However, a reason for J. P. Morgan to be associated with software development and design is a unique product called MPI/PC Report that the institution introduced in 1986. MPI/PC Report seeks to exploit a niche in the issuing and paying agency services market that allows Morgan to offer reporting services that are superior to those of the competition, but at radically reduced prices. Specifically, companies use the product to generate sophisticated financial and analytical reports on their commercial paper programs.

Commercial paper is one of the largest financial debt securities in use by institutions today, with a total market size of over $500 billion. Commercial paper is short-term promissory notes that are sold by issuers to investors to handle cash flow needs. To monitor the amount of commercial paper outstanding, and to generate detailed analytical reports, issuers rely on issuing and paying agents (that is, the banks responsible for creating the debt security) to provide them with a reporting service. Most bank systems, however, limit issuers to relying on expensive mainframe computer resources to generate reports. These expenses can exceed $100,000 per year. With MPI/PC Report, however, issuers use a PC-based software package that allows issuers to generate reports using the processing powers of their own PCs. The Commercial Paper Management Group at Morgan made the decision to develop and write a PC-based product in 1985 to lower issuer costs and to enable Morgan's clients to use PCs, which were becoming more commonplace in the business environment. The system design, analysis, and programming effort was completed within nine months, and the product was launched in August 1986.

MPI/PC Report does two basic operations. First, it retrieves the commercial paper issuance data from Morgan's mainframe computer and downloads it to the issuer's PC.

Second, it uses this downloaded information to generate reports offline. Selling for $2,500 with a $250-per-month usage fee for the basic system, this package is substantially cheaper than the mainframe alternative. Currently, the product is used by over 100 *Fortune* 500 clients, some sovereign governments (e.g., Canada and New Zealand), and numerous foreign issuers. Since the product was introduced it has generated over $1 million in revenues for the Commercial Paper Management Group, while offering flexibility to Morgan's clients.

Morgan has not rested on its laurels, however. In the first quarter of 1990, the bank introduced the second release of MPI/PC Report, which was totally redesigned. The new version is written entirely in the C programming language and has several added features to enable issuers to take advantage of hardware and software developments (e.g., local area networks and pop-up window screens). Additionally, Morgan is already looking into expanding the product to include other debt securities, such as certificates of deposit and medium-term notes.

Source: Jeffrey Rothfeder, "Bank-Developed Software Transforms Lackluster Service into a Profit Leader," *PC Week*, November 24, 1987, pp. 66, 70; and Morgan Guaranty Trust Company of New York, a subsidiary of J. P. Morgan & Co., Incorporated, 1990.

not understand any human language without some form of translation. From our discussion on bits and binary numbers in Chapter 2 on hardware, you know that the computer "thinks" in terms of on/off switches that we know as bits. In other words, the language of the computer is in the binary number system. So, to be understood by the computer, human language must be translated into these binary numbers. The computer's binary language is referred to as **machine language,** a very specific language that details every operation of the computer as a series of 0's and 1's.

Because every type of computer is different, each has a different machine language. Programming in machine language would be very inefficient, however, because the programs would have to be changed whenever they were transferred to a new computer. For this reason, **high-level languages** were developed. These languages are English-like in that programmers use English words combined with a specific grammar. The languages have also been standardized to some degree, so that a program written in a high-level language on one type of computer *may* not have to be totally rewritten when used on a different type of computer. The most commonly used high-level languages have such names as BASIC, FORTRAN, COBOL, C, and Pascal. This wide diversity of high-level languages came about because no one language could satisfy every need. Some are business languages, some are teaching languages, and some are scientific languages. In addition to these traditional high-level languages, many data base management packages have a programming language associated with them that allows automization of the search and rearrangement of data bases. dBASE is a popular data base management package for PCs that comes equipped with a powerful programming language.

If the computer understands only machine language and we write in high-level languages, how does the computer ever understand our programs? The answer is that some type of translation between the two levels of languages is

```
 File    Edit    Run    Compile    Options    Debug    Break/watch
                              ═══════ Edit ═══════
     Line 1      Col 17  Insert Indent          Unindent * C:EXAM2.Q1
Program Averages;
Uses crt;
type
     Stringtype = string[20];
var
   Inputfile: text;
   Name: Stringtype;
   Height: Integer;
   Ppg: Real;
   Count72,Count78,Count79,CountAll:Integer;
   Ppg72,Ppg78,Ppg79,PpgAll: real;
   SumH, AverageHt: real;
procedure Initialize;
     begin
     Count72:=0;Count78:=0;Count79:=0;CountAll:=0;SumHt:=0;
     Ppg72:=0;Ppg78:=0;Ppg79:=0;PpgAll:= 0;
     Clrscr;
     Assign(inputfile,'player.dat');
                              ═══════ Watch ═══════

 F1-Help  F5-Zoom  F6-Switch  F7-Trace  F8-Step  F9-Make  F10-Menu
```

High-level programming languages, such as Pascal, combine English words with specific grammar rules.

To help you understand the evolution of information systems, the figure shown depicts a time line on which we have given rough placements of the recognition of each type of information system. Remember that these time placements are very approximate and that, in some cases, a type of information system was in existence some years before it was recognized as a separate and distinct type.

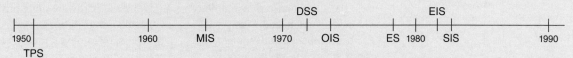

Time line of evolution of information systems

required. Utility software performs this task, converting the high-level language down to a corresponding machine-language program.

Regardless of the high-level language in which the program is written, the programmer must be able to translate correctly the logic developed in the design phase into a working program, first by learning the vocabulary and syntax (grammar) of the language and then by studying how various logical situations are handled in that particular language. The entire software development process is covered in detail in Chapter 16 and in Appendix B on programming in BASIC.

REVIEW OF KEY POINTS

1. An information system is a combination of user, hardware, and software that supports managerial decision making. A computer-based information system uses the computer to process data into a form usable by management.

2. A system is a group of elements organized for the purpose of achieving a particular goal. It is made up of input, processing, output, and feedback operations, with a boundary separating the system from its environment.

3. Five types of information systems are commonly found in all organizations—the transaction processing system (TPS), the management information system (MIS), the decision support system (DSS), the executive information system (EIS), and the office information system (OIS).

4. In any organization there are three levels of managerial decision making—operational, tactical, and strategic—with each needing a different type of information. Thus each type of information system is important to a different managerial level of the organization.

5. The TPS is usually associated with operational decisions, while the MIS is associated with both operational and tactical decisions.

6. The DSS is used by middle- and upper-level managers to help

make their decisions; the EIS is a personalized presentation system used by strategic managers.

7. Two other important types of information systems are expert systems (ES) and strategic information systems (SIS). In the ES, the computer serves in the role of an expert; in the SIS, the computer uses the information available within the organization to try to create a competitive advantage.

8. The systems life cycle describes the steps a system goes through from design and creation to implementation and maintenance.

9. Systems analysis and design is a seven-step process used to solve problems in a company's computer system by developing a new system or modifying an old system.

10. A systems analyst, the key figure in the systems analysis and design process, acts as a go-between for users and information professionals or vendors.

11. In the systems analysis and design process, the analyst first defines the problem and does a feasibility study. The analyst then creates a logical design for a solution to the problem, which is converted into a physical design. Next, the hardware and software are acquired or programmed as necessary to develop the needed information system. Finally, maintenance is important to ensure that the information system continues to perform as expected.

12. When software for the information system cannot be purchased, it must be designed and computer programs must be written to implement the design.

13. Computer languages are used to execute the instructions needed to accomplish a task or solve a problem on a computer.

KEY TERMS

algorithm
batch processing system
boundary
computer-based information system (CBIS)
data base
data base management system (DBMS)
data flow diagram
data processing
decision support system (DSS)
direct conversion
environment
executive information system (EIS)
expert system (ES)
feedback
geographical information system (GIS)
high-level language
information system

input
machine language
management information system (MIS)
model
office information system (OIS)
output
parallel conversion
processing
program flowchart
programmable decisions
pseudocode
real-time processing
strategic decisions
strategic information system (SIS)
structured approach
system
systems analysis and design
systems analyst
systems flowchart

systems life cycle
tactical decisions
top-down approach

transactional processing
transaction processing system (TPS)

1. Discuss how an information system is important to some club or organization to which you belong. How might this information system be converted into a computer-based information system?
2. Discuss the difference between a computer-based information system and data processing.
3. List the managerial levels of any organization.
4. List the five information systems commonly found in most organizations. Discuss how information systems are used in colleges or universities to support the managerial system.
5. Discuss the importance of the transaction processing system. Name the three types of transaction processing systems.
6. Discuss the importance of the management information system for any organization. What managerial level(s) would most likely use the output from this system?
7. What level(s) of management would most benefit from a decision support system?
8. Why is the executive information system referred to as a "personalized presentation system"?
9. How does an office information system support the various levels of management?
10. Discuss the rules and knowledge that might be incorporated in an expert system for a subject in which you are an "expert."
11. How are strategic information systems used in organizations?
12. List the seven steps of the systems analysis and design process. Why is this referred to as a systems life cycle?
13. Why is the systems analyst needed in this process?
14. In what step of the system analysis and design process is programming carried out?
15. What is the purpose of an algorithm in the programming process? What is pseudocode and how is it used?

5

An Introduction to Computers and Society

Having discussed computer hardware, software, and systems in the first four chapters, we will now address the interaction between people and computers. This discussion will examine the impact, both positive and negative, that computers have had on people. This will be followed by an introductory discussion of computer crime and data security, including the various types of crimes that involve computers. Next is a discussion of personal privacy and health issues in the use of computers. Then the various careers available to individuals with training or an interest in either mainframe or personal computers are noted and, finally, future trends in computer use are reviewed. These topics will be covered in more detail in Block Five.

STUDY OBJECTIVES

After reading this chapter, you should be able to

- discuss the impact that the computer has had on various segments of our society;
- recognize the types of problems that occur when people interact with the computer in the workplace;
- describe health problems that have been reported by frequent computer users;
  discuss the various types of computer crime, including those that involve copying software for personal computers;
- discuss the depersonalization of society that can occur with the use of computers;
- describe the types of careers available in the computer industry;
- note some of the trends in computer use that have been predicted for the future.

SMART WORKERS FOR SMART MACHINES

A decade ago, many workers worried that they would be replaced by robots and computerized manufacturing equipment. However, in some cases exactly the opposite has occurred—workers not only have *not* been replaced by machines but many have found that their jobs have been made more meaningful by the introduction of smart machines. This has come about because workers are being given more responsibility and authority to deal with problems or to make production-line decisions that were once reserved for supervisory personnel. Workers do more than just run machines; they spend large parts of their time collecting and processing data on quality control, inventory, and shipments. The result of this change is an **informated factory,** where machines not only perform some operations, but they supply workers with information on processing operations.

As an example of this type of change, consider General Electric's Salisbury, North Carolina, factory. At this plant, which is highly automated, it was decided in 1984 to cut factory floor bottlenecks by giving workers the information and power to make decisions to keep the manufacturing process running. A machine operator with a problem, for example, now can talk directly to manufacturing engineers about solutions to the problem or can order parts for the machine without prior approval of management. Workers also serve on committees to hire new workers in the plant.

From 1985 through 1988, General Electric's pairing of smart workers with smart machines resulted in a tenfold decrease in delivery time, a reduction in employee turnover, a reduction by two-thirds in the number of hours per production unit, and an increase in General Electric's market share. Since 1988, concrete figures have not been available on the effect of these measures; however, plant management believes that the workers are continuing to assume more and more responsibility for running the plant. Each year, they have exceeded production goals and reduced production cost.

Source: Doron P. Levin, "Smart Machines, Smart Workers," *The New York Times,* October 17, 1988, pp. 25–29, as updated in interview with Rick Fior of General Electric, November 14, 1991.

Workers at this plant are often authorized to make production and scheduling decisions without checking with their supervisors.

While a great deal of attention is often paid to hardware and software, the human aspect of the "age of smart machines" is all too often ignored. However, as just discussed in the box, organizations that recognize the need for change in the way workers interact with computers are realizing tremendous increases in productivity and are making the workers' jobs more interesting and rewarding. Because the interaction between people and computers is such an important topic, this chapter is devoted to the many and varied ways that people react to and with computers. As with all chapters in this introductory block, this chapter serves two purposes. First, it introduces the person–computer interface and, second, it acts as a lead-in to a later block of chapters, which discusses these topics in more detail.

This discussion of the interaction between people and computers will be divided into four sections:

1. the impact of the computer in the workplace, including health-related issues;
2. data security and computer crime;
3. the impact of computers on personal privacy;
4. computer careers now and in the future.

Each of these topics is discussed in detail in Block Five, Chapters 18–20.

THE IMPACT OF THE COMPUTER IN THE WORKPLACE

In the workplace there are many situations in which people come into contact with computers. In situations like the one described at the beginning of this chapter, where "smart workers" are working with smart machines, this interaction has been positive. However, there are also negative interactions between workers and the computers that they use to carry out their work.

The use of computer terminals is fast becoming commonplace in offices of all types.

A wrist brace helps relieve this data entry operator of some of the musculoskeletal problems associated with computeritis.

On the positive side of computers in the workplace is a reduction in many of the more boring or monotonous tasks. Office personnel who once took dictation with pencil and paper and transcribed the information on a typewriter have been transformed into **information specialists**—people who work with personal computers to perform such wide-ranging tasks as word processing, data base management, and spreadsheet analysis. As a second example, consider the automobile workers who once had to perform the dirtiest job in the automobile industry—arc welding. They have now been retrained to repair the robots that took their place. They, too, are information specialists, but of a different variety.

However, on the negative side is a group of workers who suffer from a malady known as **computerphobia**—the fear of computers. The malady (also known as *cyberphobia* or *terminal phobia*) is thought to occur in about 30 percent of students and workers forced to contend with the computer for the first time. The symptoms of computerphobia are nervousness, uneasiness, anxiety, and tension when the affected individual is confronted with a computer. The causes of computerphobia are described as fear of change, fear of machines (especially machines such as computers that are capable of highly sophisticated tasks), fear of breaking the computer, frustration with a machine that tends to stop for unknown reasons, fear of job loss, discomfort with the impersonal nature of computers, and an inability to use the keyboard. Several studies have revealed that some computerphobes even leave a company that is in the process of computerization and join a company that has not yet gone through the process. Some people even change professions to avoid using computers. This problem has been blamed on the fact that the current work force is the first to have to come to grips with computers. The problem is slowly disappearing as younger people who have grown up with computers and video games move into the work force.

Another potential problem with the computer in the work place is the **video display terminal (VDT).** This display can be either a personal computer or a terminal tied into a mainframe or minicomputer, and it has become a fixture in offices throughout the United States. These terminals allow the user to access and process data, display and print the results, and make decisions based on the results. As a result, the VDT is an important facet in the office of both today and the future. However, for the individual who uses a VDT over a long period of time, there may be health hazards associated with the radiation from the screen, the eye strain from watching the screen for long periods each day, and the muscular and joint problems resulting from the rigid posture associated with the use of the keyboard. In fact, a new job-oriented syndrome called "computeritis" has been associated with day-in/day-out use of the keyboard. **Computeritis** involves extremely painful musculoskeletal problems that can keep workers off their regular jobs for months at a time.

The study of work-related problems is known as human factors engineering or ergonomics. **Ergonomics** can be defined as the study of the relationship between the productivity of machines and the comfort of the people using them. When ergonomics are applied to the various body positions required in the use of a VDT, the types of keyboards used, and the other factors involved in the use of a VDT, a more healthful and productive working environment usually results.

For the organization and the individual, another problem involving the computer is unemployment due to automation of many tasks. Examples of this include the use of robots to replace workers in the automobile, electronics, and supply industries. These robots take over many of the dirtiest, most dangerous,

A more healthful and productive workplace often results when ergonomic principles are applied to the design of computer equipment.

and most boring jobs in these industries. While many of the individuals displaced by the robots do find other, more responsible positions in the same company, like those discussed at the beginning of this chapter, tens of thousands of workers may lose their jobs due to automation during the 1990s. This displacement has already occurred in the automobile industry, where the U.S. companies have responded to the Japanese competition by attempting to reduce labor costs through automation. The future holds additional opportunities for the application of automation to many industries, and the effect on the work force is yet to be determined.

DATA SECURITY AND COMPUTER CRIME

In the fall of 1988, over 6,000 computers at universities and military labs were "infected" with a "computer worm" sent over a network by a high-tech vandal. This so-called **computer worm** was a computer program that replicated itself over and over after being transmitted on a computer network. While this particular worm brought many computers to a grinding halt by taking up large amounts of internal memory, it did not destroy valuable records. However, another type of computer program called a **computer virus** has wiped out entire disk storage systems. Worms and viruses are just one type of computer crime. Sometimes money is stolen or data are stolen or the computer itself is attacked. The dramatic increase

Desktop forgers are using desktop publishing equipment to modify checks, credit card receipts, academic transcripts, and a variety of other documents for illicit purposes.

in the use of computers of all sizes now requires business and government to determine ways to provide security for their computers and data.

While the personal computer is often seen as the cause of many computer crimes, many of these same problems existed when individuals used terminals tied into institutional computers to steal funds or to destroy data. In fact, the 1988 worm attack was sent over a mainframe network. It is true, however, that the personal computer has made access to computers much easier. It has been suggested that any computer with a telephone connection is vulnerable to an incursion regardless of the type of security system devised to protect it. The annual cost of computer crime in the United States has been estimated to be in the range of $3 to $5 billion.

Computer crime can be defined as the theft of money, merchandise, data, or computer time using a computer or the unauthorized incursion into computer data files. As we have discussed, computer crime can take a number of forms, including the following:

- Manipulation of company financial records to steal funds from the company. This type of crime can involve employees of the firm or individuals from outside the firm.
- Theft of merchandise by manipulating the inventory records to hide the loss of the merchandise or by charging the merchandise to a fake account or to another customer's account.
- Theft of company data. Company consumer data, customer lists, and computer programs are common targets for data theft.
- Use of the company computer for personal purposes. This includes using the computer to develop computer programs of a personal nature or using the computer for "moonlighting" as a consultant.
- Damage to the computer or to data storage by an angry employee or ex-employee. This can include physical damage to the hardware, destruction of mass storage devices such as disks or tape, or damage to the programs that control the computer.
- Incursions into the computer programs or files or unauthorized use of the computer by individuals who are doing it for the "fun of it" or for the challenge of breaking into the computer.
- Unauthorized use of or destruction of voice mail systems.

Individuals who specialize in breaking into computers are often referred to as "hackers." The term **hacker** was originally applied to anyone who would spend many hours at the computer "hacking" programs, that is, learning how they work. In fact, many of today's leaders in the computer industry started out as hackers who wanted to make computers do more. Unfortunately, the term has recently taken on a negative connotation due to the harm many of these people have caused. For example, the individual who sent the worm across the country in 1988 was a hacker who was just trying to see if it could be done. Unfortunately, a bug in the program caused it to replicate itself throughout all available memory.

Examples of computer crimes show up almost every day in the national media, but in many other cases these crimes go undetected, unreported, or unpunished. Some cases of computer crime that have involved a great deal of money or have been well publicized include a computer-based currency fraud that cost a West German automobile company nearly $480 million, the theft of more than $20 million from a California bank through electronic funds transfer, the diversion of at least $2 million from bettors at a dog track in Florida by a group of employees using the track computers, and the incursion into NASA computers and U.S. military networks by a group of West German hackers using international phone links.

A problem in prosecution of computer crime is that until recently there were no laws appropriate to the crimes. It was a case of using outdated laws to prosecute high-tech crimes. This situation has been rectified to some extent by new laws at both state and federal levels. One sticky question remains regarding incursion into a computer when no harm is done. Is this a crime? Many state courts and legislatures have ruled that it is.

Some experts have blamed management for the lax security that enables these crimes to be carried out so easily. The most common security measure involves using special passwords to keep intruders from using the computer. Unfortunately, easy-to-remember (and easy-to-guess) passwords are often chosen, and as a result, computer security is easily breached.

Software Piracy

Most of the computer crime discussed so far involves incursions into or theft from institutional or business mainframe computers, since these are the computers that contain the large quantity of records and calculations usually needed for the crime to be profitable. Another type of computer crime that involves personal computers almost exclusively is **software piracy.** PC software is copied and used without payment to the company that developed it. Persons copying software that they did not purchase are probably violating *at least* one of various U.S. copyright laws. One survey indicated that software piracy results in lost sales of between $1.2 billion and $2 billion annually in the United States alone. Also, 40 percent of the software used on personal computers is believed to have been obtained illegally. The ease of theft comes from the need for users to be able to **backup** the software disks as protection against the primary disk being damaged by a power surge, power outage, or the like. If software companies make their disks so that they cannot be copied, then the disks also cannot be backed up. As a result, users may not buy them.

In the past, the solution to software piracy was **copy protection,** which kept products from being copied even for backup purposes. The companies would send backup disks to registered owners of their software or would limit the number of backups that could be made from the original or master disk. Another antipiracy measure required that the master disk be used at some point in the package startup process. While these measures worked in some cases, there was always someone who could devise a way around these protective measures. As a result of the many problems associated with copy protection, most PC software is sold today without any copy protection. Software companies hope that most of their users are honest and will not steal software by copying disks.

A more detailed discussion of computer crime and security problems will be given in Chapter 18.

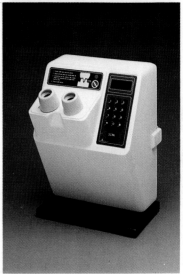

In one method of computer security, a computer compares the pattern in the potential user's retina with the patterns of valid users, which are stored in its memory.

COMPUTERS AND PERSONAL PRIVACY

In his well-known book *1984,* George Orwell describes how the society of Oceania can be totally controlled by the Party through the control of information. Although computers are never mentioned in the book, it has been assumed that it would be impossible for the Party to control the society unless it used computers to collect and store needed information. The year 1984 has passed, and it is obvious that America is far from becoming like Oceania. However, some of Orwell's ideas in *1984* about the collection and storage of data on citizens have indeed come to pass. We do not currently have a national **data bank** that contains the names of and records on every citizen of the United States, but recent surveys indicate that many people are concerned about the amount of information stored in many small, private data banks.

At the national level, there are numerous data banks: The Social Security Administration maintains data files on all individuals who pay taxes into or receive benefits from Social Security, the Internal Revenue Service keeps records on all taxpayers, the Department of Agriculture keeps track of farm incomes, and the Secret Service stores information on threats to the president. At last count in 1982, it was reported that the federal government maintained an average of 15 files on each American. Undoubtedly, other files have been added since that time. The Federal Bureau of Investigation is one of the largest holders of data, with records on over 25 million individuals who have been arrested, regardless of whether they were actually convicted of a crime.

At the state level, a 1982 study by New York State's Committee on Open Government determined that state agencies operated over 1,700 data banks on New York citizens. These data banks contain such things as voter registration

At FBI headquarters in Washington, D.C., employees use computers to sort and match over 184 million fingerprints on file there.

lists, driver's licenses, car registrations, state income and property tax records, and building permits. State and local police keep records on offenders within their jurisdiction and are quite willing to share this information with other law enforcement agencies.

In the private sector, a growing number of data banks contain data on most Americans alive today. This information may be as crucial as the credit bureau records that can affect your search for a car loan or a job or as seemingly innocent as a magazine mailing list. Private data banks also house your school records, your memberships in unions or other professional organizations, and your record of political contributions. Credit card companies keep track of your payment record, banks retain information on the checks you write, telephone companies record the numbers you have dialed, and insurance companies have a large amount of data on your driving record and medical care. In fact, the data collection industry is now a $1-billion-a-year industry.

The problem with all these data banks is that while they may be innocent enough individually, taken together they can be used to portray a fairly complete, though perhaps not altogether accurate, portrayal of each of us—our habits, our tastes, and possibly our religious and political beliefs. Before the age of computers, it was very difficult to search through all the data banks to collate all the information on a single individual, but now it is fairly easy using a single key identifier such as a Social Security number. The linking of two or more individual data banks to match information from separate data banks is more than a possibility; it is being done now. The Selective Service System performs matches to check student loan records against its registration records to ensure that the loan applicant has registered for the draft. The Internal Revenue Service attempts to detect tax fraud by comparing reported income against data maintained by various business information services to determine if an individual is living beyond his or her means. While both these matching programs are legal, there is concern about potential abuse through the interaction of data banks, especially when the right to confidentiality has not been guaranteed or has been waived.

Compounding this problem is the fear that much of the information included in these data banks is erroneous, either through errors in data collection or through improper entering of data into the data bank. Horror stories abound about people being declared dead by some agency while they are in fact very much alive. One attempt to remove fraudulent individuals from the rolls of disabled persons receiving Social Security benefits led to many cases of truly disabled people losing their only source of income.

While all these problems with data banks that include incorrect data or that are being used for purposes for which they were not intended are worrisome, what do they have to do with personal privacy? To see the relationship, let's define privacy as control over personal information. Under this definition, it is obvious that the inability of the individual to control what goes into these data banks and how this information is used is indeed an intrusion into personal privacy. Since 1970, numerous federal statutes have been enacted to give the individual more control over the information that goes into these data banks, and all 50 states now have laws that protect computer records. However, the continuing technological changes tend to make these laws outdated as soon as they are passed. This entire issue will be discussed in more detail in Chapter 19, when we address the topic of computers and personal privacy again.

Computer Monitoring of Workers

With so many people using computer terminals and PCs in their jobs today, it is not surprising that employers are monitoring the workers' productivity on those computers. In this application of computers, workers are monitored to ensure that production is maintained at an acceptable rate. For example, a telephone operator may be monitored to determine that a set number of callers per hour is being served, or a data entry clerk may be monitored to quantify his or her production level. At one time, monitoring was strictly a mainframe concern since PCs were primarily stand-alone computers, but with the proliferation of PCs linked to networks, monitoring of work on the smaller computers has become more prevalent.

There are various estimates on the extent of monitoring. The Congressional Office of Technology Assessment estimates that between 25 and 35 percent of all service workers using computers are monitored, and a labor union representing many communications workers estimates that over 6 million workers are being monitored each year.

Numerous questions are unresolved about the constitutionality of this practice, since it may violate workers' Fourth Amendment rights to security of "their persons, houses, papers, and effects, against unreasonable search and seizure." In addition, many labor organizations feel that such practices fail to account for the many different situations a worker may encounter during the day. It is also believed that monitoring may actually be counterproductive because it may increase a worker's stress level, resulting in lower efficiency and increased turnover rates. Several bills have been submitted in Congress to restrict the use of monitoring, but, at this writing, no action had been taken on any of them.

Computer monitoring of telephone operators is becoming more prevalent as companies seek to ensure that production is maintained at a predetermined level.

Problems with the Computer Depersonalizing Society

One of the common complaints about computers is that they precipitate a depersonalization of society. This is the other side of the privacy question. It appears that instead of always invading our privacy, computers may also ignore our individuality or modify a user's personality. In the first case, the increased use of bar codes, banking machines, computerized billing, and the like may tend to ignore the "people" side of business. For example, the use of bar codes in grocery stores for pricing and inventory control has been shown to reduce checkout times and stocking costs, but it also can cause problems when the wrong price has been entered into the store computer. Many people are also uncomfortable with the bar code because they cannot determine the price by simply looking at the product; they must find the shelf sticker and perform a price comparison. There are even "self-serve" bar code readers that allow shoppers to check themselves out, totally bypassing the human aspects of shopping.

One of the most frustrating experiences is trying to straighten out an incorrect bill that was prepared by a computer. Numerous comedians have used this situation as material for their monologues, but when it happens to you, it is not funny. As we have said before, this problem is not usually the fault of the computer (which is often the reason given for the problem) but rather the people working with the computer. This problem can occur in the programming of the computer or in the data entry. Either way, to straighten out the problem, you must contact the right person. Writing letters to the computer usually has no effect!

In the second case—computers modifying users' personalities–studies have shown that patterns of human interaction are modified by the way in which people use computers. Just as living with other humans teaches us certain ways of interacting with people, working with a computer tends to modify our behavior patterns. Apparently, the more a person works with a computer, the more he or she becomes intolerant of ambiguous, digressive, or tangential behavior and prefers simple yes–no answers. Some heavy computer users have been observed to put a high premium on efficient communication and to avoid people who talk slowly or in general terms.

Personal Computers and Information Flow

The data banks just discussed are all maintained by mainframe computers, as they require considerable internal and external storage. The personal computer is thought by some to be on the other side of the personal privacy coin; that is, personal computers are the individual's way of gaining access to information and communicating with other users via telecommunication systems like CompuServe and Prodigy. Without control of information, no government can hope to control its people, and wherever personal computers and telecommunications devices are sold freely, information becomes an uncontrollable entity. Recent examples include the 1989 demonstrations by Chinese students in Bejing, where fax machines were a primary source of information to the outside world,

> They [computer compulsives] prefer to communicate with people who are "system literate" so as to transfer information quickly.
>
> *Craig Bond, psychologist*
>
> Quoted in Jeremy Rifkin, *Time Wars* (New York: Henry Holt, 1987).

> The overwhelming impact of the PC is to empower individuals against large organizations.
>
> *George Gilder, author of* Microcosm *and senior fellow at the Hudson Institute*
>
> Quoted in "What the PC Means to Me," *Computer World,* August 5, 1991, p. 55.

ANOTHER VIEW

James E. Katz

James E. Katz is a sociologist with Bell Communications Research and is the author of such books as *People in Space.* The following discussion is quoted from an article by Mr. Katz and provides an opposing view of the effect of technology on privacy:

[A] technological development enhancing personal privacy is the public key-coding procedures. These allow ordinary citizens to communicate with one another in practically total secrecy. Anyone having access to a phone line, a modem, a personal computer, and some software can telecommunicate instantaneously via electronic mail with any other person in the world who has the same technology. Their communication can be so highly encrypted that it would take the most powerful computers in the world a century of computing time to break the code. That is a big step in personal privacy. In addition, a variety of protective systems are emerging that will prevent anyone but an authorized person from access to particular computer files. Unlike the paper records that historically have been used, and can be read by nearly anyone into whose possession they fall, files under these [computer] security systems will self-destruct rather than allow themselves to be compromised.

Source: James E. Katz, "Telecommunications and Computers: Whither Privacy Policy?" *Society,* November/December 1987, pp. 81–86.

PC HELPS THWART SOVIET COUP

One of the most dramatic stories of 1991 was the failure of the Soviet coup in August of that year. Russian president Boris Yeltsin, the leader of the anticoup group, was greatly aided in his efforts by an IBM PC and a Hewlett-Packard laser printer. The coup leaders had managed to deny Mr. Yeltsin access to newspapers and broadcast stations, but they failed to consider the impact of a ten-year-old PC, a laser printer, and a telephone.

The IBM PC was used to create newsletters that were printed on the laser printer and then distributed to thousands of Yeltsin supporters who surrounded the Russian parliament building. The same PC was also combined with the telephone to send electronic copies of the flyers all over the Soviet Union and to Western countries. It was also used to receive electronic messages from such supporters as British Prime Minister John Major. The messages were immediately interpreted and distributed to the supporters. The PC provided Yeltsin with a form of free press that the coup leaders forgot about!

Source: Bill Husted, "Comrade PC Saves the Day," *Atlanta Journal-Constitution*, August 21, 1991, p. C-2.

Boris Yeltsin used a PC and laser printer to create his own news source during the attempted coup.

and the 1991 Soviet coup attempt (see box), where use of a PC allowed Russian president Boris Yeltsin to communicate with both his supporters and with the outside world.

CAREERS IN COMPUTERS

So far in this chapter we have discussed some of the problems that arise from the interaction of computers and people. At one point we said that unemployment caused by automation could be one of these problems. However, there has also been a tremendous increase in computer-related occupations during the past decade. While many of these jobs have occurred in the more traditional main-

frame or minicomputer areas, a great number of jobs have opened up strictly in relation to the use of personal computers. Since this topic will be discussed in detail in Chapter 20, here we will simply provide an overview of the types of jobs open in the computer field.

In the mainframe/minicomputer area, the jobs that are available include (but are by no means limited to) such positions as information system manager, systems analyst, programmer/analyst, data base specialist or manager, telecommunications specialist, software engineer, network specialist, computer operator, and service technician. With the exception of the last two positions, all these positions require some degree of specialized training on the type of system being used in addition to a postsecondary education in the general area of computers or data processing. The last two positions usually require extensive knowledge of the computer system being used plus training in the specialized occupation.

Table 5-1 shows the starting salary ranges for experienced professionals in those positions just mentioned that require postsecondary education. In most surveys, managers state that the employment background and systems or technical background of the applicant are the most important criteria for hiring. Communication skills, education, and enthusiasm are also high-priority qualities.

In the personal computer field, with the increasing use of PCs in all types of organizations, there is a corresponding need for individuals to support and

TABLE 5-1
Starting Salary Ranges for Experienced Professionals

IS manager	$68,000–91,000
Systems analyst	37,000–48,000
Programmer/analyst	32,000–42,000
Data base analyst	38,000–50,000
Telecommunications specialist	40,000–55,000
Software engineer	38,000–53,000
Network specialist	38,000–51,000

Source: Adapted from Robert Half and Accountemps Salary Guide, 1991, Robert Half International, Inc., 1990.

maintain the smaller computers. This is in addition to the continuing need by the large personal computer hardware manufacturers and software companies for systems and applications programmers. In organizations with many PCs, three areas of particular need are end user support, network support, and maintenance. End user support includes all efforts that help end users do their job better using a PC. Network support includes installing and maintaining local area networks composed of PCs. Finally, all PCs will eventually need some type of maintenance, whether it is fixing a stuck key, installing a circuit board, or replacing a bad hard disk. Positions like these do not always require the level of formal education that might be required in a mainframe/minicomputer company since the important requirement is a knowledge of the specialized nature of the product.

Another source of employment in the personal computer field is with the growing number of dealers who sell computer hardware, software, and supplies. It is hard to find a town of any size that does not have at least one computer store. These stores need knowledgeable salespeople, service technicians, and sometimes, programmers to handle the demand for their products. This network

PERSON WITH CP "GOES TO WORK" USING COMPUTER

Even though she has had cerebral palsy since birth and has been unable to control the movements of her arms and legs, Barbara Clements has used her home computer to find a job. She works for the Regional Consortium for Education and Technology reading computer-related magazines and summarizing articles that may be of interest to members of the consortium.

Barbara controls her computer by pressing its keys with a foot-long pointer that is attached to the top of an aluminum head brace she wears. While she's not fast—seven to eight words a minute—she gets the job done. Barbara also manages the consortium's electronic bulletin board and transmits article summaries over it once they are completed.

She found her job the same way she does her work—by linking up with the consortium's office computer and telling it about herself. After a few weeks of corresponding with her prospective supervisor, Carl Hoagland, she asked him for a job. He hired her, and they worked out an arrangement where Barbara works from her home on a part-time basis. Now, after over six years on the job, she continues to draw rave reviews about the quality of her work. In the words of Hoagland, "Barb has more capabilities than just data entry. She can read as fast as you or I can. And she's an excellent writer."

Barbara Clements, who has cerebral palsey, works from her home, thanks to her computer.

Source: Ellen Futterman, "Computers Give Jobs to Disabled," *St. Louis Post-Dispatch,* January 20, 1986, p. A-5, as updated by author in interview with Carl Hoagland, November 3, 1991.

of computer dealers has become such an important link in the personal computer market that a series of trade shows has come into existence to bring hardware and software companies together with dealers. COMputer Dealer EXchange (COMDEX) shows are held throughout the year in the United States, Europe, and Japan, and it is not uncommon to have over 50,000 exhibitors, dealers, and journalists attend.

Finally, the proliferation of PCs in business has resulted in an increasing need for consultants to advise potential users on merits of one system over another. In addition, for those persons interested in teaching, the training field (preparing users to get the most from their personal computer system) is wide open.

FUTURE TRENDS IN COMPUTER USE

In the fast-paced and rapidly changing computer world, it is difficult to predict exactly when various events will happen. But they usually come sooner, not later! One trend is the increasing number of machines that are being made smart. For example, experiments with "smart cars" that will guide their drivers are now underway. By the end of the century, we may all be driving cars with built-in intelligence, yet as recently as 40 years ago, while automobiles and telephones were commonplace, there were fewer than ten computers anywhere in the world. As late as 1981, when the original IBM PC was introduced, there were only 200,000 computers of any kind in the United States. Since then, however, over 70 million personal computers have been sold. Not only has the use of computers proliferated, but the speed and memory of computers has also increased, and they have become cheaper. For example, today an IBM PS/2 sells for much less than the original IBM PC of 1981, but it is ten times faster and has over

New computer hardware and software products are often unveiled at the annual COMDEX show.

1,000 times more memory. If you had asked a computer professional for an opinion on the potential growth of the personal computer in 1981, he or she probably would not have predicted the success for this machine that we see today. However, even with the unpredictability of future computer use, some trends seem well established in computer hardware and software.

Trends in Computer Hardware

The key trend in computer hardware has been "smaller, faster, and cheaper," and this trend is expected to continue and even accelerate. Mainframes are shrinking to the size once reserved for minicomputers, and personal computers are as fast as the mainframes of ten years ago. Much of this change is the result of the ongoing research in microchip technology, which has given us the ability to pack more and more electronic elements into less and less space. Today, research is progressing into manipulating molecules to reduce the size of computer elements even further. In addition, recent advances in the field of **superconductivity** (the capability for electricity at low temperatures to flow without any resistance) have increased the possibility of using it to dramatically increase the speed of computers.

At the supercomputer level, an industry is constantly seeking ways to build faster computers. Much of this research involves finding shorter wiring paths, which would reduce the amount of time needed for information to flow between the parts of the computer. A great deal of research is going into the development of **massively parallel computers** that are capable of performing many different operations at the same time and, thus, greatly speed up the processing of data into information. In addition, research is ongoing in the field of **neural networks**—computers that can learn how to solve a problem from examples rather than having to be specifically programmed.

In personal computers, the trend is toward using 32-bit processors such as the Intel i486 chip and the Motorola 68000 series of chips. These chips permit much faster processing and access to larger amounts of internal memory. Intel and other chip companies are working on 64-bit CPU chips that would give the PC supercomputerlike capabilities.

Trends in Computer Software

As discussed in Chapter 3, the trend in software is toward the use of graphical user interfaces (GUI) as a way of making software easier to use. This is true primarily at the PC level, but there is also research into using the same type of interfaces for minicomputers and mainframes. All popular PC packages are being rewritten to run with a graphical interface.

Another trend in mainframe software packages has been the emulation of personal computer packages (word processors, spreadsheets, and so on) on the mainframe. This has been done by writing packages that work like the PC packages but take advantage of the increased power and storage on the mainframe or by moving PC packages to the mainframe. For example, WordPerfect, the current best-selling PC word processor package for IBM compatible PCs, is now available for mainframe systems as well as for the Apple Macintosh series of computers. It is highly probable that this trend will continue as software com-

Hypercard allows users to locate information through multiple access paths.

panies move to combine the ease of use often associated with PC packages with the power and storage capacity of a mainframe.

In the world of educational software, a great deal of work is ongoing in using authoring languages to create educational systems that are both easy to use and exciting. An **authoring language** is a computer package that enables the user to create a sequence of interactive learning activities where the user uses a mouse to click on a "hot button" on the screen to answer a question or seek additional information. An example of an authoring language is HyperCard for the Apple Macintosh. It has been used to develop many educational programs, including a system called KonjiMaster, which teaches students how to draw Japanese konji characters.

Artificial Intelligence

Probably the most exciting possibility in computers today and in the future is artificial intelligence. **Artificial intelligence (AI)** is produced when computer hardware and software systems are combined in such a way as to exhibit some level of human intelligence. Because the term *AI* has such a broad definition, it has been applied to many different types of computer systems. For this reason, you will see the term in several chapters of this text. Among other things, AI has been applied to robotics; to expert systems (systems that help managers

Artificial intelligence was popularized in the movie *2001: A Space Odyssey* in the form of the talking computer HAL.

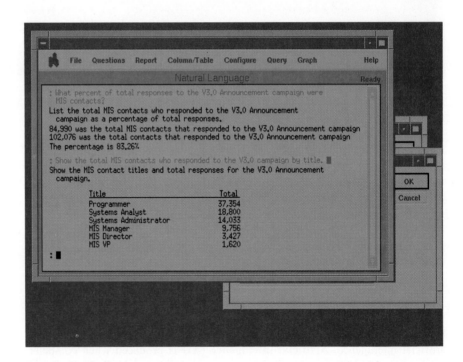

Users may request information using natural language instead of special codes, making software more user friendly.

make decisions); and to systems that can listen and understand, read printed material, generate speech, help solve problems, and so on. To many people, AI is the most important area of computer research today. However, other writers feel that there is no such thing as AI, since intelligence is a strictly human quality.

One application of AI that may have a more profound effect than other applications is "softer software"—software that is much easier to use than what is available today. One such area of research is determining the capability of a computer to understand **natural languages,** such as English rather than sometimes cryptic computer languages. Also dependent on AI are voice-input computers, pen-based computers, and **virtual reality,** which seeks to make computer and human interaction transparent. It is envisioned that virtual reality might be achieved through a high-tech bodysuit that senses its wearer's body movements and translates them to the computer. In many ways, AI is being used to make computers "people literate" rather than forcing people to become computer literate!

While still in its infancy, AI is one of the fastest-growing high-tech areas. Many companies are spending large amounts of money either to develop AI systems or to purchase systems developed by other companies. However, no one is close to developing a computer system like the fictional HAL from the movies *2001: A Space Odyssey* and *2010: The Year We Make Contact.*

**HAL: Good afternoon, Gent-le-men. I am a HAL 9000 computer. I became operational at the H.A.L. labs in Urbana, Ill., on the 12th of January 1992. My instructor was Mr. Langley and he taught me to sing a song. If you'd like to hear it, I can sing it for you.
Astronaut: Yes, I'd like to hear it, HAL. Sing it for me.
HAL: It's called "Daisy" . . .**

From Arthur C. Clarke, *2001: A Space Odyssey.* (New York: New American Library, 1968).

REVIEW OF KEY POINTS

1. The interaction of computers and society has brought many benefits but has also brought some problems.

2. The four main ways in which people and computers interact are (a) through computers in the workplace, (b) when computers are used to commit crimes, (c) when computers affect personal privacy, and (d) when computers create new career opportunities.

3. Computers in the workplace can affect workers by creating new jobs, causing unemployment, creating potential health hazards, and causing psychological problems for workers who fear computers.

4. Computer crime can involve theft of money, merchandise, time, or data; destruction of hardware, software, or data; or the incursion into a computer "for fun."

5. Personal computer software piracy occurs when software is copied illegally.

6. Computers threaten personal privacy because they are so efficient at searching out and matching elements from individual data banks. Computer monitoring of workers is another area that potentially invades personal privacy.

7. Computers have the potential to depersonalize society by removing the face-to-face human contact from many everyday actions or by modifying the personalities of users.

8. Personal computers act as safeguards to personal freedom by allowing us to communicate with other users and to exchange information freely.

9. Careers in computers are available for people who understand

and can work with mainframes, minicomputers, or personal computers. The many computer-oriented careers have varying educational requirements.

10. There are many openings for people with education or experience in working with personal computers.

11. Future trends in computer hardware are toward smaller, faster, and cheaper computers. Trends in computer software include moving personal computer software to mainframes, using authoring languages to create educational presentations, and developing the exciting field of artificial intelligence.

KEY TERMS

artificial intelligence (AI)
authoring language
backup
computer crime
computeritis
computerphobia
computer virus
computer worm
copy protection
data bank
ergonomics

hacker
informated factory
information specialist
massively parallel computers
natural languages
neural networks
software piracy
superconductivity
video display terminal (VDT)
virtual reality

1. Name the four types of interface between society and computers.
2. Discuss possible health problems arising from the use of VDTs. What is computeritis?
3. What psychological problem can arise for workers who are uncomfortable working with computers?
4. How can computers create new jobs and at the same time create potential unemployment? How does the informated factory relate to this seeming contradiction?
5. What does the science of ergonomics have to do with computers?
6. Why is it sometimes very easy for a criminal to gain access to a mainframe computer? What is a computer virus?
7. Explain the term *software piracy.* Why is it a problem for both the software company and the personal computer user?
8. List as many data banks as you can that you think may have your name included in them.
9. In what ways could data from two or more of the data banks you named in the previous question be matched?
10. What is computer monitoring and what does it have to do with personal privacy? Why does it now include PCs as well as mainframe terminals?
11. Name two ways in which you have experienced the depersonalizing effect of computers. How can a computer modify a user's personality?
12. Discuss the ways in which a personal computer can be used to increase the information flow to individuals.

13. Check a local newspaper or your college or university employment service and determine what salaries are being paid for two of the positions listed in Table 5-1.

14. Visit a local computer store and determine which of the jobs mentioned in this textbook are actually being carried on there.

15. What is artificial intelligence? Discuss how it might be used to develop "softer software" or natural languages.

BLOCK TWO

The Details of Hardware

In Block One, Chapter 2 presented an introductory discussion of hardware. Block Two will now cover the details of hardware: Chapter 6 will cover the central processing unit (CPU) and internal memory, Chapter 7 input/output, and Chapter 8 secondary storage. Each chapter will begin with a review of the material covered in Chapter 2 and then will enlarge upon the earlier discussion with a detailed coverage of particular material. We present material on computers of all sizes.

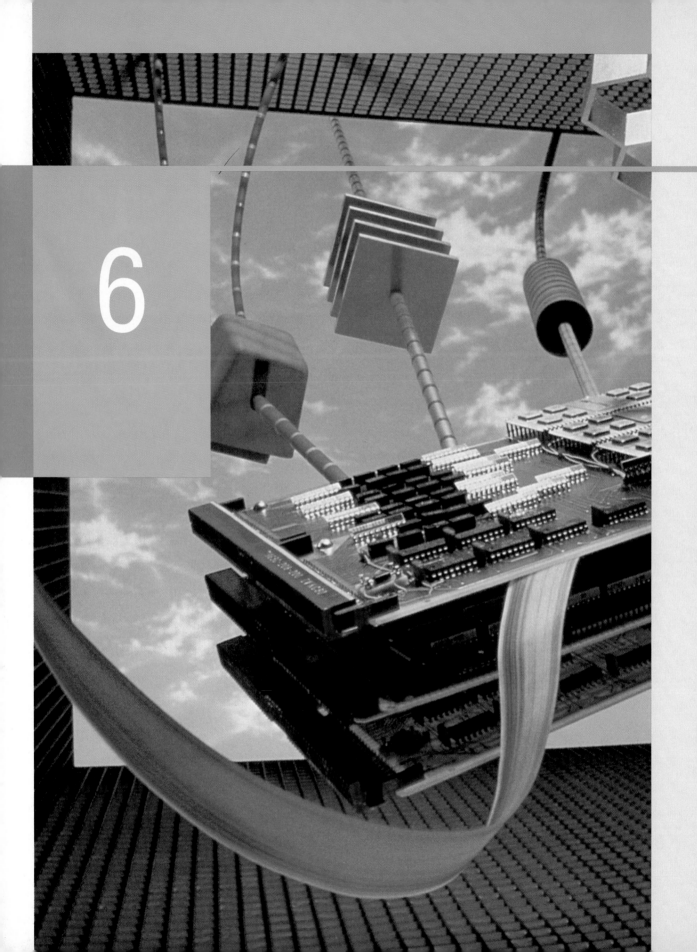

The CPU and Internal Memory

This chapter continues the hardware discussion begun in Chapter 2, concentrating on the processing and internal memory functions within the computer. The material begins with a detailed look at the conceptual computer. The parts of the CPU, along with the process of program execution, will be considered—including a discussion of temporary memory devices in the CPU. A second look at internal memory includes RAM and ROM as well as other types of memory chips. The makeup, construction, and uses of the miniature electronic device known as the chip will be considered in words and pictures. Finally, robots and androids will be discussed.

STUDY OBJECTIVES

After reading this chapter, you should be able to

■ understand the transfer of information into, within, and out of the computer;

■ describe the subdivisions of the CPU and the process of executing a program;

■ discuss registers in the CPU and the concept of a computer word as it relates to computer processing;

■ describe various types of chips used in PCs;

■ discuss parallel processing;

■ understand the makeup of RAM and ROM as well as other types of memory chips;

■ describe the construction process for chips and explain how they have affected both our lives and the development of computers;

■ discuss the types of robots available today and their problems and potential.

CHIPS DIRECT MUSCLES TO WALK

> I could do the same with a wheelchair, but I would rather walk, even if it takes a lot longer and expends a lot more energy. I think it's important.

Erik Kondo, patient using Parastep,® Shepard Spinal Clinic

Quoted in "They're Back on Their Feet," *The Atlanta Journal-Constitution*, June 11, 1991, p. F-4.

In over 10,000 accidents a year in the United States, individuals suffer spinal cord injuries that leave them paralyzed. It has been estimated that over 250,000 persons in the United States suffer from paralysis. Even though the spinal cord of a paralyzed person is broken and signals cannot reach the legs, the nerves and muscles in the individual's legs may still be functional. With **functional electrical stimulation (FES),** which uses computers to stimulate functional muscles, these individuals may be able to walk again.

Research in FES has been conducted for over 20 years, and now, as the result of research carried out by Daniel Graupe, Ph.D., at the Michael Reese Hospital and Medical Center in Chicago, an FES system has been developed and introduced commercially. The system is called Parastep®, and it consists of a Walkman-size microcomputer, a series of electrodes, a power pack, and a specially designed walker. The microcomputer and battery are worn at the user's belt, and the electrodes are attached to the skin of the legs. The walker provides balance and stability to the user when he or she is standing or walking. The patient controls electrical signals from the microcomputer to his or her leg muscles through a keyboard on the belt pack or through switches on the walker.

Costing $15,000, Parastep® is the first system of its kind that does not require users to wear heavy braces or surgically implanted electrodes. In trials at 15 hospitals, patients have been able to use the system for up to two hours a day and have been able to walk as far as 350 feet. The system benefits the users psychologically, it helps them increase muscle and cardiovascular strength, and in getting them back on their feet again, it reduces the risk of their developing blood clots and bed sores. Patrick Maher, director of marketing for the company that distributes Parastep®, has been using the system since 1983. He uses it for 20-minute intervals both at home and work. The hospital trials suggest that Parastep® may allow paralyzed patients a degree of freedom not now possible.

Source: Jan Gehorsam, "They're Back on Their Feet," *The Atlanta Journal-Constitution*, June 11, 1991, p. F-4.

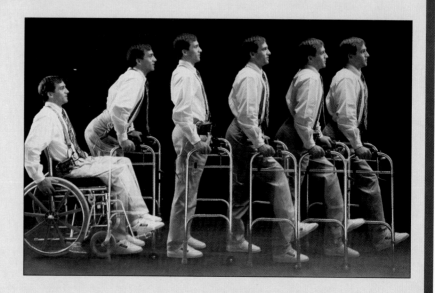

ParaStep® helps paralyzed people walk again.

In Chapter 2 we introduced the **conceptual computer** to explain how a computer works. That conceptual computer had an input unit, a processing/internal memory unit, a secondary storage unit, and an output unit. In the box example of the computer chip directing the contraction of muscles, the processing/internal memory unit handles a simple form of input from a switch on the walker and sends the output to the muscle. There is no monitor or secondary storage. This demonstrates the crucial fact that, while input, storage, and output devices are needed for many computer applications, the key element in any computer is the processing/internal memory unit, which will be discussed in some detail in this chapter.

To help you understand the important role of the processing/internal memory unit, in Figure 6-1 we have expanded the conceptual computer and added more detail. The computer's **central processing unit (CPU)** is divided into the **arithmetic–logic unit (ALU)** and the **control unit (CU).** The control unit converts the user's processing instructions into commands to the computer, and the ALU performs the actual processing within the computer. Recall from Chapter 2 the analogy of the ALU and CU to two clerks who handle the processing within the CPU. Figure 6-1 also shows the internal memory, input, secondary storage, and output units.

FIGURE 6-1
A Second Look at the Conceptual
Computer

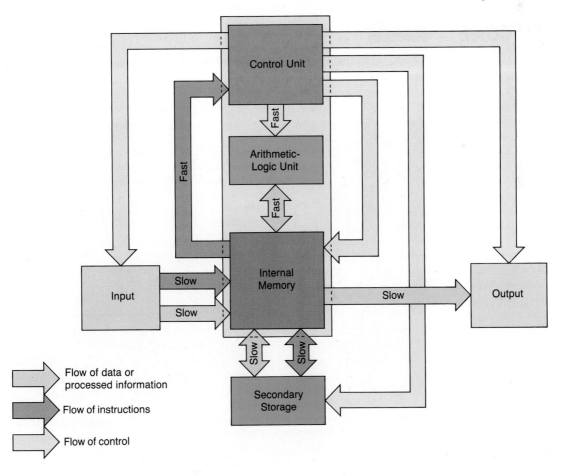

THE CONCEPTUAL COMPUTER REVISITED   151

Flows of data, instructions, control, and results into, within, and out of the computer are detailed in Figure 6-1. Data and instructions first go from the input unit into the internal memory unit. This transfer of data and information is labeled "slow," because data must be entered into the input unit and then transferred into the computer. In general, input and output are slower than processing operations.

From the internal memory unit, the instructions are transferred to the control unit, which directs the activities of all other units. The control unit directs the transfer of data to the ALU from the internal memory unit for the actual processing within the ALU. Under control of the control unit, a two-way transfer of data, results, and instructions occurs between the internal memory unit and secondary storage. The results of the processing in the ALU are then sent to the internal memory unit, where they are output under directions of the control unit. The transfers of instructions and data within the CPU and between the CPU and the internal memory unit are considered "fast" because they are either on a chip or between chips. On the other hand, the transfer of instructions, data, and results between the internal memory unit and the secondary storage unit is "slow," along with the flow of results to the output unit, because these flows involve electromechanical devices, such as disk drives. Any flow of control is "fast."

Our discussion of the workings of the conceptual computer applies to both mainframes and personal computers. The differences between the two types of computers involve speed and storage, which depend on the type and number of chips in the CPU and internal memory units.

THE CPU UP CLOSE

It is the ALU that actually processes *all* the data that passes through the CPU. The ALU processes data with arithmetic operations, such as addition and sub-

Integrated circuit boards are an important part of computers of all sizes.

traction, and logical (true/false) operations, which compare two numbers to determine if they are equal or unequal. These are the only operations the ALU performs, but they are sufficient to accomplish all computer tasks.

The control unit manages the operation of the computer, including synchronizing operations, controlling the flow of data into the computer, and providing commands to the ALU. A **clock** sends out electrical pulses at a set rate to synchronize the operations of the control unit. All instructions, data, and control commands are transferred between the control unit, the ALU, and the internal memory along a communication system called the **system bus.** Figure 6-2 shows the relationship of the system bus to the control unit, the ALU, and the internal memory unit.

The control unit and ALU combined on a chip are referred to as a **microprocessor.** Personal computers usually have only one such chip to serve a single user, whereas mainframes have multiple microprocessor chips. The microprocessor is the key element that distinguishes one computer from another.

Using Registers

Within the CPU, there is a high-speed type of memory called a register. A **register** is a temporary holding place for a particular instruction, data item, or piece of information. These fast storage areas help the computer perform the actual data processing. Different types of registers exist for the various operations that are executed from program instructions. Often, more than one of some types of registers may be used in a computer. The following types of registers are used:

- A storage register, which is a temporary holding area within the ALU, stores information to be transferred to or from internal storage.
- An address register holds the addresses of the data to be transferred from the internal memory unit.
- An accumulator register holds the results of any processing that takes place within the ALU.
- An instruction register holds an instruction in the control unit before it is decoded.

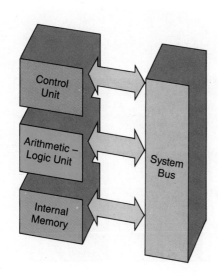

FIGURE 6-2
Computer Units and the System Bus

- A program counter register holds the address of the next instruction to be executed.
- A general-purpose register can be used for any type of operation or storage.

Only one instruction or operation can take place at a time in a register, but that operation can be done extremely quickly. However, the number of registers in a computer is limited, seldom exceeding 20 for the largest mainframe or 14 for the most powerful personal computer.

Executing a Program

The control unit and the ALU work together to execute the instructions of the program, which are stored in the internal memory unit along with the data. The storage system for instructions and data is very much like a series of post office boxes. Each instruction is stored in a particular storage location, which is defined by an **address.** However, only one instruction or data item can be stored at a given address in memory. Figure 6-3 demonstrates the concept of a computer's storage locations, some of which contain data.

To execute a program, the computer must go through the **fetch, decode, and execute process;** that is, the computer fetches an instruction, decodes that instruction, then executes the instruction. A typical instruction might be "move the contents of memory location 1001 to the storage register." The steps in this process are shown in Figure 6-4, where the circled numbers correspond to the steps in the summary of the fetch, decode, and execute process that follows:

Step 1: Fetch address of instruction from internal memory along the communication path called the **address bus.**

Step 2: Fetch and decode the instruction and have any needed data sent to the ALU along the **data bus.** The instruction is not destroyed, so this is called a **nondestructive fetch.** The decoded instruction is stored in the instruction register, and the data are stored in the storage register.

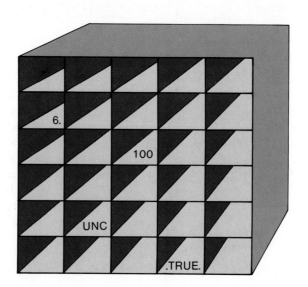

FIGURE 6-3
Storage Locations within a Computer

FIGURE 6-4
Execution Process

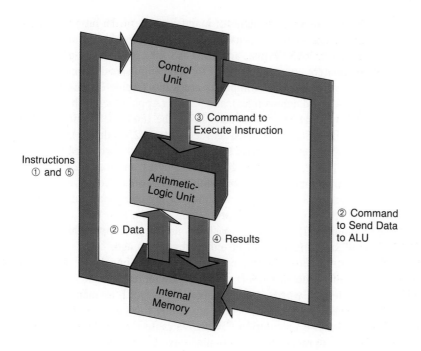

Step 3: Send a command to the ALU along the **control bus** to carry out the decoded instruction using data retrieved earlier. Store the results in the storage register.

Step 4: Send the results of the ALU operation from the storage register to internal memory. This writes over previous information in RAM, so this is called a **destructive replacement.**

Step 5: If more instructions remain, go back to step 1; otherwise, terminate execution.

In this process, steps 1 and 2 occur during **instruction-time (I-time),** whereas steps 3 through 5 occur during **execution-time (E-time).**

To speed the process, the control unit anticipates the next instruction that the program counter register may need, and it tries to store the instruction's address. If the program encounters a change in the instruction sequence, the program counter is reset to the new instruction.

Computer Words

In a computer, the **bit** is the smallest unit that corresponds to a switch being on or off. A binary value of 1 corresponds to a bit when the switch is "on," and a value of 0 corresponds to a bit when the switch is "off." While a bit corresponds to a switch within the computer, the actual processing is performed with a combination of bits called a computer word. A **computer word** is the number of bits that can be held by the registers and processed as a single unit. The size of the computer word affects the processing speed of the computer. For example, a computer with a 32-bit word will process data faster than a computer with a 16-bit word, all other things being equal, since twice as much data are being processed in a single operation.

Different sizes and types of computers have different sizes of computer words. IBM mainframes, including the ES/900 and 4300 series, use a 32-bit word size. The UNIVAC 1100 series of mainframe uses a 36-bit word, and Control Data Corporation mainframes use a 60-bit word size. Most minicomputers—including the DEC VAX, Prime, and IBM AS 400 series—use a 32-bit word size. Supercomputers use a 64-bit word for their high-speed computations.

Word sizes for personal computers are 8 bits (Apple IIe and IIc), 16 bits (IBM PC, XT, AT, and compatibles), and 32 bits (Apple Macintosh, Commodore Amiga, and a wide range of computers using the Intel 80386 and 80486, also referred to as the i486, chips, such as the IBM PS/2 Model 95). Recall from Chapter 2 that 8 bits equal 1 **byte.** In terms of bytes, the word length for an 8-bit computer is 1 byte; for a 16-bit computer, 2 bytes; and for a 32-bit computer, 4 bytes. Personal computers that work with 32-bit words offer several important advantages over the 8- and 16-bit machines: They can process a larger chunk of data at one time, yielding high processing speeds; also they can access an increased amount of RAM. These machines are rapidly approaching the speed and storage of small mainframes of only a few years ago.

While computers perform numerical calculations using **fixed-length words** (8, 16, or whatever number of bits), they represent instructions and text with **variable-length words.** In a variable-length word, as many bytes as are needed to represent instructions or text are strung together. Fixed-length words provide fast numeric calculations, while variable-length words provide the needed flexibility to represent instructions or text. Computers have the flexibility to use either type as needed.

Personal Computer CPU Chips

For PCs there is a wide variety of CPU chips in use today, including the Motorola 6502 chip used in the Apple II series, the Intel 80xxx (8088, 80286, 80386, i486, and so on) series of chips used in various IBM compatible computers, and the Motorola 68000 series of chips used in Apple Macintosh and Commodore Amiga computers. While the Intel 80xxx series of chips is upwardly compati-

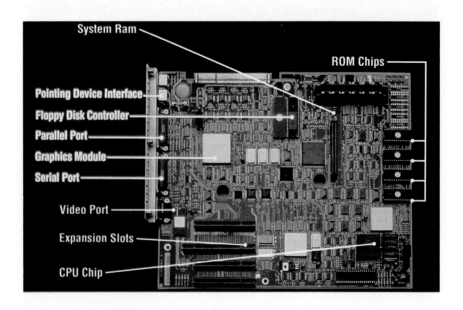

The IBM PS/2 computer planar board contains various types of chips, including the CPU, RAM, and ROM chips and the disk and video controllers.

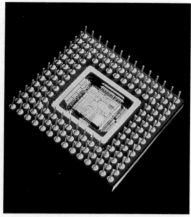

The Intel i486 chip (right) runs current applications up to 20 times faster than the original 8088 chip (left).

ble—that is, software that will run on the 8088 will also run on the higher-numbered chips—there is no compatibility between this series of chips and the other two types of Motorola chips. In fact, there is no compatibility between the chips used in the two types of Apple computers.

As mentioned earlier, mainframe computers such as the IBM ES/9000 and 4300 series, as well as most minicomputers, use a 32-bit word length. This allows the processing of information at a greater speed and the accessing of greater amounts of memory than in personal computers that use either an 8- or a 16-bit word length. Now, with the introduction of the Intel 80386 and i486 32-bit chips, the power and speed of a mainframe can be brought to the desktop. In addition to increased speed for current applications, 32-bit chips offer the capability of running new applications software in up to 4 Gbytes (billions of bytes) of memory and of running multiple applications software programs concurrently.

In terms of speed, a personal computer using the i486 can run current applications software at least 15 to 20 times faster than the original IBM PC using the 8088 chip. The capability of the 80386 and i486 chips to run multiple applications means that a user would have the equivalent of several IBM ATs running inside a computer based on one of these chips. Computer-aided design, manufacturing, and engineering; artificial intelligence systems; very large data bases; and very large spreadsheets are existing types of software that will benefit greatly from being run on PCs using these chips.

To speed up arithmetic operations, it is possible to add a special chip called a **math coprocessor** to the computer. This chip takes over from the CPU to handle the various arithmetic operations needed in many mathematical calculations. The biggest difference between the 80386 and i486 chips is that the latter chip has the coprocessor chip built into it.

Parallel Processing

Since the time of von Neumann and the stored program, most computers have been **serial machines,** which process data sequentially. That is, they can perform only one operation at a time. Each operation involves retrieving data from memory, making a calculation, sending the results to memory, and then starting the process over again. This creates a bottleneck, because the computer must wait for the previous calculation to be completed before the next one begins. Serial data processing, therefore, restricts computers because it seriously hampers speed and limits a computer's ability to process some types of problems. Supercomputers, on the other hand, avoid these restrictions because they process data in a parallel manner. **Parallel processing** allows a computer to simultaneously perform multiple calculations, because multiple CPUs simultaneously execute multiple instructions. Clearly, parallel processing can be much faster than serial processing, since it is capable of executing multiple instructions in the same amount of time it takes serial processing to execute a single instruction. Figure 6-5 illustrates the difference between serial and parallel processing.

There are two main types of supercomputers: **parallel-data computers,** which simultaneously perform the same operation on many different data items; and **parallel-process computers,** which divide a problem into many small parts that are each solved by a separate processor.

Until recently, supercomputers were used strictly for making complex calculations and were available only to a few researchers working with the military or NASA. Now however, a desktop-size supercomputer that sells for less than $100,000 is available. As supercomputers become increasingly more available,

FIGURE 6-5
Comparison of Serial Processing and Parallel Processing

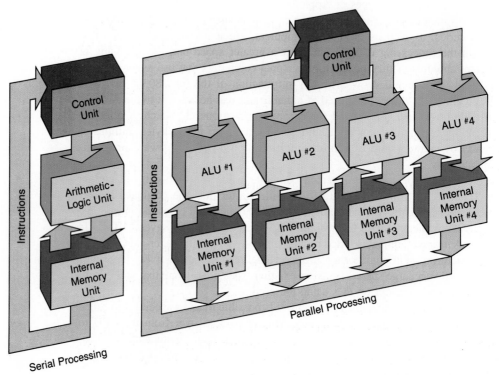

researchers in many fields are using them to solve diverse, difficult problems. For example, supercomputers have created models for the simulation of black holes, thunderstorms, tornadoes, wind shear over an airplane wing, and acid rain over the United States and Canada. During the Gulf War, a supercomputer was used to plot the courses of individual Scud missiles to enable coalition forces to locate the launchers in order to destroy them.

In many cases, the supercomputer processes tremendous amounts of research data. In other cases, it solves a large number of complex equations and then provides results in a graphical form for humans to assimilate. It is estimated that supercomputers can work 10 *million* times faster than the first computers built just a little over 40 years ago.

INTERNAL MEMORY

If the CPU is one-half of the computer's brain, the other half is **internal memory,** also referred to as **main memory,** or **primary storage.** Here, the list of instructions—the program—is stored along with the data. The two primary types of internal memory are RAM (for **random-access memory**) and ROM (for **read-only memory**). In **ROM,** information is stored in binary with a permanent series of switches in the chip. In **RAM,** storage is accomplished by the use of "flip-flops," miniature transistors on a chip that act as switches to store the information in binary form. Each bit of information corresponds to one transistor (switch), which is turned on if the bit equals 1, or left off if the bit equals 0.

Read-Only Memory

As discussed in Chapter 2, ROM is **nonvolatile** (permanent) **memory** that handles many important tasks. One of these tasks is to provide the computer with instructions during the startup, or **booting,** process. Since the ROM is devoid of information when the computer is turned on, the computer must load its first few instructions from ROM without help from the user. Usually, these instructions tell the computer to go to secondary storage to load the information from the system disk. Booting a mainframe is a complicated procedure, but booting a personal computer is quite simple. For example, booting the IBM 3090 series of mainframe computers can take up to 30 minutes, while booting a PC requires only that the user insert the system disk and turn the computer on. Figure 6-6 shows the booting process for a personal computer.

Another important role for ROM is that of **character generator.** Each keypress or instruction from software is relayed to ROM, which then supplies the appropriate character to be displayed on the screen. This dramatically speeds up the process of displaying text since all the necessary characters are quickly found in ROM rather than having to be generated from scratch as they are in graphics displays. In some computers, like the Apple Macintosh, the ROM contains various instructions for graphics and for input devices such as the mouse. Some computers are also using ROM for permanent storage of various popular software packages. A problem with this use of ROM is that the ROM chip must be replaced to update the software. Because the instructions on the ROM chip are permanent, they are often referred to as **firmware** to differentiate them from the software instructions that the user places in RAM.

THE FASTEST COMPUTER

The Thinking Machines Corporation, led by MIT graduate Danny Hillis, has been developing a parallel-process supercomputer since 1984. Recently, the corporation's multiprocess supercomputer won the title of fastest computer in an independently sponsored competition. The supercomputer runs at an almost unbelievable *5.2 billion* instructions per second.

It functions somewhat like the human brain, which is composed of innumerable neurons that process and convey information and are always in communication with one another. Similarly, the Thinking Machines Corporation's supercomputer has up to 16,000 individual processing chips that can send billions of messages back and forth, owing to specially designed software that allows the processors to communicate with each other. Thinking Machines' newer versions of the supercomputer claim speeds of up to 1 *trillion* instructions per second, which by far, is faster than any other supercomputers previously available.

Uses for the parallel-process supercomputers include image processing, document retrieval, and fluid dynamics. American Express has ordered two of Thinking Machines' supercomputers to enhance customer service by speeding the collection billing data for both merchants and card holders.

Source: Michael Alexander, "Parallel Computer Wins FLOPS Race," *Computerworld,* March 25, 1991, p. 20; and "Thinking Machines Thinks Big," *Computerworld,* November 4, 1991, p. 12.

Random-Access Memory

When considering computer memory, people usually think of random-access memory (RAM)—so named because any part of RAM can be accessed in the same amount of time as any other part. RAM is the memory that the user can access for writing programs or storing data and software. RAM is extremely fast memory but, unlike ROM, it is not permanent. In RAM, the miniaturized transistors on the memory chip must be maintained in an "on" or "off" state by a constant electrical current. Once the current is removed by turning the computer off, the transistors lose the information that was stored there. For this reason, RAM is termed **volatile memory.**

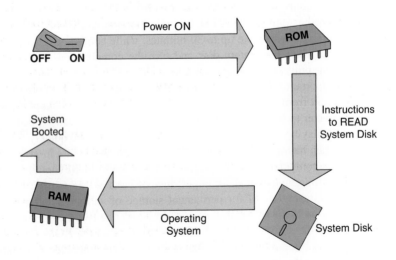

FIGURE 6-6
Booting Process for a Personal Computer

ANOTHER VIEW

Gene Amdahl

In 1970, Gene Amdahl, the chief architect of the IBM System/360 computer, left IBM to found his own company to build IBM compatible mainframes. Since that time, Amdahl has been a leader in developing mainframe computers. In this discussion, he and an associate, Jon Shiell, comment on the difference between mainframes and personal computers.

Amdahl: In the mainframe context, a CPU is a great deal more than an arithmetic unit and a memory access. In a mainframe CPU, you have an enormous array of I/O [input/output] capabilities handled automatically.

There's a separate I/O system, but a mainframe CPU is designed in such a way that it's thoroughly integrated with the I/O capability. There aren't any workstations that have this kind of architecture.

Shiell: In a mainframe, you have almost as large a processor handling I/O as doing instructions. The main deficiency of the current generation of microprocessors is that they don't do I/O well. For workstations or PCs that's fine.

Amdahl: But, if you're assuming that a small system is going to serve a single individual, then there's a limit as to how much you can do with the system. The memory systems on the most powerful PCs are pale emulations of memory on large systems.

Source: "The Mainframe Perspective," *MIPS*, March 1989, pp. 54–55.

Gene Amdahl has been a pioneer in the development of mainframe computers for over 20 years.

The amount of RAM in a computer system is discussed in terms of Kbytes. In Chapter 2 we said that 1 **Kbyte** is equivalent to 1,024 bytes. The contents of the actual memory chips used for RAM are measured in Kbits. One **Kbit** is the equivalent of 1,024 bits. Currently, memory chips have either 256 Kbits, 1 megabit (1,024,000 bits), or 4 megabits of memory.

The amount of memory on a chip is measured in powers of 2 (1,024 bits $= 2^{10}$). Therefore, the memory addresses are also expressed in powers of 2. The actual addressing of a memory location from the CPU is beyond the scope of this discussion, but the process of locating 1 bit out of a block of 64 bits is shown in Figure 6-7. In this diagram, the row address and column address are expressed in binary. For example, the bit in row 5 and column 3 would have the address 0101 0011, with the row address shown first and the column address shown second.

RAM chips come in two types: dynamic and static. **Dynamic RAM (DRAM)** uses one transistor switch and a tiny storage device called a capacitor to store one bit of data. The capacitors must be energized hundreds of times each second to continue to hold the information. This is the type of RAM that is used in most PCs. On the other hand, **static RAM (SRAM)** uses transistors that do not require constant energizing, so it is faster than DRAM, but it is also more expensive. Data can be accessed from SRAM in approximately 35 nanoseconds, whereas the access time for DRAM is around 80 nanoseconds. For PCs,

> **We figure that in almost all application environments, we'll get a cache hit [find the needed data] 90 percent of the time.**
>
> *Bob Burnett, Zenith Computers*
>
> Quoted in "Memories Are Made of This," *Personal Computing*, January 1990, pp. 84–90.

FIGURE 6-7
Addressing Storage Locations

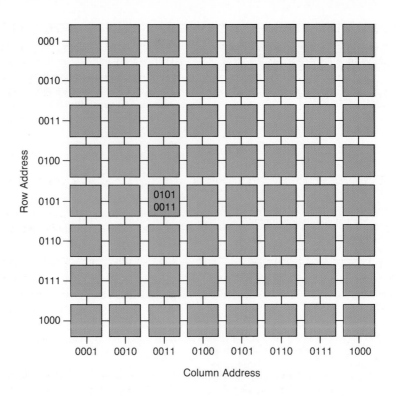

RAM chips once had to be individually installed. Today, memory chips are incorporated on a plug-in board called a SIMM (single inline memory module).

DRAM is usually used for main memory, because it is less expensive and takes up less space. SRAM, on the other hand, is much faster, so it is often used for the very fast temporary memory that is called a **cache memory.** When both DRAM and SRAM are used, the slower main RAM storage shifts data and information to the cache memory before the CPU needs it. When the CPU requires the data and instructions, they are retrieved from cache faster than they could

This 8-meg memory board uses 1-meg SIMMS (single inline memory modules).

have been retrieved from primary RAM storage. This usually results in a faster form of memory transfer and processing. Figure 6-8 shows the process of using cache to speed processing.

Because RAM is volatile, some personal computers, especially laptop models, now come with battery backup, which can retain the contents of memory for several hours—even after the computer is turned off.

PC Memory

There is often some confusion about the amount of internal memory in IBM compatible PCs that use the MS-DOS operating system. The first 640 Kbytes of RAM is termed **conventional memory,** and it is the only memory that MS-DOS was designed to recognize when it executes a program, including itself. This restriction exists regardless of how much actual RAM the PC contains. The RAM between 640 Kbytes and 1 Mbyte is called **upper memory.** This means that the upper memory of a PC with at least 1 Mbyte (1,024 Kbytes) of RAM is 384 Kbytes. Upper memory is normally reserved for software required by hardware devices, such as monitors or network linkages. However, with MS-DOS 5.0 and other memory manager programs, it is possible to move some types of software to upper memory and thereby free portions of conventional memory for other software.

All RAM between 1 and 32 Mbytes is referred to as **extended memory.** Conventional RAM plus any RAM up to 8 Mbytes is referred to as **expanded memory.** Because expanded memory was developed for MS-DOS, many popular MS-DOS–based software programs have been written for expanded memory. Unfortunately, these programs cannot use extended memory (any RAM above 1 Mbyte) unless they are used in conjunction with a **memory manager,** which is a utility-type software. With a memory manager, extended memory emulates expanded memory. However, PCs using the OS/2 operating system or the Windows operating environment can use extended memory directly. Figure 6-9 shows the relationship among conventional, upper, extended, and expanded memory on an IBM compatible PC that uses MS-DOS.

Other Types of Memory

RAM and ROM are the two most important types of memory in the computer, but other types of memory chips have many useful purposes. In some cases, these other memory chips attempt to combine the better points of both RAM and ROM.

Two memory chips that attempt to have the best of RAM and ROM are **PROM** chips (**programmable read-only memory**) and **EPROM** chips (**erasable programmable read-only memory**). The PROM chip is like a ROM chip

> When we set the upper limit of PC-DOS at 640K, we thought nobody would ever need that much memory.
>
> *William Gates, Founder and CEO, Microsoft Software*
>
> Quoted in "Give Me Power," *Infoworld,* April 29, 1985, p. 5.

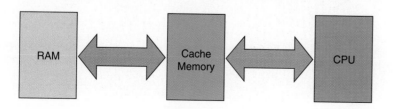

FIGURE 6-8
Use of Cache to Speed Processing

FIGURE 6-9
Types of PC Memory

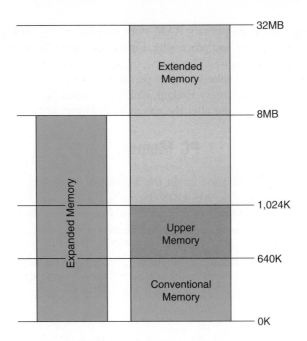

except that the instructions are not built in at the factory. The chip's user can "burn in" the chip's special instructions. Once the user does this, the chip is like any ROM chip directing applications in a specific area, such as manufacturing, agriculture, or health. A common use of PROM chips is to boot PCs attached to a network. Various types of PROM are used in popular video games, such as Nintendo. The game information is programmed onto the ROM chips by the game manufacturer.

The EPROM can be extremely useful in experimental work when the user is uncertain about the instructions that should be placed on the chip. The

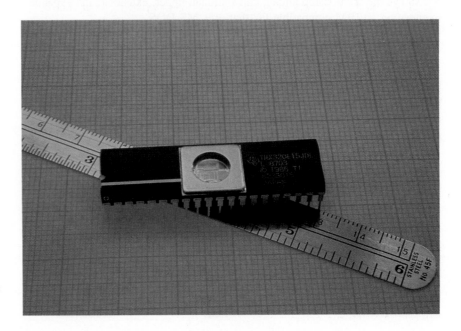

Erasable, programmable, read-only memory chips can be erased by ultraviolet light directed through the special window at the top of the chip.

EPROM chip can be *erased* by exposure to ultraviolet light and then reprogrammed as many times as needed. For example, the instructions on a read-only chip that is used to control a piece of farm machinery may be changed several times before the user has full control of the machinery.

THE AMAZING CHIP

As mentioned in Chapter 1 in our discussion of smart machines, the **chip** is probably the single technological advance that most profoundly affects the world today. Just as the transistor was developed to replace the vacuum tube, the chip was developed to solve the problems inherent in attaching a transistor to a circuit board. The chip is faster, smaller, and cheaper than either the vacuum tube or the transistor. It also has lower power requirements and a much higher degree of reliability. For example, vacuum tubes required tremendous amounts of electricity and generated large amounts of heat, resulting in one tube failing every 15 minutes! Table 6-1 compares the speeds of these devices.

While the chip first came to prominence when it was used to reduce the size and cost of calculators, it and the smart machines based on it have changed our entire way of life. As we enter the last decade of the twentieth century, each day seems to bring a new smart machine into our homes, jobs, health care, education, and recreation. Here are some examples:

- Microwave ovens, cellular phones, VCRs, automatic cameras, CD players, camcorders, and television sets all use chips to direct many of their operations.
- Digital watches use chips to keep time and dates and to perform numerous other functions.
- Arcade-type games, whether in the public game room, handheld, or on the home video screen, all depend on chips.
- Checkout operations at grocery stores use computerized bar code readers to compute costs and print an itemized receipt.
- Robots depend on special-purpose chips for their "brains" to perform the desired operations.
- Automobile manufacturers use chips to control a car's engine by monitoring fuel flow, air–fuel mixture, and timing. Some cars have chips connected to sensors that can be hooked up to a diagnostic computer for service.

> **The microprocessor has brought electronics into a new era. It is altering the structure of our society.**
>
> *Robert Noyce and Marcian (Ted) Hoff, Jr.*
>
> From Paul Freiberger and Michael Swaine, *Fire in the Valley: The Making of the Personal Computer* (Berkeley, Calif.: Osborne/McGraw-Hill, 1984), excerpted in *Popular Computing,* October 1984, p. 103.

TABLE 6-1
Comparison of Computer Speeds

Type of Device	Operations per Second
Electromagnetic relay	100
Vacuum tube	1,000
Transistor	10,000
Integrated circuit	1,000,000
Very-large-scale integration	10,000,000

The vacuum tube used in the first computers compared in size with the chip used in modern computers: Each chip can perform the duties of thousands of vacuum tubes, will last longer, and generate far less heat.

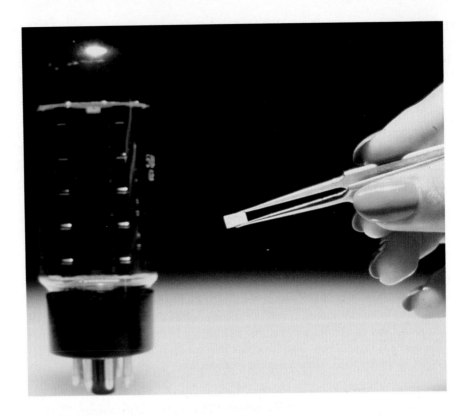

(Left) Programmable wristwatches use chips to keep time and to handle a number of other built-in functions. (Right) Autofocus cameras such as the Pentax P2-1 use chips to handle the computations necessary to focus the camera on the desired subject.

- Talking devices, including soft drink machines and cars, depend on a speech synthesizer chip to generate their conversation.
- New medical applications for chips, such as the one discussed in the box at the beginning of this chapter, direct the operations of artificial limbs and control muscles.

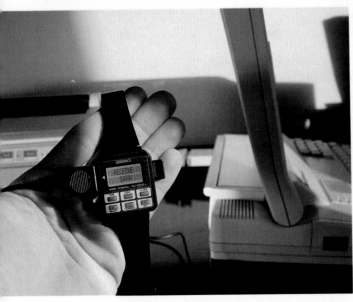

HOT ROD CHIPS

Some of the most important elements in modern automobile engines are smaller than a thumbnail and are seldom, if ever, mentioned in a car advertisement—microprocessor chips. Today, anyone wanting to fine-tune an engine must know something about computers in addition to how to use a wrench, because Detroit auto makers have been installing computer chips in their cars since 1981.

The "engine management" chips were designed to reduce emissions and improve fuel efficiency. Horsepower, however, suffered until a few computer experts analyzed the chips. They discovered that the chips were engineered with the average driver, who uses low-octane fuel, in mind. By modifying the programming of the processors that control engine timing and gear shifting, they produced a chip that appeals to drivers who prefer more power. The so-called superchips, which replace factory-installed chips, run on high-octane gasoline to increase an engine's horsepower by 10 to 30 percent. There are various types of superchips (some improve gas mileage, whereas others increase horsepower), but the average price is $130.

The downside is that replacing a factory-installed chip with a superchip negates the car's warranty and may violate the Clean Air Act, which was recently amended to require that high-performance parts meet the emissions standards for the car in which they are used. Superchip manufacturers are striving to redesign their chips to conform with the code. Meanwhile, however, some 40,000 superchips are sold annually in the United States by half a dozen firms.

Source: "Hot-Rod Hackers," *Time,* November 11, 1991, p. 96.

As we approach the end of the twentieth century, we will undoubtedly find many more applications of the chip to make our lives easier. As Microsoft CEO Bill Gates stated, It's a "new digital world order."

The Making of a Chip

The chip is made of miniature transistors and circuits and is as small as $\frac{1}{8}$ inch on a side. When seen through a microscope, the surface of a chip looks like an aerial view of a modern metropolis, with streets running between buildings and plazas. The "streets" in the chip are the connecting wires, and the "buildings and plazas" are the transistors. Figure 6-10 demonstrates dramatically how small a chip is by comparing its size with that of a ladybug. In picture 1, the ladybug is shown sitting on a 3-inch wafer of chips that have not been separated in the production process. In pictures 2 through 5, the magnification increases. Picture 6 shows that the "wires" on the chip are the same width as the hairs on the ladybug's leg!

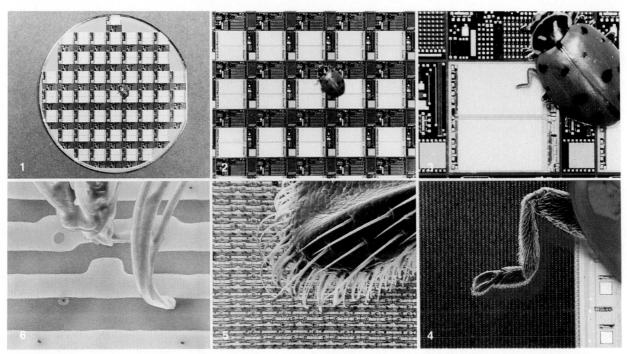

FIGURE 6-10
Comparison of Ladybug to Chip

The chip is an **integrated circuit (IC)** made up of a "sandwich" of interconnected layers of various elements on a silicon wafer. The first integrated circuits were made in 1959, when a transistor and its associated circuits were etched onto a semiconductor. A **semiconductor** is a mineral—such as germanium or silicon—that conducts electricity only under certain conditions. Since 1959, the integrated circuit has evolved from the 1-transistor IC to the current 1,000,000-transistor chip referred to as very-large-scale integration (VLSI). Between these two extremes are small-scale integration (SSI), medium-scale integration (MSI), and large-scale integration (LSI).

Before a chip can be manufactured, it must be designed by a team of engineers. Performed manually, this process could take years of work. Today, the computer can speed up the design process through computer-aided design (CAD). One type of CAD combines standardized sections of a chip to yield a custom design. Another CAD program, called a silicon compiler, can design the chip from scratch based on a description of the required functions.

After the chip is designed, engineers develop a **photomask,** which resembles a photographic negative. The photomask is used to control the process of building the chip's transistors and conductive lines. A tube of silicon that is 3–5 inches in diameter is sliced into wafers, which are processed into many chips. Using the photomask as a guide, engineers coat each silicon wafer with a chemical called a **resist** to build up each layer of the chip. The desired circuit patterns are then projected onto the resist, which acts as a photographic film, recording each layer of the circuit. Next, areas of the wafer are exposed when sections of the resist are chemically dissolved. This entire process can be performed as many as 12 times to create the desired circuitry. Between these steps, impurities are implanted in the silicon to create the transistors that control the flow of electricity.

Wafers treated in this fashion are placed in an oven to allow the impurities to sink to the appropriate layer of the chip. The chips are then separated by a diamond saw and tested to determine if each chip performs as designed. Sometimes, less than 50 percent of a batch of chips is acceptable for use. A "good" chip is then placed in a plastic carrier called a **dual inline package (DIP),** which protects the tiny chip and is the means by which the chip is connected to a circuit board.

HELP FOR NURSES FROM HELPMATE

If you have ever been hospitalized, you know that nurses and other health professionals can use all the help they can get. Now, in ten different hospitals, nurses are receiving help from a $4\frac{1}{2}$-foot-tall HelpMate robot built by Transitions Research, Inc. This robot performs many of the tasks that often take nurses away from their primary task of caring for the sick, including transporting dietary items, sterile supplies, pharmaceuticals, and blood and human liquids from the operating room. At Danbury Hospital in Danbury, Connecticut, a HelpMate prototype named "Rosco" has been delivering dinner trays for the dietary department since 1987.

The HelpMate robot does not require any type of fixed guidance system. Instead, the hospital's floor plan is in the robot's memory, and it is able to calculate distances between walls and intersections to guide it. This type of navigation is combined with vision, sonar, and radio frequency. For example, Rosco controls elevators by using radio frequency remote control. When the HelpMate robot senses a nonmoving obstacle, it stops and computes a course around the obstacle; for moving obstacles, such as patients or staff members, Rosco simply stops, allows the person to move, then continues on his way. When the robot arrives at its destination, it uses 1 of 16 messages to tell its human user what to do next.

Transitions Research, Inc., hopes eventually to sell HelpMate for home use and is designing a companion robot for outdoor work.

Sources: "HelpMate Is on the Way," *Electronic House,* April 3, 1989, p. 4; and interview with Gay Bogardus, director of marketing, Transitions Research, Inc., November 14, 1991.

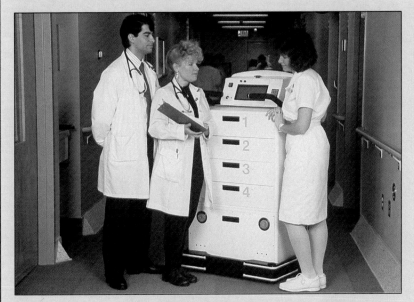

The HelpMate android is being used in several hospitals to relieve medical personnel of such nonmedical tasks as carrying food to patients who missed the regular mealtime.

BITS OF HISTORY

History of the Chip

Until 1990, most people credited Ted Hoff, an employee of Intel Corporation, with inventing, in 1971, the first true microprocessor chip. However, on July 17, 1990, nearly 20 years after Hoff's chip was developed, Gilbert Hyatt, an independent inventor, won a 20-year-old battle to obtain a patent for a computer-on-a-chip that he invented in 1968.

Hyatt's patent has broad implications for established chip manufacturers such as Intel, Motorola, and Texas Instruments, because they may have to pay royalties to Hyatt to use the technology on which he holds a patent. Most chip manufacturers admitted that the announcement was a surprise to them and said they were unaware of the existence of such a patent claim. The validity of Hyatt's patent, however, is being contested in court, and no immediate effect on the chip industry is expected.

Notwithstanding the Hyatt patent, the origins of the chips used in today's computers can be traced to 1959, when Jack Kilby of Texas Instruments and Robert Noyce of Fairchild Semiconductor simultaneously developed the first integrated circuit (IC). Noyce and another scientist, Gordon Moore, formed the Intel (for INTegrated ELectronics) Corporation in 1968. Since then, Intel has become a leader of the chip industry. Then, as mentioned, in 1971, Intel developed a microprocessor chip named the Intel 4004. Even though the 4004 could work with only 4 bits at a time (compared to the 16- and 32-bit machines so common today), it was revolutionary in design and gave rise to the family of Intel chips that are such an important part of personal computers.

When the microprocessor was introduced, Intel thought sales of

Intel 4004 chip.

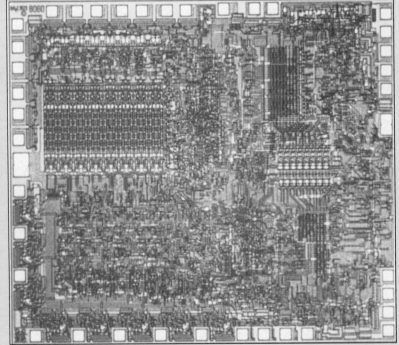

Gilbert Hyatt, independent inventor of the microprocessor chip.

memory chips would increase, because the microprocessor can't run without chips. However, with the introduction of the first general-purpose microprocessor chip, the 8080, it became clear that this new chip would be of revolutionary significance. Intel and other companies then began developing improved versions of the 8080, including the Intel 8085, the Motorola 6800, and the Z80 from Zilog (a company formed by scientists leaving Intel).

Currently used chips that were developed from the original 8080 chip are the Intel 80xxx series and the Motorola 68000 series. Table 6-2 shows the Intel family tree, with date of introduction, word size, and speed of each chip. Of these, the 8088 chip had the most impact, because it was used in the original IBM PC. However, the 80386 and i486 chips, with their mainframe-like power, may have greater long-term impact.

> **Instead of making [the Intel 4004 microprocessor] act like a calculator, I wanted it to function as a general-purpose computer programmed to be a calculator.**
>
> *Marcian Ted Hoff, Jr.*
>
> Quoted in "The Making of a Microprocessor," *Lotus,* March 1986, p. 74.

TABLE 6-2
Intel Family Tree

Processor	Date	Word Size	Instructions per Second
4004	1971	4	60,000
8080	1974	8	290,000
8086	1978	16	333,000
8088	1979	8/16	333,000
80286	1982	16	2,660,000
80386	1985	32	6,000,000
i486	1989	32	50,000,000

Intel 8080 chip.

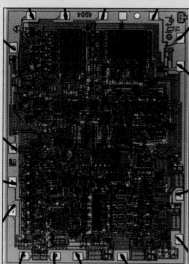

Ted Hoff, Jr.

Robotics and the Chip

The more stultifying, demeaning, and downright dangerous human activities will be taken over literally by a new slave class—mobile, sensate, service robots.

*Joseph F. Engelberger,
Transitions Research
Corporation*

Quoted in G. Bylinsky, "Get Ready for a Robot Butler," *Reader's Digest,* January 1988, pp. 157–162.

One of the most exciting areas of chip use is in the field of **robotics,** that is, the use of machines to perform work. Currently, robots are used extensively by the automobile industry to handle heavy, dirty, or dangerous tasks such as spot welding or materials handling. They are also used in the electronics industry to help build calculators, by performing the same precision task time after time. In each case, the robots that are being used are a far cry from the walking, talking C3PO robot of *Star Wars* fame. An industrial robot is little more than a mechanical arm controlled by a microprocessor chip to perform a specified set of tasks using instructions built into a ROM chip. While not very cute, these robots have had a big impact on the automobile industry; the Japanese companies have used them to gain an advantage over the more labor-intensive U.S. companies.

In robotics, chips direct the actions of a robot by sending the robot the instructions it needs to perform the desired actions. PROM (programmed ROM) chips are useful for this purpose because an individualized set of actions can be programmed into a chip. The chip converts the programming into directions for the robot. If a robot needs a new set of actions, the PROM chip can be replaced by a new PROM that contains the new instructions. One important fact to remember about the use of chips with robotics: A human must create the list of instructions for the chip before it can be used to direct the robot.

It is possible that robots will be used in such areas as hospital care (see box on page 169), security, commercial cleaning, and support of elderly, infirm people. Handling these tasks will require "smart" robots, that is, robots that can see where they are going, note obstacles, and take action to avoid them. Another name for a smart robot that has a built-in microprocessor and is able to move around is **android.** A key problem that must be solved before androids will be

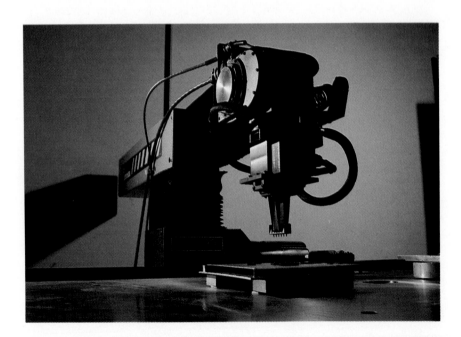

Robots are often used to handle the tedious yet delicate job of inserting electronic components into sockets on the circuit board. The computer that controls these robots can be reprogrammed to perform a new sequence of actions.

widely used is that of three-dimensional sight. Without this, robots will not be able to move around in a crowded hospital hallway or a small apartment.

1. The flow of information into, within, and out of a computer combines with the CPU and internal memory to make the whole computer.
2. The CPU is made up of the control unit (CU), the arithmetic–logic unit (ALU), the clock, and the system bus.
3. To execute a program, the CU must fetch an instruction, decode it, fetch the necessary data, and pass this to the ALU for execution.
4. Both the CU and the ALU use registers for fast, temporary storage.
5. The computer word is the number of bits the computer CPU can process as one unit.
6. Internal memory is made of ROM, which is permanent memory burned into a chip, and RAM, which is temporary memory that uses transistors to store information. RAM is volatile; ROM is not.
7. Other types of memory chips are PROM (programmable ROM) and EPROM (erasable programmable ROM) chips.
8. Current RAM chips can store up to 1 megabit, with chips holding up to 4 million bits possible in the future.
9. Parallel processing allows supercomputers to avoid the bottleneck that is created when only one instruction at a time can be carried out.
10. The two types of RAM are dynamic and static: Dynamic RAM requires constant refreshment of the transistors and capacitors; cache memory uses static RAM as a way to speed up processing.
11. A chip is a semiconductor device that uses pure silicon as a base on which to build a network of transistors and conductor lines.
12. Manufacture of a chip involves a process of repeated etchings and addition of impurities to form the necessary components.
13. Robots are devices that use computer brains to perform repetitive tasks. Androids are robots that can move around.

KEY TERMS

address	cache memory
address bus	central processing unit (CPU)
android	character generator
arithmetic–logic unit (ALU)	chip
bit	clock
booting	computer word
byte	conceptual computer

control bus
control unit (CU)
conventional memory
data bus
destructive replacement
dual inline package (DIP)
dynamic random-access memory
    (DRAM)
erasable programmable read-only
    memory (EPROM)
execution-time (E-time)
expanded memory
extended memory
fetch, decode, and execute process
firmware
fixed-length word
functional electrical-stimulation
    (FES)
instruction-time (I-time)
integrated circuit (IC)
internal memory
Kbit
Kbyte
main memory
math coprocessor

memory manager
microprocessor
nondestructive fetch
nonvolatile memory
parallel processing
parallel-data computer
parallel-process computer
photomask
primary storage
programmable read-only memory
    (PROM)
random-access memory (RAM)
read-only memory (ROM)
register
resist
robotics
semiconductor
serial machines
static random-access memory
    (SRAM)
system bus
upper memory
variable-length word
volatile memory

REVIEW QUESTIONS

1. Explain the flow of information within the conceptual computer. Why are some flows considered "fast" and others "slow"?
2. List the components of the CPU. Give the purpose of each.
3. List and give the purpose of three registers in the CPU.
4. Discuss the fetch, decode, and execute process in a computer.
5. What is the difference between a nondestructive fetch and a destructive replacement?
6. What is a computer word? What are the common word lengths in personal computers? In mainframes?
7. How are individual bits accessed in RAM? For the example given in Figure 6-7, which bit corresponds to location 44?
8. In what ways are RAM and ROM different? How do PROM and EPROM differ from RAM and ROM and from each other?
9. What is the booting process? How is ROM used in this process?
10. What is parallel processing? How does it speed up computer processing? What are the two types of parallel processing?
11. What are the two types of RAM? How do they differ, and what is their relationship to cache memory?
12. What are the four types of memory used in MS-DOS–based

PCs? What range of memory does each cover?

13. Discuss the chip production process. Why are impurities introduced into the silicon?

14. How are robots used in industrial situations? What part do PROM chips play in this process?

15. What is an android, and how does it differ from an industrial robot?

The Making of an Integrated Circuit

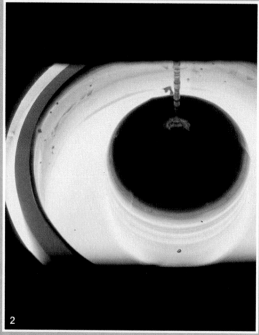

1. This is the raw material (trichlorosilane) from which silicon wafers are made.

2. Here, we see the interior of a furnace for growing silicon crystals.

3. The refining process results in a silicon ingot.

4. These are known as epitaxial (having orientation controlled by the crystal substrate) silicon wafers.

5. The ingot is sawed into wafers, which are then polished.

6. An epitaxial furnace, such as this, deposits epilayers on the wafers.

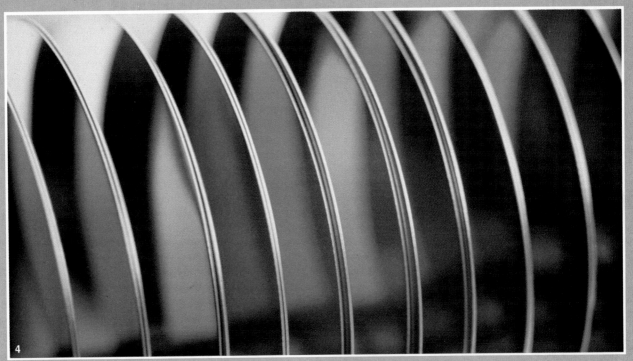

7

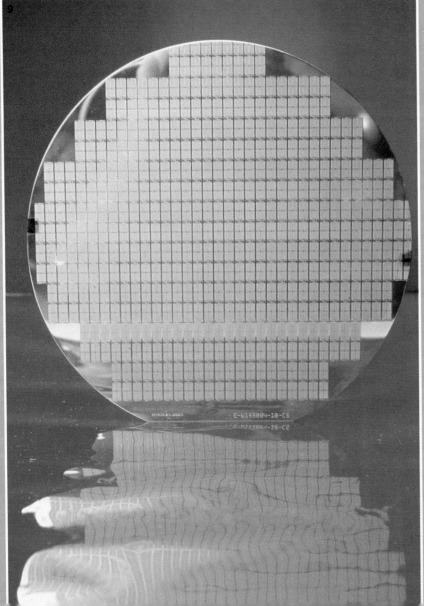

7. Some of the processes involve putting materials on top of the wafer, while others involve putting impurities into the silicon (to give it different electrical properties).

8. These men are discussing the photo mask for a silicon chip. A blowup of the mask is behind them.

9. The mask's pattern is projected onto the silicon wafer through a layer of photosensitive material. The pattern is printed on the wafer, and then the wafer is developed.

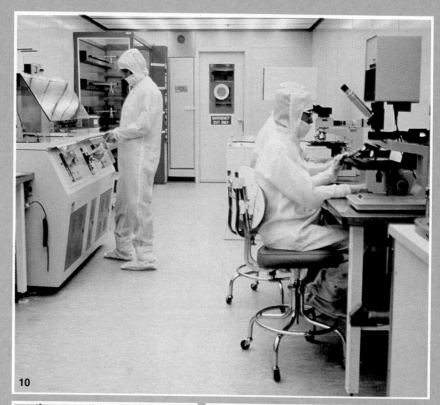

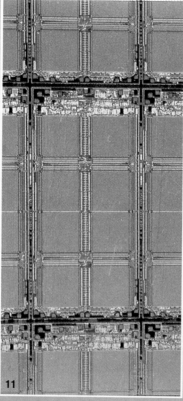

10. Here, the photosensitive material is removed, and all but the required circuit pattern is etched away.

11. This blowup of a wafer shows the result of the etching process.

12. At various steps, the wafer is visually inspected and electronically tested.

13. Individual chips in wafers are separated by a diamond saw, and defective chips are removed.

13

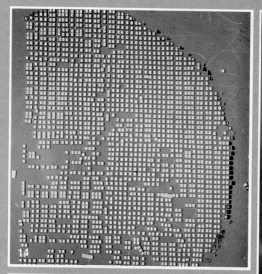

14

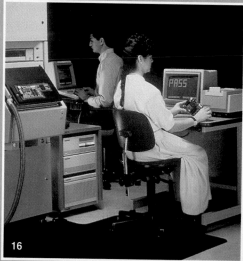

16

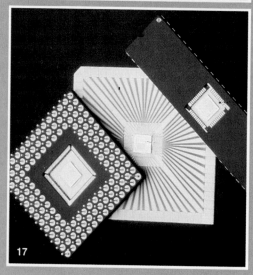

17

15

14. This is the silicon wafer after it is separated into transistors.

15. The chip is attached to a "package," with individual wires between the chip and the package.

16. After packaging, each individual integrated circuit undergoes a final set of electrical tests.

17. The result of these processes is integrated circuits, ready to use in a supercomputer or a microwave oven.

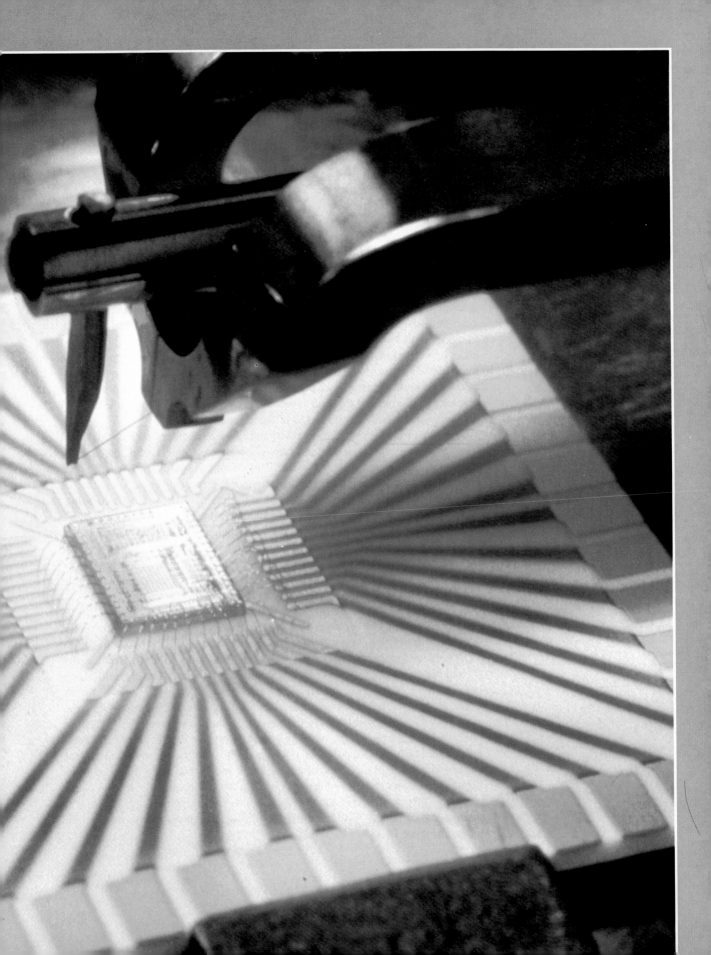

The Binary Number System

Every attempt to automate calculations must solve the problem of representing the numerical values. On the abacus, these values are represented by beads on a series of strings. In mechanical calculators, the values were represented by gears and wheels. As a value was input, a wheel was turned to a certain position to represent that value. If a second value was added to the first, the wheel turned enough to represent the addition. If the result of the addition was larger than 10, a second wheel turned to show the tens position, and so on. On a mechanical calculator, multiplication was treated as repeated addition, subtraction as the reverse of addition, and division as repeated subtraction. In all cases, the decimal number system (base 10) was used in the calculations.

If the abacus uses beads on a wire to represent numbers, and a mechanical calculator used wheels and gears, how does an electronic calculator or computer—with no moving parts—work? This question would be very difficult if we tried to answer it using the decimal number system. However, computers do not have ten fingers, so they do not need to use the base 10 system of counting. Any number, as it is used by a computer, is determined by the key characteristic of electricity—it is either "on" or "off." Mechanical wheels have any number of positions for digits, but electricity can accommodate only two digits, which correspond to the electrical states of on and off. Consequently, the base 2, or **binary,** number system is used for counting in an electronic computer. Table BN-1 shows how the numbers 1–10 are represented in binary.

To represent a number in binary in the computer, a series of switches is needed to turn the electricity on and off. Figure BN-1 shows how the computer represents the decimal value of the number 9 internally. The first and fourth switches are "on," causing the first and last light bulbs to glow. Because the second and third switches are "off," their bulbs remain dark. The only difference between these bulbs and computers, in terms of switches, is the *type* of switch used. In one of the first computers, electromechanical relays provided the switching, but they were slow and required constant adjustment. Next, vacuum tubes were used as switches, but they generated a great deal of heat and tended to burn out during calculations. In 1947, the solid-state transistor was developed and could be used as a switch with great speed and low heat and power requirements. Transistors came to be known as "flip-flops," because their state could be changed from off to on and back to off by the simple application and removal of electrical current. A flip-flop is similar to a switch that would control the light bulbs in Figure BN-1.

TABLE BN-1
Binary Representations of Decimal Values

Decimal Value	Binary Representation
0	0
1	1
2	10
3	11
4	100
5	101
6	110
7	111
8	1000
9	1001
10	1010

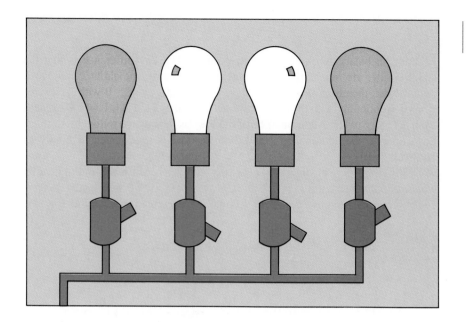

Conversion Between Binary and Decimal

Often, the number system that the computer understands (binary) must be converted to the form that humans understand (decimal), and vice versa. Converting from binary to decimal is easy if we use the powers of 2 combined with positional notation. Some powers of 2 are as follows:

$$2^0 = 1 \qquad 2^2 = 4 \qquad 2^4 = 16$$
$$2^1 = 2 \qquad 2^3 = 8 \qquad 2^5 = 32$$

We can determine the decimal equivalent of a binary number by computing the product of each binary digit and its corresponding power of 2. For example, let us convert the binary number 110101 to decimal. Multiplying the rightmost binary digit by its power of 2 gives us $(1 \times 1) = 1$. Moving from right to left and summing the results of the multiplications, we get the following:

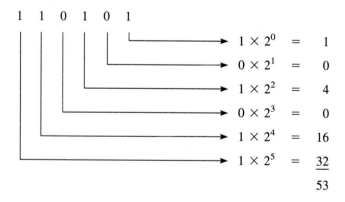

$$
\begin{array}{ccccccll}
1 & 1 & 0 & 1 & 0 & 1 \\
\end{array}
$$

$$1 \times 2^0 = 1$$
$$0 \times 2^1 = 0$$
$$1 \times 2^2 = 4$$
$$0 \times 2^3 = 0$$
$$1 \times 2^4 = 16$$
$$1 \times 2^5 = \underline{32}$$
$$53$$

In this case, 110101 in binary equals 53 in decimal.

Binary Arithmetic

Addition in binary is like addition in decimal. The key difference is that the addition rules are much simpler to remember. In binary, the digits 2 and above do not exist; therefore, $0 + 0 = 0$, $0 + 1 = 1$, and $1 + 1 = 0$ with a carry of 1 or 10. Continuing with these rules, we get $1 + 10 = 11$; $11 + 1 = 100$ because we must carry twice. Addition in binary is easy as long as we follow these rules. For example, the addition of 2 and 3 in decimal is represented in binary as $10 + 11 = 101$.

Multiplication in binary is also very simple, because the multiplication table has only four entries: $0 \times 0 = 0$, $0 \times 1 = 0$, $1 \times 0 = 0$, and $1 \times 1 = 1$. The multiplication of 3 and 3 in decimal is represented in binary as follows:

$$
\begin{array}{r}
11 \\
\times 11 \\
\hline
11 \\
11 \quad \\
\hline
1001
\end{array}
$$

Subtraction and division are simply the reverse of addition and multiplication, respectively.

If arithmetic is so easy in binary, why don't we use it instead of the decimal system? The shortcoming with binary is the same as that with Roman numerals—expressing even moderately large numbers requires many digits. For example, expressing the value 99 requires only two digits in decimal, but it requires seven digits in binary—1100011. Representing large numbers with many digits is a problem for humans, but it causes no problem for computers, which have many switches to handle the necessary positions.

Another Representation of Binary

Because a number in binary is cumbersome to work with when the number of digits becomes large, other ways of representing binary numbers have been developed for human use. The best known of these is the **hexadecimal,** or base 16, number system. Because this system is based on a power of 2, conversion between the hexadecimal number system (also referred to as *hex*) and the binary number system is fairly easy. As a result, hex is used to represent the binary number system in many mainframes and all personal computers.

The hexadecimal system uses the digits 0 through 9 and the letters A through F to represent binary numbers. The conversion from binary to hex divides the binary number up into groups of four digits, with each hex digit representing four binary digits. Table BN-2 shows the correspondence between hex digits and combinations of binary digits.

With Table BN-2, it is easy to convert a binary number to hex: We simply assign a hex digit to each 4-bit section of the binary number. For example, let's convert the binary number 110110100 to hex. The binary number is divided into 4-bit groups. Zeros are added on the left, if necessary, to ensure that the first group contains four digits. In our example, 110110100 is divided into 4-bit groups of 0001 1011 0100, where we have added three zeros on the left. This corresponds to 1B4 in the hexadecimal number system.

TABLE BN-2
Binary to Hexadecimal Conversion

Binary Digits	Hexadecimal Digit	Binary Digits	Hexadecimal Digit
0000	0	1000	8
0001	1	1001	9
0010	2	1010	A
0011	3	1011	B
0100	4	1100	C
0101	5	1101	D
0110	6	1110	E
0111	7	1111	F

In Chapter 2, we discussed the use of ASCII and EBCDIC to represent characters in binary. Since both of these are 8-bit codes, they use one byte to represent each character. As a result, each character can be easily represented by two hex digits. For example, the letter L in ASCII is 01001100 in binary. This converts to 4C in hex, which is much more compact than the binary equivalent for representing the characters.

Because the amount of memory in a computer is expressed as a power of 2, it is very convenient to use hex notation to represent these addresses. In Figure 6-7 there were only 64 memory locations, so we can represent each address with two hex digits. For example, the bit in row 5 and column 3 would have address 0101 0011, or 53 in hex. With this approach, 256 bits can be addressed with two hex digits (00 through FF). Similarly, 65,536—or 64K—bits can be represented with four hex digits.

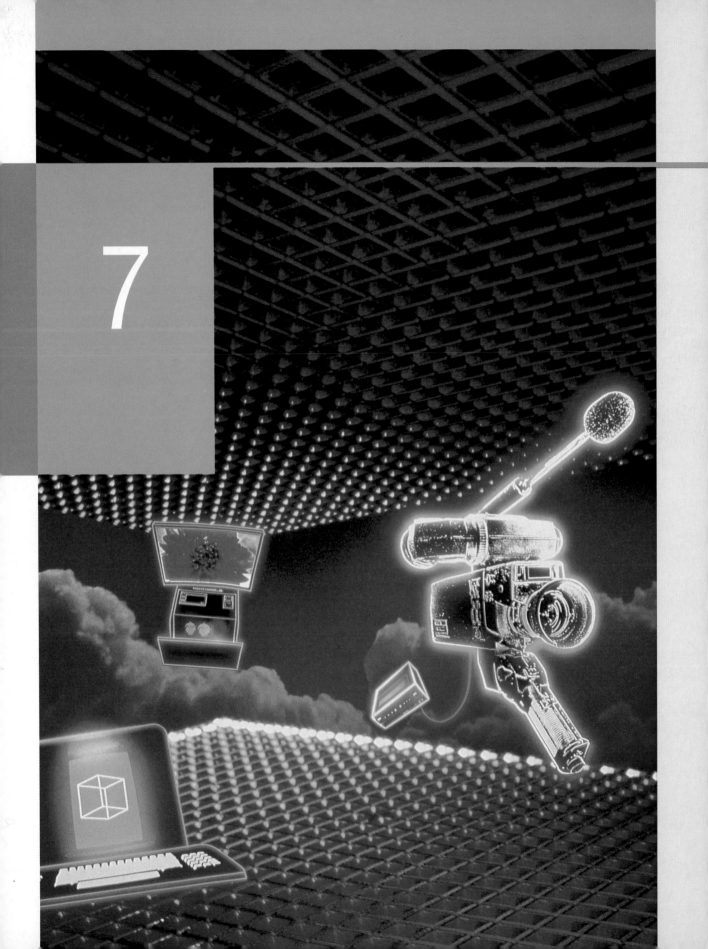

7

Input/Output Considerations

Expanded coverage of input and output begins with a look at how input and output affect the computer's efficiency. Commonly used input devices, including the keyboard, the mouse, and the light pen, are explained in detail. We will also consider the problems and potential of voice recognition and handwritten input. Barcodes and other devices used for directly entering information into computers will also be described. The chapter will then discuss output devices for both mainframes and personal computers. Various types of monitors are examined, as are the leading types of printers.

STUDY OBJECTIVES

After reading this chapter, you should be able to

- understand the importance of input and output to the use of the computer;
- discuss the data entry problem and its possible solutions;
- understand the differences between various types of keyboards;
- understand the use of the mouse, trackball, touchscreen, and light pen for computer input;
- describe the use of voice recognition and handwritten input devices;
- recognize data entry devices in the workplace and the marketplace;
- explain the differences between various types of monitors;
- recognize the differences in the output from various types of printers;
- discuss the various types of nonimpact printers, particularly the laser printer.

TRACKING PRISONER'S MOVEMENTS WITH BAR CODES

In jails across the United States, correctional authorities are faced with a bureaucratic headache—the need to keep track of each inmate's movement, both inside and outside the jail. Jails must keep these records to defend themselves against potential inmate grievances or lawsuits that allege unfair treatment. For example, an inmate might charge that he or she was held in a cell for several weeks without recreation or library privileges.

To perform this recordkeeping operation, jail personnel must manually record each inmate's name and cell location and the time of day that each inmate moves to or from his or her cell. At the end of each day, the handwritten data must be keyed into a computer by data entry operators. For a metropolitan jail with over 1,000 prisoners, each of whom may leave his or her cell five or six times a day, the process of reading the handwritten reports and entering the data can take between 40 and 60 hours a week. Even then, errors in recording or entering the information may render it almost useless.

Many jails have begun using bar-coded wristbands to track their inmates in an effort to eliminate this nightmare of recording and entering data. In this process each inmate is assigned a bar code similar to those used in grocery stores and library checkout operations. Each time an inmate leaves his or her cell, jail personnel can scan the wristband with a portable scanner, which then stores the time and inmate data. At the end of the day these data are input directly from the portable scanner into the jail computer in a fraction of the time required by manual data entry methods and with few, if any, errors.

This system has been tested or implemented with good results at the Los Angeles County Jail; Arapaho County Jail in Englewood, Colorado; and at the Dekalb County Jail in metropolitan Atlanta. A similar system has been implemented at the Veteran's Administration Medical Center Hospital to match patients with various medical samples, tests, and charges.

Source: Donna Williams-Lewis, "Jewelry for Jail: Bar-code Wristbands Track Inmates' Movements," *The Atlanta Journal-Constitution,* April 2, 1989, pp. 1C, 10C, as updated by the author, November 1991.

> I think it's going to be a very successful way of helping prison systems and other institutions keep track of people.
>
> *Debra Ratzman, new products manager, Precision Dynamics Corp.*
>
> Quoted in "Jewelry for Jail," *The Atlanta Journal and Constitution,* April 2, 1989, p. 10C.

THE IMPORTANCE OF INPUT AND OUTPUT

For a computer to store and manipulate numbers and symbols, it must always be able to receive its instructions and data. And for the storage and manipulation to be useful, there must be some way for the computer to send the processed information back to the user. This process of instructing the computer, feeding it data, and receiving processed information back is referred to as **input/output,** or simply **I/O.** Without input and output, the computer would have no way of receiving instructions as to what it should be doing, no way to receive the data that it is to process into information, and no way to send this information to the human user. Because input and output are so essential to the use of the computer, this chapter will be devoted entirely to the various methods that are used for this process.

The I/O Bottleneck

As discussed in the box at the beginning of the chapter, input (and output) can cause large problems for computer users. In that case, the transfer of handwritten data on jail inmate movements to the computer was requiring one and sometimes two full-time data entry operators per week with no guarantee of the accuracy of the data being input. The bar-coded wristbands solved a great deal of the input problem. Unfortunately, the data entry problem cannot always be solved as easily as in that case.

Because I/O requires human interaction either to input the instructions and data or to receive and interpret the output, I/O is the *slowest* part of the computer process and often causes a bottleneck in the efficient processing of data into information. I/O is slow relative to the blinding speed of the CPU and internal memory or even to the slower transfer of information to and from secondary storage. A proficient data entry operator working at a keyboard may be able to input instructions and data at the rate of 75 words per minute or about 8 characters per second. Compare this input rate to the millions of operations per second that can be carried out by the CPU! The slower rate of input can hold up the CPU since it cannot process data or instructions until both have been input.

IRS data entry operators enter tax data from the keyboard; the data are then stored on disk.

191

In addition to the potential for delaying processing in the CPU, it is possible that errors will occur during the entry of data and instructions. These two considerations are referred to as the **data entry problem.** The first half of this problem—the slow rate of data entry—is solved in a variety of ways, including use of a storage area called a **buffer** within the computer to store input. Data are then transferred from the buffer to the internal memory as needed. Another way to keep the slow rate of input from holding up processing is to enter data onto disk and then transfer the data to the CPU as needed. This transfer from disk to internal memory is faster than the original data entry process.

The second half of the problem—errors on input—is handled via a process called **verification** in which the data are entered a second time and compared to the original entries to check for discrepancies. Data are also **edited,** or checked for reasonableness. For example, are the values in the correct range, or were the correct number of digits entered?

On the output side, the rate at which information is output to a monitor or printer is limited by the speed at which the information can be displayed on the screen and digested by the user, or by the speed of the electromechanical printer putting the letters on the paper. While information can be displayed at what seems like lightning speed (up to 1,600 characters per second), a human reading 100 words per minute can digest information at the rate of only *10* characters per second. Yet the fastest printers can output information on paper at the rate of approximately 26,000 characters per second. And while this may seem fast, it still pales in comparison to the speed of the CPU.

INTERACTIVE INPUT DEVICES

We begin our discussion of input by considering *interactive* input devices, that is, devices like the keyboard, mouse, and light pen that can be used to interact with the computer to enter commands and data, to make selections from a menu, or to choose a portion of the screen for magnification. On the other hand, input devices such as the bar code readers discussed in the box at the beginning of the chapter are *direct* input devices that automate the data entry process. In this section we will discuss the keyboard and other interactive devices and also the current, state-of-the-art voice input. Direct input devices—those devices that input data without any interaction—will be discussed in the next section.

Keyboards

A computer input device that has been used for almost as long as computers have been in use is the keyboard. As discussed in Chapter 2, a **keyboard** is a configuration of keys arranged in a manner similar to that on a typewriter. While a typewriter transfers a user's keystroke as a letter on paper, a keyboard—whether on a mainframe terminal or a personal computer—is meant to electronically transmit the symbol (letter, digit, or special character) corresponding to that key. Keyboards for computers transmit information to the CPU by sending a binary code (for example, 01000001 for A, 01000010 for B, and so on) to the computer's CPU. Keyboards serve a similar purpose for transmitting data to disk or tape. Most keyboards have a **type-ahead buffer** that stores data typed by the user even when the computer is not ready to accept it. The data are then transmitted when the computer is ready for it.

The binary codes used to transmit characters from the keyboard to the computer represent the upper- and lowercase letters of the alphabet, the 10 numeric digits, and 34 punctuation marks and special characters. They also can be used to represent control characters such as backspace, line feed, and carriage return. Figure 7-1 shows a keyboard for the popular IBM 3270 series of mainframe terminals that have been used since the mid-1970s. Note that this keyboard is very similar to the IBM compatible keyboards shown in Chapter 2.

Most personal computer keyboards have between 60 and 105 keys, depending on whether they have a numeric keypad, function keys, and special-purpose keys. In Figure 7-2 we show the keyboards of two of the more popular personal computers: the Apple Macintosh SE and the IBM PS/2 Model 30.

Looking at these two keyboards, you will notice that the Macintosh keyboard layout is different from that of the IBM. These differences mean that using a different keyboard may require the user to adjust to a new arrangement of keys to perform the same actions.

FIGURE 7-1
Mainframe Terminal Keyboard

FIGURE 7-2
(Left) Apple Macintosh SE Keyboard. (Right) IBM PS/2 Model 30 Keyboard.

The Mouse

Various studies of managers and executives have found that resistance to computers often arises out of an uneasiness with the keyboard. Managers who have not used a keyboard since school (if then) may be anxious about relearning keyboard use. As a result of these studies, manufacturers have developed alternate input devices to make computer use less threatening.

A highly publicized alternative input device is the **mouse.** The device is so named because it is about the size of a mouse and has a tail-like cord that connects it to the computer. When combined with appropriate software, the mouse is a powerful input device that frees the user from dependence on a keyboard. By moving the mouse across a flat surface, the user moves the cursor and selects the various functions for execution by the computer.

The mouse is available in both electromechanical and optical forms. The electromechanical mouse has a ball in its base, which makes contact with two wheels inside the mouse. As the ball moves, so do the wheels, signaling the CPU to move the cursor in the same direction. The optical mouse moves around on a grid. A minicamera records the mouse's position on the grid and transmits the information to the CPU, which then moves the cursor to match the mouse's position on the grid. In either case, one or more buttons on the top of the mouse are pressed to signal the user's commands to the CPU when the cursor is located in the desired position.

Although the mouse is useful for moving the cursor without a keyboard, it becomes a powerful input device when matched with a **graphical user interface (GUI).** A GUI uses pictures, or **icons,** of the available operations to speed up the selection process. The use of icons is based on the **desktop metaphor,** which views the computer as a desk equipped with a file cabinet, telephone,

People who are unfamiliar with a computer keyboard often find the mouse easier to work with.

scratch pads, wastebasket, and so on. Each item actually appears on the top or side of the screen, and the user can access the related function by selecting an icon with the mouse. For example, on the mouse-driven Apple Macintosh software, the user selects a trash can to delete a file from the work area. Using this system, the user can create, send, file, or discard messages, graphs, charts, and other documents by simply pointing at the appropriate icon.

Use of the mouse is not restricted to the Apple Mac series. The IBM PS/2 series of computers is configured to work with a mouse, as well as the keyboard; and mouse products are now sold for use with IBM compatible PCs. As could be expected, Steve Jobs—the inventor of the original Macintosh—included a mouse with his NeXT workstation as a primary means of controlling the cursor. Now, it is possible to use a mouse as an input tool for all PCs.

Another device that works almost like the mouse is the trackball. The **trackball** is essentially a mouse turned upside down so that the user controls the cursor on the screen by rolling a plastic ball with the fingertip or wrist. To execute commands with a trackball, one or more buttons are pressed, much as is done with a mouse. Trackballs may vary in size, but most are approximately the size of a standard desk calculator and may be mounted on either side of the keyboard. For handicapped people who may have difficulty pressing keys on a standard keyboard or using a mouse, the trackball may be the answer since it is not necessary to move the entire arm to use it. For example, a man who lost three and a half fingers in an industrial accident thought he would have to give up his engineering drawing career. However, with a trackball he is able to use his remaining finger to spin the ball and control the cursor to use a computer-aided drafting package. A trackball is standard equipment on the Apple Macintosh Portable Computer.

The icons on the left side of this screen are used to select operations to be executed.

The trackball can be used in a confined space where it would be impractical to use a mouse.

Other Interactive Input Devices

A host of other interactive input devices is now available to make a user's data entry job easier. Three important ones are the touchscreen, the light pen, and the graphics digitizing tablet.

With the **touchscreen** the user simply points at an area on the screen to give the computer a command or to retrieve some type of information. Touchscreens are becoming very popular for use in situations where a computer is necessary but computer literacy is not required of employees. These situations include point-of-sale, training, and process control systems. Restaurants are finding that touchscreen systems are very useful, because they allow service people to quickly enter orders. McDonald's is even working on a system that allows customers to enter their own orders on a touchscreen. Process control touchscreen systems enable employees with little training to control sophisticated processes. An interesting application of touchscreens is found in the casino industry. A single system can be reconfigured to display a variety of games from which the player can select.

There are a number of technologies available to enable the computer to determine where on the screen the user is pointing. The most popular system uses a plastic membrane over the screen. When the membrane is depressed, a circuit is closed, and a signal that identifies the screen location is sent to the CPU. Another system uses pure glass that vibrates when it is pressed. The glass can be pressed harder than the plastic membrane can be, so the computer

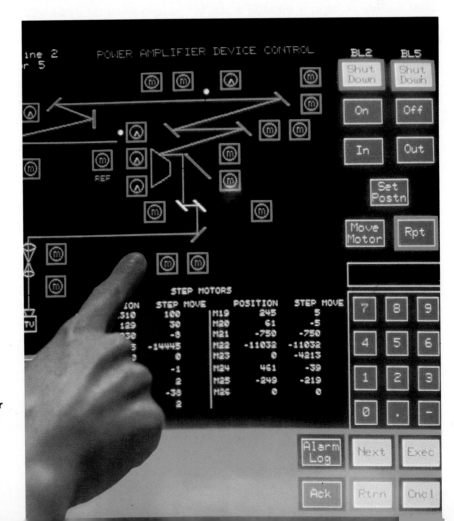

These touch controls are on a laser fusion screen, helping further the research of the Los Alamos fusion project.

responds more quickly. As with the mouse, a touchscreen cannot work without software that is designed for it, rather than for a keyboard. Without appropriate software, all touchscreen systems are useless.

The **light pen** is like the touchscreen in that the user selects from a menu on the screen by pointing at an option. However, the technology of the light pen is different from that of the touchscreen. The light pen takes advantage of the fact that every lighted spot on the screen is being constantly refreshed. When the pen is pointed at the screen, the computer can detect exactly which spot is giving off light at that moment. This difference in technology means that a light pen is much more accurate than a touchscreen. This accuracy has allowed the light pen to be used for over 25 years for computer-aided design (CAD). In CAD, the user can point the pen at a very specific part of a structural design either to obtain a more detailed plan of that part or to change the design. The pen can also be used to add or delete lines from the drawing or to select different colors for the drawing. While the touchscreen and the light pen are extremely easy to use, continually raising your pointing arm to the screen can eventually be very tiring.

Since humans are not used to looking at one surface (the screen) and drawing on another surface (the desk), the **graphics digitizing tablet** has become a popular medium for making precise freehand drawings. The membrane surface of the digitizing tablet transmits the pattern to the computer through thousands of switches that make contact whenever the pad is touched. Pens for graphics

The light pen, which is useful for many engineering and scientific applications, allows the user to point at an area of the screen and have that area expand, rotate, or otherwise change.

This digitizing pad allows the user to transfer drawings and charts from paper to the computer by tracing them with the pointing device.

tablets can be either blunt-tipped or ink-filled. While blunt-tipped pens are good for tracing images onto the pad, ink-filled pens should be used for freehand drawings so the artist can see what is being drawn.

Voice Recognition Input

In the best of all possible worlds of data input, the computer would be able to understand spoken commands and to read typed or handwritten data. Although computer recognition of typed data using scanners (which is discussed in a later section of this chapter) is becoming a common form of input, systems that understand spoken or handwritten input are still in their infancy. Both voice and pen-based systems face problems that are significantly greater than those encountered with character recognition of typewritten input.

A commercially feasible **voice recognition system** would have to address the following problems: The system would require a large number of words (5,000 to 10,000). It would have to recognize the speech pattern of each user and each user's speech pattern under a variety of conditions. Stress, for example, can alter a user's voice pattern. It would have to distinguish between speech and background noise. Telephone ringing, for example, can interfere with the system. And it would have to determine when one word stops and another begins. For example, it would be extremely difficult for a computer to understand the difference between "this guy" and "the sky" because of the similarity in the way they are spoken. Similarly, whereas we can understand "D'yawannagoouttanight?" as being "Do you want to go out tonight?", it would be extremely difficult for a computer to detect the separate words and decode the speech to form a meaningful sentence.

There are four important types of voice recognition: (1) one speaker/discrete speech; (2) one speaker/continuous speech; (3) multiple speakers/discrete speech; and (4) multiple speakers/continuous speech. The first type is the sim-

CREATING 3-D MODELS WITH A DIGITIZER

In the popular movie *Terminator 2: Judgment Day,* the cyborg performs many amazing body feats that, obviously, are impossible or too dangerous for a human actor. Many of the cyborg's actions were programmed using three-dimensional digitizing—the scan and capture of a three-dimensional object in digital form.

As dramatically demonstrated in *Terminator 2,* human movement can be digitized, and the resulting digital image can be manipulated in many different ways. The same technology is being used to help doctors save burn victims, police find lost children, and engineers develop artificial limbs.

Digitization of three-dimensional objects is accomplished with laser scanning technology. A laser circularly scans an object, such as a subject's head, in about 15 seconds. The image is transferred to a computer, where it is manipulated. This technology has been applied in dozens of areas, ranging from medicine to fantasy—as in the example of *Terminator 2: Judgment Day.* Applications of 3-D digitizing include the following:

- Planning plastic and reconstructive surgery using 3-D images;
- "Aging" missing children using 3-D images (see box on page 12);
- Redesigning toys using computer-aided design (CAD) to work with a scanned image of a 3-D prototype to avoid costly reworking of the physical model;
- Designing better fitting helmets, masks, earphones, and optical systems for U.S. Air Force fighter pilots using a digitized image of each pilot's head and face.

Looking ahead, it seems as if uses for 3-D digitization will be limited only by the imagination of potential users.

Source: Clinton Wilder, "Digitizing Enters Third Dimension," *Computerworld,* September 2, 1991, p. 14.

Three-dimensional digitizing was used in the making of the movie *Terminator 2: Judgment Day* to show this T1000 cyborg performing a seemingly impossible feat.

plest. The computer is programmed to recognize a series of commands, such as "RUN" or "EDIT," for one user's voice. This type of speech recognition system is the most widespread and is being used in many specialty areas involving "hands-busy/eyes-busy" jobs. For example, a 1,000-word system has been developed for radiologists to use in dictating reports. Such systems are possible because they use very limited vocabularies. There are several PC-based systems of this type, including IBM's VoiceType with its 7,000-word vocabulary. You can even buy a voice-command system for less than $200 to program your VCR.

Voice recognition systems for one speaker/continuous speech must be able to distinguish when one word stops and another begins. This restricts the vocabulary of the system, and the user must train the system to recognize his or her

This computer operates a page turning device upon the verbal command of the user.

unique speech pattern by speaking to it. For example, Dragon Systems markets a discrete speech system with a 30,000-word vocabulary, but its continuous speech system has only a 2,000-word vocabulary. The third system must recognize a word, regardless of who speaks it. This is a much more complex system than is the one speaker/discrete speech type, because the computer must recognize many pronunciations of the same word. As a result, speaker-independent systems cost much more than do single-speaker systems, and their vocabularies are more restricted.

Finally, there are few workable systems of the fourth type because of the extreme complexity involved in programming a system to understand continuous speech from multiple speakers. However, in such a fast-moving field as voice recognition, anything is possible. For example, Apple has demonstrated a system called "Casper" that accepts continuous speech from multiple speakers.

Pen-Based Systems

Handwriting recognition systems are also in their infancy. These systems use a notepad-size computer with a special screen and stylus combined with pattern recognition software. Market researchers think that pen-based computers could become the hottest technology to hit the computer world since the original PC was introduced over ten years ago. They predict that 250,000 pen-based notepad systems will be sold in 1992 and that 2 million a year will be sold by 1995. A pen-based system offers what many users have long wanted—a system that allows them to input information by writing, much as they would on a sheet of paper. The written information is transferred to a desktop computer through a hookup, thereby avoiding the use of heavy disk drives. Potential users and applications include the following:

- Police writing reports or tickets (see box);
- Insurance adjusters filling out forms and drawing pictures of accidents;
- Surveyors collecting data;
- Food service workers taking food and beverage orders;
- Students taking notes in class and then downloading additional information from the professor's electronic blackboard after class.

In handwriting recognition systems, the user enters data into the computer by printing or writing on the screen with a stylus that emits a faint signal from its tip. The movement of the pen is digitized, like that performed with the graphic digitizers discussed earlier in this chapter, and the screen becomes dark wherever the stylus touches. Pattern recognition software then recognizes the letters, numbers, punctuation marks, and special symbols and stores them in memory for processing. Handwritten data, signatures, and sketches can be digitized without a keyboard or mouse. The software can be taught to recognize the user's handwriting, so that any handwritten symbols, including shorthand and scientific notation, can be converted to text within the computer. The screen on a pen-based system also can interpret a user's control signals, such as tapping to present a document on the screen or flicking the bottom of the page to go to the next page. It is even possible that illiterate workers could use such a system by simply marking the appropriate boxes. As with voice recognition systems, pen-based computing is changing rapidly as new systems are introduced.

I don't think anybody feels comfortable using a keyboard in a business meeting or in social situations.

Mitch Kapor, founder of Lotus Development Corporation

Quoted in "Is the Pen Mightier than the Keyboard?" *Lotus,* August 1990, p. 10.

DIRECT DATA ENTRY

While interactive input with a keyboard or other device is a very common method of data entry, direct data entry methods are also very important. Methods such as bar codes, optical character recognition, magnetic ink character recognition, and point-of-sale systems account for a tremendous amount of data being input to computers each day. In addition, financial transaction terminals are becoming a common device for banking transactions.

Bar Codes

Probably the most widely used direct input device is the **bar code.** Bar codes are combinations of light and dark bars that are coded to contain various types of information depending on the application. In grocery stores, bar codes are used for pricing and inventory purposes; in libraries, they are used to identify library users and books. And, as discussed in the box at the beginning of this chapter, bar codes are beginning to be used in the human services area to identify inmates and patients.

The most common bar code is the Universal Product Code (UPC) used on almost all grocery products. This code has three widths of bars and spaces and is set up so that there are two bars and two spaces per character. Figure 7-3 shows a bar code for one such product. Note that there is a series of digits that correspond to the bars, which in turn correspond to the type of product, the brand, and the particular item. This bar code is for a grocery product (chocolate syrup) made by Hershey Chocolate. Other products by the same company will have a different item number, and different manufacturers will have different company codes.

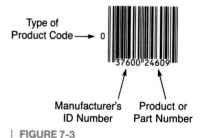

FIGURE 7-3
Bar Code Example

POLICE TESTING PEN-BASED SYSTEMS

In San Jose, California, all law enforcement officers may soon be carrying a pen-based notepad computer in addition to a service revolver and nightstick. The San Jose Police Department is testing two pen-based systems outdoors. Indoor tests were successful and provided some interesting insight into the practical use of pen-based systems.

Initial tests showed that pen input rapidly processed information from data fields requiring brief information, such as name, address, and age. The handwriting recognition system was slow, however, in converting lengthy descriptions into text. The officers found the delay bothersome and requested the use of keyboards to input longer descriptions. Pen input was also found to be very useful for creating crime scene diagrams and composite drawings, where tapping a box produces a menu from which such features as hair color and height can be selected.

For the outdoor tests, several modifications have been made to the system, including creating a "blank page" on which the officer can write without the system performing any handwriting recognition. This, combined with a lightweight keyboard, will allow the officers to write notes about the crime and crime scene and then transcribe them on the keyboard.

It is hoped that the information from the pen-based notepad can then be uploaded to the police department's main record management system computer. If this can be done, a tremendous amount of time would be saved by not having to key in the over 100,000 reports generated each year by the department's nearly 1,000 officers.

Source: Interview with Officer Tony Weir, San Jose Police Department, December 6, 1991; and James Daly, "San Jose First to Use Gridpad," *Computerworld*, January 21, 1991, p. 37.

This handwriting recognition system is able to interpret the police officer's instructions written on screen.

As the Universal Product (bar) Code is read, the information is converted to a series of digits and transmitted to the store's computer, which finds the price and sends it back to the cash register. At the same time, the store's inventory records are adjusted to reflect the sale of the product. In this way, the bar code is used for both pricing and inventory. The pricing is updated by store personnel, who enter new prices into the computer. This process of updating prices can cause problems if the incorrect price is entered or a special sale price is not entered. However, this type of checkout error is a human error, not a computer error.

There are other types of bar codes, different from the UPC, that are used for specialized purposes, but in each case bars and spaces are used to represent the information to be input. Bar codes can be read by a special laser device on the checkout counter at the grocery store or by a bar code reader often referred to as a **wand.** Each reader device works by bouncing a light beam off a bar code pattern and then measuring the reflected light. This measurement is then converted into data that are sent to a computer that determines the type of item and the price and sends them back to the point of sale. One reason for the increasing use of bar codes for a multitude of purposes is their low error rate. It has been found that with high-quality printing a bar code may be scanned with an error rate of *less* than 1 in 10 million.

> **A government study found that humans make one mistake for every 300 items they enter; the error rate for bar codes is something like one in 3 million.**
>
> *Bonnie Stamper, president of Bar Code Systems*
>
> Quoted in ''The Bar Code Revolution,'' *The Atlanta Constitution,* October 2, 1990, pp. B1–B2.

Optical Character Recognition

Another method of coding data to be electronically entered into the computer is **optical character recognition (OCR).** In OCR, a reader is passed over a document to determine the symbols present. So that the reader can pick up the correct symbols, they are usually typewritten using a special style (font) of type. A common high-volume use of OCR systems is to read the customer information on the billing forms we return with our credit card, utility, and other payments. Since these forms are prepared by computer in a specific font, the OCR system

(Left) Bar codes greatly decrease the time necessary to check out books from libraries. (Right) This bar code reader registers the price of the item while at the same time providing inventory and marketing information to store management.

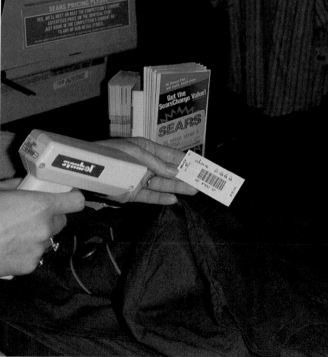

FIGURE 7-4
OCR Font

0 1 2 3 4 5 6 7 8 9
A B C D E F G H I J

has no problem reading the information from them. Figure 7-4 shows a type of font often used by commercial OCR systems like those that read billing information.

Another major user of OCR is the U.S. Postal Service. The Postal Service uses OCR to read the last line of typed addresses, including the ZIP code. If the ZIP code matches the address, then the letter is sorted to the carrier; if it does not match, or if the address is handwritten, the letter is kicked out of the system for action by a worker. A very common use of OCR with which you may be familiar is computerized scoring of tests using an **optical mark reader (OMR).** OMR picks up the black pencil marks on a special answer sheet and compares these to the correct answers.

Because OCR error rate is about 1,000 times higher than that of bar codes, many retailers, who at one time used OCR for pricing and inventory control, are now switching to bar codes. For example, Sears, one of the country's largest retailers, moved from an OCR-based pricing and inventory system to a bar-code system. However, the combination of improved OCR software and high-quality **scanners,** which translate a page of a document into an electronic form, has resulted in the reality of a computer being able to "read" typeset or typewritten documents. This capability can greatly relieve the monotony and strain of key-boarding information from a document into the computer. Scanners are also an important component of a desktop publishing system where they are used to

Automated letter sorting on optical character readers (OCRs) such as this has become the cornerstone of the U.S. Postal Service's mail processing program.

convert drawings and photographs to an electronic form that can be electronically "pasted" into a book or magazine. This subject will be covered in more detail in Chapter 10.

Scanners commonly come in two sizes: full page and handheld. If you need to scan entire pages of a document, then a full-page scanner is needed. These look and work much like a copier, except that the output goes into the computer rather than onto a hard copy of the document. Handheld scanners are less expensive than full-page scanners and are more flexible because they can be used to scan just a portion of a page.

Magnetic Ink Character Recognition

Magnetic ink character recognition (MICR) is used to process bank checks. The bank's identification code, the check writer's account number, and the amount of the check are printed in magnetic ink at the bottom of the check. The check can then be processed by machine and routed to the proper bank. The bank identification number and account number are preprinted on the check, but the amount of the check must be keyed in by a human operator who determines the amount of the check. This step takes time and can introduce errors into the data entry process. IBM recently announced a system that uses a scanner to combine OCR with MICR to read and print the amount of the check. Figure 7-5 shows a check with MICR codes.

Point-of-Sale Systems

We have already discussed two point-of-sale (POS) systems—bar codes and touchscreens—but the POS systems are becoming prevalent in many other ways, too. In addition to bar codes or touchscreens, a POS can be a cash register that is connected directly to a mainframe or minicomputer or an IBM PC compatible cash register linked to a personal computer via a communication cable.

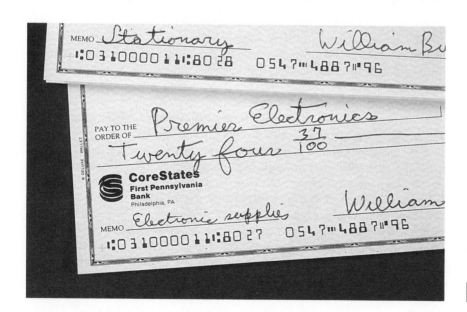

FIGURE 7-5
Check with MICR

Regardless of how a POS system is set up, it has many advantages for retailers, keeping them constantly updated on inventory so they will know which products are selling and which are not, what to push, and what to discount. Using inventory reports generated daily, retailers can avoid tying up working capital in unneeded inventory. A POS cash register system usually generates customized sales slips and handles multiple forms of payment, but it can also handle some accounting functions and develop mailing lists from a customer data base. With the more sophisticated of these systems, it is possible to integrate the cash register with the bar codes or with a touchscreen system.

Financial Transaction Terminals

In addition to using POS terminals in many stores, more and more of us are becoming familiar with the use of various types of **financial transaction terminals.** Undoubtedly, the most widespread of these is the **automated teller machine (ATM)** used to carry out our banking business at a location away from the bank or when the bank is closed. At an ATM, the user inserts a bankcard with a magnetic strip into the machine and presses numbers on a keypad to enter a **personal identification number (PIN).** If that PIN matches the information on the card, the user can then make selections from a menu and enter dollar amounts to be withdrawn or deposited. If money is being withdrawn, the ATM checks with a computer network to ascertain that the funds are available.

Other financial transaction terminals include machines that check if the amount of a credit card purchase will put a user over his or her credit limit, and "debit card" systems that work like credit cards except that they automatically and immediately transfer the money from the user's bank account to the store's account. All of these uses of financial transaction terminals are examples of the growing emphasis on **electronic funds transfer (EFT)** throughout the world's economy.

OUTPUT DEVICES ▬▬▬

As we have said several times, without output all the computer's processing is of little use to us: We must have some type of output. Usually this comes in one of two forms—the display screen or the printed page. Another common form of output involves sending the computer information to either magnetic tape or disk secondary storage. Then this information can be displayed or printed later as needed, used as input for another program, or sent to other users. Usually, output to tape or disk is in the form of **files** that are given a name. This will be discussed more in Chapter 8, on secondary storage.

In the world around us, computer output also sends commands and information to other electronic or mechanical devices, such as rocket engines, security devices, home appliances, and even, as discussed in Chapter 6, muscles of the body. This type of output, while usually unseen, goes on all around us in the many smart machines that we use daily. For example, the chip in a computerized automobile ignition is constantly sending output to the carburetor that controls the fuel mixture for maximum gas mileage. Similarly, the computer that controls the climate at a large shopping mall is constantly measuring the air temperature and humidity and sending signals to the air conditioning system based on the measurements.

RENEWING YOUR LICENSE WITH A TOUCHSCREEN

For automobile drivers in California, renewing a driver's license may become much easier, thanks to a new touchscreen system. The pilot system, which is being tested in several Department of Motor Vehicles (DMV) offices around the state, is housed in a kiosk that looks and acts like an automated teller machine. The applicant first keys in his or her driver's license number and then begins to respond to the touchscreen display to answer questions stored on a laser disk. In addition to text-based questions found on traditional driver's license exams, the system also displays short videos illustrating typical traffic situations and asks the applicant to answer questions that relate to the video clip.

After the applicant answers all test questions, the system scores the test, gives the applicant the opportunity to change his or her address or other personal information, and collects the license fee from the user's credit card. Only at this point does the DMV clerk become involved in the process by administering an eye exam, snapping a photo, and issuing a license to those applicants who have passed the test. Previously, the clerk also had to hand out the test, score it, change personal information, and accept payment— tasks now handled by the new touchscreen system.

While the new system certainly could shorten the tedious process of renewing licenses, the long-term goal of the DMV is to automate the entire process. However, before this can be done, important security concerns must be addressed, including ensuring that the person taking the test is actually the one applying for the license. The California DMV is considering a fingerprint scanner to check the identity of the applicant as one way to accomplish this.

Source: James Daly, "License Renewal Goes Self-serve," *Computerworld*, October 1, 1990, p. 39.

Touch screens are being used for driver's license renewal.

Another type of output that is becoming more common is audio output. As the touchtone phone becomes more than just a device for dialing another party's number, systems are being developed that allow you to touch additional digits based on your needs or interests. In essence, you are using the touchtone phone as an input device that results in either a computer-generated or a computer-compiled voice providing you with the required information. In the first case, a computer chip actually generates the voice; in the second, words spoken by a human are pieced together to give you information or directions.

While both output to other machines and audio output are certainly important, we will concentrate on display and printed output since these are the forms used by most applications software and programming languages.

Display Output

In the early days of computers, output from a computer often came from either a dedicated printer or, for interactive purposes, a teletype printer (similar to those once used in a newsroom) combined with a keyboard. The user could type commands and receive responses from the computer over the teletype. These devices were very slow, however, and dreadfully loud. Another common early form of output was a modified IBM Selectric typewriter. While somewhat faster than a teletype and not as loud, it still left a lot to be desired. Fortunately, both these devices have been superseded by the video monitor or, simply, monitor.

The **monitor** is a televisionlike device on which the output from the computer is shown. Because the monitor, like a television, uses a cathode ray tube to display images, it is sometimes referred to as a **CRT** (for **cathode ray tube**). When the monitor is a part of a terminal tied into a mainframe or a computer network, it is also referred to as a **VDT** (for **video display terminal**). Regardless of what it is called, the monitor is used to display both the output from processing and, in conjunction with a keyboard, the instructions or data that are being input to the computer. For example, at the same time that this text is being composed at the keyboard with a word processor, it is being shown on the screen where it can be read and changed if necessary. Later, the same screen can be used as an output device to display the results from a software package.

Virtually all computer output can be shown first on a screen if a user desires. On a mainframe, a user may want to check the output before "dumping" it to a high-speed printer (to be discussed later), while on a personal computer, the user may look at the entire output before having it printed. In either case, the monitor is an important output device; without it, using a computer would be very difficult.

Both color and monochrome monitors are widely used with personal computers.

The monitor works in much the same manner as a television screen: One or more electron beams are generated from cathode ray tubes or "electron guns." As the beams strike a phosphorescent compound (**phosphor**) coated on the inside of the screen, the energy of the collision causes a dot on the screen called a **pixel** to light up. The electron beam sweeps back and forth across the screen so that as the phosphor starts to fade, it is struck again by the beam and lights up again. If the phosphor fades too quickly, a condition known as "flicker" occurs as the phosphors blink on and off. If the phosphor remains lighted too long after it is struck, then annoying shadows may appear on the screen. Figure 7-6 shows the operation of a monitor.

Monitors are available in monochrome or color versions. **Monochrome monitors** use one color for the background and a different color for the foreground text; **color monitors** are able to display multiple colors. If the monitor displays color, then three electron guns are used to light three types of phosphor that display the colors red, green, or blue. Monitors of this type are often referred to as **RGB** (for red, green, blue) **monitors.**

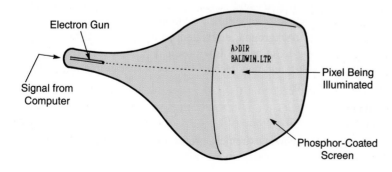

Electron Gun

Signal from Computer

A>DIR
BALDWIN.LTR

Pixel Being Illuminated

Phosphor-Coated Screen

FIGURE 7-6
Operation of Monitor

Full-page and double-page
monochrome monitors are often
used for desktop publishing
applications.

One way to measure the quality of the monitor is by its resolution. **Resolution** is defined as the number of horizontal pixels and vertical pixels relative to the size of the monitor. For two monitors of the same size, the monitor with the higher number of pixels has the higher resolution and a sharper picture. Today many color monitors have a resolution of 640 pixels horizontally by 480 pixels vertically. Newer monitors can display 1,024 pixels by 768 pixels, and the resolution of monitors is being improved every year. Chapter 10, on word processing and graphics, will take up in some detail the topic of text and graphics display on personal computer monitors.

Monitors come in a wide range of sizes depending on their intended use. Portable PCs usually have screens that are $4'' \times 9''$ while many monitors for desktop computers measure $12''$ to $14''$ on the diagonal. Mainframes and workstations may have monitors that measure $19''$ or more on the diagonal.

A type of monitor that has become popular as more laptop computers come into use is the flat-screen display. Because CRT monitors must have an electron gun, they must have a distance of over one foot between the gun and the screen, causing them to be fairly large and bulky. **Flat-screen displays** avoid this bulk and size by using one of several technologies to allow a screen that is less than one inch thick. The most popular current technology for flat-screen displays is the same **liquid crystal display (LCD)** technology used for pocket calculators and digital watches.

LCD technology uses a thin layer of liquid crystal molecules placed between two sheets of glass and separated into sections. An individual liquid crystal molecule is made opaque when a voltage is applied to it, resulting in a dark spot on a light background, equivalent to a pixel in a CRT monitor. Flat-screen displays using LCD have a low power requirement so they can be used in the laptop portables, and new technology is constantly improving the quality of this type of display.

TYPES OF PRINTERS

While output on a screen is extremely useful, the printed page—or as it is often called, **hard copy**—is a necessity in most situations. The teletype and IBM

Selectric printers used with early computers provided hard copy as the only form of output. Today, printers are used in addition to monitors to provide hard copy for either mainframes or personal computers. We will discuss various types of printers used with both types of computers.

Printers are broadly classified as **impact printers** or as **nonimpact printers.** An impact printer uses a hammer to strike a ribbon soaked or coated with ink to force ink onto the paper. Typewriters are a manual form of impact printer.

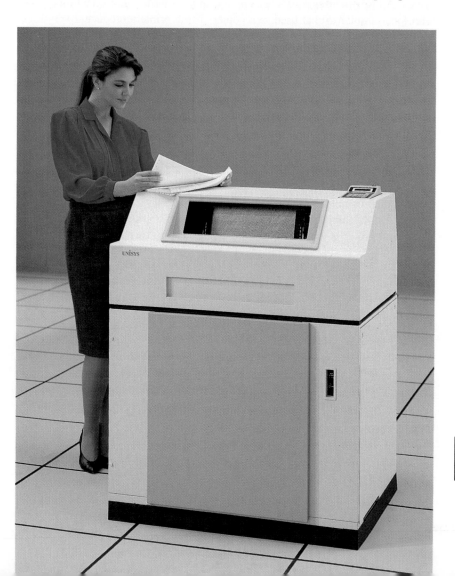

The high-speed line printer is needed to keep up with the tremendous computing speeds of mainframe computers.

211

Because impact printers use a mechanical hammer to form letters, they tend to be noisy. On the other hand, impact printers work without special paper and can print multiple copies using carbon paper or carbonless multiple-copy forms.

Nonimpact printers use some method other than a hammer strike to create a character or an image on the paper. These methods include thermal, ink-spray, and laser technologies. Nonimpact printers are often fast and quiet, but cannot work with multipart paper. We will now discuss printers of both types.

Mainframe Printers

Historically, printers associated with mainframes have been impact printers that use a chain, band, or series of cylinders to hold the letters and position them over the paper. All three of these types of printers are high-speed printers that can often print an entire line in one motion. For example, in a **chain printer** the letters and digits are attached to a chain that rotates between two pulleys. As a symbol comes by the proper position on the paper, a series of hammers strike the ribbon and paper to form the character. In all three cases, it is a fairly simple operation to change the typestyle (font) by changing the band or chain. Figure 7-7 shows a chain printer.

The current state-of-the-art mainframe printer is the nonimpact laser printer. A **laser printer** uses a laser light beam to "write" dots on a drum coated with toner similar to that used in a copier. These printers produce a very-high-quality print since they use 240 or more dots per inch to form the letters. They can also create letters of different sizes and fonts to produce output on standard $8\frac{1}{2}'' \times 11''$ paper instead of the much wider, bulkier computer paper. Because they print an entire page at one time, laser printers are often referred to as **page printers.** Mainframe laser printers can print up to 380 pages per minute to handle the high volume of output required to satisfy the needs of the multiple users of a mainframe. Figure 7-8 shows the operation of a laser printer.

Personal Computer Printers

For personal computers, the dot matrix printer is a widely used type of impact printer. A **dot matrix printer** uses a printhead with a group of 9, 18, or 24 rigid wires arranged in a vertical line. As the printhead moves across the paper, the

FIGURE 7-7
Chain Printer

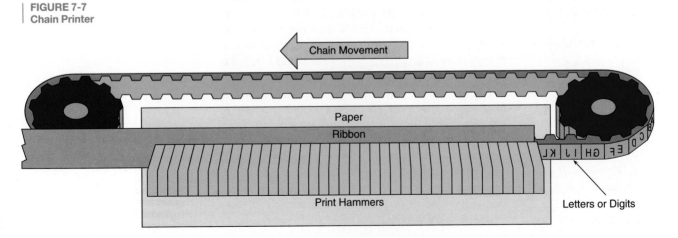

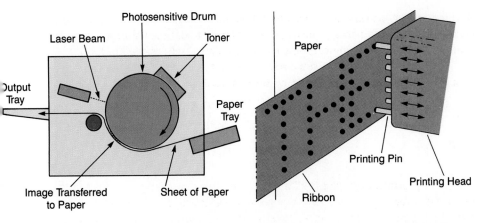

Photosensitive Drum

Laser Beam · Toner

Output Tray · Paper

Image Transferred to Paper · Sheet of Paper · Paper Tray

Printing Pin · Printing Head · Ribbon

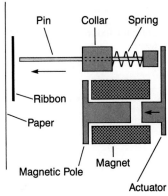

Pin · Collar · Spring

Ribbon

Paper

Magnetic Pole · Magnet · Actuator

FIGURE 7-8 (left)
Laser Printer Operation

FIGURE 7-9 (center, right)
Dot Matrix Print Mechanism.

wires strike the ribbon and the paper, creating a matrix of dots to form a letter. Obviously, the more dots per symbol, the higher the quality of output. Figure 7-9 demonstrates the operation of a dot matrix printhead.

Dot matrix printers have both advantages and disadvantages for personal computer users. Their advantages include high speed (over 200 cps—characters per second—are possible) and reasonable price (many are available for less than $300). One way a dot matrix printer is made faster is with **bidirectional printing.** The printer uses a small amount of RAM memory as a buffer to store temporarily a line of information that is then printed from either side of the printer, that is, forward and backward consecutively. Another good point about dot matrix printers is that the font and point size (the shape and size of the letters) may be changed by the software; it is not necessary to change the printhead to achieve a different number of characters per inch (10 or 12), to boldface or to italicize, or to underline. All these variations can be handled by the software's directions to the printer. At one time, a disadvantage of a dot matrix printer was that the quality of the print was not good enough for formal correspondence or for most business purposes. With the new 24-pin printers, however, dot matrix output is barely distinguishable from that obtained with a typewriter, and so is called **near-letter-quality output.**

A major disadvantage of dot matrix printers is the noise they make due to the impact action required to impress ink onto the paper. Placing the printer in an acoustical cabinet will reduce this somewhat.

Another type of printer that can be either impact or nonimpact is the **thermal printer,** which uses heat to "burn" an image into the paper. If the printhead actually touches a special type of paper to form a letter, then the printer is an impact thermal printer. On the other hand, if the wires melt a polymer on a ribbon, releasing a drop of ink, the printhead never comes in contact with the paper, making the printer nonimpact. Thermal printers are fast and initially inexpensive. However, if heat-sensitive paper is required, it can be expensive and is not acceptable for business purposes since the print tends to fade over time. Thermal printers have only a small share of the printer market, but many are being used in conjunction with laptop portable computers.

In addition to the nonimpact thermal printer, two other popular nonimpact printers for personal computers are ink-jet printers and laser printers. **Ink jet printers** form dots on paper by spraying the ink from a row of tiny nozzles. Ink jet printers have several advantages over impact dot matrix printers. First, they are quiet; since there are no moving parts and no hammer striking paper, there

is no noise. Second, they are fast, achieving speeds of up to 270 cps. Finally, since there are no moving parts in the printhead, the life of the mechanism is expected to be five times longer than that of a dot matrix printer. Disadvantages of ink jet printers are that since there is no hammer to make an impression on a carbon, multiple copies cannot be made; on some models the ink may run; and the cost is somewhat higher than for impact dot matrix printers (but lower than for laser printers).

Laser printers are becoming very popular for use with personal computers as well as mainframes. While essentially a nonimpact dot matrix printer, a laser printer can crowd enough dots into a small space to create a very high-quality output, the standard output for personal computer laser printers being 300 dots per inch (dpi). In terms of speed, a laser printer is very fast and is measured in *pages per minute* rather than characters per second. Available personal computer laser printers range in speed from over 30 pages per minute for the most expensive printers down to 4 pages per minute for the least costly printers. Laser printers are flexible in that they can print various fonts as well as printing graphics. They also are very quiet, making no more sound than the average photocopier. This is an important consideration in an office crowded with personal computers and printers.

One shortcoming of laser printers is their cost. Laser printers start at around $700 and go up to over $10,000. In addition, like copiers, they require toner that can cost over $100 for every 2,000 to 3,000 pages.

To give you an idea of the different qualities of print that are available for various types of personal computer printers, Figure 7-10 compares the output obtained from a dot matrix printer to that obtained from a laser printer. Note that in 9-pin dot matrix output the dots in some letters are easy to see—particularly in the "x." Also notice the high-quality print associated with a laser printer.

An important use for laser printers is in the rapidly expanding area of desktop publishing. In **desktop publishing,** graphics and text are integrated and

Before the laser printer, many computers were write-only devices: You put your information in and then waited a few years for it to print it back to you.

*John H. Meyer, president,
Ventura Software, Inc.*

Quoted in "View from the Top,"
Personal Computing, October 1989,
p. 270.

!"#$%&'()*+,-./0123456789:;<=>?@ABCDEFGHIJKLMNOPQRSTUVWXYZ

Dot Matrix Print

!"#$%&'()*+,-./0123456789:;<=>?@ABCDEFGHIJKLMNOPQRSTUVWXYZ

Laser Print

printed on a laser printer. Newsletters, books, magazines, and other documents can be quickly and inexpensively created in this manner. The computer lab manuals that accompany this textbook were created using desktop publishing. Chapter 10 will cover desktop publishing in more detail. Even though the resolution of a laser printer is one-quarter that of typeset documents (300 dpi, versus 1200 dpi for typeset material), laser printers are being used to create very good-looking documents.

Color Output

The increasing use of color monitors has increased the demand that hard copy output also be in color. Color output can be achieved in one of four ways—dot matrix printers, ink jet printers, plotters, and laser printers. The color dot matrix printers use the same impact approach as with black-and-white output, except that a multicolored ribbon provides the color. By moving the ribbon and making multiple passes, the dot matrix printer can produce up to 16 colors.

Multiple-pen plotters can produce colorful graphs and charts on a variety of media, including paper, transparencies, and vellum.

BITS OF HISTORY

The "Father" of the Mouse

To find the origins of the mouse, we have to go back to the almost prehistoric (in computer terms) year of 1963, when Doug Engelbart published a paper on how to augment human intellect through the use of the computer. This paper was almost 20 years ahead of its time in its description of such unknown concepts as personal workstations, networks of users communicating with one another, and word processing. Based on this paper, Engelbart received a grant to try out some of his ideas for using computers.

Among the many ideas that Engelbart's group explored to help people use the computer was the mouse. It was a pointing device that people found they could use easily without special training or other special equipment. The name came from the small size and the tail-like cord leading to the computer. The original mouse was made of wood and had a single button for sending commands to the computer, but soon the number of command buttons was increased to three.

The first computer to use the mouse was the Xerox Star, which was developed at the Xerox Palo Alto Research Center (PARC) and released in 1981. An alumnus of PARC then worked for Apple to develop the Lisa computer, which was the direct predecessor of the very popular Macintosh. Today, the mouse has become widely used with IBM compatible PCs as an input device for many different types of software.

Source: Steven Levy, "Of Mice and Men," *Popular Computing,* May 1984.

ONE

Douglas Engelbart—the inventor of the mouse and of other tools and techniques that augment the human mind—is shown here using an early version of the mouse.

Ink jet color printers use the same principle as black-and-white ink jet printers, except that multiple inks are used. Most color ink jet printers use up to seven bright colors, which the printer can mix by making multiple passes. A problem with color ink jet printers is that special paper may be required to avoid bleeding of colors.

Plotters have been used for over 20 years to draw graphs and charts. **Plotters** have pens that move across the paper to trace out the pattern of the graph or chart. When several pens are used, multicolor graphs and charts can be developed. Plotters can be used on paper, vellum, or transparencies to produce colorful charts and graphs. Although a plotter can be used to reproduce something

Color laser printers can produce hard-copy versions of computer art.

other than a chart or graph, drawing charts and graphs is what the machine does best.

Color laser printers that work on the same general principles as the black-and-white laser printers are also becoming more available for general-purpose color printing. As you would expect, they produce a much higher-quality output than any other type of printer with the possible exception of the plotter. However, they are also expensive.

REVIEW OF KEY POINTS

1. Input and output are necessary parts of any computer system.
2. Data entry is a problem because of the time needed to enter large amounts of data into the computer and because of the errors that can occur in this process.
3. The keyboard converts a keystroke into a binary code that is sent to the CPU of the computer. Keyboards tend to differ among different computers, and each requires the user to spend some time becoming accustomed to it.

4. The mouse is the most popular alternative tool for computer input. It controls the cursor on the screen and can make selections from a menu. Touchscreens, graphic digitizer pads, and light pens are alternative forms of input.

5. Voice recognition is a form of input that is very useful in specialized situations. The general use of this technology for continuous speech still appears to be a thing of the future.

6. Bar codes, optical character recognition, and magnetic ink character recognition are methods used commercially to speed data entry. Point-of-sale systems can be very helpful to retailers in managing their inventory. Financial transaction systems have made electronic funds transfer a highly convenient reality.

7. The two major forms of output for computers are display monitors and the printed page.

8. Monitors can be either monochrome or color. Monochrome monitors use one color as the background with a reverse color as the foreground. Color monitors use RGB technology to provide numerous colors.

9. Monitor resolution is measured by the number of horizontal and vertical pixels a monitor can display relative to the size of the monitor.

10. Flat-screen displays use LCD technology to provide a thin, flat screen for laptop portables.

11. Printers are either impact or nonimpact. Chain printers are widely used impact printers for mainframes. Laser printers are popular nonimpact printers for mainframes.

12. For personal computers, dot matrix printers are the most popular type of impact printers. Dot matrix printers are fast and flexible but cannot provide letter-quality output.

13. Nonimpact printers for personal computers include some types of thermal printers, ink jet printers, laser printers, and plotters. Laser printers are fast, flexible, and quiet, but they are more expensive. They are used for desktop publishing to output high-quality documents.

14. Laser printers and plotters are used to produce high-quality color computer output.

KEY TERMS

automated teller machine (ATM)	file
bar code	financial transaction terminal
bidirectional printing	flat-screen display
buffer	graphical user interface (GUI)
cathode ray tube (CRT)	graphics digitizing tablet
chain printer	hard copy
color monitor	icon
data entry problem	impact printers
desktop metaphor	ink jet printer
desktop publishing	input/output (I/O)
dot matrix printer	keyboard
edit	laser printer
electronic funds transfer (EFT)	light pen

liquid crystal display (LCD)
magnetic ink character recognition
   (MICR)
monitor
monochrome monitor
mouse
near-letter-quality output
nonimpact printer
optical character recognition (OCR)
optical mark reader (OMR)
page printer
personal identification number (PIN)
phosphor
pixel

plotter
printer
resolution
RGB (red, blue, green) monitor
scanner
thermal printer
touchscreen
trackball
type-ahead buffer
verification
video display terminal (VDT)
voice recognition systems
wand

1. Discuss the importance of input and output to a computer system. Can you imagine a system without one or the other?

2. What is the data entry problem? Name two ways to solve this problem.

3. How does a keyboard send information to the CPU?

4. What are the two types of mouse devices available as alternative input devices for personal computers?

5. What is the difference between a touchscreen and a light pen? Why is appropriate software important for any type of alternate input device?

6. Look at a product with a UPC bar code on it: What are the company code and the item code for this product?

7. What does *RGB* stand for? What does it have to do with monitors?

8. What does a monitor resolution of 640×400 mean? Is this better than 320×200? $1,024 \times 768$?

9. What are the two major categories of printers?

10. Why do we say that a dot matrix printer is fast and flexible?

11. What is "letter-quality" print? Is it possible to achieve this quality of print with a dot matrix printer?

12. Why are thermal printers defined as both impact and nonimpact?

13. What are the three major types of nonimpact printers? Which is often used with laptop portables?

14. Why is the laser printer important to desktop publishing?

15. Which printers can be used to produce high-quality color output?

8

Using
Secondary Storage

Our discussion of hardware in Chapter 2 mentioned the need for secondary storage. In this chapter, we will review secondary storage and discuss the use of magnetic tape and magnetic disks as secondary storage devices for both mainframes and personal computers. This discussion will include information on the use of floppy and hard disks for personal computers. We then cover the important concept of backup as it applies to disk storage. Finally, the chapter will cover the use of optical disks.

STUDY OBJECTIVES

After reading this chapter, you should be able to

- understand the importance of secondary storage for both mainframes and personal computers;
- discuss the various types of files used on secondary storage;
- explain how information is stored on a reel-to-reel tape in a mainframe environment;
- discuss ways in which a disk is used to store information for a mainframe computer;
- describe the various methods to organize data and information on secondary storage;
- understand the storage organization of a floppy disk;
- recognize the storage capacities of different types of floppy disks;
- discuss the importance of backup for secondary storage;
- explain how optical disks are used for secondary storage.

FLYING FOR FED EX

As one of the world's leading full-service, all-cargo carriers, Federal Express operates a large fleet of Boeing 727 and 747 and DC-10 and MD-11 freighter aircraft. To train its pilots for this fleet of planes better, Federal Express has implemented a PC-based system that uses magneto-optical (M-O) disks to provide the trainee with graphical images. An M-O system combines the best characteristics of magnetic and optical storage in a single storage system.

In the Federal Express system, pilots sit at a workstation with two display monitors that are connected to an 80386-based PC that can provide graphics from the M-O disk to one or both of the screens as needed. The trainee can work through about 20 different subject areas on the airplane stored on the optical disk, with one monitor showing the actual panel on the airplane and the other showing a schematic of the same panel. Both monitors are equipped with touch-panel screens, allowing the trainee to simulate operation of the control panels by simply touching the onscreen buttons. When the trainee opens a switch on the simulated control panel, the schematic on the other screen shows what is occurring on the airplane as a result. Digitized audio records, also stored on the optical disk, provide narration for the trainee. Once the trainee has gone through all the systems, the system provides a series of real-life technical problems to be solved.

The stored graphic images and digitized audio recordings used in the Federal Express training system consume gigabytes of secondary storage, yet must be accessed very quickly for the system to provide the required realism. To handle this need for storage and speed, a magneto-optical disk system proved to be a workable alternative. For even greater speed, large segments of RAM internal storage are used to hold information that has been transferred from the M-O disk system prior to its being needed by the training system. In addition to the speed and storage capacity, this system allows easy replacement of disk cartridges. To handle the operating system and system utilities, a hard disk system is also utilized at each workstation.

Source: Steve Cummings, "Optical's Vast Expanses," Mass Storage Supplement to *PC Week*, March 15, 1988, pp. S17–S19, as updated by the author in interviews with Federal Express, 1991.

Pilots able to fly any number of types of airplanes help Federal Express ensure that its packages arrive overnight.

In the box about Federal Express, secondary storage is a key part of the training system. Magneto-optical (M-O) disks are used to store the images and text. M-O systems combine these two forms of storage to give users the best qualities of both. As we discussed briefly in Chapter 2, secondary storage is nonvolatile memory outside of internal memory that is important to any type of computer system since all computers need more memory than is available internally. In addition, the volatility of internal memory means that when the power to the computer is turned off, anything stored there is lost.

Various devices are used for secondary storage, including magnetic tapes, magnetic disks, and optical disks. Some of these devices can be written on and read from by the user; others can only be read from. There are various types of each device. For example, disks for PCs come as both metallic hard disks and plastic floppy disks.

Using Files

To have a better understanding of **secondary storage,** it is helpful to understand how the data or information is stored on the secondary storage device. The terminology describing the storage is similar, regardless of which storage device— tape or disk—is being used. In most cases, the data or information is stored as a **file,** which is defined as *any collection of meaningful material to which a name can be attached.* For example, a list of the names of the members of a college computer club would be considered a file, to which we might attach the name MEMBERS. This name indicates that this file is the membership file.

Files can be subdivided into **records.** If a file is analogous to a standard manila file folder, then the records are analogous to the individual items stored in the folder. For example, if we have a file folder containing membership information forms, then the forms are equivalent to records. Records are often subdivided into individual units of information called **fields.**

Files can be classified according to the type of material stored in the file, the form in which the material is stored, and the way the material is accessed. When classified by type of material stored, the files can be either program files or data files. A **program file** is made up of the list of instructions or program statements for a computer program, while a **data file** contains data that are used in programs. The membership file would be considered a data file, and a computer program that would arrange the data alphabetically would be a program file.

Material may be stored on files in either text form or binary form. **Text files** (also known as **ASCII files** on personal computers) are files that are composed of text in a readable form. **Binary files** usually are program files that have been translated into a binary (0–1) form that can be executed directly by the computer.

Recall from Chapter 2 that magnetic tape and disk are the primary forms of secondary storage for all sizes of computers. Tape is a **sequential storage device,** which means that the records are physically stored in the same order that they are accessed. Records stored sequentially must be accessed one after the other; the user or software cannot skip around among the records. Disk storage is a **direct-access storage device (DASD),** which means that any record may be accessed at will. With magnetic disk, it is possible to jump around from record to record.

MAGNETIC TAPE

A popular form of secondary storage for both mainframes and personal computers is magnetic tape. **Magnetic** (or simply, **mag**) **tape** is a thin Mylar® tape from $\frac{1}{2}$ inch to less than $\frac{1}{4}$ inch wide. The tape is coated with ferrous oxide (purified rust), on which information is recorded in binary form by selective magnetization of spots on the tape. Magnetic tape is available in two primary forms: reel-to-reel tape that resembles the reel-to-reel audio tape used with high-quality recorders and cartridge tape.

A **tape drive,** which we need to use any type of magnetic tape, performs two key operations. First, the information is transferred to and from the tape with a **read/write head,** which encodes the magnetic signals on the ferrous oxide tape coating. The tape must be able to move across the read/write head. In cartridge tape systems, the tape remains entirely within the plastic case. After the plastic case is inserted in the drive mechanism, the tape is moved between the supply and storage reels by a motor in the tape drive. For reel-to-reel systems, a storage reel is part of the tape drive, and the supply reel is removable for storage elsewhere.

At one time magnetic tape was used for sequential processing of data into information. For example, payrolls and grade rolls were processed sequentially using magnetic tape. In these examples in which all names must be processed one at a time, either to compute the amount of pay for the period or to update the grades on the students' transcripts, sequential processing is appropriate.

Tapes are cataloged in a tape library so a particular tape can be found easily when a user requests it.

However, today, little or no processing is done using magnetic tape—almost all of it is performed using disk storage. For that reason, the primary purpose of magnetic tape is to provide **backup** in case there is a problem with the disk drives that results in data loss. A common backup policy using tape has two parts: First, each transaction that is processed on disk storage is also copied to a **transaction log tape;** second, all files from disk storage are copied to a **backup tape** once each week. This way, if there is a problem with the disk drives, the data can be restored by using a combination of the backup tape and the transaction log tape. The topic of backup is discussed in more detail on pages 240–242.

A second use of magnetic tape is **archival storage.** In this form of storage, data and programs that are used infrequently are archived to tape and, if necessary, retrieved at a later time. This saves disk storage space and cost.

Reel-to-Reel Tape

The oldest form of secondary storage currently in use is **reel-to-reel tape,** which is widely used in mainframe and minicomputer applications. Probably more data and information are stored on this form of secondary storage than on all other forms combined. Reel-to-reel tape is usually $\frac{1}{2}$ inch wide and 2,400 feet long and is classified by the density and the number of tracks on the tape. The **density** is measured linearly by the number of **bits per inch (bpi)** on the tape. However, since an entire byte (8 bits) can be encoded across the tape, the density in bits per inch is equivalent to bytes per inch. At one time, common densities were 800 and 1,600 bpi, but today, most tapes have a density of 6,250 bpi. With this density, a reel-to-reel tape can hold over 100 million bytes for a cost of less than $20.

A reel-to-reel tape must be loaded onto a tape drive before it can be accessed by the user.

The **tracks** on the tape are parallel magnetic lines that run the length of the tape on which binary information is stored. The most common number of tracks is nine. On some mainframes, information is stored on the tape in EBCDIC (Extended Binary Coded Decimal Interchange Code), an 8-bit code for storing or transferring information in binary form. ASCII (American Standard Code for Information Interchange) is used for other types of mainframes as well as minicomputers and personal computers.

The ninth track on a nine-track tape is for a **parity bit,** which is used for error checking. The parity bit is added during the write process to make the number of one bits across the tape equal to an odd or even number, depending on which standard is used. During the read step, the number of one bits is checked to make sure they match the parity (odd or even) used. A tape with odd parity means that the total number of one bits across the tape is always odd. Figure 8-1 shows a section of nine-track tape with the letters UGA coded on it in EBCDIC. Assuming odd parity is used in this example, a bit is added to the parity track (labeled "P") to make the number of bits in the letter "U" equal an odd number. Because the letters "G" and "A" already have odd numbers of bits, they do not need a parity bit.

Note in Figure 8-1 that the tracks are not numbered sequentially. This ordering places the most commonly used tracks (0, 1, 2, 3, and P) in the middle of the tape and the least used tracks on the outside of the tape. This minimizes wear and tear on the tape. Because an entire byte is encoded on the tape in one operation, reel-to-reel tape is a **parallel storage device.**

FIGURE 8-1
Magnetic Tape Section

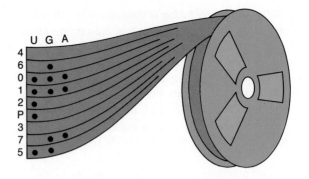

Individual records on the tape can be blocked or unblocked. **Blocked records** are combined into a physical unit that is then read by the tape drive. A block of records, also called a **physical record,** is the actual amount of tape read by the tape drive at one time. Each block is made up of **logical records.** For example, on a tape that contains a mailing list, each block could have three logical records—each consisting of a name, street address, and city and state. The space between blocks is the **interblock gap (IBG).** The tape drive starts and stops at each interblock gap.

In **unblocked records,** each physical record corresponds to only one logical record, and logical records are separated by interrecord gaps. The read or write process from the tape is slowed down because the tape drive stops more often. Figure 8-2 shows two tapes with the same information. However, one tape is blocked in groups of three logical records, and the other tape is unblocked. Note that the blocked tape can store more information than the unblocked tape in the same space.

A special reel-to-reel tape drive is needed that can move the tape past the read/write head at speeds of up to 300 inches per second. Such high speeds are necessary to handle the large amounts of information stored on tapes and provide a **transfer rate** of 1.8 Mbytes per second. Figure 8-3 shows a diagram of a tape drive. The large loops on either side of the read/write mechanism are in vacuum chambers. If the tape ran at normal atmospheric pressure, air resistance to the sudden surges in speed would break the tape.

Most computer centers have a tape library run by a special librarian who manages tape storage. When a computer operator must mount a particular tape on the tape drive, he or she obtains that tape from the librarian.

FIGURE 8-2
Blocked and Unblocked
Magnetic Tape Sections

Blocked

Interblock Gap	UGA	UNC	UF	Interblock Gap	UCLA	USC	UT	Interblock Gap

Unblocked

Interblock Gap	UGA	Interblock Gap	UNC	Interblock Gap	UF	Interblock Gap	UCLA	Interblock Gap

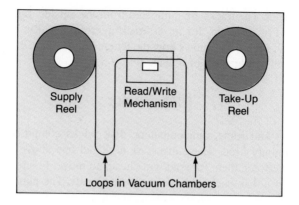

FIGURE 8-3
Reel-to-Reel Tape Drive

Supply Reel

Read/Write Mechanism

Take-Up Reel

Loops in Vacuum Chambers

Cartridge Tapes

Reel-to-reel tapes are currently being replaced by **cartridge tapes,** which can hold more data than reel-to-reel tapes can for less money and with faster transfer rates. The newest cartridge tapes are approximately 5 inches square and can store the equivalent of six reel tapes for a cost of only $5 each as compared to almost $20 for reel tapes. Cartridge tapes are $\frac{1}{4}$ inch wide, but they have more tracks than a reel tape has, and they have a transfer rate of 9 Mbytes per second. Cartridge tapes are also easier to use because you simply insert the cartridge as you would an audio tape. The use of cartridge tape systems will be discussed in more detail later in this chapter when backups for personal computers are covered.

MAGNETIC DISK

A **magnetic disk** is a metal or plastic disk coated with ferrous oxide. As with magnetic tape, a bit pattern may be magnetically coded onto the ferrous oxide. Because the disk spins like a record in the **disk drive,** the read/write head can reach any data on the disk directly rather than sequentially. For this reason, magnetic disks are direct-access storage devices.

The magnetic disk can be compared to a compact disk in that both are flat platters and both are used to transfer information. The read/write head on the magnetic disk drive is analogous to the laser light on the compact disk player in that both can be moved directly to the information that is being transferred. For the compact disk, the laser light is moved to the audio selection, whereas for the magnetic disk, the read/write head is moved to the file of interest. Similarly, both types of disks have concentric tracks on which information is stored. There are important differences, however, between a magnetic disk and a compact disk. First, information on the magnetic disk is stored in a magnetic form, whereas it is stored as pits in the surface of a compact disk. In addition, the laser light on a compact disk can only transfer information *from* the disk, but the read/write head on a disk drive can not only read information from the magnetic disk but also write the information onto the disk.

Bits are stored serially around each concentric track on a disk. The number of tracks depends on the size of the disk. For example, large metal disks used for mainframes may have 400 tracks and be 14 inches in diameter. A plastic disk for a personal computer may have as few as 40 tracks or be less than 4

IBM 3490 mainframe cartridge.

inches in diameter. The tracks are numbered from the outside to the inside starting with zero. For example, for an 80-track microfloppy disk, the tracks are numbered 0–79. Figure 8-4 shows how the letters "UGA" in EBCDIC form are stored on the outermost track of a disk.

Disk Packs

For mainframes and some minicomputers, **disk packs** composed of up to 11 disks are commonly used. These disks are arranged one above the other with enough space between them for read/write heads to move. Figure 8-5 shows the configuration of a disk pack with the read/write heads. The number of disks in a disk pack is related to the number of read/write heads in the disk drive. Information is written on both sides of each disk, with the exception of the top and bottom surfaces of the disk pack. A disk pack with 11 disks has 20 sides and 10 read/write heads, each of which can transfer information to the sides above and below. Only one read/write head is active at a time, but the transfer of information is so fast that all heads appear to work at once. A disk pack can be transported, but it must be protected by a special container that covers the entire pack. When it is used, the disk pack is placed in the disk drive and the container is removed.

The disks rotate at 3,600 revolutions per minute (140 miles per hour), and the read/write heads "float" (or "fly") above or below the disk on a cushion of air. The distance between the head and the disk is 35–100 micro-inches (0.0000035 to 0.0000100 inch). If the head encounters dust or smoke particles,

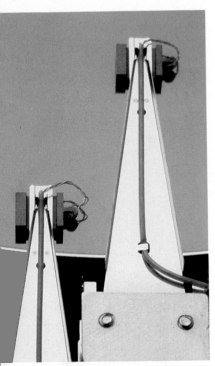

Read/write heads such as the ones shown here are used to transfer information to and from the high-speed disks.

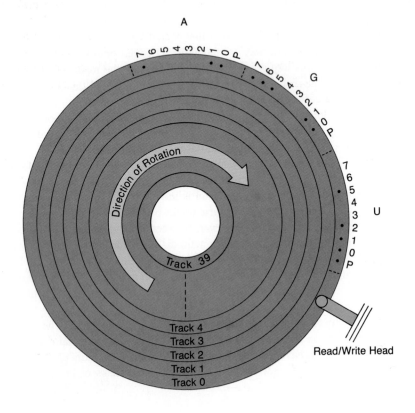

FIGURE 8-4
Disk Storage

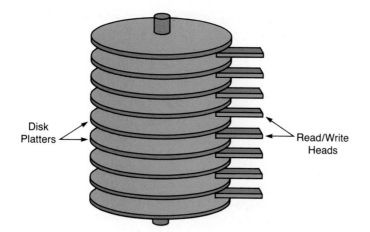

FIGURE 8-5
Configuration of a Disk Pack

Disk Platters

Read/Write Heads

a **head crash** may result. The cushion of air is interrupted and the read/write head makes contact with the disk, digging a furrow in the outer layer and destroying the data stored there. The relative size of dust and smoke particles compared with the space between the head and the disk is shown in Figure 8-6. Given the problems that dust and smoke particles can cause for a disk pack, the environment in a computer center is highly regulated, with constant air conditioning and rules prohibiting smoking around the disk drives.

In a disk pack, all tracks with the same track number on all sides of the disks are precisely aligned above one another. All tracks with the same track number make up a vertical **cylinder.** Information that requires more than one track (a common occurrence) is written on other tracks in the *same cylinder* rather than on the same disk. All read/write heads move together, and they are automatically on the same cylinder at any one time. After one head finishes transferring information to a track, another head simply transfers information to the same track on another disk, and the read/write heads do not need to move. When all tracks in a cylinder are full, the heads are moved to a new cylinder. The cylinder concept of disk storage is shown in Figure 8-7.

Transfer times to or from a disk are:

seek time, or the time to move the heads to the correct track;
rotational delay time, or the time to wait for the appropriate section of the disk to come under the head;
transmission time, or the actual time to transfer the data.

> **If you scale everything down at mass and velocity, that [read/write] head [of a hard disk] represents a 747 flying at Mach 4 an inch off the ground.**
>
> *Jim Mahon, engineering vice president, Seagate Technologies*
>
> Quoted in "The Amazing Winchester," *Popular Science,* October 1982, pp. 88–90.

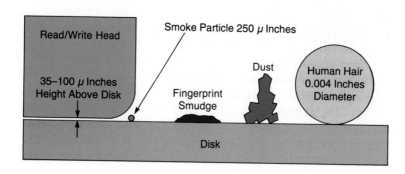

Read/Write Head

35–100 μ Inches Height Above Disk

Smoke Particle 250 μ Inches

Fingerprint Smudge

Dust

Human Hair 0.004 Inches Diameter

Disk

FIGURE 8-6
Separation of Disk and Read/Write Head

Source: Digital Equipment Corporation.

FIGURE 8-7
Cylinder Concept of Disk Storage

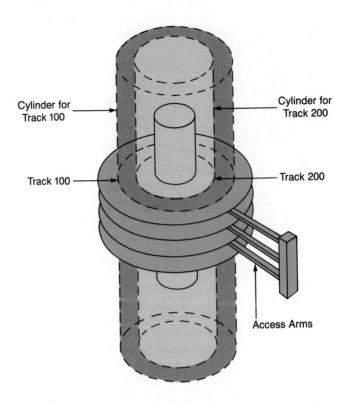

Because seek time is minimized if the heads are kept at the same position, the cylinder approach to storage is quite effective. Figure 8-8 shows the process of reading or writing information from or to a disk.

File Organization Methods

Three methods of physically organizing files on secondary storage devices are commonly used: sequential access, direct access, and indexed sequential access. All three methods can be used on magnetic disk storage, but only the sequential-access method can be used on magnetic tape. By its very nature, tape is a **sequential storage device,** and records must be processed in the same order that they are physically stored. On the other hand, magnetic disk is a **direct-access storage device (DASD),** and records can be processed in any order.

Sequential-access file organization is used whenever the records will be accessed in the same order in which they are physically stored. Many times, this order is in an ascending sequence that is based on the contents of some field. For example, payroll files may be stored in ascending order of employee number or last name. Sequential access is often used to produce reports for which every record must be processed or for processing activity files that store collected data.

In **direct-access file organization,** any record can be accessed *directly* as needed. However, to find a record, the computer must have the record's address on the disk. One method of finding a record's address is to first identify the primary key. The **primary key** is one field (or combination of fields) that uniquely distinguishes a record from all other records. In a payroll file, the employee number may be used as the primary key since it is unique to each employee. For a student grade file, the Social Security number is often used for

FIGURE 8-8
Read/Write Process for a Disk

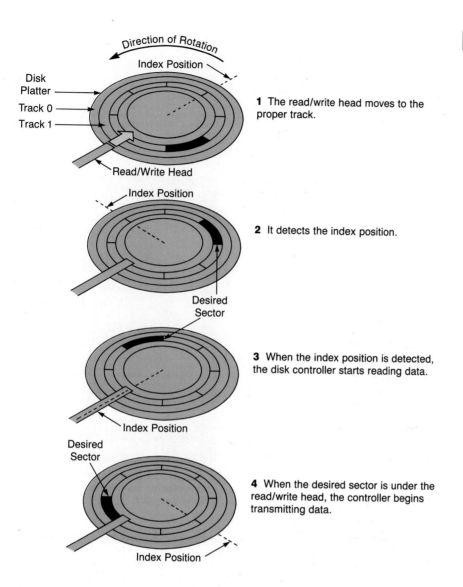

Direction of Rotation

Index Position

Disk Platter

Track 0

Track 1

Read/Write Head

1 The read/write head moves to the proper track.

Index Position

2 It detects the index position.

Desired Sector

3 When the index position is detected, the disk controller starts reading data.

Index Position

Desired Sector

4 When the desired sector is under the read/write head, the controller begins transmitting data.

Index Position

the same reason. Nonunique fields, however, can be used as **secondary keys.** For example, an employee's department number can be used as a secondary key if a listing of all employees by department is desired.

Once a primary key is identified, the next step is to find the corresponding record's location, or **address,** on the disk. There are two types of addresses: absolute and relative. A record's **relative address** gives its position relative to all other records. The computer's operating system converts this relative address to an **absolute address,** which is used to find the record on the disk. The difference between the relative address and the absolute address is similar to the difference between a description of where someone lives and his or her street address. A description of "the fourth house on the right from the end of the street" is a relative address, and 130 Pinehill Road is an absolute address.

In computer terms, a relative address is expressed in terms of the position of the record from the beginning of the group of records being processed. This position is also known as its **record number.** On the other hand, an absolute

SMALL DISKS TO THE RESCUE AT ARKWRIGHT

Arkwright Mutual Insurance in Waltham, Massachusetts, insures high-risk industries. With several thousand large companies as clients, the disk storage equipment required to make millions of records available to Arkwright workers was becoming unmanageable.

The traditional 14-inch disk drives, each the size of a refrigerator, were jamming the 2,300-square-foot computer room. There was no more space in the computer room, but the need for additional storage was growing yearly. To solve this problem, the company adopted an innovative new approach to disk secondary storage—it installed **redundant arrays of inexpensive disks (RAID).** This technology replaces the larger disk packs with a "gang" of $5\frac{1}{4}$-inch disk drives similar to the ones used in personal computers.

Arkwright's system currently includes one 4-gigabyte (Gbyte) system and one 24-Gbyte system and is supplied by EMC Corporation. Each system is composed of multiple disk drives, each of which can store 1 Gbyte of data. This system takes up one-third the floor space of the larger disk packs and costs one-third as much. The new system has enabled Arkwright to remove seven disk pack systems and has resulted in a 40 percent decrease in online processing time. It has also resulted in the elimination of a weekend shift of operators who carry out backup and other follow-up processing operations.

A recent update of the system now allows any one of the multiple disk drives to be taken offline for maintenance without taking the entire array of disks offline. Officials at Arkwright are very happy with the new system.

Source: Interview with Brian Johnson of Arkwright Mutual Insurance Company; and Gary McWilliams, "Small Disks Can Save a Lot More than Data," *Business Week,* December 24, 1990, pp. 43–44.

Arkwright Mutual Insurance's RAID system takes up one-third the space of the old storage system.

---

address is expressed as the cylinder and track (which specifies the surface) on which the record is located. It is also necessary for addressing purposes to subdivide the tracks into **blocks,** which are the smallest addressable units on the disk. For example, a record's absolute address might be expressed as

Cylinder 10
Track 5
Block 2

Most software uses the relative address of the record, and the operating system finds the record via its absolute address. To find a record's relative address on disk, hashing is often used. In **hashing,** the primary key is converted by a formula to a relative address for the record. A popular hashing scheme for a numeric primary key is the **division/remainder procedure.** In this procedure, the primary key number is divided by the prime number closest to but less than the number of storage positions on the disk, and the remainder is used as the relative address. For example, if we assume that there are 1,000 storage locations on a disk that will be used to store a file, then we would divide the primary key by the appropriate prime number—997—and use the remainder as the relative address. If the record has a primary key of 3,275, then this value is divided by 997, and we obtain a remainder of 284. This indicates that the record is stored in relative address position number 284.

When two records end up with the same relative address, the second record is placed in the storage location immediately next to that of the first. Then, when the primary key is hashed but the desired record is not found in that location, it can be found in the next relative location. Because of the possibility of such *collisions,* a hashed data file can only be 70 to 80 percent full. Other hashing schemes handle key fields made up of letters and symbols.

Indexed sequential access methods (ISAM) for organizing files on magnetic disk combine direct and sequential access methods by using indices that point to the location of sections of records. The records in each section are in sequential order. This storage organization is analogous to the method used in telephone books for storing names, addresses, and phone numbers. In a telephone book, a primary key may be the full name plus the address, because this information is usually unique. Showing the names of the first and last persons on each page at the top of the page allows a user to go directly to the page that contains the desired name and then begin a sequential search. The same procedure is used with the indexed sequential access methods on a computer disk, except that the primary key field is used to locate the area on the disk where the sequential search begins. Using this method is faster than the simple direct-access file organization method of processing numerous records, but it is more flexible than sequential-access methods.

SECONDARY STORAGE FOR PCs

For personal computers, secondary storage comes in three forms: floppy disk, hard disk, and cartridge tape. We will discuss the first two of these in this section. Cartridge tape will be discussed in the section on backups, because backup is its primary purpose for personal computers.

Floppy Disks

For personal computers, the floppy disk is the most common form of secondary storage. **Floppy disks,** also called **diskettes,** come in sizes of $5\frac{1}{4}$ inches and $3\frac{1}{2}$ inches (8-inch diskettes were, at one time, used for minicomputers and dedicated word processing computers, but their use has been almost discontinued). The smaller, $3\frac{1}{2}$-inch floppy disk is commonly referred to as a **microfloppy disk.** Both sizes are made of plastic, but while the larger size is flexible neither size is really "floppy." In fact, the microfloppy is encased in a rigid cover that protects the entire disk from dust and other contaminants. Figure 8-9 shows the makeup of both sizes of floppy disks, with the various parts pointed out.

Both sizes of diskette have a **head window,** which is the area of the diskette that is in contact with the read/write head of the disk drive. Over the head window, the microfloppy has a spring-loaded metal shutter that is pushed back when the diskette is inserted in the disk drive. The head window on the $5\frac{1}{4}$-inch floppy is uncovered, and users must be careful not to get oil from their fingers or other contaminants on the diskette. In both cases, the disk drive's read/write

Floppies were the first low-cost breakthrough satisfying users' needs for on-line memory.

James Adkisson, president, Insite Peripherals

Quoted in "View from the Top," *Personal Computing,* October 1989, p. 260.

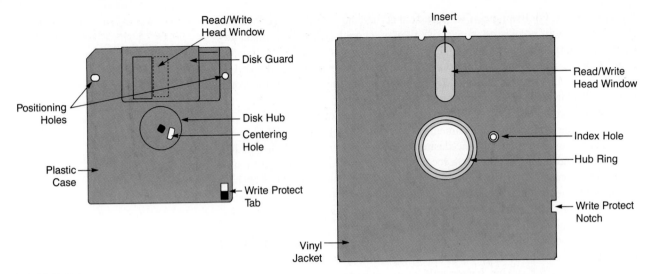

FIGURE 8-9
Floppy Disks

head actually rubs against the floppy disk rather than flying above it, so the rotation speed of 300 rpm is less than a tenth that of a disk pack.

For the 5¼-inch floppy, the **hub ring** is where the disk drive clamps onto the diskette and rotates the disk. This occurs automatically when the diskette is inserted in the disk drive on the personal computer and the drive door is closed. The hole in the vinyl cover of the diskette is the **index hole;** it is used to indicate to the computer where the disk is in its rotation. There is another hole in the plastic disk itself so that, when the inner and outer holes match up, a light can shine through the combined hole and activate a photoelectric cell underneath the diskette. This signals the computer that the index hole has passed, and the position of the desired information can then be determined from this information. There is also a **write-protect notch,** which, when covered by a piece of opaque tape, will not allow information to be written onto the disk. This is a security device that keeps data on the disk from being destroyed by new information being written over it.

For the microfloppy, different mechanisms replace the hub ring, index hole, and write-protect notch used on the 5¼-inch floppy. Instead of a hub ring and an index hole, the microfloppy has a metal hub with a hole in it that is engaged by the disk drive. The position of this engagement of the disk drive with the hub determines the position of the disk in its rotation. Instead of a write-protect notch, the microfloppy uses a sliding tab that can be opened to write-protect the disk. When the tab is moved to uncover the hole, no information can be written onto the diskette.

Since personal computers use only one floppy disk at a time, rather than a group of platters as in a disk pack, the cylinder storage system discussed earlier is not appropriate here. Instead of the cylinder system, a sectoring system is used. The tracks on the disk are divided into **sectors,** and the number of sectors on the diskette depends on the type of diskette and the operating system. A typical sectoring of a diskette is shown in Figure 8-10.

The sectoring plan shown in Figure 8-10 is called **soft sectoring** since it is dependent on the machine being used and the software system that manages the disk, called the **disk operating system (DOS)** (to be discussed in more detail in Chapter 9). Soft sectoring is currently used on all personal computers.

Often, both 3½-inch and 5¼-inch floppy disk drives are used on the same computer.

(Bottom left) The original IBM XT and compatible computers use a 360K, 5¼-inch floppy disk. (Right) The IBM AT and compatible computers use a 1.2M, 5¼-inch floppy disk.

FIGURE 8-10
Diskette Sectoring

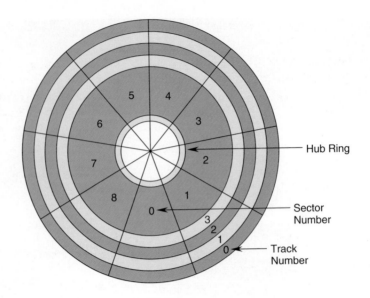

The process by which the disk operating system soft-sectors the disk and records codes on the diskette to identify each track and sector is called **formatting.** The disk must be formatted before it can be used. For example, the $3\frac{1}{2}$-inch microfloppy disk used on many IBM compatible PCs has 80 tracks and 18 sectors. Each track-sector has 512 bytes, so the total storage capacity of the diskette on one side is $18 \times 80 \times 512$ bytes = 720 Kbytes. Since this is a double-sided diskette, it can hold a total of 1.44 Mbytes.

In the process of formatting, a list of the diskette's contents called the **file allocation table (FAT)** is recorded on a specific sector and track. The disk controller (part of the personal computer's hardware) and the DOS use the FAT to locate the programs and files so that the read/write head can move to the proper position on the disk.

Laptop computers such as this one often use a 720K, $3\frac{1}{2}$-inch microfloppy disk for secondary storage.

Storage Capacities

As we said earlier, floppy disks primarily are made in two sizes: $3\frac{1}{2}$ inches in diameter—the microfloppy—and $5\frac{1}{4}$ inches in diameter. In both cases, data are stored on both sides of the diskette. Within these two sizes, there are different storage capacities, depending on the density used to store data on the disk. The density of the diskette is determined by the disk's number of bits per square inch. Currently, there are two categories of density: double and high. High-density diskettes store more data than do double density. Diskettes are commonly described by density abbreviations, with "DD" or "2D" indicating double density and "HD" indicating high density.

The storage capacities of the two sizes and two densities of diskettes used on IBM compatible computers are shown in Table 8-1 along with an example of the machine on which such diskettes are commonly used.

In each case in Table 8-1, the storage capacity is for a formatted disk; that is, the amount of storage available after the required formatting process, which uses some of the disk storage for the directory information. The same diskette can be formatted to have more or less storage space depending on the computer and the disk operating system. This is why a Macintosh can format a double-density microfloppy to have 800 Kbytes of information instead of the 720 Kbytes on the IBM PS/2.

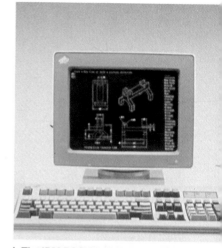

The IBM PS/2 Model 80 is one of many personal computers that use the 1.44M, $3\frac{1}{2}$-inch microfloppy disk.

TLC FOR FLOPPIES

Even though floppy disks are pretty tough storage devices that do not require a great deal of special care, they still must be protected from some environmental hazards. While many of these cautions pertain only to older, $5\frac{1}{4}$-inch floppies, care must also be taken in working with the microfloppies. Remember that the diskettes are made of plastic and use a magnetic field to store data. Here are a few rules for using diskettes:

- Don't bend or try to fold the diskette.
- Don't store the diskette in extremely high temperatures or let it be exposed to direct sunlight.
- Store the diskettes in a vertical position.
- Don't lay the diskette on the television or other appliances that create a magnetic field, as this will destroy the data.
- Don't use magnets to secure diskettes to a bulletin board. (Don't laugh—this has been done with disastrous consequences.)
- Avoid touching the disk surface with your fingers and keep other contaminants (such as pizza sauce) off the surface.
- Do not attempt to clean the surface of the diskette with any type of cleaning fluid. This can prevent the disk drive from properly reading information stored on the disk.
- Don't expose the disk to static electricity—such as that caused by a combination of dry air and carpeting—as this can destroy the data on the disk.

TABLE 8-1
Floppy Disk Storage Capacity

Density	Size	Storage Capacity	Typical Machine
Double	$5\frac{1}{4}''$	360 Kbytes	IBM PC XT
High	$5\frac{1}{4}''$	1.2 Mbytes	IBM PC AT
Double	$3\frac{1}{2}''$	720 Kbytes	Toshiba Laptop PC
High	$3\frac{1}{2}''$	1.44 Mbytes	IBM PS/2 Model 80

> **One impact of high-capacity floppies will be the low-cost distribution of software and data.**
>
> *James Adkisson, president, Insite Peripherals*
>
> Quoted in "View from the Top," *Personal Computing*, October 1989, p. 260.

It appears that the current trend is toward increased use of microfloppies relative to the older $5\frac{1}{4}$-inch floppies. All laptop computers now use this size of disk, and the trend toward it was undoubtedly accelerated by IBM's decision to use this size of disk on its PS/2 series. The convenience and security of the microfloppy has also made it the first choice of many users of other types of machines. Being able to stick the microfloppy in your shirt, blouse, or jeans pocket or in your purse without fear of damage gives it clear advantages over the larger floppy disk.

Another desirable feature of the microfloppy is its increased storage capacity. Special preformatted microfloppies with storage capacities of 20 Mbytes—comparable to a hard disk of only a few years ago—are now available. These microfloppies require their own drive system, which works only with them. These super-high-density microfloppies may soon become very important for transporting large amounts of data and software.

Hard Disks

"There is never enough storage." Personal computer users have been saying that for at least ten years! Certainly that statement is true for someone who tries to use a floppy disk for a large-scale business application. Current state-of-the-art spreadsheets, data base management systems, and integrated systems have pushed floppies beyond their limits. The increasing complexity of the software requires additional storage space, and larger problems are solved every day with these packages. In many instances, problems that at one time could be solved only on mainframes are now solved on personal computers, but multiple floppies must be used to handle the storage requirements of these sophisticated problems. The user must switch floppies in and out as needed by the package. Obviously, growing storage requirements are a real problem.

To meet this increased need for secondary storage, the hard disk has been developed. The **hard disk**—or "Winchester," as it is also called—is similar to the disk packs used by mainframes. It is metallic rather than plastic and can rotate at the high speeds associated with disk packs.

The differences between a hard disk for a personal computer and a disk pack for a mainframe are size, number of platters, and the manner in which each is enclosed. A hard disk is usually $5\frac{1}{4}$ or $3\frac{1}{2}$ inches in diameter versus 14 inches for a disk pack, and it has only one or two platters compared with eleven for a disk pack. The hard disk and its drive are usually built into the personal computer with an air filtration and movement system, whereas a disk pack depends on a special drive and a special environment. Because the hard disk and drive are enclosed, they can be used in nonair-conditioned environments that would

| The Apple Macintosh uses an 800M, $3\frac{1}{2}$-inch microfloppy.

cause a disk pack to crash. Compared with floppy disks, the data or software on hard disks can be accessed many times faster, and the storage increases from a maximum of 1.44 Mbytes to over 100 Mbytes.

To rotate at 3,600 rpm, a hard disk must use a flying head and be sealed in a protected environment to keep dust, smoke, and hair out of the drive. For this reason, most hard-disk systems cannot be removed from their drives. Removable hard-disk cartridges are currently available on the market, but their percentage of the market is less than 10 percent of total sales of storage equipment.

A recent innovation in the use of hard disks is the hard-disk card. A **hard-disk card** is a combination of a hard disk that stores at least 20 Mbytes and the controller card that is needed to control the transfer of information to and from a hard disk. A hard disk is normally inserted in one of the disk drive locations and the disk controller card is inserted in one of the slots on the primary computer circuit board. The hard-disk card combines these two operations, providing the needed secondary storage with a minimum of effort on the part of the user.

"WINCHESTER"

The 30–30 Hard Disk

Many theories try to explain why a hard disk is referred to as a "Winchester" hard disk. The most likely reason is in the design of the first

IBM hard disk in 1973. The first hard disk had two platters, or disks, each of which held 30 Mbytes. Hence, it was a 30 + 30 Mbyte drive. This storage capacity led designers to refer to the hard disk as a "30–30," which in turn reminded someone of the famous Winchester 30.30 rifle. Eventually, the Winchester nickname was applied to the first hard disk. The name has since been applied to any brand of hard disk.

Flash memory is another new development in secondary storage for PCs. Flash memory technology arranges nonvolatile memory chips, which act as another disk drive, onto a credit-card-size circuit board. Flash memory provides much faster access time than a disk drive does, but it is more expensive. Experts predict, however, that use of flash memory will increase in the future.

Figure 8-11 shows the relationship between the amounts of storage on various types of secondary storage for personal computers in terms of the number of pages of text that can be stored on each storage device.

BACKUPS

In the use of secondary storage, the concept of backup is extremely important. Whether magnetic tape or disk is used, some alternate form of storage should be available with a current copy of the material in secondary storage in case of loss of the primary storage device. In a mainframe environment, a tape backup is often made daily of the disk packs that contain user secondary storage. If a tape drive is not available, then a second disk pack may be used. If a backup does not exist and the system disk pack crashes, the data on the disk pack are probably not recoverable.

Backups of magnetic tape are commonly made and then stored in a building apart from the primary tape library. Although a tape does not "crash," it can eventually become unreadable due to everyday wear and tear. A backup can help a user avoid the pain and suffering of reading individual files from a worn-out tape.

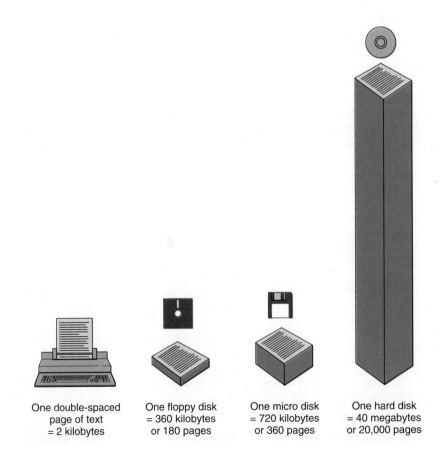

One double-spaced page of text = 2 kilobytes

One floppy disk = 360 kilobytes or 180 pages

One micro disk = 720 kilobytes or 360 pages

One hard disk = 40 megabytes or 20,000 pages

FIGURE 8-11
Secondary Storage Capacities

Backup for Personal Computers

Backup for a personal computer is just as important as backup for a mainframe. The difference is that a computer center does not perform the daily backup procedures. Consequently, the user must make periodic backups for programs. Failure to back up information on a personal computer has the same effect, but on a smaller scale, as failure to back up a disk or tape on a mainframe. In this section, we discuss backup procedures for personal computers.

For backup using disk secondary storage, most personal computer systems have a procedure for copying the contents of an entire disk to a backup disk. In this approach, the simplest backup system consists of a working copy of a disk and a backup copy. However, a second backup copy should also be made, because a power surge or blackout could catch both the working copy and the backup copy in the machine at the same time. If a second backup does not exist, the data on both the working copy and the only backup copy could be lost.

In a business setting, a definite policy on backups is needed, including a **backup hierarchy,** in which three or four disks are rotated and the oldest disk becomes the new master disk after each backup. This policy is similar to the use of a second backup, except that the third and fourth backups do not always contain the most recent copy of the material. However, they do provide a margin of safety if both the working copy and the backup copy are lost. A hard (printed) copy of the latest version of the data or program should always be kept in case *all* the disks are lost at the same time. In this case, the information could still be keyed in from the keyboard.

Backing up a hard disk is made somewhat more complicated by the fact that most hard disks in use today cannot be removed from the computer. Recall that they are sealed inside their drives to keep dust and smoke away from the read/write head. To back up a hard disk, a separate recording device is needed. The least expensive method of backing up a hard disk is to use the floppy disk drive that accompanies most hard disk drives on personal computers. This approach works well if only a few files or documents must be copied at each session. However, to back up even a small hard disk, say, 40 Mbytes, would require over 55 microfloppy disks of 720 Kbytes each. While floppy disks are

> ## If the backup does a restore only once in the life of a [network hard disk], you've gotten your money's worth.
>
> *James Jones, local area network administrator for Amoco Research*
>
> Quoted in "Backup Software Saves the Day (and Money) for Amoco," *PC Week,* March 23, 1992, p. 101.

Reel-to-reel tapes are very important for backup of mainframe secondary storage.

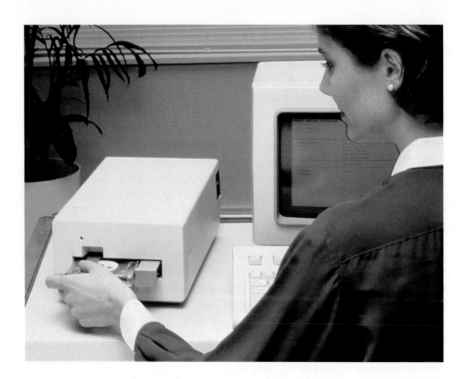

fairly inexpensive, actually performing this backup would be a very tedious task. Fortunately, there currently are numerous floppy disk backup systems on the market that can be used to back up only the most recently changed files rather than the entire hard disk.

Another popular backup method is a tape backup device called streaming tape. **Streaming tape** uses a tape cartridge such as those discussed earlier and a tape drive that "streams" the tape by the tape head at a high rate of speed as all information on the disk is output in a continuous flow. As one cartridge is filled up, additional cartridges can be swapped into the tape drive. With streaming tape, it is possible to copy the contents of a 40-Mbyte hard disk in a short period of time. Backup is extremely important for local area network (LAN) file server hard disks that store more than 600 Mbytes of data and information.

Other methods of backing up a hard disk include using a Bernoulli drive (a proprietary form of large floppy disk), a removable Winchester hard disk cartridge, or high-capacity microfloppies, as they become more available.

OPTICAL DISK STORAGE

One of the most exciting possibilities for secondary storage is the use of optical storage media. With **optical storage media,** a laser light beam burns pits of information into the surface of a shiny disk. Then another laser, in an optical disk drive, reads the information from the disk. Currently, there are four types of optical storage media: optical (laser) disks; compact disk read-only memory; write-once, read mostly disks; and erasable optical disks.

Laser Disks

Laser disks have been in use for several years for storing text, audio, and video information. One side of a typical record-album–size laser disk can show 30 minutes of motion video or 54,000 individual video scenes with a much higher quality than a videocassette recorder. These scenes can be pages of a telephone directory, pages from a retail catalog, pictures meant to amuse and inform— such as at Walt Disney's EPCOT Center—or training devices for soldiers or technicians to learn the operation of a sophisticated weapon or machine. When used with a computer, laser disks can provide tremendous amounts of storage of video, text, and digital information. If information is stored in a digital form, a laser disk has storage capacity in excess of 1 Gbyte (1 billion bytes), which is roughly equivalent to 500,000 pages of text. However, all forms of optical disks suffer from the same problem—slow access times compared to currently available magnetic disks.

CD-ROM

The storage equivalent of the popular CD audio medium is **compact disk read-only memory (CD-ROM),** which is 4.72 inches (120 mm) in diameter. CD-ROM can store up to 650 Mbytes of information—the equivalent of 900 microfloppy disks at 720 Kbytes each. This means that the entire text of the *Encyclopædia Britannica* can be stored on a single disk! CD-ROM is prerecorded and designed for easy replication and economical distribution of software programs and data bases. It is forecast that, in addition to being used for the mass distribution of data bases, CD-ROM will eventually dominate the computer

> I bought CD-ROM and I'm sold on it. I don't advocate that CD-ROM totally replace the hard-copy document. But, maybe we can print 5,000 instead of 20,000, and we'll have less to ship and store.
>
> *Ron Kercheval, Army Corps of Engineers' Printing and Publications Management Office*
>
> Quoted in "Knowledge in Hand," *PC/ Computing,* February 1990, p. 68.

The transfer of paper documents to optical disk is reducing the staggering amount of paper and improving processing efficiency and productivity in today's offices.

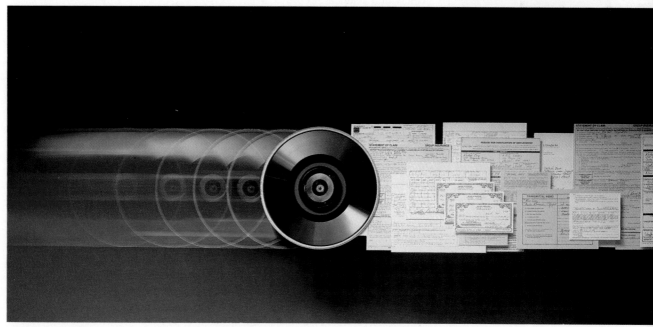

Optical disks and CD-ROM are important forms of read-only secondary storage.

markets for mass distribution of such information as encyclopedias, medical data, and statistical data. Examples of such information that is already available on CD-ROM include summaries of the literature on biomedicine; data on social science, law, and economics; and a data base of articles on psychology and behavioral sciences.

Write-Once, Read Mostly Disks

Write-once, read mostly (WORM) disks are meant to be written once, usually by the user, and then only read from. One use of a WORM disk would be to store historical papers on a disk, thereby speeding up the retrieval of older information while at the same time reducing the paper clutter. For example, a library might wish to do away with its microfilm storage of newspapers. The pages of the newspapers could be scanned with a page scanner and converted to a digital form on the WORM disk. This information would never be changed, but could be read as many times as needed.

Erasable Optical Disks

The primary shortcoming of the forms of video disk discussed previously is that they primarily "read only." Once the information has been burned into a video disk, it cannot be erased, because the pits in the surface of the disk cannot be changed. However, the technology of **erasable optical disks** has been developed to the point where the NeXT workstation computer developed by Steve Jobs comes standard with a 256-Mbyte erasable optical disk drive. In addition to the

Among the many technical innovations on the NeXT computer is its erasable optical disk drive.

tremendous storage capacity on a single disk—equivalent to 328 Macintosh 800-Kbyte microdisks—the erasable optical disks are removable, meaning that for $50 a disk, users can have as much storage as they need.

Erasable optical storage uses a combination of magnetism and optical principles known as **magneto-optical technology** to write, read, and erase the disks.

SAVING BETS ON A WORM

In most of the United States, the practice of bookmaking—that is, private individuals taking bets on sporting and horse racing events—is illegal. However, in Nevada it is a perfectly legitimate profession and is regulated by the Nevada Gambling Commission. Traditionally, bookmakers (also known as *bookies*) in Nevada used the "pen-based" system to take bets; gamblers wrote their bets

on slips of paper and passed them to the bookie. This process had few controls since numbers could be altered or deleted, and bets could be written after a game had started.

When the commission decided that all race and sports betting had to be computerized, many bookies had to decide how to meet this requirement. One bookie, Vic Salerno of Leroy's Horse and Sport Palace, decided to create a computer system that would meet his and other bookies' needs. Salerno wanted a system that would not look like a computer and would prevent the possibilities of gamblers changing their bets. The resulting system uses WORM (write-once, read mostly) optical storage combined with a personal computer and appropriate

software. Bettors hand their numbers to clerks who give them computer-generated slips. Gamblers can also place their bets themselves using an optical character reader.

This WORM-based system allows each race and sports bet to be entered into the system. This, in turn, allows the manager to use a PC to see instantly every payout entered by a cashier and how his or her bets compare to those of other cashiers. It is also possible to access information about any bets placed in the previous eight months.

This system has been so successful that at least 65 of the 72 legal bookmaking operations in Nevada have installed the same type of system.

Source: James Daly, "WORM Big Winner for Bookies," *Computerworld,* July 15, 1991, p. 40.

BITS OF HISTORY

The Magnetic Drum

The predecessor of the disk for secondary storage was the magnetic drum, a cylinder whose surface—like that of magnetic tapes or disks—is covered with ferrous oxide. The surface of the drum is divided into tracks, each of which has four channels on which spots can be magnetized to represent one bit. In this way a half-byte, also called a "nybble" (really!), can be coded across each track in a manner similar to that for magnetic tape. In fact, we can think of a magnetic drum as having strips of four-track magnetic tape wound around it, with each strip representing a track on the drum. The magnetic drum has a stationary read/write head for each track on the drum. As the drum spins, the read/write heads transfer data to and from the surface of the drum. The address of information is determined by the track on which it is coded and its position on the track. Because the read/write heads are always in place over each track, a drum has no seek time, but it still has rotational delay time while the head waits for the proper part of the drum to arrive. A schematic diagram of a magnetic drum secondary storage device appears here. Magnetic drums have been replaced completely by magnetic disks because of the disk's greater storage capacity and reduced time to find and transfer information.

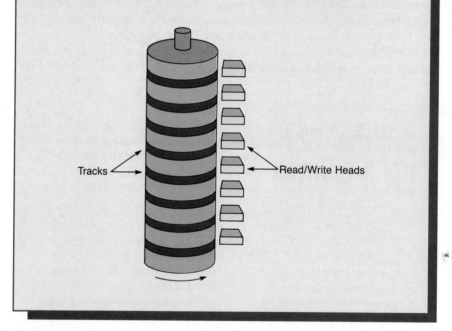

Tracks   Read/Write Heads

As mentioned earlier, this approach is somewhat slower than the current high-speed Winchester disks. For example, the seek time on the erasable optical disk used in the NeXT machine is 92 milliseconds (thousandths of a second) as compared with less than 20 milliseconds on the fastest magnetic hard disks. However, once the information is found on the disk, the time needed to transfer information from the disk to internal memory is about the same as with a hard disk.

1. Secondary storage is necessary because internal memory is both volatile and limited in size. The two most important forms of secondary storage are magnetic tape and magnetic disk.

2. Magnetic tape is a sequential-access device (SAD), whereas magnetic disk is a direct-access storage device (DASD).

3. Magnetic tape comes in two forms: reel-to-reel and cartridge tape. Reel-to-reel tape is currently the most widely used, but cartridge tape is becoming more widely used.

4. Both reel-to-reel and cartridge tape use a binary format for storing information on tape. Both types are very important for backing up computer disk storage and for archival purposes.

5. Magnetic disks for mainframe computers come as disk packs that use multiple disks for storing information from mainframes and are organized into cylinders of information.

6. File storage on disk secondary storage can be organized one of three ways: sequentially, directly, or indexed sequentially. Files that are organized sequentially can be processed one at a time. Files on magnetic tape must be organized sequentially.

7. In direct-access storage, every record has an address. A common approach to finding this address is to use hashing on the primary key to determine the relative address from which the operating system determines the absolute address. The division/remainder hashing method is often used on a numeric primary key.

8. The indexed sequential access methods (ISAM) combine direct-access and sequential storage principles using disk storage.

9. Personal computer storage comes in the form of floppy disks, hard disks, and cartridge tape. Floppy disks come in two sizes, $5\frac{1}{4}$ inches and $3\frac{1}{2}$ inches, with the latter being referred to as a micro-floppy. Storage is organized into sectors of information, and amounts vary depending on the density.

10. Hard disks that store over 80 Mbytes of information are commonly used in personal computers today.

11. Whether working on a mainframe, minicomputer, or personal computer with either tape or disk, backing up secondary storage (making an extra copy) is always very important. Cartridge tapes are often used for personal computer backup.

12. Optical disks can store large amounts of data. A laser disk can store up to 1 Gbyte of information, whereas CD-ROM can hold up to 600 Mbytes. Write-once, read mostly disks allow the user to store information on a disk to be read many times. True erasable optical disks using magneto-optical technology offer computer users a high-volume, portable storage medium.

absolute address
address
archival storage

ASCII files
backup
backup hierarchy

backup tape
binary files
block
blocked record
bytes per inch (bpi)
cartridge tape
compact disk read-only memory
    (CD-ROM)
cylinder
data file
density
direct-access file organization
direct-access storage device (DASD)
diskette
disk operating system (DOS)
disk pack
division/remainder procedure
field
file
file allocation table (FAT)
flash memory
floppy disk
formatting
hard disk
hard-disk card
hashing
head crash
head window
hub ring
indexed sequential access method
    (ISAM)
index hole
interblock gap (IBG)
laser disk

magnetic disk
magnetic (mag) tape
magneto-optical technology
microfloppy disk
parallel storage device
parity bit
physical record
primary key
program file
read/write head
record
record number
redundant arrays of inexpensive
    disks (RAID)
reel-to-reel tape
relative address
rotational delay time
secondary key
sector
seek time
sequential-access file organization
sequential storage device
soft sectoring
streaming tape
tape drive
text files
track
transaction log tape
transmission time
unblocked record
write-once, read mostly (WORM)
    disk
write-protect notch

REVIEW QUESTIONS

1. List the two reasons secondary storage is necessary for either a mainframe or a personal computer.

2. Explain the use of records on files to store information. Classify files by the type of material and the form of the material stored on secondary storage.

3. Why is magnetic tape still an important form of secondary storage? What type of access is possible with magnetic tape? Why?

4. What is the difference between blocked records and unblocked records? How do they relate to physical records and logical records?

5. What is the difference between reel-to-reel tape and cartridge tape for mainframe computers?

6. If there are 200 tracks on each disk of a disk pack, how many cylinders are there on the disk pack?

7. Describe the difference between sequentially and directly orga-

nized files on magnetic disk. How do indexed sequentially organized files work?

8. Explain the difference between the cylinder and sector methods of storage for disks.

9. How can the same disk have differing amounts of storage on two different computers?

11. Why is the microfloppy becoming a more important form of secondary storage?

12. Why is backup an important procedure for users of personal computers? What type of device is often used to back up a hard disk?

13. What is a hard card? Why is it used instead of a hard disk system?

14. List the four types of optical disks being used today. Which is the oldest?

15. What is CD-ROM? How does it differ from a WORM disk?

In Chapter 3, you were introduced to the different types of software—systems software, utility software, and applications software. We begin this block by covering the most important element of systems software—operating systems—in more detail. We will then expand upon the preliminary discussion of the six important types of applications software packages for personal computers given in Chapter 3.

Chapter 9 will cover both mainframe and personal computer operating systems in more detail. Chapters 10–13 will cover packages for word processing, graphics, financial analysis (spreadsheets), accounting (both business and personal), data base management, and telecommunications and networks. Tutorials on MS-DOS are presented in Appendix A. Separate lab manuals contain tutorials on both the educational and full-scale versions of popular commercial software packages.

An Overview of Operating Systems

As we discussed in Chapter 3 on software, it is impossible to run applications software without an operating system. For this reason, it is useful to understand how operating systems work before we go into the various types of applications software. Operating systems for mainframes will be discussed first, followed by a section on MS-DOS, OS/2, and UNIX—the most commonly used personal computer operating systems that will work for different types of computers. Each system will be discussed in some detail, with attention given to the hardware that is compatible with that operating system. We will also cover the concept of operating systems that run on only one type of computer as well as RAM-resident software and operating environments such as Windows 3. A tutorial on using MS-DOS for IBM compatible personal computers is given in Appendix A.

STUDY OBJECTIVES

After reading this chapter, you should be able to

- understand the functions of operating systems on all sizes of computers;
- discuss the terminology of mainframe operating systems;
- explain how a mainframe operating system handles multiple users and multiple tasks;
- describe the purpose of channels, buffers, and preprocessors on a mainframe computer;
- recognize differences in mainframe and personal computer operating systems;
- list the functions of a personal computer operating system;
- discuss the terminology of personal computer operating systems;
- name the three most common operating systems for personal computers and explain the differences between them;
- discuss the most popular proprietary operating systems for PCs;
- explain the use of operating environments and RAM-resident programs.

MAKING THE DESERT BLOOM WITH OS/2

OS/2 was the best choice for this system because of its graphical user interface that fully integrates point-and-click technology, dialogue boxes, and robust graphics capability.

Dennis Runo, Customer Automation, Inc.

Quoted in "OS/2 Makes the Water Flow, Changing Desert to Farmland."

Controlling the flow of water diverted from the Colorado River is crucial for the Palo Verde Irrigation District of southeastern California and western Arizona. With too much water, fields can become flooded; with too little water, crops wither and die. Until 1990, the system of ditches, gates, and pumps created in the 1970s was controlled by a teletype-like system that required an operator to enter cryptic commands that sent radio signals to a network of remote control units. Each remote control unit, in turn, controlled three or four separate gates or pumps. The remote control units also collected data on water level, gate position, and pump status. Based on the information gathered by the remote units, water was distributed to farmers who pay a water toll, which is based on the number of acres that are irrigated.

Beginning in 1988, a new system was developed to control the flow of water. It uses an IBM PS/2 Model 80

personal computer and the OS/2 operating system. This operating system was chosen by the software developer because of its graphical user interface, which is called the Presentation Manager, and its capability to run multiple tasks concurrently. Operators now use a mouse to initiate all configurations and controls. They also view the system status via color-coded graphics. For example, if there is a ditch failure, the screen flashes red to alert the operator to close a gate to avoid loss of water. Because the OS/2 system has been so effective, the water district is now planning to automate the system of gates and pumps, which would allow the PC to automatically, without operator intervention, take whatever action is required to prevent water loss.

Source: Jennifer Curry, "OS/2 Makes the Water Flow, Changing Desert to Farmland," *PC Week*, April 16, 1990, pp. 69, 80; and interview with Dennis Runo of Customer Automation, Inc., Phoenix, Arizona, December 6, 1991.

The OS/2 system controlling the Palo Verde Irrigation Districts water flow has an easy-to-use, graphical-user interface.
Source: *PC Week*, April 16, 1990, pp. 69, 80.

It has been called the computer's "traffic cop," "office manager," "nervous system," and "chauffeur." *It* is the computer's operating system. In the boxed insert, the OS/2 operating system for IBM compatible personal computers is discussed. This operating system allowed the software developer to write software with a graphical user interface that made the operation of the irrigation system easier and more efficient. For any computer, the **operating system** is a collection of software programs that manages the tasks that are performed concurrently in the computer, regardless of whether the computer is a mainframe, minicomputer, or personal computer. For example, the operating system must monitor the keyboard to determine when a key has been pressed to provide input to the computer. It must also manage the video screen and printer to provide output from the computer. The operating system controls the operation of secondary storage to transfer data back and forth between secondary storage and main memory. On mainframes and minicomputers, the operating system is responsible for additional tasks that cannot be performed on a personal computer. A mainframe or minicomputer operating system manages many different hardware sites and terminals and ensures that users have the proper user identification to access the computer. A mainframe operating system also handles the very important task of allocating resources to multiple users. Finally, the operating system for any size of computer controls the execution of applications programs.

The primary differences between the operating systems for mainframes and those for personal computers are the number of users and the complexity of the peripheral devices to be managed. Mainframes usually are multiuser

> ## An operating system is just a vehicle to run an application.
>
> *Tim Paterson, creator of the first version of MS-DOS*
>
> Quoted in "An End to the DOS Dynasty," *PC Week,* July 29, 1986, p. 52.

Personal computer operating systems usually support only one user at a time.

machines, while most personal computers are single-user machines. There are exceptions, especially in the case of personal computers, for which multiple-user systems are becoming available. Mainframes must manage a large number of disk and tape drives, input devices, and printers, while a personal computer system usually has only one or two disk drives and a printer. As a result of these differences, mainframe operating systems are extremely large programs that require a maintenance staff of **systems programmers** to maintain them. On the other hand, personal computer operating systems are less complex and must be able to operate without any day-to-day maintenance.

Another difference between mainframe and personal computer operating systems is that operating systems for mainframes are all *proprietary* and will work on only one variety of machine. For personal computers, there now exist *generic* operating systems, which will run on many different types of personal computers. Some personal computers are set up to run multiple operating systems to take advantage of a larger variety of software. While there are still proprietary operating systems for personal computers, the trend is toward the use of generic systems.

Functions of the Operating System

In Chapter 3, the operating system was depicted as the core of an "onion," with outer layers made up of utility software and applications software. The operating system is the core of the "onion" because it is the least visible form of software in a computer. It can require many commands but does not require data. There is no visible output from an operating system to either the screen or the printer except when an error occurs, in which case an error message is shown on the screen. Even though it is usually invisible, the operating system is crucial to the operation of the computer.

As measured by the number of moving parts, [the IBM] System/370 [mainframe] operating system is undoubtedly mankind's most complex single creation.

Gary D. Brown, author of System/370 Job Control Language

Quoted in "Workhorse Operating Systems Square Off," *Computerworld,* January 4, 1988, p. 18.

Systems programmers are responsible for maintaining a mainframe operating system.

The functions of the operating system can be summarized as follows:

- provides an interface between the user and the computer;
- controls access to the machine;
- works with ROM to start up, or "boot," the computer;
- schedules an efficient use of the CPU while eliminating the need for human intervention;
- manages data and information in internal memory;
- manages files on secondary storage, making them available as needed while providing security to multiple users;
- executes other computer programs;
- manages peripheral devices such as printers, disk drives, and tape drives.

We will look first at mainframe operating systems and then at operating systems for personal computers.

MAINFRAME OPERATING SYSTEMS

In any computer system, the processing unit always works much faster than the input and output operations. For this reason, an important task of the operating system is to manage the processing and input/output (I/O) operations in such a way that the slow speed of the I/O operations does not hold up the processing operations. This is especially important for a mainframe on which multiple users must be served and the processing for one user must not wait for other users' I/O. In the early days of computers—that is, pre-1960—the computer could run only one job at a time. A "job" included the program and the pertinent data. Both would be entered into the computer on cards, paper tape, or magnetic tape. Once that job was completed, a new job could be loaded and run. This process wasted a lot of time by causing the CPU to be idle while each job was entered and the output printed.

One way that a mainframe computer is able to run multiple jobs without the I/O interfering with processing is to run the jobs concurrently. In this context, *concurrently* does not mean *simultaneously,* since the CPUs in all computers (other than supercomputers using parallel processing) still can process only one job at a time. What *concurrent* means is that the computer has multiple activities in process at the same time. The CPU processes part of one job, then part of another, then part of a third, and so on until the CPU has worked on all of them, at which point it returns to the first job to work on it again. In concurrent processing, the CPU may process the same job multiple times since multiple passes may be required to finish the job. At the same time that the CPU is processing parts of multiple jobs, a secondary processor is handling the input and output operations. This frees the main CPU from this slow task and keeps the overall processing from being slowed down. Thus, many more jobs can be executed in the same period of time than if the CPU had to wait for an entire job to be input, processed, and output before the next job could be handled. Figure 9-1 shows the concurrent processing operation in action.

In Figure 9-1, JOB1, JOB2, and so on designate the job that the CPU is working on at any one time, while I/O1, I/O2, and so on designate the job that is going through input/output at each point in time. Note that in concurrent processing, at no time is the CPU waiting for I/O to take place.

When a computer is running concurrent jobs, it must manage numerous activities, including accessing the disk drives, tape drives, high-speed printers,

Mainframe computers can handle processing concurrently for numerous users.

FIGURE 9-1
Concurrent Processing

| I/O-1 | JOB1 | JOB2 | JOB3 | JOB1 | JOB2 | JOB3 | JOB4 |
| | I/O-2 | I/O-3 | | | I/O-1 | I/O-4 | |

→ Time

Concurrent Execution

user terminals, and both centralized and remote job entry sites. The disk and tape drives are used for secondary storage and are accessed as needed by the CPU and internal memory. The printers are used for printed output. The user terminals allow user interaction with the computer, with input coming from a keyboard and output going to a video screen.

In addition to being entered at terminals from which users work interactively with the computer, jobs are also entered in the batch mode. In the **batch mode,** an entire job is entered at one time from disk or tape. There may be multiple batch entry sites, called **remote job entry (RJE) sites.** These sites are *remote* because they are separate from the main computer center and they handle job entry through cards or tape. Each RJE site also has a printer to produce printed output.

It is not unusual for the operating system of the computer to support multiple terminals and RJEs concurrently. The jobs are placed in a **queue** (waiting line) to be executed according to their level of priority. The CPU will execute several batch jobs concurrently with the jobs entered from the interactive terminals by allocating processing time to the various jobs. The operating system gives each active job an extremely small amount of CPU time, called a **time-slice,** during which a portion of the job is executed. The next job is then given its time-slice and so on until all jobs are executed. Since the CPU will return to each job three or four times per second and since modern mainframe CPUs can

This printer makes up an RJE site that could be part of, say, the university computer system in your state.

accomplish a great deal of work in a short period of time, the user is usually not aware of any delay. Figure 9-2 shows the various types of devices and terminals that can be tied onto a mainframe.

How Does the Operating System Do It?

From the foregoing discussion it should be obvious that the operating system for a mainframe must manage a very large number of operations and devices. The major unit of the operating system is called the **supervisor program.** This is a program that is loaded into internal memory when the computer is started up. The startup process is commonly referred to as **booting** the computer (so named because just as bootstraps help you get your boots on, booting the computer helps it find its first instructions). Instructions on the ROM chip tell the computer where to look for the supervisor program so it may be loaded into memory. Each type and size of computer has its own booting procedure, but booting a mainframe requires more steps and takes longer than does booting a PC.

FIGURE 9-2
Devices Operating from a
Mainframe

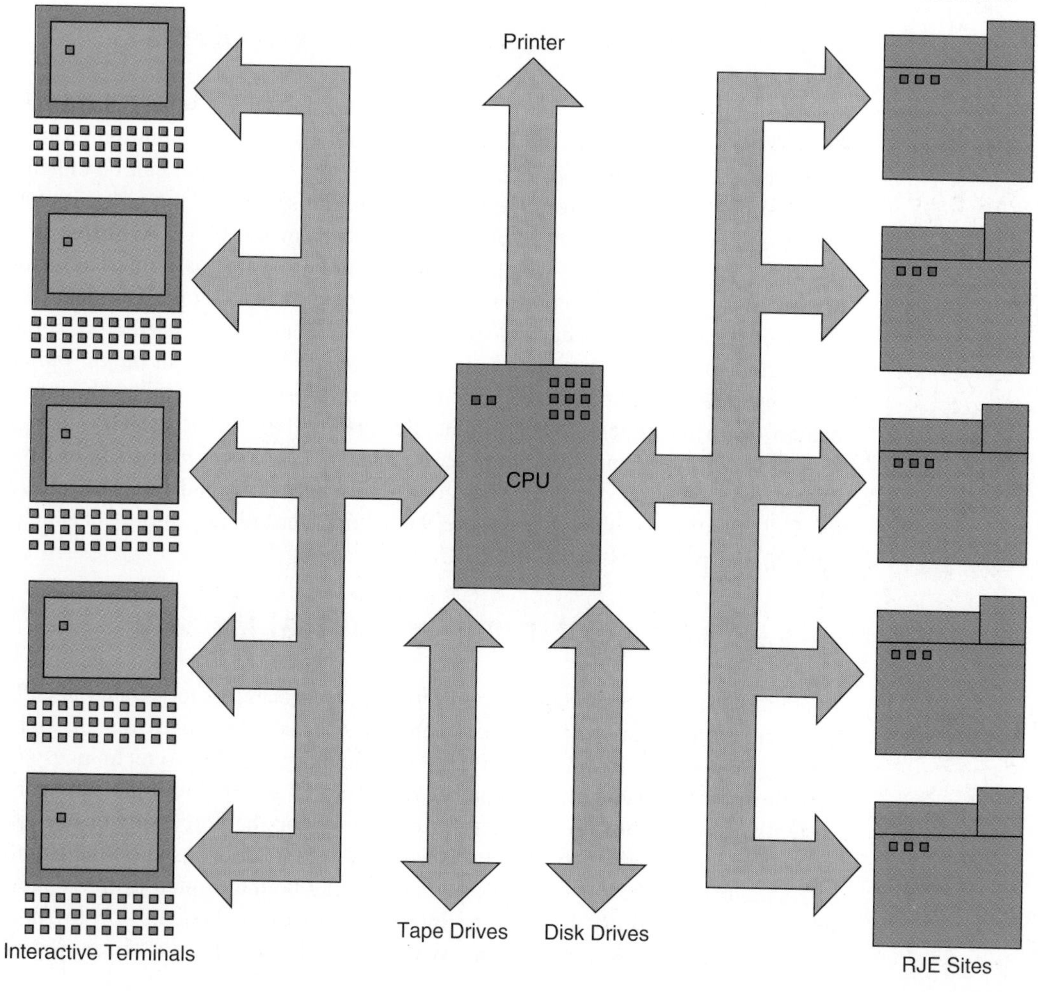

Printer

CPU

Interactive Terminals

Tape Drives   Disk Drives

RJE Sites

Once the supervisor program is loaded into memory, it remains there at all times, performing various tasks. First, it loads other parts of the operating system into internal memory as they are needed. It also supervises both the loading of applications programs into internal memory and their execution. For example, to run an accounting package, the supervisor determines where the accounting package is stored on disk. It then directs the disk drive to read that portion of the disk and to transfer the contents to internal memory. Once they are in internal memory, the actual programs in the accounting package may be executed.

While an applications program is being executed, the operating system also monitors the keyboard for instructions and data, supervises the disk drives to read and write data to and from them, and sends output to the monitor and printer without further instructions from the user.

To tell the operating system what must be done, the user must give it a series of commands. With mainframes, these commands are often combined to form what is called the **job control language (JCL).** JCL uses a combination of terms and symbols to tell the operating system what actions the user wants carried out. The JCLs for different computers are as varied as the computers themselves. The most widely used job control language is IBM JCL, which is required to accomplish almost any task on an IBM mainframe computer.

Channels, Buffers, and Preprocessors

While the CPU is concurrently processing multiple jobs, several hardware devices are used to isolate the CPU from the relatively slow input/output process. These are channels, buffers, and preprocessors. A **channel** can be either a small computer separate from the CPU or a special section of the CPU. It controls the input/output process without direction from the CPU. A **buffer** is a section of internal memory, which may be separate from the main internal memory, that acts as an intermediate storage area for input or output. The data that are input at human or mechanical speeds is stored in an *input buffer* before being transferred to internal memory at electronic speeds. Similarly, an *output buffer* stores processed information from the internal memory before sending the information on to the much slower printer. Because of the buffer, the CPU is not slowed down by the input/output process. Finally, a *front-end processor,* or **preprocessor,** is a small computer that controls the terminals and RJEs to relieve the CPU of this responsibility. Figure 9-3 depicts the relationship of channels, buffers, and preprocessors to the CPU.

System Interrupts and Virtual Memory

In addition to the use of channels, buffers, and preprocessors to isolate the CPU from input/output tasks, two other techniques speed the processing of high-priority jobs and seemingly increase internal memory. These two techniques are system interrupts and virtual memory. When the CPU runs multiple jobs concurrently, it often must use a **system interrupt** to stop the processing of one job to run a higher-priority job. Priority is assigned by the CPU based on the length or source of the job. For example, a long job may be interrupted to run a short job, or an applications job may be interrupted to run a systems job to fix a problem with the operating system. With a system interrupt, the processing of

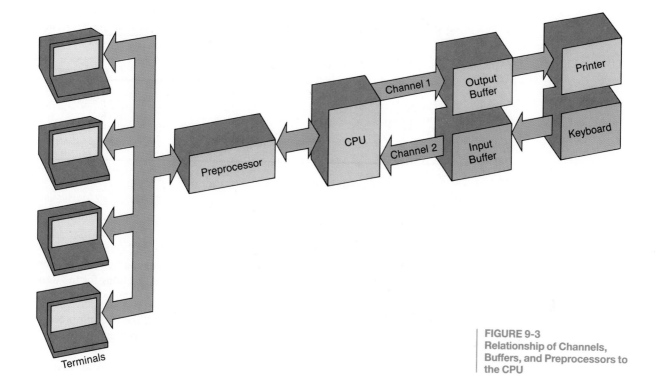

FIGURE 9-3
Relationship of Channels,
Buffers, and Preprocessors to
the CPU

one job is suspended, and internal memory is partitioned into sections. This action separates data and instructions for the interrupted job from those of the higher-priority job. This same partitioning technique is utilized when time-slices are used to run multiple jobs.

Virtual memory is a technique used to increase the apparent memory of a computer. The concept of virtual memory began with mainframe computers in the mid-1970s. In this procedure, the internal memory is divided into pages, or sections, that match equal-size sections of memory on disk. The internal memory is exchanged, or *swapped,* with the disk or virtual memory when needed. As long as the processing needs only data or instructions that are currently in internal memory, it proceeds as usual. However, when the needed information is on disk, a page is swapped into main memory. The CPU tries to "think" ahead to determine which pages from virtual memory will be needed next. As a result, the apparent memory is greater than the actual internal memory without great loss of processing speed. Virtual memory is used in most mainframes today and greatly enhances the ability of these machines to run multiple jobs at high speeds. Virtual memory is also being used with the 80386- and 80486-based personal computers to expand their memory capacity.

PC OPERATING SYSTEMS

Operating systems for personal computers share the same characteristics as mainframe operating systems, but, as we noted earlier, personal computer operating systems are primarily single-user systems. At one time, all PC operating systems were also single-tasking systems (that is, they could work on only one job or "task" at a time), but today the move is toward multitasking PC operating

TABLE 9-1
Comparison of Operating System Features

Feature	Type of Computer	
	Mainframe	*Personal Computer*
Machine use	One brand of computer	Many brands
Number of users	Multiple	Single
Number of tasks	Multiple (concurrent)	Single/multiple
Support	Systems programmers	User/consultants

systems. Table 9-1 compares the mainframe and personal computer operating systems.

Before going into specific PC operating systems, we will consider personal computer operating systems in general. Like mainframe operating systems, personal computer operating systems perform four important functions for the user:

1. *Handle the startup or booting process.* For a PC, the booting process is usually very simple, often requiring the user merely to insert a disk and turn on the computer.

2. *Control the hardware.* The keyboard, mouse, video screen, secondary storage, modem for communications, printer, and any other hardware devices are all under the control of the operating system. Because the operating system controls this portion of the process, the user can easily add new peripheral devices such as a hard disk without having to learn a lot of new commands.

3. *Interpret the user's commands.* When the user types in a command like COPY, the **command interpreter** determines what these keystrokes mean and sends a message to the appropriate utility or applications program to carry out the command. If there is an error in spelling or if an unknown command is entered, an error message is displayed to the user. When the requested procedure is complete, the operating system looks for new instructions from the keyboard (or other input devices).

4. *Maintain a* **file allocation table (FAT)** *on secondary storage.* Computers are heavily dependent on disk secondary storage, and must be able to save files to disk and retrieve them later. The FAT makes this possible.

These four operations of a personal computer operating system are demonstrated in Figure 9-4.

Because most personal computers use disks for secondary storage, the name **disk operating system (DOS)** is almost always used to describe the operating system of a personal computer. For each file, the DOS file system uses a unique name that the user supplies and then uses for future retrievals. The list of the files on the disk is known as the **disk directory.** Figure 9-5 shows a disk directory for a commonly used DOS.

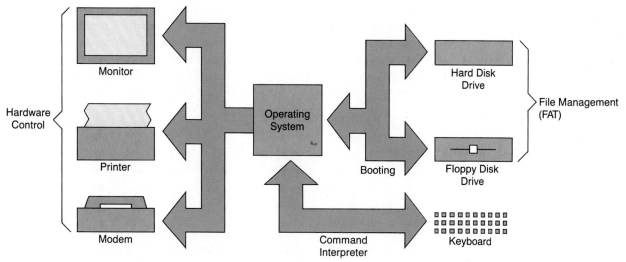

FIGURE 9-4
Functions of a Personal
Computer Operating System

Generic Operating Systems

The operating system is important to the computer because *everything* that runs on the computer depends on it for instructions. For this reason, the capabilities of a computer depend, to a large extent, upon the capabilities of the operating system. It is also true that different brands and types of personal computers that use the same DOS can run the same applications software. This is very different from a mainframe environment, in which each operating system tends to be very different from all others and applications software must be written to run on specific brands and types of machine. The need for a single DOS to run the

```
A:\-> dir

 Volume in drive A is MSWARE1-400
 Directory of  A:\

RESUME          24751    1-20-90    1:04p
PRESNTED 390     5558    1-01-80    1:40a
RAGSDALE VPI     2827    1-22-90   10:05a
FLAATL   CHR     4119    1-01-80   11:49a
MISC             2842    2-27-90    6:03a
WORDPROC DOC     2268    4-17-90    4:20p
CHRISLTR 221     3050    2-21-90   12:50a
RESUME   290    26852    2-27-90    6:07a
SUMMARY  90      2955    1-01-80    8:10a
PUBS     390    10758    1-01-80    1:36a
DRAFT    DAT      528    3-02-90   12:29a
DATA1    DAT      528    3-02-90   10:35a
EXAM2    F88     3484   11-14-88    6:51a
PROJECTE INP      936    3-02-90    5:58a
PLAYER   DAT      230    3-07-90   12:08a
MS815            3286    2-18-88   12:08p
FIG3-13  PIX     2317    4-19-90   12:06p
        17 File(s)    256000 bytes free

A:\->
```

FIGURE 9-5
Disk Directory

same applications software on different personal computers has led to the development of **generic operating systems.** There currently exist three common generic disk operating systems and several others that are not so well known. The three are MS-DOS (Microsoft DOS), from Microsoft; OS/2 (Operating System/2), from Microsoft and IBM; and UNIX, originally developed by AT&T. These systems can be broadly identified by three characteristics:

1. the number of tasks that may be run concurrently under the operating system;
2. the number of machines the operating system will support;
3. the types of computers on which the operating system can be used.

As we said at the beginning of this section, at one time almost all PC operating machines were single-user, single-task systems. Even today, the predominant PC operating system—MS-DOS—is of that type. However, the other two systems—UNIX and OS/2—go beyond this to offer either multitasking or multiuser control or both, similar to the control offered by mainframe operating systems. Even MS-DOS has been expanded to handle some multitasking in versions starting with 5.0 and through operating environments such as Windows. MS-DOS and OS/2 can be used only on IBM PS/2s and IBM compatible PCs, whereas UNIX is not restricted by type of machine. OS/2 is further restricted to computers that use the Intel 80286, 80386, or 80486 (now commonly referred to as the i486) CPU chips; it will not run on the original IBM PC, PC XT, or compatibles that use the Intel 8088 or 8086 CPU chips. Table 9-2 summarizes this information.

MS-DOS

Today, the most widely used operating system for PCs is **MS-DOS.** It was first used on the IBM PC, under the name "PC-DOS." MS-DOS and PC-DOS are often jointly referred to simply as "DOS." MS-DOS was chosen in 1981 as the operating system for IBM's entry into the personal computer market, which immediately stamped MS-DOS as an industry standard operating system for 16- and 32-bit IBM compatible computers. IBM's choice of MS-DOS also had a great deal to do with the emergence of Microsoft Corporation as one of the world's leading developers of PC software. Currently, at least 10 million people use MS-DOS as their computer operating system, and a vast majority of all applications packages in existence today will run on MS-DOS.

Like most software, MS-DOS has undergone several revisions since it was first released. These versions were numbered sequentially, that is, 1.0, 2.0, 2.1,

TABLE 9-2
Comparison of Generic PC Operating Systems

Operating System	Number of Tasks	Number of Users	Machine
MS-DOS	One	Single	IBM PS/2 or IBM compatible PCs
OS/2	Multiple	Single	Computers using the Intel 80286, 80386, or i486 chips
UNIX	Multiple	Multiple	Not restricted

(Top) This IBM compatible PC runs under the MS-DOS operating system. (Center) This IBM PS/2 Model 80 computer runs under the OS/2 operating system. (Bottom) This RISC System/6000 Powerserver 320 computer runs under the UNIX operating system.

3.0, 4.0, 5.0, and so on. Each subsequent version added new features and power to the operating system. For MS-DOS, the most commonly used versions are those numbered between 3.0 and 5.0. Versions 4.0 and 5.0 departed from the earlier, strictly command-driven form to offer either a menu-driven or a command-driven structure. DOS 5.0 also added a full-screen program editor and the capability to swap between programs.

There have been many predictions that MS-DOS would be superseded by other, more "modern" operating systems such as OS/2. However, there is little evidence that this will occur any time soon, especially with the continued release of updated versions. In addition, the release of Windows has solved many of the problems with MS-DOS.

Regardless of the version being used, the user must know or at least understand some of over 50 MS-DOS commands. Most of these commands can be input from the keyboard *interactively* or selected from a menu, but some are **batch commands** that can be combined into a program that will execute the commands sequentially. All interactive commands are entered at the **prompt,** which signals that the computer is awaiting a command.

MS-DOS is divided into two sets of commands: the **internal commands,** which are stored in RAM as a part of the booting process, and the **external commands,** which are located on disk storage. Since they are stored in RAM, the internal commands can be accessed immediately by the CPU. The external commands must be read from floppy or hard disk storage as needed.

Commonly used internal MS-DOS commands include COPY, for copying files from one disk to another; TYPE, for displaying the contents of a text file; and DIR, for listing the contents of a disk or section of a disk. Commonly used external MS-DOS commands include FORMAT, which prepares a disk to receive files, and DISKCOPY, which copies the entire contents of one floppy

Beginning with Version 5.0, MS-DOS has a menu-driven option.

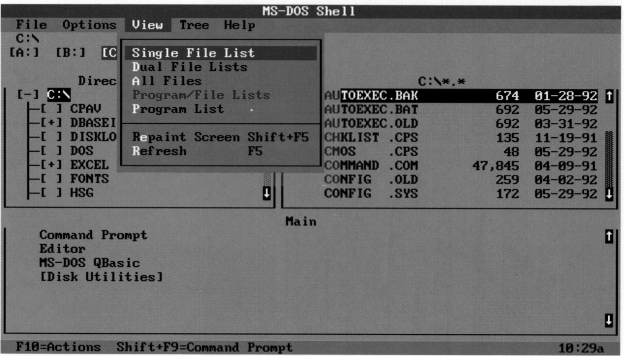

disk to another. These and other MS-DOS commands will be discussed in detail in the MS-DOS tutorial in Appendix A.

Subdirectories

As long as personal computers had only floppy disk drives, keeping up with files was relatively easy: Each original $5\frac{1}{4}$-inch floppy held a maximum of 360 Kbytes of storage. However, when hard disk drives holding megabytes of information came into widespread use, working with all the files on a hard disk became a problem. To rectify this, MS-DOS was modified to allow the user to break up the files into **subdirectories.** Each subdirectory can be given a name and can be thought of as being analogous to a separate floppy disk. This **hierarchical** or **tree structure** divides a long list of files into several shorter lists that are easier to keep track of.

As an example of the use of subdirectories, assume that a college professor stores on disk both the chapters for a book she is working on and exams for the courses she teaches. If the book has 20 chapters and she has created 25 exams at one time or another, with one file for each book chapter and one for each exam, then there would be at least 45 files on the disk. With a single directory on the hard disk, it would be difficult to look through all the files to find a particular chapter or exam. However, a tree structure with one subdirectory for book chapters and one for exams would allow the professor to look much more easily for a desired chapter or exam. MS-DOS has commands that allow the user to create subdirectories or to switch between subdirectories. Other PC operating systems have similar commands to work with subdirectories. Figure 9-6 shows how such a tree structure would appear.

OS/2

On April 2, 1987, IBM and Microsoft jointly announced the development of OS/2—the operating system that would "succeed" the almost "ancient" MS-DOS. Created in 1981 to run the then new IBM PC, MS-DOS has gone through several upgrades. Yet even with all its upgrades, MS-DOS has remained primarily a command-driven operating system aimed at running a single task or job. Also, without the use of memory management software, MS-DOS can use only 640K of RAM, regardless of the memory capacity of the machine.

> **[OS/2 2.0] is a better DOS than DOS, a better Windows than Windows, and a better OS/2.**
>
> *Lee Reiswig, general manager of IBM's system software development effort*
>
> Quoted in "The New OS/2: Impressive Rival for Windows," *The New York Times,* October 27, 1991, p. 8.

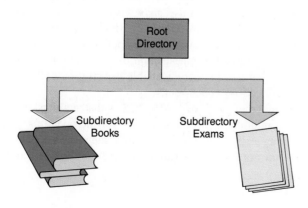

FIGURE 9-6
Tree Structure

The new system, named **OS/2,** provides users with a **graphical user interface (GUI)** called the Presentation Manager, allows for the use of up to 16 Mbytes of RAM, and runs multiple tasks on personal computers using the Intel 80386 or i486 chips.

OS/2 has gone through several stages of development, culminating in the recently released OS/2 2.0. This latest version of OS/2 was written to run only on 80386- and i486-based machines, and it features a Macintosh-like graphical interface and the capability of running multiple MS-DOS applications concurrently.

While MS-DOS continues to be the operating system of choice for many people who use PCs based on the Intel 80386 or i486 chips, many analysts believe that OS/2 will come to be used on many of these types of machines. This move to OS/2 is likely to be driven by three considerations: limited access to RAM with MS-DOS, trends toward graphical interfaces for all types of software, and the desire of many PC users to be able to carry out multiple tasks concurrently. As noted earlier in this section, without the use of programs like Windows or the so-called "DOS extenders," MS-DOS users can only access 640K of RAM, regardless of the amount of RAM on the PC and the size of the program being executed. This limitation is an inherent feature of MS-DOS and is a very real limitation to "power users" who work with very large programs. OS/2 is designed to take full advantage of the memory capacities of the Intel 80386 and i486 chips, so it can address up to 16 Mbytes of memory—almost 30 times that available with MS-DOS.

A widespread movement in computing is toward a graphical interface in which a mouse is used to point to **icons** that represent the desired action and to press one or more mouse buttons. If the user knows the meaning of the icon, then it is not necessary to learn any operating system commands. For example, if a file folder represents a file and a trash can represents the erasure of a file, the user can erase a file by pointing to the file folder and then "dragging" it to the trash can. This type of operating system interface was pioneered by the Apple Macintosh, and its ease of use has caused many IBM compatible PC users to ask for the same type of interface on their PCs. In response, a graphical interface called the **Presentation Manager,** similar to the interface on the Macintosh, is incorporated into OS/2 and, as discussed in the opening box, is important to many users.

As noted earlier, MS-DOS is primarily a single-task operating system. This was acceptable to PC users as long as they worked with slow PCs and floppy disk systems. Now, with the heavy use of high-volume hard disks and faster processors, PC users are finding that they need to be able to work on multiple tasks concurrently. For example, a user may wish to use telecommunications to transfer files concurrently with working on a word processing package. Users also want to be able to switch around among applications without actually exiting any of the applications. The introduction of the Intel 80386 and i486 chips will make multitasking more widely available because these chips can be used to run multiple applications concurrently.

A key advantage of OS/2 over MS-DOS is that multitasking is a part of OS/2. This allows multiple applications written for the operating system to run concurrently as long as there is sufficient internal memory. The latest version of OS/2, 2.0, can run applications written for OS/2, Windows, and MS-DOS concurrently.

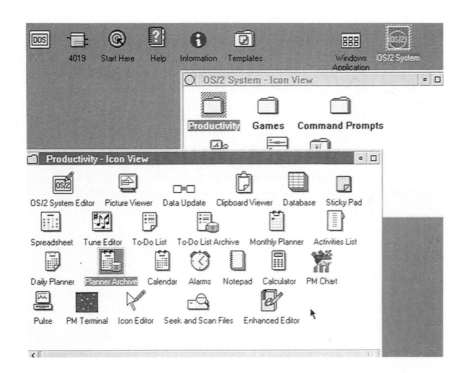

When multiple tasks are being processed, the OS/2 Presentation Manager allows them to be displayed simultaneously on the screen.

UNIX

MS-DOS and OS/2 are both single-user operating systems that can control only one machine at a time. The third generic PC operating system, **UNIX,** is a multiuser, multitasking operating system. UNIX was originally developed by AT&T for use on its own minicomputers, but has since been modified to be used on all sizes of computers, from supercomputers down to some of the more powerful personal computers that have sufficient memory and disk space. Because UNIX is a multiuser system, it is the most widely used operating system for controlling systems of workstations. IBM has also developed a version of UNIX called AIX, for use on its midsize and mainframe computers.

Microsoft has developed a version of UNIX called XENIX, which will run PCs using the Intel series of chips. Apple also has developed a version of UNIX that will run on its more powerful Macintosh computers. Finally, as discussed in the box on Steve Jobs, a version of UNIX with a graphical interface was developed for use on the NeXT computer. This interface has been licensed by IBM for use with its version of UNIX.

The reason UNIX can be used on many different sizes and types of computers is that it is written in two parts. One part is written in a high-level (English-like) language that can run on various types of computers. The second part is written in a low-level language that is specific to the type of computer. This means that only the low-level language portion must be rewritten to convert the UNIX program to run on a new computer. Another attractive feature is that UNIX can run other operating systems as a job. For example, it is possible to run MS-DOS as a task under UNIX and then to run applications written for MS-DOS as subtasks.

> A lot of people criticize UNIX, but my question is, what out there is better for multitasking/multiuser?
>
> *David Carlson, senior vice president of information systems, K mart*
>
> Quoted in "UNIX Jumps Into the Breach," *Computerworld,* May 20, 1991, p. 100.

STEVE JOBS AND THE NeXT COMPUTER

On April Fool's Day of 1976, Steve Jobs and Steve Wozniak founded the Apple Computer Company to sell the personal computers they were building in a garage. For nine years, Jobs served in various positions with the company, including president and chairman of the board, as it grew into a giant in the personal computer field. During this time, he was instrumental in developing both the extremely popular Apple II and Macintosh lines of computers, the latter being notable for its graphical user interface and easy-to-use operating system.

In 1985, Jobs left Apple to found a new company—NeXT, Inc. Three years later, on October 12, 1988, Jobs introduced a high-performance personal computer called the NeXT computer. It was originally aimed at the academic market but has since been modified for use in nonacademic situations. The NeXT is based on the Motorola 68040 chip—the same series of chip used in the Macintosh.

While the NeXT contains several technological innovations, including a 256-Mbyte erasable and removable optical disk, a 2.88-Mbyte microfloppy disk drive, and a new chip technology that gives "mainframe performance," possibly the greatest long-term contribution of the NeXT will be its operating system. The NeXT uses a variation of the UNIX operating system with a graphical user interface called NeXTStep. Although UNIX has long been known for its power, especially for multiple users and multitasking, it has also been criticized for being difficult to use. The graphically oriented NeXTStep offers an easier way to use the power of UNIX. In fact, IBM thought so much of NeXTStep that it has licensed its use on its UNIX-based machines.

Major software applications have been modified to run on the NeXT computer using the NeXTStep operating system. These include packages from Lotus, WordPerfect, and Oracle. Possibly, the crucial new application that will lure new users to NeXT is the Improv spreadsheet from Lotus Development Corporation. Designed specifically for the NeXT, Improv is said to clear up some complications associated with using spreadsheets by using English commands rather than a numerical syntax.

Source: James Daly, "Job's NeXT Unveils Do-or-Die Systems, Software," *Computerworld*, September 24, 1990, p. 7.

Lotus' IMPROV software has a graphical-user interface and pull-down menus.

Source: Lotus Corp.

Steve Jobs

UNIX is a very complete system, offering hierarchical file structures and the ability to send data from one program to another through a system called *piping*. In **piping,** the output from one program is "piped" to another program, for which it becomes the input. This very powerful feature allows programs to be combined to solve complicated problems. UNIX also has over 200 utilities that can perform almost any task a user could desire. These utilities can be joined together through piping to handle many operations. To the knowledgeable user, this wealth of commands and utilities can be very useful.

A problem that has limited the widespread use of UNIX is that the command structure can be somewhat difficult to learn. Systems like NeXTStep from NeXT, Inc., are aimed at providing a special interface that will make UNIX easy for beginners to use. Another reason often given for the lack of widespread acceptance of UNIX is the many variations of this operating system that exist today. Currently, there is a great deal of discussion as to what version of UNIX should be the "standard," and at least two groups of companies are competing to have their version accepted as the standard.

Proprietary Operating Systems

While MS-DOS, OS/2, and UNIX may be purchased separately from the computers they control, several computer manufacturers use **proprietary operating systems** for their computers. These are operating systems that are closely tied to the computer on which they run. Currently, the most popular proprietary operating systems are those for the Macintosh and the Apple II. Other systems include the Commodore and Amiga lines of computers.

The Apple II series of computers uses a chip—the Motorola 6502—on which MS-DOS and OS/2 will not work. This is not surprising; since the original Apple II was built *before* either of those operating systems were developed, its operating system was developed specifically for the Apple II series. While it is possible to purchase special hardware to rectify this problem, most Apple users

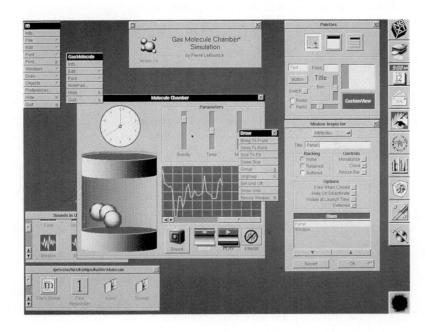

The NeXTStep graphical interface for the UNIX operating system, with icons and windows, is an important feature of the NeXT computer.

have continued to use Apple DOS (or its more recent version, ProDOS). This operating system is aimed at the student and the home user and is fairly easy to use compared to MS-DOS, OS/2, or UNIX. At the same time, the Apple II operating systems do not offer the power and capabilities of these generic operating systems.

Of the operating systems currently available, possibly the easiest to use is the Macintosh operating system. This system provides icons, a mouse, and pull-down menus for selecting commands, enabling the user to concentrate on the job to be accomplished rather than on how to get the computer to do the job. Files are stored in folders, which are analogous to MS-DOS subdirectories. To retrieve a file, the user makes the mouse move the pointer to a folder, clicks the mouse to "open" the folder, and then clicks the mouse a second time to retrieve the file. This Macintosh operating system has a unique approach to applications software in that when a data file is retrieved, the appropriate applications software is also retrieved and executed. For example, if the user retrieves a spreadsheet file that was created with Excel, then the Excel package is also retrieved and executed. This is the reverse of many MS-DOS applications in which the user executes the applications software package first and then retrieves a file.

Executing other tasks on the Macintosh is also very easy using the icon and mouse system. Recall our discussion in the section on OS/2 of the deletion of a file on Macintosh. In the case of tasks requiring multiple operations, the user may need to pull down a submenu to expose an expanded list of commands. Again the mouse is used to position the cursor over the appropriate command in the submenu, and the button is pressed to carry out the task. Figure 9-7 shows the Macintosh operating system in use.

Many popular applications packages have been rewritten to run using the Macintosh operating system. The ease of use of the Macintosh operating system was the primary reason that Microsoft and IBM put so much effort into developing similar interfaces in the OS/2 Presentation Manager and Microsoft has

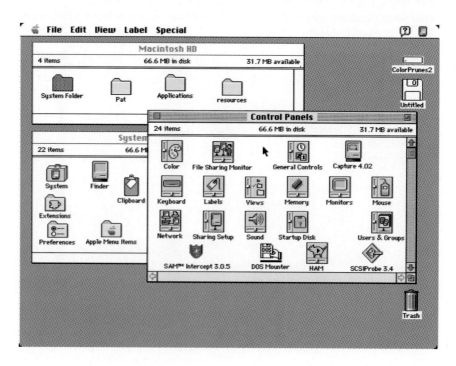

FIGURE 9-7
Macintosh Operating System

placed such emphasis on Windows. In response to these moves by Microsoft and IBM, in 1991, Apple released a new version of the Mac operating system, called System 7, which offers numerous improvements over previous versions.

Local Area Network Operating Systems

As more and more organizations are moving to local area networks (LANs) composed of PCs, there has been an increasing interest in LAN operating systems. **LAN operating systems** operate at a level above the basic operating system (usually MS-DOS) to allow users to access software and files on the file server. At the same time, the LAN operating system must also ensure that software licenses of commercial software are not being violated by having too many users accessing a package or by users illegally copying software. In addition to the LAN operating system's primary function of managing the file server, it must allow users access to printer facilities; provide security against unwanted users accessing the network through a system of account IDs and passwords; and add communication capability between the PCs. Currently, the three most popular LAN operating systems are Netware from Novell, which is the most popular system; LAN Manager from Microsoft; and Banyan Vines. Figure 9-8 shows a menu system on a LAN running under Novell Netware.

OPERATING ENVIRONMENTS AND RAM-RESIDENT PROGRAMS

In our discussion of PC operating systems, we have placed a great deal of emphasis on multitasking and easy-to-use graphical interfaces. However, the most widely used PC operating system—MS-DOS—is primarily a command-driven operating system that was designed to be used on a single machine for a single task. Fortunately, ways have been found to get around these shortcomings of MS-DOS to implement such features as graphical interfaces and multitasking. Graphical interfaces and multitasking are being incorporated into a type of software known as an *operating environment* that acts as a "shell" around MS-DOS. Another type of software called a *RAM-resident program* offers a form of multitasking. While these are not operating systems, they are related closely to operating systems, so we will discuss each briefly in this section.

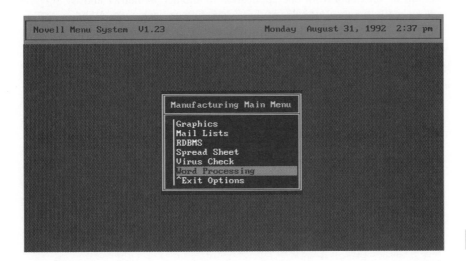

FIGURE 9-8
LAN Menu System

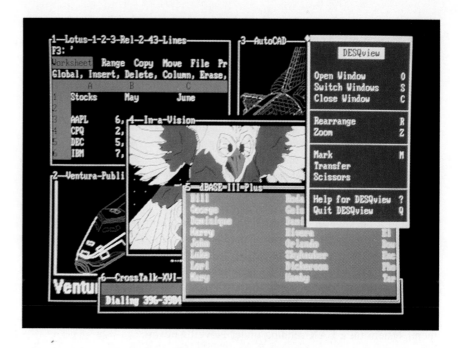

Operating Environments

An **operating environment** (also called a **shell**) is a software application that works with MS-DOS to provide one or more of the following additional features: a graphical user interface (GUI), the capability to run multiple tasks concurrently, and the capability to use onscreen windows to view the output for programs that are running concurrently. Figure 9.9 shows how an operating environment is situated between the applications software and the operating system.

These operating environments are sold like applications programs and include such packages as Microsoft Windows 3.0/3.1, DESQview from Quarterdeck Office Systems, NewWave from Hewlett-Packard, and Ensemble from GeoWorks. In addition to making the use of MS-DOS easier, these systems can give users fast access to their programs, and they allow them to switch applications or shift data from one application to another. Windows and DESQview are currently the most popular of these operating environments. Windows offers all three of the features described, whereas DESQview is aimed primarily at multitasking and displaying output in onscreen windows.

Windows

Windows 3.0 was introduced in May 1990, and since its introduction, it has become the single largest-selling application package in the short history of personal computers. In its first 18 months, *4 million* copies of Windows 3.0 were sold. Windows offers a GUI that many users find easy to use. The basic interface for all programs is the desktop, on which users work with icons that represent applications and files. There are also "groups" of applications and files that are contained in resizable windows.

In addition to allowing users to "point-and-click" to access application programs and utilities, all programs written for Windows display the same menu

```
         Applications
           Software
      Operating Environment
       Operating System
           Hardware
```

FEASTING ON WINDOWS AT TACO BELL

Taco Bell has a legal department, as do all large corporations, that makes wide use of both personal computers and mainframes. At this national fast-food chain, the legal department has moved to improve the personal productivity of its staff by installing Windows on its IBM compatible personal computers.

Although Macintosh computers are widely used throughout Taco Bell, the corporation's legal department uses IBM compatible personal computers and, thus, had to retain its MS-DOS compatibility while moving to a graphical user interface. To do this, a Windows application called deskMinder, a desktop manager, was installed. deskMinder presents the user with a graphical desktop onscreen, complete with drawers, shelves, telephone, clock, and other items. Icons were also added for a word processor, spreadsheet, data base management package, and corporate mainframe.

With this system, in addition to accessing the software packages, the user can select the computer icon to access the mainframe or the telephone icon to dial external sources such as a legal data base.

deskMinder also made many Windows utilities, such as the calculator and calendar, more accessible by creating onscreen buttons for them. Today, with Windows and deskMinder on their PCs, the 40 staff members of Taco Bell's legal department can have a graphic user interface while retaining MS-DOS compatibility.

Source: Ben Myers, "Taco Bell Feasts on deskMinder's Accessibility to Windows," *PC Week,* September 16, 1991, p. 121.

Taco Bell installed the deskMinder desktop management software in their legal department to improve productivity.

FIGURE 9-10
Multitasking in Windows 3.0

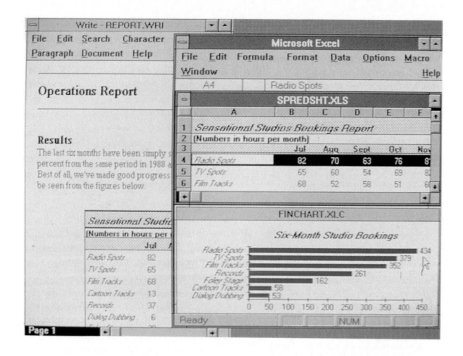

bar with menu choices at the top of the screen, a scroll bar at the right, and arrows to reduce or expand the application's window. Non–Windows-based programs usually do not have these consistent features. For example, help is accessed in 1-2-3 by pressing the F1 function key but is accessed in WordPerfect 5.1 by pressing the F3 function key. Users can run several Windows applications simultaneously, cutting and pasting data among them. In late 1991, Windows 3.1 was introduced as an improved version that cleaned up some of the problems found in the earlier version.

A disadvantage of Windows is that existing MS-DOS programs must be rewritten to take advantage of its many features, and this is not always an easy task. For example, it took the WordPerfect Corp. well over 18 months to create WordPerfect for Windows. However, almost all popular MS-DOS packages will soon be rewritten to work with Windows, if they have not already been rewritten. A second disadvantage is that Windows cannot run on all hardware because it requires at least an 80286 machine with a hard disk and a minimum of 2 Megabytes of memory. However, even an 80286 machine is still often too slow to adequately run Windows, and most experts recommend at least an 80386 machine to take full advantage of all of Windows's features. Figure 9-10 shows two applications running concurrently on *Windows*.

RAM-Resident Programs

Another way of getting around some of the restraints that MS-DOS puts on the personal computer is RAM-resident programs. A **RAM-resident program** is an applications program that once run is, as the name implies, resident in RAM until the computer is turned off. The RAM-resident program "hides" in a part of RAM that is not used by the operating system or any application program. By remaining in the background, it does not interfere with other programs that are run in the foreground. However, it can be called up as needed to overlay the existing application with one or more windows in which a function is executed.

The first example of a RAM-resident program, and still one of the most popular, is Sidekick from Borland. This is a utility software application that the user activates into the foreground by simultaneously pressing the Ctrl and Alt keys on an IBM compatible PC keyboard. When these two keys are pressed, a menu "pops up" over any existing software on the screen. From this menu, the user can choose to view a calendar, use a text editor, use a calculator, use a dialer to dial a phone number, view an ASCII table, set up the Sidekick system, or exit Sidekick. It is possible to use more than one of these applications simultaneously with multiple windows on the screen. The text editor can also be used to "cut and paste" information from the screen for later use in other programs. Figure 9-11 shows the Sidekick Time Planner.

There are numerous RAM-resident programs besides Sidekick, and it is possible to load more than one such program into RAM at one time as long as there is no conflict between the programs. For example, many of the photographs of computer screens, including Figure 9-10, used in this book were "captured" from the screen by a RAM-resident program that can convert a screen image into a digital form on disk. Other RAM-resident programs can capture a series of keystrokes and play them back when needed. As you go further into using the computer, you will certainly find a use for a RAM-resident program.

A shortcoming of RAM-resident programs is that they can occasionally interfere with the operation of a foreground program or with each other. When multiple RAM-resident programs are being used, they sometimes must be loaded into memory in a specific order. Also, it is not always possible to remove a RAM-resident program from memory without rebooting the computer.

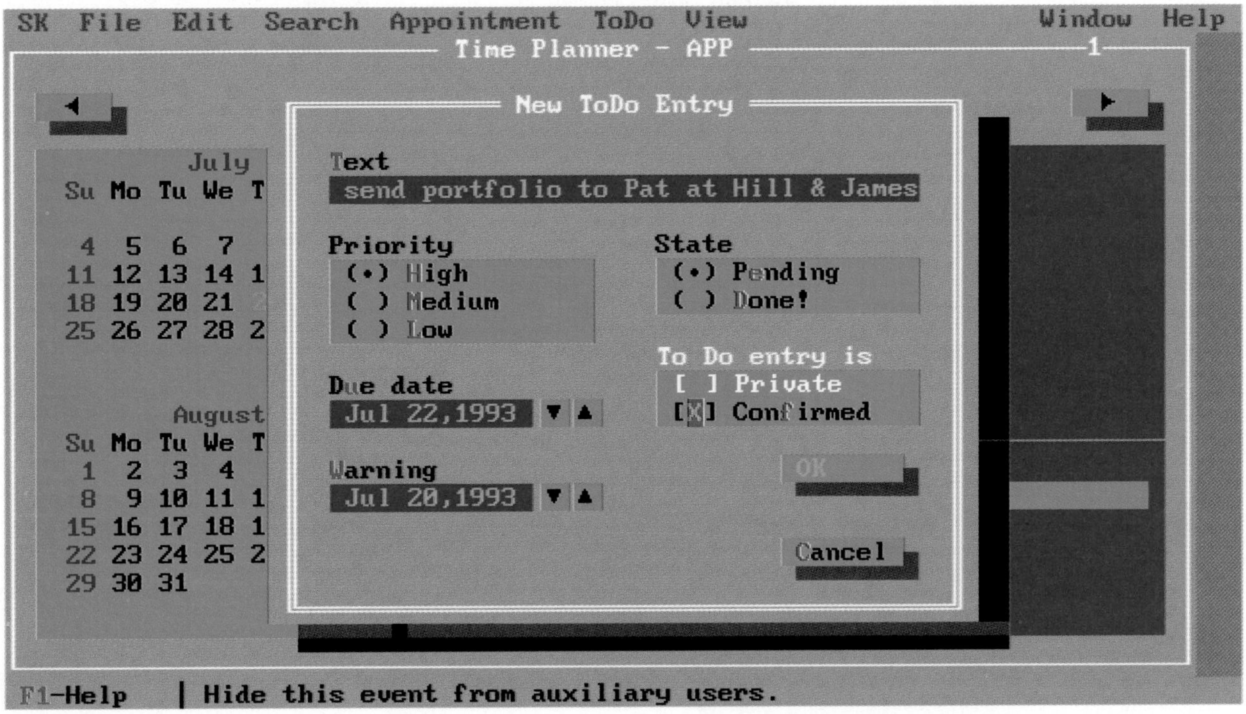

FIGURE 9-11
RAM-Resident program

BITS OF HISTORY

Operating Systems

Mainframe Operating Systems

Before 1960, computers were set up to execute or "run" one application program at a time. Only after one job had been input, executed, and output could the next job begin. This process wasted a lot of time by causing the CPU to be idle while each job was entered and the output printed. To avoid this wasted CPU time, the first operating systems were written to allow for concurrent execution of jobs. In this way, the CPU would never be idle and the number of jobs completed would be greater. The overall effect of this approach was a dramatic increase in the amount of work that could be performed by the computer.

The first operating systems were written not by computer companies, but by groups of computer users called SHARE in 1958 to 1959. The computer companies initially considered themselves to be hardware vendors only and did not become involved in writing software. However, once it was established that an operating system would enhance computer sales, the user-designed systems were purchased and developed by the hardware companies. The first operating system that allowed multiple users and concurrent jobs was the Master Control Program for the Burroughs 5500 series of machines in 1964 to 1965. This was followed by the operating system for the IBM 360 series of machines (OS-360), which, with the addition of many enhancements, has remained in use for IBM mainframes since 1966.

Personal Computer Operating Systems

Pre–MS-DOS In the early 1970s, a computer scientist named Gary Kildall was consulting for the semiconductor manufacturer Intel, developing compilers to convert high-level languages into machine languages. In the process of working on languages for desktop computers, he discovered a need for an operating system to run all these languages on the same machine. To continue his work, he developed the first operating system for personal computers, which he named CP/M (for Control Program/Microcomputers). As other computer scientists and hobbyists heard about CP/M, Kildall began to get requests for it. To meet this need, in 1974 he and his wife formed a company, Digital Research, to market the product. CP/M was the first operating system for small computers and allowed users to develop a program to suit a particular operating system rather than a particular machine. As a result it became a best-seller, with over 15,000 programs written for it at one point.

Other pre–MS-DOS operating systems included those developed to control the operation of the Apple II, Commodore, and Amiga computers.

The Burroughs 5500 series of computers was the first to accommodate multiple users and concurrent job execution.

MS-DOS Shortly after Intel first offered the 16-bit 8086 chip in 1979, a small hardware firm called Seattle Computer Products needed an operating system for an 8086 product under development. To satisfy this need, it developed an operating system called QDOS (for Quick and Dirty Operating System) with an eye to making it as compatible as possible with CP/M. This operating system was renamed 86-DOS and licensed to Microsoft for development of 16-bit software to run on Intel chips. Microsoft eventually bought the system, renamed it MS-DOS, and later licensed it to IBM for use on the original IBM PC as PC-DOS.

UNIX The oldest operating system for small computers, UNIX was developed in 1970 by Bell Labs (now AT&T) for use on its in-house minicomputers. When personal computers became popular in the early 1980s, UNIX was modified to run on these smaller computers. It has since been licensed to other companies, such as Microsoft, to be sold for 16-bit computers under the name XENIX. IBM has a version called AIX, and a version of UNIX is the operating system used on Steve Jobs's NeXT computer.

OS/2 The newest PC operating system, OS/2, was developed jointly by Microsoft and IBM and announced in April 1987. Designed as a successor to MS-DOS that offers multitasking and expanded memory management, OS/2 has gone through various stages of development leading up to the current version. Currently, OS/2 offers an easy-to-use graphical interface and robust multitasking capabilities.

Macintosh The graphical interface approach of the Macintosh operating system is based on work done in the 1970s at the Palo Alto Research Center (PARC) of Xerox (the same people who were involved in the development of the computer mouse). Of central importance at this laboratory was finding ways to make the computer easier to use rather than requiring the user to become an expert on a given machine. It is said that Steve Jobs—a co-founder of Apple Computers—visited this center in the late 1970s, saw what they were doing, and decided that this same approach should be used for future Apple computers. The people at Apple adapted the earlier work to develop the operating system on the Lisa computer and then on the Macintosh computer.

(Left) Gary Kildall, founder of Digital Research, developed the CP/M operating system—the forerunner of MS-DOS. (Right) Andrew Hertzfeld was one of the architects of the original Macintosh operating system.

1. All types of computers need operating systems.
2. An operating system performs various important functions that allow the user to execute utility and applications programs.
3. Mainframe operating systems must manage terminals and batch systems, using a supervisor program that calls in other parts of the operating system as needed.
4. Channels, buffers, and preprocessors are hardware devices that help to isolate the CPU from the input/output functions.
5. Currently, most personal computer operating systems are aimed at single users performing single tasks.
6. Personal computer operating systems control the hardware, interpret the user's commands, and maintain a file system on secondary storage.
7. Generic operating systems can run on many different computers; proprietary systems run on only one.
8. The most widely used generic operating systems for personal computers are MS-DOS, OS/2, and UNIX.
9. Of these three, OS/2 and UNIX are multitasking operating systems, and UNIX can also control multiple machines. OS/2 has a graphical user interface (GUI).
10. Apple is one of several computer manufacturers that use proprietary operating systems, with the Apple Macintosh offering an extremely easy-to-use, icon-based operating system.
11. Local area network operating systems are becoming more important as more organizations use LANs.
12. Operating environments and RAM-resident programs allow an MS-DOS user to circumvent some of the difficulties of that operating system. Microsoft Windows is an extremely popular operating environment.

KEY TERMS

batch command
batch mode
booting
buffer
channel
command interpreter
disk directory
disk operating system (DOS)
external command
file allocation table (FAT)
generic operating system
graphical user interface (GUI)
hierarchical structure
icon
internal command
job control language (JCL)

LAN operating system
MS-DOS
operating environment
operating system
OS/2
piping
preprocessor
Presentation Manager
prompt
proprietary operating system
queue
RAM-resident program
remote job entry (RJE) site
shell
subdirectory
supervisor program

system interrupt
systems
systems programmer
time-slice

tree structure
UNIX
virtual memory

1. Name the functions of an operating system.
2. How does a mainframe operating system differ from a personal computer operating system?
3. In a computer system, how is concurrent execution different from simultaneous execution?
4. How does the computer run concurrent jobs with no perceptible loss of speed for each job? What is a time-slice?
5. What is an RJE site? Why is it needed?
6. What is the purpose of the supervisor program?
7. What is JCL? How is it used?
8. What is the difference between a channel, a buffer, and a preprocessor?
9. How does a mainframe operating system use a system interrupt? How does it use virtual memory?
10. What are the functions of a personal computer operating system?
11. What is the difference between a generic operating system and a proprietary operating system? Which does a mainframe use? Why?
12. Name the three most commonly used generic operating systems for personal computers.
13. Which operating system is primarily a single-user, single-task operating system?
14. Which operating system is primarily a single-user, multitask operating system? Which can be used to control multiple machines and multiple tasks?
15. What functions does an operating environment perform? What is a RAM-resident program?

10

Word Processing, Graphics, and Desktop Publishing Packages

We noted in earlier chapters that the computer can work with symbols as well as numeric data. In this chapter, we discuss computer software packages for processing words and pictures. These packages are commonly known as word processing, graphics, and desktop publishing packages. Word processing packages enable the user to format a document in a desired form, enter text to create a document, edit the document to reach a final version, and save and print the final version of the document. If additional changes are needed, the word processing package allows them to be made with ease. Graphics packages are used to create pictures to present ideas. Four types of graphics packages will be discussed, including analysis graphics, presentations graphics, computer-aided design, and paint packages for developing computer art. The importance of hardware in selecting and using graphics packages will also be covered. Finally, we discuss a type of software package—desktop publishing—that combines features of word processing and graphics packages to produce near-typeset-quality documents on laser printers.

STUDY OBJECTIVES

After reading this chapter, you should be able to

- understand how the key operations of a word processor make this type of computer package superior to a typewriter;
- describe the process by which a document is formatted;
- discuss the word processing text entry and editing operations in the creation of a document;
- distinguish between the replace mode and the insert mode for word processing packages;
- describe the process by which a document is saved and printed;
- list and discuss other important word processing operations, including block-action commands, search and replace, and spellchecking;
- recognize the key concerns in selecting a word processing package for a personal computer;
- understand how a computer creates graphic images;
- discuss the difference between character and bit-mapped graphics;
- list and discuss the four types of graphics packages that are commonly available on computers;
- explain the importance of hardware in the selection and use of a graphics package;
- discuss the use of desktop publishing to create near-typeset-quality documents on laser printers.

TRYING SOMETHING NEW

Publishing Books at Clarke Central High

Desktop publishing has revolutionized the capabilities of small print shops and offices which previously had to rely on high-cost professionals to do specialized work in typesetting and design. The revolution continues with multimedia and the widespread use of color.

Albon "Buddy" Woods, printing and photography instructor, Clarke Central High School, Athens, Georgia

Quoted in interview with author, March 30, 1991.

Albon "Buddy" Woods is the printing and photography instructor at Clarke Central High School in Athens, Georgia. He had just begun experimenting with desktop publishing when the author of this textbook called him in November 1988 to ask him to publish, on a tight schedule, a computer lab manual. Although Buddy had never published anything as complex as a lab manual, he agreed to give it a try. Using an IBM compatible PC, laser printer, and Ventura desktop publishing package, he and the author were able to convert word processing text and screen-captured graphics into a complete product by the following February.

Since that first success with desktop publishing, Buddy has expanded his operation to produce several books for the same publisher, including two additional versions of the lab manual, two versions of a programming book, and the software tutorial section of another book.

With the money the school earned from these projects, Buddy expanded Clarke Central High's computer facilities: It now has four i486-based PCs, all with large, high-resolution monitors. In addition, the school now has three laser printers, one that produces output equal to that of a commercial typesetting machine; two scanners; optical character reading (OCR) software; and an ink jet printer for color output.

With the new equipment, Buddy and his students have completed numerous other jobs, including two family history books, each with over 300 pages and 600 photos; brochures for a local firm; sports brochures; graduation programs; and programs for Black History Week for the school district. Some of his students now use desktop publishing to layout the school newspaper and yearbook. Since the first project, over 200 Clarke Central students have experienced desktop publishing.

When Buddy was asked to comment on desktop publishing, he said, "It's easy to overdesign a project by including too many fonts or design elements. The rule should be 'keep it simple.'"

Source: Interview with author, March 30, 1991. Reprinted with permission of Mr. Albon "Buddy" Woods, Printing & Photography Instructor at Clarke Central High School in Athens, Georgia.

Buddy Woods uses the Ventura desktop publishing package for his work in and out of the classroom.

In our initial discussions of computer usage, we described computers as **symbol processors** capable of storing and manipulating symbols. While computational work is an extremely important aspect of computer use, manipulating characters and creating pictures are growing uses of the computer. In fact, studies have shown that word processing is the number one use of personal computers. On the other hand, generating graphics to represent ideas is fast becoming one of the most exciting uses of computers today. Computer graphics are used extensively for games; animation and special effects in movies; analysis of business, scientific, and engineering data; presentation of ideas to groups; design of industrial and electronic equipment; and artistic purposes. In both word processing and graphics, the computer is helping to facilitate the communication of ideas from the user to other people. And, as discussed in the box, desktop publishing is being used more and more often to combine words and pictures into a professional-quality document that can be printed on a laser printer.

For word processing, graphics, and desktop publishing, we will not discuss the operation of any one package in detail. Instead, we will present the key ideas and functions that are common to all such packages. Tutorials on the use of commercial word processing and graphics packages are presented in separate lab manuals available with this textbook.

WORD PROCESSING PACKAGES

Software packages with names like WordPerfect, WordStar, and Microsoft Word are all examples of word processing packages for personal computers. These and many other **word processing packages** allow the user to define the form of a document, input and modify text using a keyboard, and then print the document.

The four key operations of a word processing package are

- defining the form of the document;
- entering a document from a keyboard;
- editing (modifying) the document;
- printing the document.

Two of the most popular word processing packages are WordPerfect and Microsoft Word.

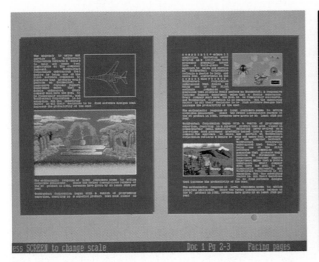

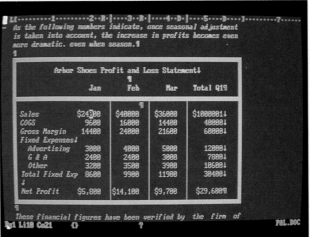

All word processing packages offer these same operations; the deciding factors between packages are most often the ease of using a particular package and the manner in which the operations are carried out. Other differences involve price, specialized features, documentation, and the amount and type of technical support offered after the package is purchased.

Defining the Form of the Document

Usually, before a document can be entered from the keyboard, its form must be defined. This process is known as **formatting,** and it involves entering values for left and right margins, tab stops, vertical spacing (single, double, or other spacing), number of lines per page, and number of characters per inch. For example, a user may format a document to double space each 56-line page, with left and right margins of 1 inch each. If ten characters per inch are selected, then these margins would be ten characters per inch per side.

Once these parameters have been defined, the user usually sees a blank screen, except for a **status line** at the top or bottom of the screen that provides information about the current status of the screen. An example of a status line for WordPerfect 5.1 is shown Figure 10-1. Note that the status shows that this is Document number 1 (of 2) and that the cursor is on Page 1, Line 1, Position 10 (the left margin) of the document.

Another common formatting decision concerns the right margin. With word processing packages, the left margin is always justified; that is, the text always lines up on the left. The user may also decide to have the right margin justified. **Right justification** means that the word processing package adds extra spaces within the lines to make the ends of the lines line up on the right margin. This may not be shown on the screen, but will occur when the document is

Doc 1 Pg 1 Ln 1" Pos 1"

FIGURE 10-1
WordPerfect Status Line

printed. As examples of documents with and without right justification, Figure 10-2 shows the same section of the Gettysburg Address printed under each condition.

A feature that more word processing packages are including is the capability to display the document on the screen in exactly the same form it will have when it is printed. This is known as *What You See Is What You Get* and is referred to as **WYSIWYG.** This is an important feature for onscreen creation of documents because the user can see clearly what the document will look like when it is printed.

Entering Text

For a word processor, as for a typewriter, the text must first be entered from a keyboard. But even as early as the text entry stage, the word processor has a very useful function called *word wrap.* In **word wrap,** the user simply enters text and lets the computer worry about whether there is enough room for a particular word on the current line. If the computer decides that a word will not fit on a line, it moves the word to the next line. The typist needs to use the Enter key only at the end of each paragraph.

Editing Text

The ability to edit (modify) text easily is an important and useful characteristic of a word processing package. **Text editing** in its simplest form means replacing, inserting, or deleting characters from existing text. With most word processors, editing means much more than this. For example, blocks of text can be deleted, copied, or moved to other points in a document, or copied or moved to an entirely different document. The editing function on a word processor also allows the user to search for a string of characters or even to replace that string with another string.

To accomplish the editing operations requires a way of controlling the blinking square of light or underline called the **cursor,** which designates where the computer is expecting text to be entered or deleted. It is also necessary to be able to give the word processor commands to carry out insertion, replacement, or deletion of text; to work with blocks of text; and to search for strings of text.

Cursor Control   Recall from our discussion of keyboards in Chapter 2 that several keys are specifically for cursor control. The **cursor control keys** with Up and Down arrows move the cursor one vertical line at a time; the keys with

FIGURE 10-2
Unjustified and Justified Printed Documents

```
Four score and seven years ago, our
forefathers brought forth on this
continent a new nation, conceived in
liberty, and dedicated to the
proposition that all men are created
equal. We are now engaged in a great
civil war testing whether that
nation, or any nation so conceived,
can long endure.
```

```
Four score and seven years ago, our
forefathers brought forth on this
continent a new nation, conceived in
liberty, and    dedicated to    the
proposition that all men are created
equal. We are now engaged in a great
civil   war   testing   whether   that
nation, or any nation so conceived,
can long endure.
```

Left and Right arrows move it one character at a time in the direction of the arrow. Holding down any of these keys will cause the movement to repeat. Moving the cursor either up or down off the screen results in an action known as **scrolling,** in which new material appears from that direction. The **PgUp** (page up) and **PgDn** (page down) keys provide larger vertical movements and often are used to scroll to a new page of the document or to a new **video page,** which is the amount of text that can be seen on the screen at one time. The effect of the **Home** and **End** keys depends on the word processing package being used. For some word processing packages, the gray plus and minus on the right side of the keyboard can also be used for larger up and down movements.

Entering Commands   The method of entering commands depends greatly on what word processing package is being used. Some packages, such as Word-Perfect, use the function keys—either by themselves or in conjunction with the Ctrl, Shift, and Alt keys—to send commands, while other packages, such as WordStar, use the Ctrl key in conjunction with letter keys. One of the most difficult parts of learning a new word processor is learning the command structure; this is probably one of the reasons that many longtime users appear to be reluctant to change word processors.

Composition houses use specially designed word processing terminals for typesetting documents of all kinds.

Replacement or Insertion of Characters   This is performed in either the **replace mode** or the **insert mode.** In the replace mode, characters that are entered at the cursor location replace or type over the existing characters. In the insert mode, characters entered at the cursor location push existing text to the right. Because of this typeover or pushover action, the replace and insert modes are also referred to as the **typeover** and **pushover modes.** On most word processors, the Ins key is used to *toggle* or switch between these two modes. For example, if the insert mode is on, then the user inserts text by locating the cursor where the insertion is to be made and then entering text, pushing existing text to the right. In this same situation, the user would replace characters at the cursor by first pressing the Ins key and then typing over the existing text. Either mode continues until the Ins key is pressed again.

Deleting Material   To delete material, we place the cursor over the character to be deleted and press the Del (delete) key. If the delete key is held down, characters to the *right* will be pulled under the cursor and deleted. This will continue until the Del key is released. After an insertion or deletion, the text is **reformatted** automatically to account for the removal of text—that is, the text is moved to fill out lines to the margin.

With most word processors, we can also delete text to the *left* of the cursor by using the **Backspace key,** which works like the Del key but in the opposite direction.

Even though we have discussed insertion and deletion as parts of the *editing* process, both of these procedures are also used during the *text entry* process to modify text as it is being entered. The edit operation can be used to correct errors or to add or delete text at any time while material is being entered.

Block-Action Commands   The user can delete a large amount of material simply by holding down the delete command keys. With a large section of text, however, it is easier to perform a block-action command to accomplish this task. In a **block-action command,** the user first defines a block of text. The cursor is then positioned at the beginning of the block and the block-define command is given. The same procedure is performed at the end of the block of text. After a block is defined in this way, a series of actions can be performed on the block, including the deletion of the entire block. We could remove a sentence from a paragraph by defining it as a block and giving the appropriate block-delete command.

Another block-action command is in the text block movement. This process is also called **cut-and-paste,** because using a block-action move is the same as cutting out a block of material from a manuscript and pasting it down somewhere else in the manuscript. For example, a user might decide that a particular paragraph should be located somewhere else in a document. With block-move commands, the paragraph could be lifted from its current location and shifted to the new spot. A block of text can also be copied to other locations in the document or to entirely different documents. A block of text used in many locations is referred to as **boiler plate material,** because it can be used over and over again. The boiler plate is copied to those other locations with a block-action command. Figure 10-3 shows a block being marked and then deleted.

Search   Most word processors can search for the occurrences of a word or some sequence of characters. In this operation, the user defines the desired word

TWP: WHAT A RELIEF

From the time that she began working in the Department of Management Science and Information Technology at the University of Georgia in 1977, one of Linda Keith's primary jobs has been typing highly technical or mathematical papers. Initially, Linda used a typewriter with interchangeable printheads to convert the professors' handwritten manuscripts into a typewritten form. This would often result in the paper going back and forth several times between the writer and Linda for retyping until all of the symbols and equations were represented exactly. Even after several typings, Linda would still have to make liberal use of "whiteout" to correct

T-Cubed reduces the amount of work necessary to produce a final mathematical manuscript.

errors. The introduction of word processors helped to some extent since the text did not have to be retyped each time. However, most word processors did not handle mathematical symbols and equations very well; Linda still had to type those on a typewriter.

Today, Linda uses a technical word processor (TWP) called T-Cubed (produced by TCI Software) to create mathematical and scientific papers. This TWP makes it much easier to type

equations and to include mathematical or scientific symbols, providing the needed symbols or even enabling Linda to create her own. "What You See Is What You Get" onscreen creation of equations allows her to be sure the equation is being entered correctly. And, of course, they can be easily changed when a professor modifies the paper or adds new material.

Source: Interview with the author, 1991.

Revising	T3 Demo		Full	Keyboards	Same as keys		Same as keys
Pg 16:1	Pos 1 29 +0.0		.50 in	Line format	Single Space		H 0 D 0

Benchmark 6:
Allen F. Henry, *Nuclear Reactor Analysis*, MIT Press, Cambridge, Mass, 1982, 495, equation 11.4.19, subequations 4 and 5.

$$iB_r\left[\tilde{a}^n_{k\ell}\right] \equiv \frac{1}{2}\left(h_{n-1} + h_n\right)\int_0^R 2\pi r\,dr\left[\rho^{n*}_k(r)\right]\frac{d}{dr}\left[\Psi^n_\ell(r)\right],$$

$$\left[\mathcal{D}^n_{r,k\ell}\right]^{-1} \equiv \int_0^R 2\pi r\,dr\int_{z_n^- - \frac{1}{2}h_n-1}^{z_n^+ + \frac{1}{2}h_n}\left[\rho^{n*}_k(r)\right]\left[\mathcal{D}^{-1}(r,z)\right]\left[\rho^n_\ell(r)\right],$$

Benchmark 7:
E. I. Guendelman and Z. M. Radulovic, "Infrared Divergence in Three-Dimensi Gauge Theories", *Physical Review. D (Particles and Fields)*, American Physic 30, No 6, 15 Sept 1984, page 1347, Figure 13.

This benchmark requires three symbols used in the Feynman diagrams which are not supplied with the standard release system. However, you can use the T³ font edi these symbols very quickly.

11:41 am ⬜⬜⬜⬜⬜ ACN3

and then enters the appropriate command to initiate the search. When the defined word is found, the computer positions the cursor over the word and waits for user action. An extension of this process is the **search and replace** operations, in which the user defines both the object of the search and a replacement word. A search and replace operation is commonly used to find misspelled words in a document and to replace them with the correct words. For example, if a user suspects that the word *compiler* has been spelled *compilor* throughout a document, the simple procedure of the search and replace operation could be used to correct this error. The object of the search is the word *compilor,* and the replacement word is *compiler.*

Most word processors can perform a **wildcard search,** which locates a word when only part of the word is known. For example, assume that both *insure* and *ensure* are used in a document and that the user wishes to search for both

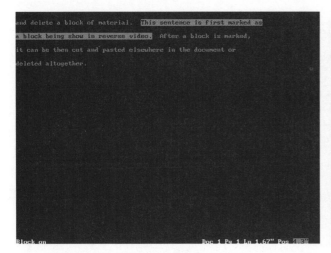
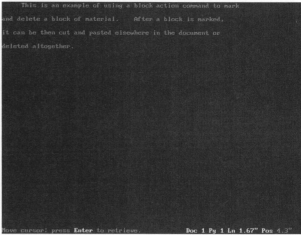

FIGURE 10-3
Block-Action Command to
Delete Material

of these words. The user substitutes a special character, such as *?,* for the first letter. The computer would then search for *?nsure* to find all occurrences of both *insure* and *ensure.*

The insertion, deletion, block movement or copy, and search and replace operations make the editing function a useful part of word processing. Editing really sets a word processor apart from a typewriter.

Other Text Entry and Editing Operations

In addition to the text entry and editing operations discussed so far, most word processors can perform many operations, including centering, boldfacing or underlining text, and indenting entire paragraphs. It is also possible to include subscripts, superscripts, headers or footers, and footnotes in the document and to paginate it automatically.

Centering allows the user to center a line of text between the margins as it is being entered or after it has been entered. A good example of WYSIWYG is the display of **boldfaced** or <u>underlined</u> words on the screen. Many word processors are being written to work under Windows to take advantage of its WYSIWYG capabilities. Windows word processors can show different types and sizes of fonts as well as graphics on the screen. Figure 10-4 shows WYSIWYG in one such Windows word processor.

In **paragraph indentation,** one or both margins of a paragraph can be indented. This feature is useful for documents in which long quotations must be indented but changing the margins for each quotation would be awkward. With technical or mathematical papers, it is important to be able to include subscripts (S_1) or superscripts (2^{10}) in the document to create equations and mathematical or chemical formulas. Inclusion of **headers** or **footers** (text that is displayed at the top or bottom of each page) is an important feature when copyright notices or other information must be included on each page of the text.

For writers of research papers, the capability of a word processor to handle the numbering of **footnotes** for references is very useful. When the paper is printed, the package also allocates the proper spacing at the bottom of the page for the footnotes cited on that particular page. An especially useful footnoting

FIGURE 10-4
WYSIWYG Word Processing
under Windows 3.0

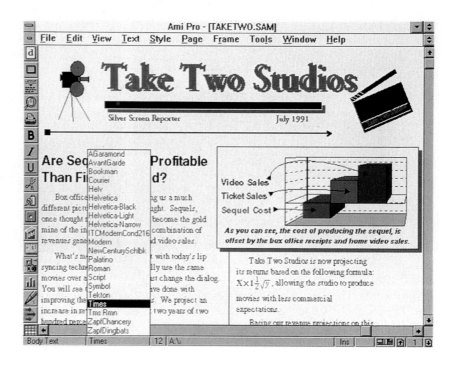

feature is the capability of the word processor to renumber footnotes when new references are added.

Automatic pagination of documents allows the user to include a page number automatically on each page of the text. Most packages will allow the user to select the position of the number on the page and the type of number (arabic or roman) to be used.

Saving and Printing a Document

Once a document has been formatted, entered, and edited, the next steps are to save the document to secondary storage and then print it. It is always a good idea to save the document first—before printing it—so that if a problem occurs during the printing process the document is still saved on secondary storage. In fact, it is a good idea to save the document at several points during the document creation process.

Printing requires a special type of software known as a printer driver. A **printer driver** converts the special characters that the word processing software has inserted in the document—for underlining, boldface, subscripts, and so on—into instructions that the printer can use. For some word processors, these **printer codes** show up on the screen next to the plain text; in others, the material itself will actually appear boldfaced, underlined, or subscripted on the screen. While many printers need specific drivers, others are able to use drivers written for one or the other of the two most popular types of printers—Epson or IBM. Word processing software usually comes with a driver for these two types of printers as well as drivers for various other types of printers. Before printing a document, the user selects a printer driver. Usually this selection needs to be done only once, and the same driver will work for all future documents. Figure 10-5 shows the printer codes for a document in WordPerfect 5.1.

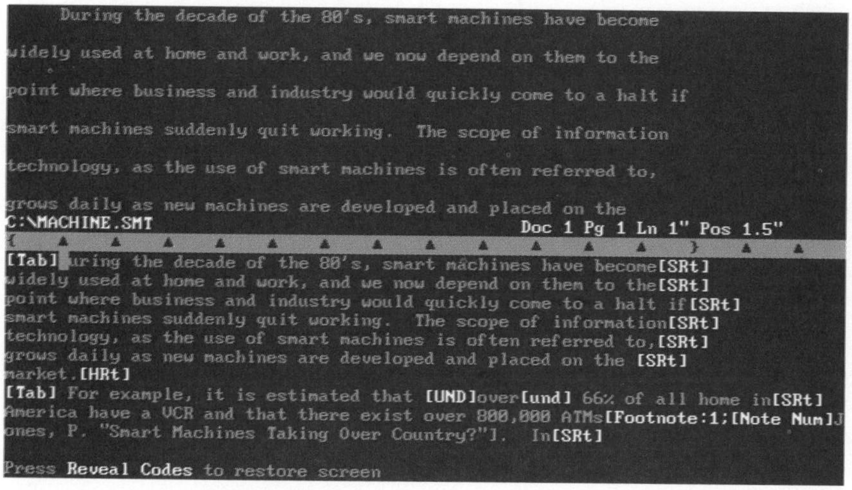

FIGURE 10-5
Printer Codes in WordPerfect 5.1

Another feature of word processing packages relating to printing is the use of print spoolers. A **print spooler** enables the user to print one document while working on another. This software uses the slices of time between keystrokes to have the CPU print the document. This is a very useful feature when several documents (letters, reports, and so on) are being prepared at the same time.

Other Operations

In addition to text entry, editing, formatting, and printing, there are many special features available on most popular word processors. Among the more popular of these are a speller and thesaurus, mail-merge, outlining, document translation, and macros. A **speller** checks the spelling in a document by consulting an electronic dictionary of commonly used words and alerting the user when a word is entered that is not in the dictionary. Words may not need to be changed—for example, if they are personal names or technical terms—and it is usually possible to add special words to the dictionary. Figure 10-6 shows the speller for WordPerfect in operation. In this case, it has highlighted the word *thse* as possibly being misspelled and has provided a suggested correction.

One problem with depending too much on a speller to find misspelled words in a document is that the speller will *not* find words that are spelled incorrectly in the context in which they are used. For example, if *their* is used when the correct word is *there,* the speller will not recognize the error. For this reason, a speller should never be used as the sole proofreader of any document.

An electronic **thesaurus** provides synonyms and, possibly, antonyms for specified words. Unlike the speller, the thesaurus usually requires that the user select a word for which synonyms and antonyms are desired before invoking the thesaurus. Figure 10-7 shows the thesaurus for WordPerfect providing synonyms for the word *fool.*

> **The word processor with language, spelling, and grammar checkers became a way to make communications more personal and more effective.**
>
> *Camilo Wilson, chairman and CEO, Lifetree Software*
>
> Quoted in "View from the Top," *Personal Computing,* October 1989, p. 260.

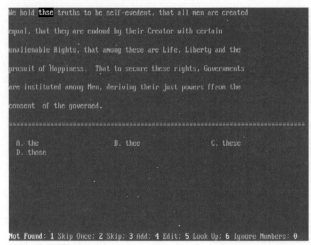

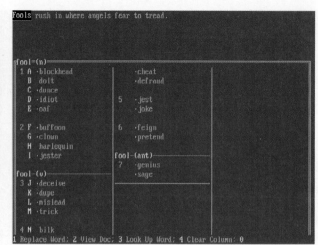

FIGURE 10-6 (left)
Word Processing Speller

FIGURE 10-7 (right)
Word Processing Thesaurus

Mail-merge is a function that allows a word processor to be used to prepare form letters. The letter is prepared in the same manner as any other document, except that the inside address and salutation are left blank. The names and addresses are then entered into another file, one after the other. Upon a command from the user, the two files are merged with a name and address being added to each letter as it is printed.

Since most writers do an outline before beginning the actual writing of a document, some word processing packages now include an **outline processor.** The outline processor helps the user plan the project by automatically numbering the various levels of the outline.

Another useful feature of a word processor is the **document translation** function that converts documents from other word processing packages. For example, WordPerfect can convert WordStar files into a WordPerfect format.

In word processing packages, a **macro** is a sequence of commonly used keystrokes to which the user assigns a name. The computer then executes the keystroke sequence whenever the user invokes the macro. For example, the sequence of keystrokes to save a document and exit the package might be named Alt-S and would be executed anytime the user presses the Alt and S keys simultaneously.

SELECTING A WORD PROCESSOR

Word processing software comes in many different forms, ranging from very complex to fairly simple and likewise varying in price from $500 down to less than $100. To select the package that fits your needs you must decide what the package will be used for, what type of computer it will be used on, and how much money you can spend. Keep in mind that word processing is probably the most personal of all types of PC software, with no one package defining the market. For this reason, you can choose from a wide variety of packages. Also, if you ask two friends who use different packages to tell you which is better, you will probably receive two different answers. Word processor users are often very loyal to "their" package and will advise you to use the same one they do. For this reason, it is extremely important to define your needs and try out the packages that appear to fit your criteria. By doing this rather than buying a best-seller or one that is recommended by a friend, you have a better chance of being satisfied with your purchase.

If you are going to be doing math or scientific word processing, then you need to purchase a specialized word processor like the one discussed in the box on page 290. If you wish to combine word processing with desktop publishing, then you should look for a package that will allow you to incorporate graphics as well as multiple fonts and type sizes. Finally, if you have no special needs, then almost any package may be adequate.

Be sure that your computer has the amount of memory needed for a particular package. If you are going to be using a WYSIWYG-oriented package, be sure you have the correct type of video system. Also, while in some cases there are different versions of the same package for the Apple Macintosh and IBM compatible computers, they are not the same package and cannot be switched between machines. Finally, note that although price is not always a good indicator of the features that are available with the package, less costly packages usually cannot afford the same level of online telephone help as may be available with more expensive packages such as WordPerfect. Table 10-1 shows some popular word processors for both the Apple Macintosh and IBM compatible computers.

In selecting a word processor or any other personal computer software, it is extremely important that you try out the package before purchasing it. Insist upon being able to sit down with the software at a computer of the type that you will be using and try sample applications of your choosing. To help in the selection of software packages (and hardware, too), there are numerous computer magazines that review software and hardware. Some of the magazines are directed toward a particular type of computer; others are more general. Table 10-2 lists some of the more popular computer magazines and the particular computer, if any, toward which each magazine is directed. Virtually every piece of software available on the market has been or will be reviewed in at least one of these magazines. These reviews can help a potential buyer determine whether a particular package fits his or her needs.

There also exist various surveys of software that keep track of the top-selling packages. These surveys appear weekly and monthly in newspapers and computer magazines and are useful in determining the most popular software.

On the Apple Macintosh, word processing has always been able to include graphics and various fonts and to show the result on the screen.

TABLE 10-1
Popular Word Processing Packages

Package	Machine	List Price	Use
WordPerfect	IBM	$495	General/DTP
Microsoft Word	IBM	495	General/DTP
WordStar	IBM	495	General
Ami Pro	IBM/Windows	N/A	General/DTP
PC-Write	IBM	$ 89	General
EXP	IBM	299	Technical
Lotus Manuscript	IBM	495	Technical
Mac WordPerfect	Mac	395	General
Microsoft Word	Mac	395	General/DTP

TABLE 10-2
Computer Magazines

Magazine	Computer Orientation
Byte	General
Creative Computing	General
InfoWorld	General
MacWeek	Apple Macintosh
MacWorld	Apple Macintosh
PC/Computing	General
PC Magazine	IBM and compatibles
PC Week	IBM and compatibles
PC World	IBM and compatibles

Remember, though, that a popular software package may not suit your needs, so don't select software on the basis of its popularity.

GRAPHICS PACKAGES

If word processing packages are used to communicate ideas via words, then **graphics packages** communicate ideas via pictures. These pictures are designed by the computer software to present material in a form that is easy to understand and easy to work with. For example, graphics on supercomputers have been used to represent such diverse physical relationships as the amount of light coming from parts of a distant galaxy, to the effect of a steam pipe breaking within a nuclear power plant, to the reconstruction of a tornado to reveal unexpected downdrafts. The combination of color, three-dimensional representations, and motion can reveal the effect of changes in data over time in a way that would otherwise not be possible. In these cases, a supercomputer is needed to handle the mass of data and the calculations that must be made to represent the relationships as a picture. However, mainframes and personal computers can be used for similar graphic analyses that require less computational effort.

Graphics packages can also be used for artistic purposes, to produce dramatic and beautiful pictures. Graphics is a very exciting area in computers, with new and different uses emerging almost every day. For example, many of the special effects in *Terminator 2: Judgment Day* were created using computer graphics. Similarly, graphics are being used to analyze baseball pitches on TV.

Types of Graphics

There are four types of graphics packages currently in use on both mainframes and personal computers: analysis graphics, presentation graphics, computer-aided design (CAD), and paint packages. **Analysis graphics** are used to help analyze data to determine if patterns exist or to gain a better understanding of

Computer graphics in films are not a novelty anymore.

Nancy St. John, executive producer at Industrial Light and Magic

Quoted in "Moviemaking Abracadabra," *Computerworld*, June 25, 1990, p. 39.

With high-resolution monitors, it is possible to use graphics in such areas of scientific research as genetics, microbiology, and medicine. It is also possible to design automobiles, tools, and space shuttles using computer graphics.

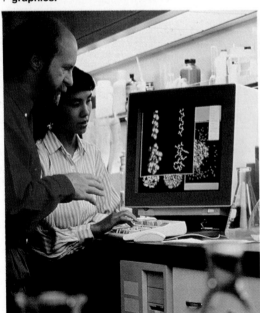

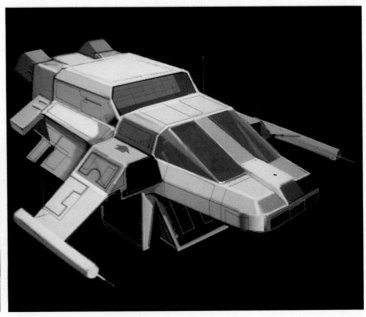

A.D.A.M.: A COMPUTERIZED ANATOMY BOOK

One of the most important courses in any medical program is human anatomy—the structure of the human body. Historically, students have learned anatomy through textbooks, slides, and cadavers. However, now a new software package called A.D.A.M.—Animated Dissection of Anatomy for Medicine—may replace all these learning tools. With A.D.A.M., the student can actually dissect, without a cadaver, any part of the human body without worrying about making mistakes.

The A.D.A.M. program uses an optical disk that stores information about the human body. The disk generates high-resolution graphics of various parts of the human body, and the graphics are displayed on either an Apple Macintosh or IBM compatible PC. Users can choose to watch a simulation of a complete pathology example or an unlimited number of dissectible views and animations of common surgeries. It is possible for students to peel the skin and muscles, layer by layer, to see deep within the body or to use the mouse as a scalpel to simulate an incision into the body. With a color printer, users can prepare a printed version of the screen.

In addition to the obvious uses of A.D.A.M. for medical students, other groups are also interested in it. For example, insurance companies have shown an interest in this system, because it allows a physician to "walk" a patient through an entire operation. That way, the patient has a better understanding of the procedure and, therefore, is less likely to initiate a lawsuit against the doctor or hospital after the surgery. Similarly, companies that make medical items, such as artificial hip joints, may wish to equip their salespeople with this system to demonstrate to the physician–consumer how the product works.

Source: Bill Husted, "New Computer Program Handles Medical Needs," *Atlanta Journal-Constitution*, May 30, 1991, p. G2.

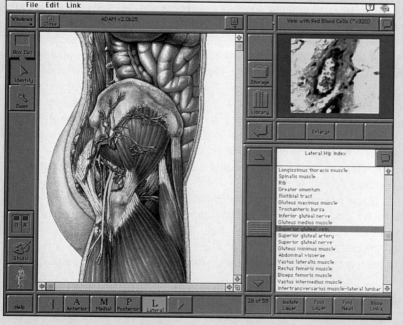

Animated Dissection of Anatomy for Medicine (A.D.A.M.) software eliminates some of the need for animal dissections.

the data. The results of an analysis graphics package are primarily charts and diagrams and usually are not meant to be used for presentations. When the impact on the audience is important, **presentation graphics** are used. These are usually full-color graphics, sometimes in three dimensions, that are meant to vividly portray an idea to an audience. The use of presentation graphics is growing rapidly—up to 36 percent in 1990 alone—as more organizations find ways to use them. If the object is to use graphics to design a building or an electronic or mechanical device, then **computer-aided design (CAD)** is needed. Using CAD, an engineer, architect, or draftsman can greatly reduce the time necessary to develop a blueprint for an electronic or structural design. Finally, if the objective is to use a computer for artistic purposes, then a **paint package** is needed. With such a package, the user may pick a type of "brush," choose colors from a "palette," and then use the cursor to draw on the screen.

We will discuss each of these types of packages in some detail. However, first we will explain how graphics are created and discuss the importance of hardware in graphics.

Understanding Graphics

To understand how graphics work, look at a picture in a newspaper. These *half-tone* pictures are made up of black dots on a white background. The black areas are completely covered with dots, and the gray areas are a mixture of dots and white background. Graphics on a computer screen work exactly like the half-tone picture in the newspaper except that the background is usually dark and the dots are light colored. Each dot corresponds to a **pixel** or picture element on the screen that is turned either on or off. The letters of the alphabet, digits, punctuation marks, and graphics symbols all are formed this way. Figure 10-8 demonstrates how the letter A and a rectangle can be portrayed on the screen using pixels.

If the dots are controlled individually, the graphics are said to be **bit-mapped,** and the on–off condition of each pixel corresponds to the on–off condition of a bit in internal memory. The number of dots on a screen determines the **resolution** of the screen, with the lowest resolution screens in use today having 320 pixels horizontally and 200 pixels vertically. High-resolution monitors have 1,024 horizontal pixels and 768 vertical pixels. High resolution becomes important when the user attempts to draw complex figures. Without high resolution, figures may be ragged and have a "stair-step appearance" on the screen.

If the dots on the screen are controlled as a group, the graphics are called **character graphics.** Special symbols are combined to create bar charts, borders around the screen, boxes, and the like. However, character graphics cannot be used to create any type of picture. The symbols used in character graphics correspond to various ASCII characters, as shown in Figure 10-9. Some early com-

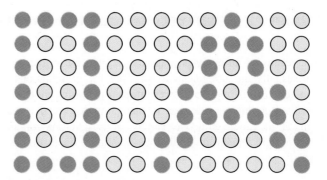

FIGURE 10-8
Dot Representation

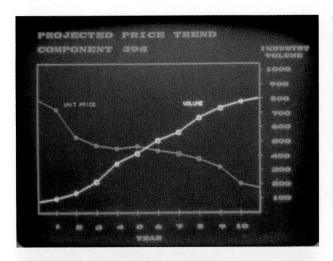

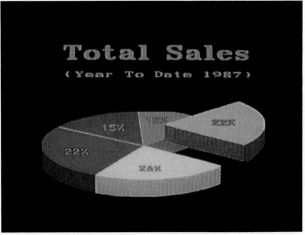

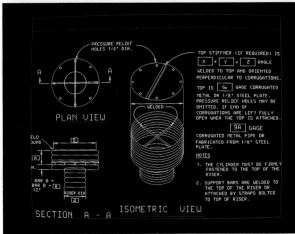

(Top left) When researchers are studying trends, they find that line graphs are a highly practical, informative type of analysis graphics. (Top right) "Exploded" pie graphs in multiple colors are often used in presentation graphics. (Bottom left) Computer-aided design (CAD) is commonly used to create engineering designs. (Bottom right) Paint packages can be used to create elaborate works of art.

puters could work only with character graphics, but today virtually all computers can work with both types of graphics. Character graphics are often used to create boxes and borders in software packages.

The Hardware Connection

Of all the packages commonly used on personal computers, graphics packages are most dependent upon hardware. This is true at both the mainframe and personal computer levels. With mainframes, very powerful graphics chips are used to generate the desired picture. Quite often, special graphics workstations using graphics chips and extremely high-resolution monitors are connected to mainframes.

For personal computers, different chips are more or less suited to displaying graphics. For example, the Motorola 68000 series of chips used by the Apple Macintosh, Commodore Amiga, and NeXT series of computers supports very-high-resolution graphics, while the Intel 8088 and 80xxx chips used in IBM compatible computers, including the PS/2 line, can support only character graphics, unless additional graphics hardware is added.

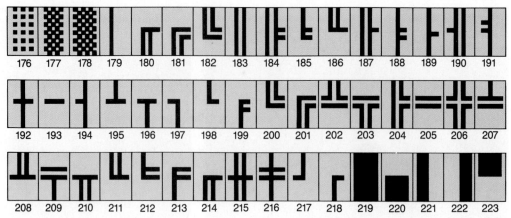

| 176 | 177 | 178 | 179 | 180 | 181 | 182 | 183 | 184 | 185 | 186 | 187 | 188 | 189 | 190 | 191 |

| 192 | 193 | 194 | 195 | 196 | 197 | 198 | 199 | 200 | 201 | 202 | 203 | 204 | 205 | 206 | 207 |

| 208 | 209 | 210 | 211 | 212 | 213 | 214 | 215 | 216 | 217 | 218 | 219 | 220 | 221 | 222 | 223 |

FIGURE 10-9
Character Graphics Symbols

For IBM compatible computers based on the Intel 8088 and 80xxx chips (80286, 80386, and i486) to work with bit-mapped graphics, an additional piece of hardware is needed. This is a **graphics adapter board,** which supports color and graphics and is installed in one of the slots in the back of an IBM compatible PC. To understand the hardware–graphics relationship on the PCs that use the Intel chips, we need to look at five commonly used options: the Hercules Graphics Card and monochrome display, the Color/Graphics Adapter (CGA) and CGA display, the Enhanced Graphics Adapter (EGA) and EGA display, and the Video Graphics Array (VGA) and VGA or multiscanning display, and the Super VGA system.

The Apple Macintosh has long been used to create outstanding graphics.

A photograph has been digitized on the Macintosh and displayed on the screen.

When the original IBM PC was introduced in 1981, it was sold with a text-only monochrome (single-color) monitor. Many users still prefer this type of monitor because of the high-quality text it supports, but, without an add-in board, it cannot show even monochrome bit-mapped graphics. The needed add-in board, called a **Hercules Graphics Card,** was introduced in 1982 and enables the display of high-resolution (720 × 348 pixels) monochrome graphics on the monochrome monitor.

The first board that was developed to display color graphics was the **Color/Graphics Adapter (CGA),** which, when combined with an RGB color monitor, would show low-resolution graphics (320 × 200 pixels) in four onscreen colors. In response to a need for higher-resolution graphics and more colors, the **Enhanced Graphics Adapter (EGA)** was created in 1984. When this board is combined with an Enhanced Color Display monitor, medium-resolution graphics (640 × 350 pixels) can be shown in 16 onscreen colors.

Introduced at the same time as the PS/2 line of IBM computer in 1987, the **Video Graphics Array (VGA)** differs from previous graphics adapters in several ways. First, instead of being digital like all previous video systems, VGA is analog like a television screen. This allows the VGA system to show up to 32 shades of 8 colors, whereas EGA could show only bright and soft shading

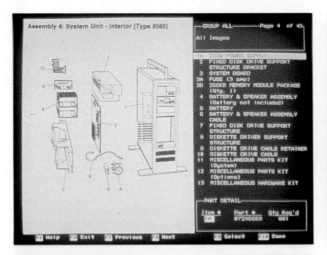

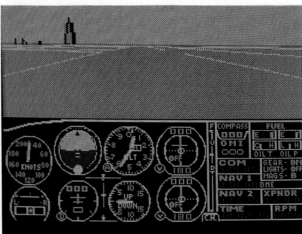

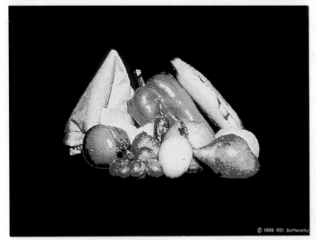

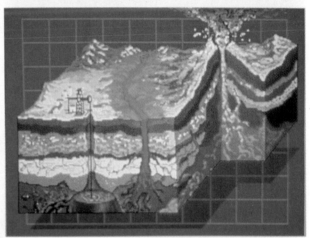

(Top left) Hercules systems can display high-resolution graphics in one color. (Top right) CGA video systems can display medium-resolution graphics in four colors. (Bottom left) EGA video systems can display high-resolution graphics in up to 16 colors. (Bottom right) VGA video systems can display high-resolution graphics in up to 256 colors.

XGA, the very latest video system from IBM, surpasses even the VGA in high-quality resolution and number of colors.

of its 16 colors. Second, the resolution is increased up to 640 × 480, offering high-quality text and graphics. A VGA board can use a VGA analog monitor, or a **multiscanning monitor** that can show display analog VGA, or any of the digital graphics adapters.

The newest and most expensive video system for personal computers is the **Super VGA system,** or XGA on IBM systems. This system provides a resolution of 1,024 × 768 pixels and 262,000 colors from which to choose to display 256 colors on the screen. Figure 10-10 shows the letter R as it is represented by the various video systems.

Selection of the appropriate graphics adapter and monitor for your purposes will be discussed in more detail in the Guide to Buying a PC, pages 411–429, at the end of Chapter 13.

As mentioned earlier, there are four types of graphics packages: analysis graphics, presentation graphics, CAD, and paint packages. All four types are available for both mainframe and personal computers, but we will consider in detail only those that are available on the personal computer. Graphics workstations connected to mainframes and minicomputers provide higher-quality graphics than do PCs, but they are also much more expensive.

> **[Super VGA] will be the next standard for the high-end computer market, and eventually the standard for all graphics applications.**
>
> *Michael Castro,*
> *senior industry analyst for*
> *Dataquest, Inc.*
>
> Quoted in "IBM Touts XGA as New High-End Graphics Standard," *PC Week,* November 5, 1990, p. 8.

A CLOSER LOOK AT GRAPHICS PACKAGES

FIGURE 10-10
Examples of Video Systems

Souce: From *PC/Computing*, October 1989, p. 225. Diagrams by Mary Ellen Zawatski.

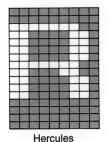

Hercules

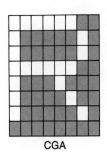

CGA

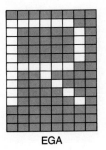

EGA

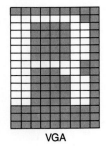

VGA

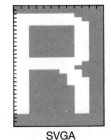

SVGA

Analysis Graphics

Analysis graphics are those that help a decision maker understand or analyze the data. Since the computer is capable of handling large amounts of numerical data and the human mind is able to conceptualize pictures better than numbers, analysis graphics help us understand the numerical data. Thousands of pages of numerical data can be reduced to a single picture to reveal relationships that might otherwise go unnoticed.

On personal computers, the emphasis for analysis graphics has been in business, so they are also often referred to as **business graphics.** Common uses include pictorial representations of sales, budgets, or expenses, or comparisons either over time or between different groups at the same time. A personal computer is well suited for this type of graphics because of its immediate access.

Most analysis graphics are created with spreadsheet packages like Lotus 1-2-3. These graphics include bar graphs, stacked-bar graphs, pie graphs, scatter diagrams, and line graphs.

A **bar graph** uses vertical or horizontal bars to compare quantities; the length or height of the bar represents each quantity. For example, monthly regional sales could be compared using a bar graph. **Stacked-bar graphs** place multiple quantities on the same bar.

A **pie graph** can be used to compare parts of some overall quantity (budget, income, etc.), for example, regional sales for a year, with the regions divided into slices proportional to their sales. A **scatter diagram** can be used to compare two groups of data, for example, the number of salespeople in each region compared to the sales in that region. Finally, a **line graph** can be used to show trends over time, for example, to show the trend of total sales over the last five years. The incline or decline of each line segment demonstrates the change in values on the vertical axis for each unit change on the horizontal axis. Figure 10-11 shows a Lotus 1-2-3 spreadsheet along with a bar chart created

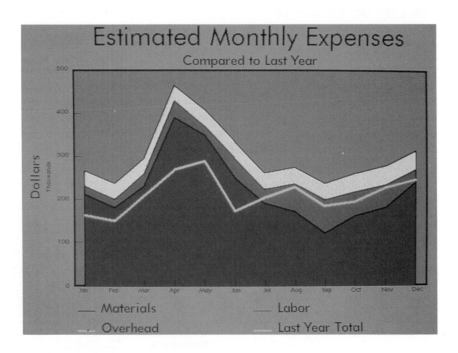

Lotus 1-2-3 Release 3.0 can display graphics generated from data in the spreadsheet.

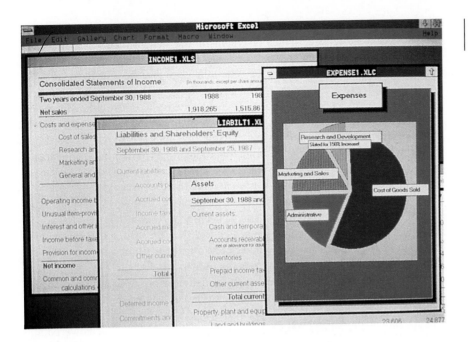

Microsoft Excel can display graphics simultaneously with the spreadsheet data.

from this spreadsheet. Note the use of color to differentiate parts of the graph. Each release of a new spreadsheet seems to bring better, more colorful graphs, including three-dimensional capabilities.

Presentation Graphics

While analysis graphics are used to help the user understand data, presentation graphics are used to present results to others. Consequently, they must have a much more "professional" look to deliver the message with a "punch." The actual graphs used in presentation graphics may include those used in analysis graphics, but they are much more elaborate: They use more colors to add emphasis to key points in the graph, and three-dimensional graphs are frequently used

FIGURE 10-11
Spreadsheet (left) and Analysis Graphics (right)

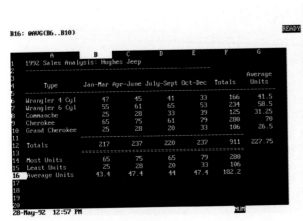

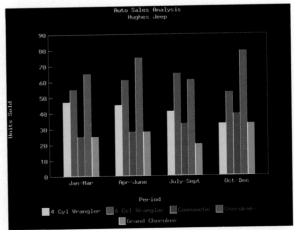

to compare more than two variables or to add depth to a picture. Another strategy is to combine different types of graphs on the same screen.

Using a presentation software package to create a slide or overhead presentation can dramatically reduce the time it takes to prepare a well-thought-out presentation. Some presentation software now allows each graphic to be handled as if it were part of a series of slides or makes it easy to create reference notes about each slide as it is prepared. This software can be divided into three types: charting, diagramming, and drawing. A **charting package** shows the relationship between sets of numerical information. Many times these packages generate enhanced graphics from the information on a spreadsheet. Figure 10-12 shows a pie chart created by Charisma, a presentation charting package.

A **diagramming package** works with shapes to graphically display a set of facts, such as organizational charts, schedules, or office layouts. Usually a series of shapes is assembled on the screen and then the size, location, and orientation of these shapes are manipulated. The third type of presentation package is the **drawing package,** which allows the user to add lines to the shapes, usually with a mouse as an input device. It is also possible to add motion to the output from a presentation package to achieve some degree of animation if the output is being shown on monitor. Popular presentation software packages include Harvard Graphics, Micrografx's Charisma, Freelance, and Powerpoint.

While a black-and-white dot matrix or laser printer is usually sufficient for hard copy of analysis graphics, a jet printer, a laser printer, or 35mm slides are needed to obtain a hard copy for presentation graphics. A color ink-jet printer uses different colored inks that are "shot" on the page to form the multicolored graph. Color laser printers are replacing black toner with multicolors.

The most common method of producing 35mm slides of a screen image is to "capture" the image on disk using special software and then have the image converted to film or slides by a company specializing in that technology. These service bureaus can also produce hard copy of the screen. Many of the screen shots in this textbook were produced using this technology.

Computer-Aided Design

CAD (for computer-aided design) has been in use on mainframes and minicomputers since the 1960s for design of airplanes, automobiles, semiconductor chips,

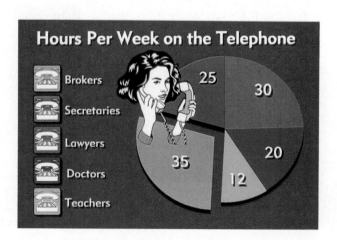

FIGURE 10-12
Presentation Graphics

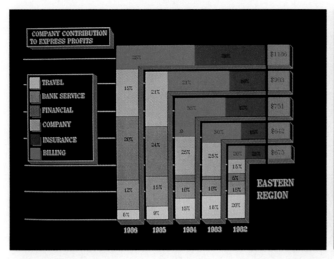

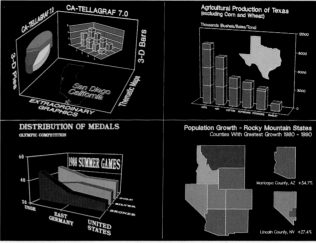

Both PCs (left) and mainframes (right) can be used to generate interesting presentation graphics.

buildings, and the like. With CAD, an engineer or designer can look at a particular design in detail or from a different angle. Frequently, a light pen is used to point to the specific part of the design that is to be enlarged or rotated. Special large screens are often used with CAD to allow the designer to see every detail of the object he or she is working with. Up until 1984, most CAD packages were used in a mainframe environment and cost in the $100,000 range. Now, as the computing power and storage capacity of PCs have increased, so too have the number and variety of PC CAD programs, with some now costing as little as $500. These lower-priced systems are moving CAD into many new areas. For example, some dentists are now using CAD to help fabricate porcelain fillings. In 1991, $333 million was spent on CAD hardware and software.

With a CAD package, a series of commands enables a designer or an architect to create and manipulate designs based on a series of graphics objects called **primitives** (points, lines, circles, and so on). Once a primitive is selected to be used, the user places it on the screen by using a mouse or other pointing device or by specifying the *X* and *Y* coordinates of the location. While the design may not be drawn a great deal faster with CAD than with paper and pencil, it can be revised much faster with the CAD package. Removing a line, room, or gear from a paper drawing can require redoing the entire picture, but CAD can do it with only a few keystrokes. Objects also can be easily moved, copied, or magnified with CAD, and the dimensions of a drawing can be computed by the computer rather than with a ruler.

The user may also create new designs by drawing with a stylus or **puck** onto a digitizer tablet or may use previously entered designs from a library in secondary storage. A joystick or mouse can also be used to create designs on the screen or to move the cursor to make menu selections. Figure 10-13 shows the use of CAD in an engineering design.

Paint Packages

If you are interested in the beauty that can be created with graphics, then you need a paint package. This type of software allows the user to manipulate pixels to produce freehand or combination freehand and library drawings of various

Both black-and-white and color plotters are used to provide a printed version of CAD graphics.

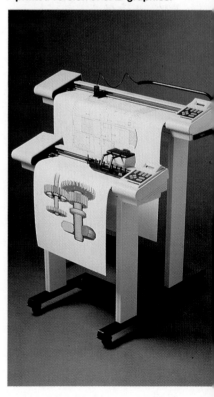

FIGURE 10-13
Use of CAD

shapes, colors, and textures. "Library" shapes are various geometric shapes (circles, squares, etc.) that are available in internal memory. With a paint package, the user has control over the screen through the cursor, and, depending upon the type of graphics available with the hardware, pictures may be "drawn" or "painted" using a mouse or other input device. There are also palettes of colors to choose from or groups of textures to use in "filling" areas on the graph. Shapes can be enlarged, reduced, or distorted as needed to meet the user's needs. The resulting picture can be saved as one of the standard graphic file types such as Paintbrush (.PCX) or Tagged Image Format File (.TIFF). These files can then be imported into documents as needed. With modern personal computers using bit-mapped graphics and a color monitor, the results can be amazing.

The paint package that really started the expansion in this field was MacPaint, for the Apple Macintosh, which was introduced in 1984. Even though it was originally available only in black and white, the results that were obtained with MacPaint were amazing. Other manufacturers soon jumped into this market for both the Macintosh and IBM compatible computers. It is now possible to obtain a paint package in color for almost any computer that can support bit-mapped graphics. Figure 10-14 shows the results of using various paint packages.

DESKTOP PUBLISHING

Possibly the most exciting trend in computers today is what is known as desktop publishing. **Desktop publishing** is the use of personal computer hardware and software to create and publish newsletters, advertisements, magazines, books, and so on, at a fraction of the cost required for commercial typesetting. For example, the computer lab manual that accompanies this textbook was desktop published using a popular package—Ventura Publishing from Xerox.

ENGINEERING WITH CAD

CAD is an important tool of many large industries, but it can also make a small company more profitable. For example, Grecon Manufacturing Co., a small engineering and consulting company, depends heavily on a PC-based CAD system to design automated production operations. In fact, Grecon's use of CAD led to a dramatic change in the way the company does business. Originally, Grecon was a metalworking shop, and the owner, Gregory Roberts, used a CAD system for many purposes: to design parts for production, analyze customer orders and blueprints before turning them over to machinists, and measure the least-cost size of sheet metal blanks required to produce a finished part. Mr. Roberts discovered, however, that his design skills with the CAD system were in sufficient demand for him to specialize in the engineering and design side of the business.

Today, Mr. Roberts designs production devices that automate secondary manufacturing operations. For example, if two metal plates are to be joined by a spring as part of a production process, Mr. Roberts uses CAD to design a production device that will automatically insert the spring. He does this by using CAD to draw the device to scale and then using the computer to check any problems with the design. If necessary, he subcontracts the actual production of the device to a third party. Designing a part correctly the first time, before it goes into production, is crucial to profitably creating a part. As Mr. Roberts puts it, "A mistake in designing the part costs you three times the amount of money—not just double—because you have to spend the time to undo the mistake and then to make the part over again." For Grecon, VersaCAD is a great help in avoiding these costly mistakes.

Source: John Pallatto, "CAD System Makes a Profit," *PC Week*, February 24, 1987, pp. 51 and 57, and author's interview with Mr. Roberts, December 10, 1991.

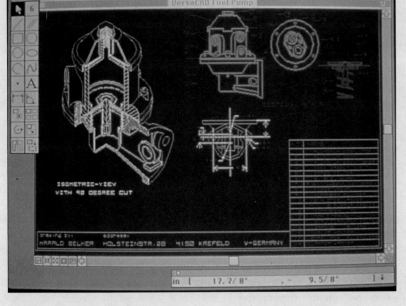

VersaCAD is one of several popular CAD packages that can be used for sophisticated design work on a personal computer.

Just in its infancy, desktop publishing can trace its beginnings to the Apple Macintosh personal computer, which allows text and graphics to be combined on the screen. The Macintosh also can handle proportional spacing like that used in printing this textbook, different type fonts, and various type sizes. In **proportional spacing,** different letters are given different amounts of space. By combining graphics with proportionally spaced text, and then printing the result on the Apple LaserWriter printer, people found they could create professional-looking documents ranging from in-house newsletters to magazines and textbooks. The desktop publishing market has grown significantly over the last five

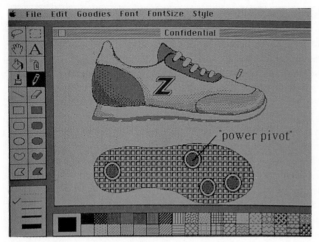
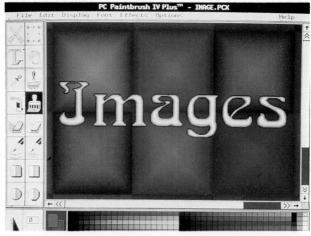
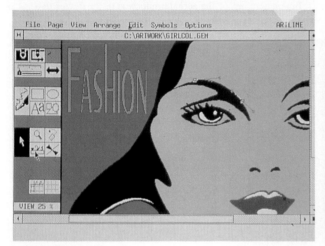

FIGURE 10-14
Some Paint Package Creations.
(Clockwise from top left)
MacPaint; PC Paintbrush IV Plus;
DeluxePaint, enhanced version
on a 20-inch color monitor; GEM
Artline.

years. In 1991 alone, almost $200 million of hardware and software was sold for use in desktop publishing.

The key elements of a desktop publishing system are a personal computer, a word processing package, a graphics package, a desktop publishing package, and a laser printer. It is important to remember that the desktop publishing package must be capable of importing the results of the word processing and graphics packages. An important part of a desktop publishing package is the **page description language (PDL),** with the most widely used page description language being Postscript from Adobe. The PDL is crucial to the success of desktop publishing since it handles the important operation of combining text and graphics into a final page format that fits the needs of the user. Another useful element is **clip art**—previously created art images—that can be imported into a document.

Current Methods

To understand desktop publishing fully, we first need to look at the steps involved in commercially publishing a newsletter or book:

> **Electronic publishing provides not just the artistic freedom we read about, but economic and scheduling freedom as well.**
>
> *John H. Meyer, president,*
> *Ventura Software, Inc.*
>
> Quoted in ''View from the Top,''
> *Personal Computing,* October 1989,
> p. 270.

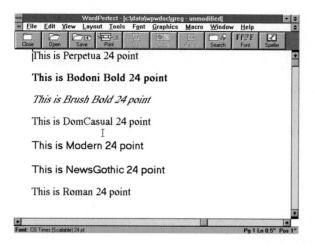

1. The document is created on a typewriter or with a word processing package.
2. A commercial typesetter sets the document in long columns of text called *galleys*.
3. The galleys are proofread and corrected.
4. A production artist "pastes up" the corrected galleys into pages, leaving spaces for photographs and drawings.
5. The completed pages are sent to an offset print shop for final reproduction.

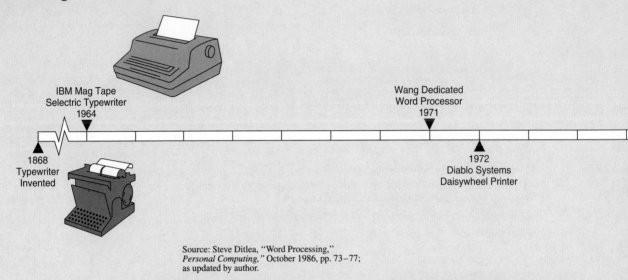

In the final production process, the print shop combines the pages of text and the various graphics elements into a single film overlay. This film is then used to produce a plate for the printing press that will produce the final pages. The cost of the typesetting and paste-up operations alone run anywhere from $50 to $250 per page.

Publishing with a PC

The steps that replace the commercial methods just discussed with a personal computer are these: The user

1. creates a document with a word processor;
2. creates a **stylesheet** with the desktop publishing package. The stylesheet assigns fonts and type sizes to the various elements of the document, defines the margins, and in general specifies the format of the document;
3. flows the text from the word processor into columns on the page;
4. inserts graphic elements;
5. prints the completed pages using a laser printer.

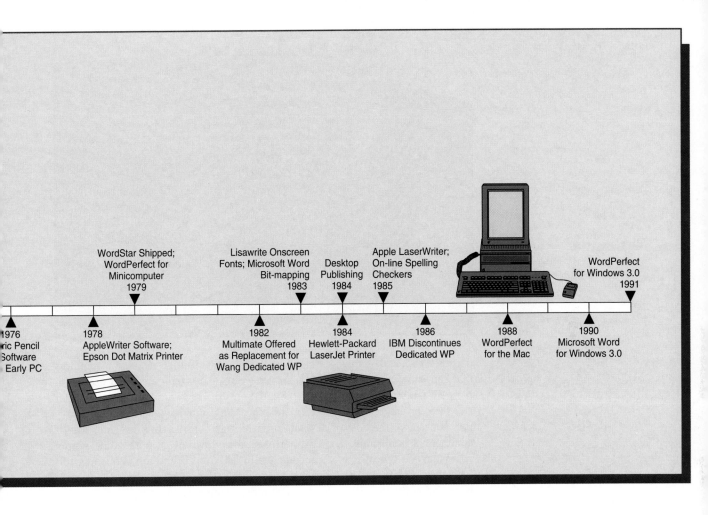

During step 3, holes or **frames** for graphics can be left in the text, and drawings, photographs, or graphic images created with graphics packages can be transferred to the page in the desired shape and orientation. It is for this step that a system that supports WYSIWYG is crucial; otherwise the user cannot see the appearance of the completed page in order to adjust the positioning of various elements and to decide on the size and style of fonts, the italics, boldfacing, headlines, and so on. Figure 10-15 shows a page being electronically "pasted up" on a computer screen.

In step 5, a laser printer is used because it can output text and graphics at 300 dots per inch. While this is less than the 1,200-dots-per-inch quality possible with commercial typesetting equipment, it is acceptable for many purposes. The printed pages can be used as camera-ready copy for creating a plate that will be used in the printing process, or, if only a small number of copies is needed, they can be printed on the laser printer.

In addition to needing a laser printer for output, users need a high-resolution graphics display to distinguish between various fonts and an **image scanner** for converting graphics, drawings, or photographs to a graphic form that can be included with the text. In addition to the popular combination of Apple Macintosh PC and LaserWriter printer, 80386 or i486 IBM compatible computers can be combined with any number of laser printers for desktop publishing

FIGURE 10-15
Example of Desktop Publishing

purposes. Special graphics systems that include very-high-resolution monitors that can show an entire $8\frac{1}{2} \times 11$–inch page on the screen are often used with these systems. Even considering the initial cost of hardware (personal computer and laser printer) and software (word processing, graphics, and page-composition packages), the cost of desktop publishing is considerably less than that of commercial publishing. The cost per page goes down even more as the startup cost is spread out over more documents. In addition, if desktop publishing follows the same road as previous personal computer applications, the cost of hardware and software will come down as more companies enter the market.

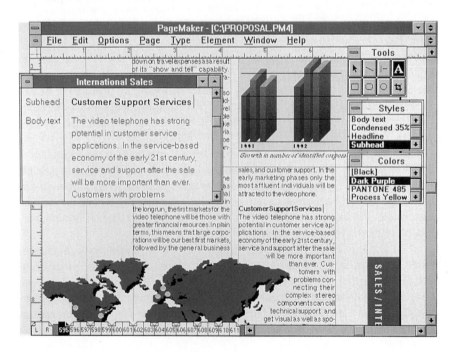

PageMaker software is one of the most popular desktop-publishing packages.

With an appropriate combination of computer hardware and software, image scanner, and laser printer, it is possible to create near-professional-quality documents.

1. Word processing, graphics, and desktop publishing packages help the user communicate ideas to other people.

2. Word processing is divided into formatting the document, entering and editing text, and saving and printing the document.

3. Formatting consists of setting up the margins, the tab stops, the vertical spacing, the right justification, and the number of characters per inch. WYSIWYG means that the text appears on the screen as it will when printed.

4. During text entry, word wrap is a useful feature that speeds the process.

5. During editing, the insert (push-over) mode and replace (type-over) mode can be used to insert or replace text. Deletion and backspacing can be used to delete existing text.

6. Other text entry and editing capabilities include using block-action commands to delete, copy, or move blocks of text; search or search and replace for finding and editing strings of text; center-

ing text; paragraph indention; pagination; and use of macros.

7. Printing consists of converting the electronic form of the document to hard copy, and it requires printer driver software.

8. Other labor-saving devices on a word processor include a speller, a thesaurus, mail-merge, outlining, and macros.

9. Graphics packages use the picture elements, or pixels, to display pictures on the screen. Graphics can be character or bit-mapped, depending on whether or not each pixel is individually controlled.

10. Graphics are hardware dependent: The quality of the graphics displayed depends on the CPU chip used and the add-on hardware included in the system.

11. There are four types of graphics packages: analysis graphics, pre-

sentation graphics, computer-aided design (CAD), and paint.

12. Analysis graphics display the results of data analysis using bar graphs, pie graphs, line graphs, or scatter diagrams.

13. Presentation graphics present material graphically and dramatically to someone besides the user. For personal computers, such graphics include chart, diagramming, and drawing packages.

14. CAD is used to facilitate and improve the design process, while paint packages enable the user to design art on a computer.

15. In desktop publishing, the user creates publishable documents by combining word processing and graphics packages on a personal computer with page composition software and a laser printer.

KEY TERMS

analysis graphics
automatic pagination
Backspace key
bar graph
bit-mapped graphics
block-action command
boiler plate material
boldface
business graphics
centering
character graphics
charting package
clip art
Color/Graphics Adapter (CGA)
computer-aided design (CAD)
cursor
cursor control keys
cut-and-paste
desktop publishing
diagramming package
document translation
drawing package

End key
Enhanced Graphics Adapter (EGA)
footers
footnotes
formatting
frames
graphics adapter board
graphics packages
headers
Hercules Graphics Card
Home key
image scanner
insert mode
line graph
macro
mail-merge
multiscanning monitor
outline processor
page description language (PDL)
paint packages
paragraph indentation
Pg Up key

Pg Dn key
pie graph
pixel
presentation graphics
primitives
printer codes
printer driver
print spooler
proportional spacing
puck
pushover mode
reformatted
replace mode
resolution
right justification
scatter diagrams
scrolling

search and replace
speller
stacked-bar graphs
status line
stylesheet
Super VGA system
symbol processors
text editing
thesaurus
typeover mode
Video Graphics Array (VGA)
video page
wildcard search
word processing packages
word wrap
WYSIWYG

1. How are word processing and graphics packages similar? Dissimilar?
2. What four operations are performed on a word processor? How does word wrap speed text entry?
3. What does WYSIWYG have to do with formatting?
4. What is the difference between the insert mode and the replace mode in editing? Why are they termed *pushover* and *typeover?*
5. What does "cut-and-paste" mean in a word processing package? What does "block-delete" mean?
6. Why are imbedded print commands and printer drivers needed to print a word processing document?
7. Discuss the purposes of spellers, mail-merge, outlining, and macros in a word processor.
8. What is the difference between bit-mapped and character graphics? Which is used the most now?
9. How are graphics depicted on the screen? What is a pixel?
10. What is the hardware connection for graphics packages? What type of graphics will an IBM compatible PC display without additional hardware?
11. List the various types of graphics adapters used on IBM compatible PCs. Which have the lowest resolutions? The highest resolutions?
12. Name the four types of graphics packages. Discuss a commonly used application for one of these.
13. What graphs are used most often for analysis and presentations?
14. Why do we say that desktop publishing combines word processing and graphics into a single application?
15. What hardware and software items are needed for desktop publishing?

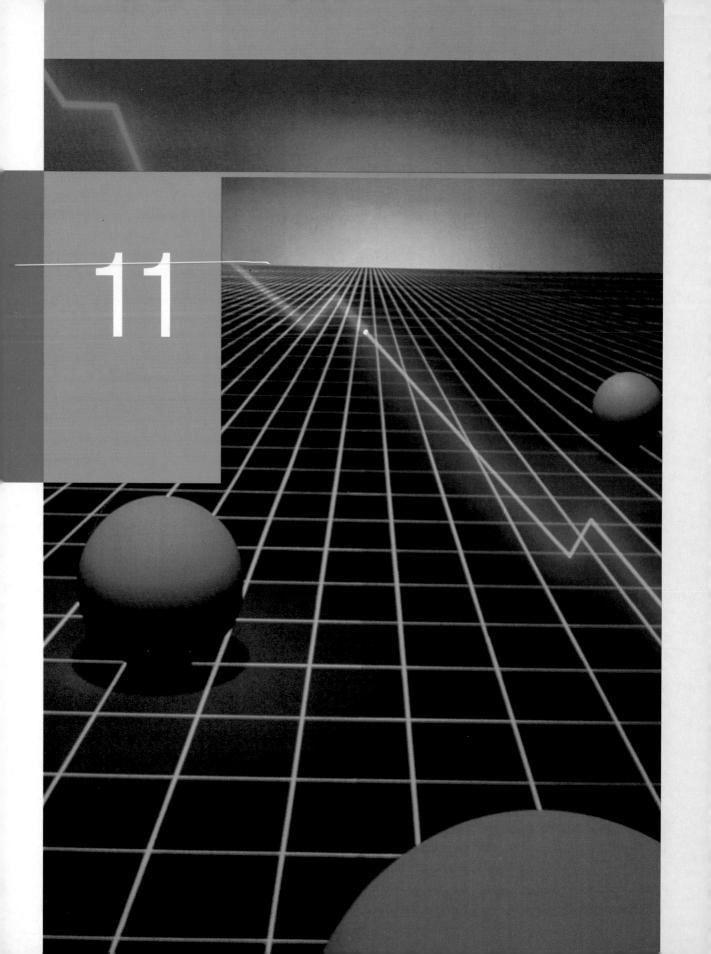

11

Financial Analysis and Accounting Packages

Since financial matters are very important to both individuals and companies, there exist numerous software packages to manage and analyze financial information. These packages can be broadly divided into two types: financial analysis and accounting. Financial analysis packages—or, as they are also called, spreadsheets—allow a user to analyze data in a tabular format and determine what will happen if either the data or the assumptions change. Integrated packages, which combine operations such as data base management and graphics with spreadsheets, are powerful extensions of the spreadsheet. Accounting packages are divided into those for businesses and those for individuals. Business accounting packages are designed to track the financial status of a firm, while personal accounting packages are meant to help manage an individual's finances. Business accounting packages have separate package elements for such operations as general ledger, accounts receivable, accounts payable, payroll, order processing, and inventory control. Personal accounting packages include functions for managing investments, preparing income taxes, and managing personal finances.

STUDY OBJECTIVES

After reading this chapter, you should be able to

- recognize financial software packages for computers;
- explain how a spreadsheet works and describe the types of entries used in a spreadsheet;
- discuss the various functions available on many spreadsheets;
- understand how a spreadsheet can be used for planning budgets and making forecasts;
- discuss the concept of an integrated package as it relates to spreadsheets;
- list and discuss the various types of packages that are available to the individual for managing personal finances;
- explain personal budgeting packages and how they may be used to track an individual's finances;
- understand the purpose of business accounting software and the modules that go into a business accounting package.

SURVIVING IN KUWAIT ON 1-2-3

It was impossible. We had no clue how much food we had or how long it would last.

Dr. Robert Morris, dental consultant to the Kuwaiti government

Quoted in Lynda Radosevich "A Template for Survival," *Lotus,* July 1991, pp. 28–29.

Dr. Robert Morris

When Dr. Robert Morris first heard in August 1990 that Iraq had invaded Kuwait, where he was working as a health care consultant, he assumed that he and other Westerners would be allowed to leave routinely. However, his assumption proved wrong, and he and 20 other non-Kuwaitis found themselves in hiding. His PC and a copy of Lotus 1-2-3 became crucial to the group's survival.

When it became clear to Dr. Morris and the rest of the group that the invading Iraqis were not going to let them leave, they decided to hide in an abandoned apartment house in downtown Kuwait City, from where they formulated security policies to avoid Iraqi army patrols and sought to secure a food source. They contacted Kuwaiti restaurants to obtain bulk food shipments. However, when they had trouble keeping track of the amounts of food and its location, Dr. Morris created a spreadsheet to handle the task.

The spreadsheet tracked the amount and types of food received, the storage location of each type of food, and the average daily consumption required to sustain the group. It also computed the number of days they could exist if no more food was acquired. Much of this information was coded, in case it fell into Iraqi hands. It took Dr. Morris three days to create the spreadsheet but only five minutes to update it each night after the midnight delivery had been distributed.

The food was distributed in amounts and types that provided each person with a nutritionally balanced diet of 1,800 calories per day. The spreadsheet became the focal point of the group as each member came to offer comments or suggestions on a daily basis.

As it turned out, all the food was not needed. Most members of the group were allowed to leave the country in December when Iraq released Western hostages.

Source: Lynda Radosevich, "A Template for Survival," *Lotus,* July 1991, pp. 28–29.

INTRODUCTION TO FINANCIAL PACKAGES

Shortly after computers were first available on a commercial basis, large corporations and institutions discovered that a computer could be very useful for handling finances, since storing numerical data and then quickly adding and subtracting them are natural applications of computers. Initially, only large companies could afford computers—mainframes. As personal computers have become widely available, however, financial management by computer has become possible for small companies and individuals as well.

Financial management software for mainframes and minicomputers has been developed for use by institutions and companies that deal with large amounts of data. On the other hand, there exist financial management software packages for all varieties of computers that both small companies and individuals can use to manage their finances. Software for the various sizes of computers is necessary because of the differences in the needs of users. For example, a mainframe could handle the payroll for a large university, a government agency, or an automotive assembly plant. Toward the other end of the computer use spectrum would be the small, family-run interior decorating store with two part-time employees. In this case, a personal computer with a hard disk could handle the inventory control and accounting needs very easily. Finally, the individual who wishes to use a computer to keep track of finances and tax records would be able to use almost any personal computer on the market today with a disk drive.

Since a financial management software package intended for use on a mainframe is primarily developed for a specific type of mainframe, we will concentrate on the software that is available for the wide range of types and brands of personal computers. There are three broad categories of financial management software, and among the three of them, all the functions listed earlier can be accomplished. The three broad categories of software we will discuss are financial analysis packages (often referred to as spreadsheets), personal financial management packages, and business accounting packages.

A **spreadsheet** can be used for almost any financial management operation, but its greatest applications are in the areas of analysis, budgeting, and forecasting. With a spreadsheet package, it is possible to set up an entire budget or sales forecast and then determine the results of making changes to one or more of the anticipated values. In the box at the beginning of this chapter, a spreadsheet was used to analyze a food "budget" to ensure that the western hostages would have sufficient supplies. A forecast of the future needs of the hostages was a part of the analysis.

Personal financial management packages are aimed at helping the individual keep track of finances. The three major operations carried out by this type

1-2-3 has made the investment business more complex. We analyze a lot more structures.

Henry Ford, vice president, Merchant Banking Group, Bankers Trust Co.

Quoted in "Where 1-2-3 Makes Deals in a Hurry," *Lotus,* June 1989, pp. 52–55.

```
D30: {H13 Bold} U [W11] 32000                                    MENU
Worksheet  Range  Copy  Move  File  Print  Graph  Data  System  Enhance  Quit
Retrieve  Save  Combine  Xtract  Erase  List  Import  Directory  Admin
```

	INCOME	ANNUAL	MONTHLY	%
	Salary #1	$35,000	$2,917	39%
	Bonus #1	0	0	0%
	Salary #2	32,000	2,667	36%
	Bonus #2	4,000	333	5%
	Estimated Stock Options	12,000	1,000	14%
	Dividends	1,400	117	2%
	Interest	625	52	1%
	Tax Refund	1,200	100	1%
	Other: Summer Rental	2,400	200	3%
	Other:			
	TOTAL INCOME	$88,625	$7,386	100%
	EXPENSES	ANNUAL	MONTHLY	%
	Charitable Donations	$700	$58	1%

Personal Budget 1992

26-Mar-92 04:13 PM

Families can use financial software on a personal computer to monitor their investment portfolio.

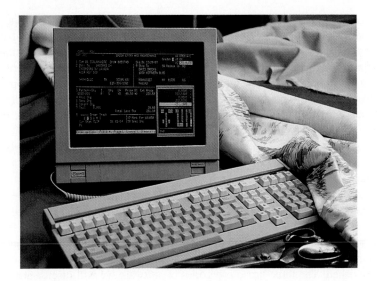

Small businesses have come to depend on personal computers to handle much of their accounting and financial work.

of software are personal accounting (classifying and summarizing all financial transactions during a month), investment analysis, and tax planning. Each of these will be discussed later in this chapter.

A **business accounting package** usually has several modules or software elements, each of which handles a single task involved with tracking the financial health of the firm. Modules for such operations as payroll, accounts receivable, accounts payable, and inventory control are often included. Business accounting packages will be discussed in more detail in a later section of this chapter.

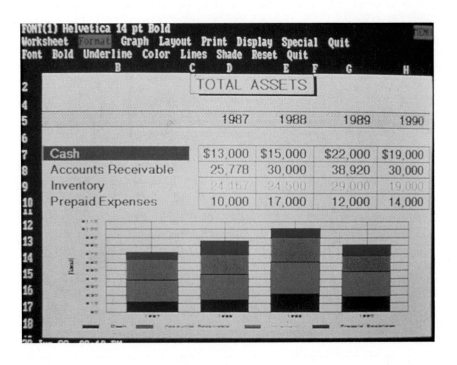

Spreadsheets like Lotus 1-2-3 are used for financial analysis by individuals and by companies of all sizes.

The explosion in the use of personal computer software packages can be traced directly to the introduction in 1979 of VisiCalc, the first spreadsheet for the Apple II computer, developed by a group of Harvard and MIT students. Since that time, numerous packages containing many variations and improvements on VisiCalc have been released. These packages include Lotus 1-2-3, Microsoft Excel, Quattro Pro, PlanPerfect, and SuperCalc[5] for IBM compatible PCs and Microsoft Excel and 1-2-3 for the Apple Macintosh. Spreadsheets are one of the most popular types of computer package in use, with an estimated 3 million packages sold in 1991 alone. Lotus 1-2-3, alone, is the all-time best-selling computer applications package. PC spreadsheet packages have been rewritten to run on minicomputers and mainframes to give the users of these larger machines the machines the capabilities of these packages. Similarly, MS-DOS–based spreadsheet packages are being rewritten to run under the Windows operating environment, as well as on the Macintosh. In addition, a spreadsheet called Improv has been written specifically for the NeXT computer. It takes full advantage of NeXT's graphical nature.

Spreadsheets have also been used for many purposes other than financial analysis. Professors use them to keep electronic gradebooks, and scientists use them to model physical systems, analyze data, and plan processes. Some of the most popular spreadsheet packages combine the spreadsheet with data base and graphical operations that allow users to work with all three at one time. Finally, integrated packages that add word processing and telecommunications to the spreadsheet–data base–graphics combination are becoming increasingly popular.

However, regardless of the name of the package and the operations that have been added to it, the general concept of using a table of numbers to represent budgets, sales forecasts, and so on remains the same. The name *spreadsheet* originated with the accountant's ledger pad, with printed row and column lines. The budget or sales forecast figures were entered in pencil on this "spreadsheet"; whenever a value was changed, all values had to be recalculated by hand. Before discussing the computerized spreadsheet packages, let us consider a manual spreadsheet in more detail, in the following budgeting example.

Jill Bradley is a recent college graduate who has taken a position with a local computer store as a salesperson/consultant. In this position, Jill will receive a salary of $700 per month plus a commission of 6 percent of her gross sales. Out of this combination of salary and commission, payroll taxes and health insurance of $250 per month are deducted to arrive at her "take-home income." The manager has told Jill that most employees have sales of about $10,000 their first month and that the sales volume usually increases by 5 percent per month for the next two months. After the first three months, the rate of increase in sales differs from employee to employee.

Jill's estimates for the first month's income and expense values are shown in Table 11-1. Jill has to pay $300 a month to rent an apartment that she shares with a co-worker. Also, she has bought a new car that carries a monthly payment of $150. While these expenses are **fixed,** in that they do not change from month to month, Jill also has **variable expenses** for food, utilities (electricity and telephone), fuel for her car, and miscellaneous expenses.

Jill also wants to save as much as possible over the next three months to purchase a high-quality compact disk player and speakers. The cost of the CD

TABLE 11-1
Estimated Income and Expense Values

Item	Estimated Value
Commission	$ 600 (0.06 × $10,000)
Salary	$ 700
Net Income	$1,050 ($600 + $700 − $250)
Rent	$ 300
Car Payment	$ 150
Food	$ 250
Utilities	$ 150
Gas	$ 50
Other	$ 100

system is $500, so this is the minimum Jill wants to save over the three months. Summing rent, utilities, food, car payment, gas, and "other" expenses and subtracting this amount from the take-home income gives the amount Jill will be able to save each month. While this sounds complicated in text form, it is very easy to see in tabular form, as shown in Table 11-2. The remainder of our discussion of the functions of a spreadsheet will depend on this case, so be sure you understand it.

In Table 11-2, we have assigned letters to the various quantities to show the relationships among the various values, and we have marked estimated values (like utilities) with an asterisk (*) since these values are subject to change. We have also shown the formulas used to compute dependent values. For example, we used the equation C = 0.06 × MS to show the commission (C) to be equal to 0.06 times monthly sales (MS). Finally, we have shown the monthly sales for July to be $10,000, with increases of 5 percent each month in monthly sales for August and September. Note also that the total of Jill's savings for the three months starting with July is only $242. Based on this budget, it will take Jill more than three months to save enough money to buy the CD system. How-

TABLE 11-2
Jill Bradley's Budget in Tabular Form

Item	Month			Totals
	July	August	September	
Monthly Sales (MS)*	$10,000	$10,500	$11,025	$31,525
Commission (C = 0.06 × MS)	600	630	662	1,892
Base Salary (BS)	700	700	700	2,100
Net Income (NI = C + BS − 250)	1,050	1,080	1,112	3,242
Rent (R)	300	300	300	900
Car Payment (CP)	150	150	150	450
Food (F)*	250	250	250	750
Utilities (U)*	150	150	150	450
Gas (G)*	50	50	50	150
Other (O)*	100	100	100	300
Expenses (E = R + CP + F + U + G + O)	1,000	1,000	1,000	1,000
Savings (S = NI − E)	50	80	112	242

ever, if her sales are higher than average, then her take-home pay and amount saved will increase.

Let us now analyze the effect of changes in assumptions in the spreadsheet. In other words, we can ask some "What if?" questions to determine the effect of changes in Jill's anticipated values. Note that changing Jill's monthly sales has the greatest effect on the spreadsheet since this value controls the amount of commission, the net income, and the level of savings each month. For example, to see how changing Jill's monthly sales will affect the spreadsheet, assume that instead of selling the "average" sales volume of $10,000 the first month, Jill sells $11,000 worth of goods. The effect of this change is shown in Table 11-3.

Note in Table 11-3 that the increase in monthly sales from $10,000 to $11,000 for the first month also increased the forecast sales for August and September. This occurred because each of them is based on the first month's sales. These increases, in turn, increased each month's Net Income and Savings values in such a way that a 10 percent increase in monthly sales actually resulted in a 78 percent increase in the total savings after three months!

According to the revisions in Table 11-3, Jill is much closer to saving enough to buy the CD system after three months. But what if food expenses are greater than expected and a heat wave during this period drives up the cost of utilities? On the other hand, what if Jill has a greater than 5 percent increase in sales volume in August and September? These and many other such "What if?" questions might be checked with this spreadsheet. However, doing it with pencil and paper would very quickly become tedious, especially if the number of months was extended to include an entire year or if the number of expense categories was increased.

Before the VisiCalc spreadsheet package was introduced, a manager in a large company would assign a staff member the task of manipulating a spreadsheet with paper and pencil. The time required to work with the spreadsheet manually was too great for a busy manager. For small firms, it was not possible to perform even this manual manipulation because of the time and effort it involves. With the advent of the electronic version of the spreadsheet, the

> **PC technology permits me to efficiently carry out tasks that I once would have delegated and then repeatedly reviewed in pre-PC days.**
>
> *Don M. Lyle, president,*
> *Emerald Systems*
>
> Quoted in "View from the Top,"
> *Personal Computing,* October 1989,
> p. 252.

TABLE 11-3
Revised Jill Bradley Budget

	Month			
Item	*July*	*August*	*September*	**Totals**
Monthly Sales (MS)*	$11,000	$11,550	$12,128	$34,678
Commission (C = 0.06 × MS)	660	693	728	2,081
Base Salary (BS)	700	700	700	2,100
Net Income (NI = C + BS − 250)	1,110	1,143	1,178	3,431
Rent (R)	300	300	300	900
Car Payment (CP)	150	150	150	450
Food (F)	250	250	250	750
Utilities (U)*	150	150	150	450
Gas (G)*	50	50	50	150
Other (O)*	100	100	100	300
Expenses (E = R + CP + F + U + G + O)	1,000	1,000	1,000	1,000
Savings (S = NI − E)	110	143	178	431

ager of any size of firm can now personally do this manipulation quickly and easily. And since having the manager involved in this process usually leads to better planning and forecasting, better management should result.

Setting Up an Electronic Spreadsheet

Conceptually, an **electronic spreadsheet** on a computer works exactly like the manual spreadsheet we showed earlier. However, once the values and the formulas that carry out the relationships among the values are entered, the computer takes care of recalculating all affected values when one value changes.

A spreadsheet is made up of horizontal **rows** identified by numbers, and vertical **columns** identified by letters. The intersection of a row and a column is called a **cell** and is identified by the row number and column letter. Movement from cell to cell in a spreadsheet is handled via the **cell pointer,** a rectangle highlighted in **reverse video.** Figure 11-1 shows a blank Lotus 1-2-3 spreadsheet (also referred to as a **worksheet**), with the cell pointer located in cell A1 (row 1 and column A). Rows and columns are also pointed out in this figure. The cell pointer can be moved with the cursor control keys (or, for some packages, a mouse).

One of three entities can go into a cell: a label made of letters and digits, a number called a value, or a formula that shows the relationship between cells containing values. A **label** is any combination of letters and numbers that describes the contents of a row or column. It is not meant to be used in any sort of calculation. The months at the top of each column and the items on the left of each row in the Jill Bradley spreadsheet are examples of labels. **Values** are numbers, either positive or negative, with or without a decimal. They may be placed in any cell and then used to make other calculations. The original values

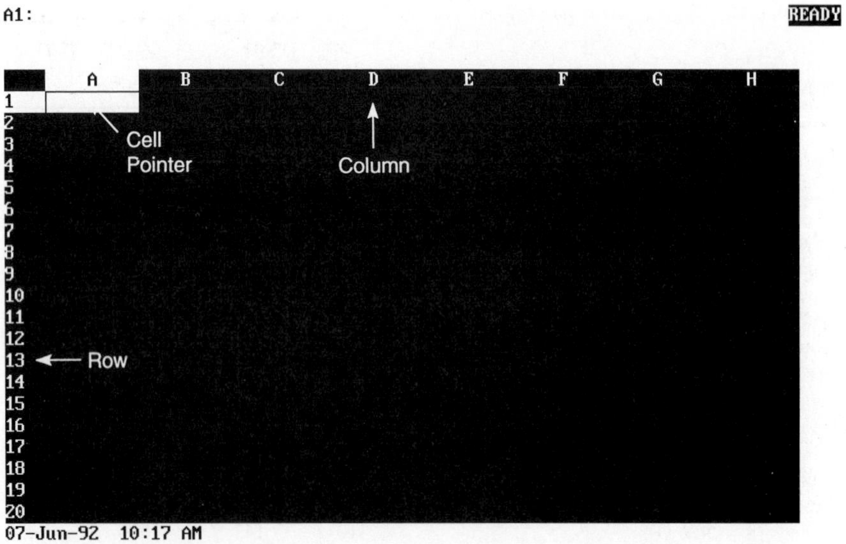

FIGURE 11-1
Blank Lotus 1-2-3 Spreadsheet

for sales, base salary, rent, car payment, and so on in the Jill Bradley spreadsheet are examples of values. **Formulas** are combinations of cell identifiers, constants, and arithmetic symbols. Calculation of the commission amount is handled through a formula.

Using this notation, we can set up Jill Bradley's budget in electronic spreadsheet form by entering labels and values into the blank spreadsheet in Figure 11-1. Entering the labels and values is simply a matter of moving the cell pointer into the cell where the entry is to be made and typing the label or value. The entry does not actually appear in the cell while it is being entered. Instead, it appears on an **edit line** above or below the spreadsheet during the entry process and then in the cell after the Enter key is pressed. Figure 11-2 shows the Jill Bradley spreadsheet after labels and values were entered. A label and a value are pointed out in this figure.

Note in Figure 11-2 that row 1 is used for the column headings and column A is used for the item names. Note also that column A is wider than the other columns in Figure 11-2 to allow for the length of the labels in this column. The column width can be changed for either the entire spreadsheet or individual columns. Changing the column widths for the entire spreadsheet is an example of a **global change;** changing the column width for an individual column is an example of a **local change.**

While labels and values are important elements in a spreadsheet, the formulas are the key elements that make it a powerful analytic tool: They represent the assumptions underlying the spreadsheet and they carry out the calculations. When a formula is entered in a cell, the value calculated by the formula is displayed. Table 11-4 shows the meaning of various symbols in spreadsheet formulas. These operations are arranged in the order in which the computer will carry them out, that is, grouping, raising to a power, multiplication and division, and addition and subtraction.

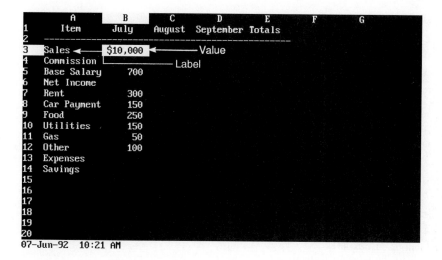

FIGURE 11-2
Electronic Spreadsheet with
Labels and Values

TABLE 11-4
Symbols Used in Spreadsheet Formulas

Symbol Name	Symbol	Operation
Parentheses	( )	Grouping
Caret (Shift-6)	^	Raising a number to a power
Asterisk	*	Multiplication
Slash	/	Division
Plus sign	+	Addition
Minus sign	−	Subtraction

It is important to understand that **cell identifiers** such as A10, B2, and so on are used in formulas wherever possible so that any change in the values in those cells will automatically be reflected in the formula. For example, in the Jill Bradley spreadsheet, cell B4 contains the July commission value, which is equal to 6 percent of the July sales in cell B3, so the formula 0.06*B3 would be entered in the B4 cell. If the sales value entered in B3 is $10,000, the result of this formula would be $600. If the sales value changes, the commission value will also automatically change. Figure 11-3 shows the entry of this formula in the Jill Bradley spreadsheet. Note that the formula is shown in the Edit line but the result appears in cell B4.

The next step is to enter the remaining formulas into the spreadsheet. As in the entry of labels and values, the cell pointer is moved to the proper cell and the formula is entered. For example, to enter the formula for July Net Income in cell B6, we move the cell pointer to B6 and enter the formula +B4+B5−250 there (the first + is used to show that this is a formula, not a label). Whatever values are in the cells in the formula will be used to calculate the value in the

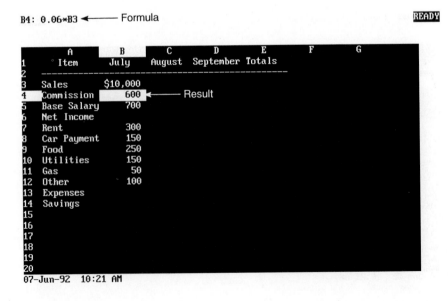

FIGURE 11-3
Entry of July Sales Commission Formula

B6 cell. The other formulas that must be entered in the July column are for Expenses, in cell B13, and for Savings, in cell B14. The formula in B13 is +B7+B8+B9+B10+B11+B12 and the formula in B14 is +B6−B13.

The formulas for the corresponding August and September cells will substitute C and D, respectively, for B in each of the formulas for the July cells. In addition, the August and September Sales values will be calculated with formulas that represent the 5 percent expected increase in sales volume each month. For August, the formula in cell C3 will be 1.05*B3; for September, the formula in cell D3 will be 1.05*C3. The formulas in the Total column will be the sum of each row. For example, the total of the sales volumes will be in cell E3 and will be equal to +B3+C3+D3. The formulas for other rows in this column will be the same except for a change in the row number. For example, in cell E4, the formula will be +B4+C4+D4.

After we enter each formula in the appropriate cell, we obtain the spreadsheet shown in Figure 11-4. Note that this electronic spreadsheet is similar to Table 11-2.

Working with an Electronic Spreadsheet

Now let's try changing some anticipated values on this electronic spreadsheet. Assume that July sales, instead of being $10,000 as was expected, are $11,000. Changing all the entries by hand would be tedious since the August and September sales values are also affected, as well as the net income and savings values for all three months. With an electronic spreadsheet, however, it's very easy. All we need to do is move the cursor to the B3 cell and change the value in that cell. The resulting spreadsheet is shown in Figure 11-5 and is the same as that shown earlier as Table 11-3.

E3: (C0) +B3+C3+D3   READY

	A	B	C	D	E	F	G
1	Item	July	August	September	Totals		
2							
3	Sales	$10,000	$10,500	$11,025	$31,525		
4	Commission	600	630	662	1,892		
5	Base Salary	700	700	700	2,100		
6	Net Income	1,050	1,080	1,112	3,242		
7	Rent	300	300	300	900		
8	Car Payment	150	150	150	450		
9	Food	250	250	250	750		
10	Utilities	150	150	150	450		
11	Gas	50	50	50	150		
12	Other	100	100	100	300		
13	Expenses	1,000	1,000	1,000	3,000		
14	Savings	50	80	112	242		
15							
16							
17							
18							
19							
20							

07-Jun-92 10:24 AM

FIGURE 11-4
Jill Bradley Spreadsheet with Formulas Added

FIGURE 11-5
Jill Bradley Spreadsheet with
New Sales Value

B3: (C0) 11000   READY

```
          A         B         C          D          E        F         G
   1    Item      July     August   September   Totals
   2  ------------------------------------------------------
   3  Sales      $11,000   $11,550   $12,128   $34,678
   4  Commission     660       693       728     2,081
   5  Base Salary    700       700       700     2,100
   6  Net Income   1,110     1,143     1,178     3,431
   7  Rent           300       300       300       900
   8  Car Payment    150       150       150       450
   9  Food           250       250       250       750
  10  Utilities      150       150       150       450
  11  Gas             50        50        50       150
  12  Other          100       100       100       300
  13  Expenses     1,000     1,000     1,000     3,000
  14  Savings        110       143       178       431
  15
  16
  17
  18
  19
  20
```
07-Jun-92   10:26 AM

With an electronic spreadsheet, it is easy to test various assumptions, as we have done with Jill Bradley's budget. In the final case, the amount available in savings after three months is still not quite enough to purchase the CD system, but it is much closer than before. Using a spreadsheet in this way, Jill can test the effect of a change in any of her original anticipated expense figures. The same is true in many business situations in which managers want to test assumptions in the process of developing an annual budget or forecasting the coming year's income.

Common Spreadsheet Features

Although commercial spreadsheet packages all differ in their ease of use and scope, most spreadsheets share a group of features. To understand the power of spreadsheets, we should discuss each feature briefly. Spreadsheets usually have the following capabilities:

Microsoft Excel is a very popular spreadsheet for use on the Apple Macintosh.

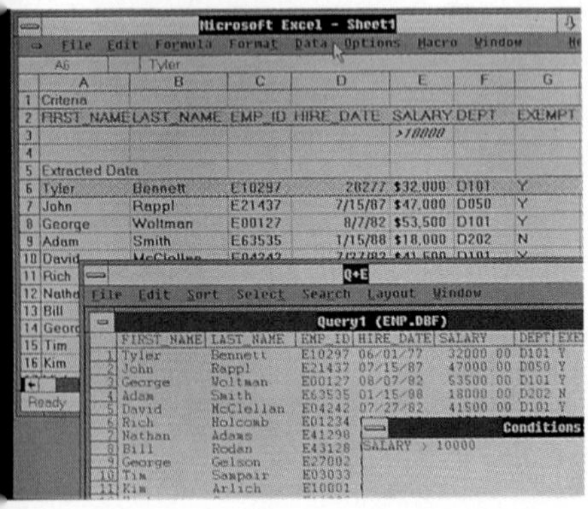

- Copy the contents of one cell or a group of cells—called a **range**—into another location.
- Move the contents of a range of cells to another location.
- Insert or delete a row or a column.
- Format the rows and columns to take a desired form.
- Work with ranges of cells.
- Save a spreadsheet to a disk or load one from a disk.
- Print an entire spreadsheet or just a part of a spreadsheet.
- Use windows that allow the user to look at two parts of a big spreadsheet.
- Include functions that perform specialized operations.
- Perform a series of operations using macros.

TRACKING HEALTH COST WITH A SPREADSHEET

For all levels of government, tracking the skyrocketing cost of providing health and social services is an important part of controlling costs. In San Mateo County in Northern California, this task falls to the county controller's Health and Welfare Claiming Department, which is responsible for monitoring and filing claims for many county departments, including Social Services, Mental Health, Public Health, and Drug and Alcohol Abuse.

The department must process the hundreds of claim forms required by the state and federal governments. Until 1990, staff members often worked overtime to manually complete the government-supplied health and welfare claim forms. They used typewriters to transfer the data received from the hundreds of program facilities to the government forms and then spent weeks checking the forms for accuracy.

To reduce the cost of completing and checking the claims forms, the department's manager, George Lumm, moved much of the claims operation to Lotus 1-2-3 Release 3.1 in 1990. He chose this package because its graphical capabilities allowed him to duplicate on the computer the government forms and then copy the data from his spreadsheet, where calculations are performed automatically and error free. Lumm, single-handedly, was able to do the same operations his entire staff of seven had done manually, and Lumm did it in one-tenth the time.

Lumm chose Lotus 1-2-3 Release 3.1 also for its data linking capabilities, which allow him to compare data electronically from different spreadsheets. For example, by using linked spreadsheets, he can compare the amounts of money that the mental health facilities received in a given period from the state, insurance companies, Medi-Cal, and Medicare. He can also determine how much time was spent on each patient to compute the cost per unit of service.

Source: "Spreadsheets Add Up for County," *Government Technology,* February 1991, p. 47.

> **The benefits my group derives by being able to duplicate state forms in 1-2-3 are enormous.**
>
> *George Lumm, San Mateo County*
>
> Quoted in "Spreadsheets Add Up for County," *Government Technology,* February 1991, p. 47.

- Create and display graphics based on spreadsheet data.
- Perform data base operations on the rows of the spreadsheet.

When an entry in one cell of a spreadsheet is to be the same as that in another cell, the *copy* command may be used to make the value or formula the same in both cells. When a formula is involved, a relative copy of it can be made. A **relative copy** uses the same formula structure in the new cell, but changes the formula to match the location of the new cell. For Jill Bradley's budget spreadsheet, the values in each row were summed to generate a Total column. Each formula is the same except for the row number. The relative copy of the first row formula—that is, B3 + C3 + D3—would be inserted into each cell of the last column but the row numbers would change. *Moving* the contents of one cell to another is similar to copying, except that the original cell is empty after the move.

If Jill Bradley wanted to know how much she could save in two months rather than three, she could *delete* the September column and the spreadsheet would recalculate all values based on only the first two months. The September component of any formula would be given a value of zero in the spreadsheet calculations. Similarly, if Jill decided to save for an additional month to buy the CD player, she could *insert* a column for October after September and then use the copy command to enter the correct values and formulas.

To make the spreadsheet appear a certain way, a user can *format* the spreadsheet. Formatting can move all values as far to the left or right as possible in a cell for a pleasing appearance. It can also be used to add commas in large numbers, to place negative values in parentheses, or to treat all numeric entries as dollar amounts with two places to the right of the decimal point. Formatting also includes changing individual column widths. The Jill Bradley spreadsheet in Figure 11-5 was formatted as currency with no places to the right of the decimal point.

The copying, moving, formatting, and printing operations can also be applied to a group of cells called a range. A range of cells can be made up of a part of a row, a part of a column, or a rectangle of cells. For example, a range copy would define a group of cells as a range and then copy this range to a designated location in the spreadsheet. It is also possible to move, format, and print a range of cells.

It may be necessary or useful to *save* a spreadsheet to a disk for future reference. For example, if an incomplete spreadsheet is saved, the user can *load* the spreadsheet at some later point and begin work again. A spreadsheet template may also be saved on disk. A **template** is a skeleton spreadsheet that matches a particular application. For example, the labels and formulas from Jill Bradley's budget could be used as a template. When new values are input for salary, rent, and so on, the template provides the formulas needed to calculate the values for the blank cells.

> **In automating the process of cranking out numbers, business plans, and forecasts [with spreadsheets], people are producing analyses 50 to 100 times more frequently than when they used only paper.**
>
> *Said Mohammadioun,*
> *president, Samna*
>
> Quoted in "View from the Top," *Personal Computing*, October 1989, p. 266.

```
      H       I       J       K       L       M       N       O       P       Q      ◀
1  Wee-B-Dry Corporation: Lease Versus Purchase Decision (Page Two)                   ▶
2  =============================================================                       ▲
3                                                                                      ▼
4        ------- OWNERSHIP COSTS AND DEDUCTIONS  -------          LEASE VALUE          ?
5     INTEREST       DEPREC-              TAX  AT LOAN PU LOAN  LEASE  PU LEASE
6  YEAR EXPENSE MAINT  IATION TOTAL SAVINGSOUTFLOW OUTFLOW PMT (AT)  PMT
7    1  2,000 2,000  4,000  8,000  2,720   4,556   4,556   4,620   4,620
8    2  1,672 2,000  6,400 10,072  3,425   3,851   3,501   4,620   4,125
9    3  1,312 2,000  3,840  7,152  2,432   4,844   4,004   4,620   3,683
10   4    916 2,000  2,300  5,216  1,773   5,503   4,134   4,620   3,288
11   5    480 2,000  2,304  4,784  1,626   5,650   3,859   4,620   2,936
12   6      0 2,000  1,156  3,156  1,073   6,203   3,852   4,620   2,622
13
14  =============================================================
15                                       $30,607 $23,905 $27,720 $21,274
16
17
18
19
20
20-Jul-92  08:36 PM
```

An important use of spreadsheets is to help managers make decisions involving financial questions.

Once a spreadsheet has tested various assumptions and is formatted to a desired form, some or all of the spreadsheet can be printed. The part of the spreadsheet that is printed depends on the commands given. A user can have just one cell printed, or the entire spreadsheet.

When a spreadsheet's rows and columns cannot all appear on the screen at one time (the number of rows and columns differs from package to package and machine to machine), the **windowing** feature of the spreadsheet is useful. In this situation, the user can see two different parts of a spreadsheet at the same time. *Windowing* can be vertical, which shows two sets of columns, or horizontal, which shows two sets of rows. As an example of the use of windowing, assume that Jill Bradley's budget spreadsheet covers 12 months rather than just 3 months. With a spreadsheet this large, **horizontal scrolling** moves the columns off the screen on the left as more columns are viewed on the right. When this occurs, the row labels are no longer visible, and the values in the right-hand columns are not easily identified. With windowing, the user can see the labels in the left-hand window and the monthly columns in the right-hand window on the screen at the same time. Figure 11-6 shows the result of using windows to view the labels in column A simultaneously with the June and Totals columns for Jill Bradley's budget. In this figure, the left window contains the row labels in column A and the right window contains columns M and N. It was assumed in this yearly budget that Jill's July sales were $11,000 and that sales initially increased 5 percent per month for the first two months but increased by only 2 percent per month for the months October through June. Note that with even these small increases in sales, Jill had a sizable total sales, net income, and savings by the end of the year.

To help the spreadsheet user make many common calculations, such as finding sums and averages and making financial calculations, spreadsheets have a set of **functions.** These are essentially a group of built-in formulas for carrying

```
N3: (CO) @SUM(B3..M3)                                          READY
```

	A		M	N	O	P	Q	R
1	Item	1	June	Totals				
2	-----------	2	----------	----------				
3	Sales	3	$14,493	$155,343				
4	Commission	4	870	2,081				
5	Base Salary	5	700	2,100				
6	Net Income	6	1,320	3,431				
7	Rent	7	300	900				
8	Car Payment	8	150	450				
9	Food	9	250	750				
10	Utilities	10	150	450				
11	Gas	11	50	150				
12	Other	12	100	300				
13	Expenses	13	1,000	3,000				
14	Savings	14	320	431				
15		15						
16		16						
17		17						
18		18						
19		19						
20		20						

```
07-Jun-92  10:34 AM
```

FIGURE 11-6
Budget Spreadsheet with Windowing

out specific operations. For example, to find the sum of a series of cells in Lotus 1-2-3, we would use the @SUM function; to find the average, we would use the @AVG function. In addition to these simple functions, there are statistical, financial, mathematical, date and time, data base, and character string functions. In 1-2-3, we use them by entering the @ symbol (the "at" symbol), the function name, and the range of cells to be included. For example, let's say we want to find the total savings after three months. Instead of placing the formula +B3+C3+D3 in the E3 cell, we can use the function @SUM(B3..D3). The ellipsis (..) shows that the function should sum everything in row 14 between columns B and D.

Frequently, a user will want to perform the same series of actions or commands a number of times. To facilitate this repetition, most spreadsheet packages allow the user to save the series of actions or commands under a name. The unit of actions or commands is referred to as a **macro**, and the user can perform the same operation again simply by giving the name of the macro. For example, an instructor may wish to find the sum of a series of quiz grades, subtract the lowest grade, and then find the average of the remaining values. The instructor can do this for one student, save the keystrokes as a macro with a name of QUIZAVE, and then use this macro for all the other students.

A powerful function of almost all current spreadsheets is the capability of converting the data from one or more columns or rows of the spreadsheet into graphs. The most common graph options are bar, line, pie, and stack-bar graphs and scatter (x−y) diagrams. Titles, legends, and labels may also be added to the graph to facilitate an analysis of the spreadsheet data.

Another useful spreadsheet operation is data base management. The rows of the spreadsheet are treated as records of a data base, so it is possible to sort entries or search for records with specific characteristics. Spreadsheets also contain a special set of data base functions that allow you to perform a variety of

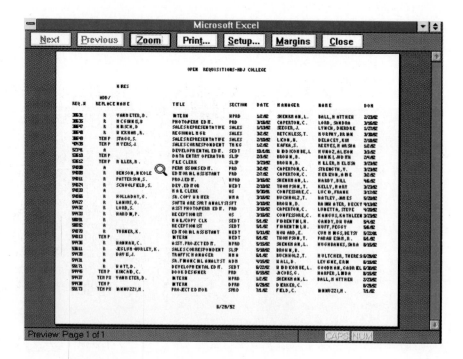

Some spreadsheet software features WYSIWYG screen layout.

operations, such as summing or averaging only those rows that meet a specified criterion.

Most new versions of spreadsheet packages include three new features: presentation graphs, WYSIWYG (What You See Is What You Get), and linking capabilities. Presentation graphs with three-dimensional graphics and elaborate titles and labels are becoming common in many packages. Similarly, multiple type sizes and fonts, which are displayed on the screen, are being added to spreadsheet packages. Finally, **spreadsheet linking** capabilities allow the user to link data and formulas to multiple spreadsheets, so that a change in one

NOT JUST FOR FINANCES

Spreadsheets as "Electronic" Gradebooks

With the availability of spreadsheets, many college instructors are replacing their traditional gradebooks with a spreadsheet equivalent. There are several good reasons to make this replacement: A blank spreadsheet with appropriate labels and formulas can be used over and over again for different grading periods; corrections can be made easily when errors in exam scores are detected; the spreadsheet's mathematical functions can be used to compute averages and other values; and the data base facilities can be used to sort the students by name alphabetically or by some numerical value.

As an example of using a spreadsheet as an electronic gradebook, consider the situation faced by the author in teaching 300 students in an Introduction to Computer class for which students attend both a lecture

For a large class especially, an electronic gradebook saves valuable time and helps to ensure accuracy.

section and a computer laboratory section each week. There are three lab instructors, all of whom use the same spreadsheet form to record scores for the students in their sections. This spreadsheet form has columns for each student's name, ID number, quiz scores, exam scores, and project scores, along with formulas to compute total and average scores for each student's overall grade and for each quiz, exam, and project. Because five quizzes are given during the term and only the four highest scores are retained, the @MIN function is used to determine the lowest quiz score, which is then subtracted

from the total of the five quiz scores. The @SUM function is then used to sum the quiz scores, exam scores, and project scores to find the total for the term. The spreadsheets for all 11 sections are combined into one massive spreadsheet, and the students are sorted alphabetically by name to match the university grade rolls. With the @IF function, the total scores are converted into letter grades, which are then transferred (by hand!) to the university grade rolls. While this is still a big job, it is much easier than doing the same job with traditional paper and pencil gradebooks.

```
H7: [W5] @IF(F7>895,"A",@IF(F7>795,"B",@IF(F7>695,"C",@IF(F7>595,"D","F"))))   READY
```

	A	B	C	D	E	F	G	H
1		CS 101						
2		Fall Semester 1992						
3								
4								
5	Student Name	Student #	EXAM ONE	EXAM TWO	FINAL	TOTAL		Grade
6								
7	ADHERN, D.	9503	275	250	385	910		A
8	ARMENTO, S.	8199	225	235	361	821		B
9	BAXLEY, S.	7868	200	173	325	698		D
10	BRIGHT, T.	3898	195	280	309	784		C
11	BROWN, G.	2407	285	217	387	889		B
12	BRUN, R.	0812	235	216	326	777		C
13	CHAX, G.	0713	220	236	263	719		C
14	DRAZLE, M.	7768	295	289	285	869		B
15	HOWLETT, J.	6010	185	132	356	673		D
16	KEVLAR, S.	8423	145	184	216	545		F
17	LOWRANCE, K.	5841	200	151	329	680		D
18	MCCORMICK, J.	4905	195	290	376	861		B
19	MILLMAN, M.	3428	215	253	352	820		B
20	CHANANA, P.	1850	225	239	278	742		C

```
07-Jun-92  10:46 AM                                        CALC        CAPS
```

spreadsheet is transferred to other spreadsheets requiring the same value or formula. More powerful spreadsheets, such as Microsoft Excel and Lotus 1-2-3 Release 3.1, can simultaneously display multiple-linked spreadsheets.

Integrated Packages

The popularity of spreadsheets has led software companies to create packages that add other packages to the spreadsheet. The first such package was the extremely successful Lotus 1-2-3, which included graphics and data base management functions along with the spreadsheet. After 1-2-3 came the **integrated package,** which allowed a user to do even more work with only one package. Examples of integrated packages for IBM compatible PCs are Symphony from Lotus, Framework III from Ashton-Tate, Enable OA from Enable, First Choice from Spinnaker Software Publishing Corporation, and Microsoft Works, which is also made for the Apple Macintosh.

These packages all have spreadsheet, data base, word processing, graphics, and telecommunications functions. Each package works differently, but all have the same objective—*to allow users to do all their processing in one package with a common interface and command structure.* For example, it is possible with an integrated package to begin writing a report, decide a graph is needed, switch to the graphics part of the integrated package, design the graph, then move the graphic into the report. With integrated packages, any change in one part of the package is immediately known to all other elements of the package. For example, if the results of a spreadsheet are being included in a graph and the values of the spreadsheet are changed, the graph will also reflect the changes.

Purchasing a Spreadsheet and Integrated Packages

When shopping for a spreadsheet package, you should know that all choices for IBM compatible PCs have been standardized on the Lotus 1-2-3 file format, that is, .wk1 files. This means that no matter which spreadsheet you choose, it will work with spreadsheets developed on another package. Price probably will not be a determining factor in your decision because most packages cost about the same: They list for about $500 to $600 but usually can be purchased for considerably less from a discount dealer. SuperCalc[5], however, is quite a bit less costly. With this in mind, your choice of spreadsheet will depend on your hardware and on whether you are using the Windows operating environment. Several packages run on virtually any PC. They include Quattro Pro from Borland, SuperCalc[5] from Computer Associates, PlanPerfect from WordPerfect Corporation, and Lotus 1-2-3 Release 2.4. However, Lotus 1-2-3 Release 3.1 and Microsoft Excel require an Intel 80386 or i486 computer.

For PCs running under the Windows operating environment, there is Lotus 1-2-3 for Windows and Microsoft Excel. Both packages use the Windows graphical interface, high-quality graphics, and multiple text fonts, but as we mentioned, they require a CPU with either the Intel 80386 or i486 chip. Other spreadsheets are being rewritten to run under Windows and may be available at the time this text is published. Macintosh users can choose between 1-2-3 for the Mac and Microsoft Excel.

Integrated software packages can be divided, roughly, by price into two categories: high end and low end. At the high end are the packages that sell for

1-2-3 for Macintosh will open the door to a whole new set of users who have never used 1-2-3.

Jim Manzi, president and CEO of Lotus 1-2-3

Quoted in "1-2-3 and the Mac Finally Click," *Lotus,* October 1991, p. 33.

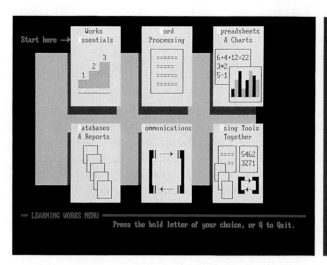

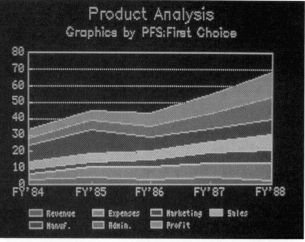

(Left) Microsoft Works. (Right) First Choice.

more than $600. For IBM compatible PCs, these include Framework, Symphony, and Enable. At the low end are the packages that sell for less than $200. They include for IBM compatible PCs, First Choice and LotusWorks from Lotus. Microsoft Works is available for both the Macintosh and IBM compatible PCs and can interface Microsoft's spreadsheet package, Excel. The low-end packages are very popular today among two groups: first-time users and laptop computer users. First-time users can have all their software in one package with a single interface. Laptop users find that a low-end integrated package fits very nicely their fairly inexpensive portable computer. At the high end, sophisticated users are discovering that there are more features in the later versions of these packages than there were in earlier versions.

Lotusworks enables us to serve those users in small businesses, home offices, and education with an extremely capable, cost efficient, all-in-one solution.

Tim McManus, director of marketing for integrated software at Lotus Development

Quoted in "Integrated Software for Entry-Level Users," *Lotus Quarterly,* Fall 1990, p. 3.

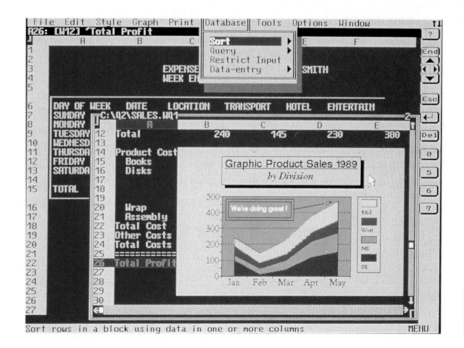

Quattro is capable of annotating graphs that can be displayed simultaneously with the spreadsheet data.

Unit sales of low-end packages increased 46 percent between 1989 and 1990, whereas sales of the high-end packages increased only 5 percent during the same period.

PERSONAL FINANCIAL MANAGEMENT PACKAGES

Personal financial management is a popular use for a personal computer. Studies have shown that close to 50 percent of all personal computer owners use their computers for some sort of financial management. Personal financial management packages fall into three major categories: personal budgeting (accounting), tax planning and preparation, and investment analysis. **Personal budgeting packages** allow a user to perform a number of tasks on a computer, including the following:

- Assign checks to various expense classifications and keep a running total of each budgeted amount.
- Record checks as they are written and then use the computer to do a bank reconciliation (comparing the checkbook balance to the bank balance).
- Track tax-deductible expenses as they occur and sum them at the end of the tax year.
- Provide a calculation of net worth.
- Keep an inventory of home furnishings and valuables.

Tax planning and preparation packages may be used to keep tax records throughout the year and determine the effects of financial decisions as they are made throughout the year. At year-end, a tax package can help in the preparation of state and federal income tax returns. Such packages can be useful if the user knows the tax laws well and is in a financial situation that could benefit from careful tax planning. However, annual software updates are needed because the government constantly modifies the tax code.

Investment analysis packages may be stand-alone packages or they may be tied into a national data bank that updates the information in the package. Portfolio management and security analysis are two basic types of investment analysis software. Portfolio management software is primarily a stand-alone package that helps the investor manage a list of stocks, bonds, mutual funds, treasury bills, and so on. Such packages can also determine the effect of selling a stock by calculating the gain or loss and the resulting tax effect. Security analysis software is usually tied into a national data base that updates the prices of a selected list of securities to aid the investor in making investment decisions.

Although the tax preparation and investment analysis software are designed for a specific group of users, the personal budgeting software can be used by almost anyone.

Personal Budgeting Software

While double-entry bookkeeping is the standard form of accounting for most companies, most individuals use a single entry for each expenditure. This is called single-entry bookkeeping, checkbook accounting, or cash-basis accounting. For each expenditure or deposit, the individual enters a check number, the person or institution to whom the check is paid or the source of the deposit, and

THE ELECTRONIC TAXMAN

Recent years have seen increasing numbers of professional tax preparers sending electronic tax returns instead of bulky paper returns. In a program begun for the 1985 tax year, the Internal Revenue Service is accepting digital submission of certain tax filings; in 1990, the IRS started accepting electronically submitted tax returns from every state in the nation. While this program includes only those income tax returns that involve a refund and those submitted by a person or company approved by the IRS, the process promises to speed refunds to taxpayers and to result in fewer errors and reduced paperwork for the IRS. Currently, a paper tax return must be opened, numbered, and sorted before data entry operators read and key in the figures on each return. While most errors can be blamed on the taxpayer or the tax preparer, some errors do occur in the data entry process. It usually takes two weeks for the IRS to process a paper return.

In contrast to the paper return process, with electronic returns the IRS does not have to key in all the forms, make corrections, store the paper returns, or try to decipher a taxpayer's handwriting. The IRS can also electronically transfer a refund directly to the recipient's bank account. The IRS hopes that the software used to digitally prepare tax returns will catch many of the errors that go unnoticed during the submission of the paper return. The result for the taxpayer? The IRS has said that digital returns can result in a refund in as few as 17 days—as compared to 10 weeks for a paper return. However, there is a cost. The IRS estimates the cost of filing electronically is between $5 and $50.

With all of these advantages to both the IRS and the taxpayer, many commercial tax preparation firms are getting set up to handle digital returns. An H & R Block spokesperson said that many of its employees will be among the over 40,000 professional preparers using the electronic filing program.

Sources: Steve Rosenthal, "The Taxman Goes High-Tech as IRS Accepts Electronically Filed Returns," *PC Week,* January 27, 1987, pp. 111–113; and Kathy Kristof, "Does Filing Taxes Electronically Make Sense?" *LA Times,* March 10, 1991, p. D4.

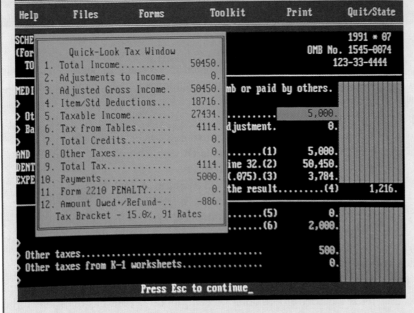

Tax preparation software is becoming very popular with individuals who prepare their own federal income tax returns.

the amount in a checkbook ledger. The person keeps a running balance in the checkbook, which shows the current level of funds in the bank account. At the end of each month, the individual compares the balance shown in the checkbook with the balance provided by the bank. The individual must first modify the bank balance by subtracting checks that have not cleared and adding deposits that have not cleared and then compare this modified balance to that in his or her checkbook.

One welcome feature of personal budgeting packages is their ability to help users balance the family checkbook quickly and easily.

To reduce the time and effort involved in personal accounting, numerous software packages have become available. While each is different in some way, they all have similarities:

- A user can set up a budget with some number of accounts.
- Each check that is written is entered with a number or name that matches an account in the budget.
- A running total is kept of all expenditures in each account.
- At the end of the month, the actual expenditures in each account are compared with the budgeted amounts.
- Also at the end of the month, the software can be used to reconcile the check returns.

The central problem of personal finance software is that people won't use it if it doesn't save time.

Scott Cook, founder and president, Omtiot (maker of Quicken personal budgeting package)

Quoted in "What's New in Personal Finance Software," *Personal Computing,* January 1989, p. 131.

Most such personal budgeting packages use completion screens to prompt the user for the needed information. A **completion screen** has questions to be answered and places for category names and amounts to be entered. Usually, these packages ask the user to define income and expense categories and to enter budgeted amounts.

A second common type of completion screen is the transaction screen. A **transaction screen** prompts the user to enter the actual income and expenses. This screen may request such information as the check number (or other code), the date, a description of the transaction, whether it is an income transaction or an expense transaction, the amount, and the category from the budget screen into which this transaction falls. Another characteristic of personal budgeting packages is that they can show a monthly income and expense summary that compares actual amounts to budgeted amounts.

Personal accounting packages can help keep track of an individual's or even a small business's finances. In addition to the screens discussed earlier, some software can generate reports involving check reconciliation, assets, liabilities, credit cards, and summary reports. Also, an entire group of packages is now available that has the primary purpose of writing checks. The user enters all the information necessary and the computer generates checks that are printed on the user's printer.

Selecting Personal Budgeting Software

When selecting personal budgeting software, you should answer several questions to determine which package is most suitable for your needs. First, how easy is the package to use and how flexible is it? It should be easy to enter and edit transactions. Second, what is the capacity of this package? If the package handles only 50 checks a month and the user normally writes more than 50, the package will not be useful. Third, will the package print checks? For those who write a large number of checks, this may be an important feature. Fourth, can the package suitably search for and report transactions? This function can be important if the user must recall previously entered transactions. Finally, can the package track and report tax-deductible transactions, and will it interface with a tax program? This feature can make tax preparation much easier.

If you are trying to decide whether to purchase personal budgeting software, and you do not own or have access to a computer and printer, you should also know that it will be difficult to justify buying the hardware, because it will probably cost far more than the amount of money you can save by using personal budgeting software.

BUSINESS ACCOUNTING PACKAGES

Tracking the inflow and outflow of money is crucial to the management of a business of any size. This tracking operation is referred to as **accounting.** High interest rates and the increasing complexity of the tax laws emphasize the importance of the accounting function to businesses. Because of the importance of accounting and the large amounts of data involved, for almost 30 years large corporations and institutions have used mainframe computers to handle this function. When minicomputers and personal computers were developed, accounting packages were among the first packages made for these smaller computers. Today, many commercial accounting packages are available for standard accounting systems. Many small software companies get their start by developing packages for special situations in which a company could not use a standard package.

Six major operations exist within business accounting—general ledger, accounts receivable, accounts payable, payroll, order processing, and inventory control. Usually, each operation is developed as a module. A **module** is a separate program that performs a specific task and shares data with the other modules to lead to an integrated system. Let us take a closer look at each accounting operation.

The **general ledger** is the record that contains all the firm's financial transactions. The term **double-entry bookkeeping** originated here, because each transaction must be recorded twice, once as a **credit** to some account and once as a **debit** to some account. For example, the purchase of a delivery truck for

$10,000 is recorded in two accounts: The asset account is debited for $1,000, and the cash account is credited for the same amount. All business accounting software packages have some form of general ledger module.

The **accounts receivable** module of a business accounting software package keeps track of money owed to a firm and when payments are due. Some packages generate sales reports on sales volume and print reminders that can be sent to past-due accounts. The software also ages the various accounts from current status to past due to uncollectible. Most firms must track credit accounts, so all business accounting software packages have some form of accounts receivable module. This module accounts for all money that is owed to the firm. Figure 11-7 shows the opening screen for an accounts receivable summary from a typical business accounting software package.

The **accounts payable** module of a business accounting software package monitors the money the firm owes its suppliers. Because creditors may give some form of discount if bills are paid before the due date, an accounts payable module can save money as well as ensure that all bills are paid. An accounts payable module can also print checks to suppliers and generate reports on amounts paid to each supplier. Like the general ledger and accounts receivable modules, the accounts payable module is found in all business accounting software packages. Figure 11-8 shows an accounts payable screen from an accounting package.

To speed payment of employee wages, a **payroll** module is commonly included in business accounting software packages. This module computes employees' gross wages due from regular-time work, overtime, and tips. It then determines the deductions from the wages for taxes, Social Security, health insurance, union dues, and so on. After subtracting the deductions from the gross wages, the payroll package can then print a check for each employee. At the end of each tax year, a payroll package can also generate the W-2 forms for employees based on the total wages for the year.

The **order processing** module helps the retail or wholesale operation by making sure that customers' orders are filled in a timely manner. With this mod-

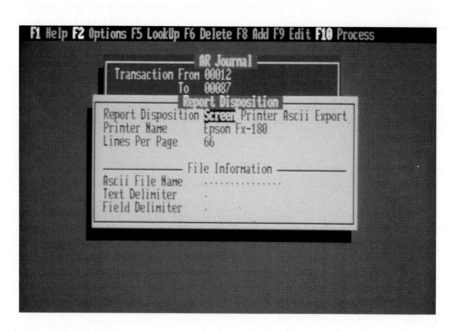

FIGURE 11-7
Opening Screen of Accounts
Receivable Summary

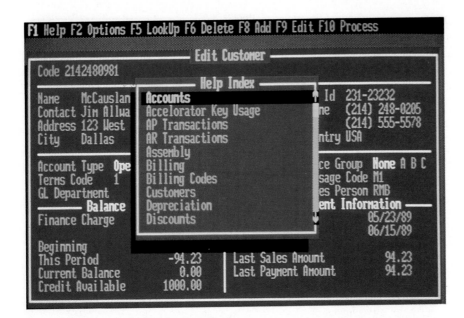

FIGURE 11-8
Accounts Payable Screen

ule, orders can be received, entered, and managed. Once the order is entered, the module can print an order confirmation for the customer and the packing slip used to select the ordered goods. If out-of-stock goods are input, the module generates an order to replace these items. If standing orders exist, the order processing module prints a reminder that these orders should be filled.

Along with order processing, the **inventory control** module manages the flow of goods into, within, and out of the firm. Inventory is the storage of raw materials, work in process, and finished goods. An inventory module keeps track of the numbers of items that are kept in inventory at any one time. It is not unusual for even a small company to have over $100,000 tied up in inventory.

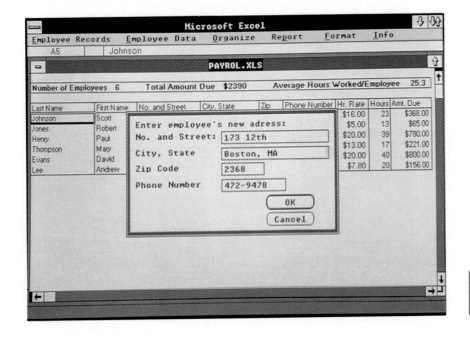

Even spreadsheet packages, such as Excel from Microsoft, can be set up to act as payroll modules in an accounting system.

BITS OF HISTORY

It All Began with VisiCalc

[VisiCalc] was the catalyst that launched the personal computer out of the hobbyist garages and into small businesses.

Paul Saffo, research fellow, Institute for the Future

Quoted in "Looking at VisiCalc 10 Years Later," *Personal Computing,* November 1989, p. 233.

If there was one event that made the public aware that the personal computer was indeed a "mind tool" that could make work easier, it was the introduction of VisiCalc. By allowing the recalculations to be done on a personal computer, this software package relieved the user of the drudgery of constantly recalculating by hand the many values in budget and forecasting tables. VisiCalc allowed a user to enter the values once, tell the software what formulas to use to make the calculations, and then let the computer do the work. This was such a revolutionary idea that 200,000 copies were sold in the first two years on the market. Since VisiCalc was initially available only on the Apple II computer, it is also credited with selling 20,000 of these machines.

The history of VisiCalc is a classic story of one person trying to find a way to make a task easier. In this case the person was Dan Bricklin, who in 1978 was an MBA student at Harvard. Harvard uses the case method of teaching in its MBA program, and this involves using spreadsheets. Bricklin got the idea of computerizing this process. Even though a Harvard professor told him the idea would never work, Bricklin enlisted the aid of an MIT student, Bob Frankston, to program the project and named the finished product VisiCalc, for VISIble CALCulator. Another Harvard MBA, Dan Fylstra, also became involved—in the marketing of the finished product.

The success of VisiCalc spawned many other "Calcs," the most successful of which are Lotus 1-2-3 and Excel. Although VisiCalc is no longer on the market, having been purchased by Lotus Development Corporation, it is clearly the "grandfather" of all current spreadsheets.

Bob Frankston.

Therefore, the inventory module can be a key element in the management of a firm's resources.

Selecting and Using a Business Accounting Package

Why does a company use a specialized accounting package rather than a spreadsheet? Although a spreadsheet is a flexible financial tool that can be used for a wide range of applications, accounting packages also have a wide range of uses. The answer to the question depends on the size of the firm and the consistency of the applications. If the firm is small or the applications vary a great deal, then a spreadsheet probably could be chosen. On the other hand, accounting packages are a necessity for most firms, because the same operation is carried out many times. Such repetition on a spreadsheet would be very tedious.

Another advantage of accounting packages is that they are usually *menu driven.* A menu-driven package is easier to use because a user need only answer the questions shown on the screen. Many packages have an **error trapping** mechanism that keeps a user from entering an incorrect type of data. For example, if the package requests an employee's name and the user tries to enter the number of hours worked, the package would flash an error message and refuse to accept the input.

Business accounting software packages can be very complex because they perform so many tasks. Users should read the documentation carefully before proceeding, since one step may affect the next. Because of the complexity of the accounting packages and of the accounting function in a firm, a great deal of thought must be given to the selection of a package. The package should match the firm's accounting system. If a firm's accounting system does not match a standard software package, the firm has two choices: Have an accounting package written to match the company's accounting system or change the accounting system to match an available software package. Having a software package specifically developed for an existing system can be a time-consuming and expensive process with no guarantee that an acceptable package will result. On the other hand, changing the accounting system to match an existing package may seem like a radical solution. However, the user is guaranteed a computerized accounting system that works as expected. Recent decreases in the prices of accounting systems have made it possible for a small company to buy a package and try it out for an outlay of less than $200.

REVIEW OF KEY POINTS

1. Software packages for handling finances are very popular programs for personal computers.
2. The following three types of packages can be used to manage or analyze finances: spreadsheets, personal financial management packages, and business accounting packages.
3. A spreadsheet allows a user to use a table of numbers, labels, and formulas to analyze relationships between the values.
4. Spreadsheets are commonly used to analyze data and to work with budgets and forecasts.
5. Once a spreadsheet has been created with labels, values, and

formulas, the user can ask "What if?" questions by changing values to determine the resulting changes in other values.

6. Common operations on spreadsheets include copying or moving ranges of cells, printing some or all of the spreadsheet, saving or loading the spreadsheet, and using functions and macros.

7. Integrated packages combine spreadsheets with other software packages.

8. The three types of personal financial management packages are personal budgeting, investment analysis, and tax planning and preparation.

9. Personal budgeting packages are used to help individuals track their expenditures and compare these payments against a budget.

10. Investment analysis packages are used to help individuals analyze and manage investments in various types of securities.

11. Tax planning and preparation packages can help individuals plan their tax strategy and prepare income tax returns.

12. Business accounting software packages are designed to keep track of a company's finances.

13. Modules in most business accounting packages include general ledger, accounts receivable, accounts payable, payroll, order processing, and inventory control.

KEY TERMS

accounting
accounts payable
accounts receivable
business accounting package
cell
cell identifier
cell pointer
column
completion screen
credit
debit
double-entry bookkeeping
edit line
electronic spreadsheet
error trapping
fixed expense
formula
function
general ledger
global change
horizontal scrolling
integrated package
inventory control
investment analysis package

label
local change
macro
module
order processing
payroll
personal accounting package
personal budgeting package
personal financial management
    package
range
relative copy
reverse video
row
spreadsheet
spreadsheet linking
tax planning and preparation package
template
transaction screen
value
variable expense
windowing
worksheet

1. Why is a financial analysis package also referred to as a "spreadsheet"?

2. What three types of elements can be entered in a spreadsheet? How do they relate to each other?

3. How can a spreadsheet be used to ask "What if?" questions of a budget or forecast?

4. What is a *cell* in a spreadsheet? How is a cell location denoted?

5. Why are cell locations, rather than values, used in formulas?

6. What is "windowing" in a spreadsheet? Why is it useful?

7. What is a relative copy? What is a range?

8. How is a template used with a spreadsheet? How do functions make working with a spreadsheet easier?

9. Under what circumstances could a spreadsheet be used instead of a business accounting package? Instead of a personal accounting package?

10. What problem can occur in the use of a tax planning and preparation software package?

11. What is the difference between double- and single-entry bookkeeping?

12. How does a personal budgeting package differ from a business accounting package?

13. Why are there different modules in a business accounting package?

14. In a business accounting software package, what is the accounts receivable module? The order processing module?

15. Why is *error trapping* important in a business accounting package?

12

Data Base Management Packages

Because the management of large amounts of information is crucial in many situations, the use of a data base is extremely important. This chapter presents the general concepts and terminology of data base management software, beginning with a discussion of the use of fields, records, and files for storage and manipulation of information. Types of data base management software are discussed and the differences between file processing systems and data base management systems are emphasized. The various operations that are common to all file processing systems are explained. The three types of data models—relational, hierarchical, and network—for data base management systems are then discussed and demonstrated. Finally, data base management packages for personal computers are discussed and suggestions are madc for selecting and purchasing data base management software for personal computers.

STUDY OBJECTIVES

After reading this chapter, you should be able to

- discuss the importance of data bases and data base management software;
- understand the concepts and terminology of data bases, including fields, records, and files;
- discuss the differences between file processing and data base management systems;
- understand the various operations available on file processing systems;
- describe the use of indexing and pointer systems for sorting data base records;
- explain the differences between relational, hierarchical and network data models;
- describe three common operations for working with a relational data base management system;
- discuss the use of SQL with relational data base systems;
- list some popular data base management packages for personal computers and differentiate file management systems from data base management systems;
- understand the facts that affect the selection of a data base management package for a personal computer.

DATA BASE HELPS FIGHT ON AIDS

In the fight against Acquired Immune Deficiency Syndrome (AIDS), the computer has become an important weapon for researchers in their search for drugs that might be effective in deactivating the Human Immunodeficiency Virus (HIV) that causes AIDS. Studies have shown that inhibiting the HIV enzyme, called a protease, deactivates the AIDS virus; therefore, researchers have been looking for a chemical compound that will match and thus cripple the enzyme.

The traditional approach to this type of research would involve randomly testing thousands of chemicals, a time-consuming process that would not guarantee that a suitable chemical would be found. Instead, scientists at the University of California at San Francisco used three computer programs to search the Cambridge Crystallographic Data Base for molecules that mirror the HIV enzyme. The data base contains structural images of more than 60,000 existing drugs.

The first program narrowed the search to 10,000 possibilities. The second program, called Dock, then searched for chemicals whose shape would fit an indentation in the HIV enzyme. Dock reduced the list of possible chemicals to 200. A stereo image of each chemical was produced by the third program, Midas Plus. This enabled the scientists to reduce the list to 20 chemicals, including Haldol, a psychotropic drug that doctors often prescribe to their patients who suffer from schizophrenia.

The researchers were encouraged by their discovery that Haldol closely matches the HIV enzyme. However, they also determined that the drug would have to be administered in doses 1,000 times that of normal—enough to kill a patient—to block the HIV virus. Although Haldol is not an immediate "cure" for individuals suffering from the HIV virus, it provides researchers with a starting point in developing a chemical compound that is less toxic than Haldol but effective in blocking the HIV enzyme.

Source: Michael Alexander, "Fight Against AIDS Takes to the Screens," *Computerworld,* July 1, 1991, p. 17.

INTRODUCTION TO DATA BASE CONCEPTS

For as long as humans have been keeping records, they have been storing information. Usually, the information has been stored in a manner that makes specific elements easy to find. The information may be stored as phone books, dictionaries, encyclopedias, stock quotes in the newspapers, mailing lists, and lists of batting averages for major league baseball players. Cooks often use 3- by 5-inch index cards to store recipes; students use them to store term paper notes. You undoubtably can think of other ways to store information; but in every case, it is organized in a form that is easy for the user to retrieve.

A collection of information stored on a computer is referred to as a data base; specifically, a **data base** is *any collection of information stored on a computer and arranged in such a way that the information can be easily manipulated and retrieved.* Data bases are often used to access particular pieces of information or to rearrange the information in some order. For example, when a mailing list is stored as a data base, it is possible to output only those names in certain ZIP codes or to output the entire list in numerical order by ZIP code. In the box on p. 350, a data base facilitates the search for a drug that will help in the fight against AIDS. The information in a data base can be output as a summary, or a report can be generated based on the collected information.

As mentioned, before the era of computers, information was stored as lists, on index cards, in file folders, in filing cabinets, and so on—and in many cases it is still stored in these forms. However, these nonelectronic forms can involve a great deal of paper or card shuffling for any summary information or report to be obtained. Because the computer is a machine that stores and manipulates information electronically, **data base management software** can do the same work more easily and in less time than humans. Data base management software can be used to create the data base, enter information into the data base, and then rearrange the data base or retrieve desired information from the data base. The information that is retrieved can then be output in a report format if desired.

In this chapter, we will discuss data base terminology and types of data bases, and then give an example of the creation and use of a PC data base. Finally, we will discuss the need for larger data bases and the various approaches used to work with them.

Data Base Terminology

Like any field of study, data base management has its own specific terminology that defines the various elements and operations used in working with data bases.

Many college libraries now have computers to search for books and articles by author, title, or subject.

The first concept to be considered is the data hierarchy. The **data hierarchy**—the way data or information is organized in the computer—is made up of fields, records, files, and data bases. In this section, we provide an overview of this terminology, starting with the concept of a field.

A single fact or data item under consideration is called a **field.** Examples of fields include a name on a mailing list, a part number, or a sales amount. Fields are usually identified within a file by a **field name** that is unique to that field. For example, we might have a field called SALES_AMT to refer to a sales amount field. A collection of fields that pertains to a single person, thing, or event is termed a **record.** For example, we might have a transaction record that contains numerous fields, including sales invoice number, customer name, date of purchase, product number, sales amount, and salesperson number. A related collection of records, all having the same fields, is referred to as a **file.** For example, a mailing list file would have a record for each person on the mailing list, with each record having the same fields but having different names and addresses on each record. Figure 12-1 shows a mailing list file with the fields and records pointed out.

Finally, if we have multiple files that are accessed together to generate needed information, then we have a data base. For a company that maintains a mailing list file, the data base might also have a sales file that contains the customer name and information on previous sales—including the date and amount of each transaction and the person responsible for the sale—and an inventory file that contains the product numbers and the current price and number of units in stock of each product. By accessing the data base made up of these files, we can generate various reports, including one that shows which products are being sold by which salesperson to which customers. This information could be helpful in deciding whether to hire an additional salesperson and, if so, where he or she should be located.

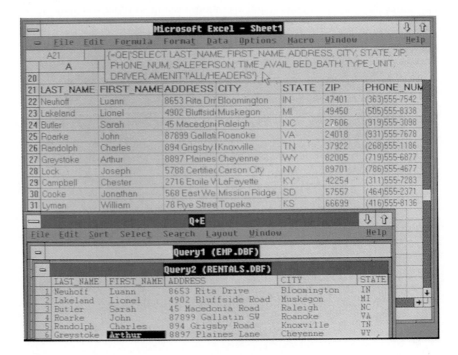

A popular use for computerized data bases is to set up mailing lists.

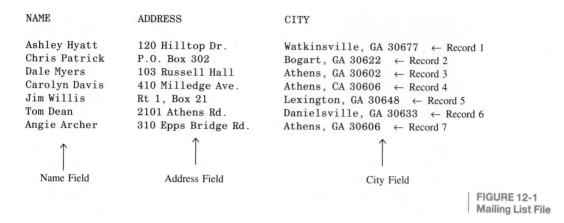

NAME	ADDRESS	CITY	
Ashley Hyatt	120 Hilltop Dr.	Watkinsville, GA 30677	← Record 1
Chris Patrick	P.O. Box 302	Bogart, GA 30622	← Record 2
Dale Myers	103 Russell Hall	Athens, GA 30602	← Record 3
Carolyn Davis	410 Milledge Ave.	Athens, CA 30606	← Record 4
Jim Willis	Rt 1, Box 21	Lexington, GA 30648	← Record 5
Tom Dean	2101 Athens Rd.	Danielsville, GA 30633	← Record 6
Angie Archer	310 Epps Bridge Rd.	Athens, GA 30606	← Record 7
↑	↑	↑	
Name Field	Address Field	City Field	

FIGURE 12-1
Mailing List File

Figure 12-2 shows the concept of a data base made up of a mailing list file, a transaction file, and an inventory file.

Types of Data Base Management Packages

Computer software for working with data bases can be broadly divided into two groups—file processing systems and data base management systems—with the primary difference between the two types of packages being the number of files the package can manage. A **file processing system (FPS)** can work with *only* one file at a time, while a **data base management system (DBMS)** can work with multiple files. An FPS can work with many types of lists including mailing lists, membership rolls, customer lists, and parts lists. Many data base management packages for personal computers are designed to work with single files. However, whenever the needed information appears on different lists in separate files, a DBMS must be used. Mainframe data base management software is almost always of the multifile variety (DBMS) since mainframes are used to work with very large and sophisticated data bases. As PCs are becoming more powerful and have larger amounts of secondary storage, multifile data base management systems are being used on them as well. In the next section we consider file processing systems. Data base management systems will be taken up in a later section.

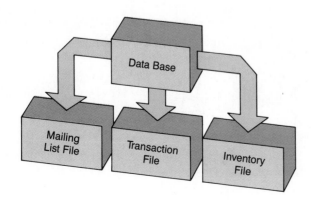

FIGURE 12-2
Data Base

File processing systems are often used to maintain up-to-date records on retail inventories (left) and to control patient records in hospitals (right).

Another institution that has benefited greatly from the use of data bases is the city or county blood bank.

As we said earlier, one of the two types of data base management package is the file processing system—or, as it is also known, a **file processor.** File processing systems are important because almost all organizations, regardless of size, require some form of recordkeeping that involves lists. In some cases, these records are simply lists of the members or employees of the organization; in larger organizations, the records go into great detail about the people, products, or services involved in the organization. Before computers, the only way to keep these records was on cards, on paper lists, or in folders in filing cabinets. When information was needed from these records, someone had to go through the cards, lists, or folders manually to collect the information.

Today, file processors are essentially electronic forms of these record-keeping systems that allow the user to go through the file quickly and easily. These software packages work with one file made up of many records to organize the information and to generate reports. File processors are often used on personal computers when the list management operations can be restricted to one file. Some of the more popular file processor packages for personal computers are RapidFile; Professional File; the data base manager in Lotus 1-2-3; and a shareware package, PC-File. dBase III PLUS, one of the most popular data base management packages, is often used as a file processor even though it is capable of working with multiple files.

Operations Using a File Processor Package

All data base management packages that include file processors have some operations in common: the file management operations and report generator operations. The **file manager** controls the actual creation of the file, including giving it a name, setting up the structure of the file with its fields, and entering data into the file. The file manager also handles file manipulation tasks such as sorting (rearranging) the file according to some field and searching for records that meet some criterion. It is also possible for the file manager to output only those

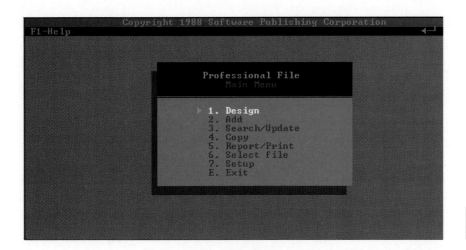

Professional File from Software Publishing Co. is an easy-to-use file processing system.

COMPUTERIZED HITMAN HELPS LA POLICE

A couple of years ago, we could have spent days going through unsolved cases and we may never have found the one. The killer probably would have walked.

Lt. Edward Hocking, Los Angeles Police Department

Quoted in "Police Have Their Own 'HITMAN': Computer File on Killings," *Los Angeles Times,* February 20, 1988, p. cc/Part II.

When Los Angeles police detectives need information on a homicide or suspected killer, they go to HITMAN— Homicide Information Tracking Management Automation Network. HITMAN is a data base management package that catalogs information about homicides in metropolitan Los Angeles, which number approximately 1,000 per year. HITMAN originally ran on a personal computer, but as its size continued to grow, it was moved to a mainframe. Currently, HITMAN contains over 7,000 records. Each record can contain over 100 fields, and detectives can search many fields simultaneously.

With HITMAN, detectives can electronically track individuals who are suspected of being involved in not only murder but other criminal activities such as prostitution, drug dealing, and gang-related or domestic violence. The data base provides the police with a list of suspects that has been narrowed by such factors as weapon, neighborhood, race, and motive. It is especially useful in finding a serial killer's MO (*modus operandi,* or mode of operation), because it can merge information from multiple crimes.

Another important use of HITMAN is linking new information to unsolved crimes. Frequently, individuals arrested in jurisdictions outside Los Angeles provide information about crimes that occurred in LA. The new information, regardless of how brief or seemingly insignificant, is entered in HITMAN, which performs the link function. Many homicide cases have been solved in this way. For example, a prisoner in Texas confessed that he had robbed and killed someone in Los Angeles several years before his arrest in Texas. He did not know the name of his victim or even the neighborhood in which he committed the crime, but he did remember that he shot the victim in the face several times and that he threw the body in a dumpster next to a bar. Texas authorities gave the information to LA police, who fed it into HITMAN, which linked the details to those of unsolved homicide cases and found only one case in which a victim with face wounds was found in a dumpster behind a bar. Case closed.

Without HITMAN, detectives would have had to spend several days manually searching case files to link the data. The suspect probably would have been released for lack of evidence before the detectives could manually link the new information to the unsolved crime.

Source: Jill Stewart and Boris Yaro, "Police Have Their Own 'HITMAN': Computer File on Killings," *Los Angeles Times,* February 20, 1988, p. CC/Part II; and interview with Los Angeles Police Department, December 11, 1991.

---

records that match a desired characteristic. For example, the first three fields of a file can be output for all records that meet some criterion.

The **report generator** handles the output of some or all of the fields either in the original order or in a sorted order with appropriate headings and a specific format. It can also be used to sum or average the contents of one or more fields.

Operations within the file manager and report generator functions include but are not limited to the following:

- creating the data base file;
- defining the structure of the file in terms of the fields;
- using a data entry screen in entering the information in each record;
- listing records on the file in some desired order;

- searching for a particular record or listing all records on the file with some special characteristic;
- creating the report format to be used;
- outputting the information in the desired report format.

The best way to understand these operations is to actually set up and use a data base. To do this, we will look at a data base example that involves a familiar situation—a professor's grade roll. There will be four fields: student name, student Social Security number, number of absences, and quiz average.

Creating the Data Base File   With the data base management software, creating the data base file is usually very easy—often requiring only that a unique but meaningful name be assigned to the file. In the case of the student data base, the professor might assign a name of STUDNTDB.

Defining the Structure   To work with this student data base, the professor must determine the type of information that will go into each field. This is known as creating the **data base structure**—defining the data base fields in terms of the field names, widths, and types.

The field name is a unique name given to each field in the data base. For example, the professor might use field names of NAME for the student names and SS_NUMBER for the student Social Security numbers. For many data base packages, field names must be made up of only letters, digits, and underscores.

The **field width** is the number of positions needed to store the information in each field. In our example, a field width of 20 should be satisfactory for the student name field; a field width of 11 (nine digits and two dashes) is needed for the student Social Security field.

The **field type** is the type of information that will be stored in that field. The allowable field types depend on the package being used, but four common field types are character, numeric, date, and logical. A **character field** can store any type of information but *cannot* be used for any type of calculation, while a **numeric field** can store numeric information and also can be used for making calculations. Numeric fields often designate the number of decimal positions that can be included in the value, or whether the field can include decimals at all. A **date field** can store only a date in dd/mm/yy format while a **logical field** can only be true or false (or yes or no). Table 12-1 shows the field names, field widths, and field types for the student grade data base. Table 12-2 shows the information that will be entered for this class. If the field type is numeric, the number of decimal positions is also shown. Note that while both the ABSENCES field and the QUIZ_AVE field are numeric, the ABSENCES field

TABLE 12-1
Structure for STUDNTDB Data Base File

Field Name	Field Width	Field Type	Decimal Positions
NAME	20	Character	
SS_NUMBER	11	Character	
ABSENCES	3	Numeric	0
QUIZ_AVE	6	Numeric	2

TABLE 12-2
Student Data Base Information

NAME	SS_NUMBER	ABSENCES	QUIZ_AVE
McCormick, Charles	999-89-1234	4	63.40
Deplant, Susan	999-40-2773	4	82.00
Factor, Ben E.	999-04-3043	3	74.90
Quay, May	999-99-1532	2	91.50
Fields, Samuel	999-09-0744	0	94.25
Boat, Rhoda	999-21-9876	2	48.50
Hyatt, Ashley	999-80-2269	1	85.50
Monk, Chip	999-13-4321	0	57.90

has zero decimal positions (sometimes referred to as an **integer field**) and the QUIZ_AVE field has two decimal positions (sometimes referred to as a **real field**). Be aware that the decimal point may be included in the field width of a real field and that the absolute maximum number of digits or letters to be entered should be considered when the field width is selected.

Entering Information   To enter the information in the data base, we commonly use a data entry screen. A **data entry screen** prompts the user to enter information for each record through a series of "fill-in-the-blank" questions that are shown on the monitor screen. Usually, the field name will be shown with the cursor next to it in a blank area in which the information for that field is entered. After the professor enters the information for a particular field and presses the Enter key, the cursor moves to the next field and awaits entry of information in that field. When all information for a record is entered, a blank data entry screen is shown for the next record.

Listing the File in Some Order   Once the information is entered in the data base, the records may be listed in the order in which they were input or the file may be rearranged or sorted according to some field. Figure 12-3 shows the student grade data base listed in the order in which it was input.

It is very common, in a data base file containing names, to sort alphabetically by name. Figure 12-4 shows the student data base listed alphabetically. The same data base can be sorted on another field if the professor wants it in another order. For example, the grade data base can be sorted from the highest QUIZ_AVE to the lowest. We will discuss the process of sorting in more detail in a later section.

Listing Particular Records   A very important operation with any data base is the process of finding records that meet some criterion. This may involve matching a single record or listing a group of records that meet the criterion. In our example, the professor may wish to see the record for the student "Hyatt, Ashley" or the records of all students with fewer than three absences. In either case, the data base management software will search the data base for records meeting the criterion and then list them on the screen or on the printer. Figure 12-5 shows a listing of students with fewer than three absences.

It is also possible to perform more complex searches by combining two or more fields. For example, the professor may want to list all students with

NAME	SS_NUMBER	ABSENCES	QUIZ_AVE
McCormick, Charles	999-89-1234	4	63.40
Deplant, Susan	999-40-2773	4	82.00
Factor, Ben E.	999-04-3043	3	74.90
Quay, May	999-99-1532	2	91.50
Fields, Samuel	999-09-0744	0	94.25
Boat, Rhoda	999-21-9876	2	48.50
Hyatt, Ashley	999-80-2269	1	85.50
Monk, Chip	999-13-4321	0	57.90

NAME	SS_NUMBER	ABSENCES	QUIZ_AVE
Boat, Rhoda	999-21-9876	2	48.50
Deplant, Susan	999-40-2773	4	82.00
Factor, Ben E.	999-04-3043	3	74.90
Fields, Samuel	999-09-0744	0	94.25
Hyatt, Ashley	999-80-2269	1	85.50
McCormick, Charles	999-89-1234	4	63.40
Monk, Chip	999-13-4321	0	57.90
Quay, May	999-99-1532	2	91.50

FIGURE 12-3 (left)
Listing of Student Data Base

FIGURE 12-4 (right)
Alphabetical Listing of Student Data Base

fewer than three absences *and* a quiz average greater than 80. The result of this search is shown in Figure 12-6.

Finally, it is possible to list records depending on a computation involving numeric fields. For example, our professor has a policy of subtracting the number of absences from the quiz average, and wants to see a listing of all students with a resulting modified quiz average greater than 90 to determine which students will receive a grade of "A." That is, the professor wants a listing of students who meet the requirement QUIZ_AVE − ABSENCES > 90. This listing is shown in Figure 12-7. Note that May Quay, who had an average of 91.50 before the absences were subtracted, was not listed in Figure 12-7 because her two absences dropped her modified quiz average below 90.

Generating Reports While a simple listing of records may be acceptable in many cases, other situations require a more formal report from the data base. Most data base management packages have a report generation function built into the software. This function may allow for special formats or headings, the summing of fields, and the creation of new columns by combining existing

FIGURE 12-5 (left)
Listing of Students with Fewer than Three Absences

FIGURE 12-6 (right)
Listing of Students with Fewer than Three Absences and Quiz Average Greater than 80

NAME	SS_NUMBER	ABSENCES	QUIZ_AVE
Quay, May	999-99-1532	2	91.50
Fields, Samuel	999-09-0744	0	94.25
Boat, Rhoda	999-21-9876	2	48.50
Hyatt, Ashley	999-80-2269	1	85.50
Monk, Chip	999-13-4321	0	57.90

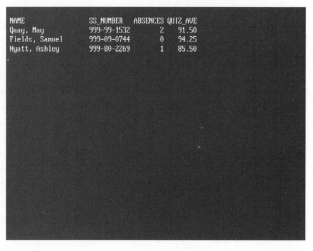

NAME	SS_NUMBER	ABSENCES	QUIZ_AVE
Quay, May	999-99-1532	2	91.50
Fields, Samuel	999-09-0744	0	94.25
Hyatt, Ashley	999-80-2269	1	85.50

```
NAME            SS_NUMBER  ABSENCES QUIZ_AVE
Fields, Samuel  999-09-0744       0    94.25
```

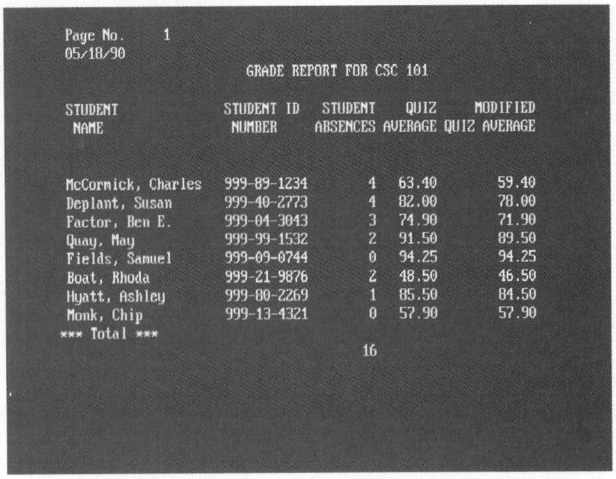

```
Page No.    1
05/18/90
                        GRADE REPORT FOR CSC 101

        STUDENT         STUDENT ID  STUDENT    QUIZ    MODIFIED
         NAME            NUMBER    ABSENCES AVERAGE QUIZ AVERAGE


    McCormick, Charles  999-89-1234      4    63.40      59.40
    Deplant, Susan      999-40-2773      4    82.00      78.00
    Factor, Ben E.      999-04-3043      3    74.90      71.90
    Quay, May           999-99-1532      2    91.50      89.50
    Fields, Samuel      999-09-0744      0    94.25      94.25
    Boat, Rhoda         999-21-9876      2    48.50      46.50
    Hyatt, Ashley       999-80-2269      1    85.50      84.50
    Monk, Chip          999-13-4321      0    57.90      57.90
    *** Total ***
                                        16
```

FIGURE 12-7 (left)
Listing of Students with
QUIZ_AVE − ABSENCES >90

FIGURE 12-8 (right)
Final Report for Student Data Base

columns. A report thus created is essentially a template for the output of some or all of the data base. The professor may wish to use more descriptive headings in the final report, find the total number of absences for the class, and create a new column that subtracts the number of absences from the quiz average. Figure 12-8 is a report showing this result. Note the difference between the QUIZ AVERAGE column and the MODIFIED QUIZ AVERAGE column, which resulted in three students dropping a letter grade on a 60−70−80−90 scale.

More on Sorting a Data Base

As we mentioned earlier, an important operation in working with a data base is **sorting,** or rearranging the information in some specific order. The resulting list is in either ascending or descending order (ascending order is the default on many data base managers) based either on the alphabetical or numerical sequence, depending on what is in the key field. When the student data base is listed alphabetically, it is sorted in ascending order based on the alphabet. It could also have been sorted in descending order according to the QUIZ_AVE field to list the students from highest to lowest quiz average.

Usually, the computer does not sort information by actually rearranging the records on the disk. Physically rearranging data base records to create a new, sorted file is a very slow process, and the new file must be used anytime a sorted version of the data base is needed. Instead of physically sorting the data, the computer can handle the rearrangement process via **indexing,** which is a system of using record numbers to keep track of the record locations. A **record number** refers to the physical position of the record in the list. Indexing schemes are usually implemented by a **pointer system,** wherein the value of a given pointer denotes the location of the *next* record in the indexed ordering. Such a system avoids the need for a search through the record numbers to find the *next* record in the indexed ordering. It also allows additions and deletions to be incorporated easily into the ordering: The computer simply changes the pointers. As an example of a pointer system in use, consider again the STUDNTDB data base file shown in Table 12-2, which we have listed again as Table 12-3 with the records numbered. In this case, the alphabetical ordering can be expressed through a

TABLE 12-3
Student Data Base Information Using Pointer System

Record Number	Pointer	NAME	SS_NUMBER	ABSENCES	QUIZ_AVE
1	8	McCormick, Charles	999-89-1234	4	63.40
2	3	Deplant, Susan	999-40-2773	4	82.00
3	5	Factor, Ben E.	999-04-3043	3	74.90
4	–	Quay, May	999-99-1532	2	91.50
5	7	Fields, Samuel	999-09-0744	0	94.25
6	2	Boat, Rhoda	999-21-9876	2	48.50
7	1	Hyatt, Ashley	999-80-2269	1	85.50
8	4	Monk, Chip	999-13-4321	0	57.90

pointer system. This alphabetical ordering is shown in Table 12-3, with the pointer system in a separate column.

To use the pointer system shown in Table 12-3, we must first know that record 6 is first in the ordering. Note that there is no pointer to record 6 since nothing points to it. Note also that no pointer follows record 4 since it is the last record in the ordering and points to no other record. To use the pointer system to determine the alphabetical ordering, go first to record 6. The pointer value from 6 is 2, so 2 is the next record. Go to record 2 and note that the pointer value is 3; go to record 3 and its corresponding pointer, and so on, down to record 4, the last record in the ordering. This procedure yields an alphabetical ordering of 6–2–3–5–7–1–8–4 in terms of record numbers.

If a record is added to or deleted from a data base that is using a pointer system, only the pointers need to be changed to reflect this. For example, if Sue Dodd adds the class late, her information would become record 9. Then the pointer system for an alphabetical order would become 6–2–9–3–5–7–1–8–4, since Dodd comes before Factor (record 3) and after Deplant (record 2). Only the pointers for records 2 and 9 would be affected by this change. The new pointer system for this ordering is shown in Table 12-4, with the added record and changed pointers highlighted.

TABLE 12-4
Modified Student Data Base Information Using Pointer System

Record Number	Pointer	NAME	SS_NUMBER	ABSENCES	QUIZ_AVE
1	8	McCormick, Charles	999-89-1234	4	63.40
2	9	Deplant, Susan	999-40-2773	4	82.00
3	5	Factor, Ben E.	999-04-3043	3	74.90
4	–	Quay, May	999-99-1532	2	91.50
5	7	Fields, Samuel	999-09-0744	0	94.25
6	2	Boat, Rhoda	999-21-9876	2	48.50
7	1	Hyatt, Ashley	999-80-2269	1	85.50
8	4	Monk, Chip	999-13-4321	0	57.90
9	3	Dodd, Sue	999-83-6900	2	74.50

Advanced Features

In addition to the features just discussed, which are common to all file processing systems, some packages offer the capability of combining fields from separate files and combining commands into programs. In the first case, for example, we might want to combine the student grade information in STUDNTDB with other grade information, say, student grades on projects, which is kept in another file. As long as the two files have at least one field in common, we can create a third file by combining fields from records that have the same entry in the common field. In our situation, if the student Social Security number is common to both grade files, we could match Social Security numbers to create a new file that contained some or all the information in the two existing files.

In the second case—creating files made up of commands—file processing systems offer the capability to have the package run through an entire series of commands for the data base file. These file processing programs are often referred to as **command files,** and they greatly extend the power of these packages. Figure 12-9 shows one such command file that uses dBASE III PLUS to create a list of student names and quiz averages.

The newest version of dBASE, dBASE IV, goes a step beyond command files. It also has an applications generator that allows the user to create menus to tie together forms, queries, and reports without having to actually write a program.

DATA BASE MANAGEMENT SYSTEMS

As we discussed in the previous section, file processing systems are very useful for working with lists of information that can be contained on a single file. They are often very easy to use and can be quite inexpensive. Frequently, however, information is needed that is stored on multiple files. For example, a college or university could have one file for the registrar's office with application and admissions data similar to the file discussed earlier, another file with housing information, and still another file for the financial aid office with information

```
*********** Program STUDENT *************
SET TALK OFF
SET ECHO OFF
* Select data base file
USE STUDNTDB
?
? "Student Name          Quiz Average"
?
* The program loop ends when end of file is reached
DO WHILE .NOT.EOF()
     ?NAME,QUIZ_AVE
* Skip to next record
     SKIP
ENDDO
RETURN
```

FIGURE 12-9
dBASE Command File

Colleges may use several different data bases to store various types of information about students.

on scholarships and loans. When information is stored on separate files, accessing the various elements is not an easy task and fundamental questions about data redundancy, data integrity, and data dependence are raised.

Data redundancy is the repetition of the same data on different files. The college or university offices mentioned earlier may have separate files containing much of the same information, for example, name, Social Security number, address, and so on. Such redundancy is costly in terms of money required to collect and process the data for computer storage and in terms of computer storage itself.

The second problem mentioned, **data integrity,** is closely related to data redundancy. When the same information is stored in multiple files throughout an organization, any change in the data must be made in *all* files. For example, a student's change of address has to be entered in all the university files mentioned earlier. A change missed in only one file can lead to severe problems for the users of the data and for the person referred to by the incorrect data.

Whenever different departments in an organization collect, process, and store information, it is altogether possible that they will use different software to perform this operation. One department might use a computer language like COBOL to create its files on a mainframe computer, another department might use a file processing package to do the same operation on a personal computer, and still another department might use a minicomputer to process and store information. When this occurs, there is a problem with **data dependence** between the software and the files. The files of one department are incompatible with the files of another department and, as a result, it is often very difficult to combine the information from the two files.

Taken together, the problems of data redundancy, data integrity, and data dependence mean that any effort to combine files from different departments can be a very painstaking task. Consider again our example of the three departments at a university or college. If a college administrator wished to write a report on the number of students who were accepted who also requested financial aid and on-campus housing, the process of collecting the necessary data from three different files created by three different departments could be quite slow and awkward.

The solution to the problems that result from each department in an organization creating its own files is for the institution to install a data base managed by a DBMS. A data base management system will create all files with the same software, and this software will be used by all units to access the data base. Further, a file processing system that can handle only one file at a time will not be acceptable for the demands of working with a data base made up of numerous files, so we will need a data base management system that can manage multiple files.

Data Models

In working with data base management systems, the user has a choice of how the data will be organized on the data base. Three **data models** have been developed for organizing the data base: the hierarchical data model, the network data model, and the relational data model. In a hierarchical data model, there is a hierarchy from top to bottom, with each lower-level element linked to only one upper-level element. In a network model, there is also a hierarchy, but a lower-level element may be linked to multiple upper-level elements. In a relational model, a series of tables is used to show the relationships between the data elements. Figure 12-10 shows each of the data models schematically.

Each of the three models has been implemented in various commercial DBMSs, and each has its strong and weak points. We will give a brief overview of each data model and show examples of each.

The Hierarchical Data Model

The **hierarchical data model** can be used to handle situations in which data elements have an inherent superior–subordinate relationship in that every data element has one and only one **parent** or owner but a parent may be linked to

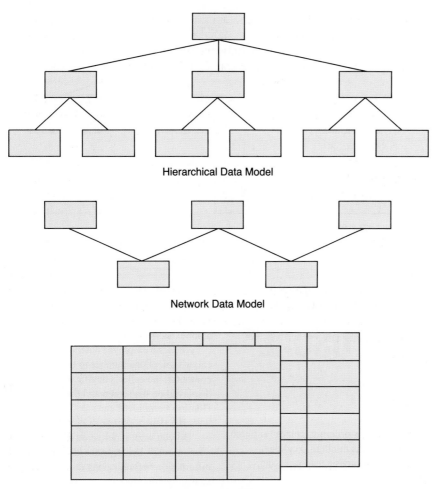

FIGURE 12-10
Schematic of Various Data
Models

Hierarchical Data Model

Network Data Model

Relational Data Model

multiple lower-level elements called **children.** Such linkages are referred to as
one-to-many and **one-to-one relationships;** a parent (the "one") is linked to
many children or to one. A hierarchical model is similar to the charts that organizations use to describe their superior–subordinate relationships. As an example of the use of a hierarchical data model, consider a data base made up of
family names, the cars owned by family members, and any outstanding parking
tickets on each car. Figure 12-11 shows how this automobile data base would
be represented as a hierarchical data model.

Note in Figure 12-11 that the family name is the highest-level data type,
the automobiles are the next level, and the parking tickets for each automobile
are at the bottom. There is always only *one* upper-level data element for any
number of lower-level elements. This is a one-to-one or one-to-many
relationship.

The Network Data Model

If there are **many-to-many relationships,** the **network data model** can be used,
which allows each data element to have more than one parent. The hierarchical

FIGURE 12-11
Hierarchical Data Model for
Automobile Data Base

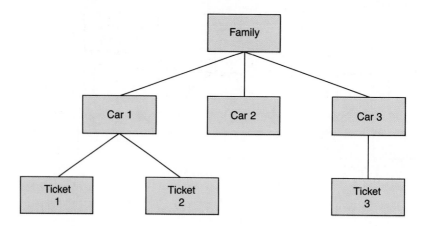

"I'LL HAVE THE USUAL"

It seems that ordering a pizza for home delivery is as familiar to college students as buying textbooks and studying for exams. Now, Domino's Pizza has a data base system called OASIS that makes it even easier for students and other pizzaphiles to indulge.

The next time you call Domino's to place an order, an employee may request your telephone number and then simply ask if you want "the usual." This is possible because OASIS, which is installed on each store's UNIX-based personal computer, gathers information about the store's customers. Types of information the data base stores include the customer's address, favorite toppings, number of pizzas usually ordered, method of payment, and special requests, such as delivering the pizza to a dorm room. The data base also knows if the caller is telephoning from a number that has been used by someone who refused to

pay for a pizza or by a prankster who, for example, requested pizza delivery to a nonexistent address.

When the employee enters the caller's telephone number in the store's computer, the caller's buying habits are displayed on the screen and the Domino's employee can ask, "Do you want the same toppings as last time?" or "Do you want it delivered to your dorm room?" Drivers have all this information before leaving the store. If a customer does not want to provide his or her telephone number, the system allows the employee to key in the order rather than pull up the information from the customer data base.

In addition to speeding the order process for both the customer and the Domino's employee, the OASIS system automates order preparation and delivery by creating a "door slip" when an order is taken. The slip tells the pie maker exactly what the customer ordered and tells the driver exactly where to deliver the pizza. Further, OASIS provides Domino's management with the demographic characteristics of each store.

Source: "New Domino's Computer System Could Help the Company Avoid Those Noids," *The Atlanta Journal-Constitution,* September 11, 1989, p. C14; and interview with Domino's on December 12, 1991.

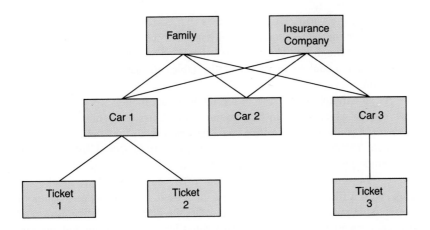

FIGURE 12-12
Network Data Model for
Automobile Data Base

model described previously is actually a special case of the network model in which the number of parents per child is restricted to one. Figure 12-12 shows how the network model could be used to represent the automobile data base when another upper-level data element has been added—the insurance company that insures each automobile.

In the network data model for the automobile data base, each automobile now has *two* parents: the family that owns the cars and the insurance company that insures the cars.

The Relational Data Model

While the hierarchical and network models use a tree or a network structure to show the linkages between fields, the **relational data model** uses a table structure. These tables—or, as they are also called, **flat files**—have columns that

Data base software on mainframe computers helps brokers on the New York Stock Exchange manage the tremendous number of transactions that take place each trading day.

correspond to the various fields and rows that correspond to the records. Each row must have the same number of columns, and the same specific format must be followed throughout. The word *relational* comes from the capability of a relational data model to relate all of the tables to each other to find needed information.

As an example of the use of a relational data model, we will use another situation with which you may be familiar—an admissions office at a college or university. Assume that this office has a data base with four fields: an applicant name field (NAME), a Social Security number field (SSNUMBER), a high school grade point field (GPA), and a Scholastic Aptitude Test (SAT) score field. With just these four fields, the admissions office has been able to handle applications with a file processing system of the type discussed earlier. Assume that now the college admissions committee wants the admissions office also to consider recommendations that have been written for each applicant and any extracurricular activities in which the applicant was involved in high school. In both cases, the number of fields needed to store this information is unknown. All applicants must have two recommendations, but they may have more. Similarly, the majority of applicants will have at least one extracurricular activity, but most will have several. Using a file processing system to handle this data base would lead to many empty fields or to not enough fields. In this case, a data base management system capable of handling multiple files is needed.

Figure 12-13 shows the three tables necessary to represent the admissions data base. The table in Figure 12-13a contains the NAME, SSNUMBER, GPA, and SAT fields; the table in Figure 12-13b contains the SSNUMBER and RECOMMENDATION fields; and the table in Figure 12-13c contains the SSNUMBER and ACTIVITY fields. Horizontal and vertical lines have been drawn in

To research the bloodlines and race records of approximately 1 million thoroughbred horses before making a purchase, many horsebreeders use Bloodstock Research, an online data base service.

NAME	SSNUMBER	GPA	SAT
Stafford, Phyllis	999-23-4321	3.65	1270
Box, Rip	999-31-9776	2.95	1080
Maxwell, Danny	999-99-1234	4.00	1390
Triesch, Martha	999-88-1532	3.50	1250
Campbell, Lange	999-14-3143	2.75	890
DeVane, Samuel	999-19-1744	2.90	980
Roth, Susan	999-74-3343	4.00	1500
Patrick, Ashley	999-89-2269	3.10	1270

FIGURE 12-13a
Applicant Table

SSNUMBER	RECOMMENDATION
999-23-4321	Ben Dyer
999-99-1234	Andrew Seila
999-99-1234	Ron Armstrong
999-99-1234	Robert Brown
999-14-3143	Ann Scott
999-74-3343	Chris Jones
999-74-3343	Roscoe Davis
999-89-2269	Ralph Stam
999-89-2269	Dane Marshall
999-89-2269	James Cope
999-89-2269	Carol Calbos

FIGURE 12-13b
Recommendation Table

SSNUMBER	ACTIVITY
999-99-1234	Football
999-99-1234	Basketball
999-99-1234	Computer Club
999-23-4321	Chorus
999-74-3343	Cheerleader
999-89-2269	Computer Club
999-89-2269	Swimming
999-14-3143	Volleyball

FIGURE 12-13c
Activity Table

the tables in Figure 12-13 to show the row and column nature of the relational data base. The Social Security number, which is common to all three tables, is the factor that determines the relationship between the various tables. When multiple tables are used, the number of recommendations and activities is not limited by the number of fields, as it might be in a file processing system, and there are no blank fields. A relational data base management system provides much more flexibility to add a new table of information related to the existing tables.

For the relational data base management system to use this combination of tables to find the information on a particular individual, it must go through a two-step process. First, a search procedure is used to find the name of the individual in the first table; the corresponding Social Security number is noted. Then, using the Social Security number, the file manager goes to the other tables to find the corresponding information. To do this the file manager needs a data dictionary. The **data dictionary** contains information about the data base,

By placing medical records in a data base, medical professionals can help ensure proper disease diagnosis and provide higher-quality patient care.

including the number and names of the fields, the location of the various fields in the tables, and the relationships between the tables. The data dictionary is a necessity for proper documentation of the data base.

Two important operations in the use of a relational data base management system are the SELECT and JOIN operations. The computer uses the SELECT operation to create a new table by choosing only those rows from a table that have a desired attribute. The JOIN operation allows a user to create a new table from two existing tables by combining rows that meet some criterion. For example, if we wanted to create a table made up of those applicants from the first table who had a GPA greater than 3.0, we would use the SELECT operation to find all rows from the main applicant table that meet this criterion. The resulting new table is shown in Figure 12-14. We could then use the JOIN operation to combine the activities with the information in this table. Figure 12-15 shows the result of this second operation.

Another useful operation is the PROJECT operation, which allows a user to choose which fields from a table to use in creating a new table. The PROJECT operation can be combined with the SELECT and JOIN operations as needed to manipulate the tables in a relational data base.

Comparing the Data Models

While you probably feel more comfortable with the relational data model since we constantly work with tables of one sort or another, it is good to know that the hierarchical and network models exist and have an important role in data

NAME	SSNUMBER	GPA	SAT
Stafford, Phyllis	999-23-4321	3.65	1270
Maxwell, Danny	999-99-1234	4.00	1390
Triesch, Martha	999-88-1532	3.50	1250
Roth, Susan	999-74-3343	4.00	1500
Patrick, Ashley	999-89-2269	3.10	1270

FIGURE 12-14
Result of Using SELECT
Operation

NAME	SSNUMBER	GPA	SAT	ACTIVITY
Stafford, Phyllis	999-23-4321	3.65	1270	Chorus
Maxwell, Danny	999-99-1234	4.00	1390	Football
Maxwell, Danny	999-99-1234	4.00	1390	Basketball
Maxwell, Danny	999-99-1234	4.00	1390	Computer Club
Roth, Susan	999-74-3343	4.00	1500	Cheerleader
Patrick, Ashley	999-89-2269	3.10	1270	Computer Club
Patrick, Ashley	999-89-2269	3.10	1270	Swimming

FIGURE 12-15
Result of Using JOIN Operation

A data base system in a local pharmacy can help the pharmacist improve customer service and monitor possible harmful drug interactions.

base management. The hierarchical model, used extensively on mainframes and minicomputers, is based on the standards set by a computer industry group called CODASYL (Conference On Data Systems Languages), while the relational model has been used on personal computers for some time and is becoming more popular on mainframe computers.

Hierarchical and network models offer some advantages over the relational model: They have less data redundancy and require less computer time. On the other hand, the relational model tends to be the more flexible of the three, because new tables can be created as needed using the SELECT, JOIN, and PROJECT operations. With the other two models, all of the structure in the data base must be defined as it is being created. Many users also find the relational model the easiest to understand and use. The trend in data base models is definitely toward increased use of the relational model on both personal computers and mainframes.

Examples of hierarchical and network models on mainframe computers are the IDMS and IDS systems; DB2 from IBM is a relational DBMS for mainframe computers. On personal computers, dBASE III PLUS and dBASE IV and R:BASE 5000 are popular relational data base managers, and KnowledgeMan/2 is a network product.

Interfacing with a DBMS

To use any of the commercial data base management systems, the user must learn the command structure that interfaces with the software system. Some popular personal computer data base managers have developed interfaces that are very easy to use, while many of the mainframe systems require either a programming language or a special **query language** to access the software. One such query language is the Structured Query Language (SQL), which is an inherent part of a relational data base and can be used to work with relational data bases on any size computer. An additional advantage of SQL is that it was originally designed to work in multiuser environments, so it can be used with workstations and in the increasing number of PC-based networks. As evidence of the increasing popularity of SQL, it is now included as a part of dBASE IV.

An example of a query using SQL is shown in Figure 12-16. This set of statements requests a list of the names, grade point averages, and SAT scores for all applicants with GPAs greater than 3.0. This list is output in alphabetical order.

Personal computer data base management packages like the very popular dBASE III PLUS and dBASE IV have their own query language in the form of commands that can be entered interactively from the keyboard or combined into a series of instructions that takes the form of a computer program. For example, Figure 12-17 shows the dBASE III PLUS series of commands; the period in

FIGURE 12-16
Example of SQL

```
SELECT NAME, GPA, SAT
FROM APPLICNT
WHERE GPA > 3.0
ORDER BY NAME
```

```
. USE APPLICNT INDEX ALPHA
. LIST NAME, GPA, SAT FOR GPA > 3.0
```

FIGURE 12-17
Example of dBASE Commands

front of the command is the dBASE III PLUS user prompt. The first statement requests that the dBASE file name APPLICNT, which has been indexed alphabetically, be used, and the second statement lists the desired fields for records that meet the GPA criterion.

Because both the mainframe and dBASE III PLUS query languages require the user to develop a *logical procedure* to perform the desired task, they are referred to as **procedural languages.** If the user can perform the desired task by simply answering questions from the software, then the language is **nonprocedural.** Procedural languages are analogous to command-driven software and nonprocedural languages are like menu-driven software. dBASE III PLUS and dBASE IV also have a nonprocedural, menu-driven command system that allows the user to answer questions instead of entering commands.

Some systems go beyond a nonprocedural language structure to use a natural language. As the name implies, a **natural language** allows users to enter

> **You can spend an awful lot of money on a program, but if it doesn't do what you need it to do, it's a waste of money.**
>
> *Marlise Parker, small business consultant*
>
> Quoted in "The Perfect Small Business Data Base," *PC Today,* June 1992, p. 17.

DBMS software may contain a natural language query feature.

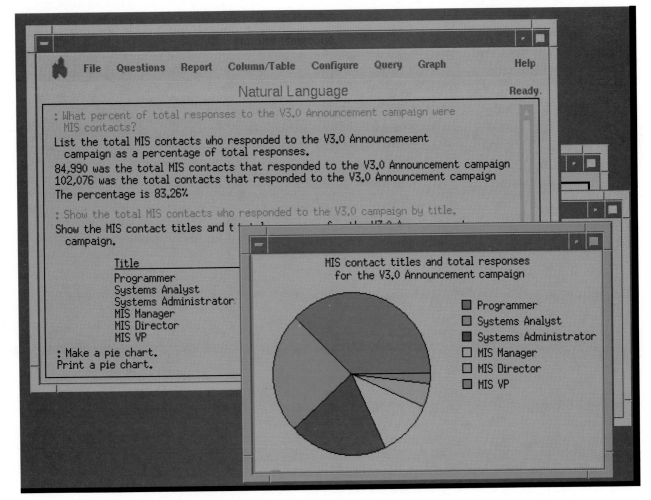

LEARNING A FOREIGN LANGUAGE WITH HYPERTEXT

Data bases are primarily used to provide users with needed information. The information is usually stored in fields, records, and files, and specific commands are used to retrieve the information. A form of electronic information retrieval that is becoming more popular, however, is provided by hypertext.

Hypertext allows its users to navigate a data base more freely, because it is largely free of the constrictions imposed by traditional data bases. Unlike traditional data bases, hypertext stores information in discrete nodes or groups that can be reached from any other node. This is possible because hypertext's author created links within the system. The system links, in turn, allow the user to link *anything* in the document, including words, phrases, or specified strings in the file. Therefore, navigation within the data base is motivated by the user's mental connections.

As an example of the application of hypertext to a familiar situation, consider the often painstaking process most high school and college students go through to learn a foreign language. Traditionally, students learn a language's grammar rules and vocabulary before they progress to reading blocks of text. Now, a computer system called Transparent Language uses hypertext to enable a beginning foreign language student to read popular text material almost immediately.

This is possible because the software allows students to translate the

> It [Transparent Language] would make an excellent program to present to our foreign language methods classes to acquaint them with the really fine technology that has become available for second language acquisition.
>
> *Prof. Genelle Morain,*
> *Language Education*
> *Department, University of*
> *Georgia*
>
> Letter from Genelle Morain to author.
> April 5, 1992.

commands in their own "natural language." Examples of this are the Clout system for R:BASE 5000 and the Q&A data base management package. A natural language version of the procedural commands shown in Figures 12-16 and 12-17 might be

```
Show the NAME, GPA, and SAT of all students with
GPA greater than 3.0
```

text as they read. The text is presented at the top of the computer screen, and the student positions the cursor on a line, word, or phrase that he or she wants to translate. The translation, grammatical structure, and verb tense of the selected word or passage appear in a window at the bottom of the screen; therefore, if the reader does not understand a portion of the text, a quick look at the bottom of the screen explains its meaning. The system includes various texts or stories and a linguistic data base for each text. The data base was created by language experts, who entered information at the rate of 5 hours per page, and includes five languages—English, Spanish, French, German, and Latin.

This method of language learning is based on a linguistic theory called "comprehensible input," which proposes that people learn a language better by having repeated encounters with real words in real text, in the same way children learn new words from their parents, than by traditional systems. For example, school administrators traditionally set aside an entire year for high school students and a semester for college students studying Latin to translate the *Aeneid;* but with the Transparent Language hypertext system, the *Aeneid* can be read in a few hours.

Source: Daniel J. Lyons, "Program Eases Learning of Foreign Languages," *PC Week,* October 21, 1991, p. 203.

```
┌─────────────────────────Original-Language Text─────────────────────────┐
│ EL SOMBRERO DE TRES PICOS                                              │
│                                     ◆                                   │
│      XI                                                                 │
│                                                                         │
│      --Dios te guarde, Frasquita...  --dijo el corregidor a media voz, │
│ ≡ apareciendo bajo el emparrado y andando de puntillas.             ≡ │
│      --¡Tanto bueno, señor corregidor!  --respondió en voz natural,    │
│ haciéndole mil reverencias--.  ¡Usía por aquí a estas horas!  ¡Y con el│
│ calor que hace!  ¡Vaya, siéntese su señoría!...  Esto está fresquito. ¿Cómo│
│ no ha aguardado su señoría a los demás señores?  Aquí tienen ya preparados│
│ sus asientos...  Esta tarde esperamos al señor obispo en persona, que le ha│
├──────Word Translation───────────┬─────────Phrase Translation──────────┤
│ appearing                       │                                     │
│                                 │                                     │
│          ────────────────Sentence or Clause Translation──────────────┤
│ appearing under the grapevine, walking on tip-toe.                    │
│                                                                         │
│                                                                         │
├─────────────────────────────────┬───────────────────────────────────┤
│ Present participle. If used as a noun, it │ Infinitive: aparecer        │
│ is a gerund.                              │                             │
│                                           ├───────────────────────────┤
│                                           │ Esc=Menu    Location: 4-1 │
└───────────────────────────────────────────────────────────────────────┘
```

Because there are two separate and distinct types of data base packages for PCs—file processors and data base management systems—it is important to decide first which type of package is needed. The user should know how much data is involved, how many fields may be needed, how big the fields will be,

BITS OF HISTORY

The Origins of Hypertext

There are so many ways that computers can help you get stuff out of your mind so you can study it and look at it; hypertext is going to be a big part of that development.

Douglas Engelbart, inventor of the mouse

Quoted in "What's All the Talk about Hypertext, Anyway?" *PC Week,* October 6, 1987, pp. 60, 69.

Hypertext, although new to most computer users, actually predates the use of computers. The notion of hypertext was proposed by Vannevar Bush, President Franklin D. Roosevelt's science advisor, in a 1945 *Atlantic* magazine article entitled "As We May Think." Bush's words were prophetic, and he actually developed plans for an electromechanical hypertext machine that would allow users to store and retrieve virtually any amount of information as well as shift quickly between documents stored on microfilm. However, he did not give it the name we use now. That came 20 years later, when computer visionary Ted Nelson coined the term *hypertext,* which he described as "nonsequential writing."

Early hypertext systems were created in the late 1960s by Doug Engelbart, the inventor of the mouse, at the University of Illinois, where at least one actual hypertext application ran on an IBM mainframe. Then in the 1970s, a hypertext system called NoteCards was developed by researchers at Xerox. Hypertext remained a largely hidden concept, however, until the release in 1987 of the HyperCard software system by Apple for use on the Macintosh. HyperCard contains hypertext among its broad array of information management and programming capabilities.

Source: Paul Karon, "What's All the Talk about Hypertext, Anyway," *PC Week,* October 6, 1987, pp. 60, 69.

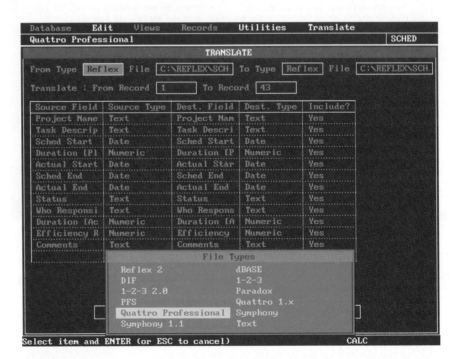

This RapidFile file processor software can be used in conjunction with a number of other packages, as shown in the window at the bottom of the screen.

and what kind of reports will be required. Prices for file processors range from "almost free" packages that are available from various bulletin boards to over $100 for packages with more power and options, such as Professional File and RapidFile. Relational data base management systems such as Paradox, dBASE IV, and R:BASE are usually much more costly, with prices exceeding $500.

1. A data base is a collection of information arranged for easy manipulation and retrieval. Data bases are found all around us.

2. Data base packages are aimed at manipulating information and outputting it in the form of reports.

3. The data hierarchy is made up of fields, records, files, and data bases. A record is made up of information in the fields, and a file is a collection of records all having the same fields. A data base is made up of one or more files.

4. The field width is the number of positions taken up by a field. Field names are used to identify fields on a record.

5. The two primary types of data base management packages are the file processing system (FPS) and the data base management system (DBMS). An FPS is used for working with a single file; a DBMS can work with multiple files.

6. File processing systems create the data base file, set up its structure, manage data entry, and handle file manipulation tasks. Then the information can be output as lists or as more formal reports.

7. Common file processor operations include sorting the records, searching for a given record, and listing a group of records.

8. Because physical sorting of data base records is very slow, pointer systems are used to perform the sorting process through indexing.

9. More advanced file management operations include merging two files that share a common field and writing command files made up of data base commands.

10. Data base management systems, which work with a data base made up of multiple files, help eliminate problems with data redundancy, data integrity, and data dependence on software.

11. Data models are utilized to organize the information in a data base. The most widely used data models are hierarchical, network, and relational.

12. A hierarchical data model works with one-to-one and one-to-many relationships in a tree structure. A network data model is like a hierarchical data model except that it allows many-to-many relationships.

13. A relational data model uses tables to model the data base. These tables, called flat files, are related by having a field in common.

14. Procedural and nonprocedural languages are used to interface with a DBMS. Now, natural languages are also being used to access a data base.

15. Selecting a data base package requires a great deal of planning: The user's needs and knowledge should be carefully matched to the appropriate package.

character field
children
command file
data base
data base management software
data base management system
 (DBMS)
data base structure
data dependence
data dictionary
data entry screen
data hierarchy
data integrity
data models
data redundancy
date field
field
field name
field type
field width
file
file manager
file processing system (FPS)
file processor

flat file
hierarchical data model
hypertext
indexing
integer field
logical field
many-to-many relationship
natural language
network data model
nonprocedural language
numeric field
one-to-many relationship
one-to-one relationship
parent
pointer system
procedural language
query language
real field
record
record number
relational data model
report generator
sorting

1. What is a data base? What is the relationship of a data base to files?

2. What is a data base management package?

3. What are the elements of a file? How are they ordered? What are the field width and field name?

4. What is the difference between a file processing system and a data base management system?

5. What are the first two steps involved in using a file manager to work with a data base file?

6. How is information entered in data base management software?

7. How is indexing used to speed up the sorting process? What is a pointer system?

8. Name two advanced features found in many file processing systems and discuss their functions.

9. Name three problems that can occur when separate files exist within the same organization. How can a DBMS help eliminate these problems?

10. List the three data models. Which does not support a many-to-many relationship between fields?

11. Why is the concept of a table important in a relational data base? What is the "JOIN" function for a relational data base package and why is it such a useful operation?

12. Why is a relational data base package more flexible and more powerful than a file processing package? If you were going to set up a membership list of a student

organization, what type of package would you choose? Why?

13. What is SQL? Why is it becoming more popular for working with data bases?

14. What is the difference between a procedural language and a non-procedural language? How are natural languages being used in data base management packages?

15. Name four points that the user should consider when selecting data base management software for a personal computer.

13

Telecommunications and Computer Networks

Combining a computer with a communications link for two-way communications with other computers is called telecommunications, and two or more computers linked together form a computer network. In this chapter, we will cover the related topics of telecommunications and computer networks, including the use of local area networks, which are restricted to a single location, and wide area networks, which may cover the entire globe. The use of PCs for accessing online services and data base vendors, interacting with other users, sending mail via telephone lines, telecommuting, and buying goods and services will be examined. The hardware and software needed to communicate using a PC are also discussed, and some directions for the future are covered.

STUDY OBJECTIVES

After reading this chapter, you should be able to

- understand the many opportunities that telecommunications offers users of personal and mainframe computers;
- discuss computer networks in general;
- distinguish between a local area network (LAN) and a wide area network (WAN);
- list reasons why a LAN can be useful;
- describe the three types of LANs that are commonly used;
- discuss the three types of wide area networks;
- list and discuss the various ways in which a personal computer can be used to communicate with other computers;
- describe how a modem and communications software enable a personal computer user to telecommunicate;
- distinguish between an online service and a data base vendor;
- explain how electronic bulletin boards and electronic mail operate;
- discuss telecommuting and the use of videotex;
- understand the importance of integrated services digital network for the future of telecommunications.

PCs JOIN THE MARINES

We train like we fight. When we go into the field we just unplug [the personal computers] from the wall and go.

Major Robert A. Coates, USMC

Quoted in "PCs in the Trenches," *The Atlanta Journal-Constitution*, May 2, 1989, pp. C1–C2.

When the U.S. Marines were mobilized for Operations Desert Shield and Desert Storm, they packed personal computers for communications along with their rifles and other supplies. The same PCs that you can purchase at the corner computer store were outfitted for war with software able to quickly organize, retrieve, and communicate information on battlefield conditions.

During a battle, large-scale troop movements are directed from division headquarters, which is usually a mile or more behind the front lines. Traditionally, communication with the front has been through couriers, telephone, and radio, all of which have disadvantages. Couriers may be shot or captured, and voice communications over telephones or radios can easily become garbled. Even within division headquarters, there is a great deal of noise and confusion, which may interfere with a commanding general's communication with staff officers.

To solve these problems, the Marines in Saudi Arabia used both radio and cable communications media to set up 20 mobile local area networks (LANs) in various desert locations for communications. They used many innovative methods to keep the PCs cool. In fact, the LANs were repeatedly taken apart, moved, and put back together as various marine units shifted locations. In this way, they created a truly mobile telecommunications system in the middle of the desert.

Documentation about front-line conditions and requests for supplies could be transmitted to division headquarters in seconds, which was far more efficient than it would have been to read a list of conditions or items into a radio. The speed of the communication also prevented the enemy from obtaining a fix on the transmitter.

For transmitting information from a LAN to Marine headquarters in Quantico, Virginia, two mobile data centers on trucks were used. These centers included a minicomputer, a front-end processor, disk drives, and high-speed printers. Data from the mobile data centers were communicated to Quantico via satellite.

Source: Robert Snowdon Jones, "PCs in the Trenches," *The Atlanta Journal-Constitution,* May 2, 1989, pp. C1–C2 and as updated December 1991.

Marines will be using computers and telecommunications extensively in any future military conflicts.

One of the most interesting topics in information systems today is that of tele-communications. **Telecommunications** may be broadly defined as *the electronic transmission of information.* This transmission of information can include voice, data, and pictures. Voice transmissions have been with us since Alexander Graham Bell invented the telephone well over 100 years ago, and radio and television transmissions have become common occurrences over the last 50 years, so these are not new areas. However, the electronic transmission of data between computers is a newer use of telecommunications, dating from the 1960s. Computers and communications have become so intertwined that any communications company that hopes to compete in a national or international market must also be involved with computers—and similarly, computer companies must be into communications.

Almost daily, we read and hear of innovations in this field, for example, teleconferencing, voice and electronic mail, electronic bulletin boards, satellite links, fax machines, fiber optics, and information banks. The military use of computers to ensure that correct information and instructions flow between the front lines and the command post (discussed in the box) is just one of many telecommunications examples that are frequently discussed in newspapers and magazines and on television. It seems that new forms of communications are springing up as quickly as new ways are found to use telecommunications. For example, the **compound document,** which combines written, voice, and computer communications to express an idea clearly, is becoming a popular method of sharing ideas.

Because telecommunications is such a broad topic and could easily take up an entire book by itself, we will restrict this chapter to a discussion of the transmission of data between computers and the use of fax machines.

Computers transmit data over a variety of communications links. (Left) Microwave towers are very important in telecommunications for transmitting voice and data. (Right) Fiber optic cables are replacing the older copper cables because of increased transmission speed and capacity as well as much reduced size.

Types of Telecommunications

Using communications allows companies to collect and disseminate information quickly while optimizing the management of resources.

Dennis Hayes, president, Hayes Microcomputer Products, Inc.

Quoted in "View from the Top," *Personal Computing,* October 1989, p. 258.

Twenty years ago, telecommunications involving computers usually consisted of the use of "dumb" terminals to send instructions and data to the mainframe. A **dumb terminal** and a PC look somewhat alike in that each has a keyboard and a monitor. However, the dumb terminal was so named because it had no CPU or secondary storage. Its sole purpose was as an input/output device for the mainframe. As information systems have grown, so too has the need for much more sophisticated telecommunications systems. While there is still a great need for terminals linked to a mainframe, they quite often are "smart" terminals or PCs that allow the user to carry out some processing at the terminal and to use the mainframe for more complicated or time-consuming operations. PCs are often made to work like mainframe terminals through **terminal emulation** hardware and software.

In addition to terminals linked to mainframes, there is a need for **computer networks** that use telecommunications to link two or more computers together and allow them to share data, to spread out the processing chores, or to serve as huge repositories of information that is available to users. Examples of computer networks include

- banking networks in which one bank card can be used at many automatic teller machines over a widespread area;
- message networks that allow people to use computers to send and receive mail electronically;
- U.S. Department of Defense computer networks that allow users in numerous universities and research centers to exchange results and data;
- airline, car rental, and hotel computer networks that enable travelers to make reservations from anywhere in the country;
- corporate computer networks that transfer the results of data processing operations between corporate locations;

Commonly used networks include (left) banking networks that allow us to withdraw money from an ATM hundreds of miles from home and (right) airline reservation networks that enable us to make reservations for several different airlines with one telephone call.

- commercial information networks—like CompuServe and Prodigy—that serve many roles for individual users, including making different types of information available, acting as a mail drop, and providing an electronic bulletin board;
- PC-based networks that allow individuals to share software, files, and peripherals as well as to communicate with each other.

Computer networks can be wide area networks or local area networks. **Wide area networks** can range in scope from a few city blocks to almost global; **local area networks** are usually thought of as being restricted to a single location. Local area networks also usually involve telecommunications between PCs and are very important in office information systems.

Individuals are also using PCs to search for information, to communicate with other PC users, and to obtain "free" software. Equipped with a PC, a modem, and communications software, a PC user can access commercial information sources, computer bulletin boards, and electronic mail services.

Facsimile Machines

A widespread use of telecommunications technology that does not always involve a computer is the use of **facsimile machines** or, as they are commonly called, **fax machines.** Fax machines are rapidly changing the way we work by making it very easy and quick to send *any* type of document around the corner, across the country, or even around the world. To use a fax machine for telecommunications simply involves dialing the telephone number of the receiving machine and feeding the document into the sending machine; at the same time, the document is reproduced by the receiving machine at another location. The document can be typed or handwritten, can contain pictures, or can be any combination of these. Fax machines are especially useful for sending documents that require signatures, something that is not possible with electronic or voice mail. Over the past five years, facsimile transmission of documents has grown tremendously, with an estimated 1.5 million fax machines in use in the United States today. In fact, the growth in the number of easy-to-use facsimile machines has led to a decline in the use of overnight mail.

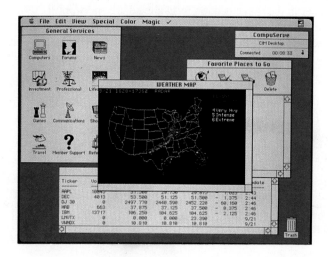

Commercial information networks such as CompuServe offer a tremendous variety of information.

Facsimile uses a scanner to digitize very thin strips of the document (0.005 to 0.01 inch wide) and convert the result into binary. The binary pattern corresponding to the document is then converted into telephone signals and transmitted over telephone lines. At the receiving end, the telephone signals are converted back to binary, which is then used to create on a blank sheet the same black-and-white pattern that was on the sending document. This process is shown in Figure 13-1.

Communications Media

Information transmitted over networks travels over various media, including twisted pairs, coaxial cable, fiber optics, and microwaves. **Twisted pairs** of copper wire are like those used in much of the existing telephone system. **Coaxial cable** is the type of cable used to transmit cable television signals into your home, whereas **fiber optic cable** is the newest medium and consists of thousands of glass fiber strands. **Microwaves** are high-frequency radio transmissions that can be sent between two earth stations or between earth stations and communications satellites, the method commonly used to transmit television signals. Twisted pairs are commonly used only for slow, **voice-grade transmissions,** whereas the other media are used for much higher-speed **broadband transmissions,** which can transmit large amounts of data.

LOCAL AREA NETWORKS

Since the introduction of the mainframe computer in the early 1950s and the personal computer in the late 1970s, computers have rapidly become a fixture in organizations of all sizes, ranging from General Motors and the U.S. government down to the neighborhood hardware store and homeowner's association. Whenever there are two or more computers in an organization, there are also many times when the organization would benefit if the computers could work together to share data and information. As a result, a great deal of interest has been generated in the subject of linking computers together, regardless of whether they are in the same location or on different continents. Computers linked together in the same location form a local area network (LAN); computers located in different geographical locations form a wide area network (WAN). We will discuss local area networks in this section and wide area networks in the next.

FIGURE 13-1
The Facsimile Process

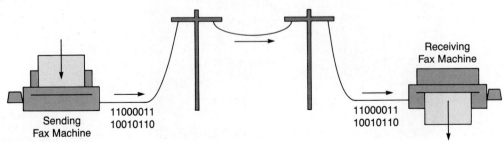

Sending Fax Machine

11000011
10010110

11000011
10010110

Receiving Fax Machine

Uses of LANs

Local area networks can be useful for those frequent situations in which computer users wish to share information, secondary storage, peripheral devices, or a data base. For example, a user may wish to send another user information in the form of a document, a graph, or a spreadsheet analysis. Without a local area network, the usual way to do this is to physically share a floppy disk. This is cumbersome and the disk can become damaged and unreadable. Using a LAN, the user can simply send the information over the network to the other user without having to store it on disk.

A part of the concept of sharing information in a LAN is electronic mail. Using **electronic mail** (also called **E-mail**) on a network involves sending documents, pictures, and messages to one or more persons. The user simply turns on the terminal or PC, enters the proper commands, types in the document, gives the names of those persons who are to receive it, and presses a key. Instantaneously, a message that "mail is waiting" appears at the proper terminals or PCs. If the recipient is working at the terminal at that time, he or she can read the mail immediately; otherwise, the message appears on the screen the next time the terminal or PC is turned on. No more going through the hassle of typing the document; making copies; addressing envelopes; remembering to send the letters; and then waiting for the recipient to receive, read, and reply. With electronic mail, the recipient can receive the message and respond immediately. Figure 13-2 shows electronic mail being sent over a local area network that uses personal computers.

Enabling users to share secondary storage, peripherals, software, or a data base is another way that a local area network can be very useful. By sharing a single hard disk drive, all users have access to certain information, while other information may remain specific to a given computer within the network. This hard disk is usually referred to as a **file server,** because it contains files that all users may access. These files may be data files or software packages, and the user can usually access them just as if they were on a local hard disk. In the

> ## File servers are going to blow the doors off traditional mainframes.
>
> *Larry Boucher, CEO of Auspex Systems, Inc.*
>
> Quoted in "Rethinking the Computer," *Business Week,* November 26, 1990, p. 119.

(Left) Local area networks are often used in colleges and universities to allow students and faculty to use software and printers or to send messages from one to the other. (Right) The terminal displaying this screen from Microsoft Windows 3.0 is linked up to a LAN.

FIGURE 13-2
Electronic Mail over Local Area
Network

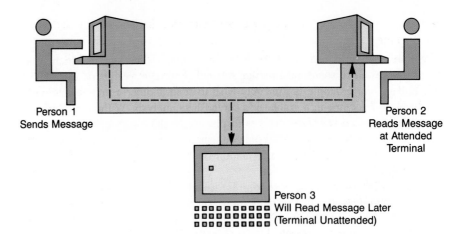

case of a package, the user can retrieve it to his or her machine, load it into RAM, and execute it just as if it were located on the local machine. In some cases, the PC may not even have any disk drives, depending totally on the file server for disk access. These **diskless workstations** make access to software and data easier to control, thereby improving the security of the system.

In terms of sharing peripherals, having one high-speed letter-quality or laser printer or a flatbed plotter in the network that can be accessed by all PCs saves equipment costs. Instead of each PC having its own printer or the user having to carry a floppy disk to the PC that is linked to the printer, print jobs can simply be sent to the print queue to be printed in their turn. Similarly, sharing a single data base gives all users access to the data base information. In most cases, the users can access the data base but cannot change it, thereby ensuring the security of the information. Figure 13-3 shows how information, secondary storage, peripherals, software, and data bases can be shared in a local area network.

A PC on a LAN can not only share files, software, and hardware resources with other PCs on the same LAN but can communicate through gateways and

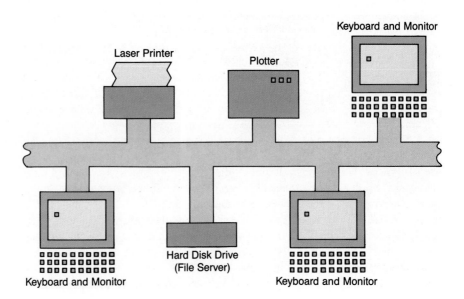

FIGURE 13-3
Sharing Information, Secondary
Storage, Peripherals, and Data
Bases in a LAN

bridges with other types of computers and with other LANs. A **gateway** is the combination of hardware and software that connects two dissimilar computer networks. A gateway allows a LAN user to access a mainframe network without leaving his or her PC. Similarly, a gateway between a LAN and a WAN enables a LAN user to send E-mail over the WAN. For example, the author of this textbook was able to use a gateway to communicate from his LAN with a colleague in Australia over the WAN.

A **bridge**, on the other hand, connects two similar networks. For example, if two LANs are connected with a bridge, the users of each LAN can access the other network's file server without making any physical changes to their data.

The proliferation of local area networks in organizations has led to a trend called **downsizing,** which occurs when a LAN replaces a mainframe or minicomputer system. Companies downsize for several reasons. First, a mainframe system is much more expensive than a PC network. Second, a mainframe's cost makes it inflexible because a company may be unwilling to change the system once it is up and running, which soon renders the system obsolete. Third, PCs are usually much easier to use than mainframes, and they are becoming even more so with the advent of such graphical-based systems as the Macintosh and, for IBM compatible PCs, Windows.

Classification of LANs

Local area networks can be classified according to the topology of the network. Basically, there are three topologies of LANs: star, bus, and ring. In the **star network,** a **host computer** has multiple "slave" computers connected to it. Since the host controls all **data communications,** any communications between any two computers must be routed through the host computer. If the host fails, then the entire system goes down. Terminals linked to a minicomputer form a star LAN.

A **bus network** has computers that tie into a main cable or **bus,** with no one central computer; the failure of any one computer does not affect the overall performance of the network. To send a message to another computer requires only that the software be able to signal the correct computer to receive the message. An example of a bus network is the popular EtherNet system.

In a **ring network,** all computers are treated the same and any communications between two computers must be processed by any intervening computers. To avoid having the system go down when a single PC fails, ring LANs often have ways to drop the single PC without interfering with the operation of the LAN. IBM's Token Ring Network is a good example of a ring network. Figure 13-4 shows the diagrams of the star, bus, and ring networks.

Since users may not know when another user is sending information over the network, there must be some way to control access. Two procedures are often used to control the sending of information from computer to computer. In a **token sharing network,** a special bit pattern called a **token** is sent to each computer sequentially around the network. Only the computer that has the token at a given instant can transmit. In a **multiple access network,** such as a bus network, all computers are free to transmit at any one time, but collision-detecting software must be in place to control those cases in which two or more computers are trying to transmit at the same time. Figure 13-5 shows the operation of the token ring LAN.

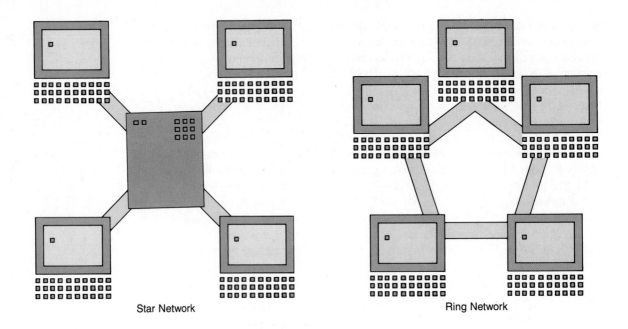

Star Network

Ring Network

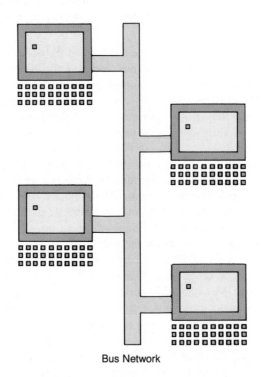

Bus Network

FIGURE 13-4
Star, Bus, and Ring Computer
Networks

LANs can also be classified by their configuration; that is, LANs can be designated as file-server, client-server, or peer-to-peer configurations. Currently, the most popular configuration is the **file-server configuration** in which the files are stored on a central hard disk but local PCs do most of the processing. However, the **client-server configuration,** in which the processing burden is on the central computer, is becoming more popular. In this configuration, the server

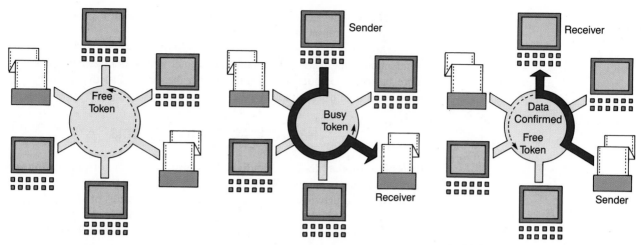

FIGURE 13-5
Operation of Token Ring LAN

computer is often dedicated to a single purpose, such as a data base engine or communications. This leads to an entirely different approach to networking, where users share the processing device, as well as files or peripherals.

Finally, the **peer-to-peer configuration** is often used for smaller networks in which the emphasis is on users sharing files. With the peer-to-peer configuration, each computer can function as both a server and a workstation, instead of as a single dedicated file server. This configuration is significantly cheaper

LAN BRINGS GOODWILL TO THE GAMES

A 120-node LAN was crucial to the success of the 1990 Goodwill Games in Seattle. The file server LAN was involved in all aspects of the games, from administration and security to reporting and broadcasting. Running on an 80386-based file server with a 660-megabyte hard disk and a laptop data base server, the network handled such tasks as overall games administration, connecting reporters and broadcasters speaking five languages, transmitting

scripts from Turner Broadcasting System (TBS) writers to television host Larry King, and checking the identity of the 2,200 full- and part-time TBS workers. There was also a mainframe gateway that allowed LAN users to retrieve event results from the mainframe used by games officials.

The network used the Novell LAN operating system to manage the 120 PCs connected by twisted-pair wiring. Additional remote users could access the network via modems. With the exception of two custom-written applications, off-the-shelf commercial applications were used on the Goodwill LAN. These applications included an E-mail package, Excel and Word for Windows from Microsoft, Lotus 1-2-3, and WordPerfect.

Source: Stuart J. Johnston, "Goodwill Games Prove LANs Aren't Toys," *Infoworld,* August 6, 1990, p. 31.

The days of the LAN as a toy are over.

Walter Toucher, systems coordinator for the Goodwill Games LAN system

Quoted in Stuart J. Johnston, "Goodwill Games Prove LANs Aren't Toys," *Infoworld,* August 6, 1990, p. 31.

than either the file-server or client-server configuration, but it is not well suited for heavy-duty transaction processing.

The future of local area networks appears very bright, with a great deal of attention being paid to them and to computer networks in general. More and more personal computers are being used in the office, and the advantages of tying them together are rapidly being realized.

Network Operating Systems

LANs that use the file-server configuration must have a **network operating system** that manages the interaction between the various local PCs and the central file server. The network operating system has many features of single PC operating systems, because it, too, must manage disk access, file storage, and memory use. In addition, the network operating system must control access to the server—that is, determine who can log onto the server to use its files. As security becomes more important and more and more of an organization's data reside on the file server, it becomes more crucial for the network operating system to protect data yet allow authorized individuals to log onto the system. Network operating systems are also discussed in Chapter 9.

WIDE AREA NETWORKS

While local area networks are in the process of becoming extensively used in the office, wide area networks have been around for many years—in the form of long-distance telephone networks. Today, as the need for transferring data and information between computers over long distances grows, wide area computer networks are also becoming very important for business, industry, and government. There are basically three types of wide area computer networks in use today: academic and research networks, private networks designed to provide communications between a company's host computer and the employee's and customer's terminals, and value-added networks.

All these wide area computer networks use a special form of telecommunications called packet switching. In **packet switching,** the terminals are linked to the host computer through interface computers. The host computer breaks up long messages into data units called **packets,** which are then given to the interface computers to transmit through the network. The terminal at the destination receives the packets and then reassembles them into a copy of the original message. Figure 13-6 shows a schematic of a typical packet switching network.

Academic and Research Networks

Various wide area networks are used to facilitate interaction between universities and other research institutions. In many cases, the networks allow users on smaller systems to communicate. The biggest such WAN is called Internet, which connects 500,000 computers on 5,000 networks in 33 countries. A subnetwork of Internet is BITNET, which is an electronic mail system subscribed to by over 1,500 colleges, universities, and other academic and research institutions. With BITNET, a user at one of the network's subscribing institutions,

Ninety percent of the people I deal with are on E-mail.

Nicholas Negroponte, director of the MIT Media Laboratory

Quoted in "Electronic Mail: Ready for the 1990's," *Lotus,* February 1990, p. 7.

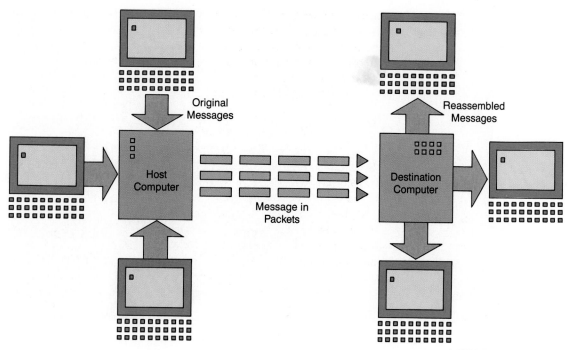

FIGURE 13-6
Packet Switching Network

or **nodes,** can send electronic mail to a user at another subscribing institution if he or she knows the other user's network address, PMCK@UGA, for example. This is very useful for professors or researchers, because they can send messages, letters, or even papers to colleagues throughout the United States, Europe, and the Middle East.

A WAN called ARPANet (for Advanced Research Projects Agency Network) was set up by the U.S. Department of Defense to link defense-oriented researchers. ARPANet spans the United States. Its success encouraged the development of several related networks, including NSFNet (National Science Foundation Network), which links many subnetworks of research universities.

Finally, MCI Mail is a commercial electronic mail system that allows subscribers to send messages electronically across the country.

Private Networks

When a private company wants to set up a wide area network to connect its mainframes or to link its own or outside terminals into its mainframes, it must decide the type of telecommunications media that will be used: standard or wide area telecommunications service (WATS) lines, a dedicated private line leased from a telephone company (called a **leased line**), or satellite communications. This decision will depend on the number of transmissions to be made and the quality and speed required of the transmissions. Some computer networks require high-quality, high-speed lines on a frequent basis, making the use of leased lines or satellite transmissions economical. Other networks will find the use of standard, low-speed, voice-quality lines adequate and economical.

In addition to selecting the type of transmission facility, a company using a private network must decide whether it will manage the telecommunications

```
Date:       Tue, 14 Jul 1992 09:19 CST
From:       NFPKP@DUCVAX.TEXAS.EDU
Subject:    Re: Summer Issue of National Forum
To:         PMCKEOWN@cbacc.cba.uga.edu


Patrick:

Did you get a reply to your message?  We had your article typeset and it is
on the way in the process, but we are not completed here...may be 2-3 more
weeks at least before issue is out...

Sorry for not getting back to you before now.  Let me know if you have not
seen galleys of your article....I believe Mary Lister has already sent
them to you, has she not?

Advise,
Stephen W. Brown
```

 +/- <F5>─mark <Del> Copy Forward Headers Move Print Reply eXtract ────── 5%

Professors and researchers at universities and research centers worldwide can send and receive messages electronically using electronic mail.

function itself or hire an outside telecommunications company. This management role includes determining the speed and routing of transmissions and the error-checking mechanisms used to ensure that data are correctly transmitted.

Value-Added Networks

The third alternative for wide area networks is value-added networks. **Value-added networks (VANs)** are public networks that are available by subscription and provide their clients with data communications facilities. The company that runs the VAN assumes complete responsibility for managing the network, including providing conversion between different systems. In addition, VANs often offer other services, such as multiple terminal sessions, electronic mail, and access to network data bases. In a sense, a VAN adds value to the data by ensuring that it reaches its destination with little effort on the part of the subscriber.

A VAN works for its subscribers by providing connections or **ports** to its wide area network through a local telephone call. Once the subscriber accesses the network, data are routed between the local terminal and a long-distance host computer that is connected to the network by a leased line. By using communications channels that are shared among many users, these public data networks take advantage of economies of scale to provide these services at an acceptable cost to their clients. In some cases, it is also possible to forward data from one VAN to another to reach a destination computer that is not linked to the user's VAN. Figure 13-7 depicts a value-added network.

This network control center manages and monitors Tymnet's public (VAN) network worldwide.

FIGURE 13-7
Value-Added Network

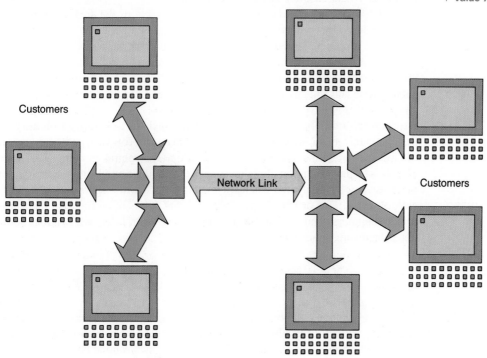

Customers

Network Link

Customers

Examples of VANs include Infonet, Tymnet, GTE Telenet, CompuServe, and AT&T Information Services NET. In some cases, a company will subscribe to multiple VANs—to ensure that its clients will always have a network available to them through a local telephone call and to take advantage of lower rates in different markets.

Computer Networks and DDP

Networks are important in the area of **distributed data processing (DDP),** which attempts to place computing power as close as possible to the point of actual information processing, as compared to the centralization of computer resources. Using the evolving telecommunications technology, DDP networks are capable of connecting mainframes, minicomputers, and personal computers together. DDP allows a computer-based information system to be designed to match organizational structure, to support unique business strategies, and to provide a more natural use of information systems.

How does DDP work? As an example, assume that a manufacturing plant firm has one central administrative office and several plants located in different parts of the country. A mainframe in the administrative office handles data processing that involves the firm as a whole. Minicomputers and PCs at each manufacturing plant handle the processing for that site. The smaller computers are linked to the mainframe by some form of communications link that allows them to obtain information from the mainframe and send back the result of the processing handled locally. The mainframe stores the company's primary data base, and the smaller computers have local data bases, or **distributed data bases,** that are separate from the primary data base. The smaller computers can also access the primary data base for needed information.

DDP has certain obvious advantages. The users of the smaller computers are not held up by competing for access to the mainframe; at the same time, the mainframe's processing load is reduced. In addition, local users can customize software to fit their individual needs and can develop their own computer-based information systems. At the same time, they can interface with the central computer. These advantages often result in lower costs for the organization as a whole.

On the other hand, problems with DDP include lack of data security of the communications links, inconsistency between the software and hardware at the local sites and the software and hardware at the central computer, and possibly less technical support at the local sites than at the central site. The hardware inconsistency is aggravated when users attempt to interface personal computers with the mainframe or with local minicomputers. Users often find that their personal computers cannot "talk" to the mainframe or transfer data without additional hardware or software.

Electronic Data Interchange

The use of computer networks in business for **electronic data interchange (EDI)** is growing. EDI allows computers to exchange electronic transmissions of data and information and, therefore, automate much routine business between retail stores, distributors, and manufacturers. Instead of sending paper documents, such as purchase orders, invoices, bills of lading, shipping slips, and so forth, back and forth through traditional communication channels, EDI allows companies to transmit the same information electronically between their computers. By combining EDI with point-of-sale inventory systems, a computer at a retail store can automatically order goods, based on sales, from its supplier. The supplier, in turn, can automatically ship the goods to the retail store and electronically transmit the appropriate document. EDI greatly reduces human involvement in the ordering and shipping process, thereby reducing costs and speeding service.

TELECOMMUNICATIONS ON THE PERSONAL COMPUTER

One of the most popular uses of the personal computer is for telecommunications, either with a mainframe or with another PC. Using a PC, a modem, and communications software, the user can access a wide range of information sources, goods and services, and other PC users. The uses of the PC for telecommunications fall into five broad categories: accessing information sources, interacting with other users, using electronic mail, telecommuting, and using videotex. Before going into these in detail, we will briefly discuss the concepts and terminology of PC telecommunications.

Personal Computer Telecommunications Concepts and Terminology

To understand how a computer can send and receive data and information, first recall that the information in a computer is stored and manipulated in the form of bits. A **bit** is *an electronic pulse (one) or the absence of a pulse (zero).* Before the information in this electronic form can be transmitted, it usually must be translated into a form that the communications linkage can accommodate. This translation process has two steps: conversion of data from parallel to serial form and conversion of digital data into an analog form.

To understand the first step, note that, within the computer, data are stored and processed in a **parallel form**—16, 32, or 64 bits at a time, depending on the type of computer. On the other hand, data being transmitted must be sent one bit at a time in what is called **serial form.** To understand the difference, think of parallel form as bits marching through the computer 16, 32, or 64 abreast and serial form as the same bits moving in single file. The computer's **serial port** converts parallel data into a serial form for transmission or converts serial data back into a parallel form.

The second step of the translation process involves converting the data, which are now in a serial form, from the binary "on–off" state that is used in the computer into an **analog equivalent** that can be telecommunicated. The word *analog* refers to a physical relationship that represents data. The physical relationship is an electrical wave form that the communication link can carry. For example, to be sent over an ordinary telephone line, information must be converted to an audio form; that is, a one-bit is translated into one tone and a zero-bit into another tone. The translation from binary to the analog form of data is carried out by a device known as a **modem.** The name *modem* comes from

Prodigy (screen shown right) has proved to be a popular form of telecommunications for all family members.

the conversion of digital data into analog data through a process known as MODulation and the reverse process known as DEModulation.

When a bit is modulated, it is converted into a particular wave form. There exists one frequency that represents the digit 0 and a second frequency to represent the digit 1. When these frequencies are demodulated, they are converted back into a 0 or a 1. Figure 13-8 demonstrates the process of sending information from one computer to another over telephone lines.

Data can be sent between computers in one of two modes: synchronous or asynchronous. In **synchronous communications**, large numbers of characters

are sent as a block, whereas in **asynchronous communications**, the characters are sent one at a time. Synchronous communications are much faster but also require more expensive equipment. Most communications between two PCs or between a PC and a larger computer are asynchronous and involve only the purchase of an inexpensive modem and appropriate software.

Asynchronous communications modulate and demodulate ten bits, usually the first seven bits of the ASCII representation of a character, *plus* three other bits. Only seven ASCII bits are needed because they are enough to represent all characters of the alphabet. The three additional bits are the start bit, parity bit, and stop bit. The **start bit** is before each character and signals the computer that

FIGURE 13-8
Communication between Computers

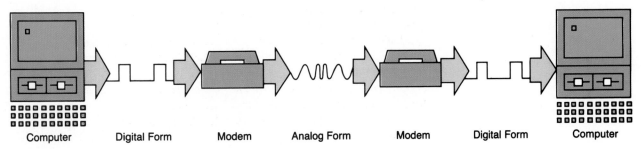

| Computer | Digital Form | Modem | Analog Form | Modem | Digital Form | Computer |

a character is coming. A **parity bit** is immediately after the character and checks the number of 1-bits in the character to see if the computer correctly received the character. If even parity is specified, there should be an even number of 1-bits in the signal; similarly, if odd parity is specified, there should be an odd number of 1-bits. Finally, the **stop bit** is after the parity bit and notifies the computer that the previous character is complete. Characters are always preceded and followed by strings of 1's that fill the gaps between characters. If necessary, all eight bits for a character may be used by dropping the parity bit.

Figure 13-9 demonstrates three different representations of the letter A (1000001 in ASCII) as it is transmitted over a telephone line. In all three representations, the following have been added: a start bit of zero at the beginning of the character, a parity bit of one (even parity) after the character, and a stop bit of one at the end of the bit-string. The first representation is in binary form. Next, the bits are shown as square waves before entering the modem and then as audio waves after the modulation. In all three representations, the part that represents the character is shown in a box to distinguish it from the start and stop bits. Demodulation is simply the reverse of this—sound waves are converted into pulses that are equivalent to the character representation.

The speed at which modems can send and receive information is measured by the number of **bits per second** (bps) that can be transmitted. For modems used with personal computers, rates of 1,200, 2,400, and 9,600 bps are the standard. Since each character in asynchronous communication is equivalent to 10 bits, a rate of 1,200 bps is approximately equal to 120 characters per second. Modems can be either **internal** or **external,** depending on whether they are installed inside the computer or connect to the serial port and sit outside the computer. Most modems now have the capability to dial or answer your phone

Binary Representation of Letter A

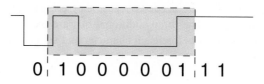

Digital Equivalent of Binary Representation

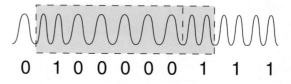

Analog Representation After Modulation

FIGURE 13-9
Demonstration of Modulation
Process

(known as **autodial** and **autoanswer**), to hang up the phone if a busy signal is reached, or even to dial a second number if the first is busy.

If you are buying a modem, a crucial consideration is **Hayes compatibility,** that is, whether it uses the same commands as a Hayes modem. The communications system in Hayes modems has become an industry standard, so it is important to ensure that any modem you purchase is Hayes compatible.

When a modem is used to connect a terminal or personal computer to another computer, the communication can be in one of three modes: simplex, half-duplex, or full-duplex. When the communication is possible in only one direction, the **mode** is **simplex.** Communication between computers is in the **half-duplex mode** if only one computer can send information at any one time. On the other hand, the communication is in the **full-duplex mode** if both computers can send information at the same time. Half-duplex is like a bridge that allows only one car to cross at a time; full-duplex is like a bridge that allows cars to cross in both directions simultaneously. When half-duplex is used, one computer sends and the second receives, then the second sends and the first receives. When half-duplex is used, the screen of the sending computer usually will show the same signal that is being transmitted, but when full-duplex is used, the receiving computer will send the signal back to the screen of the sending computer. Thus, with full-duplex the user can check the accuracy of the signal being received by having it sent back to the originating computer. Most communications involving personal computers use the full-duplex mode. Figure 13-10 shows half-duplex and full-duplex communication between computers.

The final consideration for a modem is what is known as the protocol for the communication. The **protocol** is the set of rules that the two computers will follow in sending and receiving information. With the continuing standardization of modems, this has become much less of a consideration than it once was.

A personal computer is not capable of sending or receiving information without special instructions. The **communications software** used to carry out telecommunications on a PC is another type of "personal productivity" software in that it allows the PC to be used for many tasks, including dialing telephone numbers, answering calls, sending and receiving data and information over the telephone line, and accessing other computers. Software packages like ProComm Plus, PC-Talk, and Crosstalk are all examples of communications software that allows the PC to communicate with other computers.

Now that you know a little bit about the technology of PC communications, we can turn our attention to the five primary uses of a PC for communications: accessing information sources, interacting with other users, using electronic mail, telecommuting, and videotex.

FIGURE 13-10
Types of Computer
Communications

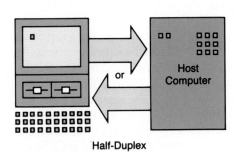

Half–Duplex

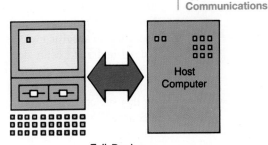

Full–Duplex

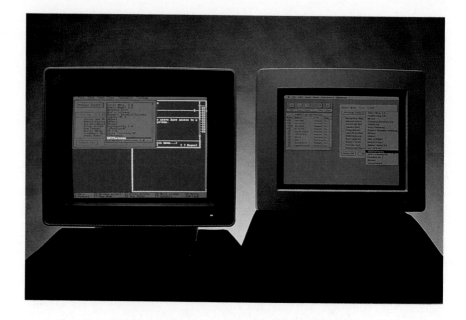

Accessing Information Sources

One of the oldest uses of telecommunications is to obtain information from the various data bases that have been available on a commercial basis since 1972. Information can be obtained from online services, from data base vendors, or directly from the data bases. There are currently over 3,500 data bases that can be reached from a personal computer.

Online services are companies that provide computerized information to their subscribers. Users can reach the online services through a local call or a toll-free (800) number. The services offer a wide range of information, including a general information category of the type found in an encyclopedia. They also offer news services, newspaper articles, business and financial information, stock market quotes, magazine articles, airline schedules, and medical information. Most of them also provide such services as electronic mail, special interest groups (SIGs) on various topics, and gateways into other electronic services such as the American Airlines reservation service and the Official Airline Guide. These online services have an initial subscription charge plus hourly charges that vary according to the time of day and the number of bps. The most popular online services are CompuServe, with close to 600,000 subscribers; GEnie, with over 100,000 subscribers; and Prodigy, with over 1 million subscribers.

Data base vendors offer many full-text data bases from newspapers, magazines, scientific journals, and so on. They also offer data bases with only bibliographic citations, abstracts, or summaries. Data base vendors also tend to specialize in specific topic areas. For example, Lexis offers data bases that cover federal and state court decisions, and the Dow Jones New/Retrieval tends to specialize in business news. Once in a specific data base, a PC user can specify a subject, such as "computer," and then receive a list of all available references on this subject. The information is taken from among the many data bases that are stored in each service. In some cases, the full article may be accessed; in others, only a bibliographic listing and a summary of the article are available. There is often overlap between data base vendors since they do not actually

> **CompuServe's greatest effect on PC technology has been to marry software to information access.**
>
> *Charles W. McCall, president and CEO, CompuServe, Inc.*
>
> Quoted in "View from the Top," *Personal Computing,* October 1989, p. 248.

CompuServe's computer facility shows the multiple mainframe computers and secondary storage equipment needed to support this enormous information service.

create the data bases but purchase them from outside companies who collect and compile the information.

Costs for using one of these encyclopedic data base services are charged by the hour and can range from $25 an hour to $300 an hour. This may seem expensive, but remember what the user receives for that cost. When the user initiates a search for a topic, it is possible that *every* reference to that topic will be found in 15 minutes! Compare this with a search in the library that could take days to complete, and you will see why these services are well worth the cost. Examples of data base vendors include BRS, Dialog, Dow Jones New/ Retrieval Service, Lexis, Nexis, and WestLaw.

The actual data bases that may be accessed through an online service or a data base vendor are quite varied. And in some cases, the user may access the data base directly without going through one of the data base services. Table 13-1 will give you an idea of the types of data bases that are available.

Interacting with Other Users

Just as the personal computer enables users to obtain information from mainframe computer data banks and information services, it may also enable them

Using a modem in conjunction with a personal computer and communications software, a user can research almost any topic in an encyclopedic data base over the home telephone line.

TABLE 13-1
Examples of Online Data Bases

Data Base	Topics Covered
Dun's Market Identifiers	A directory of 2 million U.S. businesses
Forbes 500 Annual Directory	A ranking of the 500 largest U.S. companies
Business Periodical Index	An index to articles from 476 legal periodicals
CENDATA	Economic and demographic data on 200 countries
Career Placement Directory	Resumés in over 200 occupations
Books in Print	Over 1 million bibliographic references
Insurance Data Bases	Laws relating to insurance
AP Online	News stories from the Associated Press

Source: Scott Spanbauer, "On-line Services and Data Bases," *PC World,* October 1988, pp. 200–202.

THE "WIRED" CAMPUS

Students at Drew University in New Jersey are "wired" to each other, to faculty members, to the library, and to the world through a communication and information network that connects all offices and dorm rooms. So that all students can take advantage of this network, they are provided with a PC that is paid for with part of their tuition. The network includes a data network, voice system, and broadband network. The data network links the academic computing system, the library, all PCs on campus, and external networks that provide electronic mail, data base, and information services. The voice system provides enhanced telecommunications facilities, including voice mail. The broadband network provides every student room and classroom on campus with high-speed video (TV) and data transmission.

Drew students and faculty are using these networks in many ways. Voice and electronic mail are widely used for assigning and submitting coursework and research projects. Voice mail is widely used for class announcements, including updates, reminders, and other timely notifications. E-mail is used by many members of the Drew community to communicate not only among themselves but, at no additional cost, with faculty and students at other institutions. The broadband network enables Drew faculty members to include educational broadcasts in their courses.

The network technology available at Drew is also used in more innovative ways. For example, students discovered that they could create a "chain" voice mail message, which resulted in the creation of a 60-minute version of "The Twelve Days of Christmas" as students added a new verse each time the message was forwarded. In another case, the network was responsible for saving a Drew student's life. The student used her computer to communicate regularly with a friend in Ithaca, New York. When she communicated that she was depressed and had taken drugs and alcohol, the Ithaca student contacted administrators at Drew, who immediately located the Drew student and provided emergency care.

Source: Drew University press release, September 1991.

to interact directly with other users. This interaction can take place in one of two ways: through a bulletin board service or through participation in a tele-conference. In a **bulletin board service,** a user, club, or corporation combines a computer with one or more telephone lines, a modem, and a type of communications software that allows users to call in and "post" messages on the electronic bulletin board for other users to see. Both CompuServe and Prodigy have national bulletin board facilities, and there are an estimated 30,000 local bulletin boards around the country. Local bulletin boards get along quite well with a personal computer, while the national bulletin boards require the speed and storage capabilities available only on mainframes.

One of the most popular uses of a bulletin board—whether a national one or a local one sponsored by a user's group—is the exchange of public domain

software. This is software that has not been copyrighted and so can be copied without violation of copyright laws. Exchanging software (or other information) involves **downloading** and saving the software. If software is being sent from the user's PC disk to the host computer, it is being **uploaded.**

Since the mainframe host computers of national services like CompuServe and Prodigy can serve multiple users simultaneously, conferences or other multiple-user sessions can take place on these services, ranging from informal "gab" sessions to formal, long-term conferences on a particular topic. For formal teleconferencing, it is possible to have a real-time conference or a delayed conference. In a **real-time conference,** all participants are actually logged onto the system at the time of the conference. In a **delayed conference,** the comments of the participants are stored sequentially as they are entered. In the latter case a conference can go on for months, with participants taking whatever time they need to formulate replies to comments already made by others. Normally, a real-time conference would be used to address a pressing topic that requires a quick resolution, while the delayed conference might be used for philosophical or policy questions that do not require immediate decisions. Teleconferencing has also become popular as a means of training employees in widely separated locations around the country.

Electronic Mail

Just as electronic mail is very useful within the organization and over wide area networks, it is also useful for communications on a PC. In fact, PC users often have access to the same wide area network mail services as are available to mainframe users. In addition, PC users can use the electronic mail services of such operations as CompuServe and Prodigy, which offer the facility to communicate with other subscribers through their electronic mail services. A subscriber can send a "letter" to another subscriber by "addressing" it to the recipient's account number.

> **A lot of people are able to talk at once without stepping on toes.**
>
> *Robert E. Johnson, director of research and business development, Phelps Dodge*
>
> Quoted in "At These Shouting Matches, No One Says a Word," *Business Week,* June 11, 1990, p. 78.

Telecommuting

One of the very first forms of telecommunications involved using a portable terminal to call back to a mainframe in order to work on some project. The introduction of the personal computer made this approach easier by lessening the need for access to a mainframe. Now employees can use their personal computers at some location other than the office, store the results on disk, and then download them to a computer at work. These workers are said to be **telecommuting** to work, and in 1988, there were an estimated 27 million of them. In addition, there are now almost 15 million home-based businesses, and this number is expected to grow to almost 21 million by 1995.

Basically, there are three types of telecommuters: individuals who use their personal computers to access the office mainframe to avoid having to make a trip to the office, individuals who use their personal computers at home to continue or finish work begun at the office, and individuals who usually work on a personal computer at home full time. For the first two types of telecommuter, having a computer at home is a convenience that allows them to complete their work more quickly and easily. For the third type of telecommuter, work at home becomes a way of life.

Of course, there are problems with any of the three types of telecommuting. The mainframe user may have problems reaching a free line into the computer and may end up using the home telephone line for long periods of time. The individual who uses the personal computer at home to complete work begun at the office faces problems with accessing the data bases on the office mainframe: Often these mainframes are not set up for access from the outside, and the company's MIS department must be willing to change its policies toward outside access.

For the telecommuter who works at home the majority of the time, what may be perceived as the perfect work situation has its own set of problems involving time management and lack of interaction with co-workers and superiors in the office.

Videotex

When a new avenue of communication opens, businesses are always quick to take advantage of it for advertising and selling. The "opening" of the telecommunications avenue was no different. **Videotex** refers to a system that combines the computer, telephone, modem, and software to allow users to view and purchase various services and products. Although videotex is widely used in France, where it is supported by the telephone company, it is a relatively small industry in the United States. Several attempts have been made to start videotex companies here, with Prodigy the most recent example. It was introduced by IBM and Sears in 1988.

Prodigy's features are similar to those of CompuServe and GEnie, other information sources, but Prodigy brings colorful graphics to videotex. Currently, over 1 million people subscribe to Prodigy, but experts believe that 2.5 million individuals must subscribe to Prodigy before Sears and IBM can break even on their investment, which means that Prodigy must continue to grow if it is to become a financial success.

Prodigy offers its subscribers a number of services; for example, they can purchase such things as clothing, sporting goods, airline tickets, and computer hardware and software. They can view news stories and weather, bank at home, use electronic mail, and play games. As previously noted, Prodigy is similar to CompuServe, but it uses a colorful graphic menu system, which makes it popular among first-time computer users. Its banking and shopping features also distinguish Prodigy from other online services or data bases.

THE FUTURE OF TELE-COMMUNICATIONS

Even as this is being written, telecommunications technology is evolving even further. In fact, telecommunications is the one area that may be changing faster than computer technology! In addition to increasing the use of fiber optics and satellites as communications media, technology is evolving by replacing analog transmissions with digital (binary) voice transmissions. The transition to a digital standard called **integrated services digital network (ISDN)** will make possible the transmission of all types of signals—voice, video, data, and so on—on the same lines. Many experts expect that as ISDN becomes a standard, there will

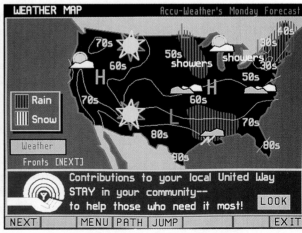

USING PRODIGY FOR TRIP PLANNING

As discussed in the text, Prodigy is now one of the most widely-used electronic information sources in the United States. It is also a videotex service on which members can purchase goods. And, as the author discovered, it can be very useful for planning an overseas trip.

Prodigy was used in several ways to plan a trip for four (the author's entire family) to Australia in the summer of 1991. It helped us find the least expensive airfare from the United States to Australia and between cities within Australia. We checked weather forecasts in Australia, and, through the Prodigy Travel Club bulletin board, we discussed travel options with members who had been to Australia.

For airfares, we accessed the Eaasy Sabre airline guide to find the lowest fares. Had we chosen, we also could have purchased the tickets through Eaasy Sabre. Even after we purchased the tickets, however, we were able to obtain a refund from the Australian airline, because a random check of the airline guide showed that the company had reduced its fare from Sydney to Cairns after we had purchased our tickets.

By tracking Australia's winter weather patterns on the Prodigy weather service, we were able to decide which types of clothes to pack. The weather service was especially important because it correctly predicted that an extended warm spell in Sydney would end before our arrival and that cold and wet conditions would prevail while we were in Sydney.

By leaving queries on the Prodigy Travel Club bulletin board, we obtained much useful information about hotels, restaurants, tours, and so on. These queries were answered by members who had been to Australia, or as it is known to Prodigy members, the "Land of Oz." In some cases, E-mail was used to carry on extended correspondence regarding specific questions.

be a tremendous increase in the use of home-related information services, resulting in turn in users having better access to the large institutional data bases discussed earlier in this chapter. Another direction of future growth is **wireless LANs,** that is, local area networks that use radio waves for transmission of data rather than wires.

REVIEW OF KEY POINTS

1. The electronic transmission of information is known as telecommunications.
2. Two or more computers tied together with communications links form a computer network.
3. A popular form of telecommunications that does not always involve computers is the use of the facsimile (fax) machine.
4. Local area network (LANs) are personal computer networks at a single location. They can facilitate the transfer of information and the sharing of secondary storage devices, peripherals, and data bases.
5. Popular types of LANs are ring, star, and bus.
6. When computer communications are required over long distances, wide area networks (WANs) are used. There are three types of WANs: specialized networks, private networks, and value-added networks (VANs).
7. Distributed data processing (DDP) uses small computers to handle local processing and to relieve the central mainframe of

some processing chores. Electronic data interchange (EDI) allows companies to electronically order and pay for raw materials and finished goods.

8. A computer can be combined with a telephone, a modem, and communications software to allow the user to communicate with other users and computers.

9. Important uses of telecommunications include finding information, interacting with other users, sending and receiving electronic mail, shopping and banking by computer, and working from home using a computer.

10. CompuServe, GEnie, and Prodigy are online services that offer the user many telecommunication functions.

11. Data base vendors provide access to a large number of data bases and are a wide-ranging source of information.

12. A user can interact with users at other locations through electronic bulletin boards and teleconferences.

13. Electronic mail enables a computer user to send messages and documents over long distances instantaneously and to communicate more efficiently with other users in the same office or local network.

14. The number of individuals working at home has increased with the availability of personal computers and communications packages.

15. Communications software and services enable people to use the computer for such everyday activities as buying goods and services, carrying out their banking, and managing their stock portfolio.

16. The future of telecommunications appears to be in the implementation of the integrated services digital network (ISDN), which will use an all-digital communications system.

KEY TERMS

analog equivalent
asynchronous communication
autoanswer modem
autodial modem
bit
bits per second (bps)
bridge
broadband transmission
bulletin board service
bus
bus network
client-server configuration
coaxial cable
communications software
compound document
computer network
data base vendor
data communication
delayed conference
diskless workstation

distributed data processing (DDP)
distributed data base
downloading
downsizing
dumb terminal
electronic data interchange (EDI)
electronic mail (E-mail)
external modem
facsimile machine
fax machine
fiber optic cable
file-server configuration
full-duplex mode
gateway
half-duplex mode
Hayes compatibility
host computer
integrated services digital network (ISDN)
internal modem

leased line
local area network (LAN)
microwave
modem
multiple access network
network operating system
node
online service
packet
packet switching
parallel form
parity bit
peer-to-peer configuration
port
protocol
real-time conference
ring network
serial form

serial port
simplex mode
star network
start bit
stop bit
synchronous communication
telecommunications
telecommuting
terminal emulation
token
token sharing network
twisted pairs
uploading
value-added network (VAN)
videotex
voice-grade transmission
wide area network (WAN)
wireless LANs

REVIEW QUESTIONS

1. Define *telecommunications*. What is a compound document?
2. What is the difference between a "dumb" terminal and a "smart" terminal? What is "terminal emulation"?
3. Give an example of a computer network other than those listed in the text.
4. How is fax communication like PC communication? How is it different?
5. How are computer networks differentiated by size? Which type of network would normally be found in a college or university?
6. Give three reasons why a LAN is useful. What does a file server have to do with the use of a LAN?
7. Describe three commonly used types of LANs and give an example of each.
8. Describe the three types of wide area networks. Why is packet switching used in these networks?
9. What are the advantages and disadvantages of DDP?
10. List the five main categories of use of the PC for telecommunications.
11. List the steps necessary to send data and information between computers. Why are start and stop bits necessary in asynchronous communications?
12. Discuss the difference between simplex, half-duplex, and full-duplex modes of communication between computers. What is a protocol used for?
13. What is the difference between an online service and a data base vendor? Give an example of each.
14. List the advantages and disadvantages of telecommuting. Name three services that Prodigy can provide.
15. What does ISDN have to do with the future of telecommunications?

A Guide to Buying a Personal Computer

Since the early 1980s, personal computers have been a subject of great interest, and more and more individuals and businesses are entering the world of PCs by buying their first personal computer, while others are upgrading old computers or buying additional computers. It has been estimated that at the end of 1991, over 100 million PCs were in use in the United States alone.

Many of these PCs are used in business to help companies save money and increase profits, but the number of them used in homes is growing. Surveys show that over one-third of U.S. households (17 million) have a personal computer, and by the end of the century, statisticians believe that the average home will have more PCs (2.2) than children. Your reading this textbook indicates that you, too, may soon be in the market for a personal computer—if you do not already own one!

Because there are so many makes and models of personal computer to choose from, purchasing a computer tends to require more research on the part of the prospective owner than the comparable purchase of, say, an automobile or a television. Another complicating characteristic of personal computers is that they are not all equally effective in handling the different tasks for which computers are commonly used. For example, one machine might be great for running educational software but not have the speed or memory to handle business-related tasks such as working large spreadsheets or data bases. The computer you purchase should suit your computing needs in the same way that the type of vehicle (car, van, truck, sports car, etc.) you buy fits your transportation needs.

Because your needs are particular to you and the computer that suits your needs may not suit those of another person and vice versa, directing you to one brand of computer over another would not be a sound approach. Instead, we will describe a five-step process for selecting a personal computer. The brand of computer you actually choose will depend on the results of this procedure and the prices available to you.

STEP-BY-STEP PURCHASING PROCEDURE

The five steps for buying a computer system are these:

1. Define the tasks for which you will be using your personal computer.
2. Determine which software will accomplish these tasks.
3. Determine which hardware systems will support the software you selected in step 2.
4. Find suppliers that can provide the hardware and software selected in the previous steps.
5. Purchase the software and the hardware system.

Personal computers promise an incredibly positive impact on productivity, economy, and quality of life in corporate America, in small offices, homes, schools, and home offices.

*John Roach, chairman,
Tandy Corp.*

Quoted in "The Pace of Change in Corporate America," *Personal Computing*, October 1989, p. 240.

This procedure assumes that you have already learned enough about computers to know what they can and cannot do and that you are able to define the tasks for which a computer will be useful to you. These may include managing your finances, handling correspondence or writing papers, managing a business, or learning to program. Then, whatever your needs are, you can determine what software packages will meet your computing needs. There is such a wide variety of software available today that this step requires the most time and research; you will probably end up with a list of software from which you must make a subjective choice. Selecting the particular software package that meets your needs greatly narrows the choice of computers, since not all computers will run all software. With this reduced range of computers to choose from, you can select suppliers who carry both the software and the hardware you're considering. We will discuss each of these steps in detail.

An important concept to remember about buying a computer is that the original purchase of hardware and software is just the beginning; you can purchase additional software packages as you find additional uses for the computer, or you can add hardware devices to expand the capabilities of the computer system. For example, a buyer planning to use the computer for managing finances may decide to add a data base management package or a high-quality printer to enhance the use of the computer. Following the purchasing procedure just outlined will help ensure that you purchase an expandable computer system. By planning ahead, you avoid being locked out of the future.

STEP ONE: DEFINING YOUR NEEDS

All too often—perhaps because it is "the thing to do"—people purchase computers before they have clearly defined their needs. But as the personal computer is a tool, it is crucial to define what you will use it for before moving any further into the personal computer market. You would not normally buy an expensive woodworking tool, such as a lathe or a table saw, unless you needed it for your business or hobby. The same should be true of a computer.

Because the computer is such a versatile machine—capable of being used for word processing, financial management, publishing, education, and so on—most people find that they have multiple needs. To help in the decision process, you should rank these needs according to which computer application you use the most. This will help you determine the most appropriate computer and so avoid over- or underbuying.

(Top left) Personal computers are used at home for education and games. (Top right) Macintosh computers are becoming very popular for use in schools. (Bottom) Today it is almost impossible to find an office that does not have at least one personal computer.

Types of Computer Needs

Most people find that their computer needs fall into one of the following three broad categories:

1. personal
2. school related
3. work related

Personal uses of the computer include home budgeting, correspondence, tele-communications, and volunteer activities.

School-related computer use includes writing papers, doing research with electronic data bases, writing computer programs, and using computer software to complete assigned homework and projects. It may also include using packages that provide math drill, computer-aided instruction, and SAT/GRE review to prepare for college and graduate school entrance exams.

Finally, work-related computer use includes bringing work home from the office to complete on a personal computer, using the computer to carry out activities from a home office, and using the computer to manage a small business.

STEP TWO: SELECTING SOFTWARE

Once you have determined your computer needs, the next step is to look for software that will meet those needs. Remember that without software the computer is nothing but a collection of silicon chips and electronic components. For this reason, you should select the software first. In selecting software, you should try to match your needs and your level of computer experience with the software rather than just buying the most popular package on the market. For example, while there are several popular word processing packages that sell for close to $500, there are also numerous less expensive, less sophisticated word processing packages that may easily handle home correspondence or short papers. If you are going to use the software to prepare a senior or graduate thesis, then you will probably need a more sophisticated word processing package to handle the volume and complexity of the work.

Methods of Selecting Software

There are several ways to go about selecting software: You can read articles or reviews about the software, discuss software with members of a user's group, visit a computer store and explain your needs to a salesperson there, and—possibly the best of all—actually use the software at work or school. In many cases, your research into computer software may require you to take advantage of more than one of these research avenues.

Reading Articles and Reviews Some of the better-known computer magazines, listed in Table 10-1, often review individual packages, listing specific capabilities and drawbacks. Occasionally, a computer magazine will review an entire class of software, comparing the available packages on a feature-by-feature basis. Looking through back issues of these magazines, you will find reviews of software packages for almost every need imaginable. Often, general-purpose magazines and newspapers also have periodic columns discussing various software packages, usually at a less technical level than the discussions in computer magazines.

Visiting a User's Group   You may be able to find information on various packages by visiting a computer user's group meeting and asking questions of members. You can find out meeting times of user's groups by calling a computer store or watching for notices in the newspaper. At a user's group meeting, you can talk to experienced users about problems they have faced, look at the types of software they use, and, possibly, try out some software and hardware in a friendly environment. Most members of a user's group are very happy to show off their hardware, software, and computer expertise to a novice.

Visiting a Computer Store   Visiting a computer store can be very helpful if you can talk with someone who is knowledgeable about your specific computer need. To ensure that you will be able to talk to this person, call ahead and make an appointment. Once at the store, you should be able to have the salesperson walk you through the use of the packages that you think will fit your needs. To make this "test use" worthwhile, bring some data for the type of problem for which you will use the software. Ease of use and applicability to your problem are two important criteria for deciding whether a software package fits your needs. This demonstration should also include a review of the user's manual and any other documentation that comes with the software. If you have difficulty reading the user's manual and other documentation, then this package may not fit your needs.

> **Today's emphasis on the entrepreneur and the small business is due, in part, to the PC.**
>
> *Art Afshar, president,*
> *Micro Express*
>
> Quoted in "View from the Top,"
> *Personal Computing,* October 1989,
> p. 262.

A computer store is a good place to discover the great potential of a PC.

Actually Using the Software   Without a doubt, the best way to decide which software package to purchase is to experiment with several of them in a work or school environment.

Software Support

A crucial consideration in selecting software is the degree of support that is available from the vendor or software developer. At one end of the support spectrum are those companies that offer unlimited free technical support for their products over toll-free (800) telephone lines. At the other extreme are those companies that offer no support at all or require you to pay for the call as well as for each minute of help they provide. Obviously, software that comes with the first type of support is preferable to other types, but sometimes, if you must have particular software, you simply must pay for the support. Buying software that offers no telephone support at all is a risky proposition at best!

STEP THREE: SELECTING HARDWARE

After you have determined your software needs, the next step is to select the hardware that will run the software. Since not all computers will run all software, this is an important matching process. Computers differ in the number of bits that they can manipulate (16 or 32), the amount of memory they have (640K, 1 Mbyte, or more), and the operating system that directs the computer operations (MS-DOS, OS/2, Windows, or proprietary). Just as it is impossible to insert an Atari cartridge in a Nintendo game computer, it is also impossible to run MS-DOS software on an Apple Macintosh and vice versa. Some typical examples of each type of computer are shown in Table PC-1.

When discussing a personal computer, we need to recall its component parts. Shown originally as Figure 2-3, these include the central processing unit (CPU), the keyboard, the video screen, secondary storage, a printer, and, possibly, a mouse and modem. These are shown again as Figure PC-1.

Since the keyboard and the CPU come with the computer, the decisions facing the computer buyer usually involve the amount of internal and secondary storage, the type of video system, the type of modem, the type of printer, and the expandability of the system.

Selection of CPU, RAM, and Secondary Storage

As software has become more sophisticated and users have found more reasons to process and store data on a computer, requirements for CPUs, RAM, and disk storage have increased. Users today find that they need fast CPUs, large amounts

TABLE PC-1
Some Popular Computers

Type	Operating System	Bits	Examples
AT compatible	MS-DOS/OS/2	16/32	Compaq, Dell, ZEOS
PS/2	OS/2/MS-DOS	16/32	IBM PS/2 Model 80
Macintosh	Proprietary	32	Mac SE, Mac II

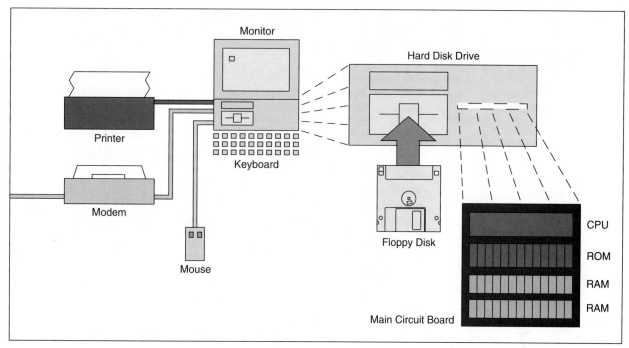

Monitor

Hard Disk Drive

Printer

Keyboard

Modem

Floppy Disk

Mouse

CPU

ROM

RAM

RAM

Main Circuit Board

FIGURE PC-1
Personal Computer System

of RAM, at least one floppy drive, and a hard drive. In choosing a PC, you should consider the CPU's **clock speed.** Clock speed measures in **Megahertz (MHz)** the CPU's top processing speed. It is to a CPU what horsepower is to an engine; all other things being equal, the higher the clock speed, the faster the computer's processing capability.

The original IBM PC had a clock speed of 4.88 MHz, whereas the current i486-based computers, such as the IBM PS/2 Model 95, have clock speeds of up to 50 MHz. Still faster machines will soon be available. Macintosh computers are running at up to 33 MHz.

Intel 80386 and i486 CPU chips now come in two versions, SX and DX. The SX version transfers 16 bits of data to the CPU from RAM, whereas the DX transfers 32 bits. Although computers based on the 80386SX or i486SX chips run somewhat more slowly than those based on the DX version, they are significantly cheaper and have all the other advantages of using these chips. Given the choice between a computer based on the 80286 and one based on the 80386SX, you would be much better off, in general, with the SX version of the 80386 chip.

The amount of internal memory and secondary storage you will need depends on which software you plan to use and how you plan to use your computer. Today's PCs usually have at least 1 Mbyte of memory and often have 2 Mbytes or more. You should not consider buying a computer that does not have a hard disk drive. In choosing a hard drive, consider its **access speed,** which is the amount of time the disk requires to find and move data. Most hard disks today offer access speeds of less than 20 milliseconds—many are even faster. For many applications, a fast hard disk can make as much difference as a fast CPU. If you are using a large-capacity (60 Mbyte or more) hard drive, you should consider some form of tape backup as protection against loss of precious data and software.

For business applications, the Intel 80286 CPU, even at 12 MHz, just isn't fast enough.

Paul Rubin, director of product marketing at Dell Computer Corporation

Quoted in "Computer Technology: A Look to the Future," *WordPerfect: The Magazine,* January 1991, p. 59.

Expandability of the system is something else you should consider: How easy is it to add extra RAM to the system? Can the system be upgraded to a faster processor if one becomes available? Will the system run newer operating systems? Buying a system that is locked into its present condition may lock you out of future improvements in the computer field. Several companies are offering so-called "upgradable PCs" that allow the user to easily replace the CPU with a newer, more powerful one.

Hardware Required to Use Windows

A consideration in buying IBM compatible and PS/2 computers is their capability of running the Windows operating environment and the software rewritten for it. The absolute minimum configuration is a machine that runs the Intel 80286 CPU and has a hard disk, 2 Mbytes of memory, and VGA graphics. Even this configuration, however, is often too slow to run Windows adequately. Most experts recommend an 80386 or i486 machine with at least 4 Mbytes of RAM and "Super VGA" graphics to take full advantage of all Windows's features.

Choosing a Video System and Printer

Chapters 7 and 10 discuss video systems and printers, but let's review the options here. There are essentially three types of video systems to choose from: Hercules-compatible, VGA, and Super VGA (CGA and EGA systems are seldom available, if ever, for new PCs). Recall that the Hercules-compatible system provides high-quality text and graphics on a monochrome monitor. It is by far the least expensive of the three options. The VGA system provides high-resolution text and color graphics on either a VGA or multiscanning monitor, but the Super VGA system provides yet higher resolution. Most top-of-the-line desk-

(Left) Dot matrix printers are an inexpensive device for producing printed output. (Right) Laser printers are now widely used for producing business-quality output.

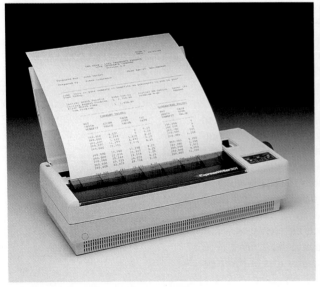

top systems sold today package the Super VGA system. (IBM PS/2 computers have this type of video system, but it is called XGA, which means eXtended Graphics Array.)

If you are considering a Super VGA system, make sure the monitor has a **dot pitch** of no more than 0.28 millimeters and that it is "noninterlaced." Dot pitch refers to the width of a dot on the screen; the smaller the dot pitch, the sharper the image. Interlacing is a technique that "paints" every other line on the monitor with each pass of the cathode ray tube; therefore, a **noninterlaced monitor** paints *each* line, which results in a sharper screen image.

Printers come in three categories: dot matrix, ink-jet, and laser. All three form characters with tiny dots, but each does so with a different mechanism. Dot matrix printers use a series of small rods that impress a ribbon to form letters on a page. Ink-jet printers, on the other hand, spray tiny droplets of ink onto the page. Finally, laser printers use a light-activated system (similar to that of photocopy machines) to create dots of ink on a page. Dot matrix printers are the least expensive of the three types and are usually fine for most school work; however, they are not usually suitable for printing formal correspondence. Laser printers are capable of producing very high-quality output, and they have become more popular since their price has dropped to below $800. Ink-jet printers are not as fast as laser printers, but they offer many of the same capabilities for less money.

Modems

Although the selection of a modem was discussed in detail in Chapter 13, we review it here. Most modems sold today are 1,200 bits per second (bps), 2,400 bps, or 9,600 bps and can be external or internal. While the 1,200-bps modems are the least expensive, many people are buying the 2,400-bps or 9,600-bps modems because of their higher speed. The choice between an internal modem and an external modem depends on the type of computer you are using and whether or not there is space for the internal modem inside the computer. In any case, remember that you will need communications software to implement the modem.

A Package Approach

With the exception of the modem and the mouse, all the components just listed are necessary to make full use of the computer and should be included when you purchase a computer. It is probably best to use a package approach to make your hardware purchase. Sometimes suppliers promise to "back order" some part of the hardware, meaning that they must order it from the factory since they do not have the item in stock. This is a somewhat risky process that can leave you unable to perform the operations for which you purchased the computer system in the first place. According to the step-by-step approach discussed here, you should view the computer system as a whole. Make every attempt to avoid having only part of it. Another problem that could arise with a new hardware model is that promised hardware devices might not be forthcoming when they are expected. If you purchase a new type of system that requires a special printer not yet available, the system will be virtually useless until the printer arrives.

Types of Computers

Besides classifying computers by operating system, number of bits, and memory size, we can also classify them by four major types:

1. IBM compatible PC
2. IBM PS/2
3. Apple Macintosh
4. Other (Amiga and NeXT machines)

IBM compatible computers are those that are compatible with IBM's original 8088-based XT and 80286 AT PCs in that they will run any software written for the XTs and ATs. IBM no longer markets the original PC, XT, or AT, but many companies, including IBM, market computers that are compatible to them and, therefore, can run the vast amount of software written for MS-DOS. Although you can still buy an 8088-based computer that is compatible with the IBM XT, most IBM compatible computers sold today use Intel 80286, 80386, or i486 chips and are compatible with the IBM 80286-based AT computer. These include the IBM PS/1 series, Compaq, Tandy, and Dell computers, as well as those manufactured by many other companies. Most of the IBM AT compatible computers cost between $750 and $4,000, depending on the type of CPU chip used and the types and number of peripherals. They are popular in business and industry, and many universities are buying them for computer labs. With sufficient RAM, all AT-class compatible computers will run Windows and the software written for it. XT compatible computers, however, will not run Windows.

IBM PS/2 computers were developed by IBM to replace the original PC, XT, and AT computers. Engineers aimed at creating a machine that other companies could not duplicate. The features of PS/2 computers vary from model to model. Some have a high-resolution video system, some are capable of running the OS/2 operating system, and they have differing internal communication systems. As with the AT compatible computers, all PS/2 machines can run software written for MS-DOS or the Windows operating environment. Many companies

(Left) The 486 Dell computer is a popular IBM compatible PC. (Right) IBM's 486 PS/2 is a popular new model.

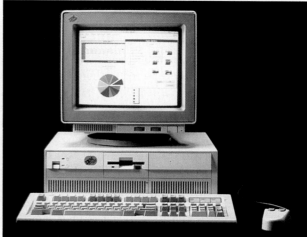

(Top left) The IBM PS/2 386 is purchased by many people to get started in computing. (Top right) The Model 55SX provides the computing power of the 80386 chip at a reduced cost. (Bottom) The Model 80 is a popular PC in many business and engineering offices.

The Macintosh Classic II (left) uses a high-quality black-and-white screen; the Mac II (right) offers the user the option of a color monitor.

and colleges and universities buy this type of computer. Popular models are Model 25, Model 30, Model 55SX, and Model 95.

The Apple Macintosh is an extremely innovative computer introduced in 1984. The first Mac combined text and graphics on a high-resolution white screen. Recent versions offer high-resolution color monitors as well as the original white screen. The Mac is without peer when it comes to creating newsletters, forms, greeting cards, and so forth. In fact, desktop publishing owes its origin to the Macintosh's unique abilities. Because of the Mac's increasing popularity, more and more software is being written for it for use in business, education, and home. In addition, it is now possible to convert some software from a Macintosh version to an MS-DOS version and vice versa with a special floppy disk drive called a "super drive." Popular lines of the Macintosh include the Mac Classic II, the Mac LC II, and the Mac II series.

The NeXT computer combines the UNIX operating system with powerful graphics and easy-to-use menuing systems.

THINGS TO CONSIDER WHEN BUYING A PORTABLE COMPUTER

It is true that all personal computers are portable, to some extent, but an entire class of extremely portable computers arose in the last half of the 1980s. While the overall market for PCs is becoming saturated, sales of easily transportable computers continue to grow at a rapid rate. There are four types of portable computers: luggable, laptop, notebook, and pocket. Size distinguishes the categories. **Luggable PCs** are at one extreme. They weigh over 10 pounds, require AC power, and are portable from desk to desk. Examples of luggable PCs are the Toshiba T5200 and the Zenith TurboSport. At the other extreme are **pocket PCs,** which are about the size of a large calculator and replace such things as traditional address books, calculators, and appointment calendars. They are battery powered and do not include a disk drive. Examples of pocket PCs are the Poquet PC, the Fujitsu System 29, and the Sharp Wizard.

Laptop PCs and **notebook PCs** fall between the two extremes. Both are full-power computers that can run on either AC power or rechargeable batteries. Laptops and notebooks are distinguishable by weight, options, and expandability. The distinction, however, is rapidly fading as computer companies steadily design portables to fit inside the average briefcase, which requires a size of approximately $8\frac{1}{2}$ by 11 inches.

Laptops and notebooks have a similar design, either "clamshell" or "lunch box," depending on the keyboard. With a clamshell design, the screen folds down over the keyboard; whereas, with the lunch-box design, the keyboard pulls out for positioning at various angles.

The Macintosh Portable, or "Mactop," and the three types of Power Book PCs from Apple Computer require special attention. The Mactop was designed to be completely "Mac-like" and will run any software designed for desktop Macintosh computers. Mactops come with a mouse, but a built-in trackball and mousebar make them truly portable. The Power Book computers are smaller than the Mactop and can run software created for either the Mac or MS-DOS.

Hints for Buying a Notebook

MS-DOS–based notebook computers are becoming the most popular portable computers among business persons and students. Tips for buying an MS-DOS–based notebook computer follow:

- Look for at least an 80286 CPU processor with as much memory as is available. If you plan to run Windows, you will need at least an 80386SX CPU and up to 4 megabytes of RAM. Make sure you can easily add an internal modem, so that you can communicate with other computers.
- Make sure the notebook PC has a hard drive and a 1.44-Mbyte, $3\frac{1}{2}$-inch floppy drive, and insist on a VGA display that will drive an external monitor. Check the visibility of the display from several angles and under different intensities of light to ensure that you can read it.
- Carefully check the keyboard to make sure it satisfies your needs. Test it by keying text and figures into documents and spreadsheets—this may prevent you from buying a keyboard that will frustrate you later.
- Look for a well-padded case and a handle on the PC. Make sure the purchase price includes a battery and charger and that the charger is small and lightweight. Do not buy a PC that does not have a low-battery light.
- Look for at least a one-year warranty and the availability of a "loaner" if the PC requires repair while under warranty.

Sources: "Buying: Making the Decision," *WordPerfect The Magazine,* July 1991, pp. 46–47; and Mary Jerome, "How to Buy a Notebook PC," *PC Computing,* June 1991, pp. 132–134.

Other computers include the Amiga and NeXT machines. The Commodore Amiga uses the same chip as the Apple Macintosh and competes with the Mac for sales in the graphics market. The NeXT computer is a Unix-based PC developed by Steve Jobs' NeXT company. Its hardware and software have many innovative features.

STEP FOUR: SELECTING A SUPPLIER

Once you have selected software and hardware, it then becomes important to choose a supplier from whom to make the purchases. Most people have three choices of where to buy computer hardware and software:

1. a local computer/software store
2. a discount computer/software outlet
3. through the mail

Each option has good points and bad points. A local computer store usually stocks a range of computer hardware and software and usually (but not always) has a staff knowledgeable about what they sell. Such a store can also offer the local touch you may need to help with problems, and for a novice in computers it can be a good place to learn about the various types of hardware and software.

On the other hand, a discount computer store is usually larger than the local computer store and may carry a wider variety of computer equipment and software at lower prices. Usually the salespeople are as knowledgeable as those at a local store about the various pieces of equipment and types of software they may have in stock and so can help you make your selection. There are even specialty discount stores for one particular type of equipment, say, printers, or just for software. On the negative side, a discount computer store, especially if it is not located in your hometown, may not offer the help you need when problems arise after the purchase.

Finally, often the least expensive way to buy computer software and hardware is through the mail. Computer magazines carry numerous advertisements for software and hardware at prices that are quite a bit lower than the list price. While it is possible to save a great deal of money by going through a mail order company, you must be well informed and experienced since you will get no help setting up the equipment or installing the software. Another point to consider about software purchased from a mail order house is that there is no way to test it before you buy it; once you have opened the package, it may be that the software cannot be returned to the company for a cash refund.

Service Factors

A key point to consider in selecting a hardware supplier is service. While a computer is usually a very trouble-free machine with few moving parts, there *will* come a time when service is needed. Perhaps a disk drive falls out of alignment or a key gets stuck; in any case, some type of repair will eventually be necessary. Most local and discount computer stores have repair services to handle such problems. Most equipment has anywhere from a 90-day to a two-year warranty that computer stores will honor on equipment purchased from them. If the equipment was purchased from another source, say, through a mail order house, you may need to return the equipment to the factory at your own expense.

It is also possible to purchase a service contract from either the seller or a third-party service company. Whether to purchase such a contract depends to a large degree on how much risk you are willing to accept and how important it is to you to know that the cost of repair is covered. In general, businesses

Discount computer stores in metropolitan areas often offer lower prices, combined with technical help.

with a large number of machines that are important to them are probably smart to purchase such an agreement.

STEP FIVE: MAKING THE PURCHASE

Once you have selected the software, hardware, and supplier, making the purchase is the final step. But first it is worthwhile to go through a checklist to ensure that you are getting a "ready-to-use" system and will not have to return to the supplier for extra items. (This checklist includes questions the supplier must answer as well as items that need to be included in the purchase.)

1. Are all printer and monitor cables included in the system or will they have to be purchased separately?
2. Are any additional interface cards or boards needed to run the printer or the monitor?

TIPS FOR BUYING BY MAIL

Before you buy computer hardware or software by mail:

- Check on the company's payment policy and determine whether you will be charged extra for using a credit card. Also find out how long you will have to wait for a check to clear before the product is shipped.
- Make sure incidental costs such as shipping and handling don't raise the price above that offered by a local supplier.
- Check if the product is in stock and ask how long the company will take to deliver it to you. If it is not in stock, determine the back-order time.
- Get a clear idea of return policies— whether the company offers an unconditional 30-day money-back guarantee or replaces defective products only. Also determine if the company will accept the return of opened software for a refund, for credit toward another product, or not at all.
- If the price is a great deal lower than that found locally, check the description carefully to ensure that you are actually getting what you want. Check to see if a local store may be willing to meet or come close to the mail order price. Remember, however, that you may have to pay sales tax locally, but may not have to through mail order.
- Make sure that the company has a toll-free (800) number and is willing to answer questions about the product in addition to accepting orders.
- Keep all records of the transaction, including the salesperson's name and *all* correspondence, in case a problem arises.
- You are entitled to a full refund if the merchandise is not delivered within 30 days of payment. If there are problems, first call the company and then write, explaining your problem in a clear, logical, polite manner. If these steps fail and you have paid by credit card, the Fair Credit Billing Act allows you to contact your credit company and have them withhold payment until the problem is resolved.

Source: Ron Bel Bruno, "Tips for Buying by Mail," *Personal Computing*, February 1989, p. 83.

3. Are there sufficient connections to be able to hook up a modem and a printer at the same time? If not, what is the cost of these interfaces?
4. Is communications software included with the modem? If not, what is the cost of software that is compatible with the computer?
5. Can you expand the system in the future by adding additional memory or disk drives?
6. Have you included in your purchase price the cost of an initial purchase of blank floppy disks, printer paper, and, if you have a tape backup system, tape cartridges?
7. If you are buying a laser printer, is the toner cartridge included in the purchase price?

ALTERNATIVES TO BUYING A NEW PC

You do not have to buy a factory-fresh PC to have use of one. You can buy a used one, or you can rent one. One advantage of buying a used PC is that the original owner, rather than you, sustained the 40 percent loss in value that occurs when a computer is removed from its box. If you rent, you will not have to make a large outlay of capital.

As the power and speed of PCs increase, PC owners often upgrade to newer, more powerful machines; therefore, used PCs are widely available. In fact, the Boston Computer Society maintains a market price index on various types of used PCs. Used machines are not only cheaper but fully set up—the first owner has already invested the hours of time required to get the PC up and running. They may not be "state-of-the-art," but that does *not* mean they cannot serve the purpose for which they were built. A used computer is like an old pickup truck; it may not be shiny and new, but it still does the job. There are things you should remember, however, if you are considering buying a used PC.

- Know what you want and thoroughly research the market prices before you shop. It is worthwhile to have the system appraised before you seal the deal.
- Thoroughly test all the equipment before you buy it. You should check each key on the keyboard to make sure each works smoothly and that none cause extraneous letters to appear. Also, test the disk drives thoroughly to ensure that the computer will boot up and copy files without difficulty.
- Unless you are somewhat of a computer expert, find a friend or hire a consultant to help you check the system.
- Watch for "hot" machines if you are buying through a newspaper advertisement. Always ask to see the original sales receipt.

PC rentals total approximately $500 million annually, and analysts believe the figure will increase 30 to 40 percent annually. Most PC rental business is short term (30 days or less), and most businesses deliver the PC to you, set it up, provide free technical support for the term of the rental, and pick it up at the end of the rental period. Rates vary, depending on machine type and geographical location. In general, however, you can expect to pay at least $100 per week or $175 per month for an 80286 machine. This may seem expensive, but if your machine has died and you have four papers due in one week, a rental machine at even twice the price could seem cheap!

Sources: Alex Randall, "How to Buy Used PCs Without Getting Ripped Off," *Computerworld*, March 11, 1991, p. 84; and Jennifer Smith, "If You Can't Buy It, Rent It," *Lotus*, May 1991, p. 18.

Once the questions in this checklist have been answered satisfactorily, you can make the purchase knowing that the system will run just as soon as it is set up in the home or office. If any answers imply that additional equipment or purchases are required, then you might need to do more research before making the final purchase.

After the Purchase

Once you have purchased your personal computer, it is always wise to "burn in" the machine immediately by running it for several hours. In many cases, components in computers will fail during the first 50 to 100 hours of operation or not at all. Turning on the computer and running a repetitive program overnight improves the chance of catching a problem while the computer is still under warranty. It is also a good idea to test the software again to detect problems not found during the test-use phase. Once the hardware "burn-in" phase is over and the software has been tested, you are ready to enjoy the use of this wonderful mind tool.

BITS OF HISTORY

A Short History of the Personal Computer

The term *personal computer* was coined by a computer scientist, Alan Kay, in a 1972 paper titled "A Personal Computer for Children of All Ages." As a result of Kay's work in this area, Xerox built a personal computer called the Alto, though they never put it on the market. Other established computer companies also considered the concept of a personal computer but decided that there was no market for such a machine. As a result, it was not until 1975 that an Albuquerque, New Mexico, company called MITS released the first personal computer in kit form. This machine, named "Altair" after a planet in the "Star Trek" TV series,

had just 1K of memory and was very slow by today's standards. MITS had 5,000 orders for the Altair after it was pictured on the cover of *Popular Electronics.* A pioneer in the field, the current computer science publisher Rodney Zaks, remarked that "Never before had such a powerful tool been invented and so few people realized what it could do."

While MITS was the first to come out with a personal computer, it was up to Apple, Radio Shack, and Commodore to popularize its use. These were among almost 100 companies that rushed to put out personal computers in the years immediately after MITS offered the first one.

An amazing success story of this period is that of the Apple Company, formed by two young Californians, Steve Jobs and Steve Wozniak, when they built the first Apple computer in their garage.

With all these infant companies competing for the emerging computer

market, Apple made a real breakthrough in 1978 when it offered a disk drive to go along with the original Apple II. This was the key addition that, along with the VisiCalc software package offered only on the Apple, allowed Apple to leapfrog over Radio Shack and Commodore into first place among the pioneer companies.

The next breakthrough came when IBM offered its PC in 1981. While not an innovation technologically, the IBM PC almost immediately became an industry standard and legitimized the concept of a personal computer. It was followed by the Apple Macintosh in 1984, the IBM PS/2 line in 1987, and the NeXT computer in 1988. These introductions have divided the industry roughly into five types of computers: IBM PS/2, IBM PC AT compatibles, Apple II series, Apple Macintosh series, and others (Commodore, Atari, NeXT, and so on).

Source: John Hillkirk, "Computer Whiz Kids Recall Magic," *USA Today,* June 18, 1984, p. B3. Updated by the author.

The original IBM PC quickly became an industry standard and made IBM a force in PC manufacturing.

In Chapter 4, we looked at a broad category of information systems that aid in the management of an organization, and we introduced five widely used information systems: transaction processing systems (TPS), management information systems (MIS), decision support systems (DSS), executive information systems (EIS), and office information systems (OIS). We also discussed expert systems and strategic information systems, and the systems analysis and design process used to develop information systems.

In Block Four we have included chapters on each of these major topics: Chapter 14 closely examines types of information systems, and Chapter 15 discusses in detail the systems analysis and design process, presenting a case study. The various tools used by systems analysts are spotlighted through this example. Chapter 16 looks at the program development portion of systems analysis and design in detail and provides a step-by-step, language-independent procedure for writing computer programs. Finally, Chapter 17 surveys the computer languages a programmer would use to write the software that supports information systems.

14

Types of Information Systems

Chapter 4 made clear the value of information in organizations today and introduced the concept of the information system as the vehicle for supplying that information to the appropriate decision maker. Chapter 14 will now review the various types of information systems discussed in Chapter 4 and then discuss each of them in detail. Included in this discussion are transaction processing systems, management information systems, decision support systems, executive information systems, and office information systems. Two other systems that contribute to the overall success of the organization but are not usually tied to a single level of the organization—expert systems and strategic information systems—will also be discussed.

STUDY OBJECTIVES

After reading this chapter, you should be able to

- understand the importance of computer-based information systems in organizations;
- describe the evolution of information systems in organizations;
- list the various transaction processing system modes;
- discuss the management information system for an organization and explain how it provides information to the manager;
- discuss the types of reports produced by a management information system and the purpose of each type of report;
- explain the parts of a decision support system and the role each plays in managerial decision making;
- describe an executive information system and discuss how it helps top-level executives make decisions;
- distinguish between an MIS, a DSS, and an EIS and discuss the role each plays in supporting decision making;
- list the functions of the office information system and discuss how it supports the information system;
- discuss the concept of an expert system and describe how the expert system may be used to improve the decision-making capabilities of managers;
- describe strategic information systems and discuss how they can be used to improve the competitive position of an organization.

COMPUTER-AIDED SCHOOL BUS ROUTING

Bus transportation is a large expense for many school districts. Reducing this cost is the objective of the Transportation Information Management System (TIMS), which all 133 school districts in North Carolina use. This personal computer-based decision support system (DSS) lets local school districts create efficient routes and schedules for their school buses.

TIMS has four modules: (1) geocoding, which digitizes the school district's street network maps; (2) transportation, which maintains all routing and scheduling information, including the location of each student; (3) optimization, which tries to identify the least costly bus routes and schedules and enables administrators to perform "what if?" analyses; and (4) boundary planning, which provides demographic data on students.

TIMS's data base contains information on the district's streets and roads, bus travel speed, student locations, bus stops, bus runs, and bus routes. The models are designed to determine how to reduce the time and distance of all bus runs based on the capacity of each bus. In tests in the Randolph County school district, TIMS reduced school bus mileage by 6 percent and was instrumental in reassigning or parking nine buses.

A widely used spin-off of the primary purpose of TIMS is the boundary planning module. This module allows administrators to plan school attendance districts based on student location information stored in the TIMS data base. It provides administrators with precise information about number of students, racial makeup of the student population, and distribution of students across grades for analyzing existing, new, or proposed attendance boundaries.

Source: Derek Graham and Jerry Shackelford, "Computer-Aided Bus Routing," *Technological Horizons in Education Journal*, November 1991, pp. 58–61.

INFORMATION SYSTEMS IN ORGANIZATIONS

Recall from Chapter 4 that an organization's information system is crucial to the organization's well-being because of the value of information. Processing, storing, retrieving, and distributing information throughout an organization requires multiple information systems. As discussed previously, **information systems** are more than just computer hardware and software; they also must include the all-important human user, and they must support the managerial decision making that ultimately determines the future well-being of the organization. In the boxed insert, the transportation information system helps school district administrators reduce school-bus costs without reducing service to students. This is an example of one type of information system—a decision support system. There are various other types of information systems that provide information in other forms to other users. We will discuss each type in this chapter.

An Overview of Information Systems

To better understand the function of information systems, consider the "ideal" integrated information system for an organization, in Figure 14-1. We say "ideal" because very few organizations have been able to integrate all the separate information systems as shown in the figure.

Figure 14-1 is a conceptual view of the way the various information systems are combined to provide needed information to users to support managerial decision making. These individual information systems include the transaction processing system (TPS), the management information system (MIS), the decision support system, the executive information system (EIS), the strategic information system (SIS), and expert systems. All are combined with a data base to form an integrated organizational information system. Note that while the office information system (OIS) is not specifically shown here, it makes possible *all* the communications linkages between the information systems and their users.

The conceptual integrated information system begins with data coming from internal and external sources. The data are prepared through the transaction processing system and then go into the internal data base via a **data base management system (DBMS).** Next, employees use the DBMS to find needed information in the internal data base—for use by the MIS to create any of various reports to management or for use by the DSS to attempt to answer a question posed by a manager. The MIS reports can be sent to the manager through the document preparation and electronic mail functions of the OIS. These reports can also be stored with the electronic storage function or sent to other persons over the external electronic mail operation.

The information in the internal data base can also be combined with information from external data bases for presentation to top-level executives through

FIGURE 14-1
Conceptual View of an
Information System

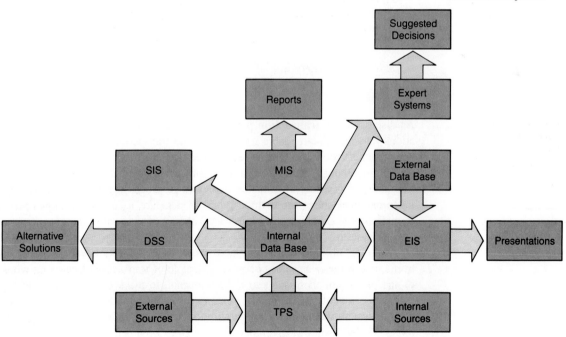

(Left) Processing remittances is an important use for the transaction processing system for many companies. (Right) A summary report such as this one is generated by the management information system that accesses a data base. (Page 437, left) Modeling complex problems on the computer is an important application of the decision support system. (Page 437, right) An executive information system provides information to busy executives in a form that they can easily use.

the EIS. The internal data base is also a source of information for the SIS and is part of the knowledge used in an expert system.

Throughout this process, the OIS supports the decision-making process at all stages by facilitating the preparation of text, sending information electronically, and filing results electronically. The actual movement of information is handled by a computer network in which computers are tied together using communication links.

While these information systems appear to work together as in the ideal integrated information system shown in Figure 14-1, such is not the case in the "real world." In most cases, if these individual information systems actually exist, they work independently. A truly integrated information system is not the reality but the goal in most organizations.

TRANSACTION PROCESSING SYSTEMS

As discussed, the **transaction processing system** converts raw data from operations into machine-readable form, stores the transaction details, processes the transactions, and, if necessary, reports the details of the transactions. A transaction processing system has data input, processing, and output functions. Many transaction processing systems are dedicated to processing accounting, sales, or inventory data, since these three types of data are used for decision making throughout the organization. Figure 14-2 shows conceptually a transaction processing system.

An example of transaction input would be sales data keyed into an electronic cash register as sales occur. An example of transaction processing would be the posting of these sales to a sales journal, to the accounts receivable file, and to the inventory records. An example of the output of a transaction processing system would be the preparation of detailed monthly statements for customers or the display of inventory items in stock on a personal computer display screen.

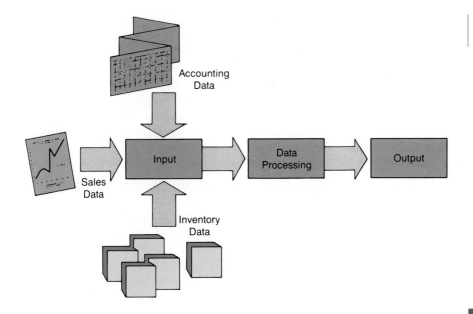

FIGURE 14-2
Conceptual View of the
Transaction Processing System

Accounting
Data

Input

Data
Processing

Output

Sales
Data

Inventory
Data

Transaction Processing Input

At one time, transaction input was handled by keypunch operators who transcribed data onto punch cards that were then fed into the computer for further processing, storage, and reporting. While that may still be done in a few cases, the overwhelming trend is toward using computer terminals to enter the data directly into the computer or onto some form of secondary storage (usually magnetic disk). While the skills needed to perform this processing are the same as for keypunching, the results are stored in a form that can be accessed more easily by a variety of computer applications.

The future of transaction input appears to be in optical character and bar code readers. The optical character recognition (OCR) devices allow written and

The volume of information is increasing exponentially; PCs are making it possible for businesses to manage that flow effectively.

*Eugene R. Kunde,
executive vice president,
Epson America, Inc.*

Quoted in "View from the Top,"
Personal Computing, October, 1989
p. 254.

printed documents to be converted into an electronic form without going through the process of having a human key in the words or data. The current state of this technology is such that many printed documents can be read, but reading handwritten documents still is often beyond the capability of these machines. Bar code input is almost error free and can be used for a variety of operations—from programming VCRs to monitoring grocery checkout to keeping up with prison inmates. While OCR will have many important applications, bar code input is fast becoming the predominant form of nonkeyboard input for transaction processing.

Transaction Processing Modes

Transaction processing systems can be classified according to the manner in which the data are input, processed, and output; that is, the TPS can use batch, transactional, or real-time processing.

In a **batch processing system,** the data from multiple users or time periods are combined, input, and processed as a batch. All the data or transactions are batched according to some common criterion, such as the type of transaction; for example, all sales returns might be processed at one time. This system is used whenever there is no immediate need for up-to-date data or when competition for scarce resources is not associated with the processing. Also, a great deal of similar data must be processed at the same time. Thus, the grade reporting output system is usually a batch processing system because the data and the type of processing are the same and there is no immediacy required. Payroll systems are usually batch systems, since they must process the same type of data once a pay period.

In **transactional processing,** each transaction is processed as it occurs; the data are processed at the time of entry rather than being held for later processing. We are all familiar with transactional processing systems at the grocery checkout counter, where we are handed an itemized receipt immediately after the items are processed. While the customer may not be aware of it, such point-of-sale (POS) transactional systems are often also updating the inventory of the items sold and keeping a running total of each type of item being sold. This information is of great use to managers in making decisions about replenishing inventory, allocating shelf space, or scheduling checkout personnel to match shopper demand.

In **real-time processing,** the processing of the transaction can actually affect the transaction itself. For example, perhaps several users are competing for the same resource, such as a seat on an airplane or a seat in a college class. In the latter case, a real-time system would be very useful because a student could know at the time of registration whether space is available in a class and whether his or her schedule has been approved.

Transaction Processing Output

Once data are input and processed, they may be stored in disk files, displayed on a screen, printed, or, most often, all three. The processing of data at this point is often just the first step; the resulting information will probably be processed several more times through summarization or in combination with other information.

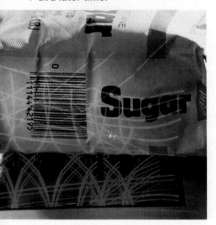

Bar code readers allow grocery stores to process transactions as they occur rather than in batches at a later time.

TPS at the FishTale Company

As an example of an online transaction processing system, consider the FishTale Company. FishTale is a wholesale distributor of fishing tackle and supplies, and has data in the form of handwritten sales invoices for all of its sales transactions for the past month. Assume that FishTale's management wants to determine which customers are purchasing the largest total dollar volume from the company and which salespeople are selling the most. The current handwritten data are not in a form that is useful to the company since they are by individual transaction and do not contain totals or summaries. Before the data can be used to answer management's questions, they must first be processed into an electronic form by the transaction processing system and stored on a file in a data base. Figure 14-3 shows this process, beginning with the handwritten sales invoices. From here the data are keyed into the computer and processed into a form that FishTale's data base system will accept. In this case, FishTale is using a batch transaction processing system. On the other hand, the company may also use a transactional processing system to keep up with its inventory, but would probably have no need for a real-time system.

MANAGEMENT INFORMATION SYSTEMS

When information systems were introduced to relieve the information overload caused by the use of computer data processing, one of the first objectives of their use was to generate reports so that managers would not have to search through reams of computer output to find needed information. As the information system grew to be responsible for report generation, management information systems came into being to handle this very important task. A **management information system** can be defined as "an integrated user-

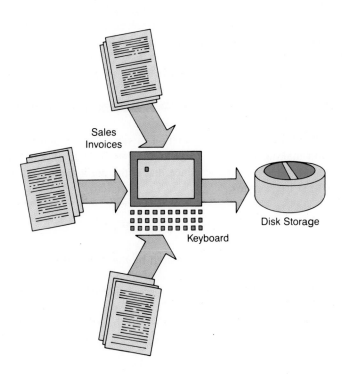

FIGURE 14-3
FishTale Transaction Processing System

SAVING MONEY AND TIME AT DENNY'S WITH POS

By their own admission, managers at the over 1,000 company-owned Denny's restaurants in 46 states spent too much time each week manually entering data into a paper-based payroll and sales system and using handheld calculators to determine totals. This process turned them into bookkeepers who often became bogged down in paperwork. As a result, they were unable to spend adequate time training employees, overseeing pricing of entrees, and handling customer relations.

To remedy this problem, Denny's began installing point-of-sale (POS) systems in its restaurants in 1989. Each system consists of three to five terminals for data input by servers, a terminal that acts as a cash register, a PC in the back office, and a printer in the kitchen. Servers at each restaurant daily enter receipts and so forth into a terminal. The information is then summarized and forwarded to company headquarters.

Benefits from this POS system were immediately measurable: Revenue increased more than 1 percent because items, such as free cups of coffee and food given to friends, that never figured into sales receipts are now accounted for. The increased revenue amounts to $10 million per year for the 1,000 stores. In addition, administrative activities decreased by about 14 hours per week per store, which amounts to annual savings of about $25 million. The time saved is spent now on customer service and other managerial activities.

The POS system has also helped Denny's gather information about new hires more efficiently and identify staffing and other problems that have the potential to hinder a restaurant operation.

Source: Charlotte A. Krause, "Denny's POS Effort," *Computerworld*, May 27, 1991, pp. 81, 84.

> **Now we have a way to measure our business in more detail within each restaurant.**
>
> *Charlotte A. Krause, director of information services, Denny's*
>
> Quoted in "Denny's POS Effort," *Computerworld,* May 27, 1991, pp. 81, 84.

machine system for providing information to support operations, management, and decision-making functions in an organization."[1] In this definition, the emphasis is on the word *support,* since that is the purpose of the MIS through the reports that it generates.

Types of Reports

Reports can take various forms as required by the different management levels in the organization. Basically, three types of reports are generated by the management information system: scheduled reports, exception reports, and demand

---

[1] Gordon B. Davis and Margaret H. Olson, *Management Information Systems,* 2nd ed. (New York: McGraw-Hill, 1985), p. 6.

reports. Each serves a different purpose for the organization, but all are important.

Scheduled reports reflect the periodic and historic information on the organization's operations. They are much like the original information produced by the transaction processing system, with the addition of needed categorization and summary information. These reports help the lowest-level manager make operational decisions to meet the objectives set by the higher-level managers.

Exception reports are generated only if some condition—usually an abnormal event—has occurred to signal the need for a report. The exception report is useful to the manager for early detection of problems, an essential part of good management. At the same time, the exception report does not overwhelm the manager with unnecessary information. For example, a management information system might generate an exception report whenever overtime pay for a given period is greater than 10 percent of total time worked. The production manager can then investigate the possible reasons for the excessive overtime. Is it due to a big production job or to poor planning? If the latter, then the production manager can address a problem that would not have been immediately evident without an exception report.

Finally, **demand reports** are specialized reports that a manager requests on a particular subject. Often this request results from unexpected information in one of the other reports from the MIS or from outside information. For example, the president of an international soft drink company may hear a rumor that the leadership of a foreign country may outlaw the use of caffeine in cola drinks sold in that country. The company president quickly requests a report from MIS on what percentage of total soft drink sales in that country would be affected by such a ban. Since this information is not of the type that can be programmed in advance, special effort will be necessary to generate the report. The staff of the MIS department must have access to a data base that can supply the needed data and produce such a report.

MIS at FishTale

Consider again the FishTale Company, which is processing handwritten sales invoices into a form that managers can use to make decisions. The handwritten data have already been processed and stored on a file in FishTale's data base. The next step is for the management information system to use the information in the data base to create reports. One such report might be a scheduled monthly report, listing the salespeople in order from highest to lowest sales and listing customers in order by sales volume. Another report might be an exception report showing the salespeople who have sold significantly less than their monthly quota. The sales manager would then want to meet with these people to determine the reasons for the low sales. In addition, because of increased competition, the sales manager may request a demand report showing the names of customers who purchased less this month than they did during the same month last year. Figure 14-4 shows the production of these reports by the management information system.

DECISION SUPPORT SYSTEMS

While various types of reports produced by the MIS provide much-needed information to lower-level managers, they often do not supply the type of information

FIGURE 14-4
Reports Produced by MIS at
FishTale

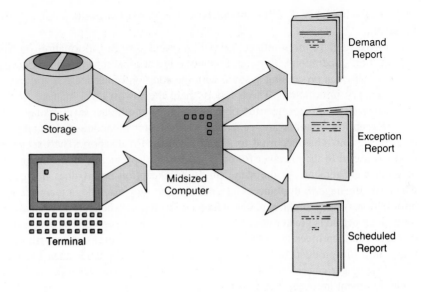

needed by middle- and upper-level managers. The lack of timely information and the inability of managers to use MIS to test the effect of a possible decision led to the development of the **decision support system.** The objective of DSS is to aid managers by enabling them, through the use of quantitative and graphical models, to find answers to questions and thereby to make better decisions.

Decision support systems have been used for such diverse activities as ski resort development, financial planning, and, as discussed in the box at the beginning of the chapter, school bus routing. The system can be as simple as an electronic spreadsheet on a personal computer or as powerful as a full-scale financial planning package on a mainframe. While most decision support systems were originally implemented on mainframes because of the additional processing power, storage capabilities, and advanced graphics available on the larger machines, DSS packages for the more powerful PCs are now in wide use.

Parts of a DSS

A decision support system has three major parts: a **data base,** from which information can be retrieved as needed; a **model base,** made up of various models that can be used to help arrive at a solution; and a **dialog base,** which handles the interactions between the manager and the computer.

The data base must be available to the decision maker so that needed information—including internal information, reports from the MIS, and external data from national databases such as Dialog and CompuServe—may be retrieved on demand. The decision maker also selects a model from the model base and combines the data and the model to develop alternative solutions. The model base is made up of a group of computer programs that will perform specific operations on the information from the data base. The various alternative solutions can then be portrayed in a tabular or graphical form. To make the DSS easy to use, the dialog base uses various software procedures that allow the decision maker to change data and models as he or she goes through the process of making a decision. For example, the user may use the dialog base to request a plot of the data on the screen. The dialog base chooses the correct model and com-

```
WHAT WE KNOW:

    SALES VOLUME IS DOWN OVERALL
    CORPORATE EXPENSES ARE UP SIGNIFICANTLY
    INVENTORY LEVELS ARE TYING UP LOTS OF CASH
    CANADIAN REGION PROFITS ARE DOWN DUE TO HIGHER OPERATING EXPENSES
    EASTERN REGION PROFITS ARE DOWN DUE TO LOWER GROSS MARGINS ON
        PRINTERS AND CAMERAS
    PRINTER AND CAMERA MARGINS ARE DOWN DUE TO HIGHER PRODUCTION
        COSTS
    CASH FLOW AND MARGINS CAN BE IMPROVED THROUGH BETTER
        INVENTORY CONTROL
    EXPENSE REDUCTION AND INVENTORY CONTROL WILL RAISE MARGINS TO
        PLAN LEVELS


WHAT WE DISCOVERED:

    A MIX OF MARKETABLE SECURITIES, SHORT TERM AND LONG TERM DEBT
        WILL BE REQUIRED TO FINANCE OUR 4TH QUARTER ACQUISITION
```

By presenting alternatives, decision support systems help managers solve complex problems.

bines it with the data to arrive at the requested plot. To a large extent, the dialog base should make the data base and model base invisible to the user by handling all the interactions. It is the dialog base that makes the DSS a truly useful tool by allowing the manager to move about freely in the DSS. Figure 14-5 shows the interaction between the user and the parts of the DSS.

Types of DSS

Decision support systems take three basic forms: general-purpose DSS, specific DSS, and DSS model generators. The **general-purpose DSS** is like an electronic spreadsheet package: The user must develop the model and then manipulate the variables to arrive at alternative solutions within a general modeling framework. At the other extreme, a **specific DSS** is developed for one specific type of problem. This usually involves writing a program in some high-level language. Finally, a **DSS generator** helps the user develop specific models by making

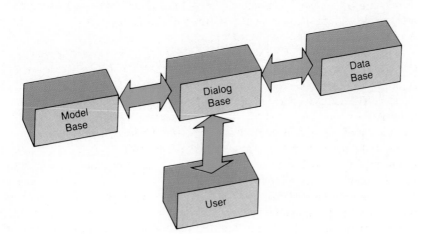

FIGURE 14-5
User Interaction with DSS

available everything that might be needed. The dialog base is usually already written in such a way that the user can modify it to ask appropriate questions and to output the needed results. The DSS generator also includes many of the most commonly used models as well as a library of commonly used mathematical and graphical operations. Finally, either the DSS generator will include the operations to set up a data base or it may be easily tied into the organization's data base or into an external information source. The DSS generator has been described as an *electronic workbench* since it is like a carpenter's workbench with all tools within easy reach. An example of a DSS generator is the Interactive Financial Planning System (IFPS) available on many mainframes for helping managers make financial forecasts and decisions.

Using Models in DSS

To provide the support that the decision maker needs to handle unstructured and semistructured problems, a system must be developed that enables the manager and/or the staff to interact with the computer online. In addition to being able to obtain information at will from a data base or from external sources, the decision maker must be able to use the software at the terminal to determine the effect of changes in the information or the effect of new information.

For these changes to be observed, a model must be developed that represents the physical, economic, or financial situation being studied. A **model** is a simplified version of reality that captures the interrelationships between important variables in the situation. Once the model has been created, the manager may then use it to answer questions. There are three primary models: forecasting, optimization, and simulation.

In a **forecasting model,** historical data, managerial assumptions, and a forecasting formula are combined to "guess" what the future may hold. For

```
               ACQUISITION FINANCING OPTIMIZATION
                         4th Quarter 1986


                                          PLAN          FORECAST
                                       ---------        ---------
       MIX OF INSTRUMENTS:

           CASH                            0%               0%
           MARKETABLE SECURITIES           0%              53%
           SHORT TERM DEBT                 0%              12%
           LONG TERM DEBT                100%              35%


       CONSTRAINT VALUES:

           DEBT TO EQUITY RATIO           1.2             1.0
           CURRENT RATIO                  2.0             2.1
           CASH                         20000           20000


       FINANCE EXPENSE                    3397            3444
```

Optimization and forecasting models are often used by decision support systems.

example, a university would like to predict the number of incoming freshmen in order to plan for dormitory space. As applications begin to arrive in the fall before the year being considered, predictions can be made about how many students will actually be enrolling. This prediction report would be based on the number and quality of applications compared to those of previous years, the acceptance rate, and the attendance rate for those accepted. While the prediction of the number of students will probably become more accurate as the beginning of the school year draws nearer, even the earliest prediction reports will enable the administration to make some plans. These early plans are then refined as the forecasts are improved each month.

In **optimization,** the user implements a mathematical technique that will determine the best possible solution to the model. The most common forms of optimization are unconstrained methods using calculus and constrained methods such as linear and integer programming. By *constrained* we mean that the range of possible solutions is restricted in some way. For example, we may wish to find the maximum profit associated with a particular product where production is constrained by the availability of raw materials, labor hours, and so on.

With **simulation,** the user enters a series of values for the variables to simulate the situation under study. Usually, simulation is done when the model that has been developed is too complex to respond well to optimization techniques or when more information on the model is needed than just the best solution. With a computer, several years of operation can be simulated in just a few seconds. Once the results are compiled and analyzed, they can be used to determine the effect of a change in one or more of the values that control the model. For example, several promotional schemes and quality levels can be simulated for several years to test their long-term effects on the company's profits.

Everything we do on a computer is simulation.

Alan Kay, Apple Fellow

Quoted in "The Revolution that Fizzled," *Time,* May 20, 1991, p. 49

By simulating battlefield conditions, a decision support system can be used to train military officers for future combat.

While many DSS systems used for either optimization or simulation are mainframe based, there are smaller DSS systems that can be used on a personal computer. In addition, combination spreadsheet–graphics packages such as Lotus 1-2-3 or Excel can be used to help a manager make decisions.

DSS at FishTale

The FishTale Company could easily use a spreadsheet to retrieve, analyze, and graph its sales data once they have been processed. If the data were entered in a spreadsheet and a forecasting model were applied to predict sales for the remainder of the year, the result could be displayed as a line graph. Figure 14-6 shows this prediction process both in a spreadsheet (left) and in a line graph (right) displaying the predicted sales levels.

EXECUTIVE INFORMATION SYSTEMS

While decision support systems are aimed at solving problems and answering "What if?" questions for decision makers in an organization, it has been found that in many cases top-level executives such as the chief executive officer (CEO) do not use the DSS. This can be blamed on a combination of two factors. First, for a DSS to be able to solve the problems for which it is designed, it must be a fairly complex combination of hardware and software; even with a friendly user interface, the individual must invest a substantial amount of time to learn how to use it. Second, the one commodity that top-level executives are always short of is time.

However, this lack of use does not mean that executives do not want to use the computer to obtain important information to be used in decision making. They just want the information system to be *very* easy to use; to provide the information in a form to which they are accustomed; to be able to access external data bases as well as internal data; and to present the information in such a way that they can easily look below the surface data to find the reasons for various results. This **executive information system,** then, becomes a presentation system that will help executives make the decisions necessary to keep the organization ahead of its competition.

FIGURE 14-6
DSS Forecasting Model at
FishTale

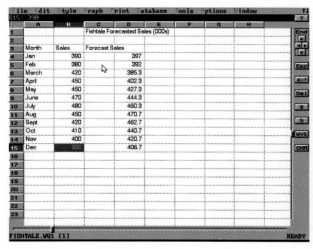

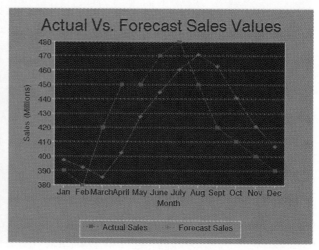

Most executive information systems combine the power and storage capability of the mainframe with the ease of use and graphics capability of the PC. Information is transferred to the PC from the mainframe or from external data bases. The executive then uses some type of pointing device, such as a mouse, to select from a menu. The keyboard is seldom used in an EIS, because the executive is usually searching for information and answers to questions rather than inputting data. Output on the PC's monitor is often in a graphics form or in a combination of graphics and tables. Crucial to the success of any EIS is the degree to which the output can be personalized to suit the style of the executive. Market researchers have found that if the information is not shown in the form to which the executive is accustomed, he or she will be uncomfortable with the EIS and will not use it.

EIS is not about executives. It's about a technology that solves a class of information problems.

David Friend, founder and chairman, Pilot Executive Software

Quoted in "Does 'E' Stand for 'Everybody'?" *Computerworld,* July 16, 1990, p. 83.

EIS at FishTale

As an example of the use of EIS, assume that the CEO of FishTale wants to compare his company's past year's sales to those of various competitors. To do this, he uses his EIS to access the reports to the stockholders of the publicly held competitors. These reports are available from financial data bases to which FishTale subscribes, and the EIS has been designed to access these data bases with several very simple instructions from the CEO. The EIS can also access the yearly sales at FishTale. The competitors' sales are graphically compared to FishTale's sales, as shown in Figure 14-7.

Using this combination of internal and external information, the CEO is better able to make decisions that will enable the company to compete more effectively in the marketplace. Also, the CEO can look beneath the summary data to try to find reasons for the sales trends.

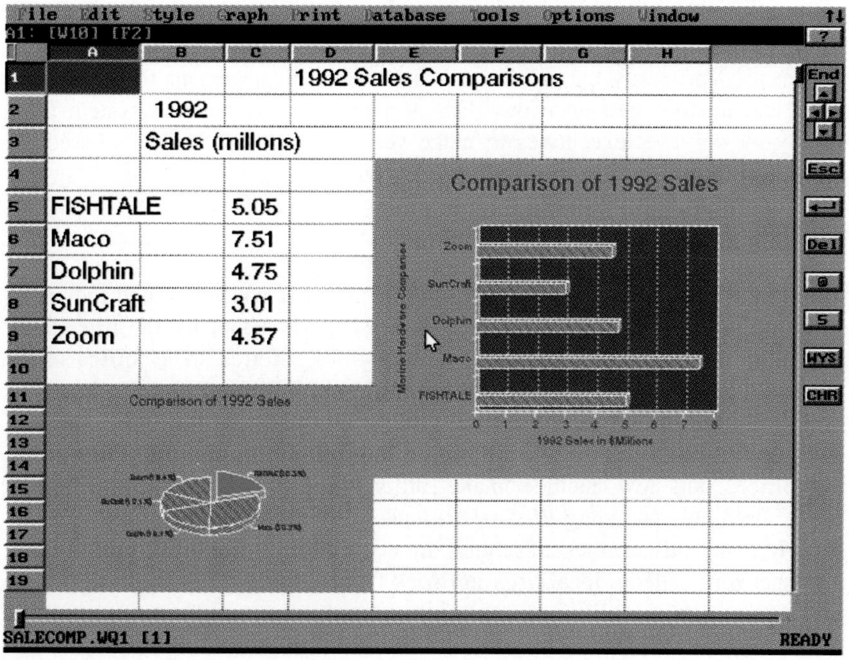

FIGURE 14-7
EIS at FishTale

Comparison of EIS to DSS and MIS

Since all three systems—MIS, DSS, and EIS—"support" managerial decision making, a commonly asked question is, Where does one stop and another begin? One way to look at this differentiation is to consider the report generation emphasis of MIS, the modeling emphasis of DSS, and the presentation emphasis of the EIS. Another way to distinguish EIS from MIS is to recognize that MIS is directed toward control through exception reporting, while EIS concentrates on problems and opportunities.

Another way to view MIS, DSS, and EIS is to link each to a different level of management. For example, MIS is used by all levels of management, but mostly by lower and middle management to make operational and tactical decisions that implement the decisions made by top management. On the other hand, DSS is often described as being used by middle management to solve problems. Finally, EIS is used by a very small group of executives and must be personalized to the individual's needs.

Another approach to differentiating between MIS, DSS, and EIS compares the type of decision that each information system supports. This approach views MIS as providing the manager with information—often in the form of reports or tables—to make **structured decisions.** An example of making a structured decision would be using a table of information to make a short-term forecast of sales or using a report of machine usage to decide how many spare parts to order. On the other hand, DSS and EIS are used to help make **unstructured decisions** in such areas as project management, budget preparation, and research and development planning. Unstructured decisions require the decision maker to use the information in different forms and to use various procedures to solve the problems that come up during the solution process.

It is not always possible to differentiate between management information, decision support, and executive information systems from a single point of view. A more general way to think about MIS, DSS, and EIS is to combine the three approaches. MIS is a report-oriented system used primarily by lower- and middle-level management for well-structured decisions. DSS is a model-oriented system used primarily by middle- and upper-level management for semistructured and unstructured decisions. EIS is a presentation-oriented system used strictly by top-level executives to make very unstructured decisions based on information gleaned from a wide range of sources.

OFFICE INFORMATION SYSTEMS

The development of office information systems in the workplace and the office has been one of the most dramatic changes brought about by the use of the computer. An **office information system**—often referred to as **office automation**—provides for the free flow of data and information throughout the organization, not just in the office. Office information systems began with the introduction of the electric typewriter, the dictaphone, and the telephone to the office, but now include many different electronic and computerized office machines, including PCs or terminals, copiers, fax machines, and scanners. In many offices, these machines are connected via a special type of computer network called a **local area network (LAN),** which is discussed in detail in Chapter 13.

A CONTROL ROOM EIS

One of the problems in the banking industry during the last decade was that bank executives were often unaware of problems. Bank managers tended to conceal delinquent loan or accounts receivable problems in the hope of solving them without involving executives. The Bank of Boston implemented an executive information system (EIS) "control room" to detect problems immediately.

A group of information systems employees conceived the control room after concluding that paperwork in a bank is no different from production flow in a factory. Taking the analogy a step further, the group decided that an EIS "control room" could alert bank executives of problem areas in the same way that it alerts nuclear-plant managers. The Bank of Boston's EIS is unique, however, because problem areas are color coded—green if there is not a problem, yellow if there is a potential problem, and red if there is a problem.

All bank managers provide control room employees with daily reports about their departments. The information is entered into the EIS. Executives can then access the EIS and check the colors of each department to determine whether any problems exist. If there is a problem, the executive can "drill" into the data base to determine how the problem arose. EIS has been a big success, and Bank of Boston executives believe that it is cost efficient. The system cost $300,000, but it has alerted executives of problems that could have cost the bank millions of dollars if they had not been detected.

Source: Robert L. Scheier, "Bank Enlists EIS in Battle to Boost Control," *PC Week*, February 5, 1990, pp. 129, 131

> ## We want to know if there is a very subtle "nuclear leak."
>
> *Peter Manning, chief financial officer, Bank of Boston*
>
> Quoted in Robert L. Scheier, "Bank Enlists EIS in Battle to Boost Control," *PC Week*, February 5, 1990, pp. 129, 131.

The important support functions of an office information system are (1) text preparation, (2) voice and electronic mail, (3) copiers and facsimile transmission, (4) electronic filing, and (5) access to internal and external data bases.

Text Preparation

The most widely used operation in an office information system is text preparation—through word processing on a personal computer or through the use of an electronic typewriter. The newer typewriters often have many word processing features built into them, allowing the typist to take advantage of the memory and editing capabilities of the PC without having to learn how to use a PC.

Regardless of whether a PC or an electronic typewriter is used, documents must be prepared from handwritten originals or dictation or by modification of another document. To speed up the process of modifying another document that is not available in electronic form, scanners are often used. **Scanners** and **optical character recognition (OCR)** systems can be used to "read" a document and convert it into an electronic form that can then be modified on a word processor.

Electronic typewriters and dictaphones are an important part of the office information system.

(Left) The facsimile (fax) machine has become an indispensable element in many office information systems. (Right) Text preparation is one of the most widely used functions of the office information system.

Voice and Electronic Mail

Communications—the lifeblood of an office—were once limited to interoffice paper memos, the mail system, and the telephone. Now there is a wide range of possibilities. **Voice mail,** for example, has extended the use of the telephone by allowing users to send, receive, store, and relay spoken messages. The messages are stored in a "mailbox" that the recipient can access at his or her convenience. **Electronic mail** does much the same for written messages and has become commonplace in many companies.

The idea of sending documents, pictures, and messages to one or more persons via the computer sounds very inviting. Just turn on your terminal or PC, enter the proper commands, type in the document, give the name of those persons who are to receive it, and press a key. Instantaneously, the message that "mail is waiting" appears at the proper terminals or PCs. Recipients can receive the message and respond immediately. Figure 14-8 shows electronic mail being sent over a local area network via personal computers.

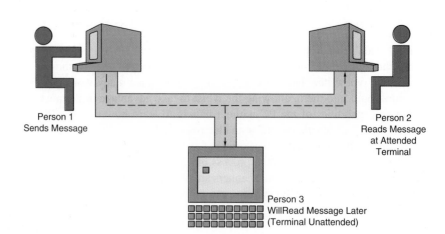

Person 1
Sends Message

Person 2
Reads Message
at Attended
Terminal

Person 3
WillRead Message Later
(Terminal Unattended)

FIGURE 14-8
Electronic Mail over Local Area Network

One very popular mainframe office electronic mail system is PROFS (Professional Office System) from IBM. On an IBM mainframe terminal, employees access the system by supplying a user ID and a password. (Employees using PCs can often use a terminal emulation program that will make their PC look like a mainframe terminal.) The PROFS main menu includes the current time, a 30-day calendar, and a menu of business communications, time management, document preparation, and search and retrieval functions. Users may also notice a "mail waiting" message at the bottom of the screen.

If a user does have mail, it may be "opened" by a single keystroke, with each message identified by sender, time received, and topic. Such messages may be viewed, then forwarded, commented on, or answered through the PROFS facility for message reply. With PROFS, users can send messages to individuals or to all the people on a distribution list. They can also schedule group meetings by entering the names of individuals who should attend, the meeting's duration, and various alternative meeting times. PROFS then searches all participants' schedules, provides a list of possible meeting times, and, once a time is selected, automatically uses the PROFS electronic mail function to notify all attendees of the time, purpose, and location of the meeting. Figure 14-9 shows electronic mail over a mainframe.

In the office, people have found that using electronic mail tends to increase the professionalism of everyone involved. Employees tend to experience less "down time" as they try to communicate on pressing issues. The amount of time spent waiting for a reply to an interoffice memo or a telephone call or waiting to see someone can be decreased significantly.

When combined with word processing on a LAN, electronic mail can make preparation of documents much more efficient. As shown in Figure 14-10, an executive dictates a document into an electronic recording device that a secretary accesses over the telephone. The secretary prepares the original document and sends it back to the executive over the LAN. The executive can print

Having an entire company on electronic mail has had a profound effect on our productivity and communications.

Trip Hawkins, president,
Electronic Arts

Quoted in "View from the Top,"
Personal Computing, October 1989,
p. 252.

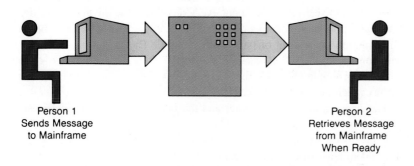

FIGURE 14-9
Electronic Mail on Mainframe

Person 1
Sends Message
to Mainframe

Person 2
Retrieves Message
from Mainframe
When Ready

FIGURE 14-10
Combining Word Processing with
Electronic Mail

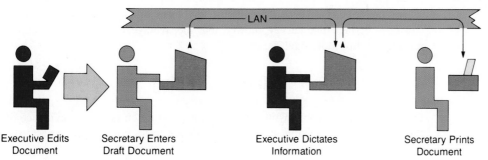

LAN

Executive Edits
Document

Secretary Enters
Draft Document

Executive Dictates
Information

Secretary Prints
Document

The Professional Office System
(PROFS) is a widely used
electronic mail system.

the document on a draft-quality (dot matrix) printer and, if needed, edit the document on his or her word processor. When the executive is satisfied with the final product, it can be returned to the secretary for printing on a letter-quality printer on letterhead stationery.

Copiers and Facsimile

Two machines that have had a tremendous impact on the office are copiers and facsimile machines. Both have been available for well over 20 years, but new ways to use them seem to come about every day. Both use the process of detecting the dark spots on a document, but while the copier immediately reproduces this information on a sheet of paper, the facsimile (fax) machine transmits the information to another fax machine down the street or across the country. Because the principle on which they operate is so similar, there are combination copier/fax machines on the market today.

The strength of both the copier and the fax machine is that documents do not have to be in any special form: They can be typed or handwritten, can contain pictures—or any combination of these. Facsimile is especially useful for sending documents that require signatures, something that is not possible with electronic or voice mail. It is more reliable than verbal communication and knows no holidays. These days almost any form of communication is being "faxed." In fact, one survey showed that the average *Fortune* 500 executive receives 50 faxes per day!

Electronic Filing

One of the major problems in offices today is too much paper. As evidence of this problem, consider that the U.S. government has a commission whose sole

task is to reduce the amount of paper that circulates through the federal bureaucracy. Organizations of all types face this paperwork problem because of the many forms, letters, documents, and reports that must be filed away in preparation for the day (which may never come) when they will be needed for reference. It has been noted that a single document may be filed in numerous places in an organization. For example, the originator keeps a copy, his or her office keeps a copy, the recipient has a copy made for his or her staff, and so on. One way to reduce this load is through electronic filing over the LAN.

In **electronic filing,** the document is prepared via word processing and is stored in secondary storage, usually on magnetic disk, for later retrieval. An extension of this is used whenever electronic mail is being used: The document being sent and any related electronic correspondence are filed together on disk. Also, a scanner can be used to convert paper documents into electronic form for electronic filing. While this sounds easy enough, there are some problems to be considered: First, there must be a system capable of identifying and retrieving a given document. Second, there must be adequate protection from loss of the document due to problems with the storage medium. Finally, there must be security against theft of or tampering with the document.

Access to Internal and External Data Bases

As we said in our discussion of information systems, having access to data bases is a very important means of supporting the decision making of managers. The office information system can make this possible by enabling users to access both internal and external data bases—the information stored in both the organization's data base and the national data bases—from their desks. Access to internal data bases is obtained with the local area network and appropriate data base management software. Access to various external data bases is handled over telephone lines.

The Future of Office Information Systems

The growth in the use of computer hardware and software in the office is expected to continue for the foreseeable future, as the technology expands to make various tasks easier and faster to perform. Continued growth is expected in the use of networks to link PCs together and to provide a convenient gateway from PCs to mainframes. The use of facsimile machines is also expected to grow, as is the linkage between PCs and fax machines, allowing text and graphics to be sent directly from the PC without having to be printed first.

OTHER TYPES OF INFORMATION SYSTEMS

■

Two very different types of information systems that are both becoming increasingly important to companies of all sizes are expert systems and strategic information systems. An expert system uses a computer to incorporate the knowledge and rules from several experts on a given subject to provide advice to managers. A strategic information system uses the information that is generated by other information systems to help the organization achieve a competitive advantage over its competitors.

Expert Systems

You probably couldn't find a single field that hasn't had an expert system developed for it.

Julie Walker, executive director, International Association of Knowledge Engineers

Quoted in "Knowledge Engineers Blend People Skills, Programming," *Computerworld*, April 13, 1992, p. 91.

Almost every organization has one or more individuals who because of their knowledge are essential to the successful operation of the organization. They are the people who can cut through superfluous details to get to the heart of any problem. Whether they are using their expertise to decide when a commercial soup is ready to be canned or to diagnose a pulmonary disease, experts use a body of knowledge and a set of "rules of thumb" to make recommendations to others who actually make decisions. While such experts are obviously important to any organization, they can also be very expensive. One study showed that the yearly cost of an engineering expert with a base salary of $54,000 would be over $122,000![2] In addition, when such an expert retires or otherwise leaves the company, his or her expertise and years of experience can be very difficult to replace.

Because they lack the creativity of a human expert, **expert systems** are being used to answer the everyday questions that would divert the human expert's time from larger problems and projects. Expert systems are one very practical facet of the rapidly growing field known as **artificial intelligence.** Before we look further into how an expert system works and what types of expert systems are available, consider these examples of expert systems:

- The first working expert system, called DENDRAL, was developed in 1965 at Stanford University. DENDRAL was developed to interpret spectrographic data to determine the structure of an organic molecule. Descendants of DENDRAL are used in laboratories all over the world.
- Using techniques learned from DENDRAL, computer scientists and doctors at Stanford Medical Center created MYCIN to diagnose

---

[2]Leilani Allen, "The Cost of an Expert," *Computerworld*, July 21, 1986, pp. 64–68.

diseases of the blood by incorporating knowledge and rules used by the doctors.

- Prospector, developed at Stanford Research Institute, is an expert system that aids geologists in exploring for minerals. This system was credited for leading to the discovery of a $100-million deposit of molybdenum in the state of Washington.
- To preserve the 44 years of knowledge and experience of the man who controlled the huge cooker ovens at Campbell Soup Co., an expert system named COOKER was developed. COOKER not only contains much of this man's factual knowledge, it uses the same rules that he would to reason through a problem with the ovens.
- To aid companies in making important financial decisions, the Financial Advisor expert system incorporates the analytic abilities of

NERSys INSTEAD OF NURSES

A significant task for all health insurance companies is processing claims, and an important part of processing claims is reviewing those that the computer system rejects because the amount claimed is "too high." Many health insurance companies employ nurses to review claims. Nurses use their expertise in medicine to determine whether extenuating circumstances may have caused a particular procedure or treatment to cost more than the insurance company allows. Veteran nurse-experts frequently move on to higher-paying positions, however, leaving insurance companies short-handed in reviewing questionable claims. To prevent this problem from occurring, Blue Cross of Western Pennsylvania developed Nurse Expert Review System (NERSys).

NERSys is a PC-based system that contains facts about over 9,000 medical

diagnoses and procedures and, most important, a blueprint for reviewing a claim. The system's software designers obtained the blueprint by asking experienced nurse-experts what strategies they used to evaluate questionable claims. NERSys can also download from the mainframe rejected claims for review.

As an example of NERSys' capability, consider a claim for a pregnant woman's routine office visit. If routine visits cost between $55 and $75 but the claim is for $125, the computer will reject the claim and send it to NERSys for evaluation. NERSys then scrutinizes the claim for references to special tests or procedures that would explain the excessive amount of the claim.

Blue Cross of Western Pennsylvania initially used NERSys to review claims involving pregnancy, which represented 10 percent of the claims it processed. Today however, the system reviews 80 to 90 percent of the rejected claims, including those involving diagnostic procedures, medical emergencies, and minor outpatient surgeries. As a result, the work load of nurse-experts has been significantly reduced.

Source: John Pallatto, "Expert System Cures the Blues," *PC Week*, December 12, 1988, pp. 35, 44; updated in an interview with Blue Cross of Western Pennsylvania, December 18, 1991.

The nicest thing about [NERSys] is that it displays messages explaining why it is recommending a claim be paid, rejected, or researched further.

Mary Jane Cherry, medical reviews director, Blue Cross of Western Pennsylvania

Quoted in "Expert System Cures the Blues," *PC Week*, December 12, 1988, pp. 35, 44.

numerous experts in finance, taxation, and other areas of business. One user of Financial Advisor was quoted as saying it even answers questions that he hadn't thought of asking!

Behind an Expert System

Most expert systems are written in such a way that the user simply inputs data and answers questions to receive various recommendations. To understand how this occurs, we need to look behind the friendly exterior of an expert system. Because experts use both a body of knowledge and a combination of experience, intuition, hunches, good guesses, and creative leaps of the mind, an expert system must in some way include many of these same features. To do this, the expert system is made up of two parts: a knowledge base and an inference engine. The **knowledge base** includes all of the facts surrounding the problem at hand, while the **inference engine** tries to include as much of the experience, intuition, and so on as possible—expressed as if–then rules. An **if–then rule** says, "If this is true, then that is also true." For example, an if–then rule for choosing a wine with dinner: If the entree is red meat, then choose a red wine.

While many expert systems are developed for specific applications, it is also possible to separate the inference engine from the knowledge base to create expert system shells. Using an **expert system shell,** an individual can easily create his or her own expert system by providing the knowledge base and the necessary information to fill in the rules in the knowledge base. Two types of expert system shells are commonly in use: example based and rule based. An example-based system allows the user to enter examples into a table, from which the shell deduces rules. The rule-based system requires the user to write the rules as program statements. An example-based system is easier to learn and use, but rule-based systems are more powerful.

A Financial Aid Expert System

To help you see how an expert system could be used, consider the financial aid office at a state university. Such offices often have scholarships to award based on the hometown of the student, his or her major, or his or her parent's employer. It is almost impossible for any one person to remember all of the possibilities, and even if such people exist, they may leave the institution and take their knowledge with them. To make it easier for students to determine if they qualify for financial aid, an expert system could be used, with rules like these:

```
IF   Student is from Washington County AND
     Student is Agriculture major AND
     Student has 3.0 grade point average OR
     Student has SAT score over 1000
THEN Student is eligible for $1000 scholarship
```

Such a series of rules could be created for a rule-based system, or a table like Table 14-1 could be used in an example-based system. In either case, the expert system would ask the student a series of questions. If the answers matched any of the rules, then the student would be informed of scholarships for which he or she is eligible.

```
Where is the student from?
 AMES

What is the student's MAJOR?
 ENGINEERING

What is the student's grade point average (GPA) ?
 3.6█
```

```
RULE 2 IF                          HOME = AMES CNF 100
MAJOR = ENGINEERING AND            MAJOR = ENGINEERING CNF 100
GPA > 3.5 AND
PARENT_EMP = LOCKHEED
THEN
AWARD = 500 CNF 100
Finding MAJOR
Finding GPA
```

```
Enter to select     ? & Enter for Unknown     /Q to quit
```

Expert systems can help students identify scholarships and other types of financial aid that they may be eligible to receive.

While still in their infancy compared to other parts of an organization's information system, expert systems are expected to grow steadily in use as more and more managers find ways in which an expert system can help them. Another impetus for the growth of expert systems will be the increased availability of people who have academic backgrounds in artificial intelligence and expert systems. A new name has even been developed for this type of specialist—**knowledge engineer.** These people are trained in extracting from experts the facts and rules they have not even attempted to verbalize before.

Strategic Information Systems

The traditional use of information systems is to automate basic operations such as payroll and to support managerial decision making, however, some forward-thinking companies are beginning to use their information systems as strategic

TABLE 14-1
Example-Based Table

Home	Major	GPA	SAT Score	Parent's Employer	Award
Wash. Cty	Agri.	3.0	********	***************	$1000
Wash. Cty	Agri.	****	1000	***************	$1000
********	Eng.	3.5	********	Lockheed Aircraft	$500
Ames	Eng.	3.5	1100	***************	$1500

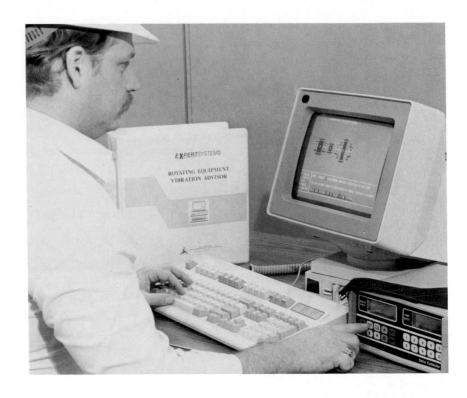

The expert system used to diagnose problems with pumps in nuclear power plants uses many rules like the one shown here.

Strategic information systems use available information to provide the organization with a competitive advantage.

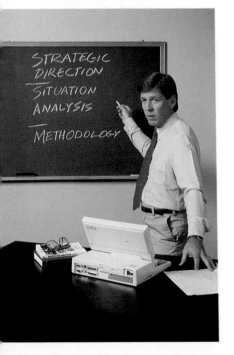

weapons in the constant battle for market share. Typically, a **strategic information system** is used to support or develop a company's competitive strategy. An SIS can be used, for example, to increase product differentiation, to help create or distribute an innovative product, and to help reduce costs in order to increase the company's market penetration.

Numerous companies have been forced out of business because they did not have what James Martin calls "strategic vision"[3] to see the result of changing technologies. Today, because information is increasingly important to every company, this strategic vision often involves the use of information. Strategic information systems can be used in many ways to help a company obtain an advantage over its competition, including using available information for new purposes, providing an early-warning system against decline in market share, finding new markets for existing products, and even redefining the mission of the organization.

In the first case a company may, as a part of its normal operations, collect information on customers; such information may then be used for purposes other than those for which it was collected. For example, a company in London was collecting names and addresses of customers who were U.S. citizens to return the value-added tax that is collected on all purchases in the United Kingdom. The company was then able to gain a competitive advantage with this information by also using it as a mailing list for catalog sales.

As an early warning system, an SIS may alert the company to declining sales in one segment of the market that portend future problems in other market

---

[3] James Martin, "Strategic-Information Systems: A Formula for Success," *PC Week,* November 28, 1988, p. 36.

segments. Being warned of this trend, the company can take action to avoid problems. This response may involve another facet of the SIS—finding new markets for existing products. The company might use the information system to determine untapped areas where the product may be sold. Another response to an early warning of declining sales may be to change the focus of the company from selling new products to servicing existing products. In any case, the SIS serves to help the company satisfy the number one goal of any organization—staying in business.

REVIEW OF KEY POINTS

1. The information system ensures that the appropriate information is available to managers for better decision making.

2. Important types of information systems are the transaction processing systems (TPS), the management information system (MIS), the decision support system (DSS), the executive information system (EIS), and the office information system (OIS).

3. Management information systems, decision support systems, and executive information systems provide managers with information they need to make decisions.

4. A TPS converts raw data into a form that can be stored on the organization's data base for use by other information systems.

5. An MIS provides managers with various types of reports, including scheduled reports, exception reports, predictive reports, and demand reports.

6. A DSS helps managers through the use of models. The DSS is made up of a data base, a model base, and a dialog base; the data base provides the data to be used in the models in the model base, and the dialog base handles the interaction between the system and the user.

7. Important types of DSS are the general-purpose DSS, the spe-

cific DSS, and the DSS model generator. A spreadsheet is a simple version of a DSS.

8. Top-level executives need executive information systems to provide information in a form to which they are accustomed.

9. While MIS, DSS, and EIS all serve to help managers make better decisions, the MIS does so by providing written reports, the DSS by interactively answering queries, and the EIS by presenting information to executives.

10. Five important functions of an office information system are text preparation, electronic and voice mail, copiers and facsimile, electronic filing, and access to internal and external data bases. Many of these functions are carried out over a local area network.

11. An expert system tries to incorporate a human's expertise into a computerized information system through the use of factual knowledge and rules that will make suggestions to the user. The factual knowledge is the knowledge base, and the rules are the inference engine.

12. A strategic information system helps the company remain competitive by providing it with information that can give it an advantage in the marketplace.

KEY TERMS

artificial intelligence
batch processing system
data base
data base management system
   (DBMS)
decision support system (DSS)
demand report
dialog base
DSS generator
electronic filing
electronic mail
exception report
executive information system (EIS)
expert system
expert system shell
forecasting model
general-purpose DSS
if–then rule
inference engine
information system
knowledge base

knowledge engineer
local area network (LAN)
management information system
   (MIS)
model
model base
office automation
office information system (OIS)
optical character recognition (OCR)
optimization
real-time processing
scanner
scheduled report
simulation
specific DSS
strategic information system (SIS)
structured decision
transaction processing system (TPS)
transactional processing
unstructured decision
voice mail

REVIEW QUESTIONS

1. Name the types of information systems that are used to help managers in organizations.
2. What part does a transaction processing system play in an information system? Name the various processing modes.
3. Name the three types of reports generated by an MIS. Explain the purpose of each.
4. What is the role of a model in a DSS?
5. Name and discuss the three ways of using a model. Which one tries to find the best solution to a problem?
6. What are the three parts of a DSS? Which one does the user interact with?
7. List the types of DSS commonly used to support managerial decision making.
8. What is the purpose of an executive information system?
9. Explain the differences between an MIS, a DSS, and an EIS. Use two approaches to differentiate between the types of information systems.
10. What is the relationship between a local area network and an office information system?
11. List the office tasks that have been automated to some degree. Which is used the most?
12. Why are expert systems included in our discussion of management information systems?
13. Name the two parts of an expert system. Which is included in an

expert system shell and which must be added by the user?

14. Create an if–then rule for the third row of Table 14-1. Then do the same for the fourth row of this table.

15. How does a strategic information system relate to the future health of an organization? In what ways can it be used to make the organization more competitive?

15

Systems Analysis and Design

In Chapter 4 we outlined systems analysis and design as a method of building information systems. In Chapter 15, by presenting a case study that demonstrates software/hardware selection, we will fill in the details of that outline. The various tools used by the analyst are discussed in the context of their use in the analysis and design process. Finally, two new approaches to systems development—prototyping and end user computing—are discussed. The thrust of this chapter is not to make you a systems analyst, but rather to make you aware of the work that goes into the development of the many information systems people encounter each day.

STUDY OBJECTIVES

After reading this chapter, you should be able to

- understand the role of the systems analyst in the systems analysis and design process;
- relate the various steps involved in the analysis and design process to the final system;
- understand the problem identification step of the process and how it differs from a solution to the problem;
- explain the purpose of a feasibility study and the outcome required for this step to be successful;
- point out the system that is considered in the analysis step;
- understand what is required in the analysis stage of the systems analysis and design process;
- understand how the systems design step differs from the acquisition step;
- explain the actions that are taken in the acquisition/programming step;
- discuss how the implementation step utilizes the output from the previous steps;
- understand the importance of the maintenance step to the performance of the system;
- explain the use of special systems analysis and design tools;
- discuss the effect of prototyping and end user computing on systems development.

LEARNING THE HARD WAY

In California, an important function of the secretary of state's office is to determine if property being used as collateral for a bank loan has already been pledged for another loan. Banks use this information to decide whether or not to make a loan. In the mid-1980s, the office decided to convert from a semiautomated mainframe information system to an optical disk-based system. The design and development of the new system went well until the implementation step. When the new system was ready to be installed, the systems analysts at the secretary of state's office and at the company supplying the new system recommended at least a 30-day period during which both systems would run concurrently. By running the two systems in parallel, the analysts would have an opportunity to fix any problems in the new system without delaying processing. However, state budget officials decided that it would be cheaper simply to shut down the old system as soon as the new system was installed, before any testing was carried out on it.

The result: As would be expected with a new optical disk system as large as the one installed in the secretary of state's office (up to 204 disks and 50 PC workstations), there were numerous implementation problems. Problems with the new system included failures of online laser printers, bugs in software, and the lengthy training period required to teach employees to use the new system. Consequently, the system ran at only 30 percent of capacity, resulting in a backlog of over 50,000 property checks causing commercial banking at the 470 banks to come to a virtual halt. At that point, the state had no choice but to bring the old system back up, at a cost to taxpayers of $500,000. The cost to banks was estimated to be in the millions of dollars.

Source: J. B. Miles, "Systems Collapse Stymies Borrowers in Golden State," *PC Week,* June 19, 1989, pp. 1, 8.

REVIEW OF SYSTEMS ANALYSIS AND DESIGN

In Chapter 4, we discussed the importance of **computer-based information systems (CBIS)**—systems that use computers to process data into information. For managers of organizations, various types of CBIS provide the information needed to make management decisions. These include the transaction processing system, management information system, decision support system, executive information system, office information system, strategic information system, and expert systems, all of which must be planned, designed, and built to fit the needs of the organization. Once built, these systems must be implemented and maintained.

As discussed in Chapter 4, the **systems analysis and design process** is used both to build or acquire new systems and to update existing systems. This process is also known as the **systems life cycle** or the **systems development life cycle.** Regardless of the name, the process may be thought of as being composed of seven steps: problem definition, feasibility study, analysis, system design, acquisition/programming, implementation, and maintenance. As discussed in the

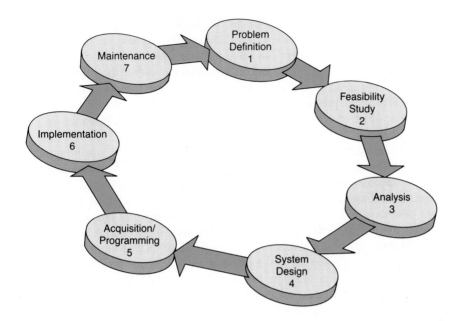

FIGURE 15-1
The Systems Life Cycle

box at the beginning of this chapter, failure to carry out any one of these steps correctly can cause the entire project to fail. In the California state government's case, the implementation step was not handled properly, leading to a costly return to the old system while the new one was fixed. Figure 15-1 shows the seven steps of the systems life cycle, and Table 15-1 lists the steps and their objectives. These steps were discussed briefly in Chapter 4; this chapter will provide details on exactly how each step is accomplished.

Individuals who perform the systems analysis and design process, called **systems analysts,** work closely with the users of the system, the programmers or software/hardware suppliers, and the managers of the organization. Each group views the problem differently, and it is the systems analyst's job to act as

> They [the California secretary of state's office] just wanted to turn the system on and have our new system running at 100 percent. That's impossible in the startup phase of a project like this.
>
> *Bob Castle, vice president of marketing, FileNet Corp.*
>
> Quoted in "System Collapse Stymies Borrowers in Golden State," *PC Week,* June 19, 1989, pp. 1, 8.

TABLE 15-1
Steps in the Systems Life Cycle

Step	Objective of Step
1. Problem definition	To define the problem to be solved or the new system to be designed
2. Feasibility study	To determine whether or not the problem can be solved within budgetary constraints and to make an initial recommendation
3. Analysis	To develop a logical description of the system being designed
4. System design	To develop a high-level physical design for the recommended system
5. Acquisition/programming	To select and acquire hardware/software or to write the needed software
6. Implementation	To install the hardware/software acquired or programmed in the previous step
7. Maintenance	To ensure that the system continues to work properly and is updated as needed

THE MYERS FURNITURE COMPANY CASE

an intermediary between the three groups. The analyst must understand the problem from the user's point of view, must also understand how the programmers or software/hardware suppliers can solve the user's problem, and, finally, must be responsible to management and make decisions within the organization's budgetary constraints. This relationship is crucial to the success of the systems analysis and design process. The California secretary of state's office case is an example in which budgetary constraints actually caused the systems analysis and design process to fail.

Several tools have been developed to help the analyst carry out the systems analysis and design process necessary to develop a new information system or to correct problems in an existing one. These include data dictionaries, data flow diagrams, and systems flowcharts. While you may not understand these terms right now, they will become more clear as we go through this chapter. To demonstrate the use of these tools in the systems analysis and design process, we will present a case study involving the conversion of an existing manual information system to a computer-based information system that produces the same result—a very common situation. In Chapter 16 we will discuss the use of systems analysis and design for another very common situation—creating software to solve a problem.

In the early 1950s, Len Myers founded the Myers Furniture Company in Charlotte, North Carolina, to build and distribute fine furniture. Because the Myers Company produced quality furniture, it enjoyed significant success in the Charlotte market. After nearly 30 years of operating in Charlotte, Len decided to expand his operation into the High Point area of North Carolina to compete with the many national furniture companies operating there. Both the Charlotte and High Point divisions of Myers Furniture are wholesale operations; however, the factory in High Point differs from the main operation in that it not only manufactures furniture but purchases furniture from subcontractors.

The High Point Division has annual sales of $5 million and 60 employees, including the plant manager, Phil Mikens; the personnel manager, Joan Bernard; the purchasing manager, Mike Stafford; the sales manager, Sonya Martin; the production manager, Jim Triesch; and 3 secretaries. The division also has a personnel assistant, who reports to Joan; two purchasing agents, who report to Phil; a customer service representative, who, along with sales agents in the field, reports to Sonya; and 4 production supervisors and a furniture designer, who report to Jim. The employees who build the furniture work four 10-hour shifts and report to production supervisors. Figure 15-2 shows the organizational structure of the High Point Division of the Myers Furniture Company.

Myers Furniture Company was recently purchased by an international conglomerate whose management considered closing the High Point Division. A recent fire caused losses that exceeded $500,000, and the division was marginally profitable, at best. When auditors for the new owner visited the High Point Division, they learned that its managers and employees know the furniture business and produce quality products, but they discovered administrative and recordkeeping problems. High Point sent its inventory and accounting records to headquarters in Charlotte once a week by mail for processing on the company's mainframe computer. There was nearly a two-week lag between the submission of the data and the return of the processed information to High Point.

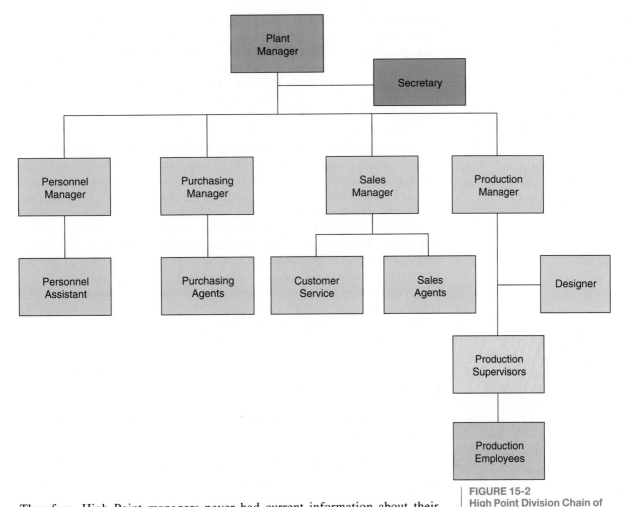

FIGURE 15-2
High Point Division Chain of Command

Therefore, High Point managers never had current information about their factory.

Because of the high quality of High Point's products, corporate management deemed the division a worthy investment and sought to design an information system that would enable the division to reduce its overhead costs and, thereby, show a profit. If the project is successful, corporate management would like to make the system a prototype for replacing Charlotte's mainframe system with either a minicomputer or personal computer network system.

To handle this project, the owners hired an outside consulting firm to perform a systems analysis of the High Point operation and recommend a plan. The consulting firm assigned an analyst to the project, and she traveled to Charlotte to learn more about the situation.

STEP 1: PROBLEM DEFINITION

For any systems analysis and design project, the first step is **problem definition.** Initially, the analyst discussed the project with the corporation's managers, who told her that they believed the High Point Division of the Myers Furniture Company was unprofitable because it lacked an efficient recordkeeping system. The analyst noted their opinions but did not make any decisions yet. Next, the analyst went to Charlotte to see the mainframe operation. She consulted with the individual in charge of processing the data received from the High Point factory and learned that the data included information about shipments to the factory and about the sales and production of each style of furniture in inventory. Processing the data involved preparing summary reports. The reports were correct but, because they were two weeks old by the time they reached the High Point Divison, they were dated. Based on these interviews and a discussion with Len Myers, the analyst felt that she understood the Charlotte operation.

Next, she travelled to the High Point Division. Phil, the plant manager, gave her a tour of the factory. The division had 1,000 pieces of furniture in 50 different styles in stock. Sales agents located throughout the eastern United States constantly called High Point to inquire about the availability of various furniture styles. Unfortunately, the sales manager could not give them accurate information, because her only source of information was the two-week-old report generated by the mainframe at Charlotte. In fact, High Point Division once lost a big sale to a major department store because of the dated inventory records. The division simply did not have an adequate method for adjusting the inventory to reflect daily activities in production, purchasing, and sales.

After the analyst toured the plant and discussed its operation with key employees, she reviewed the computer-generated reports the division received from Charlotte. The output certainly contained the information submitted from High Point each week, but it was not current, and its format made certain information on particular furniture styles difficult to find.

Over lunch, Phil further defined the problem as he saw it for the analyst. First, the new inventory control system must be easy to use and inexpensive. Obviously, the parent corporation would not want to invest large sums of money in a system for an operation it might shut down. Phil had previously suggested to corporate management that it install terminals at High Point connected by telephone lines with headquarters in Charlotte, but corporate management had not acted on his suggestion. Finally, Phil suggested that the new system should be capable of handling payroll and facilitating interoffice communication. Currently, the personnel assistant computed payroll by hand, which took most of his time, and employees communicated by telephone or memo. Phil believed that some type of electronic mail system would be very helpful.

Statement of Problem

Based on all these conversations, the analyst concluded that timing was the problem. That is, the reports were dated when the High Point Division received them; therefore, they were useless. A new system was needed that would give the managers up-to-date inventory information *and* reduce administrative costs.

The next time the analyst met with Phil, she outlined the problem as she understood it and explained to him the restrictions of a system that would solve the problem. She stated that the new system

1. must provide managers with up-to-date inventory information;
2. must be easy to use;
3. must be relatively inexpensive;
4. must be integrated with Charlotte's existing mainframe system.

After Phil heard the analyst's statement of the problem, he reiterated the ease-of-use criterion. Although the secretaries used personal computers for word processing and the furniture designer used one for computer-aided designing, none of the managers had much experience with computers. He made several other suggestions and noted that the last criterion required the cooperation of the MIS department in the home office. The analyst agreed and incorporated Phil's suggestions in a revised statement of the problem.

Statement of Scope and Objectives

The analyst prepared and submitted a statement of scope and objectives (shown in Figure 15-3) to the corporation to obtain approval for a feasibility study. She estimated that it would take the rest of the week to prepare and would cost an additional $1,500. The parent company's management team approved and told the analyst the company would not pay more than $50,000 for the project, including the $1,500 for the feasibility study and the $1,000 for the time already expended.

Note that the analyst listened to key parties and gathered enough preliminary information to determine the *real* problem with the High Point Division of the Myers Furniture Company. Analysts must ask the right questions and listen carefully to the answers. Often, an interested person's statement of the problem will also contain his or her solution to the problem. For example, Phil suggested using terminals to transmit information to the home office. The analyst listened to his suggestions for solving the problem, but she concentrated on defining the problem, leaving the solutions for a later step. In the High Point situation, the problem was not poor recordkeeping on the part of the management. It was the company's lack of an interactive, real-time inventory system, in which data are entered as they become available and results are output instantaneously at a video display terminal or printer when needed.

Statement of Scope and Objectives:
March 11, 1993

The Project: Record keeping at Myers Furniture Company–High Point Division

The Problem: Inventory updating is not current, leading to lost sales and excessive record-keeping expenses.

Project Objectives: To develop an improved method of updating inventory that will integrate with the existing system at the home office

Project Scope: The development cost of this project should not exceed $50,000.

Preliminary Ideas: Use terminals to transmit data to mainframe at home office; install a personal computer network or minicomputer network to process data locally.

Feasibility Study: In order to investigate possible improvements to the inventory record-keeping system, a feasibility study should be carried out at a cost not to exceed $1,500.

FIGURE 15-3
Statement of Scope and Objectives

Environmental Considerations

An important consideration of the analyst's problem definition is the problem environment; that is, in order to arrive at a solution, an analyst must consider circumstances that surround the problem. In the High Point example, environmental considerations included High Point management's attitude, especially toward computers. It also included the limitations corporate management placed on the solution to the problem. Recall that we said in Chapter 4 that every system has an environment. This applies to the system the analyst will propose. We also said that every system has a boundary. The analyst for High Point decided not to include the payroll problem in her problem definition. In this way, she drew the system's boundary at the inventory problem, with the payroll and inter-office communication problem part of the system environment.

STEP 2: FEASIBILITY STUDY

In the **feasibility study,** the analyst determines whether an acceptable solution to the problem exists. He or she must perform a "quickie" version of the entire systems analysis and design process. The feasibility study includes technical, operational, and economic aspects of the problem. Technical feasibility means that the technology to solve the problem exists, and operational feasibility means that the problem can be solved within any constraints that have been placed on changes in current operations. Finally, economic feasibility means that solving the problem is an economically wise decision. The systems analyst in our example used the following seven-step process in her feasibility study:

1. Clarify the scope and objectives stated in the problem definition.
2. Study the existing system.
3. Develop a high-level model of the existing system.
4. Redefine the scope and objectives.

After the problem is defined, the next steps in the systems life cycle are the feasibility study and the systems analysis.

5. Develop alternate solutions.
6. Recommend a course of action and possibly a new system.
7. Write and present the feasibility study.

To clarify the scope and objectives, the analyst interviewed Phil again and then discussed the problem with High Point's sales, purchasing, and production managers. Each interview involved the analyst's statement of scope and objectives, but she still gathered facts on the current operation. From these interviews, the analyst learned that each manager spent a great deal of time on recordkeeping and inventory-updating duties. Much of this time was charged to the company as overtime, which was a significant part of the high administrative costs experienced by this division.

Developing a Model

The study of the current system also included interviews with the secretaries, supervisors, and factory workers. The systems analyst also observed the current system, read operations manuals, and examined the records and recordkeeping procedures. With this information, she could build a model of the existing system. A **model** is *a simplified version of the system* that allows the analyst to understand the system's important parts.

Systems Flowcharts

One tool that systems analysts use to model a system is the **systems flowchart,** which demonstrates the physical elements of the system and the flow of information and control. A systems flowchart uses various symbols to represent the physical elements and arrows to show the flow of information and control. The standard set of symbols used in systems flowcharts was shown in Figure 4-9. Using the information she has gathered during her interviews and observations, the analyst can develop a systems flowchart that describes the physical operation of the current system. In Figure 15-4, only a general overview of the system is depicted, and the actual detail in each box is ignored. This kind of flowchart is useful to gain an understanding of the overall system. In Figure 15-5, the detail

FIGURE 15-4
Overview Systems Flowchart of
Existing Operation

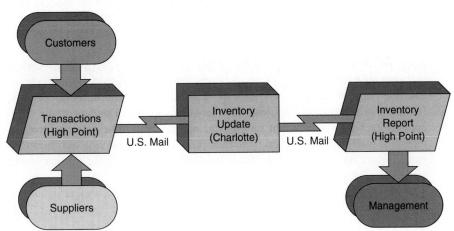

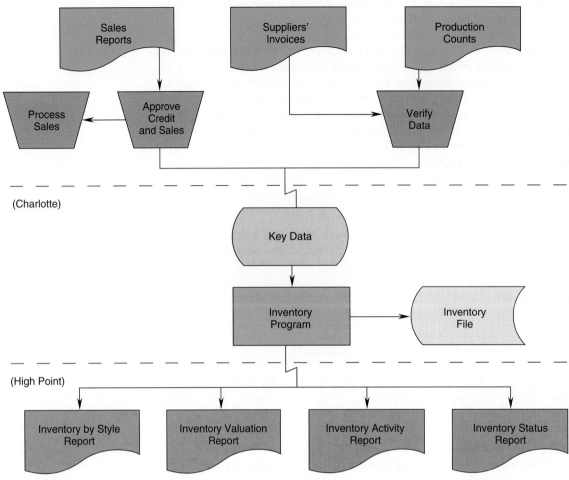

(High Point)

FIGURE 15-5
Detailed Systems Flowchart of
Existing Operation

in each box in the overview flowchart is shown. These two flowcharts demonstrate the **top–down approach** to systems analysis and design—that is, the overall system is studied first, and detail is added as the project continues.

In the systems flowchart in Figure 15-5, three copies of sales reports, suppliers' invoices for furniture received, and production counts were processed manually in High Point, but only one copy of each form remained there. The other two copies of each form were mailed to Charlotte for processing on the home office mainframe. One copy of the sales report was used to update accounts receivable (money owed to Myers Furniture Company by customers), and one copy of the suppliers' invoice was used to update accounts payable (money owed by Myers Furniture Company to suppliers). The data on the other copy of each item were input into the mainframe, where the data on furniture received, sales, and production were then processed to update the old inventory status stored on magnetic disk. After the disk was updated, four reports were sent to High Point.

The systems flowchart in Figure 15-5 gives the analyst a clear picture of the High Point Division's operations. After the diagram was explained to Phil, he agreed that it portrayed the current system. He emphasized that the most important aspect of a new system was ease of use combined with reduced record keeping and timely inventory update.

In each conference, the analyst and a manager learned something from each other. Initially, each was ignorant of the other's role. However, during discussions, each learned a great deal about the other's job and what a new system could and could not do. As a result of this process of problem definition and study of the current system, the analyst became something of an expert on High Point's current inventory system. A systems analyst must learn as much as possible at this stage in order to do a good job in the later stages of the systems analysis and design process. In fact, without a thorough understanding of the underlying concepts of High Point's inventory system, the analyst could not proceed to the next step in the feasibility study—development of alternative solutions.

Developing Alternative Solutions

The analyst can now determine whether any solutions exist for the inventory control problem defined earlier. If no solutions to the problem exist, the study is terminated, and only a small investment has been made in the problem definition and feasibility study. If only one solution exists, then the remainder of the study is dedicated to designing this one solution. Usually, multiple solutions can be found for a problem. Three types of solutions may be considered—a low-cost, "bare-bones" solution; an intermediate solution that meets all stated requirements; and an expensive solution that extends beyond the current needs. For the High Point Division of the Myers Furniture Company, the analyst developed the following three possible solutions:

1. Install terminals and a high-speed printer in the High Point office. The terminals and printer would be linked to the corporate mainframe to transmit data and receive reports. Special leased telephone lines would be necessary for this option to provide a high-quality communication link. Inventory would be updated daily, and reports would be transmitted to High Point to be printed there. This option would require software development at the home office to support it.
2. Install a personal computer on each manager's desk at High Point, and install a file server-based local area network to link new and existing PCs to a file server. An inventory package would be installed on the file server, so that data could be entered and managers could have access to up-to-date inventory data. The file server would be linked to the corporate mainframe so that the master inventory file could be updated periodically. The laser printers already used by the secretaries would be tied into the network to provide hard copy of the inventory reports.
3. Install a minicomputer-based network in the High Point office with terminals on each manager's and secretary's desk. The master inventory file would be transferred to High Point, and all processing would be handled there. A high-speed printer would also be installed.

Selecting an Alternative

The analyst first discussed each alternative with Phil and the other managers. After some consideration, the minicomputer network alternative (option 3) was dropped from consideration. Its cost, which was estimated to be over $100,000 for the hardware alone, was significantly more than the limit for the project.

The choice between option 1 and option 2 was not as clear-cut. Phil liked option 1, which would link High Point terminals to the corporate mainframe so managers could check the inventory status directly. However, other managers expressed several concerns about this option. They worried that the mainframe could be "down" during the business day, which, as headquarters in Charlotte explained to them, was why inventory reports sometimes took longer than usual to be returned. Also, this option did not provide for expanding the system to handle electronic mail or payroll. In addition, they were not sure of the level of cooperation that would be forthcoming from the Charlotte mainframe operation in developing the software needed to support the terminals in High Point. Finally, it was the consensus of the managers that option 1 was a "status quo" alternative that failed to consider the advantages of installing the most modern technology available.

After listening to all the managers' comments, the analyst prepared a rough cost-estimate analysis comparing the first two alternatives with the current system (see Table 15-2). Figure 15-6 shows a graph of the analysis. The costs in this analysis were based on the analyst's knowledge of the computer hardware and software market and on estimates of current costs supplied by High Point's managers.

Figure 15-6 clearly shows that although the current system is cheaper initially, the total costs of both the mainframe terminals and the personal computer network decrease to less than the cost of the current system in the second and third year, respectively. The comparison of the two proposed systems is not as

TABLE 15-2
Alternative Cost Analysis

	Alternatives		
	Current System	Terminals and Printer	PC Network
Estimated initial development costs			
Hardware	$ 0	$ 8,750	$26,000
Communications equipment	$ 0	$ 1,200	$ 200
Software	$ 0	$10,000	$ 9,500
Installation costs	$ 0	$ 500	$ 1,500
Total	$ 0	$20,450	$37,200
Estimated yearly operating costs			
Phone lines	$ 0	$ 3,000	$ 500
Supplies and postage	$ 1,250	$ 1,000	$ 1,000
Labor (overtime)	$ 4,000	$ 1,000	$ 250
Maintenance agreement	$ 0	$ 250	$ 2,000
Estimated lost sales and goodwill	$10,000	$ 2,000	$ 0
Total	$15,250	$ 7,250	$ 3,750
Annual cost savings	$ 0	$ 8,000	$11,500

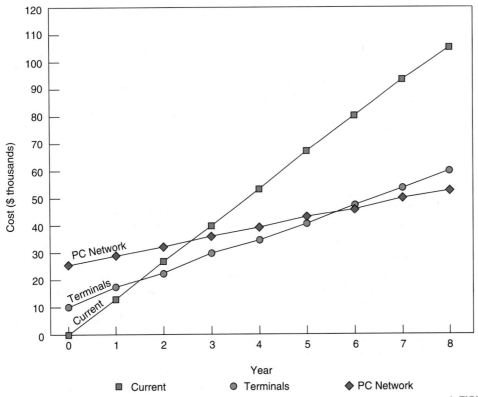

FIGURE 15-6
Cost Analysis

clear, because the PC network is initially more expensive than the mainframe terminals and remains so until the fifth year. However, if the analyst performs a **cost/benefit analysis** of these two options, she must consider, with the PC network, expandability and the views of the High Point management. The network is an infrastructure investment that provides a computing platform that takes advantage of distributed processing. For example, an electronic mail system can be added to the network, whereas no such option exists for the mainframe terminal system. So from a cost/benefit analysis, the PC network appeared superior. Based on the analyses, the analyst recommended the PC network system. Remember, this recommendation is not final; it is based only on the feasibility analysis.

Preliminary Recommendation

The analyst concluded in her feasibility report that the problem, as defined earlier, could be solved with a computer system. She then made a preliminary recommendation of a personal computer network for providing the management at the High Point Division of the Myers Furniture Company with up-to-date inventory reports. Finally, she included a rough implementation schedule, as shown in Table 15-3. The schedule will help her determine a cost estimate of the project, and it will give local and corporate management an idea of how long it will take to solve the problem. In this case, it will take less than six weeks to analyze, design, and implement the recommended system.

Based on the implementation schedule and the estimated initial cost of the personal computer network system, the analyst estimated a total cost of $50,700

TABLE 15-3
Rough Implementation Schedule

Activity	Time Required (weeks)	Elapsed Time	Activity	Time Required (weeks)	Elapsed Time
Problem definition/			System design	1.0	4.0
feasibility study	1.0	1.0	Acquisition	1.0	5.0
Analysis	2.0	3.0	Implementation	0.4	5.4

for the new system ($37,200 for computer system and $13,500 for analysis and designing—5.4 weeks at $2,500 week). Although the estimate was $700 more than the parent company wanted to spend, the analyst felt comfortable with her recommendation because of the future savings it would generate.

STEP 3: ANALYSIS

Based on the analyst's report resulting from the feasibility study, corporate management decided to proceed with the analysis and design work. If results found during the **analysis** stage indicate that the project should not be continued, management will be able to terminate it at any time up to the acquisition/programming step. Up to this point, the cost at termination will be limited to the time spent by the analyst.

In the analysis stage, the analyst will incorporate the output from the feasibility study into a more detailed study to develop a logical model of the recommended system. In this step of the process, the objective is to determine what must be done to solve the problem. The actual details of how it must be done will be delayed until the systems design step.

System Being Studied

Before we go on, it is useful to discuss a question that often arises regarding the analysis step: Which system is being analyzed? Is it the current system or is it the system that was recommended by the analyst in the feasibility study? Or, if an entirely new system is being developed, how does the analysis proceed? The answers to these questions depend on what is being done: If the current system is being converted from a manual system to an automated system, then both the current and the new systems must be analyzed to some extent. The input and output for the current system must be analyzed since any new system must use the same input to produce identical output. The new system must be analyzed as to how the input data will flow logically through the system to generate the needed output.

On the other hand, if an entirely new system is being developed, then the analyst must first develop a logical model of the new system, complete with the data to be input, the flow of data through the model, and the required output.

Regardless of which system is being considered, current or new, a logical definition of the system must take place in the analysis step. The analyst must be careful not to jump past this step into the physical definitions that take place in the system design step. Otherwise, problems can easily occur at later steps because the data and data flows within the system have not been clearly defined.

Logical Definition of System

Recall that the primary objectives for the Myers Furniture Company were redefined in the feasibility study as follows:

1. Provide current inventory information.
2. Save time and effort with recordkeeping activities.

It was also desired that the system be easy to use and expandable to other activities at a later date.

These objectives can be accomplished by means of reports to management, either in a printed form or shown on the computer screen, with additional inventory-related reports being output for study at a later date. In the analysis step, it must be determined exactly what should be included in each report. It is also necessary to develop logical models of the recommended system at both a high level and a detailed level.

To begin the analysis step, the systems analyst considered the input and output for the existing system, since the recommended system must use the same input to generate the reports. The inputs to the system come from three sources: sales reports, suppliers' invoices, and production counts. Using the inputs, the system must generate various reports to the management in High Point, as well as generating the data that must be sent to Charlotte. Table 15-4 lists some of these reports that the analyst found in her research and gives a short explanation of each. It is important that the recommended system provide these same reports.

Data Flow and the Data Dictionary

Next, the analyst developed a logical model of the recommended system that will create the desired reports using the three sources of input. Earlier, she had developed a physical model of the existing system using a systems flowchart. Now, to develop a logical model of the recommended system, she introduced another tool that is often used to depict the flow of data in the system. This analytical tool is the **data flow diagram.** A data flow diagram uses symbols to depict the sources and destinations, the processes that transform data, the data stores, and data flows within the system. These symbols were shown in Figure 4-7. Table 15-5 shows each of the four types of data flow elements for the Myers Furniture Company system, and Figure 15-7 shows the data flow diagram the

TABLE 15-4
Examples of Needed Reports for High Point Division

Report	Explanation of Contents
Picking ticket	An order for a factory worker to pick certain numbers of various styles of furniture to fill an order
Customer invoice	A statement of the number of pieces and price of furniture that is shipped
Sales report	A summary report for sales of each style of furniture
Inventory status report	A list of the number of pieces of each style of furniture currently in stock

TABLE 15-5
Data Flow Elements for Myers Furniture Company

Sources and/or Destinations	Process	Data Store	Data Flow
Customers	Process transactions and production counts	Local inventory	Transactions (receipts and sales)
Independent furniture makers		Master inventory	Production count
Factory workers	Transmit data		Processed transactions and production counts
Management	Update files		
	Generate reports		Reports
	Transmit reports		

analyst constructed as a logical model of the new system. It is important to remember that this is a *model* of *what* must be done to solve the company's problems, not *how* it is done.

After collecting a list of all reports that must be generated by the system and developing a data flow diagram of the overall system, the analyst had a good

FIGURE 15-7
Data Flow Diagram for High Point System

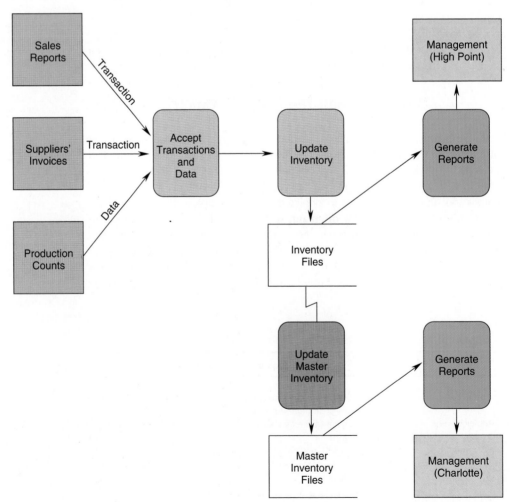

STEP BY STEP

The systems analysis and design procedure emphasizes planning for all possible situations. However, oversights may occur because the systems analyst or programmer is too close to the project. To avoid these errors, project members can use the **structured walkthrough**—a review of an analyst's or programmer's work by his or her peers. Such a review does not include management, so the developer is not evaluated by supervisors until the project is in final form. The structured walkthrough is designed to find errors in the system design or program in an atmosphere that avoids faultfinding on the part of the reviewers and defensiveness on the part of the developer. The emphasis is on helping the developer find possible problems at an early stage of development, not in the final product.

In a structured walkthrough, the developer's fellow project members help him or her analyze the project design or program. Because reviewers are provided with information on the project, they are expected to come to the walkthrough with questions in mind. In the walkthrough, the developer explains the project, giving a brief tutorial on how it will work. He or she then "walks" the reviewers through the design or program, step by step, to simulate all of its functions. During this manual execution of the project, the reviewers may develop more questions for the designer.

After the manual simulation, the reviewers summarize their joint concerns with an eye toward generating problems to be solved, rather than finding solutions. The developer must ensure that the reviewers' concerns are resolved successfully and that the reviewers are notified of the corrective action. More than one such walkthrough may be necessary to resolve major questions that may arise or to review the same project at a later stage of development.

Source: *Improved Programming Technologies: Management Overview,* IBM IPTO Support Group, Zostermeer, Netherlands, 1975, pp. 29–32.

The structured walkthrough provides a crucial review of the programmer's or systems analyst's logic and plans for the system.

TABLE 15-6
Partial List of Data Elements

Discount price	Quantity on hand
Open orders	Transfers in
Product description	Transfers out
Product number	Total month-to-date (MTD) sales
Product price	Total quantity
Quantity available	Total value
Quantity back-ordered	Total year-to-date (YTD) sales

idea what the new system must do. The next step was to analyze the data elements and data flows used to generate the reports. These analyses were done by two means:

1. the writing of a data dictionary,
2. an expansion of the overall data flow diagram into its parts.

A **data dictionary** contains information about data; that is, it is an explanation of the uses of each type of data. The data dictionary and a list of the data elements make up one part of what is known as the **formal documentation** of the analysis. The formal documentation will also include the data flow diagram for the entire system as well as data flow diagrams for each component and written reports describing these parts. This documentation will be expanded in successive steps as additional diagrams and reports are created. This documentation will be compared to the final system design to ensure that it fits the logical model. Table 15-6 lists some of the data elements that the analyst found. Each data element has one page in the data dictionary showing the data stores, data flows, and reports in which this data element can be found. Any aliases of the data element are given, as well as the form of the data. A sample data dictionary page is shown in Figure 15-8.

Next, the individual elements in the overall data flow diagram are broken down into individual parts. For example, the analyst magnified the section of the overall data flow diagram associated with production in order to show its components. As a result, a new data flow diagram was created with data stores and flows that were concerned only with production. The analyst's production data flow diagram is shown in Figure 15-9.

After the formal documentation was completed, the analyst arranged an inspection and management review to give management an opportunity to check over the data dictionary and various data flow diagrams. Once again, this was a learning experience for both parties that resulted in various changes in the items in the data dictionary and the data flow diagrams. As a result, the analyst

Name:	Quantity on hand
Aliases:	Total furniture, furniture on hand, inventory total
Description:	Amount of each style of furniture currently in stock
Form:	Numeric; maximum value = 10,000
Location:	Inventory status report, inventory valuation report, price list, inventory activity report

FIGURE 15-8
Data Dictionary Page.

came away with an even better picture of the operation in High Point. When these changes had been made, approval by the manager of the High Point Division was the last step before the logic underlying the data dictionary and data flow diagrams could be assumed to be correct. Once this was done, the analyst felt that she understood what was needed in the new system well enough to move on to designing the system.

STEP 4: SYSTEM DESIGN

The objective of the analysis step was to develop a logical view of a new system using a data dictionary and data flow diagrams, first for the system as a whole and then for the parts of the system. The **system design** step produces a high-level physical design of the new system that includes its actual parts. This type of design, often referred to as a *black box design,* shows a system that performs the needed functions, but it does not consider exactly how those functions actually work. Such a design should include a systems flowchart of the recommended system.

Recall that the systems analyst recommended that the High Point Division of the Myers Furniture Company use a file server-based personal computer network to provide a real-time online inventory system. To facilitate designing the system, the analyst developed the systems flowchart shown in Figure 15-10. It shows the various elements of the recommended system. In the systems flowchart, note that a telecommunications link is used to transmit information to the home office on a periodic basis. Using the recommended system, the home office receives the same information as before, but it is sent by telephone instead of mail. In addition, the High Point Division has its own processing system, which generates reports containing current information to High Point's managers. Although the systems flowchart does not reflect it, the PC network will also display current inventory status on each manager's workstation and allow managers to make queries about particular items or analyze the effects of pricing or purchasing decisions.

The components of the recommended system are designated only in general terms. The actual selection of make and model of hardware occurs in the next step. At this stage, the analyst did not change any of her cost estimates, because the costs and analysis of the recommended system seemed within budget.

Using the systems flowchart, the analyst then worked toward a physical design of the system, first by determining software and hardware needs. As with all computer system selection, she first defined the software needs of the proposed system.

Software Design

The next step was to design the software that would accomplish the results shown in Figure 15-10. The software requirements include updating inventory files and providing up-to-date inventory reports as well as handling the preparation of picking tickets, customer invoices, sales reports, and so on. In other words, the logical design developed in the analysis step will guide her software design. If the software is to be purchased, it will not be selected at this step, but it will be clearly defined so that various software vendors will be able to bid on the project. If customized software is a viable alternative, then it must also be

FIGURE 15-9
Data Flow Diagram for Production Count

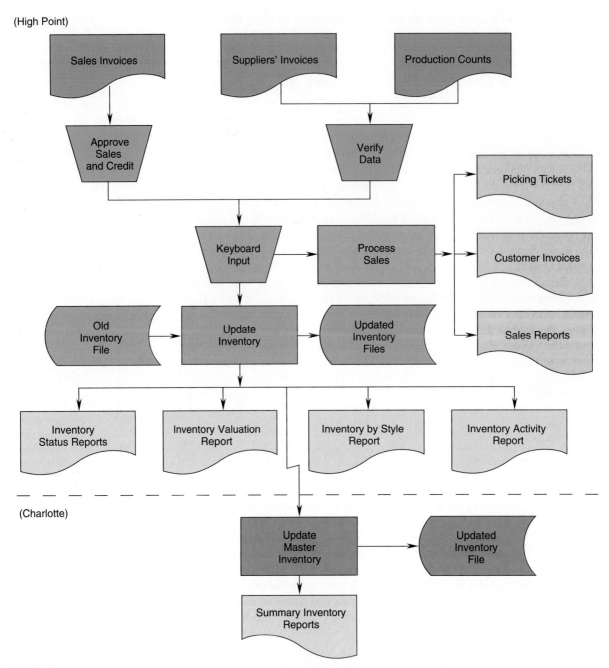

(High Point)

(Charlotte)

FIGURE 15-10
Systems Flowchart of
Recommended System

designed in this step. If both purchased and customized software are alternatives, then both must be designed in this step. The decision about whether to purchase software or program it will be made in the next step. Considering the results of the feasibility study, the analyst expected to be able to purchase commercially written software for the Myers Furniture Company. She knew that having customized software written would not be possible, given the budget limitations, so she did not pursue the design process for this alternative. For that reason, we will concentrate on developing a software design for the purchase of commercial software for the PC network. If this is found to be impossible, then the

Developing the system design requires close contact between the system analyst and the end user of the system.

Statement of Software Specifications
Myers Furniture Company Inventory System

1. The software must be able to handle the volume of inventory updating at the Myers Furniture Company and provide the needed reports, invoices, and picking tickets.

2. The software must be menu driven; that is, it must allow the user to select commands from an onscreen menu.

3. The software must have data entry screens that are easy to use.

4. The software must have a high level of error trapping to avoid the entry of incorrect types of data.

5. The software must have onscreen help screens that will aid the user whenever a question comes up.

6. The software must come with a tutorial system and must have a toll-free technical support telephone number.

7. The software must be able to create output files that can be transmitted over telephone lines to the Charlotte office.

8. The software must be available in a network version that will allow users to access inventory information from any workstation.

FIGURE 15-11
Statement of Software
Specifications

FIGURE 15-12
Statement of Hardware
Specifications

Statement of Hardware Specifications
Myers Furniture Company Inventory System

Proposed hardware requirements are

1. a file server that will run whatever software is purchased or written and will be able to handle the volume of work now being handled by the home office mainframe. The file server should have a large (at least 100 megabytes) hard disk and a tape backup. It should also have a high speed modem for transmitting files to the home office.

2. nine PC workstations that are compatible with the file server chosen. Each workstation should have its own hard disk and CPU as well as a high-resolution monitor.

3. an appropriate wiring plant to connect the new and existing PCs to the file servers. The wiring plant should also connect existing laser printers to the file server.

4. network connection cards that are compatible with the file server and PC workstations.

5. adequate support to install the wiring and to set up the file server and PC workstations.

alternative of using terminals linked to the home office will have to be considered in more detail. In a later chapter, we will look at the systems design process for customized software.

Based on her understanding of the Myers Furniture inventory problems, the analyst developed a statement of software specifications, shown in Figure 15-11. From this figure, it is easy to see that the analyst developed a physical design that incorporates both the inventory processing requirements and the High Point management's concerns regarding ease of use.

Hardware Design

Hardware design is highly dependent on software design, because hardware must be able to run whatever software is purchased or written for it. If the software will run only on a PC network using a DOS-based operating system, then it is necessary to purchase that type of network. On the other hand, if the software runs on a UNIX-based network, that type of hardware must be chosen. After developing the list of software requirements shown in Figure 15-11, the analyst prepared a statement of hardware specifications, shown in Figure 15-12, for the Myers Furniture Company.

The analyst showed these two specification statements to the High Point management team and explained the terminology. Management then approved the specifications, with one additional requirement: They wanted this system to be purchased locally from a reputable firm that would be able to provide training for the Myers Furniture Company employees and maintain the network after installation.

STEP 5: ACQUISITION/ PROGRAMMING

After the software and hardware specifications were approved by the management at the furniture operation, the analyst began researching software and hardware that would fit the requirements outlined in the systems design step. She began her search by looking for an inventory control package that would meet

SYSTEMS DEVELOPMENT PROBLEMS IN VERMONT

In 1987, Blue Cross and Blue Shield of Vermont requested proposals for a software system to handle membership, billing, and claims processing on their minicomputer system. The system would replace a claims processing contract with Blue Cross and Blue Shield of New Hampshire. After a presentation by Blue Cross and Blue Shield of Western Pennsylvania, the Vermont firm signed a $5 million contract with the Pennsylvania company. Blue Cross of Vermont felt comfortable with the contract, since the Pennsylvania firm was much larger and had given a "sparkling presentation." As a result of this confidence, Blue Cross of Vermont failed to assign sufficient inside staff to the project to check the work until it discovered that the work was hopelessly behind schedule. In fact, Blue Cross of Vermont had trusted an outside consultant to oversee the systems development work that was being carried out in its headquarters in Montpelier.

Blue Cross of Vermont's failure to assign sufficient inside staff to a large-scale systems development project contributed to Pennsylvania Blue Cross's failure to deliver programs on time. Further, because the Pennsylvania firm was required to pay system backup costs, which amounted to $250,000 a month, it convinced Blue Cross of Vermont to drop the backup contract. By March 1989, Blue Cross of New Hampshire pulled the plug of its claims processing system and left Blue Cross of Vermont with no system at all.

The failure of the systems development process, combined with the loss of the claims processing contract, caused many problems for Blue Cross of Vermont. At one time, a backlog of 238,000 claims existed—in a state with a population of only 500,000—along with a $15 million deficit in an account for future claims. To solve the problem, the company hired contract programmers, who often had to rely on verbal specifications from end users, to build a working system.

Source: Robert L. Scheier, "Botched System Transplant Induces Green Mountain Blues," *PC Week*, September 4, 1989, pp. 1, 6.

---

the needs of the furniture operation, that is, a package that would provide all data requirements as well as being easy to use. In the feasibility study, she had proposed to purchase a commercial inventory package, and she had designed the software with this in mind. If writing customized software had been a viable alternative, she would have developed software designs for both purchasing and writing the software and then decided whether to purchase or program the software—in the **acquisition/programming analysis** rather than the next step. While this was not the case in the Myers Furniture Company example, because writing customized software would have been too expensive, it is useful to consider this decision in more detail.

The Purchase/Program Decision

In general, if a package that meets the user's needs can be found, it is wise to purchase the package rather than designing and programming customized software. There are several reasons for this:

1. The cost of the software design and programming is spread out among all purchasers rather than being borne by one user alone.
2. The problems associated with finding errors in the software have (it is hoped) been solved by the software company.

In the acquisition/programming step, the software is either written or acquired, and the hardware is selected.

3. The time between purchasing a software package and putting it to use is much shorter than the time between deciding to write a program and putting it to use.
4. The cost is usually a known factor when a package is purchased, but costs can escalate when a program is being written.
5. Software companies often provide technical support to users either at no cost or for a nominal fee. They also often upgrade the software and make it available to current users at a reduced cost.

On the other hand, there are many instances in which purchased software will not meet the user's special needs. If this is the case, users have two alternatives: (1) design and program customized software (or attempt to modify an existing package) to meet the perceived needs or (2) change the way the company does business to fit an existing software package. While the first choice sounds more reasonable, remember that the time and effort required to design and program sophisticated customized software is often very difficult to gauge. Also, modifying an existing package can take longer and cost more than expected, and the original supplier of the package may not support it after it is modified. While changing the way a company does business may sound radical, doing so may be easier than having special software written. In this section, we will concentrate on the process of acquiring hardware and software. Chapter 16 discusses the programming process in detail, and Appendix B provides an introduction to programming in the computer language BASIC.

Acquiring Software

Referring to the software specifications statement, an analyst can prepare and send out requests for proposals. A **request for proposal (RFP)** is a request for vendors to bid on supplying a software package or a hardware system. This RFP must include sufficient information for the vendor to understand all of the client's needs. The analyst working on the Myers Furniture project sent RFPs to a group of vendors who specialized in developing inventory control software packages. While vendors were preparing their proposals, the analyst returned to her office.

When all proposals were in, the analyst compared the documentation for each software package to the needs of the High Point Division of the Myers Furniture Company. She selected three workable software packages and asked the vendor of each to demonstrate his or her product at a local site. To make the final decision, she asked the management team to accompany her to the demonstration site, where the vendors had installed their respective packages on the computer system and input some sample inventory data. High Point's production manager took with him examples of production, purchasing, and sales data that the software would be required to process. The sales manager took along examples of typical questions asked by sales agents, and the plant manager took some of the reports generated by the home office.

After working with the three packages, the managers agreed that the Hyatt Information Systems Perpetual Inventory System best satisfied their needs. The network version of the package cost $2,400, which was close to the budgeted amount, and the package had many features the High Point managers thought beneficial. The system would run on MS-DOS–based computers and networks, and it required 512K of internal memory in each workstation, as well as at least a 100-Mbyte hard disk on the file server to accommodate the storage needs of the High Point Division. In addition to satisfying the data requirements, the Hyatt software package satisfied managerial requirements in the following ways:

1. Ease of use: The Hyatt Perpetual Inventory System is menu driven. Options can be selected from a pull-down menu.
2. Expandability: The software package can be expanded to include other financial and accounting applications and could be easily integrated with the existing mainframe inventory system at the home office.
3. Knowledge requirements: The Hyatt system does not require knowledge of accounting principles.
4. Support: Hyatt Information Systems has an 800 (toll-free) number for user support and offers free updates to users as needed.
5. Network capability: The Hyatt system will run on an MS-DOS–based network using the Novell network operating system. Each PC workstation can access reports from the inventory package and print them on the network laser printers.

Acquiring Hardware

Based on the software requirements discussed earlier, the systems analyst began researching various network systems that would run the Hyatt inventory package. Her search for a network system was restricted by the requirements of the software package—an MS-DOS–based network with the Novell operating system. She also considered the level of training that would be available with the network and the cost of maintaining and supporting it. No provision had been made by management to hire a network supervisor to run the proposed network, so she had budgeted $2,000 annually for network support from the vendor of the network.

The analyst's research guided her decision to buy an Intel i486-based file server with 8 Mbytes of RAM and a 600-Mbyte hard disk. She also decided to use the token ring configuration for the network and to buy nine Intel 80386SX-based PCs as workstations, each with a VGA video system, 2 Mbytes of RAM, a 50-Mbyte hard disk, and a $3\frac{1}{2}$-inch floppy disk drive. She then checked with local computer suppliers in the area and found that several claimed the ability to install the network. As with the software selecting process, she sent RFPs describing the required hardware system to suppliers.

Within a week, she received bids for the network system from three suppliers. To select the system, she visited the suppliers, interviewed them, and tested a demonstration network. Based on these visits, she selected a supplier who offered 20 hours of on-site training to users. The supplier also employed a certified netware engineer who would install the network and provide support for a fee of $50 per hour after it was up and running. The supplier reserved a full day to demonstrate the network, and arrangements were made with the home office to test the compatibility of the system and the mainframe. High Point managers spent the day testing the inventory system on the network. They found the menu system easy to use, and the data entry system trapped several errors. The reports generated by the system, although not in the same format as those from the home office, provided the required information. Finally, the sales manager determined that the interactive display system worked well for answering typical sales questions. And, although an electronic mail scheduling system was not part of the proposed system, the managers tested one and agreed it would solve many of their interoffice communication problems. At the end of the day, there was consensus among managers that the system definitely would solve many of their recordkeeping and inventory problems.

The cost figures for the file server, wiring plant, nine PC workstations, network cards for new and existing PCs, Novell network operating system, and installation are shown in Table 15-7. The total package recommended by the analyst is as follows:

Hyatt Information Systems Perpetual Inventory System	$ 2,400
Network hardware and software	$34,600
Total system cost	$37,000

When the recommendations were presented to corporate managers, they noted that the overall hardware and software cost was close to that proposed in the feasibility study. They decided to go ahead with the purchase and installation of the system.

STEP 6: IMPLEMENTATION

Once a software/hardware system has been acquired or customized software has been written, the next step is to **implement** the hardware/software system.

ANOTHER VIEW

Frederick P. Brooks, Jr., on System Design

Frederick Brooks was the manager of the team of systems programmers who developed the operating system for the IBM System/360, which was the industry standard from the mid-1960s to the early 1970s. Before that he had been the project manager for the hardware team for the same system. This operating system, known as OS/360, was the result of many people working for several years to arrive at a workable system. In his book on the problems of managing software development, Brooks makes the following comments:

In most projects, the first system built is barely usable. It may be too slow, too big, too awkward to use, or all three. There is no alternative but to start again, smarting but smarter, and build a redesigned version in which these problems are solved. The discard and redesign may be done in one lump, or it may be done piece by piece. But all large-system experience shows that it will be done. Where a new system concept or new technology is used, one has to build a system to throw away, for even the best planning is not so omniscient as to get it right the first time.

Source: Frederick P. Brooks, Jr., *The Mythical Man-Month: Essays on Software Engineering* (Reading, Mass.: Addison-Wesley, 1975), p. 116.

TABLE 15-7
Network Cost Figures

Item	Cost
File server (i486 CPU, 8 Mbytes of Ram, 600-Mbyte hard disk, tape backup, and 9,600-bps modem)	$ 5,000
Wiring plant	$ 1,500
9 PC workstations (80386SX CPU, 4 Mbytes of RAM, 50-Mbyte hard disk, and VGA video system) @ $1,400 each	$12,600
12 network cards @ $500 each	$ 6,000
Novell network operating system	$ 7,000
Uninterruptible Power Supply (UPS)	$ 1,000
Installation	$ 1,500
Total network cost	$34,600

Implementation Problems

Once a system is purchased and delivered, it must be installed and tested, the staff trained, and existing data converted over to the new system. This is a very important part of the systems life cycle and must be planned very carefully. If the system is not installed and tested correctly and/or the staff is not trained properly, the new system is almost doomed to fail, for one of two reasons: Either the system will not work as proposed or the staff will avoid using it because of a fear of computers or a lack of understanding of the appropriate use of the computer.

Testing of a new hardware/software system is extremely important to ensure that the system works as designed. Problems with hardware are usually easy to find: The system either works or it doesn't. Unfortunately, testing of a software system is much more complicated, whether the software has been purchased or specially written. In either case, it is important to first test the system with data that represent the data that typically will be used on the system. If this

Implementation of new hardware and software involves a comprehensive training process for users.

test is successful, then the next test should involve "live" data, and the results on the new system should be compared to those on the existing system. This testing continues right on through the conversion process. For customized software, a special effort should be made to look for situations that cause problems with the program since the programmer may not have looked for all the ways the system might fail.

Training is an area of implementation that is all too often ignored. For an organization to receive full benefit from a new computerized system, the staff must be adequately trained on the use of the computer hardware, operating system, and applications software. If this is not done, either the staff will avoid the computer or errors can occur that may cause the organization to regret having installed a new computer system.

The *data conversion process* involves two steps. First, all data in the old system must be converted over to the new system. For the conversion of a manual system to a computerized system, all of the data currently on paper must be entered into the new system. This is often a long and tedious process, but once accomplished it will usually result in large savings in time and effort.

The second step in the conversion process is to move from the old system to the new system. Recall that in Chapter 4 we discussed the two types of conversion—parallel and direct. In **parallel conversion,** the old and new systems are run simultaneously to check that the new system works as planned; in **direct conversion,** the old system is replaced by the new system with no parallel testing. As discussed in the box at the beginning of the chapter, direct conversion may appear to be the quicker way, but parallel conversion is safer.

Implementation at the Myers Furniture Company

Before the system could be installed, the analyst, with the assistance of the managers of the High Point Division, had to determine where to place the file server for the network. Someone suggested the supply room, which had functioned once as an office and, therefore, had electrical outlets and telephone jacks. Further, it was centrally located, so it would be easy to run cables between the file server and the new and existing PCs and to the laser printers.

The analyst contacted the telephone company to install a business-quality phone line for telecommunication with the home office. She also contacted the supplier to arrange installation of the file server, cabling, and new PCs. The analyst then returned to her office to begin another project but returned to the High Point Division the day after the network was installed to test it. Too frequently, users become discouraged if problems with the computer network arise shortly after it is installed, so she wanted to check the system before she began training the management team. If she detected any problems with the network, she could work with the supplier to solve them. She also arranged all hardware and software documentation in binders and prepared a special sheet of instructions that advised employees what to do and whom to call if problems occurred with the file server or with any of the PCs attached to the network. The binders and instructions were stored near the file server.

Next, she set up the training sessions, which the local supplier offered. While High Points managers and staff experienced $2\frac{1}{2}$ days of hands-on training on the network operating system and inventory package, the analyst tested the new system's software and hardware and planned the conversion process. The conversion process at the Myers Furniture Company would involve entering into the system the inventory data that were either on paper or stored in the mainframe at Charlotte. The paper data would have to be keyed into the system, but the mainframe data could be downloaded over the telephone line to the personal computer system. Once she completed the plan for the data conversion process, she began planning the parallel conversion process. For parallel conversion, the High Point office would continue to send information to the home office for processing on the mainframe. At the same time, the data would be processed on High Point's file server. Once the data had been converted to the new system, the parallel conversion process began and continued for two months. During this time, the analyst worked on other projects at her office but was available to answer questions from the High Point Division. After two months, the conversion was complete, all processing was handled at High Point, and the new system seemed to work correctly.

STEP 7: MAINTENANCE

Maintenance of any information system includes ensuring that the system is operating correctly and correcting any problems that occur. Recall from Figure 15-1 that the systems life cycle moves from maintenance back to problem definition so that problems in an existing system can be analyzed and fixed. For hardware systems, maintenance includes repairing or replacing any parts that are found to be defective. Since a computer has few moving parts, most hardware problems occur within the first few weeks of use. Most later problems occur either with a disk drive or with printers, since both have moving parts. If a system becomes outdated, then the systems analysis and design approach described in this chapter would be used to find a replacement for the system.

Maintenance can involve both repair of hardware components and correction of software problems.

Software maintenance involves finding and correcting programming problems that have previously escaped detection. If the software is a commercial package, the company it was purchased from usually provides corrections free of charge; but if the software is customized, the responsibility for corrections will depend on the warranty provided by the programmer. Software maintenance is discussed in more detail in Chapter 16.

Maintenance at the Myers Furniture Company

The analyst had budgeted $2,000 a year for maintenance and support of the PC network. Although the hardware carried a one-year warranty that would cover any initial problems, network difficulties that were unrelated to the hardware would have to be solved by the supplier's network technician. For example, problems arising from conflicts between software would be dealt with by the technician. Because the analyst provided for maintenance and support in the PC network's operating cost, she was confident neither would create a financial problem.

The software manufacturer would maintain the software by supplying High Point with free corrections to the package. New releases of the package would be available for a nominal fee.

Postscript

The PC network system the analyst designed and implemented for the High Point Division of the Myers Furniture Company worked very well. The division was able to save money on administrative costs and have an up-to-date inventory system. Six months after the system was installed, the analyst spent another week at High Point to help managers select and install payroll and electronic mail software systems on the network.

Summary of the Systems Analysis and Design Process

To help you pull the systems analysis and design process together, we have summarized it in Figure 15-13, showing the seven steps, the decision points where management can decide whether or not to continue, the output from each step, and the tools used to accomplish the output.

OTHER APPROACHES TO SYSTEMS DEVELOPMENT

As computer users came to have increased access to the computer during the late 1970s and early 1980s, first through terminals tied into mainframes and then through personal computers, they found many new ways to use the computer to perform their jobs in a more efficient manner. At the same time that users were being afforded the increased availability of computers, the data processing departments in many organizations were finding themselves overwhelmed by users' demands for additional services. These two trends in computing were not unrelated, since as workers discovered the power of the computer, they also came to expect more from their data processing department. The increased expectations often included developing software for specific applications or making needed information available from a mainframe data base. Jobs that were

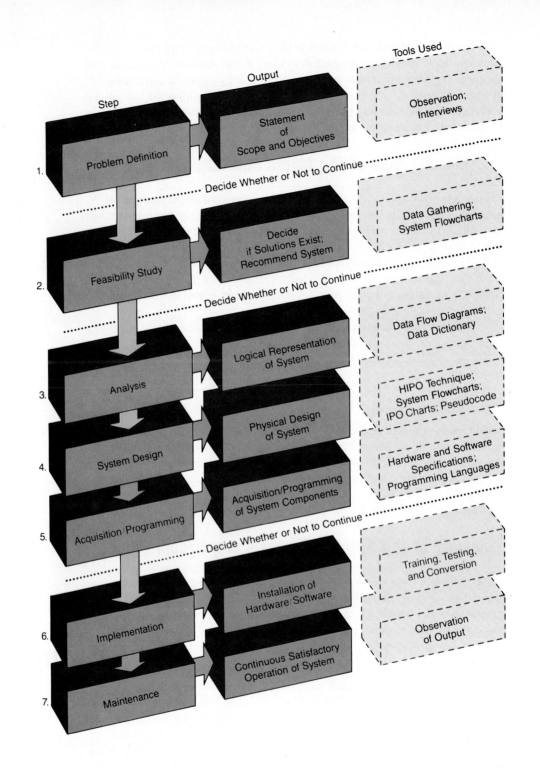

Step

Output

Tools Used

1. **Problem Definition** → Statement of Scope and Objectives — Observation; Interviews

Decide Whether or Not to Continue

2. **Feasibility Study** → Decide if Solutions Exist; Recommend System — Data Gathering; System Flowcharts

Decide Whether or Not to Continue

3. **Analysis** → Logical Representation of System — Data Flow Diagrams; Data Dictionary

4. **System Design** → Physical Design of System — HIPO Technique; System Flowcharts; IPO Charts; Pseudocode

5. **Acquisition/Programming** → Acquisition/Programming of System Components — Hardware and Software Specifications; Programming Languages

Decide Whether or Not to Continue

6. **Implementation** → Installation of Hardware/Software — Training, Testing, and Conversion

7. **Maintenance** → Continuous Satisfactory Operation of System — Observation of Output

FIGURE 15-13
Diagram of Systems Analysis and
Design Process

A DATA BASE WITH A VIEW

A t the Car Product Development (CPD) Division of Ford Motor Company, over 150 end users can access multiple sources of data with a new mainframe computer interface called VIEW, which is an acronym for Virtual Interface Engineering Window. With VIEW, end users can access mainframe data base systems, such as DB2 and IMS and various types of flat files, to create necessary reports. The system especially benefits the information systems department, because it no longer has to create a second set of information for users to access. Now, users can go directly to the data bases they need, which saves system resources.

VIEW was written in four months, in the Focus 4GL, by systems analyst Wendy Balaka. It is menu driven and allows users to easily access data bases and create reports. For example, VIEW users created 12 reports in two months. It would have taken two years to create the reports with Ford's previous system, which required systems analysts to make repeated visits to clients to ask them what they want.

Users can store report formats in their personal libraries to create and print reports on the fly or overnight. VIEW also contains a global library, which lets users share their report formats with other users. The system is available only on the CPD mainframe, but there are plans to develop a PC equivalent so PC users can access data from a mainframe and download it to a spreadsheet or word processor.

> ## It would have taken me at least $9\frac{1}{2}$ months doing it COBOL.
>
> *Wendy Balaka, systems analyst,*
> *Ford Motor Company*
>
> Quoted in Johanna Ambrosio, "Ford Gives Users a Database with a VIEW," *Computerworld*, September 16, 1991, p. 33.

Source: Johanna Ambrosio, "Ford Gives Users a Database with a VIEW," *Computerworld*, September 16, 1991, p. 33.

---

awaiting action from the data processing department created a **backlog.** This unfinished work meant that it would often take well over a year for a data processing professional to complete a user's project. By the time the project was completed it was often out of date and thus of no use to the user. It is felt that many users stopped submitting jobs to the data processing department because of the delay, creating an additional **invisible backlog** of unsubmitted, uncompleted jobs.

The frustration felt by many users at having to wait so long for the data processing department to complete projects has combined with new systems development tools to bring about the use of two new approaches to systems development. These new approaches are prototyping and end user computing.

Prototyping

In **prototyping,** the analyst or user creates a "quick and dirty" prototype of the final product, using either advanced languages or software tools. Prototyping can help the user to "short circuit" the often lengthy systems analysis and design process by skipping past the problem definition, feasibility study, and analysis steps and going directly to the design stage. The advanced languages that have

Fourth-generation languages (4GLs) are often used in prototyping a system to determine if it will suit the organization's needs.

```
OPEN(MAIN)                                      !OPEN MAIN MENU SCREEN
 LOOP
  ALERT                                         !CLEAR ALERT KEYS
  ACCEPT                                        !GET CHOICE
  EXECUTE CHOICE()
     GET_FILE                                   !GET OR CREATE A FILE
     SHOW_CALNDAR                               !SHOW THE CALENDAR SCREEN
     RETURN                                     !TERMINATE THE PROGRAM
   ..

                   EJECT('SHOW CALENDAR')
SHOW_CALNDAR PROCEDURE

CALENDAR    SCREEN      WINDOW(25,80),AT(1,1),PRE(CAL),HUE(14,0,0)
OMIT('**-END-**')
    SUNDAY   MONDAY   TUESDAY  WEDNESDAY  THURSDAY   FRIDAY   SATURDAY
      <#
    ██████████
    ██████████



CALENDAR.CLA 92:1                               LIN OVR ZON IND
```

made prototyping possible are referred to as **fourth-generation programming languages (4GLs)** because they were developed after many of the current high-level languages such as COBOL, BASIC, and FORTRAN. These 4GLs enable users to develop programs in a fraction of the time that would be needed for a typical high-level language. While programs written in a 4GL tend to be less efficient than those written in a high-level language, the increasing power and speed of computers make this less of a problem. The software tools that have helped make prototyping possible include program generators and easy-to-use data base management systems. **Program generators** allow users to generate programs in high-level languages with as little as 20 percent of the effort they would need to write the code themselves.

Prototyping often takes one of two forms. In the first, a basic system is created with a 4GL and then is expanded as the need arises. In the second, a simulation of the final product is created: The user can test the design by using the simulated product. The user's experience with the simulated product is incorporated into the design of the actual information system.

End-User Computing

With the increased availability of computing power at both the mainframe and personal computer levels has come a new breed of computer user—the end user. **End users** are non–data processing professionals who use the computer to solve problems associated with their job. End users are usually interested only in doing their own job better and are not interested in creating applications software for other users. However, sometimes an end user will do such a good job at solving his or her own problems that the solutions are disseminated to other users.

Since the late 1970s, the work of end users on the computer, which is referred to as **end-user computing (EUC),** has fast become an important part of computing in organizations. Some estimates show end-user computing as utilizing 40–50 percent of the computer resources of an organization. Other studies have shown that end-user computing is growing at a rate of anywhere from 50 to 90 percent per year. The primary reason for this increase in the importance of EUC is that end users found that they could cut down development time from months and years to days and weeks! This means that the applications developed by end users actually solve a problem while it is still a problem.

Recall that the systems analysis and design procedure is carefully thought out for solving users' problems, but it has led to a backlog of uncompleted user jobs. The end user short-circuits this process by going directly to the analysis and design steps—knowing what the problem is and not worrying about the feasibility of solving it. If the problem turns out to be one that is not easily solvable, that will become evident soon enough. The end user then combines the analysis and design steps into a single problem-solving step. Once he or she has developed an idea of how to solve the problem, the user jumps right into using an applications software package or right into developing a computer program. In so doing, the end user also combines the software design and programming steps, using the highly interactive nature of available software packages and languages. Once an application is developed that meets his or her needs, the end user seldom worries about the maintenance step, other than to solve any problems in the application as they come up.

Types of End Users

It can be said that anyone who uses a computer, either directly or indirectly, is an "end user." While it is true that the person who makes an airline reservation through a computerized service is an indirect end user, we will consider only direct end users. Direct end users—those people who have direct contact with the computer—can be further divided into data processing professionals and non–data processing professionals. From our previous definition of the end user, we are interested in only the latter group. Various studies have developed finer classifications of this group:

Type 1: Beginning end users
Type 2: Intermediate end users
Type 3: Advanced end users
Type 4: Functional support end users

Let's look at each type and see how that user might use the computer to perform a job better.

Beginning end users tend to use applications software at its lowest level and make no effort to extend their knowledge of the software beyond what they need to solve the most basic problems.

Intermediate end users have found that they can solve many more job-related problems by increasing their knowledge of the software and beginning to explore its limits.

Advanced end users are those who have pushed the software to its limit and have begun writing out their own procedures for solving complicated problems. They may even be writing computer programs to solve problems that cannot be handled with commercial applications software.

Functional support end users are "local experts" who, because of their knowledge of a particular software package or computer language, have become informal experts in computer use in their functional area. In many cases, they

Scientists and engineers are among the many professionals who are using programming languages and applications software to perform their jobs better.

end up developing software applications for their fellow workers. However, they do not view themselves as data processing professionals; rather, they feel that they are financial analysts, marketing researchers, and so on, whose primary job is to provide tools and procedures for using applications software to solve problems.

Breakthroughs in research could make end-user programming a necessity in the sciences.

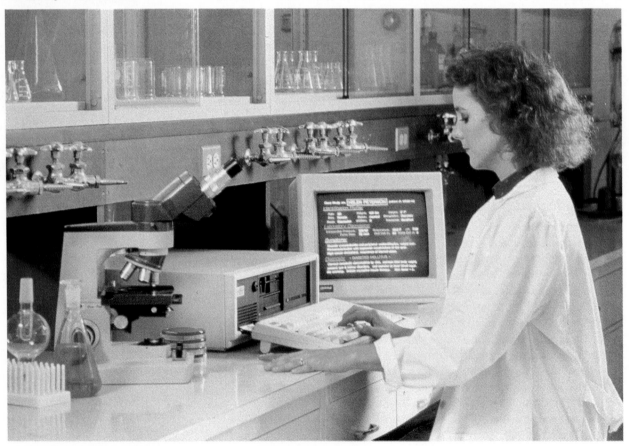

"QUICK AND DIRTY"

As Sun Microsystems unhappily found out, using the standard systems analysis and design approach to create a new information system in a rapidly changing marketplace is not always the best method. Sun—a leading manufacturer of workstations—spent three years using the conservative, sequential approach to develop a new information system. However, the company got a messy surprise around April Fools' Day of 1989 when, after months of testing, the old system was "unplugged" and Sun's new system was unable to handle a large number of new orders. This, in turn, caused Sun to be unable to plan its production, leading to a drop in revenue in the fourth quarter of that year.

Even when the conservative systems analysis and design approach works, the resulting information system may not actually solve the original problem when business conditions are changing rapidly. In cases like the one at Sun, it may be better to use a flexible, evolutionary approach to systems development or even to create a "disposable" system that is used only until a permanent system can be created and tested. In the former alternative, it is important to take tasks that would be performed sequentially in the conservative design approach and overlap them. For example, testing begins when users define their requirements for the system. As one developer said, "We can't wait nine months to have a baby anymore; we have to do it in two. And it has to come out perfect and it has to run when it's two weeks old."

In the latter alternative, the "quick and dirty" system is rushed into operation without extensive documentation, backup plans, or confirmation that it complies with all standards. The key to using disposable systems is to pick the right application, say, a one-time analysis of a new plant, and not to try to make the system permanent just because it worked for a short while.

Sources: Robert L. Scheier, "Taking the Quick Path to Systems Design," and "In a Development Jam? Try a Disposable System," *PC Week,* June 19, 1989, pp. 65, 69.

> **It is clear that the use of HOS (Higher Order Software) methodology completely changes the traditional life cycle.**
>
> *James Martin, author of more than 70 books on computing*
>
> *Systems Design from Provably Correct Constructs: The Beginnings of True Software Engineering* (New York: Prentice Hall, 1985), p. 301.

Problems with the End-User Approach

Problems with the end-user approach can result from lack of documentation or from the failure to use formalized problem-solving approaches. For example, in the first case a problem can arise when the end user develops an application that solves an important organizational problem but fails to create the documentation necessary to support the application. If the end user leaves the organization without creating the documentation, it may not be possible for another individual to use the undocumented computer application. In the second case, when end users fail to use the formalized problem-solving approaches outlined in the systems analysis and design procedure, it is possible for the end user to solve the wrong problem or use the wrong approach to solve the right problem. Because the end user often works alone, none of the evaluation procedures of the systems analysis and design procedure are included to help detect these errors before they are implemented in a computer application.

1. The systems analyst is responsible for analyzing and designing information systems.
2. A seven-step procedure should be followed to perform structured systems analysis and design.
3. Problem identification involves learning about the problems of the current system and determining its scope and objectives.
4. The objective of the feasibility study is to determine if the problem can be solved and to make an initial recommendation. Systems flowcharts can be used to help the analyst model the existing system.
5. A cost/benefit analysis and a rough implementation schedule are parts of the feasibility study.
6. The analysis step is aimed at developing a logical model of what must be done to develop a new system being studied. Data flow diagrams and a data dictionary are useful in the analysis of the system.
7. The system design step develops a high-level physical design of the new system. Systems flowcharts are useful in designing the new system. Statements of hardware and software specifications are needed to define what must be acquired in the next step.
8. In the acquisition/programming step, a decision is made whether to purchase or program software. Hardware and software systems that match the system design are acquired, and any custom software is programmed in this step.
9. The implementation step puts the system into place. This step includes installing and testing the new system and training the staff to use it. Conversion to the new system also occurs at this stage.
10. The maintenance step ensures that the new system continues to operate as it was designed.
11. To avoid the often long lead time required to develop a new system using systems analysis and design, two new approaches to system development have come about: prototyping and end user computing.

KEY TERMS

acquisition/programming analysis
analysis
backlog
computer-based information system
cost/benefit analysis
data dictionary
data flow diagram
direct conversion
end-user computing (EUC)
end-user
feasibility study
formal documentation
fourth-generation programming
   language (4GL)
implementation
invisible backlog

maintenance
model
parallel conversion
problem definition
program generator
prototyping
request for proposal (RFP)
structured walkthrough
systems analysis and design process
systems analyst
system design
systems development life cycle
systems flowchart
systems life cycle
top–down approach

1. Why would the systems analysis and design process be used to select hardware and software for a small business?
2. Why is interviewing an important tool during the problem definition step?
3. How does model building fit into the systems analysis and design process? What is the difference between a logical model and a physical model?
4. Why is the feasibility step described as a scaled-down version of the entire systems analysis process?
5. How does the analyst decide which system should be studied during the analysis step? What does the data dictionary have to do with this step?
6. What is the objective of the systems design step? What tools are used in this step?
7. In what steps can systems flowcharts be used to help the systems analyst?
8. How does the acquisition/programming step relate to the systems design step?
9. How does the acquisition/programming step differ between hardware/software selection and software development?
10. What activities take place in the installation step?
11. What are the various types of implementation? Which method is the fastest but also the riskiest?
12. What activities take place in the maintenance step?
13. Why have prototyping and end user computing come about as alternatives to systems analysis and design? What is the invisible backlog?
14. What is the difference between prototyping and end user computing? How does a 4GL fit into this?
15. What are some potential problems with end user computing?

16

Program Development

In the systems life cycle, if software must be developed rather than purchased, then one or more programs must be created. This chapter discusses the process of designing those computer programs, but does not go into the actual languages used: Because a program must first be designed before it can be written in any computer language, this discussion concentrates on the steps taken and the various tools used in planning a computer program. A case study will demonstrate the process in a real-world situation. After reading this chapter, you should be able to develop the logic needed to write a program, regardless of the programming language. Appendix B will discuss actually writing a program in BASIC to implement the procedures developed here.

STUDY OBJECTIVES

After reading this chapter, you should be able to

- discuss the relationship between program development and the systems life cycle;
- understand the step-by-step nature of designing, writing, and executing a computer program;
- describe the concept of an algorithm and explain how algorithms are important to the whole process of computer programming;
- list the steps that should be followed to write a computer program;
- recognize the various flowchart symbols used in program planning;
- understand the use of pseudocode in the program development process;
- use flowcharts and pseudocode to convert an algorithm into a form that can be programmed;
- describe various parts and types of loops as well as the ways in which loops are terminated;
- discuss the importance of structured programming to good program design;
- develop an algorithm to solve a problem and then convert that algorithm into a flowchart and pseudocode.

ALL CIRCUITS ARE BUSY

It started innocently enough: At 2:25 P.M. on January 22, 1990, a New York City computer on the gigantic AT&T long-distance telephone network somehow came to believe it was overloaded and started to reject phone calls. When other computers on the network tried to pick up the slack for the supposedly overburdened New York City computer, they, too, exhibited the same weird symptoms. Eventually all 114 computers on the AT&T network were affected, and long-distance callers using the AT&T system all across the United States began to receive a busy signal or to hear the now famous "All circuits are busy" message. The problem continued for over nine hours, during which time AT&T lost between $60 million and $75 million in revenues. Companies who depend heavily on long-distance phone service for telemarketing were also big losers on this day. Some companies even sent their employees home because they could not make needed calls.

And what was the cause of this problem in the nation's largest long-distance network? Engineers traced the problem to a single logic error or "bug" in the software used to route calls on the AT&T network. This particular bug, like many others, arose during an effort to improve an existing software system. All of AT&T's computers use the same software, so all were affected by the same problem in logic.

While software designers are always working to ensure that software is bug-free, this is not always possible. A program like AT&T's faulty switching system can contain a *million* lines of code. Even when fault-tolerant computer systems attempt to reduce runaway system failure by having modules that check on each other, the entire system can go down if all modules simultaneously suffer the same malady.

Source: Thomas McCarroll and Paul Z. Witteman, "Ghost in the Machine," *Time,* January 9, 1990, pp. 58–59.

PROGRAMMING AS A PART OF THE SYSTEMS LIFE CYCLE

Chapters 4 and 15 discussed the systems life cycle as a seven-step process for designing and implementing an information system to solve problems in organizations of all sizes. Recall that the steps in the systems life cycle are problem definition, feasibility study, analysis, system design, acquisition/programming, implementation, and maintenance. While the system design step will often involve choosing and purchasing computer hardware and software, in many cases no software exists that will fit the system design, so specific computer software must be designed and written. Remember that computer software is made up of **programs,** which are a series of instructions to the computer, and that the process of developing the correct set of instructions is referred to as **programming.**

While the decision to acquire software or to write it is made in the acquisition/programming step of the systems life cycle, the problem has been identified and analyzed and a solution designed in earlier steps. In the acquisition/programming step, once the analyst and the client decide to have software written rather than to acquire it, the physical design of the software is converted into a computer program. This chapter looks at the detailed process of developing the physical design from which the actual program can be written. As discussed in the box, a crucial step in this process is finding and correcting any errors in the programs.

The Programming Process

The most important concept to learn about programming is that it is a form of *problem solving*. There are two crucial steps in the problem-solving process. The first is to ensure that the correct problem is being solved; the second is to develop the correct logic to solve the problem.

Ensuring that the correct problem is being solved requires careful study of why a problem exists. Maybe an organization is currently handling some process manually and wants to use a computer instead. Or maybe management has a complicated mathematical or financial problem that cannot be solved by hand. Regardless of the source of the problem, first it must be clearly identified.

Once the problem has been identified, the second crucial step is to develop properly the step-by-step process—the **logic**—that will actually solve it. Many times a program fails to work because the programmer has not developed an appropriate plan for solving the problem before attempting to write the program.

Once a problem has been identified and a step-by-step process worked out, three other steps must be carried out before a working computer program actually exists: (1) incorporating the step-by-step logic in the form of a computer program written in a computer language, (2) testing the program on a computer and correcting any errors, and (3) using the final, corrected program. To summarize, the five-step process for writing a computer program is this:

Step 1: Identify the problem.
Step 2: Develop a step-by-step solution to the problem.
Step 3: Write a computer program to implement the step-by-step solution.
Step 4: Test and correct the computer program.
Step 5: Use the final version of the computer program.

Steps 1 and 2 do not involve using a computer language, but step 3, writing the program, does. Several computer languages are discussed in Chapter 17, and programming in one language—BASIC—is discussed in detail in Appendix B. As indicated in the box at the beginning of the chapter, step 4, testing and correcting the program, is an extremely important aspect of the programming process that must not be taken for granted. Finally, step 5, implementing the program, begins the actual use of the program. As discussed in the opening box, it is not uncommon for "bugs" to be found even after extensive testing has been done or when new versions of the package are created. In either case, the same programming process is used to clean up the program or to create an updated version.

Comparison of Programming Steps to Systems Life Cycle

To help you understand how the programming steps fit into the overall systems life cycle, Table 16-1 compares the steps in the two processes. Note that the

Any software upgrade or addition is a major undertaking.

Jim Manzi, president and CEO, Lotus Development Corp.

Quoted in "Software Must Work the Way People Do," *Personal Computing,* October 1989, p. 211.

(Top left) Many retail computer stores offer the general public lessons in programming. (Top right) Programming on personal computers is now being taught in many elementary and middle schools. (Bottom left) High school students can now take advanced placement (AP) courses in computer programming. (Bottom right) Labs filled with IBM compatibles, IBM PS/2s, and Apple Macintoshes are commonplace at most colleges and universities today.

problem must be defined during the first three steps of the systems life cycle. The solution is then designed in the system design step. The resulting design is programmed and tested as a part of the acquisition/programming step of the life cycle. Finally, in the implementation step, the completed software is installed. A key result from Table 16-1 is that the process of actually writing the program (program development steps 3, 4, and 5) takes place only *after* a great deal of systems analysis and design work has been done. This is an important concept— because no matter how well the program is written, the objective will not be achieved if the program is being written for the *wrong* process.

An Example: Averaging Quiz Scores

To help illustrate the programming process, we will use a case study that involves computing the average quiz score for a student in a college class. In

TABLE 16-1

Relationship Between Systems Analysis and Program Development

Systems Life Cycle Step	Program Development Step
1. Problem definition 2. Feasibility study 3. Analysis	1. Identifying the problem
4. System design	2. Developing a step-by-step solution to the problem.
5. Acquisition/ programming	3. Writing the program 4. Testing and correcting the program
6. Implementation	5. Implementing the program
7. Maintenance	

this case, each term an instructor gives five quizzes that are averaged to use in assigning a final letter grade to every student. Assume that the instructor wants to design a program to automate the processes of averaging the quiz scores. Input to the program for each student in the class will include a name and five quiz scores. The program should average these five scores. Output from this program should include each student's name, five quiz scores, and average quiz score. The program should also indicate whether a student has an average quiz score of less than 60; if the student does, the computer should output a message that the student is failing.

STEP 1: IDENTIFYING THE PROBLEM

The first step of program development—identifying the problem—is the most important, since it is virtually impossible to write a satisfactory computer program without a *clear understanding and identification* of the problem to be solved. Fuzzy thinking at this stage may cause the programmer to write a program that does not correctly solve the problem at hand, or a program that correctly solves the wrong problem, or a combination of both! Therefore the programmer *must* spend as much time as is necessary to truly identify and understand the problem. Often, only a verbal statement of the *objective* is required. Other times, it may be useful to write down the objective and other important factors of the problem. Finally, for very complex problems, it may be necessary to develop a formal written description of the problem, supported by a detailed listing of all items that must be considered in the writing of the program.

The problem identification step should include identification of the data to be *input* to the program and the desired results to be *output* from the program. Often these two items will be specified by a person or an agency other than the programmer. Much grief can be avoided if these input and output requirements are incorporated into the programmer's thinking at this early stage of program development.

When the program is complete (step 5), the programmer should always return to the problem identification step to ensure that the problem being solved is indeed the problem identified in step 1. While it may seem obvious to do this

PRISON INMATES PASS THEIR TIME WITH PROGRAMMING

At Somers Correctional Institute, Connecticut's only maximum security prison, a group of prisoners is spending time writing programs. The inmates wrote the programs not just for their use but for some of the prison's operations. For example, the group wrote programs in dBASE to automate the prison's pharmacy, track the status of prisoners for prison administrators, and monitor job and pay schedules for the 1,400 inmates at Somers.

Some prisoners were in the computer field before entering prison.

Others, however, learned computer programming through the prison's educational program. Many prisoners had not seen a personal computer before their incarceration but learned a lot in the six hours a day they spent in school. When administrators were confident that prisoners could write the programs, they began assigning projects to them, and prisoners have taken over many responsibilities associated with the prison's restricted information system.

The members of the group work six days a week, 10 to 12 hours a day. They believe they are gaining valuable experience that will help them when they are released from prison. In recognition of the group's effort, it has been designated as a tester of dBASE IV. Members believe their work is important—so important that one member of the group turned down an opportunity to move to a medium security prison, because it did not have computers.

Source: Beth Freedman, "Inmates Gain Hope, Stability Through dBASE Programming," *PC Week,* December 11, 1989, pp. 75, 77.

> **When I get out of here, I'll have experience as a programmer equivalent to four years in college in computer science.**
>
> *William Wright, inmate at Somers Correctional Institute*
>
> Quoted in Beth Freedman, "Inmates Gain Hope, Stability Through dBASE Programming," *PC Week,* December 11, 1989, pp. 75, 77.

when a program is finished, not all programmers actually do it. To avoid later frustration and problems, program results must be checked against the original program objectives.

STEP 2: SOLVING THE PROBLEM

For the quiz score averaging case, the problem identification step is fairly simple: For each student, the input is the name and five quiz scores. Output should include the name and five scores and the student's average score. If the student has an average quiz score of less than 60, a message that he or she is failing should be output. The input and output for this case are shown in Table 16-2.

Since computers can follow only very specific instructions to manipulate data, the next step in writing a program is to develop a step-by-step solution for the problem identified in the previous step. This step-by-step solution, called an

TABLE 16-2

Input/Output for Quiz Score Averaging Problem

Input	Output
Name and five scores	Name and five scores
	Average quiz score
	If average quiz score is less than 60, a message that student is failing

algorithm, expresses the logic of the program in a written form. No matter how skilled the programmer, unless he or she has a complete understanding of how to solve the problem, it will be impossible to write the algorithm successfully.

Algorithms are used quite often outside of computer programming. Perhaps the most common use is in cooking, where an algorithm is called a "recipe": a step-by-step description of the actions necessary to perform a task (cooking a main dish, vegetable, or dessert). An example of a recipe as an algorithm is shown here—in this case, making a cake from a mix.

Step 1: Preheat oven to 350 degrees.
Step 2: Generously grease and flour pan.
Step 3: Empty mix into large bowl; add 1 cup of water and 2 eggs and blend until moist.
Step 4: Beat vigorously for 300 strokes and pour into pan.
Step 5: Bake at 350 degrees until done. Cake is done when toothpick inserted in center comes out clean.

The key difference between algorithms written by humans for use by other humans and those written by humans for use by computers lies in the level of understanding that the recipient of the algorithm may be assumed to have. When an algorithm is written for human use, the user is assumed to have a certain degree of reasoning ability that will keep him or her from interpreting an instruction literally or carrying it to an extreme. For example, the cake mix instruction to "blend until moist" assumes that the cook can determine when to stop blending. Similarly, the user is assumed to know the meaning of certain terminology in the instructions or to be able to find out the meaning. For example, we know the meaning of "preheat." Computers, on the other hand, cannot reason, nor can they recognize the meaning of words that are not in their limited vocabulary. In the case of the recipe, the computer would have difficulty deciding when to stop blending or difficulty understanding what some of the other terms mean.

For computers, algorithms must be very precise. Strange things can happen when the computer does what the programmer *tells* it to do rather than what the programmer *wants* it to do! Also, if told to repeat some operation but not told when to cease repetition, the computer will continue repeating the action until the program is aborted by a command from the user or the computer operator.

It is at this step that the programmer must think in a logical fashion and learn to divide a problem into a logical sequence of small steps that a computer can understand. Many persons can state in general terms a procedure for solving a problem on the computer, but they may have difficulty breaking this general procedure into smaller steps. Unfortunately, there is no quick, easy way to learn this skill. The best way, as usual, is to start with simple examples. Further, you must learn by *doing* rather than by watching. Reading this or any other textbook or observing your professor develop algorithms is not enough; you must "get your hands dirty" and develop algorithms yourself.

Application to Quiz Score Averaging Problem

After identifying the input and output for the quiz score averaging problem, the next step is to develop an algorithm for this problem. The general procedure to find and output the average quiz score is as follows: First, input and output the student's name and quiz scores. Then, sum the quiz scores and divide the sum by five to find and output the average quiz score. Next, check to see if the average is less than 60; if it is, output a message.

While the reader may understand this statement of the general procedure, it is not yet in a form that can be used to write a computer program. We need to convert the general procedure into specific steps that make up the desired algorithm:

Step 1: Input the student's name and five quiz scores.
Step 2: Output the name and scores.
Step 3: Compute the average quiz score by summing the five scores and dividing the sum by five.
Step 4: Output this average quiz score.
Step 5: Check to see if the average is less than 60; if it is, output a message that the student is failing.

Note also that if the number of quizzes given during the term is changed, then the algorithm also must be changed to account for the different number of scores. To apply this algorithm to sample data, assume we have a student named George Burdell with exam scores of 57, 60, 55, 63, and 60. Applying the algorithm to this data, we obtain

Step 1: Input "George Burdell" and 57, 60, 55, 63, and 60.
Step 2: Output "George Burdell" and 57, 60, 55, 63, and 60.
Step 3: Sum 57, 60, 55, 63, and 60 to obtain 295; divide this by 5 to find an average of 59.
Step 4: Output the computed average of 59.
Step 5: Is 59 less than 60? Yes, so output a message that this student is failing.

Using Flowcharts

Once we have an algorithm, we are well on the way to writing a program to perform the desired task. However, we need to go one step further to ensure that the program we write will actually represent the algorithm stated previously: The algorithm must be converted to an intermediate form from which we can prepare the actual program.

The algorithm can be converted into one or both of two forms, one pictorial and one written. The pictorial form is referred to as a **flowchart** and the

written form is called **pseudocode.** We will discuss how to convert an algorithm into each form.

A flowchart is a *pictorial representation* of an algorithm, and it clearly demonstrates the flow of control that will occur in the final program. Because it often is difficult to follow this flow of control by just reading the computer program, a flowchart can help both the person doing the programming and someone else who is reviewing the program.

A standard set of flowchart symbols is used with computers. The actual flow of control is designated by arrows, which connect the symbols. We will use the set of symbols shown in Figure 16-1.

The **terminal symbol** is used to show the starting or stopping point of a flowchart—where the flow of control begins and ends. The following terminal symbol indicates the beginning of a flowchart:

Start

Terminal Symbol

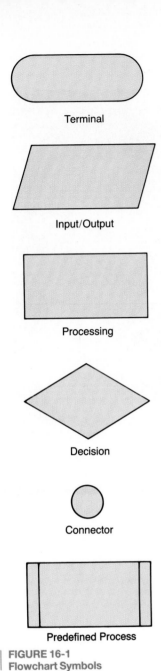

Terminal

Input/Output

Processing

Decision

Connector

Predefined Process

FIGURE 16-1
Flowchart Symbols

To communicate with the program, input and output are necessary. The **input/output symbol** can be used for either operation regardless of the input or output method. The following symbol shows that the values X and Y are input:

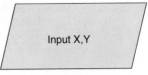

Input X,Y

Input/Output Symbol

The **processing symbol** is very important in any flowchart. It shows all calculations and often represents the operations that must be accomplished. In the following processing symbol, the quantity Z is set equal to the sum of X and Y:

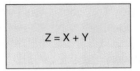

$Z = X + Y$

Processing Symbol

The **decision symbol** is used to denote that a decision must be made. Without decisions, the program's flow of control moves directly from statement to statement in the order in which the statements are entered. A decision in a computer program changes the program's flow of control. When a decision is used, direction can be changed to skip around a segment or to repeat a segment. With decisions, a program segment may be selected for execution from among two or more program segments depending on the logic of the program and the data that are input. For example, suppose that if X is greater than Y, then X is output; but if X is not greater than Y, then Y is output. The decision symbol would represent this logic as follows:

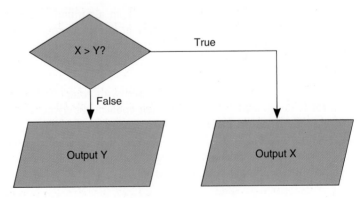

X > Y?   True   Output X

False

Output Y

Decision Symbol

If the flow of control requires that distant portions of the flowchart be connected, then the **connector symbol** is used. In the flowchart, an arrow points to a connector, which contains a number. Control is then transferred elsewhere in the program, to another connector with the same number. This symbol is useful for complicated programs that have many connections. In the example here, one alternative of a decision symbol is a connector. This connector is also shown elsewhere in the program, as follows:

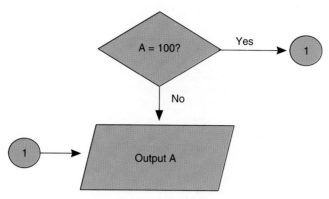

Use of Connector Symbol

In some situations, a particular procedure is included in the flow of control, but the logic of this procedure is actually flowcharted separately. When this happens, a **predefined process symbol** is used to designate a separate flowchart:

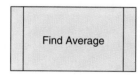

Predefined Process Symbol

To demonstrate the use of flowcharts in a familiar situation, Figure 16-2 is a flowchart of an imaginary registration process in which a student goes through several steps and decisions before (we hope!) finally creating an acceptable schedule.

Figure 16-3 is a flowchart of the algorithm of the quiz score averaging problem. This flowchart replicates the algorithm in a pictorial form that clearly demonstrates the logic of the program that will be written later. The input/output parallelogram denotes the input and output of the name and scores as well as the output of the quiz average and the "failing" message. The processing block denotes the computation of the quiz average, and the decision diamond represents the decision as to whether or not the student is failing. The start and stop ovals appear at the beginning and end of the flowchart, respectively.

Using Pseudocode

Once the logic has been expressed in a pictorial form, the next step is to express the logic of the program module in pseudocode. This involves actually writing a program in English rather than in a computer language—yet another conversion to help the programmer express the logic and to ensure that it is correct. Later, the step in which the actual computer program is written (step 3) is a translation of the pseudocode to whatever computer language is being used. Once you have written several programs, you will find that developing an

FIGURE 16-2
Flowchart of Registration
Process

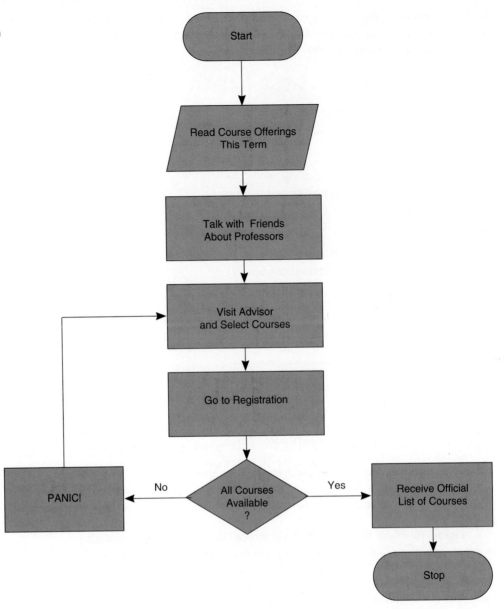

algorithm and converting it to pseudocode tend to become one and the same, with the algorithm often being written as pseudocode to begin with.

A pseudocode program is useful for two reasons. First, the programmer can use it to structure the logic of the algorithm in a written form. Second, it provides a relatively direct link between the algorithm and the computer program because the programmer uses English to write instructions that he or she can then convert into program instructions in whatever computer language is being used. Often, this conversion from pseudocode statement to computer language instruction is virtually line for line.

There are almost no set rules for writing pseudocode; it should be a personalized method for going from the algorithm to the computer program. However, the pseudocode should be a set of clearly defined steps that enables a reader

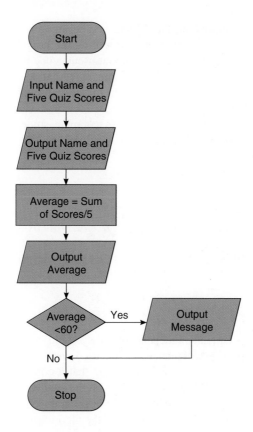

FIGURE 16-3
Flowchart for Quiz Score
Averaging Problem

to see the next step to be taken under any possible circumstances. Also, the language and syntax should be consistent so that the programmer will be able to understand his or her own pseudocode at a later time. As an example of pseudocode, assume a program is needed to compare two values, X and Y, and to output the larger of the two. The algorithm for this problem is

Step 1: Input values for X and Y.
Step 2: Check if X is greater than Y; if it is, output X and stop.
Otherwise, perform step 3.
Step 3: Output Y and stop.

A possible pseudocode for this algorithm is

```
Begin program;
Input X and Y;
If X > Y, then output X;
Otherwise, output Y;
End program.
```

In this pseudocode, the two values X and Y are input and then compared. If X is greater than Y, then it is output. If X is not greater than Y, then Y is output. Semicolons are used to denote the ends of statements in this pseudocode, but another form of punctuation may be used. It is easy to follow this program as we convert from the algorithmic form to the pseudocode form. It is also easy to see why more experienced programmers often combine the algorithm step and the pseudocode step. For the beginning programmer, however, it is worthwhile to develop the algorithm first, then flowchart the algorithm and write a pseudocode program to make the transition to writing the program easier.

The important point to remember about pseudocode is that it expresses an algorithm to the programmer in the same way that a computer language expresses the algorithm to the computer. In this way, pseudocode is like a personalized programming language.

The pseudocode for the algorithm to compute student quiz averages is shown next. Note that it follows the same logic as the algorithm and the flowchart.

```
Begin program;
Input name and quiz scores;
Output name and quiz scores;
Set quiz average = sum of quiz scores/5;
Output quiz average;
If quiz average < 60, output failing message;
End program.
```

STEP 3: WRITING THE PROGRAM

Steps 1 and 2 were language independent—they could be followed by any programmer regardless of the language to be used. At some point, however, it becomes necessary to use a specific language that a computer can understand. The success of this step depends a great deal on the quality of the previous steps. The programmer must clearly understand the program objective, the development of an algorithm, and the conversion of the algorithm to a flowchart and to pseudocode.

Every language has its own **syntactical (grammatical) form** and vocabulary. For example, in English one syntactical rule is that the subject of a sentence must agree with the verb. Computer languages also have syntactical rules and a vocabulary that the programmer must follow in the actual preparation of the program. The logic will be much the same regardless of the language, but the programmer must ensure that both the logic and the syntax of the program are correct before the program will be ready for actual use.

Almost always, the programmer handles the actual "writing" of the program by typing the program into a personal computer or terminal linked to a mainframe. Usually, some type of text editor—say, a word processing package—is used to facilitate entering the program and correcting typing mistakes.

We will leave further discussion of writing the program until we take up the details of the computer language BASIC in Appendix B. Once we have learned the vocabulary and syntax of BASIC, we should be able to convert the logic embodied in the flowchart and pseudocode into a written version of the program. Figure 16-4 shows the BASIC program statements that correspond to the flowchart symbols and pseudocode statements shown earlier.

STEP 4: TESTING AND CORRECTING THE PROGRAM

Once the program has been written, the next step is to test and correct it. This stage is referred to as **debugging**—trying to remove all of the errors or **"bugs."** This very important part of program development often takes as long as the actual design and writing steps. The best way to test and correct a program is

```
100 REM PROGRAM TO COMPUTE ONE STUDENT'S AVERAGE QUIZ SCORE
200 INPUT "ENTER STUDENT'S NAME AND SCORES" ;STUDENT$,SCORE1,SCORE2,SCORE3,
SCORE4,SCORE5
300 PRINT "STUDENT'S NAME: ";STUDENT$
400 PRINT "STUDENT'S SCORES: ";SCORE1,SCORE2,SCORE3,SCORE4,SCORE5
500 AVERAGE = (SCORE1+SCORE2+SCORE3+SCORE4+SCORE5)/5
600 PRINT "STUDENT'S AVERAGE SCORE IS: ";AVERAGE
700 IF AVERAGE < 60 THEN PRINT "STUDENT IS FAILING"
800 END
```

FIGURE 16-4
BASIC Quiz Score Averaging Program

to execute it using test data. **Test data** are data whose results are known in advance of running the program.

First, however, a command must be input that will cause the computer to translate the program into a form that it can use in processing data. English-like programming languages such as BASIC are termed **high-level languages** because they are on the language level of the programmer. For the computer to understand these high-level languages, they must first be translated into a binary form the computer understands called **machine language,** as shown in Figure 16-5. The translator itself is a software program that can change high-level statements into machine-language instructions, either one statement at a time or all statements at once. During this process, the translator checks the program for vocabulary or syntax errors. If the translator program cannot understand a statement, it displays an error message, and the programmer must correct the error before the translation can continue or begin anew. After the high-level statements have been translated into machine-language instructions with no vocabulary or syntax errors, the program can be executed.

Even though the translated program does not contain syntax or vocabulary errors, it still may be incorrect—either in the manner in which it carries out the logic or in the logic itself. To find and correct any such errors, we first need to test the program using the test data discussed earlier.

The test data are checked by hand in advance to determine the results expected from the program. Then the test data are input and the program is run. If the results from the program do not agree with the results from the hand calculations, there is an error, either in the program logic or in the hand calculations. After the hand calculations have been verified, the program logic must be

> **The best bug detector we've ever found is lots of hands-on end users.**
>
> *Frederick Gault, vice president,*
> *San Francisco Canyon*
> *Company*
>
> Quoted in "Bug-Free Code: The
> Competitive Edge," *Computerworld,*
> February 17, 1992.

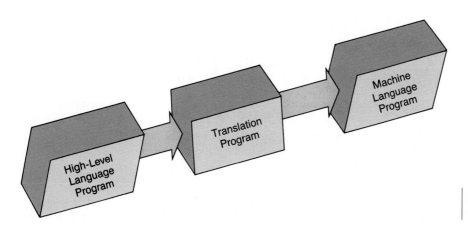

FIGURE 16-5
Computer Language Translation Process

IS "BUG-FREE" SOFTWARE POSSIBLE?

In the software development process, which is part of the systems life cycle, a crucial step is finding and correcting errors—so-called "bugs." As software becomes more complex, the process of "debugging" each program of a software package also becomes more difficult. Programmers now spend at least as much time debugging their work as they do in actually writing their programs. Nevertheless, it is generally acknowledged that bugs still exist in most commercial software. In fact, most software sold today carries a disclaimer stating, in effect, that the package is not guaranteed to work! Writing bug-free software is inherently difficult, because the logic supporting the program is inflexible. In most engineering projects, a margin of error is built into the design specifications, so a bridge, for example, usually will not collapse if an element is defective or fails. With computer software, on the other hand, *each* program instruction must be correct. Otherwise, the whole program may fail.

Examples of problems attributed to faulty software include the following:

- 1,800 automatic teller machines at a major bank in Tokyo shut down on payday.
- An airline's reservation system failed, forcing 14,000 travel agents to book flights manually.
- The air traffic control system at Dallas-Fort Worth International Airport began spitting gibberish, forcing controllers to track planes on paper.
- A bug in the Pennsylvania state lottery computer system allowed clerks to buy winning tickets *after* a drawing—about 465 winning tickets were punched out before the error was detected.
- Problems with telephone systems have included the AT&T outage in 1990 (discussed on page 504) and the disrupted service to 10 million people in five states and the District of Columbia in 1991.
- A problem with the computer system that directed the Patriot antimissile system allowed a Scud missile to hit a barracks, killing 28 U.S. service people during the Gulf War. The error, attributed to a "freak" combination of ten abnormal variables, was not detected in thousands of hours of testing.

Sources: Thomas McCarroll and Paul Witteman, "Ghost in the Machine," *Time,* January 29, 1990, pp. 55–59; Richard Pastore, "Lottery Agents Hit Jackpot, Courtesy of Systems Glitch," *Computerworld,* January 8, 1990, p. 6; and Mitch Betts, "Glitch Let Scud Beat Patriot," *Computerworld,* May 27, 1991, p. 109.

> **It [the bug in the Patriot missile system] was a one-in-a-million thing that was never detected in thousands of hours of testing.**
>
> *Col. Bruce Garnett, U.S. Army (Ret.), ex-manager of the U.S. Army's Patriot missile program*
>
> Quoted in Mitch Betts, "Glitch Let Scud Beat Patriot," *Computerworld,* May 27, 1991, p. 109.

checked. For the quiz score averaging program, when the data for George Burdell—scores of 57, 60, 55, 63, and 60—are entered, the program should output the name and the scores. It should also output an average of 59 and a message that the student is failing.

Other errors that can occur during execution include the incorrect use of data or the inadvertent request by the user that the computer perform a meaningless operation, for example, dividing by zero. The program will execute until it encounters an error; then it will stop and display a message telling why it has abnormally terminated the program execution. If possible, test data that can test all portions of the program should be chosen. If this is not done, errors in any untested section of the program will not be discovered. If an error *is* detected, then the programmer must trace through both the logic of the program and the actual language statements to find it. If a logic error goes *undetected,* the results can be catastrophic, like the problems experienced by the AT&T network described in the opening box.

STEP 5: USING THE PROGRAM

After it has been executed correctly with test data, the program is ready to be used for its intended purpose. In the program for computing the average quiz score, the names and quiz scores for each student can now be entered.

At this stage it is necessary to determine whether the results meet the objectives outlined in the problem identification step. If the program does not meet the final user's needs, then the programmer must analyze the results and the objectives to find out where they diverge. After the analysis, the programmer should trace through the program development procedure and change the algorithm, flowchart, pseudocode, and high-level program as needed to satisfy the final user.

In the quiz score averaging case, the instructor should be able to use the BASIC program to compute the average for each student by repeatedly running the program. If the program fails to work as desired, then the programmer will need to reexamine the planning and debugging processes.

LOOPS

In the flowchart and pseudocode versions of the quiz score averaging program, the algorithm works for only one student. One thing a computer does extremely well, however, is to repeat some action, say, averaging the quiz scores for many students. This type of repetition is an example of an important programming concept called a loop. A **loop** may be defined as *the process of repeatedly executing one or more steps on an algorithm or a program.* Almost all programs are used to perform some repetitive task.

In the registration process in Figure 16-2, the student goes back to the advisor whenever a course that he or she has selected is not available. If this process—selecting courses, determining if they are available, and then returning to the advisor if one or more courses are not available—is repeated more than once, then it becomes a loop. In this case it could end up being an endless loop, since a student might never be able to register for all the courses desired. At all costs, the programmer should avoid an endless loop, by putting in checks to ensure that the loop will stop. Otherwise, it will continue until the programmer or computer operator enters a command to abort the job.

Since loops are essential to any program, we must look closely at the parts of a loop, types of loops, and termination of loops. For the quiz score averaging problem, we will show two types of loops that can repeat the calculation of student quiz averages.

Parts of a Loop

To repeat some action successfully, a loop must have three parts:

1. a loop termination decision;
2. a body (the steps to be repeated);
3. a transfer back to the beginning of the loop.

These parts are pointed out in Figure 16-6.

FIGURE 16-6
Parts of a Loop

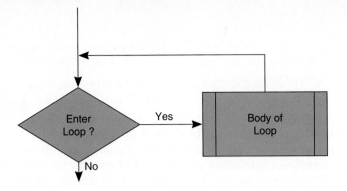

The **loop termination decision,** which determines when the loop will terminate, is always necessary because a computer will continue repeating a loop until told to stop. In Figure 16-6, the loop termination decision is represented by a decision symbol. If the condition is true, the body of the loop is executed and the loop continues, with control being transferred back to the loop termination decision. If the condition is false, control is transferred out of the loop and the loop is terminated.

The **body of the loop** is the step or steps of the algorithm that are being repeated within the loop. The body may be only one action or it may include almost all of a program. In Figure 16-6 the body of the loop is shown by the predefined process symbol.

Finally, the **transfer** back to the beginning of the loop is a means of returning control to the beginning so a new repetition can begin. In Figure 16-6 the transfer is denoted by the arrow pointing back to the decision symbol.

Types of Loops

The two basic types of loops are differentiated by the position of the loop termination decision in relation to the body of the loop. The loop shown in Figure 16-6 is called a **pretest loop,** because the loop termination decision occurs *before* the body of the loop. A loop termination decision that occurs *after* the body of the loop indicates a **posttest loop,** as shown in Figure 16-7.

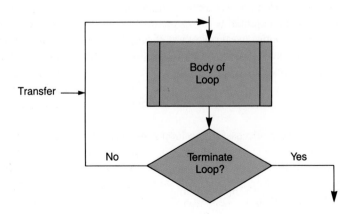

FIGURE 16-7
Posttest Loop

Termination of Loops

As stated earlier, for all loops there must be some kind of termination decision. Otherwise, the loop would continue infinitely or until it is aborted in some way. Two types of loop termination decision are commonly used: (1) comparing a repetition counter to some value and (2) checking for some value or values that indicate the end of the loop. In the first case, the number of repetitions is compared to some predefined value; when the number of repetitions reaches this value, the loop terminates. In the second case, when a value is found that matches the termination condition, the loop terminates.

Using a Repetition Counter for the Quiz Score Averaging Problem

Assume that we want to process a class of 24 students, using the same logic as for 1 student. In addition, we want to compute the class average. The professor inputs first the number of students, then each student's name and five quiz scores. The program must compute the average score for each of the 24 students and keep a running sum of these averages to compute an overall average at the end of the program. After all 24 students' quiz scores are averaged, the sum of the averages is divided by 24 to find the class average. In this case, a natural loop termination decision would be to count the number of students processed. When this count exceeds the number of students in the class, the loop terminates. The algorithm for the multiple student averaging case is this:

Step 1: Input number of students.
Step 2: Set sum of averages to 0 and student counter to 1.
Step 3: Check if student counter is less than or equal to number of students; if it is, perform step 4. If student counter is greater than number of students, perform step 6.
Step 4: Process each student.
Step 5: Add average quiz score to sum of averages and add 1 to student counter. Go back to step 3.
Step 6: Divide sum of averages by number of students and output result as "average quiz score for class."

How do the new steps in this algorithm fit the concept of a loop? In step 1 the user simply inputs the number of students in the class, and in step 2 he or she *initializes* the sum of averages to 0. This **initialization** process is necessary because computers must be told explicitly where to start summing or counting; they do not automatically know to start at 0 or 1 (or whatever value the user may desire). A student counter counts the students as their scores are processed so that the computer knows when all students have been processed. The sum of averages sums the individual student averages to compute an overall class average.

In step 3, the beginning of the loop, the computer compares the student counter to the number of students input in step 2. If the student counter is less than or equal to the number of students, the loop is continued by step 4; otherwise, the loop is terminated by step 6. Step 4 carries out the same logic as the algorithm for processing a single student's quiz scores, shown earlier on page

516. Step 5 then adds the student's average to the sum of averages, adds 1 to the student counter, and returns control to step 3. Steps 4 and 5 constitute the body of the loop.

Step 6, which occurs after the loop, handles the computation of the class quiz average by dividing the sum-of-averages value by the number of students input in step 1. We assume that the professor would *never* enter a zero number of students; if she did, an error would occur in step 6 when the computer attempted to determine the class quiz average.

We will now look at this same algorithm in flowchart form in Figure 16-8 and then in pseudocode form. In the flowchart the loop termination decision comes *before* the body of the loop, making it a pretest loop. We also have used the predefined process symbol to represent the logic involved in processing a single student (shown earlier as Figure 16-3).

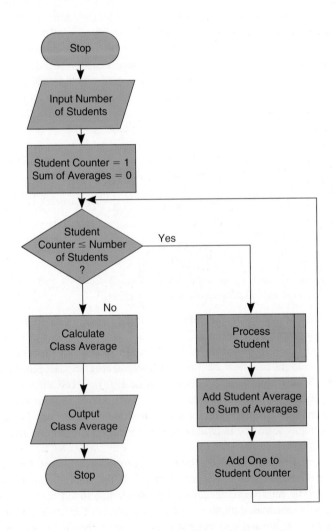

FIGURE 16-8
Flowchart for Multiple Students

In Figure 16-8 we have added an instruction that initializes the student counter to 1 before going into the loop and an instruction in the loop that increments the counter after each student is processed. In the decision block, we compare the value of the student counter to the number of students to be processed. When the value of the student counter is greater than the number of students to be processed, the loop terminates. All computer languages have standard statements that the programmer writes into the program to handle initializing and incrementing the counter and comparing it to the final value.

The pseudocode for the multiple student quiz score averaging program embodies in a written form the same logic as shown in the flowchart in Figure 16-8:

```
Begin program;
Input number of students;
Set student counter = 1 and sum of averages = 0;
While student counter ≤ number of students, repeat
the following:
  Process this student's scores;
  Add student's average to sum of averages and
  add one to the student counter;
End repeat;
Set class average = sum of averages/number of
students;
Output class average;
End program.
```

In the pseudocode for multiple students, the statement "While student counter ≤ number of students, repeat the following:" handles the loop termination and the repetition. The use of the word *while* in pseudocode characterizes this loop as a *pretest* loop since the loop will continue "while" a condition is true. The body of the loop is indented to show what is being repeated, and an "End repeat" statement shows the end of the body of the loop. If the student counter is greater than the number of students, then the loop terminates and control goes to the statement immediately following the "End repeat" statement.

To see how the logic in the flowchart and pseudocode works for three students, assume that the following data are input:

3   ←Number of students
SAM JONES 43, 62, 65, 60, 55 ←data for first student
CATHY SMITH 70, 80, 63, 67, 75 ←data for second student
BEN SIBLEY 65, 83, 87, 82, 83 ←data for third student

The number of students (three) is input first, the number-of-students counter is set to 1, and the sum of averages is set to 0. The student counter is less than or equal to 3 so the body of the loop is executed. The first student's name and quiz scores are input and output. The quiz scores are averaged to compute a value of 57. Since this value is less than 60, a message is output that the student is failing, 57 is added to the sum of averages, and the student counter increases to 2. The student counter is still less than or equal to 3, so another repetition occurs. The second student's name and scores are input and output. The second student's average is calculated to be 71, so the sum of averages

TABLE 16-3
Calculations in Loop

Step	Calculation
Before loop	Student counter = 1 and sum of averages = 0
First repetition	Student counter = 1 + 1 = 2 and sum of averages = 0 + 57 = 57
Second repetition	Student counter = 2 + 1 = 3 and sum of averages = 57 + 71 = 128
Third repetition	Student counter = 3 + 1 = 4 and sum of averages = 128 + 80 = 208
After loop	Class average = 208/3 = 69

Workstations such as this one give the programmer access to the processing power of a mainframe.

becomes 57 + 71 = 128 and the student counter is increased to 3. Because the student counter is still less than or equal to 3, the process is repeated.

The third student's name and scores are input and output. This student's average is calculated to be 80, so the sum of averages becomes 128 + 80 = 208. The student counter is now greater than 3 so the loop is not repeated and the student counter is increased to 4. Instead, the class average is computed as 208/3 = 69. This value is output and the program ends. Table 16-3 shows the calculations that are made at each step of the flowchart.

Using a Last-Record Check for Quiz Score Averaging Problem

A second common way to terminate a loop that inputs data is to use the **last-record check.** Each record that is input is checked to see if it contains a value that signals the end of the loop. This **sentinel value** must be different from any legitimate value and must be on the last record that is input.

The last-record check method is especially useful if the number of records to be processed is not known prior to execution of the program. For the quiz score averaging problem, if the number of students in the class is not known, then the loop might be terminated when a phony student's name is entered after all students' data has been processed. For example, a name of "zzzzz" might be used as a last-record check; when this name is entered, the loop terminates. Figure 16-9 shows a flowchart of this process. Since the number of students is unknown prior to execution of the program, the student counter also counts the students so the class average can be computed.

STRUCTURED PROGRAMMING

When programs become sufficiently complex to require loops and decisions, the programmer begins to need to plan the design of the program. Whether pseudocode or flowcharting or both are used, a key concept for all programmers to keep in mind when designing the actual program is structured programming. A **structured program** is written in modules or blocks and allows only one entrance to each module and only one exit from each module. When a program is designed in this way, the program logic is easy to follow and understand during the actual writing of the program. In addition, structured programs are much easier to correct than programs that have multiple entry and exit points to and from a module. Consider Figure 16-10, which shows the same three program modules in a structured design and in an unstructured design. In the unstructured

FIGURE 16-9
Use of Last-Record Check

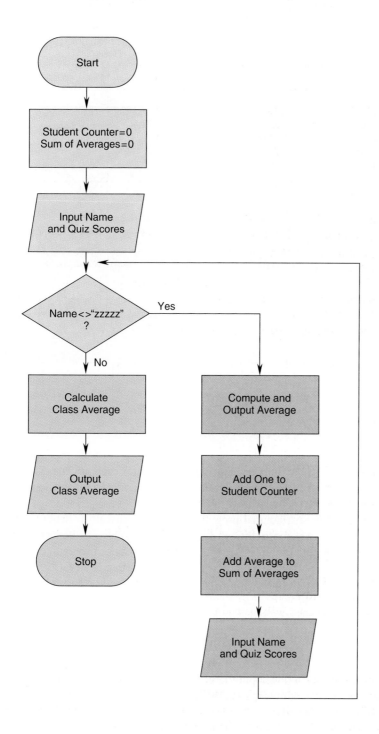

design, there are multiple entry and exit points to and from the modules; in the structured design, each module has only one entry point and one exit point.

Hand in hand with the unstructured program is the GOTO transfer statement, a statement that is carefully avoided in structured programming for two reasons. First, modern programming languages do not need the GOTO statement to form loops. Second, programmers often misuse the GOTO statement to make up for failing to plan a program sufficiently. If the statement is used, program

> **You've got to make [software development] more of a manufacturing process, with standard parts and tightly disciplined development.**
>
> *Ed Yourdan, author of more than 15 books on structured analysis and publisher of* American Programmer *magazine*
>
> Quoted in "The Call for Quality Control," *PC Week,* December 19, 1988, p. 44.

FIGURE 16-10
**Structured and Unstructured
Program Designs**

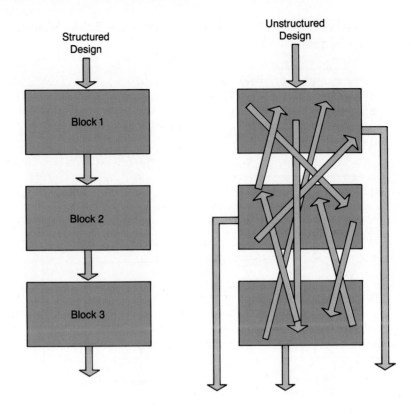

control may "jump out" of a module into another part of the program and violate the rule of having only one entry and one exit for each module. The transfers of control shown in the unstructured design in Figure 16-10 would be accomplished by the GOTO statement.

Generally, unstructured programs are more difficult to debug than structured programs, are more difficult for a reader to follow, and execute less efficiently. Further, use of the GOTO statement can cause the program to suffer from "spaghetti code." This name derives from the fact that if all GOTO statements were connected with lines to the object of the GOTO, the result would resemble a pile of spaghetti!

USING CASE

A growing trend in developing large software systems is the use of **computer-aided software engineering** (CASE). CASE is the use of software to help in all phases of system development, including analysis and design and writing the programs for the system. In the analysis and design phases, data dictionaries and diagramming programs can automate much of the paper flow. Application or code generators can automate writing the programs. CASE can also automate the documentation process, so that as new versions of the program are developed, new documentation is also created. CASE process is used for two reasons; it provides (1) rapid production of prototypes and (2) reusable structured code that can be used for other applications.

The benefits of using CASE software package—so-called **CASE tools**—include the following:

- The duration of the system's overall life cycle is reduced, because the various cyles are compressed and begin to overlap.
- Information sharing is improved, because paperbound methods are automated and stored in central information repositories. This also reduces duplicating effort.
- Users are involved throughout the process and more effort is spent on the early design stages—often the source of critical errors that are difficult to correct.
- Systems are easier to modify, because system parameters and functions are stored in a central place. When one part of a system is changed, all elements of the system that are affected by the change automatically access the new value.

A side effect of using CASE technology is that it encourages developers to concentrate on the front end of the software design procedure: the design and analysis of new applications. The result is the production of applications that require less debugging or re-engineering and get to the consumer sooner.

> **As information systems organizations retool throughout the 1990s, CASE tools will play a significant role in the process.**
>
> *James Martin, author of more than 70 books on computing*
>
> Quoted in "CASE Tools to Play a Larger Role in IS Organizations," *PC Week*, July 2, 1990, p. 45.

REVIEW OF KEY POINTS

1. Custom programming can create applications that commercial software packages are not designed to do.
2. A program consists of instructions to the computer.
3. The programming process can be viewed as a five-step procedure that overlaps with the systems life cycle.
4. Problem identification and algorithm development are crucial steps in developing the logic of the program.
5. Flowcharts and pseudocode are two means of converting an algorithm into a form that can be easily programmed.
6. After the program is written in a high-level language, it must be translated into machine language, debugged, and then implemented with actual data.
7. The loop is an important concept in programming. Two important types are the pretest or "while" loop and the posttest or "until" loop.
8. A pretest loop is required when the loop will be repeated an unknown number of times; the posttest loop can be used when the number of repetitions is known before execution.
9. All counters and sums in a program must be initialized, because the computer itself cannot set them to a desired value.
10. The computer can terminate a loop by comparing a counter to a preset value or by watching for a specific value that signals the end of the loop.
11. Structured programming uses modules to develop easy-to-understand code. The GOTO transfer statement is avoided in structured programs.
12. CASE uses software to all phases of system development.

KEY TERMS

algorithm
body of the loop
bug
CASE tool
computer-aided software engineering
  (CASE)
connector symbol
debugging
decision symbol
flowchart
high-level language
initialization
input/output symbol
last-record check
logic
loop

loop termination decision
machine language
posttest loop
predefined process symbol
pretest loop
processing symbol
program
programming
pseudocode
sentinel value
structured program
syntactical (grammatical) form
terminal symbol
test data
transfer

REVIEW QUESTIONS

1. Why is it often necessary to write computer programs?
2. Why is the first step in problem solving so important?
3. What is an algorithm? Find an algorithm in your everyday life and discuss why it fits our definition of an algorithm.
4. What does the programming procedure presented in this chapter have to do with the systems analysis process discussed in Chapters 4 and 15?
5. Why do we use pseudocode or a flowchart as an intermediate step between an algorithm and a computer program?
6. Flowchart the algorithm you found in question 3 and rewrite it in pseudocode.
7. Why is it necessary to translate a computer program into machine language?
8. Why do we use test data in the debugging process?
9. How is a loop an important concept in programming? Name a process that requires looping.

In each of the following exercises, develop an algorithm, draw the flowchart, and create the pseudocode that represents the logic needed to write a program.

10. The International Parcel Service Company delivers packages around the world. If a package is delivered by surface transportation, the charge is $0.50 per pound. Air transportation is $0.75 per pound, and C.O.D. is one of the charges plus a $5.00 service charge. Assume that the weight of the package and the type of service are to be input, and compute the final charges.
11. The water company charges a fixed fee of $3.50 if a customer uses between 0 and 175 gallons per billing period. From 176 to 500 gallons, an additional $0.02 per gallon is charged. All gallons over 500 are billed at a rate of $0.01 per gallon. If the number of gallons used is input, compute the customer charge.

12. The Dear John Implement Company sells tractors and combines. Salespeople for Dear John are paid $1,000 per month plus a commission of 5 percent of that monthly salary on tractor sales and 10 percent on combine sales. Develop an algorithm to compute the monthly pay for each employee and the total pay for all employees if the number of employees and sales for tractors and combines are input.

13. Professor Anderson has her students take some number of quizzes each term. However, this number changes from term to term. Develop the logic to input the number of quizzes to be taken and, for a given student, to input the quiz grades and compute an average.

14. Now assume that Professor Anderson allows her students to take as many quizzes as they wish (all take at least one). Develop the logic to input a student's quiz scores, count the total number of quizzes he or she has taken, and compute the student's average grade. Use a negative quiz score to signal the end of the input for this student.

15. Easy Rider, Inc., operates a fleet of taxis. The owner is considering purchasing small cars to replace the company's full-sized cabs. To help evaluate the cost of operating the smaller cars, he is running a mileage test on a prototype cab. Based on odometer readings, gasoline consumed, and the cost of gasoline, he wishes to calculate the gasoline cost per mile. Develop the logic necessary to make this computation for an unknown number of taxis if the taxi ID number, beginning and ending odometer readings, gasoline consumed, and cost of gasoline are input. Use a negative ID number to signal the end of the data.

Top–Down Design

In Chapter 16, we used flowcharts and pseudocode to design a program for a quiz score averaging problem. In the single student case, the logic was sufficiently simple that the entire logic could be displayed in one flowchart and a short pseudocode. However, when larger computer programs are being designed, the logic becomes so complex that the entire problem cannot be considered at one time. This situation is very common in the development of commercial software, which often must be divided into numerous parts for different teams of programmers to work on. When programs are too complicated to be considered as a whole, programmers use a "divide and conquer" strategy. This approach even has a special name: **top–down design.**

To accomplish top–down design, the programmer first views the program as a whole and decides how it can be divided into smaller programming blocks or modules. This is the "top-level" stage of the design process, when the emphasis is on the program's overall design. At this stage, the programmer should simply try to state the program as a sequence of steps to be carried out, giving no attention to detail but instead developing the "big picture."

Next, the individual modules in the program are developed, in a process known as "stepwise refinement." Part of the process involves ensuring that the top-level design is correct. A **module** is a section of the program that performs a specific task. If a module is too complicated to perform a specific task, then it should be divided into several smaller parts and the task performed by a lower level of module. This process of subdividing tasks continues until no more modules are needed. Most programs have at least three first-level modules: input, computation, and output. Figure TD-1 shows what a top–down design of a program can look like.

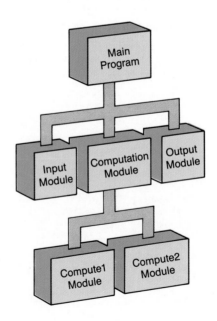

FIGURE TD-1
Top–Down Designed
Program

530

In Figure TD-1 on page 530, the main program, or module, links all first-level modules. In this case, we have an input module, a computation module, and an output module. The computation module is broken down further into smaller modules, each handling a particular computation. This form will be used as a basis for our discussion of top–down design.

The key to top–down design is that each module performs a recognizable task and should be designed and written to be correct when considered as a separate unit. Modules must also be able to communicate with the rest of the program through linkages with the main program or with other modules. In a very complex program, it is often useful to write and test each module separately before trying to test the program as a whole. If each module is correct and the main program handles the linkages properly, then the entire program has a high probability of being correct.

What is the difference between structured programming and top–down design? These two important concepts are often confused. The easiest way to keep them straight is to remember that top–down design programming is an *approach* to the design of programs that are efficient and easy to maintain, while structured programming is a *method* of implementing this design. In both concepts, blocks or modules are extremely important because they are what enable us to write top–down, structured programs.

To summarize, first a main program made up of references to modules is written. Next, each module is written, with care taken to ensure proper linkages with the main program. Then, each module is tested for correctness before the entire program is tested.

Top–Down Design Techniques and Tools

To implement a top–down design, we can use various techniques and tools, including hierarchy charts and input/processing/output (IPO) tables. **Hierarchy charts** graphically show the subdivision of the problem into smaller and smaller pieces until a program can be written to implement each piece of the package. As each module is subdivided further, the additional modules are added to the hierarchy chart. For example, Figure TD-2 shows the first-level hierarchy chart for solving the quiz score averaging problem.

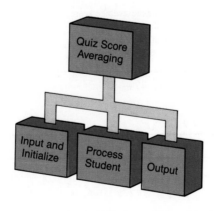

Figure TD-2 contains a module to input, a module to process students, and a module to output the class average. Obviously, we will need to divide the student processing module further.

For each module in the hierarchy chart, it is often useful to develop an **input/process/output (IPO) table,** showing the input to the module, the processing in the module, and the output from the module. Figures TD-3a, 3b, and 3c show the IPO charts for each of the modules in Figure TD-2.

Stepwise Refinement

Now that we have the first-level design worked out, we need to address the details of that design through stepwise refinement of the top-level logic. For the quiz score averaging problem, this involves working out the details of the student processing module that were not handled in the top-level design: entering and outputting each student's name and five quiz scores; averaging those scores; outputting the quiz average; checking whether the average is less than 60; and, if it is, showing a message that the student is failing. Also, since we want to compute the class average, we need to keep a running total of the average quiz scores.

The second-level hierarchy chart to represent this algorithm is shown as Figure TD-4. We have broken out the main steps into their own modules; now each module can be written in computer language. For each submodule, IPO charts would be used to determine the input, processing, and output.

FIGURE TD-3a
IPO Chart for Input Module

Input	Processing	Output
Number of students	Sum of averages $= 0$	Sum of averages

FIGURE TD-3b
IPO Chart for Student Processing Module

Input	Processing	Output
Student name	Compute average score	Name and quiz scores
Quiz scores	Failing decision	Average quiz score
Sum of averages	Add average to sum of averages	Failing message
		Sum of averages

FIGURE TD-3c
IPO Chart for Output Module

Input	Processing	Output
Number of students	Class average	Class average
Sum of averages		

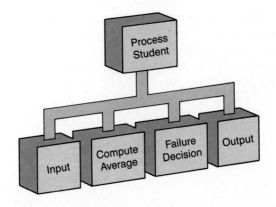

Implementation of Top–Down Design

The implementation of top–down design in a computer language depends to a large extent on the language, but all languages have a means to allow the programmer to modularize the program. In BASIC, for example, this is handled via GOSUBs. In Pascal it is done through procedures. In any case, the idea is the same: Put as much of the detail as possible in various modules, which are referred to by the main program or by other modules.

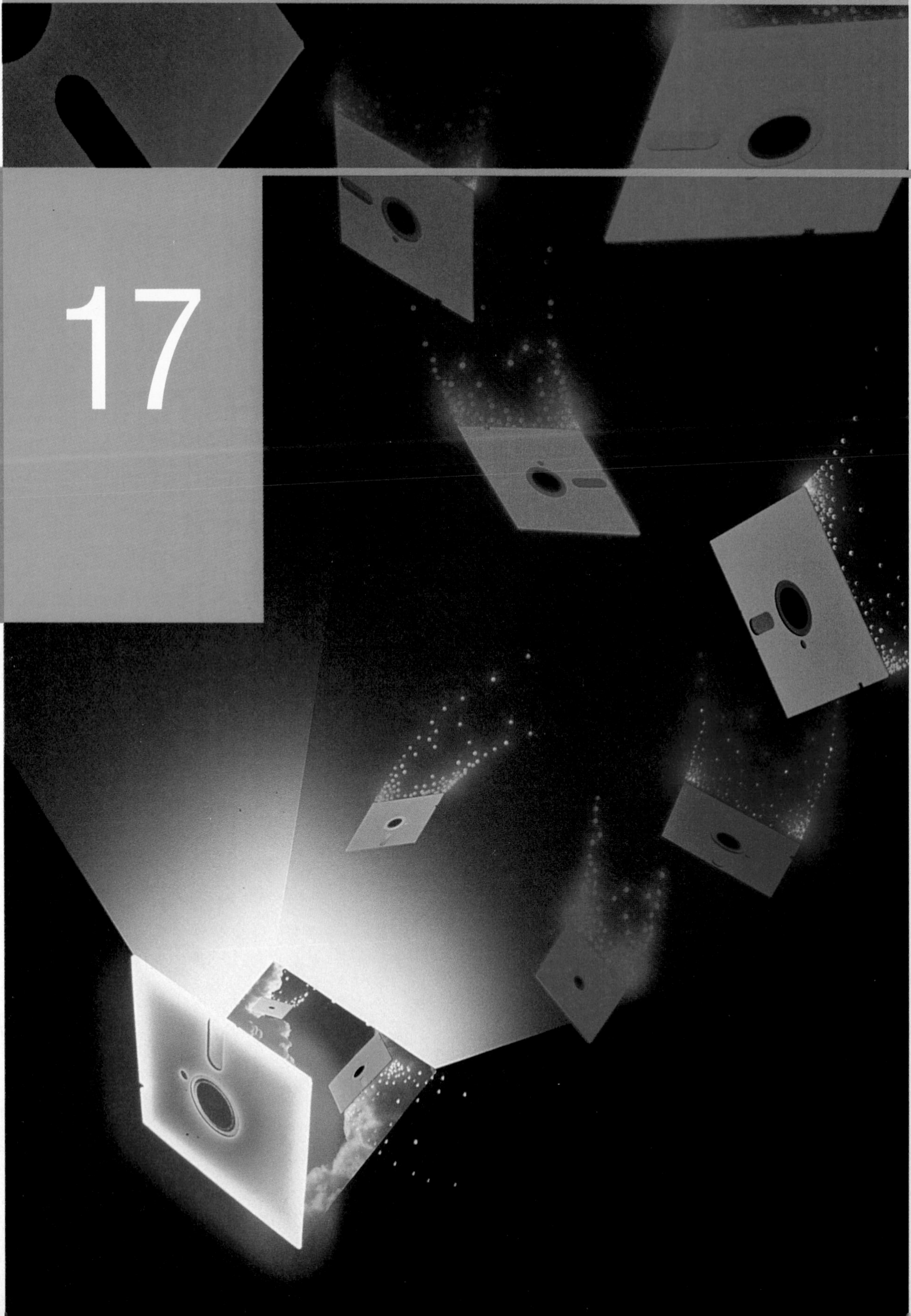

17

A Survey of
Computer Languages

Currently, the most common way to give instructions to a computer is through one of many computer languages. In this chapter we will discuss why computer languages are needed and how they may be classified—as general or special purpose, high or low level, compiled or interpreted, procedural or nonprocedural. FORTRAN, COBOL, BASIC, Pascal, C, and the dBASE language will be examined in some detail and an example of each will be shown. Several other languages will be discussed in less detail. We will also explore fourth-generation languages and the concepts of natural languages and artificial intelligence.

STUDY OBJECTIVES

After reading this chapter, you should be able to

- understand the need for computer languages for communication with computers;
- discuss the difference between a high-level language and a low-level language;
- differentiate between a compiled language and an interpreted language;
- understand the difference between procedural languages and nonprocedural languages;
- recognize programs written in FORTRAN, COBOL, BASIC, Pascal, C, and dBASE;
- list and discuss various other computer languages;
- discuss fourth-generation and natural languages and artificial intelligence.

TOOLS OF THE TRADE

Just as carpenters need tools to build a house, programmers need tools to build an information system. The difference is that carpenters' tools are of a physical nature, while programmers' tools are computer languages. And just as carpenters select a particular tool to do a particular job on the house, programmers select the computer language they will use based on the type of program to be written. The question is, How do programmers choose the necessary language for an application? There are more programming languages available today than most people could learn in a lifetime, so programmers need some rules to follow in selecting a language for a particular task. This selection process can be divided into three steps: (1) determine the application to be developed, (2) identify the features the language must have in order to deal with that application, and (3) consider the practical ramifications of choosing a particular language.

In characterizing the application being developed, a programmer should consider the size and type of application and how close to the level of the machine the language must be. One language may be great for handling very large business applications but useless for controlling a machine on a second-by-second basis. Similarly, one language may be good for doing scientific computations but not very good for producing multicolor graphics.

In choosing a language to meet the needs of the application, it is best first to list the features the application requires. These can be used to rate each available language, resulting in a short list of languages from which one may be chosen. Features might include the class of problems for which the language was designed, the clarity of the language syntax (grammar), the types of data that are supported, and the ease with which a program can be moved between machines.

After the programmer develops a short list of potential languages by comparing language characteristics to the features required by the application, the last step is to consider practical questions like how much support the language requires, whether the language is available or will have to be purchased, and how much knowledge of the language the programmer already has. Once these questions are answered, the list of languages will probably have been whittled down to only one or two choices.

Source: Gary Elfring, "Choosing a Programming Language," *Byte,* June 1985, pp. 235–240.

THE NEED FOR COMPUTER LANGUAGES

One of the first complaints heard from new users of computers has to do with learning a computer language. In most cases, a novice user is uncomfortable with having to learn a new grammar and syntax just to be able to give the computer the simplest of instructions. From previous chapters, we know that we can use computer packages to solve problems on the computer without knowing a computer language. However, if (as discussed in the box) a user needs to create a computer application for which software currently does not exist, a computer language must be chosen and learned.

Why not just give the computer commands in English as they do in the science fiction movies? To use English or any other natural language is the objective of much work that we will discuss at the end of this chapter. But for the time being one of a wide variety of computer languages must be used to communicate with the computer. English cannot be used because it offers too much ambiguity for the computer to handle. Many words in English have multiple meanings that depend upon the context in which they are used. For example, the computer would have trouble with the two commands "Choose the item on the right side" and "Do this right away." In the first case, the word *right* refers to a physical location; in the second case, the same word means "immediately." In fact, there are at least 21 meanings to the word *right* listed in an unabridged dictionary.

Because the human brain is such an amazing computer, it can decipher the appropriate meaning of a word based on the context in which it is used, but electronic computers have nothing nearly that sophisticated. Consequently, we need to use computer languages that have very restricted vocabularies and specific grammars that allow little or no possibility that the computer might misinterpret them. Because of their restricted vocabularies and definite grammatical forms, computer languages are much easier to learn than foreign languages once the hurdle of thinking logically has been cleared.

Why So Many Computer Languages?

A second question that new computer users often ask is, Why are there so many languages? There are over 200 computer languages available for use on mainframes, minicomputers, and personal computers; some even have specific dialects that depend on the type of computer being used. These languages go by such names as SLAM, dBASE, C, COBOL, Pascal, Natural, and BASIC. Some are **special-purpose languages,** developed to handle a specific task. For example, SLAM (for Simulation Language for Alternative Modelling) has been specifically designed to enable practitioners and researchers to use the computer to simulate economic or physical conditions. On the other hand, **general-purpose languages** are used to perform tasks ranging from computing payrolls to computing satellite orbits.

There are multiple languages for the same reason that a carpenter has more tools than just a hammer and a saw. While it might be possible to build a house with just these two tools, it would be easier and more efficient to use a full range of tools. Similarly, while it might be possible to write all programs in the same language, multiple languages allow us to use the most efficient language for each different programming problem. Some are better for scientific problems, some for business applications, some for working with lists, some for working with textual material. Still others were developed to be easy to learn for educational purposes. The fact that a particular language is slanted toward a particular type of problem means that it will work easily and efficiently for that problem. We cannot say that one computer language is better than all others, any more than we can say that English is better than all other languages. As discussed in the box at the beginning of this chapter, choosing the "right" language to use in writing a program is a selection process that is every bit as complicated as selecting a college or university.

The one thing that is true about computer languages but is often not true about human languages is that once you have learned a computer language, it is much easier to learn any other computer language. It does not matter which computer language you learn first; it still will be easier to pick up other languages quickly.

Classifying Languages

"Special purpose" and "general purpose" form one area of classification for computer languages, but the languages can also be classified as high level or low level, compiled or interpreted, and procedural or nonprocedural.

High-Level versus Low-Level Languages If you recall from previous discussions, a computer actually works with instructions in a binary form. While it is possible to program at this level using a so-called **low-level language,** it is an extremely tedious task. On the other hand, languages such as BASIC, which use English-like instructions that cause the computer to carry out a series of binary commands, are called **high-level languages.** They are so called because they are at the level of the programmer rather than at the level of the machine. Unless you plan to become an expert in using the computer, you will be using a high-level language for your programming.

Compiled versus Interpreted Languages As we said in Chapter 16, a computer cannot use high-level language unless another program translates the high-level language into machine language. The translation program must perform the following steps:

- Analyze the vocabulary of the high-level language.
- Check the syntax (grammar) of the program.
- Relate the names used by the programmer for various quantities to storage locations in the computer.
- Find the operations that are called for in a library of such operations.
- Generate the appropriate machine language code.

There are two methods of translating languages. If the instructions are translated one at a time as they are executed, this is an **interpreted language**. If the program is translated as a unit to form a complete machine language program that can be executed, this is a **compiled language.** An interpreted language has the advantage of alerting users to errors in statements when the statement is executed. It also allows the user to test a single statement or a group of statements before incorporating it in the program. The disadvantage of an interpreted language is that it executes much more slowly than a compiled language, because it must interpret anew each statement each time it comes across the statement in the execution of the program. The interpretation process is shown in Figure 17-1.

In a compiled-language translation, the entire program is entered before the computer attempts to translate any part of it. Once the entire high-level program is entered, it is called the **source program.** When it is compiled into a machine-language program, its machine-language form is referred to as the

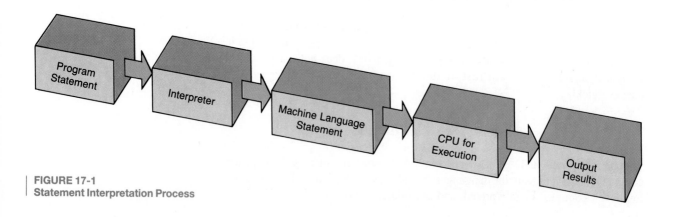

FIGURE 17-1
Statement Interpretation Process

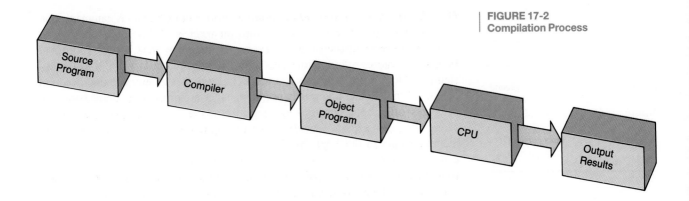

FIGURE 17-2
Compilation Process

object code. An advantage of compilation over interpretation is that a compiled program will run faster than an interpreted program once all errors have been found and corrected. However, no syntax and vocabulary errors can be found until the entire program has been entered and an attempt is made to compile it into object code. Figure 17-2 shows the compilation process.

Once the source code has been converted into object code, it must be linked to all sorts of small programs that are needed to carry out the instructions in the program. The linkage process is handled by a program known as the **link-editor,** which locates all the small, standard-procedure programs that are stored as **library routines** and links them with the object code. An example of a library routine is the task of finding a square root. This process has been preprogrammed; is kept in secondary storage, entirely separate from the program at hand; and is available to any user who needs it. The compile–link–execute process is shown in Figure 17-3.

Most high-level languages are compiled rather than interpreted. BASIC is the major exception, and there are even versions of BASIC—those available for personal computers—that can be compiled, resulting in a faster-running version of the basic program and the ability to obtain an object code. For commercial purposes, it is sometimes advantageous to sell not the source code but the object code of a package, so that it cannot be changed or copied.

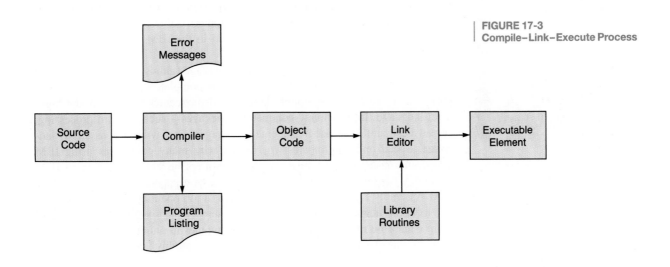

FIGURE 17-3
Compile–Link–Execute Process

TABLE 17-1
Language Classifications

Classification	Options
Purpose	Special or general
Level	High or low
Translation	Compiled or interpreted
Procedure	Procedural or nonprocedural

Procedural Languages versus Nonprocedural Languages   A language that requires the program to give instructions on what should be done and how it should be done is a **procedural language.** On the other hand, a **nonprocedural language** requires only that the user define the desired task, without a step-by-step procedure. Currently, only a few special packages qualify as nonprocedural languages; most other commonly used languages are procedural. Some data base packages offer nonprocedural languages as a means of finding information. Many computer experts consider HyperCard, the popular information management software for the Apple Macintosh, a nonprocedural language, because you can create screens and actions without worrying about developing a complete train of logic. It lets users build data bases that incorporate the Macintosh graphical user interface. HyperCard calls a file of records a "stack" (of cards), and a record is like a Rolodex card on screen. Users can customize the record with graphic images and button icons that, when clicked with a mouse, perform various data base operations.

Table 17-1 summarizes the computer language classifications we have just discussed. As we consider each language in this chapter, we comment on whether it is a compiled or an interpreted language. All languages discussed in this chapter—except machine language and assembly language—are high-level languages, all are procedural languages, and most are general-purpose languages.

LOW-LEVEL COMPUTER LANGUAGES

There are two types of low-level computer languages—**machine language** and **assembly language.** Machine language can be expressed in binary, octal, or hexadecimal numbers, and assembly language is made up of abbreviations of commands. When machine language is used, the programmer uses the binary number system or a hexadecimal equivalent to specify everything that the computer must know. With assembly language, the programmer does not use numbers for instructions. He or she still works close to the computer's level of communication, but a translation program called an **assembler** handles many tedious chores associated with using machine language.

Because low-level languages are so close to the machine, the specific language used depends on the type of computer or chip. For example, the machine or assembly language for an IBM mainframe is quite different from that for a UNIVAC computer. Similarly, the assembly language for the Motorola 68000 series of chips used in Apple Macintosh computers is different from the language used for the Intel 80xxx series of chips used in the IBM PS/2 and IBM compatible computers.

An advantage of using an assembly language (almost no one bothers with machine languages today) is that the user has complete control over the computer's inner workings. Assembly language also executes faster than any high-level language. In fact, many commercial packages—such as word processing, spreadsheet, and data base management packages—are written in assembly language. Speed and control are two reasons why many companies using IBM mainframe computers require that programmers be knowledgeable in IBM Assembly Language. (Check any metropolitan newspaper. Along with COBOL, IBM Assembly Language is often mentioned in job openings for programmers.)

On the negative side, because each assembly language is different, a program cannot be moved from one type of computer to another. An entirely new program must be written in the new computer's assembly language. Writing pro-

> **Assembly language programming is an extravagant waste of human talent and should be avoided whenever possible.**
>
> *Peter Norton, developer of the Norton Utilities software package*
>
> Quoted in "PC Languages: The Living and the Dead," *PC Magazine,* September 1983, pp. 99–101.

PUTTING THE DEAD SEA SCROLLS TOGETHER WITH HYPERCARD

Most Biblical scholars agree that the Dead Sea Scrolls are the most valuable biblical find of the century. A shepherd found the scrolls in 1947 in a cave near Jerusalem. The badly disintegrated scrolls were given to a group of biblical scholars to classify, translate, and publish. More than 40 years later, however, the group had succeeded in publishing only about one-third of the material, leaving many scholars without access to the scrolls extremely unhappy.

The researchers who controlled the scrolls released some of their research data, including a concordance of about 50,000 entries on handwritten cards. Each card contains a word from the scrolls; the fragment number, column number, and line number of the scroll on which the word appears; and the words that precede and follow the word. With this information, Martin Abegg, a researcher at Hebrew Union College in Cincinnati, created virtually complete versions of the scrolls.

He accomplished this by entering the information about each word into a data base program. He then sorted the words by scroll, fragment, and line number into a text document. Next, he imported the document into HyperCard, which "pasted" together strings of three-word segments, while deleting duplicate words. Finally, he exported the HyperCard results to a word processing package for formatting. Abegg succeeded in creating a version of the original scroll text that researchers could use to study the early first century A.D. (the period of history following the crucifixion of Jesus). When the text of the scrolls was finally released, Abegg's version was found to be very accurate.

Source: Penn Jillette, " 'Computer Expert' Cracks Dead Sea Scrolls," *PC Computing*, December 1991, p. 430, and interview with Martin Abegg.

---

grams in assembly language usually takes much longer than writing in a high-level language, because, in assembly language, the programmer must address specifically many operations that a high-level language covers automatically.

Tables 17-2 and 17-3 show machine language and assembly language programs, respectively, for the summation of the numbers from 1 to 100. The languages used here are for the 16-bit Intel 8086 chip. This chip is compatible with the Intel 80286, 80386, and i486 chips, so these programs will run on those chips.

HIGH-LEVEL COMPUTER LANGUAGES

With the advent of high-level languages and compilers, many people who did not understand the details of the computer could write programs. The first high-level language, FORTRAN, was introduced in 1956. Since then, numerous high-

TABLE 17-2
Intel 8086 Machine-Language Program

Step	Machine-Language Statement			
1	10111000	00000000	00000000	Load total register with 0
2	10111001	00000000	01100100	Load current register with 100
3	00000001	11001000		Add current register to total register
4	01001001			Subtract 1 from current register
5	01110101	11111011		If current register is not 0, then go back to step 3

level languages have been introduced, either as general-purpose or as special-purpose languages. In this section, we discuss in detail six popular high-level languages—FORTRAN, COBOL, BASIC, Pascal, C, and dBASE—in order of their introduction to general use.

As an example of each language, we will demonstrate a program similar to that discussed in Chapter 16. This program will find average quiz scores for some number of students by using the following procedure:

Step 1: Input the number of students.
Step 2: For each student, input five quiz scores and compute the average of these five scores.
Step 3: Output the student's name and quiz average.
Step 4: If the student's average is less than 60, print a message that the student is failing.
Step 5: Keep a running sum of the average scores.
Step 6: When all student scores have been processed, compute the class average by dividing the sum of student averages by the number of students in the class.

We also discuss other special-purpose languages and languages that are not as popular as the six mentioned earlier.

FORTRAN

The oldest high-level language, FORTRAN, was originally developed by an IBM-sponsored committee headed by John Backus. FORTRAN was designed to meet the needs of users in the scientific, mathematical, and engineering community who want to write programs without learning an assembly language. In

TABLE 17-3
Intel 8086 Assembly-Language Program

	Symbolic Instructions	Remarks
	MOV AX,0	;LOAD TOTAL WITH 0
	MOV CX,100	;LOAD CURRENT WITH 100
LP:	ADD AX,CX	;ADD CURRENT TO TOTAL
	DEC CX	;DECREASE CURRENT BY 1
	JNZ LP	;JUMP IF CURRENT NOT 0

fact, the acronym FORTRAN comes from the name FORmula TRANslator. FORTRAN can easily convert a user's equation or formula into a statement that the computer can execute. First released in 1956 as FORTRAN I, FORTRAN has been standardized twice by the American National Standards Institute (ANSI). ANSI is the scientific body that decides which version of a language is the standard. In 1966, the first standard version was FORTRAN IV, or FORTRAN 66; the 1978 version is FORTRAN 77. The remainder of this discussion concerns the latest version of FORTRAN, because it is available on all mainframes and is much more versatile than earlier versions. Personal computer software vendors have also released complete versions of FORTRAN 77.

FORTRAN is a compiled language. In other words, the entire program is entered before any syntax or vocabulary mistakes can be detected. On the other hand, once compiled and debugged, FORTRAN is one of the fastest (if not *the* fastest) of the high-level languages for executing program instructions.

FORTRAN was often criticized as a language that could not handle textual material and that was difficult to use when data were input from a terminal. These criticisms were true of FORTRAN's early versions. With FORTRAN 77, however, the programmer can write programs that manipulate textual material as well as carry out scientific and mathematical calculations. This version of the language also simplified data entry from a terminal.

As an example of how FORTRAN converts a formula into a program statement, consider the computation of the value of y, where $y = 5x^2 + x/8 - 10$. In FORTRAN, this equation is

$$Y = 5*X**2 + X/8 - 10$$

where * means multiplication, ** means raised to the power of, + indicates addition, / indicates division, and − means subtraction.

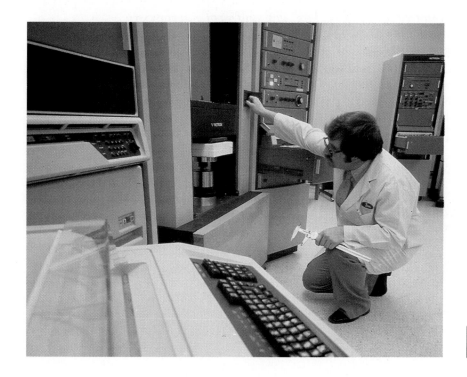

FORTRAN is especially well suited for scientific and engineering applications.

Figure 17-4 shows a FORTRAN program for computing quiz score averages for several students and the class average. Several statements in this program are noteworthy. First, statements beginning with an asterisk (*) are **comment statements** that explain the computer statements. This **documentation** is useful for explaining the program logic. The three statements that begin with INTEGER, CHARACTER, and REAL declare that the memory location names—usually referred to as **variables**—are whole numbers, characters, and decimal numbers, respectively. The DO 100 statement repeats the student input loop and counts the number of repetitions. The 100 CONTINUE statement has a numeric **label** and indicates the end of the body of the loop.

COBOL

FORTRAN I clearly was not adequate for the data processing needs of business and government. To remedy this situation, a group of computer users from business, government, and academia met with representatives of the computer industry in 1959 to discuss their computing needs. This group, CODASYL (Conference on Data Systems Languages), developed COBOL (COmmon Business Oriented Language). The "common" in COBOL refers to the ability to run the language on many different computers. Since its introduction in 1960, more software has been written in COBOL than in any other computer language, with close to *$1 trillion* worth of COBOL software now in existence.

COBOL is often used for business applications on mainframes because the language can organize and manipulate large amounts of data. Approximately one-half of the language is dedicated to file handling like that in the data base management packages. In addition to superior file-handling capabilities, COBOL

FIGURE 17-4
FORTRAN Program to Compute Quiz Score Averages

```
*  PROGRAM TO COMPUTE QUIZ AVERAGE FOR MULTIPLE STUDENTS
        INTEGER NUMSTU
        CHARACTER*30 NAME
        REAL SCORE1,SCORE2,SCORE3,SCORE4,SCORE5,QAVE,CAVE,TOTAL,CTOTAL
        CTOTAL = 0
        READ *,NUMSTU
        DO 100 I = 1, NUMSTU
           READ *,NAME,SCORE1,SCORE2,SCORE3,SCORE4,SCORE5
           TOTAL = SCORE1 + SCORE2 + SCORE3 + SCORE4 + SCORE5
           QAVE = TOTAL/5,
           PRINT *,'QUIZ AVERAGE FOR: ',NAME,' IS', QAVE
*  READ NAME AND QUIZ SCORES, TOTAL SCORES AND FIND AVERAGE
           IF(QAVE,LT,60,) THEN
              PRINT *,'STUDENT HAS FAILED'
           ENDIF
*  CHECK TO SEE IF STUDENT IS FAILING
           CTOTAL = CTOTAL + QAVE
100     CONTINUE
        CAVE = CTOTAL/NUMSTU
        PRINT *,'CLASS AVERAGE IS ',CAVE
*  COMPUTE AND OUTPUT CLASS AVERAGE
        END
```

has a sort module, which reorganizes data files. COBOL also provides arithmetic commands for addition, subtraction, multiplication, and so on.

COBOL programs are strikingly similar to English prose. This similarity was built into the language on purpose. A nonprogrammer businessperson can pick up a COBOL program and at least understand its purpose, if not all of the logic. For example, the following program segment clearly computes the gross pay for an hourly employee using either a regular-time or an overtime computation.

```
IF EMPLOYEE-HOURS ARE GREATER THAN 40
   PERFORM REGULAR-TIME-GROSS-PAY-ROUTINE,
ELSE
   PERFORM OVERTIME-GROSS-PAY-ROUTINE.
```

The use of English-like vocabulary and syntax makes a program easier to maintain. Software maintenance is an important part of a programmer's job. **Maintenance** includes fixing bugs that are discovered during program execution, adding features to the program, altering parts of the program, and performing any other activities to keep the program responsive to current needs. Maintenance of previously written programs uses an estimated 70 percent of a programmer's time. Because COBOL is easy to understand, it is also easy to maintain. COBOL is essentially a **self-documenting language,** because the user does not need comments to explain what the program is doing.

COBOL has been criticized for its wordy and repetitive nature and for the fact that in COBOL it is difficult to write a short program. These criticisms relate to the same features that are stated as advantages. COBOL was designed as a

Because of its file-handling capabilities, COBOL is the most popular computer language in business.

business language, not a programming language, and as such is not meant for all types of general programming. The newest form of COBOL, COBOL II, supports structured programming and top–down design with several new statements.

COBOL is a compiled language. Figure 17-5 shows a portion of a COBOL program for the same example shown in the FORTRAN program in Figure 17-4. Only a portion of the program is shown, because the entire program would take several pages.

BASIC

Shortly after the introduction of FORTRAN and COBOL, two professors at Dartmouth College, John Kemeny and Thomas Kurtz, devised a computer language for their students that would be easy to learn yet would retain the formula translation characteristics of FORTRAN. Kemeny and Kurtz called their new

```
PROCEDURE DIVISION.

MAIN-ROUTINE.
    PERFORM OPENING-ROUTINE
    PERFORM PROCESS-ROUTINE UNTIL STUD-ACCUM = NUM-STUDS
    STOP RUN.

OPENING-ROUTINE.
    DISPLAY " " ERASE
    DISPLAY "Please enter the number of students"
    ACCEPT NUM-STUDS, NO BEEP, TAB
    ACCEPT DUMMY, NO BEEP.

PROCESS-ROUTINE.
    MOVE 0 TO SCORE-ACCUM
    MOVE 0 TO SUM-SCORES
    DISPLAY "Please enter the name of the student . . ."
    ACCEPT STUD-NAME, NO BEEP
    PERFORM UNTIL SCORE-ACCUM = 5
       DISPLAY "Please enter a score . . ."
       ACCEPT SCORE, NO BEEP, TAB
       ADD SCORE TO SUM-SCORES
       ADD 1 TO SCORE-ACCUM
    END-PERFORM
    DIVIDE SUM-SCORES BY 5 GIVING AVG-SCORES-W
    MOVE AVG-SCORES-W TO AVG-SCORES-D
    DISPLAY STUD-NAME, "AVERAGE:", AVG-SCORES-D
      IF AVG-SCORES-W < 60
         DISPLAY "Student is failing."
      END-IF
    ACCEPT DUMMY, NO BEEP
    ADD 1 TO STUD-ACCUM.
    END.
```

FIGURE 17-5
Position of COBOL Program to
Compute Quiz Score Averages

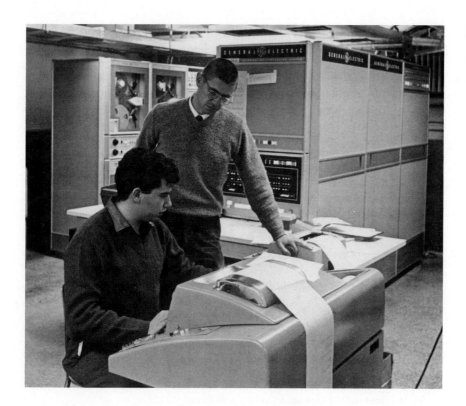

language BASIC (Beginner's All-purpose Symbolic Instruction Code). It was first used in 1964.

BASIC was a simple language, in which programs could be written with as few as seven statement types. An interpreted language, BASIC was easy for students to use because errors were signaled to the user during execution. For ease of use and simplicity, BASIC was chosen by early personal computer manufacturers. The earliest Apple and Radio Shack computers always included BASIC on cassette or disk.

The current versions of BASIC found on personal computers are far different from the simple language that Kemeny and Kurtz originally developed. Many new commands have transformed the language from a beginner's instructional language into one that can be used to write commercial software. Such advanced commands as PEEK and POKE are used either to check the contents of a single memory location or to change those contents.

Even with the new commands, BASIC is an interpreted language that is highly interactive. Programs in BASIC are easy to write and debug. A user can write one or more statements of a BASIC program and try them out before incorporating them into the program. For these reasons, BASIC is often chosen as a first computer language. However, because BASIC is interpreted, it runs much more slowly than compiled languages. (Compiled versions of the language are now available if speed is important—such as in commercial software.)

Another criticism of BASIC for personal computers—the lack of standardization of the language—has been met by the almost universal availability of Microsoft BASIC for personal computers. This language is available for the IBM PS/2 and IBM compatible computers and for the Apple Macintosh series of computers. Apple uses a different version of BASIC for its Apple II series

> ## I was appalled by [the] C [language]. BASIC is much more legible.
>
> *Mark Rossow, professor of civil engineering at Southern Illinois University*
>
> Quoted in "BASIC: Still the Solution for Non-Programmers," *PC Week*, November 4, 1991, p. 129.

BASIC AND THE FIRST PC

Why is BASIC synonymous with personal computers today? It started in the early 1970s, when two Seattle teenagers named Bill Gates and Paul Allen worked for a computer firm. Gates and Allen were among the first hackers who spent almost every waking hour figuring out how mainframe and minicomputer operating systems worked. They had convinced a Seattle computer firm to let them work on the company's PDP-10 minicomputer to solve the company's systems problems. Their success in this project made a name for them.

Two years later, after both men had tried college, they read about the first personal computer—the Altair. The Altair, which used an Intel 8080 chip, was built by a firm called MITS. Gates and Allen called MITS and proposed to develop a version of BASIC that would run on the Altair personal computer. Because they did not have an Altair computer, Allen used that computer's specifications to develop a simulated Altair on the PDP minicomputer. With only the simulated Altair, the two developed a form of BASIC that they thought would work on the real computer. Less than two months after the original contact with MITS, the software was finished, and Gates and Allen were on a plane to Albuquerque to demonstrate their Altair BASIC for MITS. In true storybook fashion, the BASIC worked the first time it was loaded on the Altair, even though Gates and Allen had never seen one before.

After this success, Gates and Allen formed a company called Microsoft to make their version of BASIC—the rest is history. Today, Microsoft BASIC is an industry standard, and the MS-DOS operating system that Microsoft developed for the IBM PC is also an industry standard for IBM compatible PCs. Who would believe that the company's founders, Bill Gates and Paul Allen, are still only in their thirties?

Source: Paul Somerson, "In Defense of BASIC," *PC Magazine,* September 1983, p. 331.

Bill Gates and Paul Allen are the founders of Microsoft and the developers of the first BASIC for personal computers.

```
110 REM STUDENTS IN THE CLASS FOR AN UNKNOWN NUMBER OF STUDENTS
200 LIST.AVERAGES = 0
300 PRINT "LISTING OF STUDENT NAMES AND QUIZ SCORES"
600 INPUT "ENTER NAME AND SCORES: ";STUDENT$,SCORE1,SCORE2, SCORE3,SCORE4,SCORE5
610 REM ENTER DATA FOR FIRST STUDENT
700 WHILE STUDENT$ <> "ZZZZZ"
800    PRINT "STUDENT'S NAME:";STUDENT$
900    PRINT "STUDENT'S SCORES:";SCORE1;SCORE2;SCORE3;SCORE4;SCORE5
1000   AVERAGE = (SCORE1+SCORE2+SCORE3+SCORE4+SCORE5)/5
1100   PRINT "STUDENT'S AVERAGE SCORE IS: ";AVERAGE
1200   IF AVERAGE < 60 THEN PRINT "STUDENT IS FAILING" ELSE PRINT "STUDENT IS PA
SSING"
1300   SUM.AVERAGES = SUM.AVERAGES + AVERAGE
1400   NUMBER = NUMBER + 1 'COUNT STUDENTS
1500   INPUT "ENTER NAME AND SCORES: ";STUDENT$,SCORE1,SCORE2,SCORE3,SCORE4,SCOR
E5
1600 WEND
1610 'ENTER DATA FOR NEXT STUDENT
1700 IF NUMBER > 0 THEN CLASS.AVERAGE =SUM.AVERAGES/NUMBER ELSE PRINT "NO  STUDE
NTS"
1800 IF NUMBER > 0 THEN PRINT "CLASS AVERAGE IS : ";CLASS.AVERAGE
1900 END
Ok

1LIST  2RUN←  3LOAD"  4SAVE"  5CONT←  6 "LPT1 7TRON←  8TROFF← 9KEY    0SCREEN
```

BASIC programs are among the easiest to write and debug.

of computers, which presents problems in the conversion of BASIC programs from Apple II-type computers to IBM compatible or Apple Macintosh computers. New versions of BASIC—with such names as Quick Basic, Turbo Basic, and True Basic—offer more features than the now standard Microsoft BASIC yet can still run programs written in the original language. These features include compiling programs, not requiring line numbers, and top–down design tools. Microsoft also included an interpreted version of Quick BASIC, called QBASIC, in MS-DOS 5.0.

PC users' almost universal understanding of BASIC is evidenced in the results of a survey by the Boston Computing Society: 80 percent of its members use some form of BASIC. The results of this survey are shown as Figure 17-6. Also, Microsoft Corp. estimates that there are 4 to 6 million BASIC users.

Figure 17-7 contains a Microsoft BASIC version of the quiz score averaging program. Note that this BASIC program has **line numbers,** which are used for identification. Line numbers can also be quite useful during the interpretation and debugging process. In BASIC, the REM statement can be used to give information about any program statement. Also, the apostrophe (') is used to begin a comment on the same line as the statement it references.

Pascal

In 1971, a Swiss computer scientist named Niklaus Wirth introduced a teaching language that he called Pascal, after the French mathematician. Pascal is now a popular language for teaching introductory computer science. This popularity is due to the fact that Pascal *must* be written in a manner that meets accepted programming standards. As a result, students never learn to write poorly designed programs.

FIGURE 17-6
Programming Languages Used

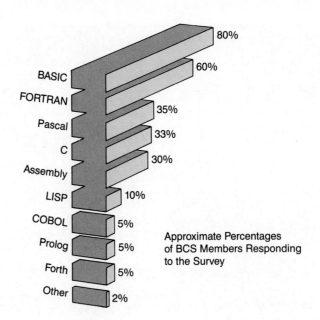

BASIC 80%
FORTRAN 60%
Pascal 35%
C 33%
Assembly 30%
LISP 10%
COBOL 5%
Prolog 5%
Forth 5%
Other 2%

Approximate Percentages
of BCS Members Responding
to the Survey

Pascal takes a clean, block-structure approach to programming, making the language easy to learn and use. Pascal is also a **strongly typed language,** which means that all variable names must be declared at the beginning of the program. The computer must be told what each variable name represents—whole numbers, decimal numbers, text, and so on. Because of this approach, the user must think through the program before it is written. In comparison, BASIC and FORTRAN are **weakly typed languages** that do not require a declaration of variable types. All Pascal programs follow the order shown here:

```
PROGRAM   program name;
VAR
            variable declarations
BEGIN
            program logic
END.
```

FIGURE 17-7
BASIC Program to Compute Quiz
Score Averages

```
100 REM THIS PROGRAM INPUTS QUIZ SCORES AND FINDS THE AVERAGE SCORE FOR
ALL STUDENTS IN THE CLASS, IT ALSO COMPUTES THE CLASS AVERAGE.
200 INPUT "ENTER NUMBER OF STUDENTS IN CLASS: ";NUMBER
300 CLASSTOTAL = 0 `INITIALIZE CLASS TOTAL TO ZERO
400 FOR I = 1 TO NUMBER `REPEAT THE FOLLOWING FOR EACH STUDENT
500    INPUT "NAME AND SCORES: "; STUDENT$,SCORE1,SCORE2,SCORE3,SCORE4,SCORE5
600    AVERAGE = (SCORE1+SCORE2+SCORE3+SCORE4+SCORE5)/5 'FIND AVERAGE SCORE
700    PRINT "STUDENT'S NAME: ";STUDENT$
800    PRINT "STUDENT'S AVERAGE: ";AVERAGE
900    IF AVERAGE < 60 THEN PRINT "STUDENT IS FAILING" `CHECK AVERAGE
1000   CLASSTOTAL = CLASSTOTAL+AVERAGE `ADD STUDENT AVERAGE TO CLASS TOTAL
1100 NEXT I
1200 CLASSAVERAGE = CLASSTOTAL/NUMBER `COMPUTE CLASS AVERAGE
1300 PRINT "CLASS AVERAGE = ";CLASSAVERAGE
1400 END.
```

ANALYZING STOCKS WITH BASIC

Many commercial PC software packages are written in Pascal or C, but it is still possible to write sophisticated software applications in BASIC. One such package is the Channel Trend Analysis program, which was written by Harry Gish to predict price changes in individual stocks. Using statistical methodology, the program tracks highs and lows of more than 4,000 stocks over a ten-year period. The program tries to find the range, or channel, in which a stock tends to remain. When a stock reaches the limit of its historical range, up or down, Gish's method assumes the stock price will move back toward the middle of its range. Users have found the methodology 85 percent accurate in predicting changes in stock prices.

Gish chose BASIC because its simplicity and flexibility make it easier to create and modify a program. This is important for the Channel Trend Analysis program, because it requires frequent modification: Whenever a stock's status changes, owing to a two for one split, for example, it is necessary to modify the progam to show the change. The program is also easy to use. A single menu accesses functions. A user can request information about a stock by entering its ticker symbol. The Channel Trend Analysis package costs at least $20,000 annually and can include weekly stock price updates. Approximately 100 financial institutions use the package, including the Star Bank Capital Management Company, which uses it in conjunction with other stock analysis software to track as many as 1,900 stocks for portfolios and market funds.

Source: Eamonn Sullivan, "BASIC Program Offers Financial Firms 10-Year Stock Analysis," *PC Week,* November 4, 1991, p. 129.

The development time in any other language [than BASIC] would just be too great.

Harry Gish, president of Channel Trends

Quoted in Eamonn Sullivan, "BASIC Program Offers Financial Firms 10-Year Stock Analysis," *PC Week,* November 4, 1991, p. 129.

Pascal programs must have a PROGRAM statement that names the program, a VAR statement that comes before the variable declarations, and a BEGIN statement that defines the beginning of the actual program logic. The program always ends with an END statement. Other BEGIN and END statements can define blocks of material within the main program.

Because of these advantages, Pascal is used for many purposes other than instruction. Commercial software is now available in Pascal, much of it written in the extremely popular Turbo Pascal from Borland International. With these additional uses of Pascal, the original language has expanded, and nonstandard forms of Pascal now exist. To remedy the need for extensions to Pascal, Wirth introduced a new language—Modula-2—that meets the needs of software developers. This new language is discussed in a later section.

Most versions of Pascal are compiled, but an interpreted, interactive version was released for the Apple Macintosh. The Macintosh version is much like BASIC in that parts of a program can be tested before they are incorporated into the main program. Figure 17-8 shows a Turbo Pascal version of the quiz score averaging program.

Note that the Pascal program allows both upper- and lowercase letters, whereas previous examples use only uppercase letters. The words in all upper-

These graphics were produced from a program written in Pascal.

case letters are **keywords,** which are part of the syntax of Pascal. The program statements after the keyword VAR are the variable declaration statements required in Pascal, and the FOR statement handles the counting loop.

Pascal also allows the names of the various quantities, such as student average and class average (variables), to be written out as in COBOL—compared with FORTRAN and some versions of BASIC, which restrict the number of letters in a name. Both characteristics make Pascal a self-documenting language. Self-documenting languages like COBOL and Pascal are easy to maintain.

FIGURE 17-8
Pascal Program to Compute Quiz
Score Averages

```
PROGRAM Average;
VAR
      Numberstudent,I,K: INTEGER;
      Studentaverage,Classaverage,Classtotal,Score1,Score2,Score3,Score4,
      Score5; Real;
      Studentname: String[20];
BEGIN
      READLN(Numberstudent);
      Classtotal :=0;
      FOR I := 1 TO Numberstudent DO
            BEGIN
                  READLN(Studentname);
                  READLN (Score1,Score2,Score3,Score4,Score5);
                  Studentaverage := (Score1+Score2+Score3+Score4+Score5)/5.;
                  WRITELN('Average for student named ',Studentname,' is '
                  ,Studentaverage);
                  IF Studentaverage < 60 THEN WRITELN('Student has failed');
                  Classtotal := Classtotal+Studentaverage;
            END
      Classaverage := Classtotal/Numberstudent;
      WRITELN('Class average is ',Classaverage);
END.
```

C

For writing operating systems, a favorite language of programmers is the C language. C was developed at Bell Labs in 1974 by Brian Kernighan and Dennis Ritchie. These two authors supposedly looked at all programming languages and chose the most desirable features of each. Like Pascal, C has a block structure. However, C differs from other high-level languages in the degree to which the computer can be controlled with the language. In a sense, C is a cross between a high-level language and an assembly language; some people refer to it as a *middle-level language.* A distinguishing feature of C is that it uses functions to perform most of its operations. **Functions** are short programs that are stored in a computer memory library, which may be accessed by the language as needed to perform specific tasks. Today, versions of C are available for all types of computers—from personal computers to CRAY-1 supercomputers.

The C language produces machine-language code that executes extremely fast, has greater control of the machine than any other language, and is easily portable. Every day more software is written in C, including much of the UNIX operating system used on computers of all sizes. Microsoft's popular Multiplan spreadsheet package is written in C. The IBM version of the HBJ software that accompanies this text is written in C for fast execution and portability.

The major criticism of the C language is that understanding a C program written by someone else can be difficult. In fact, some people have suggested that the language name stands for "Cryptic"! Critics also suggests that programs written in C should have one comment for each program statement to facilitate program maintenance. C was designed for systems programming, not for learning to program. However, with its power and speed, C is a popular language for advanced programming projects. Figure 17-9 shows the C version of the quiz score averaging program.

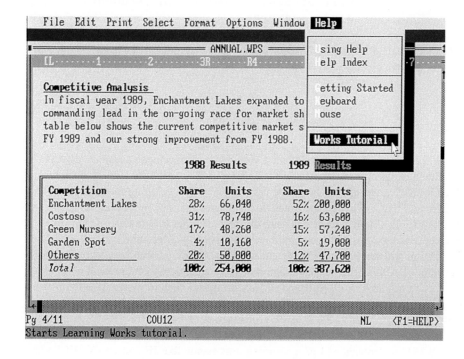

The popular integrated package Microsoft Works is written in the C computer language.

FIGURE 17-9
C Program to Compute Quiz
Score Averages

```c
*/
#include <stdio.h>
#define SCORES 5
main()
{
    char student[80];
    int number, scores[SCORES], count, classtotal = 0,
        cnt_score, average, sum, newline;
/* get number of students in class */
    printf("Enter number of students in class ");
    scanf("%d%c",&number,&newline);
/* for each student get the grades and average them */
    for(count=0; count < number; count++)
    {
        printf("Name : ");
        scanf("%80s",student);
        sum = 0;
        for(cnt_score=0;cnt_score < SCORES; cnt_score++)
        {
/* Most people don't start counting from 0 */
            printf("Score%d :",cnt_score+1);
            scanf("%d%c",&scores[cnt_score],&newline);
            sum += scores[cnt_score];
        }
        average = sum / SCORES;
        printf("Student's name: %s\n",student);
        printf("Student's average: %d\n",average);
        if(average < 60)
            printf("Student %s failed.\n",student);
        classtotal += average;
    }
/* Print the class average */
    printf("Class Average = %d\n", classtotal/number);
}
```

dBASE

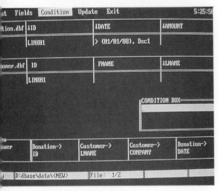

Sophisticated applications can be written in the dBASE language.

While most often thought of as a data base management package, dBASE in either of its current forms—dBASE III PLUS or dBASE IV—is also a very powerful programming language that is used for developing many applications. Created by C. Wayne Ratliff and first released in 1982 by Ashton-Tate, Inc., as dBASE II, this language has gone through various improvements. However, it has remained upwardly compatible—that is, programs written in dBASE II or III will still run on the more recent versions. Of the various languages discussed here, dBASE is the one language that is available only on personal computers.

Programs in dBASE are called **command files** to distinguish them from the actual data base files or other files used in working with the data base. Command files can be made up solely of a series of interactive dBASE commands like USE, LIST, and so on, or they can be a combination of the interactive dBASE commands and programming commands like IF and DO WHILE. The programming commands are much like those used in Pascal or BASIC and perform the same actions.

With dBASE, it is possible to create a data base file interactively and then to use a command file to work with, add to, or modify the file. In our quiz score averaging problem, the professor has created a data base file called QUIZZES that contains the student names and quiz scores. She will input this data base file to the command file, where each student's average will be computed and added to the data base. The command file will also compute the class average of all student quizzes.

dBASE has its own word processing type editor, so the user can create a command file from within dBASE and then execute the command file simply by typing DO plus the name of the command file. When executed from within dBASE, a command file is an interpreted program, but software is available that will compile a dBASE command file to make it run faster. Being able to compile a dBASE command file is essential when the applications involve very large data base files and command files made up of thousands of lines of code. Figure 17-10 shows a dBASE version of the quiz score averaging program. Note that the question mark (?) is used as a print command, the asterisk (*) and the double ampersand (&&) are used to denote comments, and the STORE TO and REPLACE commands are used to store or replace information in memory cells.

> **dBASE was different from programs like BASIC, C, FORTRAN, and COBOL in that a lot of dirty work had already been done.**
>
> *C. Wayne Ratliff, developer of dBASE*
>
> Quoted in Susan Lammers, *Programmers at Work* (Redmond, Wash.: Microsoft Press, 1986), p. 117.

OTHER HIGH-LEVEL LANGUAGES

In addition to the six languages just discussed, numerous other languages are available on mainframes, minicomputers, and personal computers. Some are

```
* DBASE PROGRAM TO COMPUTE QUIZ AVERAGE FOR MULTIPLE STUDENTS
SET TALK OFF   && TURN OFF CONVERSATIONAL DBASE
STORE 0 TO CTOTAL
STORE 0 TO NUMSTU
* INITIALIZE CLASS TOTAL AND NUMBER OF STUDENTS COUNTER
USE QUIZZES   && USE STUDENT QUIZ SCORE DATA BASE (QUIZZES.DBF)
DO WHILE .NOT. EOF()   &&CONTINUE UNTIL OUT OF RECORDS
*    FIND QUIZ AVERAGE FOR THIS STUDENT
     STORE SCORE1 + SCORE2 + SCORE3 + SCORE4 + SCORE5 TO TOTAL
     REPLACE QAVE WITH TOTAL/5
     ?"QUIZ AVERAGE FOR: "+NAME+ " IS ",QAVE
* CHECK TO SEE IF STUDENT HAS FAILED
     IF QAVE < 60
          ? "STUDENT HAS FAILED"
     ENDIF
* ADD QUIZ AVERAGE TO TOTAL AND ADD ONE TO NUMBER OF STUDENTS
     STORE CTOTAL + QAVE TO CTOTAL
     STORE NUMSTU + 1 TO NUMSTU
     SKIP &&JUMP TO NEXT RECORD
* END OF STUDENT RECORDS
ENDDO EOF
* COMPUTE AND OUTPUT CLASS AVERAGE
STORE CTOTAL/NUMSTU TO CAVE
? "CLASS AVERAGE IS ",CAVE
RETURN
```

FIGURE 17-10
dBASE Command File to Compute Quiz Score Averages

general-purpose languages, but most often they are specialized languages that make the job of communicating with the computer easier when a specific type of task must be accomplished. Once again, presentation of the languages will follow the chronological order of their introduction.

LISP

LISP (for LISt Processing) was developed in 1960, specifically for the processing of lists. It approaches everything—from sentences to mathematical formulas—as a list. LISP has been found to be very useful in the area of artificial intelligence, and was also the parent of the very popular educational language Logo (see p. 557).

PL/I

Following the introduction of FORTRAN in 1956 and COBOL in 1960, IBM developed a language that it hoped would combine the best features of the two languages. This language was called PL/I, for Programming Language/One, and was introduced in 1964. PL/I was the first high-level language designed to promote structured programming while at the same time allowing a very flexible form. It combines the scientific computation aspects of FORTRAN with the file-handling capability of COBOL, and also has extremely good text-handling capa-

LOGO is a computer language that can be learned quickly, even by preschoolers, shown here moving the "turtle" with simple commands.

bilities. Even though the language was pushed by IBM as a replacement for both FORTRAN and COBOL, it has not been as widely accepted as its developers hoped.

ALGOL

The parent of Pascal and other block languages is ALGOL (ALGOrithmic Language). This language, which was very popular in Europe in the 1960s, is similar to FORTRAN except for its structured style. It is a general-purpose language like FORTRAN or PL/I.

APL

APL (A Programming Language) is a special-purpose language used for mathematical and scientific formulas. With special symbols—like Greek letters and overstrike characters—APL can accomplish in one line what other languages might take ten lines to do. APL is also an interpreted language that is easy to use. However, it can be difficult to decipher because of its special symbols and compact form. In fact, compared with APL, the C language is very easy to read!

Logo

For ease of use, Logo probably ranks first among all languages. Preschool children learn how to move the special Logo graphics cursor around on the screen to trace patterns. The cursor, called a **turtle,** is moved via simple geometric commands. For example, the commands

```
FORWARD 60
RIGHT 120
```

instruct the turtle to move 60 steps forward and then turn right at an angle of 120 degrees. If we repeat this command three times—

```
REPEAT 3 (FORWARD 60
  RIGHT 120)
```

—the turtle draws an equilateral triangle.

Using other commands—such as GROW and EDIT—a user can draw sophisticated figures on the screen and, at the same time, learn the concept of programming logic. With more advanced commands, Logo can be used for nongraphic programming tasks similar to those performed by other high-level languages. Logo users can also generate new commands by combining available commands, so the language can expand to meet users' needs. Because Logo was developed by the MIT Artificial Intelligence Laboratory as a dialect of LISP, these commands are based on the same list processing concepts used in LISP.

Forth

Forth was originally developed in 1969 by an astronomer to control his telescopes. It is a very fast, high-level language that has a small but devoted following of users. Forth is different from other languages because it uses **reverse**

> **Underlying all advances is software technology that gets more done and is more transparent to users: structured programming in the '80s, now object-oriented programming.**
>
> *Philippe Kahn, president, Borland International*
>
> Quoted in "View from the Top," *Personal Computing,* October 1989, p. 247.

Polish notation (RPN) like that used on Hewlett-Packard calculators. In RPN, 3 4 + 5 × means to add 3 and 4 to get 7, and then to multiply this value by 5 to obtain 35. Its primary use is for controlling industrial processes and instrumentation. For example, Forth was used to control the heating, ventilation, and air-conditioning at an automobile factory.

Modula-2

Niklaus Wirth invented Pascal to teach correct programming methods. However, Pascal is also used commercially, which requires an expanded version of the language. To meet the need for an extended Pascal, Wirth developed Modula-2. This language looks very much like Pascal, but it is used for systems development.

Ada

Named for Lady Ada Lovelace—the first programmer and the co-worker of Charles Babbage—Ada was developed by the U.S. Department of Defense so that all its military software would be written in one language. Much like Pascal, Ada is a structured language. However, it has many more features than Pascal, since it is designed to meet the needs of military programmers. Because of the tremendous amount of software developed for military computers, Ada is an increasingly important language in programming.

PC-Based Languages

In addition to the many languages we have discussed earlier, there are various languages that are specific to PCs. The dBASE language is a good example. Two other examples are DOS batch files and Lotus 1-2-3 macros.

For everyday users of MS-DOS computers, the capability to group DOS commands into a **batch file** is an important asset. These batch files are the equivalent of a program in that from them, with special **batch commands,** it is possible to create loops and make decisions. A commonly used batch file is the **AUTOEXEC.BAT file** that is automatically executed when a PC is booted with MS-DOS. Other batch files can be used to create menus of applications or to execute a series of applications one after the other. Figure 17-11 shows an AUTOEXEC.BAT file, which creates a path to various subdirectories on a hard disk with the PATH command, sets up a specific type of prompt with the PROMPT command, and causes three utilities to be executed. The PATH command allows programs to be executed from any subdirectory.

Once Lotus 1-2-3 users start to create sophisticated spreadsheets, they often begin to use macros. A **spreadsheet macro** is a sequential series of 1-2-3 commands that the user determines and thereafter can put into play by pressing

All Department of Defense software development is now carried out in the programming language Ada.

FIGURE 17-11
MS-DOS AUTOEXEC.BAT File

```
PATH = C:\DOS;C:\BATCH;C:\NORTON;C:\PCUTIL;
PROMPT $p-$g
QKB
DOS-EDIT
SCRN 5
```

the few keys that represent the particular macro. Macro commands can be used to cause looping, to make decisions about which command is to be executed next, and so on. This capability turns spreadsheet macros into another programming language, giving the user much wider control over the spreadsheet. With macros, the user can generate menus or retrieve, execute, and then save multiple spreadsheet files with a single keystroke.

Since the first use of computers, the trend in computer languages has been toward making the computer do more while the programmer writes fewer instructions—for example, having one instruction from the programmer causes the computer to execute more than one internal command. We can see how far languages have evolved by noting that the first computer languages were just the binary instruction codes to the computer. The programmer entered one instruction for each command to be carried out.

The next step, assembler languages, allowed the programmer to use mnemonic commands instead of binary instruction codes. While this was a great improvement, it still required the user to know exactly how the computer worked. If we refer to binary instruction codes as a "first-generation language" and assembler languages as a "second-generation language," then all the high-level languages discussed earlier are "third-generation languages." These third-generation languages offer instructions that are a step further removed from the computer's machine code than assembler languages: Their English-like instructions are turned into machine code by interpreters or compilers. A single statement in one of these languages results in many machine-code commands. Beyond these third-generation languages—which are primarily procedural, requiring the user to develop the logic and the sequence of commands—are at least two more generations of languages. A whole range of fourth-generation languages (4GLs) are already in existence, and fifth-generation languages based on research in the area of artificial intelligence appear to be right over the horizon. While not a generation of languages, object-oriented programming systems offer a new approach to writing programs.

Fourth-Generation Languages

While high-level or third-generation languages use computer power to convert them into machine code, **fourth-generation languages (4GLs)** use this same computer power to move even further away from the machine-code level by allowing the programmer to develop applications software without having to specify each detail. The 4GL supplies much of the information that the programmer would have had to provide in a third-generation language. For example, if a programmer were creating a data entry screen using BASIC, he or she would have to worry about writing many instructions to move the cursor to various points on the screen to accept the data, accept input characters one at a time, check for terminators, and so on. On the other hand, a programmer using a 4GL would be able to create the screen using a utility program; then the 4GL would generate the machine code to display the screen when the program is run.

Another primary difference between third- and fourth-generation languages is that third-generation languages are almost all procedural, while 4GLs are closer to being nonprocedural. The programmer can concentrate on the task

Fourth-generation languages are languages that are much more powerful than COBOL or C; they enable you to build applications much faster, and with a smaller number of people.

James Martin, author of more than 70 books on computing

Quoted in "James Martin on Computing's Future: Development Stands Still for No Manager," *PC Week*, October 17, 1988, p. 57.

at hand without worrying so much about how the machine is going to do it. The user specifies what is wanted and lets the system decide how to do it.

Primarily, there are two types of 4GLs: applications tools and end user tools. **Applications tools** are 4GLs developed to create new applications quickly and easily. An advertisement for one such applications tool language, called Clarion, noted that in just a few hours a programmer using this language could build a simple onscreen monthly calendar. Besides showing the days of the month, this calendar could "pop up" an appointment calendar for any given day. To create such a calendar using a traditional language would have taken a great deal more time. Applications tools are meant to be used by experts in applications development for a wide variety of uses, often with the intent that the applications be distributed to other users.

While 4GL applications tools make an applications programmer's job easier, **end user tools** are nonprocedural packages oriented toward allowing the average computer user to solve problems without having to learn a programming language. Examples of end user tools include data base query languages that allow a user to access a data base and spreadsheet templates that create a spreadsheet for a specific application. In both cases, the user simply answers questions and enters data.

CLUB MED GOES NATURAL

With approximately 250 company-owned or -affiliated resorts, Club Med is one of the largest resort companies in the world, so a modern reservation system is an absolute requirement. For the past 20 years, Club Med has used a reservation system written in assembly language. The system, which processes reservation requests from some 1,800 terminals worldwide, was rewritten, however, in a fourth-generation language (4GL) to link into IBM's data base system, DB2.

The new system will not seem much different to users. However, it will offer several new features, including a data base containing information on about 5 million Club Med clients. One feature of this database is called the White List, which contains the names of all clients who have suffered a mishap at a Club Med resort. When a client on the White List makes another reservation, the system alerts the Club Med manager that the client's name is on the White List. The manager then presents the client with a gift when he or she arrives at the resort.

Club Med chose a 4GL called Natural to rewrite the reservation system because Natural is compatible with other applications and DB2 and because the programmers wanted to use Natural for the large project. The system was to go online in November 1992 and run parallel with the old system for six months.

Source: Rosemary Hamilton, "Resorting to New Reservation Systems," *Computerworld,* November 11, 1991, p. 31.

Object-Oriented Programming Systems

Nobody doubts that programming productivity has improved with the wide-spread use of structured programming, where users build programs by combining modules written in third-generation programming languages. However, many individuals believe that the improvement falls short of addressing all needs of complex programs. They believe that **object-oriented programming systems (OOPS),** will dramatically improve programming. OOPS uses objects—self-contained items that combine data and algorithms—that cooperate in the program by passing strictly defined messages to one another. Its methodology is easier to work with, because it is more intuitive than traditional programming methods, which decompose programs into hierarchies.

The original OOPS language was Smalltalk, which a Palo Alto research center developed in 1972, based on the ideas of Alan Kay, a University of Utah graduate student. Kay was seeking a way to implement the notion that computers work by sending messages, and he hit upon the idea of an object-oriented language. Today, both C and Pascal have object-oriented versions. The OOPS version of C is C++, which AT&T uses widely. Turbo Pascal 6.0 is Borland's version of OOPS. Undoubtedly, other versions of these languages, as well as other languages, will soon incorporate object orientation.

To understand why OOPS is an extremely valuable programming tool, it is necessary to understand that (1) all programs consist of data requiring processing and procedures for processing the data; that (2) as long as the data and procedures remain the same, the program will work; however, (3) if either the data or procedures change, the program may not work. OOPS transforms programming by binding data and procedures in objects. Users can combine the objects with relative ease to create new systems and extend existing ones. Supporters of OOPS see a world made of objects, so they believe that the use of objects to create information systems provides a natural approach to programming. For example, Borland uses OOPS to write Quattro Pro.

Fifth-Generation Languages and Artificial Intelligence

If third-generation languages are procedural and fourth-generation languages are to some degree nonprocedural, what characteristics will "fifth-generation" languages exhibit? While no definite answer is possible, most observers agree that they will become closer to everyday human languages. We have already discussed the problems associated in most human languages with the very large vocabulary, the often inconsistent syntax, the many idioms, and the general ambiguity of meaning. However, these do not stop researchers from attempting to design **natural languages,** as the fifth-generation languages are also called, to be used in giving instructions to a computer. This research into using natural languages is an important part of a larger field of research known as **artificial intelligence (AI).** There are many definitions of this field, but in general it may be thought of as building computer hardware and software systems that exhibit the same type of intelligence as humans. This includes listening, reading, speaking, solving problems, and making inferences.

In addition to developing computers that will understand natural language, computer scientists are working to give computers all the other characteristics

> **We've done three releases [of Quattro Pro] in 18 months, and that's all attributable to OOP technology.**
>
> *Gene Wang, vice president of Borland International*
>
> Quoted in "Industry Warms to OOP Concept," *PC Week,* July 29, 1991, p. 14.

of intelligence mentioned above. Two fields in which AI has already had an impact are **robotics** (Chapter 6) and **expert systems** (Chapters 4 and 14). In robotics, machines are programmed to carry out various operations; in expert systems, computers are used to provide information and advice to managers, doctors, engineers, and scientists. Another area of AI research is the use of voice input to computers. AI is considered to be of such importance that it is one of the fastest-growing high-tech areas. Many companies are spending large amounts of money either to develop AI systems or to purchase systems developed by other companies.

With a natural-language AI system, managers could access a data base simply by typing in their questions in "plain" English. The instruction "How many female employees have been hired since January 1?" would be answered with the appropriate number. This question could then be followed up by "How many are paid more than $30,000?" with no ambiguity about the group being referred to.

Several recently introduced packages for personal computer users have some degree of natural-language characteristics. These are the *Q & A* from Symantec for use on data bases, *HAL* from Lotus Development for use with Lotus 1-2-3, and *PC-IQ* from A.I. Solutions, which provides a natural-language interface for MS-DOS. One interesting feature of *Q & A* is the Teach facility. If, in the process of interpreting a user's request, *Q & A* finds a word that is not part of its built-in vocabulary, it prompts the user to teach it the meaning of the new word. Once *Q & A* believes it has determined the meaning of the command, it asks, *"Shall I do the following?"* and presents a list of procedures it has determined the user wants it to accomplish.

The HAL (Human Access Language) product from Lotus 1-2-3 enables users to enter spreadsheet commands in an English-language format. The user types in sentences, phrases, or requests, and HAL interprets them using its 2,000-

It's [PC-IQ] a pretty slick program because it puts a little more of the "personal" in personal computing.

Jim Matteson, sales representative at Associated Spring

Quoted in "DOS Interface Understands Plain English," *Computerworld,* December 9, 1991, p. 37.

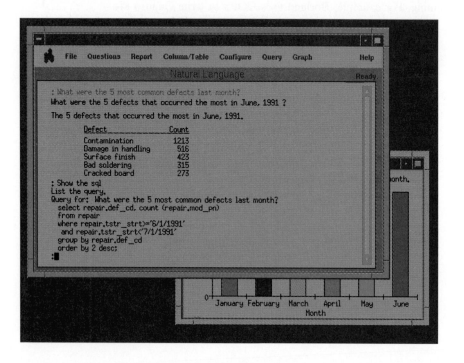

BITS OF HISTORY

Programming Languages

In the late 1940s and early 1950s, computer scientists programmed computers by connecting wires and throwing switches so that the computer could solve a specific problem. When the computer had solved one problem, the programmer changed the connections and threw a new set of switches to solve a different problem. This extremely slow and inefficient process improved with the use of binary numbers to direct the same operations. When working with binary numbers quickly became unwieldy, programmers used octal (base 8) and hexadecimal (base 16) notation to represent the patterns of zeros and ones.

Programming improved even more with the use of abbreviations for the operations previously denoted by binary or hexadecimal numbers. For example, instead of entering a hexadecimal number to designate multiplication, programmers could use a **mnemonic** abbreviation like MUL to represent the operation. However, even with mnemonic instructions, the programmer needed a detailed understanding of the computer's operations. This situation limited the access to a computer.

High-level languages using English-like vocabulary and consistent grammar were created to make computers more accessible to users without technical knowledge. These languages are the basis of many of the today's popular computer packages. The time line below shows when the various high-level languages were introduced, beginning with the first high-level language, FORTRAN.

Source: Bill Machrone, "Micro-Linguistics: Languages for the PC," *PC Magazine*, September 1983, pp. 115–27; Bernard Cole, "The Family Tree of Computer Languages," *Popular Computing*, September 1983, pp. 82–88. Updated by the author.

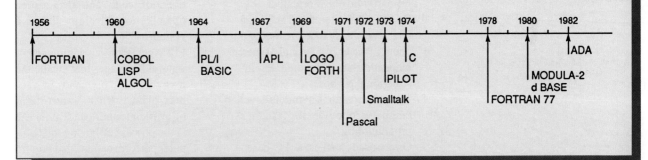

word expandable vocabulary. For example, instead of entering the cryptic /wir (Worksheet Insert Row) command to insert a row in a 1-2-3 spreadsheet, HAL will do the same thing with *insert a row*. Similarly, HAL's *total all columns* command will find the end of all columns of numeric data and insert a command to find the total of each column.

Finally, PC-IQ allows the user to enter DOS commands in plain English. For example, instead of entering "COPY A:*.DBF C:\DBASE\" as a DOS command, you would enter the command "Copy all files ending in DBF from drive A to my dbase directory." The package would respond with the appropriate DOS command, and explain what it is going to do. If the package does not understand a command, it requests more information. PC-IQ allows users to select either conversational or formal mode, according to their respective needs.

While these packages offer features that make a user's job easier, most experts agree that the development of a true natural language that will work at even a third-grade level is still in the future. Problems in developing such a system involve the need for the system to understand the world around it and be able to determine the context of a command.

1. Programmers need computer languages to communicate with computers because computers cannot understand human languages.
2. Computer languages may be classified by level, by the manner in which they are translated into machine language, and by whether or not the user must provide the logic.
3. Machine and assembly languages are low-level languages. All other languages are high level. Computer languages are either interpreted or compiled, and either procedural or nonprocedural.
4. FORTRAN is primarily a scientific language, while COBOL is primarily business oriented.
5. BASIC is an interpreted language that is very easy to learn, use, and debug. Pascal is a strongly typed language that is favored for instructional purposes.
6. The C language is a middle-level language popular for systems programming.
7. Often used just as a PC-based data base management package, dBASE also offers an extremely powerful programming language that can be used to create large applications.
8. There are numerous other special-purpose languages, each one designed to fit a particular programming need.
9. Beyond the current high-level or third-generation languages are the fourth- and fifth-generation languages. These languages will be even further from machine level and will make the process of giving commands to the computer easier.
10. Fourth-generation languages are either applications tools or end user tools, depending on the market they serve. In both cases, they use computer power to ease the user's job. Object-oriented programming systems use combinations of code and data called objects to develop software systems.
11. Fifth-generation languages—natural languages that enable the user to enter commands in very near plain English—are a form of artificial intelligence (AI). AI is the process of having the computer perform actions that require intelligence.
12. Artificial intelligence is useful in the areas of robotics, verbal commands, natural-language commands, and expert systems.

KEY TERMS

applications tool
artificial intelligence (AI)
assembler
assembly language
AUTOEXEC.BAT file
batch command
batch file
command file
comment statement
compiled language
compiler
documentation

end user tool
expert system
fourth-generation language (4GL)
function
general-purpose language
high-level language
input/process/output (IPO) table
interpreted language
keyword
label
library routine
line number

link-editor
low-level language
machine language
maintenance
mnemonic
module
natural language
nonprocedural language
object code
object-oriented programming system
   (OOPS)
procedural language

reverse Polish notation (RPN)
robotics
self-documenting language
source program
special-purpose language
spreadsheet macro
strongly typed language
top–down design
turtle
variable
weakly typed language

1. Explain why we cannot currently use a human language to communicate with a computer except in special circumstances.
2. Name four ways to classify computer languages.
3. Why are machine and assembly languages called "low-level" languages? When would an assembly language be a useful computer language?
4. What is the difference between a compiled language and an interpreted language?
5. Why does an interpreted language execute more slowly than a compiled language?
6. Why is FORTRAN often thought of as a scientific language?
7. Why is COBOL a self-documenting language?
8. Why did BASIC become the language of personal computers?
9. What is the unofficial standard version of BASIC for PCs? Name three other versions of BASIC in use today.
10. Why is dBASE often used as both a data base management package and a language for creating applications?
11. Why is Pascal the choice of many for teaching programming? What languages are similar to Pascal but are for commercial or defense purposes?
12. What are the generations of computer languages? How are they distinguished?
13. What are two types of fourth-generation languages? What is the market for each? What is OOPS?
14. Why do we say that the fifth generation of languages will be made up of natural languages?
15. What problems stand in the way of developing a true natural-language system?

Robotics and Artificial Intelligence

1. One of the most difficult tasks to "teach" a robot is to walk. This robot has been taught to walk and to step over pipes in a nuclear power plant.

2. The Ambler, developed at Carnegie Mellon University, is also a "walking" robot.

3. Personal robots that can carry out such tasks as babysitting or entertaining children are a possibility in the near future.

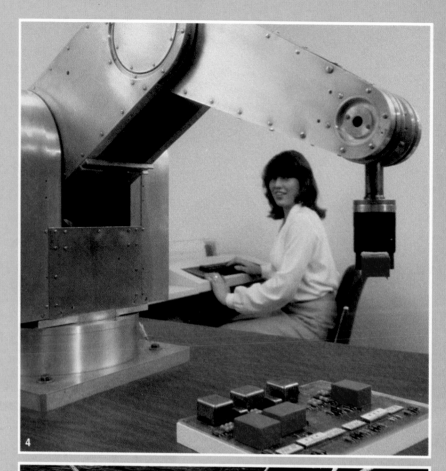

4. With a robotic "master" unit, a human operator controls this robot "slave" arm, thereby avoiding contact with hazardous materials.

5. This remotely operated undersea vehicle is being used by the U.S. Navy to neutralize bottom and moored mines. It is attached to the ship by an umbilical cable that allows it to perform extended-duration subsea missions.

6. This multifingered robot hand can handle many kinds of objects skillfully and gently.

7. Robot arms are being used in many industries to perform the dirty and sometimes dangerous task of arc welding.

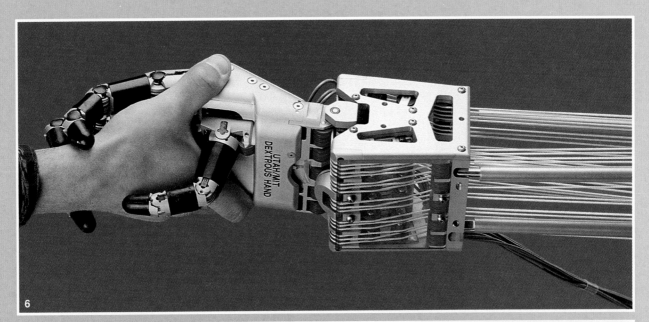

6

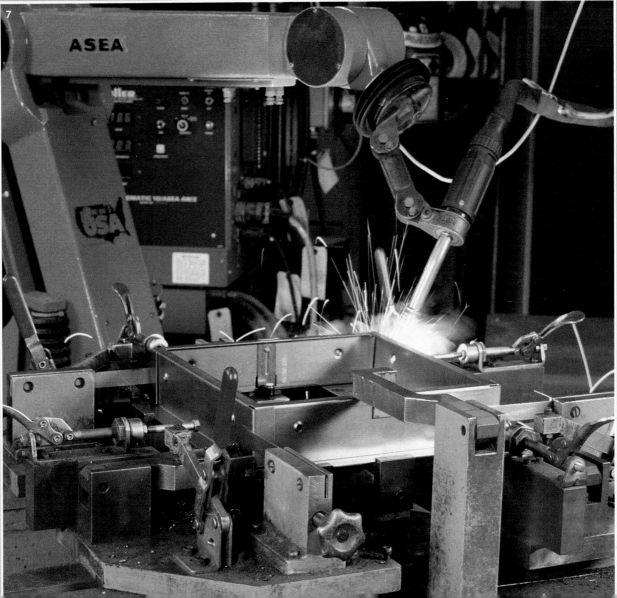

7

8. Androids—robots that can walk and talk—like the fictional C3-PO from the *Star Wars* movie series are a long way from becoming a reality.

9. With a level of precision unobtainable by surgeon's hands, "Robodoc," from the University of California, Davis, can cut bone to precisely accommodate a metal implant—a major breakthrough in orthopedic surgery.

10 This artificial intelligence screen from the UCLA AI Lab is used for teaching purposes.

11. The Command-2 computer-controlled robot arm is used with excellent results in stroke therapy.

12. These three terminals are all linked to United Airlines' expert system at O'Hare Airport and help the airline solve routing problems.

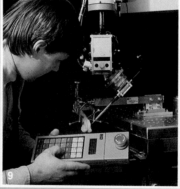

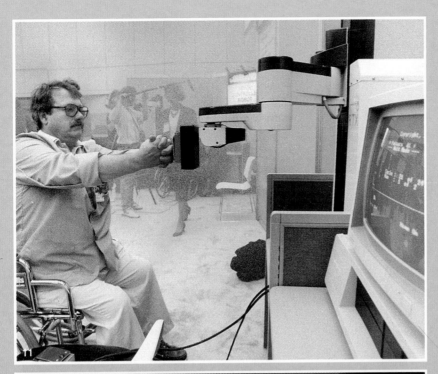

12

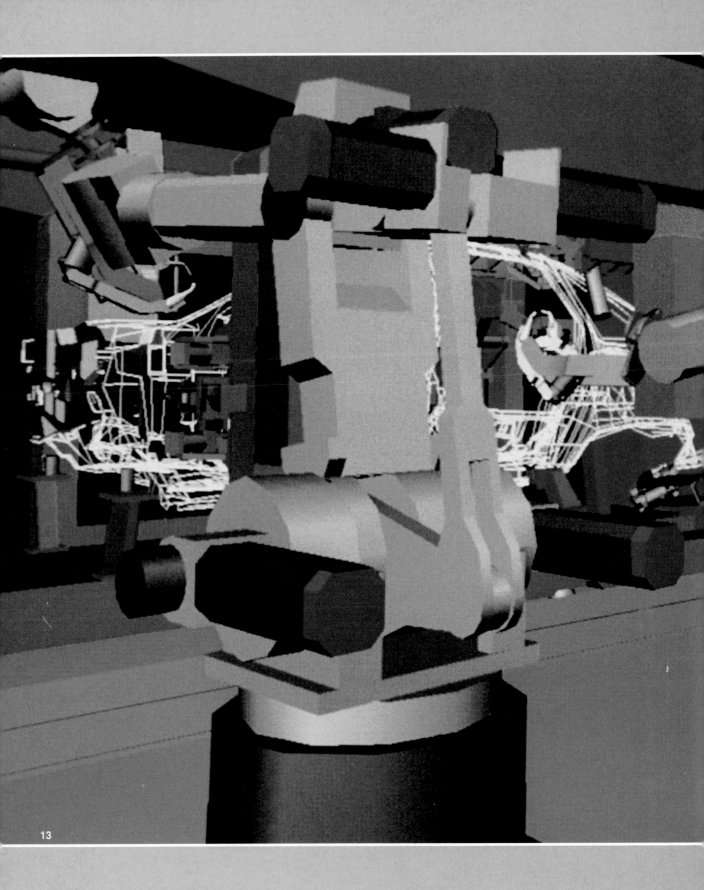

13

14

15

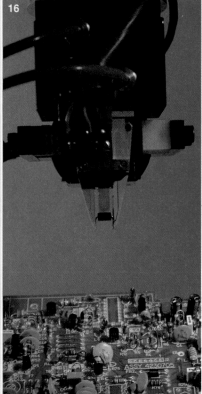

16

13. Computer simulation is now being used to test the computer programs that guide all robotic work—before they are actually installed on the robots.

14. By combining a lifting device with a robotic mobile vehicle, it is possible to automate many of the "fetch and carry" tasks in warehouses.

15. The mailmobile shown here uses robotic intelligence to distribute mail to various locations within a building without human supervision.

16. Robots that install various chips and components are very important in the manufacture of computer circuit boards.

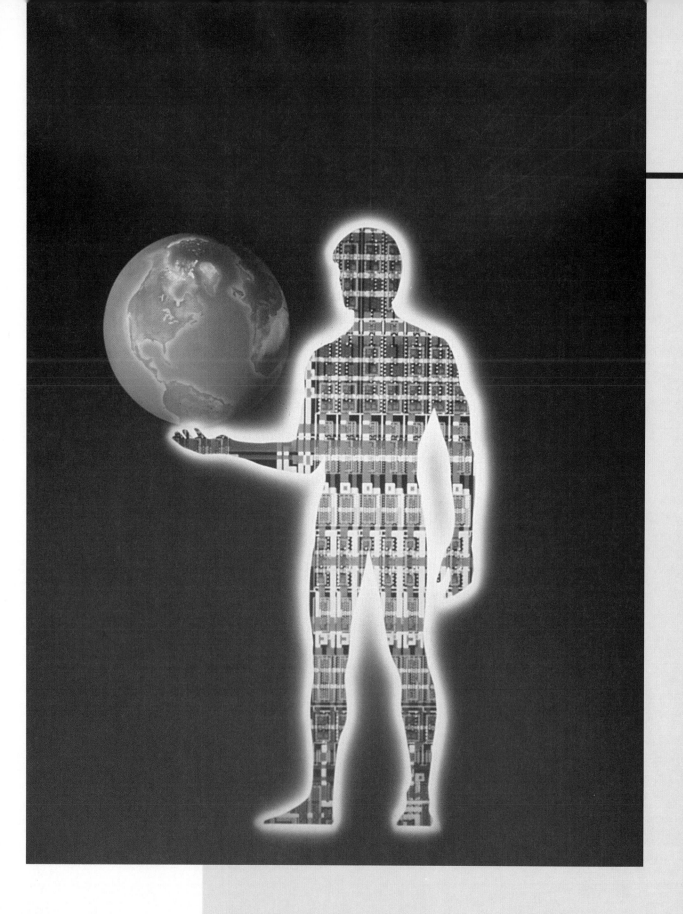

Human Aspects of Computer Use

Chapter 5 introduced some of the human and social issues of computer use, including computer crime and security problems, privacy and health issues, computer careers, and the future of computers. These topics are pursued in depth in the following three chapters. In Chapter 18, on computer crime and security, the numerous types of computer crime, as well as methods for protecting the computer, the data, and the software, are covered. In Chapter 19, on privacy and health issues, certain dangers associated with the computer's invasion of personal privacy are examined. The chapter also covers both the possible health problems associated with long-term use of a computer terminal and the science of ergonomics. In conclusion, Chapter 20 addresses the many career opportunities available in the computer field and explores the exciting future of the computer.

18

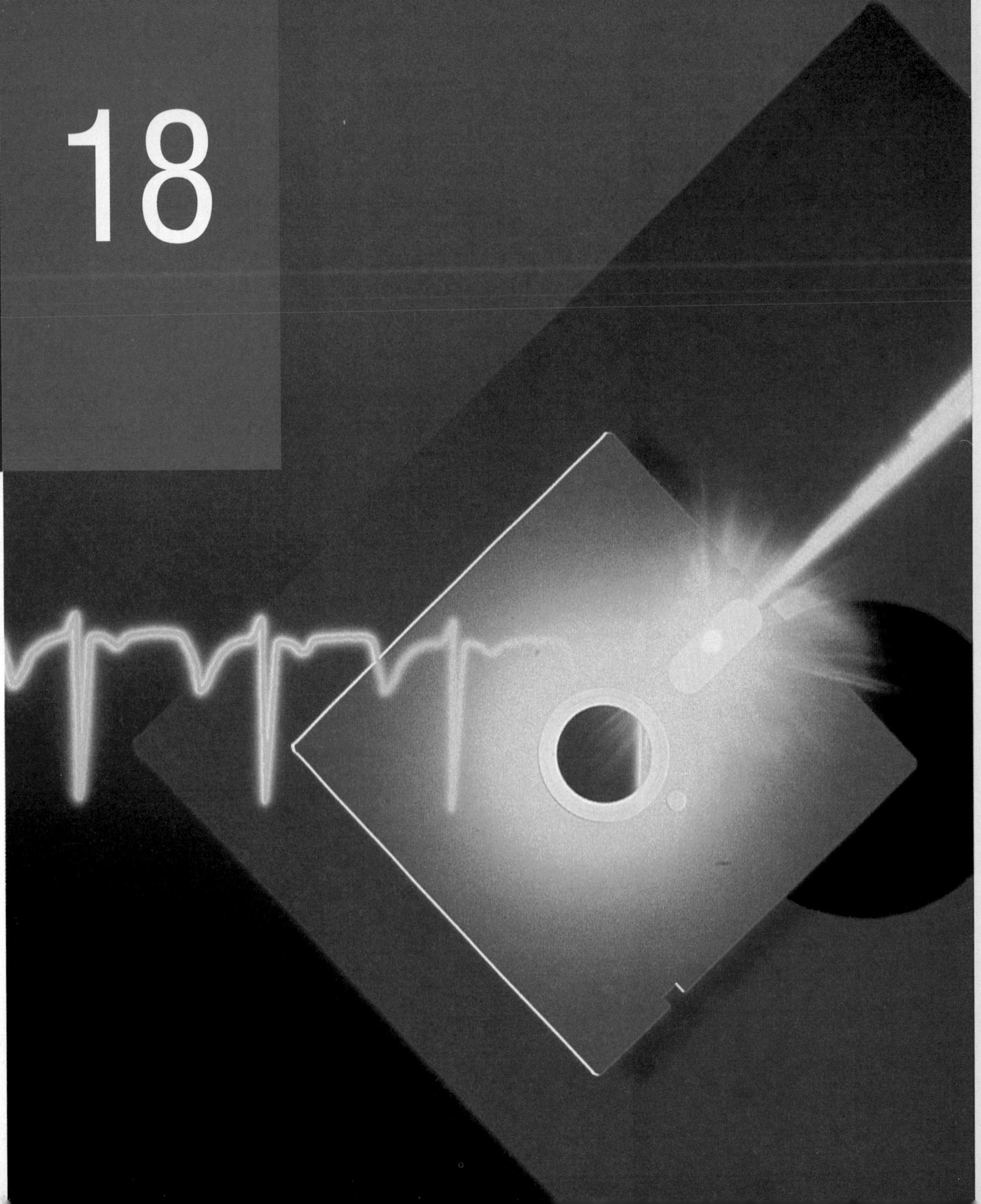

Computer Crime and Security

As they do with almost all other human pursuits, some people have discovered how to use the computer for illegal or unethical purposes. In this chapter, the two aspects of this problem—computer crime and computer security—are addressed. The first part of the chapter outlines various illegal computer practices, including attacks on the computer, software, and data and the use of the computer to steal information or money, to manipulate information, or to deceive others. The second part of the chapter then examines computer security—both physical security and data security. Finally, we investigate computer crime and computer security for the personal computer, especially as they apply to software piracy.

STUDY OBJECTIVES

After reading this chapter, you should be able to

- discuss the magnitude of computer crime and the efforts that are underway to stop it;
- list and describe the various types of computer crime, including computer viruses;
- recognize how computer crimes are committed and what type of person commits computer crime;
- discuss the legal and insurance aspects of computer crime;
- describe various security problems encountered at a computer installation;
- explain the differences between physical security and data security;
- discuss the various methods for protecting data and software;
- understand software piracy as well as physical security for personal computers.

A VIRUS IN TEXAS

On Saturday morning, September 21, 1985, a computer programmer at USPA & IRA, Inc., in Fort Worth, Texas, discovered he could not log on to the company's computer. His unhappiness at this difficulty was soon magnified when accounting personnel found out that 168,000 sales commission records had been deleted. When operators examined the log of operations, they noticed that the system had been used during the night when no one should have been in the building. The police were notified of a possible break-in, and the data on sales commissions were painfully restored from backup tapes.

The following Monday morning, within ten minutes of its first use of the day, the computer crashed. When the systems programmers studied the situation this time, they realized that the problem was more than just one of restoring lost data. They found a small control language program, composed of a single command, that would take the system down whenever a certain file was accessed. Using the day this program was created—September 3, 1985—as their guide, the systems programmers found other programs created on that day that also were designed to disrupt the operation of the company's computer. These programs were referred to by the systems programmers as "trip wires" and "time bombs," set to go off whenever certain parts of computer memory were activated. One such program was designed to wipe out two sections of memory, then duplicate itself, change its name, and execute itself automatically again one month later. This type of program is called a "computer virus" because of its ability to replicate itself within legitimate computer code. To resolve the problem of the rogue programs, the entire system had to be restored from scratch to "decontaminate" it.

Once the system was repaired, attention was turned to the source of the programs causing the problems. The leading suspect was a senior programmer who had been fired recently because he couldn't get along with other employees. Through system logs, it was determined that the programs had been entered from that ex-employee's office on September 3 with his personal ID code. Based on this and other information, the ex-employee was arrested and charged under a "harmful access to computer" Texas statute. At his trial in 1988, he claimed that someone else had entered the programs, but he was found guilty and sentenced to serve seven years probation and repay the costs the company incurred in stopping the virus—some $12,000.

Source: Edward J. Joyce, "Time Bomb—Inside the Texas Virus Trial," *Computer Decisions*, December 1988, pp. 38–43.

Donald Gene Burleson, convicted of "harmful access to a computer."

Throughout this textbook, we have emphasized the many ways in which the computer can be used as a mind tool, expanding our mental capabilities and making our work easier and our recreation more enjoyable. In the vast majority of cases, the computer is used for completely ethical and legal purposes. Unfortunately, as illustrated in the box, there also are users who have found ways to use the computer for unethical or illegal purposes. This wrongful use of computers has gained quite a bit of notoriety recently with the extensive media coverage of so-called computer viruses and with stories of various groups breaking into computers. Computer viruses are actually small computer programs that can replicate themselves with either benign or destructive results. While high school and college-age individuals who use the computer for unethical or illegal purposes are often pranksters, in many other cases people have stolen large sums of money or done great damage to the computer's data or software.

This chapter discusses the two aspects of the illegal and unethical use of computers, that is, computer crime and computer security. A **computer crime** is an illegal act that requires special knowledge of computer technology; **computer security** comprises the methods used to protect the computer, the data, and the computer user from both natural and criminal forces. We will look at the extent of computer crime and the various types of computer crime, and then we will consider the methods used to combat this type of crime.

COMPUTER CRIME

As mentioned, a computer crime is committed whenever someone uses special knowledge of computer technology to perform an illegal act. This act may be theft of money, destruction of data or software, or harmful access to the computer hardware. The total extent of computer crime in the United States is unknown because many companies are reluctant to prosecute the persons involved for fear that the general public will lose confidence in the company. Companies also worry that discussing details of the crime in open court may lead someone else to try to replicate the act elsewhere. Estimates of computer crime costs each year range from $500 million to over $5 billion. In fact, one expert in the area of computer crime contends that no one really knows what the true figure is. Table 18-1 shows some recent computer crimes in which very

TABLE 18-1
Examples of Recent Computer Crimes

Year	Crime	Estimated Cost
1988	Cornell worm	$186 million
1988	Union Bank of Switzerland	$54 million*
1986–1988	U.S. telephone access fraud	$125 million
1984	Volkswagen AG	$428 million
1982	Toronto Board of Education Credit Union	$7.8 million
1982	Saxon Industries	$53 million
1981	Wells Fargo	$21 million
1974–1978	Flagler Dog Track	at least $2 million
1973	Equity Funding	$600 million

*Foiled because of computer malfunction.

large amounts of money were stolen or the costs of repairing the damage were very high.

From Table 18-1, it is easy to see that computer crimes involve large amounts of money. In fact, the FBI has estimated that the average size of a computer crime is between $100,000 and $500,000. On the other hand, the average armed robbery nets the criminal only $6,600 and the average embezzlement is $19,000. With the potential losses so great, computer crime has become a very important topic for computer-using organizations of all sizes.

Types of Computer Crime

Computer crimes fall into five major categories:

1. manipulation or theft of data or assets;
2. direct attack on the hardware, software, or data;
3. use of the computer for conducting or planning a crime;
4. use of the computer to deceive or intimidate people;
5. unauthorized use of the computer for personal gain.

The first type of computer crime—manipulation or theft of data or assets—is probably one of the most publicized. In it, the computer is used to perpetrate a fraud so that assets or data may be stolen or data may be modified. The Volkswagen AG and Toronto Board of Education Credit Union cases listed in Table 18-1 are both examples of this type of computer crime. In the first case, in 1984 a ring of employees altered computer files to conceal the theft of over $400 million—an amount greater than the total profits for the company that year. In the second case, an employee altered computer records to conceal a series of personal loans to her boyfriend.

The second type of computer crime—direct attack on the hardware, software, or data—has earned a great deal of notoriety in the media lately, through such cases as the Texas virus trial discussed earlier and the Cornell worm case listed in Table 18-1. In the Cornell worm case, a Cornell University graduate student sent a program through a nationwide academic research network—InterNet—just to prove that it could be done. Unfortunately, the program contained an error that caused replications of the program to take over available memory in over 6,000 computers infected by the worm. The cost listed in Table 18-1 for this crime is a conservative figure based on the computer time lost and the effort required to clean the worm from these computers. Other types of attacks on computers, software, and data include theft of PCs from offices, water and fire damage to computers, and various types of rogue programs to be discussed in detail later.

An example of the third type of crime was the Flagler Dog Track case. The computer operator used the two computers at the dog track to generate bogus trifecta winning tickets. He and his friends would then cash in the fake winning tickets, reducing the true winners' take. This scheme went on for five years and was discovered only when a spouse talked too much and a bogus ticket was generated on a machine that was not in use that day. Because the leader of the group was the only one who knew how much had been stolen and he refused to talk even when convicted, the $2 million value shown in Table 18-1 is probably a very conservative estimate.

Robert Morris, Jr., was found guilty of violating federal computer-tampering laws in connection with the computer worm he created and released on a national computer network.

FLAGLER DOG TRACK

The largest computer crime of all, the Equity Funding case, was an example of the fourth type of computer crime—the use of the computer to carry out a crime by intimidating or deceiving people. In this case, a group of con artists used a computer to generate a list of over 64,000 fake insurance policyholders who ostensibly held insurance with a face value of over $2 billion. This list was then used to convince investors to buy over $600 billion in stock from an imaginary company.

The final type of computer crime, unauthorized use of a computer, is common in many offices and is probably the least reported type of computer crime. It involves personal use of the computer during work hours, at lunch, or after hours, and the types of use may range from playing games to setting up a computer service bureau or doing personal consulting on the company computer. While playing games during lunch hour may sound innocent enough, it may allow employees to use the computer for personal gain.

Another way to categorize computer crimes is by the object of the crime— that is, what the criminal wants from the crime. The National Center for Computer Crime Data (NCCCD) lists three such categories: financial gain, theft of or damage to data or software, and theft of services (telephone or computer services). A 1988 survey by the NCCCD showed that 36 percent of computer crimes involved financial gain, 20 percent involved theft of or damage to data or software, and 34 percent involved theft of services. In all categories, the survey showed that about one-third of the perpetrators were employees or ex-employees.[1] Figure 18-1 shows the result of this survey.

> [Computers] are used to store vital information, from medical records to business plans to criminal records. Although we trust them, they are vulnerable.
>
> *National Research Council report, "Computers at Risk"*
>
> Quoted in "Computers Worst Weapon, Study Says; Nation's Been Lucky for So Little Crime," *Athens Banner-Herald,* December 2, 1990, p. 2.

---

[1] Jennifer Smith, "Computer Crime," *Lotus,* June 1989, p. 18.

FIGURE 18-1
NCCCD Survey of Computer Crime

Source: Copyright 1989 by C W Publishing, Inc., Framingham, Mass., 01701. Reprinted from *Computerworld*.

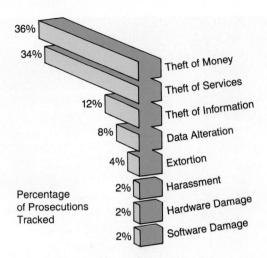

36% Theft of Money
34% Theft of Services
12% Theft of Information
8% Data Alteration
4% Extortion
2% Harassment
2% Hardware Damage
2% Software Damage

Percentage of Prosecutions Tracked

The Computer Criminal

Computer criminals may be grouped in three major categories: employees, outside persons, and organized crime. As noted in the NCCCD survey, employees or ex-employees form the largest group of computer criminals, usually because they have the easiest access to the computer. As in the Texas virus trial, the criminal may be a disgruntled employee wishing to get back at the company either by attacking the computer or by using it to steal from the company. Other times, the employee accidentally finds a way to perform an illegal act with the computer. Usually the employee will not act on this knowledge immediately but will wait until he or she finds an accomplice to help carry out the crime.

Persons outside the organization can use telephone lines to break into computers. Often referred to as **hackers,** these people are usually viewed as being interested in unauthorized access "for the fun of it." A 1983 movie, *WarGames,* portrayed a likable teenage hacker who almost started World War III by breaking into a Department of Defense computer. Although it would hardly be possible for that actually to happen, in the process of "hacking" into a computer, the potential to damage computer programs and files *is* very real. In fact, in an increasing number of recent cases, hackers have been involved in criminal activities. For example, in 1987 the German Chaos Computer Club revealed that its members had broken into NASA computers and examined some of the agency's secret files.

Usually, outside users obtain the phone number of a computer system along with a password that allows access to the system. Sometimes this information is amazingly easy to acquire. In one case, a credit bureau was including the user's access code and password on every credit report sent to that individual. When these reports were discarded, a knowledgeable computer criminal could easily find and recognize this information. A number of electronic bulletin boards have sprung up across the country, displaying phone numbers and access information for various computer systems. These "cracker boards" are often combined with electronic voice mailboxes to circulate information among would-be criminals. In the U.S. access code fraud case listed in Table 18-1 (page 579), an individual used this method to sell long-distance access codes. In 1988, when he was arrested in Denison, Texas, 2,050 access codes were recovered from his home.

Another era of criminal activity that is of growing concern to authorities is that of electronic forgery. In **electronic forgery,** desktop publishing equipment is used to create such items as phony work orders, receipts, bank checks, and even stock certificates. The equipment needed to carry out this criminal activity is fairly inexpensive—less than $5,000—and includes a PC, laser printer with typographic fonts, and scanner to capture photographs and drawings. The greatest potential for harm with electronic forgery, however, is in the creation of phony versions of everyday forms of identification, such as letters of reference, diplomas, or identification cards. In one case, forgers used a color copier to produce a large quantity of false ID cards.

Organized crime has discovered that the computer can be extremely useful in furthering its objectives. One of the biggest criminal uses of the computer is for drug cartels to "launder" money derived from the importation and sale of illegal drugs such as cocaine. These groups have found that getting drugs into the United States is easier than using the cash! American banks are required to report cash deposits of more than $10,000, so the drug leaders are very restricted in the use of their cash profits. To get around this, many criminals smuggle the cash out of the country and then deposit it in a foreign bank where secrecy is very strict. A dummy corporation with an American subsidiary is created, which then uses telecommunications to move money to a U.S. bank. The dummy corporation then "loans" the money back to the drug dealer or the American subsidiary pays him a "salary." Presently, the U.S. government is fighting this type of scheme with a proposal to require all foreign banks that do business in the United States to report cash deposits over $10,000.

The misapplications of desktop publishing are almost as numerous as the legitimate uses.

James Cavvoto, publishers of "Desktop Publishing Forgery: The Potential for Abuse"

Quoted in "Technology Leaps Raise the Specter of Forgery," *Computerworld,* March, 5, 1990, p. 44

The Crime Process

To understand fully the problem of computer crime, it is useful to look at the processes used to commit such a crime. First, let's identify all computer crimes (except physical attacks on or theft of hardware) as input crimes, possessing crimes, output crimes, or storage crimes.

An **input crime** involves changing, fabricating, or manipulating data while entering it into the machine. If a computer criminal can gain access to long-distance telephone billing data before bills are sent out, the complete statement of toll calls can be wiped clean. Similarly, a grade can be changed before it is entered on a transcript. An input crime could also involve fabricating fake suppliers to whom checks are sent or fake customers to whom merchandise is sent.

A **processing crime** involves manipulating software so that it or the data it is processing are used to steal, sabotage, or fudge results. The box at the beginning of this chapter discusses a processing crime. Another type of processing crime would be to use a program to shift small amounts of money to an unauthorized account. One such incident involved a program that rounded all interest on savings accounts *down* to the nearest penny. The difference between the rounded amount and the actual interest was then accumulated in a secret illegal account. This may not sound like a lot of money, but when the program was applied to every depositor over a period of several years, the amount accumulated was well over $100,000. Because various types of processing crimes have been important recently, a detailed discussion will follow in the next section.

An **output crime** involves the theft of processed information for resale, extortion, or personal use. A common problem is the theft of a firm's or agency's client list or inventory control output, or any other forms of information crucial to the successful operation of the organization. An example involves a former employee of an ad agency starting a new agency using the computerized client list stolen from his or her former employer.

Since the output from processing is often saved on secondary storage, the criminal may actually attempt to steal the stored results by taking a disk or tape, thus committing a **storage crime.** This is especially easy to do when PC floppy disks are left lying around the office.

Viruses, Worms, and Other Processing Crimes

In the past few years, the number and importance of processing crimes have increased dramatically. These crimes take such names as viruses, worms, Trojan

CHIP HACKERS CAUSE CELLULAR PHONE FRAUD

One of the fastest-growing consumer uses of computer chips is in cellular telephones—those portable phones that use radio waves to communicate with a local "cell" that, in turn, transmits the call to the nearest switching center. Unfortunately, modification of the chip by hackers has led to a type of fraudulent activity that cost U.S. cellular phone companies almost $600 million in 1992. The fraud is not limited to the United States, however. It is an international problem. For example, over 50,000 cellular phones were stolen in England and refitted with modified chips.

The memory chip in a cellular telephone contains a unique serial number that tells a telephone company's computer to accept the call, because a bonafide user is placing it. By using a personal computer to rewrite the software in the phone's memory chip, hackers found a way to make free calls over the cellular phone network. The modified chip fools the computer into thinking that the phone is from a different calling district. Because data bases between cellular systems are not cross-checked, the computer accepts the call. Cellular phones with bogus chips are in virtually every state and are predominantly used by cocaine traffickers and money launderers.

A California man invented the bogus chips in 1987, but their proliferation is attributed to a fellow hacker who stole the design and began creating similar chips. However, the second hacker failed to include a security provision that would force users to return the chip to him periodically for reprogramming. As a result, other hackers could reproduce the chip. A police "sting" operation eventually caught both hackers, but the damage was done. Telephone companies are working to modify their systems to forestall the use of the illegal phones, but use of them continues.

Source: John J. Keller, "Thanks to Hackers, Cellular Phone Firms Now Face Crime Wave," *The Wall Street Journal*, June 14, 1991, pp. A1, A4.

horses, time bombs, logic bombs, and trapdoors. In each case, a special computer program is inserted into the computer. Its intended purpose may be to destroy data and information or it may be to benignly display a holiday greeting.

A **virus** is a program that attaches itself to a computer program or file the computer executes. When executed, the virus replicates itself with potentially harmful results. There are over 100 viruses for IBM compatible PCs. They go by such names as "Stone" and "Jerusalem." The number of computers that have been infected by viruses is unknown, but a survey of 600 companies showed that 63 percent had experienced at least one computer virus. An official of the Electronic Data Processing Auditors Association testified before Congress that hundreds of thousands of viruses have attacked computers in recent years. Examples of such viruses include the following.

- Around Christmas 1987, a Christmas greeting program circulated on IBM's international network. In addition to displaying a greeting, the program forwarded itself to everyone on the recipient's outgoing mail list. It swamped the entire network.
- A nationwide spread of the Jerusalem virus was narrowly averted in 1990 when the Census Bureau disks containing the virus were withheld from the mail after the infection was discovered.
- The most publicized virus case involved the Michelangelo virus, which was triggered to go off on March 6, 1992. However, many computer installations took preventive measures, so only a few computers actually sustained damage.

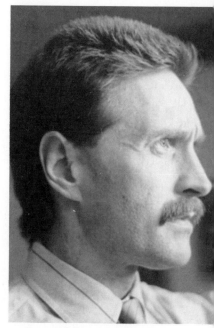

John D. McAfee is an expert on computer viruses and computer security.

The virus process is shown in Figure 18-2. Note that in this figure the virus enters the computer through pirated software, through software obtained from a friend, or over a computer network. Once in the object computer, it copies itself to the files of the operating system and then into RAM. From RAM it replicates itself and makes copies on any disks inserted into the computer or sends itself back out over the network, where the process starts over.

To combat viruses, users should avoid using software obtained from bulletin boards or acquaintances without first checking thoroughly to make sure it is clean. There are also "vaccines" available that help keep a virus from attaching itself to system software.

Viruses are probably the best known type of processing crime, but other types of processing crimes have also affected computers in many ways. A **worm** of the type unleashed on Internet's network of over 6,000 computers is similar to and often confused with a virus, because both can replicate themselves. The difference is that a virus must attach itself to another program, whereas a worm is a free-standing program that can continually execute without outside influence. A **Trojan horse** program appears to do one thing but actually does another. For example, a Trojan horse program was attached to a supposed AIDS information disk that was sent to many MS-DOS users. When the disk was used, the Trojan horse program made users believe their hard disk had been wiped out. A **time bomb** is a program timed to execute itself on a certain date, whereas a **logic bomb** executes whenever a certain command is given. Criminals often access a computer through a **trapdoor,** which is the part of the operating system that allows access to knowledgeable users.

> **The number of viruses has exploded exponentially. We used to see four or five new viruses a month. Now we see that many each week.**
>
> *Greg Drusdow of Accord, a nonprofit technological service group for the insurance industry*
>
> Quoted in "Sophisticated Virus-Fighters," *The New York Times,* March 8, 1992, p. 8 of Business Section.

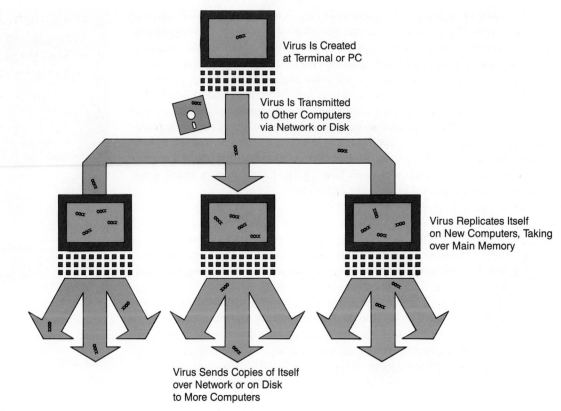

Virus Is Created
at Terminal or PC

Virus Is Transmitted
to Other Computers
via Network or Disk

Virus Replicates Itself
on New Computers, Taking
over Main Memory

Virus Sends Copies of Itself
over Network or on Disk
to More Computers

FIGURE 18-2
The Virus Process

Legal Aspects of Computer Crime

In the past, while computer criminals have tended to reap large sums of money from crimes, they usually have not spent much time behind bars when convicted—for two reasons: First, not many laws actually covered computer crime, and even when they did, prosecutors had difficulty obtaining a conviction. In many cases, the only thing stolen was information or computer time, neither of which would constitute a crime under theft laws enacted prior to the age of computers. Often the only law that came close to applying to computer crime was the mail fraud law. Even when money was taken, the thief usually got off—because he or she was young and clean-cut and had no previous record or because the jury considered the crime "victimless" since the injured party was a large corporation. In addition, the intricacies of the computer were often very difficult to explain to the judge and jury, so the prosecution may have had a hard time demonstrating how a crime was committed.

The second reason for computer criminals going unpunished was that corporations were hesitant to take action against former employees. These companies did not wish to risk the negative publicity of a trial or the appearance of not having adequate security for their computer. As a result, many white-collar computer criminals have been allowed to resign quietly from the company, in some cases moving to a similar position in another company.

To rectify the problem of inadequate laws against computer crime, the federal government and all 50 states have passed laws covering computer crime. The most recent federal laws, passed by Congress and signed into law by the president in 1986, were the Computer Fraud and Abuse Act and the Electronic Communications Privacy Act. The Computer Fraud and Abuse Act makes it a crime to damage data in any government computer or in any computer used by a federally insured financial institution (this includes most banks). It also makes it a crime to use a computer to view, copy, or damage data across state lines. Under this act, if a victim can show that at least $1,000 damage was done or that medical records were in any way damaged, the alleged offender can be prosecuted. This act also makes it a felony to set up or use bulletin boards that list individual or corporate computer passwords. Persons convicted under the Computer Fraud and Abuse Act can be sentenced to up to 20 years in prison and fined up to $100,000. The individual who sent the worm through the Internet network, Robert Morris, Jr., was convicted under this act.

The Electronic Communications Privacy Act extends the 1968 federal wiretap law to include the full range of communications technology that has evolved since 1968. This law extends to electronic communications the same constitutional protections afforded to telephone conversations. It also updates legislation to make it easier to prosecute people who violate the security of computer systems. Persons convicted under this law can be sentenced to up to ten years in prison and fined up to $100,000. Organizations convicted of electronic eavesdropping can receive fines of up to $250,000 for each offense.

Computer crime is not restricted to the United States. Other countries, such as Canada and the United Kingdom, have either enacted laws similar to those discussed earlier or are exploring other legal avenues to combat computer crime.

Insurance Against Computer Crime

Beginning with Lloyds of London in 1981, many insurance companies have been offering coverage for computer crime. In many cases, this coverage is part of a more general insurance policy, and most large corporations are covered to some degree. Unfortunately, many small businesses cannot afford coverage against damage to data or computers.

Most policies cover illegal money transfer by a third party using the computer. They also cover the cost of reproducing stolen or destroyed data as well as loss of revenue due to interruption of service. Premiums start at $25,000 per year and provide an average coverage of $10 million.

As mentioned earlier, there have been various predictions regarding the continuing increase in computer crime. We have already discussed the statistics on the average size of computer crimes. If these values are valid, then the need for insurance against computer crime may become as great as if not greater than the need for insurance against burglary or other crimes against a company.

COMPUTER SECURITY

Computer security is the protection of computer assets—including hardware, software, and data—of individuals and organizations. Given the huge losses involved in computer crime, computer security has become a very important topic for computer users of all sizes. Computer security includes the wide range of methods used to protect the computer, the data, and the computer user from natural and criminal forces. (We include natural forces because fire, water, wind, or earthquakes can be as devastating as the criminal who seeks personal gain.) Types of security range from a commonsense approach of locking doors to

PUTTING THE BYTE ON KGB HACKERS

When he found a 75-cent accounting error in his computer system, U.S. citizen Clifford Stoll's curiosity was piqued. A $1,000 mistake would not have bothered him, but 75 cents did. This error came to light in 1986 and resulted in an investigation that finally led to the arrest of three West German hackers who were working for the KGB, trying to gain access to U.S. military computers. The process Stoll followed in uncovering this spy ring displayed his expertise with computers.

Convinced that the unaccounted-for 75 cents indicated a computer break-in, Stoll tracked the intruders by himself for six months by noting every time they logged on to the computer. When he discovered that passwords were being stolen to access military computers, Stoll informed the FBI, which began to assist him in the investigation. After a year, he finally traced the intruders to Hanover, West Germany, where they were using modems to penetrate a constantly changing series of computers. Stoll couldn't locate the hackers exactly, however, because they would break their connection after only a few minutes. To keep them on the line for a longer time, Stoll planted his own Trojan horse program, comprising a mass of bogus military data and a fictitious computer network called "SDI Net." The intruders believed this to be sensitive information on the U.S. "Star Wars" program.

The Trojan horse program did the trick; the intruders stayed on for several hours reading the material, which enabled Stoll to trace the telephone call. He had also received, from a man with East European connections, a letter asking about SDI Net. Knowing the location of the hackers and using the information obtained from the letter writer, the FBI and West German authorities were able to make the arrests. The hackers had tried to access 450 computers and had successfully accessed more than 40 of them.

Source: "Spy Catcher: Sleuth Puts Byte on KGB Hackers," *Dallas Times Herald,* March 4, 1989, pp. A1, A19.

Harvard University astronomer Clifford Stoll helped the FBI track down a German computer hacker, leading to the cracking of a major spy ring.

sophisticated methods of coding data to make them unreadable to anyone other than designated users. The importance of security becomes even more evident when one considers that there are over 100,000 commercial and government computer installations across the country that exchange all types of information hourly. Add to this the daily electronic transfer of over one *trillion* dollars between banks and financial institutions in the United States, Europe, and Japan and the potential for computer loss becomes enormous. Figure 18-3 shows the results of a survey on the perceived security threats to network users.

Threats to the Computer

While unauthorized access by outside parties is the most publicized threat to a computer system's security, most experts do not consider it the most important. Research has shown that the most prevalent damage to computers and data comes from errors and omissions by employees; outside attack ranks among the least of security concerns. Other, more pressing concerns include errors in and omission of data; the actual theft of the computer and peripheral devices (printers, monitors, and so on); misuse by disgruntled or dishonest employees; and damage from fire, water, or natural disasters.

While not everyone will agree with a particular ranking of threats to computer hardware, software, and data, no one will deny that all of these items pose a threat to which security must respond. Another way to look at the security problem for computers is to consider physical security and data security. **Physical security** is the protection of computer hardware from theft or damage, whether natural or human induced, in the same way that other office equipment would be protected. **Data security** is the protection of software and data associated with the computer from unauthorized manipulation, destruction, or theft. In this section we will consider only mainframe computer security; a later section will be devoted to security for personal computers.

Physical Security

Methods of protecting computer hardware from outside forces include

- employing procedures that effectively exclude unauthorized persons from the computer center;

> **If [senior management] really understood the potential liability and the potential risks to corporate assets and to their reputations, they might shut down all networks and computer centers.**
>
> *Kenneth Weiss, chief technical officer, Security Dynamics, Inc.*
>
> Quoted in "Lay Security Invites Liability Nightmare," *Computerworld*, March 26, 1990, p. 1.

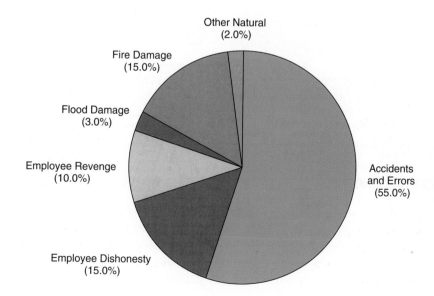

FIGURE 18-3
Users' Perceived Security Threats

Source: Executive Information Network.

- designing hardware to be tamperproof;
- protecting the hardware as much as possible from natural disasters and from fire and water damage;
- protecting the tape library.

In addition to these threats to the computer, a new physical threat comes from the increase in terrorist activity. If located in an unprotected area, a computer and tape library could easily be destroyed by a car bomb or truck bomb. It has been estimated that 60 percent of all terrorist attacks are now against computer systems. In Germany alone, 24 computer centers were bombed in one year.

Methods of ensuring physical security include locating the facility in an area that can be protected from terrorist activity; controlling entry to the computer facility; using finger-, eye-, or voice prints to identify individuals seeking entry; and, as simple as it may seem, keeping doors locked. Figure 18-4 shows a schematic of this process.

Damage from fire or water is somewhere on everyone's list of dangers, but these threats are not often treated with the respect they deserve. Like any electronic machine, the computer is always in danger from an electrical fire caused by a short circuit. Nonelectrical fires can also cause great damage if water is used to extinguish them, because water can do great damage to the delicate circuits of a computer. For this reason, the danger from water must be considered in the planning of the security system for the computer. Sprinkler systems are a

FIGURE 18-4
Physical Security Procedures

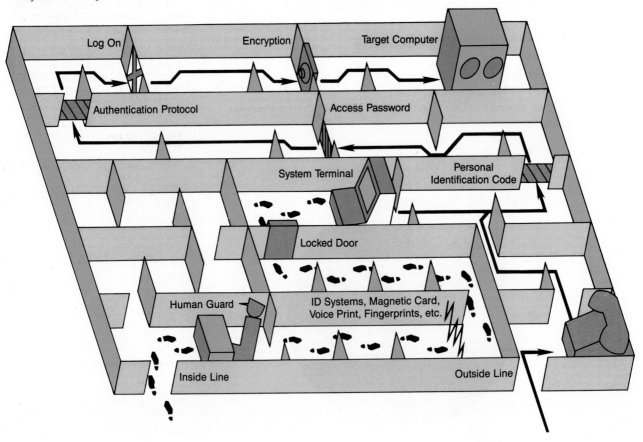

common protection against fire in most commercial buildings, but they can cause more damage to a computer than the fire itself. Several years ago, a government agency's sprinklers went off by accident, soaking the computers and causing many related problems! In addition, to avoid a complete loss of data in the event of either a natural or a human disaster, there should be a policy of regularly backing up the files on the system and storing the backups in an area physically separate from the main computer center. Recall that a **backup** is a second (or even a third) copy of a data file on a secondary storage device separate from the primary disk secondary storage.

Data Security

While physical protection of the computer is usually a matter of ensuring that unauthorized persons do not gain access to the hardware, protecting the software and data is an entirely different problem—with conflicting objectives. On the one hand, it is generally agreed that while computer hardware can almost always be replaced, an organization's data are its most important asset and may be irreplaceable. Even if data are not destroyed, having them fall into a competitor's hands can have disastrous implications for either private companies or national governments.

On the other hand, there is the objective of making the computer available and as easy as possible to use. In general, this objective has taken precedence, with the emphasis on making systems as "user friendly" as possible. When this movement toward easy-to-use systems is combined with the many other changes occurring in computers today, the data security problem becomes massive. These changes include recent technological and software advancements, the growing need to access larger and larger amounts of data, and the movement toward decentralization of computer systems.

The popularity of the personal computer has added to this problem by vastly expanding the number of people who have access to the equipment necessary to carry out computer crimes. While either a PC or a mainframe terminal

(Left) Valuable data and programs can be safeguarded through backup tapes stored in a tape library like this one. (Right) In voice imprint security, when the user speaks into the telephone, the system compares his or her voice to the speech information already stored on the card you see in this user's hand. The green graph on the computer screen compares the differences between two people uttering the same word. The blue graph charts the differences between two words uttered by the same person.

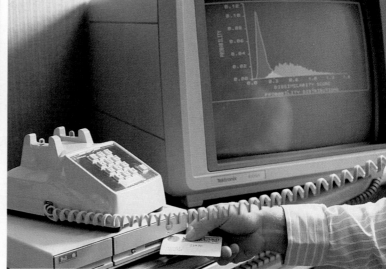

can be combined with a modem to break into computer systems, it is usually far easier to buy a PC and modem than it is to gain access to a mainframe terminal.

The primary tool for protecting access to computer systems is the password. A **password** is a sequence of letters and/or digits, supposedly known only to the user, that must be entered before the computer system can be accessed. Most people have become accustomed to using a type of password called a **personal identification number (PIN)** to access a bank account from an automatic teller machine (ATM). Unfortunately, many passwords are common words such as *test, system,* or the name of the user's child or pet. The prevalence of easily guessed passwords led one person to comment that if a system has a phone line coming into it, then the computer can be broken into! Figure 18-5 shows the methods often used to gain unauthorized access to such **dial-up computer systems.**

Any solution to the computer security problem must include methods of physically protecting the data and information stored on the computer. In addition, there must be ways to prevent unauthorized release or modification of data and information. While it is true that specially designed new hardware and software play an important role in solving this aspect of the problem, a change in the attitude of the people involved is even more important. People often do not want to go to the trouble of using multiple passwords to protect access to the computer. Given that the password is the primary method of protecting data, it is surprising how easy it is to find or guess a user's password. All too often, the password is short and has been chosen by the user to be easily remembered. For security purposes, passwords should be made up of combinations of unrelated letters and digits and should be changed every 30 days. Until top management realizes that risking data security can be costly, and until users are forced to take more care with passwords, the computer security problem will not be solved.

Data Protection Methods

Some of the tools currently being used to protect computer software and data include password policies, systems audit software, security software packages,

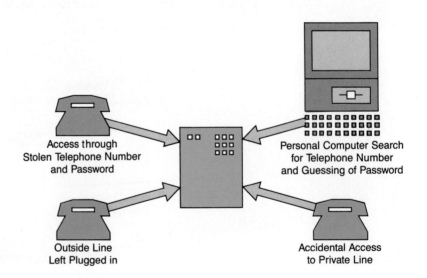

FIGURE 18-5
Unauthorized Access Methods

Access through
Stolen Telephone Number
and Password

Personal Computer Search
for Telephone Number
and Guessing of Password

Outside Line
Left Plugged in

Accidental Access
to Private Line

call-back systems, port protection devices, data encryption systems, and antivirus policies and software. **Password policies** should include not allowing users to choose their own passwords and requiring that the password be longer than four letters or digits. In addition, the user should have the password changed immediately if any evidence exists that security may have been breached. In addition, all passwords should be changed periodically to make guessing the password more difficult. Finally, if an employee is fired or leaves under less than pleasant circumstances, *all* passwords, not just the ex-employee's, should be changed. Failure to change all passwords can leave the system open for intrusion. For example, in the Texas virus trial described in the box at the beginning of this chapter, the ex-employee's password was canceled as soon as he left. However, since he had been the company's security director, he knew every employee's password and was able to log on using another password.

Systems audit software keeps track of all attempts to log on the computer, giving particular attention to unsuccessful attempts. An audit of the system log would indicate who has been on the system at any given time and therefore should reveal if an unauthorized user has been on the system. In the same Texas case mentioned, the system log showed when and from which terminal the rogue programs were entered, enabling the systems programmers to determine the probable culprit immediately.

Security software packages protect the computer system by various means. One method is to make users wait at least five seconds between attempts to enter a password. Another method requires the user to hang up the phone and redial after three unsuccessful attempts to log on. In either case, the objective is to keep a hacker or computer criminal from repeatedly guessing passwords using a computer. A similar type of security system, referred to as a **call-back system,** accepts calls and passwords from users, looks up the phone number associated with the user, and then calls the user back at that number. If the password has been stolen, the unauthorized user will not be at the correct number, so the computer will deny access.

Port protection devices provide an extra level of security that separates the user from the computer. A **port** is one of the entry lines coming into the computer; a port protection device requires the user to enter a second password to access the port. Some of these devices also camouflage the computer by answering with a simulated voice rather than with the high-pitched carrier signal

To protect computers from unauthorized access, modems often incorporate key-lock procedures such as the one shown here.

BANK ROBBERY: ATM STYLE

When you hear of a bank robbery, you usually think of a Bonnie and Clyde operation where the robbers enter the bank with masks and guns to make off with the cash. However, much more money is stolen each year through those "smart machines" known as ATMs (automatic teller machines) than in traditional bank robberies. In 1986, the last year for which data are available, U.S. banks lost nearly $40 million in various ATM scams, and customers sustained 97 percent of the loss. Such statistics are not surprising, considering there are over 350,000 ATMs in the United States; that they are available in a multitude of places, from grocery stores to race tracks to aircraft carriers; and that most of these ATMs are connected through various networks.

As an example of an ATM scam, California police broke up a gang that had more than 7,000 counterfeit ATM cards in an apartment. The alleged mastermind of the gang also had an identification key for each counterfeit card. He obtained the numbers while working for GTE Corp. as a programmer on the GTE ATM network. Even though GTE's data about their customers was encrypted, the programmer was able to find the ID key of any California customer who had ever used the GTE network. GTE had not changed the encryption password since the process was tested.

In New York, a former ATM repairman stole nearly $90,000 using a fairly simple procedure: He would stand behind a customer and watch as the individual entered his or her personal identification number (PIN). Then if the person discarded the receipt, he retrieved it and used the account data to make phony ATM cards. An $1,800 machine created the magnetic strip on the plastic card.

Source: Frank Kuznik, "The Great Cash Machine Capers," *Information Week,* April 2, 1990, pp. 44–47.

> The magnetic stripe [on an ATM card] can be on a piece of cardboard or almost anything else— because no person is going to look at it.

Benjamin Miller, publisher and editor, Personal Identification News

Quoted in Frank Kuznik, "The Great Cash Machine Capers," *Information Week,* April 2, 1990, pp. 44–47.

---

commonly used for computer communications. This keeps the system from being recognized by unauthorized computer search.

Data encryption systems are combinations of software and hardware that convert data coming out of a computer into an unreadable form for transmittal over a network. The process is one of transforming **cleartext** (a readable form) into **ciphertext** (an unreadable form) at the source computer and then back to cleartext again at the destination. The American National Standards Institute (ANSI) has developed a standard method of coding the data, called the **Data Encryption Standard (DES),** which is the most widely used encryption standard. Figure 18-6 shows an encryption system.

Antivirus policies include avoiding the use of software of an unknown origin that has not been thoroughly tested. Some **antivirus software** limits the replication of a program received over a network. Other such software prevents the virus from attaching itself to the systems software.

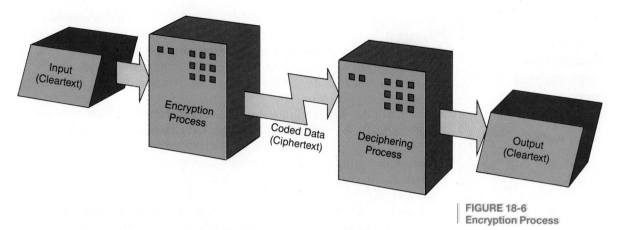

FIGURE 18-6
Encryption Process

Human Aspects of Computer Security

The role that humans play in ensuring the security of a computer system is every bit as important as the technological measures mentioned. Education is the first means of changing peoples' attitudes toward security. People must come to understand that unauthorized intrusion, no matter how innocent it may seem, is a crime punishable by a fine or imprisonment or both. Second, management must be willing to run a complete background check on each prospective employee to determine if any security problems occurred in that person's previous position. The offender in the Texas virus case had taken a new job with a telecommunications firm when he went to trial; he was found out and fired only after his picture appeared in the media!

Another way to tighten computer security is to involve users in the design of the security system. While failure to involve the users may still lead to a system that is secure, users may end up spending more time devising ways to circumvent the security measures than doing their work. Finally, users of the system need to recognize that people, not machines, have the real responsibility for computer security. The study and discussion of this aspect of computer ethics is growing in importance as the use of computers grows.

CRIME, SECURITY, AND THE PERSONAL COMPUTER

Of the crimes listed in Table 18-1 (page 579), only the telephone access code fraud case clearly resulted from using a personal computer. But, as stated earlier, the personal computer has had an impact on computer crime by enabling unauthorized users to break into computer systems using modems. In addition to being used to break into mainframe computer systems illegally, the personal computer has brought on a new group of ethical, legal, and security problems. Most of these problems revolve around the copying of commercial software, but there are also new security problems involved with the use of the personal computer in the office and with the security of PCs on a network.

Software Piracy

Before personal computers were introduced—back when mainframes and minicomputers were the only sources of computing power—users had access to whatever software was available at their computer center or whatever they had written themselves. Occasionally, they could use software at other centers through a network system, and, of course, hackers were able to avail themselves of software not available to the average user. In this environment, there was seldom the need or the facility to copy the commercial software from the computer.

All of this has changed as personal computers have become more widely used. Stand-alone PCs require a copy of a software package for each machine, rather than simply using the software available on a mainframe. To avoid the expense of buying commercial software packages for a PC, many users have resorted to the use of pirated copies. As the popularity of personal computers and their software has grown, so has the problem of people illegally copying software—commonly referred to as **software piracy.** In 1991, it was estimated that worldwide losses from copyright infringement were over $10 billion. In the United States alone, the losses amount to over $2 billion annually. The Software Publisher's Association, with over 500 members, has moved strongly against the worst domestic offenders and against retailers around the world to reduce this practice. However, some foreign countries are referred to as "one disk countries" because of the widespread software piracy they practice.

To understand how copying for personal use of commercial software and software piracy differ, it is necessary to look at the 1980 Software Copyright Act. In this act and others before it, a distinction is made between copying a piece of software for backup purposes and copying it to sell or give away. It is perfectly legal to copy a disk for backup purposes. It does not matter how many copies are made, as long as all are retained by the user. The minute a copy is given or sold to anyone else, a federal law has been broken. The penalties under this law include damages to the copyright holder, in this case the software developer, as well as loss of any profits made by the person who has copied the program. In cases of willful copying and resale, prison terms can be imposed. From a practical standpoint, enforcement of the copyright law is reserved for the most blatant offenders because of the cost of prosecution. This means that the person who copies a program and gives it to a friend is probably not going to be prosecuted, but copying and reselling a piece of software in large quantities will bring quick action by the U.S. Attorney's office. However, one must remember that the software developer has put a great deal of money and effort into creating that package and expects a fair return on the investment. Every time someone gives away a copy of the program, the developer suffers a loss. If this were to happen enough times, there would be no incentive for companies to develop software.

Another part of the copyright act permits the user to modify the program to the extent necessary to make it useful. In this case, a user may decide to change a program to meet special needs, but no matter how much it is changed, it still cannot be resold as a new product. The U.S. Attorney's office has become involved in several cases in which persons have either knowingly or unknowingly modified a package and tried to resell the result as a new product.

Physical Security for the Personal Computer

The widespread use of personal computers has added a new security problem: These machines are easily stolen unless they are secured to a heavy object such as a desk or a table. Even then, their covers can be removed and disk drives and other internal devices stolen, leaving the computer useless. While replacing a PC is quite inexpensive compared to replacing mainframe equipment, even a small hard disk can contain data and information that can be very expensive to replace. The 3M Corporation has calculated that the loss of a hard disk with 20 Mbytes of sales and marketing data will require 19 days to recreate at a cost of $17,000.[2] Floppy disks are even easier to steal when they are left lying around or are stored in an unlocked desk drawer or cabinet. Locked doors may be even more important for PC security than they are for the larger, less portable computers.

In addition to securing a PC against theft, individuals and companies must take care to protect the personal computer from environmental harm. The normal precautions taken for any piece of office equipment against fire, water, dust, and other physical damage apply. Besides these, the user must protect the computer and its data against, of all things, electricity. Too much electricity, too little, the wrong kind, or the right kind applied in the wrong manner can all cause problems. If a computer is hit by a **voltage surge,** or **spike,** in which lightning or some other electrical disturbance causes a sudden increase in the electrical supply, the delicate chips and other electrical parts can be destroyed. For this reason, **surge protectors** are recommended to protect the computer. Some of these devices are available for less than $50 and plug into a normal wall outlet. The computer and its peripherals are then plugged into outlets in the surge protector. When a surge hits the wall outlet, a circuit breaker is thrown in the surge protector and the computer and its peripherals are protected.

Too little electricity—in the form of a brownout or a blackout—can cause the loss of all data from internal memory. Since RAM is volatile and depends on a constant power source to retain the information, loss of power means loss of memory. Devices exist for continuing the power to a personal computer if electrical current is disrupted, and they are becoming important to so-called "power users"—those people who use the personal computer on a daily basis in their business or at home. These devices, called **uninterruptible power supplies (UPS),** retail for less than $300. However, if you do not have a UPS, the best defense against a power outage is frequently saving information in RAM to disk.

Another problem that must be considered in the use of a personal computer is **static electricity.** In a dry climate, walking across a rug can generate a charge of static electricity sufficient to cause significant damage to data or to electrical parts. Antistatic spray, touchpads, or special floor covers provide protection against static electricity.

Finally, plugging parts of the system into different outlets can cause explosions in the computer equipment. Occasionally, an outlet will have **reverse polarity;** when a system with normal polarity is plugged into such an outlet, an explosion may occur. Obviously, the computer parts would be damaged by such an occurrence, so a surge protector with multiple outlets should be used to connect all computer units to the same wall outlet. Figure 18-7 demonstrates the right way and the wrong way to go about this.

Static electricity can have a devastating effect. This chip—magnified 10,000 times—was subjected to 3,000 volts by human contact with the computer.

[2]Mikkel Aaland, "Preventing Computer Disaster," *Working Woman*, November 1988, p. 88.

Power supply devices can ensure that the computer continues to have an adequate supply of electricity even if there is a brownout or blackout.

Data Security for the Personal Computer

Data security for a personal computer is similar in many ways to that for a mainframe, except that normally a single user is involved. The first way for the user to protect data is to lock disks up when leaving the building. If a hard disk model is used, lockup mechanisms can be placed on the computer itself. With some operating systems, passwords can be used to protect files from unauthorized use or damage. With other equipment, the user can make information disappear from the screen by pressing a single key if an unauthorized person walks by.

Backing up data frequently is every bit as important on PCs as it is on mainframe computers. Unfortunately, PC users generally tend to put this task off as long as possible. To avoid the potentially expensive problems that can occur if the hard disk crashes or an errant command destroys all data on the disk, making backups on disk or tape should be a policy of every PC user.

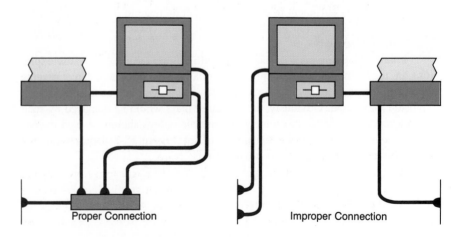

FIGURE 18-7
Proper and Improper Electrical Connections

Proper Connection

Improper Connection

Network Security

With the ever-increasing number of networks of PCs, network security is becoming an important consideration. Network security considerations combine the requirements of mainframe security and PC security. Like mainframes, networks often use passwords to control the user's access to files. Like PCs, the individual workstations on the network must be physically protected. Encryption packages for networks are similar to those for mainframes and are aimed at stopping unauthorized access to the data being sent among the terminals in the network. Network operating systems must also ensure that users cannot copy software from the file server or that there are not more users accessing a given software package than have licenses for that software. For example, if a college has purchased only ten copies of a certain package to be used on 100 network workstations, the network operating system must ensure that only ten users access the package. The network file server must also be protected with a high-quality surge protector as well as an uninterrupted power supply.

REVIEW OF KEY POINTS

1. The two aspects of the unethical or illegal use of the computer are computer crime and computer security.
2. Computer crimes involve a great deal of money, yet historically the penalties have not been very severe.
3. The five categories of computer crime are manipulation or theft of data or assets; direct attack on hardware, software, or data; use

of the computer for planning or committing a crime; deception or intimidation of people by computer; and unauthorized use of the computer for personal gain.

4. Persons who commit computer crime fall into three groups: employees, outside users (including hackers), and organized crime. Employees (or ex-employees) make up the largest element.

5. The computer crime process includes input crimes, processing crimes, output crimes, and storage crimes—depending on where in the input, processing, output, and storage process the crime occurs.

6. Processing crimes include viruses, worms, Trojan horses, time bombs, logic bombs, and trapdoors. Viruses, the most publicized of these crimes, are programs that replicate themselves in the computer's memory in either a benign or a harmful manner.

7. New laws have increased the penalties for computer crime and for eavesdropping on electronic communications. Usually, larger corporations have insurance coverage for computer crime losses; smaller companies may not.

8. Threats to the computer and data include errors and omission of data, misuse by disgruntled or dishonest employees, fire damage, water damage, and external attacks.

9. The two types of computer security are physical security and data security. Physical security protects the computer hardware, and data security protects the data and software.

10. Physical security measures include excluding unauthorized persons, building tamperproof hardware, protecting hardware from natural or human disasters, and protecting the tape library.

11. Tools to provide data security include passwords that are changed often, systems audit software, security software packages, callback systems, port protection devices, data encryption, and antivirus policies and software.

12. Software piracy—users making and distributing unauthorized copies of a software disk—is a major problem in personal computer security.

13. A personal computer must be protected from the same physical threats as mainframe computers are, but it must also be protected from theft and the problems that result from too much or too little electricity.

14. Ensuring data security for PCs involves making frequent backups of disk storage. Network security is a combination of mainframe and PC security.

KEY TERMS

antivirus software
backup
call-back system
ciphertext
cleartext
computer crime
computer security
Data Encryption Standard (DES)

data encryption system
data security
dial-up computer system
electronic forgery
hacker
input crime
logic bomb
output crime

password
password policy
personal identification number (PIN)
physical security
port
port protection device
processing crime
reverse polarity
security software package
software piracy
spike

static electricity
storage crime
surge protector
systems audit software
time bomb
trapdoor
Trojan horse
uninterruptible power supply (UPS)
virus
voltage surge
worm

1. Why have computer crimes often brought large amounts of money to the criminals who commit them?

2. Name and discuss the five types of crime involving a computer.

3. Name and discuss the three types of computer criminal. Why are hackers considered computer criminals?

4. What group of computer criminals is the most threatening to computers?

5. In what ways is organized crime using computers for illegal purposes? In what other illegal ways might they use the computer?

6. Discuss the various points at which crime can occur in the use of a computer.

7. Name three types of crime that involve the CPU and memory of a computer. What is the difference between a virus and a worm?

8. Discuss the Computer Fraud and Abuse Act of 1986. What penalties are given for computer criminals in this act?

9. How are large corporations different from small companies in terms of their insurance coverage against computer crime?

10. What two types of security does a computer need?

11. List three methods, other than passwords, that are used to protect data on a computer. Discuss one of these methods in detail.

12. Discuss the use of passwords to discourage unauthorized access.

13. How is security for a PC different from security on a mainframe?

14. Define *software piracy*. Why is this a problem with personal computers but not with mainframes?

15. Why is it necessary to protect a personal computer from too much, too little, or the wrong type of electricity? What is a UPS?

19

Computer Issues in Privacy and Health

There is no doubt that the computer is truly a mind tool that helps us do many things that we could not otherwise accomplish. However, problems arise when the computer is used to invade individuals' privacy or when computer use results in health problems for users. In this chapter, we discuss both privacy and health issues related to computer use. The computer can be used to invade our personal privacy in several ways, including reading electronic mail and using private data banks to direct sales efforts. Health-related problems associated with long-term use of computer terminals have been reported, in addition to problems resulting from the use of computer-controlled machines. The chapter concludes with a discussion about the science of ergonomics, which is concerned with the design of the workplace.

STUDY OBJECTIVES

After reading this chapter, you should be able to

- recognize the privacy and health issues related to computer use;
- understand how the combination of computers and data banks can accelerate the invasion of personal privacy;
- discuss the explosive growth of private data banks and how information stored in them is cross-matched for marketing purposes;
- describe the increased use of transactional data and how it is used to create private data banks;
- discuss the issues involved in the privacy of electronic mail;
- list the laws enacted to protect privacy;
- describe the use of electronic supervision to monitor workstations;
- discuss the various reported health hazards associated with long-term use of computer terminals or PCs;
- describe carpal tunnel syndrome and how to avoid and treat it;
- explain the health hazards associated with software errors (bugs) in computer-controlled machines;
- describe the psychological problems resulting from computer use;
- discuss the meaning of "ergonomics" as it applies to computer workstations.

"LITTLE BROTHER" IS WATCHING YOU

In December 1989, District Cablevision in Washington, D.C., hired James Russell Wiggins to fill a $70,000-a-year sales job. However six weeks later, a routine background check showed that Wiggins apparently was once convicted of cocaine possession. Consequently, he was fired. In Bossier, Louisiana, Ernest Trent, an oil rig roustabout with 15 years of experience, has applied without success for nearly 200 jobs over the past six years. His problem in finding a job seems related to a worker's compensation claim he filed against the Pennzoil Company after he injured his right arm in a job-related accident. Between 1984 and 1986, Alice Arias, a mother of four

sons, was turned down over 100 times when she attempted to rent an apartment in Los Angeles. As a result, she was forced to live in a motel and store her belongings, which the storage facility sold when she could not pay the storage fee.

Although the problems of these people seem to have little in common, they all stem from a single problem— incorrect or unethical use of personal information contained in private data bases. Instead of contending with a single, huge government data base that contains information on all citizens, we now face many small private data bases that, if combined, can provide the same information as one huge government data base. This phenomenon has been termed "little brother," to differentiate it from the infamous Big Brother that watched over the citizens of Oceania in the book *1984*.

Returning to the first case, it turned out that James *Ray* Wiggins, not James *Russell* Wiggins of District Cablevision, had an arrest record for cocaine possession. When the company requested a background check, Equifax Corporation (one of the three largest

credit bureaus) provided incorrect information. In the second case, Mr. Trent's name was entered on one or more data banks that track workers who file worker's compensation claims. Mr. Trent's experience indicates that the information contained in the data base is used by companies to determine whether an applicant has ever filed a claim, and if the applicant has, to deny work to the individual. Finally, Alice Arias had problems finding an apartment because another Alice Arias not only existed but lived on a street with a name similar to that on which Alice, of the example, lived. The other Alice had been evicted from her apartment and ordered to pay $1,400 in back rent. As a result, the innocent Alice Arias was blacklisted by landlords who subscribed to a data base that lists names of bad-risk tenants. At this writing, all three individuals have filed suit against the respective data bank companies.

Sources: Jeffrey Rothfeder, "Looking for a Job? You May Be Out Before You Go In," *Business Week,* September 24, 1990, pp. 128–129, Simson L. Garfinkel, "From Database to Blacklist," *The Christian Science Monitor,* August 1, 1990, pp. 12–13.

INTRODUCTION

In Chapter 5, we discussed some people-oriented issues common to computer use. Two issues have received a great deal of attention in the last few years— the effect of computers on personal privacy and the potential health hazards associated with the use of computers and computer-controlled machines. These two issues and the science that is devoted to finding a more healthful work-place—ergonomics—are discussed in this chapter.

The privacy issue has roots from almost 30 years ago, the mid-1960s. It became clear then that the computer can be used to solve many problems society faces but can also be used to invade privacy. As mentioned in the box at the beginning of this chapter, the major concern was that the government would use computers to invade personal privacy. In other words, the threat of "Big Brother" concerned people most. Personal privacy has always been an important issue in the United States, and not all invasions of privacy have been computer related. However, computers have made it much easier to find and collect information about individuals and organizations, which means that it is also much easier to invade privacy.

Today, on the other hand, people are more concerned about the threat of organizations and individuals using private data bases to invade their privacy. This is because almost anyone with a personal computer and modem can access a data base and retrieve information about prospective employees, tenants, or other individuals of interest.

Just as the increased use of computers has made existing problems with invasion of privacy worse, the increased use of computers in the workplace has greatly increased the potential for work-related health problems. Health problems for workers have always existed, but heavy dependence on the keyboard to input data and instructions to terminals and personal computers has created an entirely new set of health problems for workers who use these machines over long periods of time.

In the following sections, we look at the privacy issue as it relates to the security and confidentiality of computer-based information on individuals. The ethics of computer use, a related issue, is also discussed. We will then turn our attention to the health issues associated with computer use and to the use of ergonomically designed office equipment.

PRIVACY ISSUES IN THE USE OF THE COMPUTER

As we said earlier, protection of personal privacy has always been a great concern in the United States. In fact, a primary purpose of the Bill of Rights is to protect citizens from government interference. Each new technological advance in communication and computers must be scrutinized to determine how it affects privacy, whether it falls under existing privacy laws, or whether new laws are required. For example, the introduction of both the telegraph and telephone in the latter half of the nineteenth century raised questions. Would telegrams be protected by mail privacy laws, or would they be open to investigation by the authorities? Could authorities listen in on telephone conversations if protecting the public good seemed to warrant it?

There is also concern about information gathered by the Bureau of the Census. The first census was taken in 1790 and consisted of only four questions. However, by 1890, some 200 census forms contained a total of over 13,000 questions. In 1990, this number was even larger. Census information is supposedly confidential and used *only* by the Bureau of the Census for reporting statistics about the population of the country. In two instances, however, the right to privacy was abridged. First, during World War I, census records were used to locate draft evaders. Second, at the beginning of World War II, census records were used to locate Japanese Americans to remove them to detention camps. It is interesting to note that these two instances predated the introduction of computers, so a computer is not required to invade individual privacy. The computer, however, can search multiple data sources in a matter of *seconds*, whereas a manual search would require *days*.

Although the computer can be used to invade privacy, it is important to remember that it also simplifies our lives. For example, the computer, with its ability to process data quickly from one or more data bases, enables anyone with

> Consumers want it all. They want privacy, and they want the consumer society.
>
> *Alan F. Westin, Professor, Columbia University*
>
> Quoted in "Consumers Fear Threat to Privacy," *Computerworld,* June 18, 1990, p. 4.

Without computerized data bases, it would be impossible to have airline reservations systems, such as American Airlines' Sabre System.

a telephone line to make an airline reservation with any carrier for virtually any flight. It enables us to use credit cards and automatic teller machines virtually anywhere in the world. The Social Security Administration and health insurance companies would be unbelievably slow in processing claims without computers to check records. These are but a few examples from a very long and growing list of how computers and data bases have benefitted us. They have become necessary tools of modern life and should not create problems for law-abiding citizens. Invasion of personal privacy occurs when personal data bases are used inappropriately or unethically.

The National Data Bank Concept

In the mid-1960s, the Bureau of the Budget recommended setting up a national data base, or, as such a data base containing information about individuals is called, a **data bank.** The data bank would allow the government to analyze national economic trends more efficiently. Several independent studies supported the concept, but hearings before the U.S. House of Representatives in July 1966 resulted in the publication of a report entitled "Privacy and the National Data Bank Concept," which was extremely critical of the recommendation. Comments in the report demonstrate the public's concern about a national data bank: "The creation of such systems might well make the individual citizen apprehensive about exercising his rights to express controversial views and behave spontaneously."[1]

Based on this report, the federal government dropped the idea of developing a national data bank. However, this did not end the threat of using computers to invade personal privacy. For example, the Lotus Corporation (distributor of Lotus 1-2-3) and the Equifax Corporation (one of the three largest credit bureaus) developed a data bank product called MarketPlace that had all the properties of a national data bank. MarketPlace would have allowed personal computer users to access information from CD-ROM on over 120 million Americans in 80 million households. Public outcry forced Lotus and Equifax to terminate their plan to distribute MarketPlace; however, the mere fact that it was developed demonstrates the ease with which private organizations can create the equivalent of a national data bank.

Privacy Laws

The proposal for a national data bank and its subsequent rejection was the beginning of a period of legislative action on the privacy issue. This action included the following acts:

- the Fair Credit Reporting Act of 1970
- the Freedom of Information Act of 1970
- the Privacy Act of 1974

---

[1] U.S. House of Representatives, Committee on Governmental Operations, "Privacy and the National Data Bank Concept," August 1, 1968, p. 3.

- the Electronic Communications Privacy Act of 1986
- the Computer Security Act of 1987

We will look briefly at each of these laws before turning our attention to the current status of data banks.

The **Fair Credit Reporting Act of 1970** regulates some actions of credit bureaus. These private companies collect credit information on individuals who have borrowed money and on many who have not. When a person wishes to borrow money or engage in various other activities, including applying for a job, the potential lender or, in the latter case, employer, runs a **credit check** on the individual by requesting information from a credit bureau. The credit bureau sends a report, based on information it has gathered, to the company requesting the information. It is important to note that credit bureaus make little or no effort to verify the information they gather and pass on in a report. The 1970 law attempts to regulate the industry in a number of ways: It specifies to whom credit agencies can send reports; it sets time limits for reporting types of financial data; it requires credit agencies to disclose to consumers the contents of their respective files; and it makes it possible for a consumer to dispute the contents of his or her file by adding a note to it. It also requires credit agencies to use their data *only* for the purpose it was originally intended. Unfortunately, the tremendous increase in computing power since 1970 has caused widespread abuse of the last proviso.

The **Freedom of Information Act of 1970** gave individuals the right to inspect information concerning them held in U.S. government data banks. It also made certain data about federal agencies available to individuals and organizations. The latter aspect of this act has opened many files that otherwise would not have come to light.

Based on a 1973 report on privacy by the Department of Health, Education and Welfare (now the Department of Health and Human Services), the **1974 Privacy Act** attempted to correct most of the recordkeeping practices of the federal government. The act exempts various law enforcement agencies, the CIA, and the Secret Service, but in general, it applies to all other government agencies and organizations doing business with the federal government.

The most recent legislations for protecting the personal privacy of individuals in the United States are the **Electronic Communications Privacy Act of 1986** and the **Computer Security Act of 1987.** Wiretapping laws make it illegal to eavesdrop on telephone conversations and other "aural" communications; however, until the Electronic Communications Privacy Act was enacted in 1986, bits and bytes flowing between computers were not protected. This act extended the wiretap law protecting aural conversations to include communications between computers. A person convicted of electronic eavesdropping or violating the security of a computer system can be sentenced for up to 10 years in prison or fined up to $100,000. Organizations convicted of electronic eavesdropping can also be punished. The Computer Security Act of 1987 was aimed at ensuring the security of U.S. government computers. It was the government's response to concerns about security risks that might arise from its growing use of computers and information technology. Public electronic mail is protected by this act, but recent court decisions have made corporate electronic mail messages the property of the organization (see box on page 608). Proposals to change the Electronic Communications Privacy Act to protect corporate E-mail have been placed before Congress, but at this writing, no action has been taken.

WATCH WHAT YOU SAY ON E-MAIL!

For over 12 million U.S. employees, sending and receiving messages by electronic mail is a routine part of the job. Many employees assume that, like regular mail, their messages are private. However, a recent court decision ruled that employee E-mail is the property of the company and that it does not fall under the 1986 privacy act that protects public E-mail on MCI, CompuServe, Prodigy, or other services.

The case, which is under appeal, began when the electronic mail administrator at Epson America discovered that her boss was reading employee E-mail messages. When she alleged that the practice violated the privacy of employees, she was fired. In a similar case, two former employees of Nissan Motor Company filed suit against Nissan, charging that their E-mail messages were read and used against them.

Some companies maintain that E-mail messages generated by employees using company computers and stored on company hard disks are company property. They believe their position is reasonable, because employees who use E-mail to send frivolous messages or run their own businesses cut into company computer resources and processing power. On the other hand, companies such as Hallmark Cards, which has 4,500 users on its E-mail system, believe that the same rights to privacy exist with E-mail as with any other type of correspondence. Regardless of a company's initial stand on E-mail, the two lawsuits we mentioned have motivated many companies, Hughes Aircraft for one, to take a hard look at their E-mail policies.

Source: Christine Casatelli, "Setting Ground Rules for Privacy," *Computerworld*, March 18, 1991, pp. 47, 50.

> **You don't read other people's mail just as you don't listen to their phone conversations. Right is right, and wrong is wrong.**
>
> *Alana Shoars, former electronic mail administrator at Epson America.*
>
> Quoted in "Do Employees Have a Right to Electronic Privacy," *The New York Times*, December 8, 1991, p. 8.

Data Banks Today

Although the United States does not have a national data bank, numerous public and private data banks have evolved, and their number increases almost daily. The combined growth of mainframe power and storage capacity, along with the introduction of personal computers, has accelerated the computerization of data banks. The personal computer has allowed small organizations to set up data banks of clients, customers, and so on, and at the same time, communicate with mainframe data banks. Many of these are public data banks that exist for federal and state government use, but there also exist numerous private data banks. Table 19-1 provides examples of various public and private data banks, divided into broad categories.

All the data banks listed in Table 19-1 were intended for legitimate purposes. Unfortunately, there is a tendency to extend their use to other areas. Many times, the data banks are combined through a process known as **computer matching** to generate one huge data bank that allows an interested party to obtain information from two or more data banks. Computer matching takes advantage of the fact that an individual's record in one data bank will usually

TABLE 19-1
Examples of Data Banks

Category	Data Bank
Law Enforcement	FBI—National Crime Information Center (NCIC)
	Security clearances
	Defense department surveillance of citizens
Taxes and Regulatory	Internal Revenue Service
	State revenue departments
	Car and boat registration
	Professional and driver's licenses
	Hunting and fishing licenses
Human Services	Social Security registration
	Aid to Dependent Children
	Food stamps
	Veteran benefits
	Employment and unemployment registers
Financial	Credit bureaus
	Credit card companies
	Financial institutions
	Landlord listing of renters
	Insurance company policy holders
	Magazine subscription lists
Organizational	Personnel files, including intelligence, aptitude and personality tests, and supervisor appraisals
	Political party and club membership lists
	Armed forces discharge records
Medical	Hospital and doctor records
	Psychiatric and mental-health records
Travel	Airline reservations
	Lodging reservations
	Car rentals
Communications	Telephone call records
	E-mail messages

have one or more attributes in common with that same individual's record in other data banks. In many cases, this attribute is the Social Security number, which has become virtually a universal identifier for residents of the United States. The biggest user of computer matching is the federal government. Currently, over 100,000 federal computers can access more than half of the government's over 3.5 billion records. The government uses computer matching to increase efficiency. For example, individuals who have not repaid their government student loans were matched with individuals eligible for tax refunds. This enabled the IRS to collect some of the money—$544.91 per case for a cost of only $3.70—owed the government.

Most people would agree that this exemplifies a perfectly legitimate use of computer matching, but many people are still concerned about the potential for invasion of privacy. It may be reassuring to note that a recent study by the General Accounting Office found that most government agencies could not show the benefit of computer matching. Similarly, a Health and Human Services report showed that computer matching identified only 12 percent of the fraudulent cases in California. Another concern is that inaccurate information in the data base or a computer error could harm an individual. An example of this occurred when the state of Massachusetts compared the names of people on welfare roles

This group of documents and credit cards demonstrates the variety of data bases in which a person's name and other information could appear.

to names on bank accounts. If the size of the bank account was above a certain amount, that person was removed from the welfare role. Names were removed before individuals could appeal. In a number of cases, it was determined that the data were wrong, often *after* the welfare recipient lost his or her benefits.

Transactional Data

With the recent computerization of almost all travel, credit, and communication services and point-of-sale purchase systems, a new type of data, unforeseen in the 1960s and 1970s, has come about. It is called **transactional data,** which are collected from transactions requiring customer identification. Examples of transactional data include credit card receipts, long-distance call records, rental car contracts, airline tickets, and automatic teller machine transactions. These and other types of transactional data indicate such things as the types of clothes you buy, where you eat, where you stay when out of town, to where and whom you make long-distance calls, where and when you take trips, and when you withdraw money from the bank. Together, such data can paint a complete picture of an individual's life-style.

Consumers also create data about themselves and their buying habits whenever they fill out "product registration" or contest cards. This information is combined with transactional data to create private data banks. The Market-Place data bank, discussed earlier in this chapter, was going to be created from transactional data provided by Equifax Corporation to Lotus Development Corporation. The private sector can match data banks in the same way that governmental agencies match them. However, the private sector has a different

By the time [businesses are] done, they know more about you than your mother does.

Ed Mierzwinski of U.S. Public Interest Research Group

Quoted in "Your Private Life Is for Sale," *The Atlanta Journal-Constitution,* April 19, 1992, p. A-10.

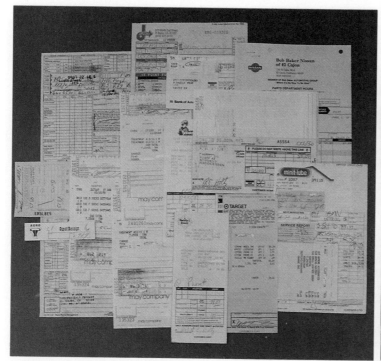

Transactional data can come from an incredible variety of sources. They are created every time a person makes a purchase with a credit card (left) or makes a reservation through a computer network (right).

objective: Private data banks are used for target marketing. In **target marketing,** advertisers use data banks to select a group of individuals who are most likely to buy their products, which allows them to spend more time and money on fewer prospects. For example, credit agencies can use their data bases to create listings of individuals with exemplary bill-paying habits and sell the lists to companies, which then send "preapproved" credit card applications to potential customers, knowing beforehand the individual is not a credit risk. Similarly, target marketing allows the jeweler at your local mall to advertise more efficiently by mailing advertisements only to individuals who live within 10 miles of the mall and have an income of at least $100,000.

As with computer matching operations, target marketing has a potential for abuse by pinpointing potential victims of fraudulent marketing schemes. For example, it would be very easy to match several data banks to create a list of elderly widows with high equity in their homes. Unscrupulous individuals could use the list to market fraudulent home equity loans. The Federal Trade Commission is investigating several such uses of target marketing, but here again, the technology has outstripped the law, for there are few regulations on using this type of data. In light of the power of transactional data, we should avoid giving people information about ourselves unnecessarily, because it could be used for purposes we never intended. For example, a common ruse used by criminals is calling individuals to "verify" a credit card number in order to steal the number.

It is worth noting that in Canada and Europe, laws provide that information may not be used for purposes other than that for which it was originally intended. In enacting such laws, both Canada and Europe have prohibited matching data banks.

TAKING ON TRW AND WINNING

Karen Porter believes she just did her job. To others, however, she is a celebrity for taking on TRW, the credit bureau giant, and forcing it to change its records. Ms. Porter, the town clerk of Norwich, Vermont, got involved with TRW in July 1991 when a local banker called her prior to granting a Norwich physician a car loan. The banker wanted to know if the physician had paid his tax debt. Karen was surprised at the call, because the doctor did not have a tax debt. On the same day, she received two similar calls. All three calls resulted from TRW credit reports that showed nonexistent tax debts.

To find out why TRW was reporting that Norwich residents had tax debts, Karen called TRW six times, but company supervisors did not return any of her calls. Consequently, she planted a story in the local paper. In response, TRW contacted her and began to remedy the problem. It seems that *all* 1,500 local taxpayers of Norwich were incorrectly identified as tax *evaders*. The problem occurred when a TRW contractor posted Norwich's list of taxpayers as tax debtors. TRW initially claimed that no damage had been done and that the problem affected only Norwich. After citizens of other towns also complained, however, TRW purged tax lien data in Vermont, New Hampshire, Rhode Island, and Maine.

Source: John Schwartz, "The Whistle-Blower Who Set TRW Straight," *Newsweek*, October 28, 1991, p. 47.

Criminal Invasion of Privacy

Even if the data bank is not intended to invade our privacy, computer criminals can use them for that purpose. Computer crime is discussed in Chapter 18; however, the privacy issue is important enough to warrant its discussion here as well. Once, the infamous "hackers" (recall from Chapter 5 that a **hacker** is an individual who breaks into computers for the "fun" of it) were the only individuals involved in this type of attack on personal or corporate privacy. However, criminals are finding they can use the computer to invade our privacy for profit. In Houston, "credit doctors" sold good credit histories to individuals who were ineligible for credit through legitimate channels. These "clients" paid up to $2,000 for stolen or fake credit histories that would make them eligible for credit. Houston police identified between $7 and $10 million in merchandise and homes bought through the use of fraudulent credit information.

Criminals and hackers invade our privacy by illegally gaining access to computers containing medical, personnel, or financial records. Although hackers do not usually destroy information, use it for personal profit, or cause harm to people or property, the potential always exists. In a case similar to the credit history scheme, hackers broke into TRW Information Services, the nation's largest credit bureau, using a stolen password. The hackers were able to look at personal data on credit histories, delinquent debts, work histories, bankruptcies, home ownerships, and Social Security numbers. This break-in is regarded as one of the first cases of a breach in a personal data system. While the data could not be changed, in some cases sufficient information existed to enable credit card fraud schemes. A case that had life-threatening potential involved an unidentified hacker in Los Angeles who broke into a hospital computer and doubled the drug doses for all ICU patients. Fortunately, the crime was discovered before any harm came to patients. Individuals involved in this type of action can be prosecuted under the Computer Fraud and Abuse Act or the Electronic Communications Privacy Act passed in 1986 (see Chapter 18, page 587).

Workplace Issues

The introduction of the computer into the workplace has brought with it a raft of new issues involving personal privacy, ethical use of the computer, protection for workers, and electronic supervision of workers. **Electronic supervision,** or **computer monitoring,** refers to the use of the computer to monitor the amount of work performed by employees using a terminal or PC. Because a terminal is connected to a central computer for entering data, making reservations, and so on, an employer can easily monitor an employee's work rate. This is accomplished by installing appropriate software in the central computer. Such software measures values such as the amount of time a telephone operator takes to answer a request, the number of keystrokes a data entry operator makes each second, or the number of errors made by users of terminals. Types of employees often monitored include secretaries, factory and postal workers, and some reservation agents. For example, the length of calls to reservation agents at Pacific Southwest Airlines is monitored to determine whether agents handle an adequate number of calls each hour. Similar software is available for local area networks (LANs) for monitoring PC users on LANs.

An employee rights organization estimated that 52 percent of the 50 million American workers using video display terminals (VDTs) are monitored in this way, and that 10 million of them are evaluated by computer-generated statistics.[2] Many employee organizations and unions believe that this sort of computer monitoring is a clear invasion of employee privacy. Unions representing office workers have filed grievances regarding this policy, and several unions and worker organizations are pressing for legislation prohibiting computer monitoring of workers. They believe it is an unfair way for management to determine productivity and pay. In addition, they believe that monitoring increases the stress level of workers, causing stress-related health problems.

However, it has also been pointed out that the key issue is the spirit in which computer monitoring is done. Management can use it as another supervisory tool or to harass workers over minor details. In the first case, computer monitoring may be viewed as an extension of existing supervisory roles. In the second case, however, it is probably counterproductive, because workers may seek ways to beat the "system."

Other workplace-oriented ethical questions involve use of the computer for purposes other than work, misuse of company data, and viewing of other users' electronic mail. In the first case, some companies encourage employees to use the computer for any purpose they wish, whereas other companies strongly dis-

> These [electronic snooping] techniques were supposed to increase efficiency in the workplace, but they're proving counterproductive.
>
> *Karen Nussbaum, chairperson of 9 to 5, Working Women Education Fund*
>
> Quoted in "Workers' Group Says Computers Used as 'Whips'," *The Atlanta Journal-Constitution,* February 16, 1990, p. A-3.

---

[2] Karen Nussbaum, "Workers Under Surveillance," *Computerworld,* January 6, 1992, p. 21.

courage it. Misuse of company data is almost always unethical, as well as a security breach. Viewing other users' electronic mail could be regarded as being similar to reading someone's U.S. mail.

Telecommuting also interests employee rights groups. Recall from Chapter 13 that **telecommuting** refers to using the computer to work at home. While telecommuting brings a new level of flexibility to many workers, some unions believe that many telecommuting employees are paid on a piece-rate basis, thereby turning the home into a modern-day "sweatshop." In some cases, such workers are not actually employees of the company and do not receive benefits such as retirement and health insurance. In most cases, employees must be better informed of the conditions of their employment and then weigh the benefits of telecommuting against those of working in the office.

HEALTH HAZARDS

In general, the use of computers has been very beneficial to society and has allowed us to do many things not otherwise possible. However, health problems may arise from long-term use of a **video display terminal (VDT)** or personal computer. Also, errors in software that control robots or medical devices have caused injury and death. In this section, we will discuss the various health hazards associated with the use of computers and computer-controlled machines. Here, we will concentrate on the problems. In a later section, we will discuss possible solutions resulting from the use of ergonomics.

VDT-Related Health Hazards

Long-term users of all types of VDTs complain of health problems, particularly of neck, arm, and back pain. Since tens of millions of people use VDTs daily for jobs requiring a high level of concentration, as well as manual dexterity, it is not surprising that complaints are forthcoming. However, the levels of complaints suggests that the problems are not just stress related. Employees most frequently complain of musculoskeletal problems, but they have also cited other problems associated with long-term use of a VDT, including visual difficulties, noise pollution, and psychological problems. Other problems are more subtle. In fact, the use of the computer has created a new dimension in occupational health and safety. With the exception of musculoskeletal problems, employee advocates and scientists do not agree on the exact effects of long-term use of VDTs, but there is sufficient evidence to consider health issues in some depth, beginning with musculoskeletal problems.

Musculoskeletal Problems

Many musculoskeletal problems are associated with the rigid posture requirements of operating a VDT and with poorly designed office desks and chairs. These problems go by several names, including **repetitive strain disorder, cumulative trauma disorder, computeritis,** and **terminalitis.** Regardless of the name, the problem is much the same: High-volume users of VDTs begin feeling aches and pains in the wrists, arms, neck, or back. These minor pains gradually become worse, until almost any motion causes pain from swollen tendons, muscle spasms, or nerve damage. Incidents of cumulative trauma disorder have been

Working at home on a personal computer—telecommuting—is now a very popular way to earn a living.

noted by workers in, for example, meat packing houses and cookie plants, but the National Institute for Occupational Safety and Health (NIOSH) attributes the large number of computer-related cases to the higher number of computers in the workplace. Such disorders comprise the fastest-growing occupational illness and now may constitute as much as 52 percent of all work-related illnesses in private industry.

Why do computers cause cumulative trauma disorder? To answer this question, we must look at how one works at a VDT: Shoulder muscles are tight in supporting the arms, and eye muscles are rigidly focused on the screen. If the typing motion is incorrect or at the wrong level, muscular pain may result. If the wrists are held at the wrong angle or rest on a sharp edge, injury to the tendons or nerves may occur. Each time a key is pressed, tendons slide back and forth in the wrist. If friction occurs, the tendon sheaths, or the tendons themselves, may become inflamed and cause pain. If the swollen tendons squeeze the arm's median nerve at the wrist, where the median nerve passes to the fingers through a narrow passage called the carpal tunnel, a painful condition known as **carpal tunnel syndrome** can occur. This process is shown in Figure 19-1.

Carpal tunnel syndrome is a potentially crippling injury that afflicts over 200,000 workers yearly and has symptoms such as pain, tingling, or numbness in the fingers, hand, or arm. With proper early treatment, over 80 percent of all cases of carpal tunnel syndrome can be reversed. Treatment usually includes a splint on the hand or anti-inflammatory medications. Severe cases, however, may require surgery. It is important that workers not ignore the early symptoms of this disease, as it can worsen to a much more severe condition.

Why do VDTs cause cumulative trauma disorder and typewriters do not? The answer lies in the way we work with these two machines: With a typewriter,

Video display terminals can be terminals tied to a mainframe, such as the one shown here.

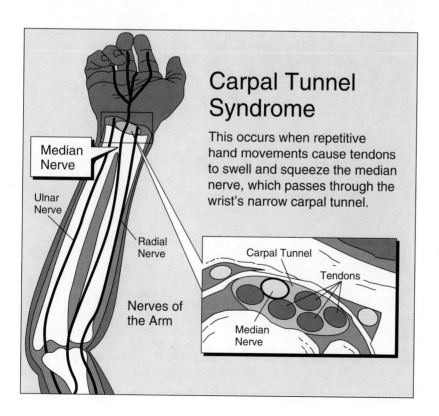

Carpal Tunnel Syndrome

This occurs when repetitive hand movements cause tendons to swell and squeeze the median nerve, which passes through the wrist's narrow carpal tunnel.

Median Nerve

Ulnar Nerve

Radial Nerve

Nerves of the Arm

Carpal Tunnel

Tendons

Median Nerve

FIGURE 19-1
Carpal Tunnel Syndrome.

Source: *The Atlanta Journal-Constitution,* December 4, 1990, p. E-7.

COMPUTER DISEASE

Judy Pasternak, a 30-year-old *Los Angeles Times* staff writer, began suffering neck pain in December 1986. She thought it was from typing on her VDT while cradling a telephone with her neck. Although she visited both a physician and a chiropractor, the neck pain became more intense and, after continued use of her terminal, migrated to her forearms. Her hands became numb and her fingers tingled. After checking around, Judy found that many co-workers had experienced similar ailments, which they referred to as "computer disease," or as Judy named it, "computeritis." To avoid aggravating the condition, Judy began changing her work habits. On the advice of the *Times* safety director, she acquired a new chair and a wrist rest to realign her posture. She also cut back on the number of stories she wrote using a VDT.

By June 1987, she felt much better. However, the neck and back pain returned the following October after she reported and typed a big story. But this time the pain was much more severe and affected her every activity. A physical therapist informed her that she had the wrist strength of an 80-year-old and would need a long period of rest and physical therapy before she could hope to return to anything approaching her previous work schedule. Along with exercising to build up her endurance, she would have to use other reporting tools and keep her use of the VDT keyboard to a minimum.

By following this regimen for over a year, Judy increased her endurance and, in early 1989, returned to an "almost" normal work schedule. She could type for periods of up to 30 minutes without suffering any pain. She then wrote a story about her experience and that of others with "computeritis." A six-month maternity leave further helped relieve the problem and, by early 1992, she was back at work full time. She controls her problem with daily exercise and monthly visits to her physical therapist. She also has a completely adjustable workstation with wrist and foot rests.

Source: Judy Pasternak, "Computeritis," *Los Angeles Times Magazine,* March 12, 1989, pp. 18–23, 42–46, as updated in an interview, January 9, 1992.

Judy Pasternak of the *Los Angeles Times*.

the range of actions is varied by inserting new sheets of paper in the machine, using an eraser or white-out to correct errors, or moving to the file cabinet to retrieve documents. With a VDT, all actions are performed by the fingers on the keyboard, with little, if any, variation in the range of actions and without moving from the terminal periodically. Because the VDT requires little movement of its users, employers often pressure workers to produce large volumes of work in a short period of time. In response to a growing interest in this problem, the first Repetitive Motion Institute in the United States was recently established in Santa Clara County, California.

The solution to problems arising from heavy VDT use lies in more ergonomically designed workplaces—that is, where tables, chairs, keyboards, monitor supports, and so on, are designed so the worker need not strain muscles and tendons—and more varied tasks to avoid constant repetition of motions. This will be discussed in greater detail later in this chapter.

Other Physical Concerns

In addition to the musculoskeletal problems discussed already, there are other physical concerns associated with long-term use of VDTs. They include radiation levels, visual disorders, and noise pollution.

In a video display terminal, the image on the screen is created by a **cathode ray tube (CRT)** that emits a stream of electrons that strike phosphors on the screen to form characters. This is the same technology that forms images on a television screen. The stream of electrons is a form of radiation, and users working less than two feet away from the screen may absorb it. Therefore, many individuals and groups are concerned with the long-term effects of exposure to the radiation, particularly for pregnant women. Spontaneous terminations of pregnancies and fetal deformities have occurred among women who are long-term VDT users, although research has not proved that radiation is the sole cause or even a contributing cause. In response to this concern, monitor manufacturers now offer low-radiation monitors for a slightly higher price than standard monitors. Various organizations continue to monitor the long-term effects of VDT radiation.

Eyestrain is a common complaint associated with prolonged use of VDTs. This presumably results from working for long periods of time at a VDT with glare on the screen caused by misplaced light sources, such as lights and windows, and failure to use a nonglare screen or screen cover. This problem can be solved by removing any reflected light sources and by using a hood to stop other reflections. When Xerox Corp. replaced direct fluorescent lights with indirect fixtures, the number of employees reporting eye focusing problems dropped from 25 percent to only 2 percent! The changeover cost $100 per employee, but improved productivity and reduced health costs more than made up for the cost. Finally, eyestrain can result from the contrast between the screen and the hard copy from which data are entered. The problem occurs because the screen usually has a dark background with light letters, whereas the hard copy usually is white with dark letters. Switching between the two can cause difficulty because it requires a quick adjustment in focus.

Increased use of personal computers has also increased noise levels in the office. The noise may come from impact-type printers, disk drives, and power supply fans on PCs. Multiple impact-type printers used on a continuous basis

The number of those suffering repetitive motion injury is increasing. Most of that increase is coming from information processing workers.

Linda Morse, medical director at the Repetitive Motion Institute

Quoted in "Repetitive Motion Institute Opens, First in U.S.," *Computerworld,* December 3, 1990, p. 73.

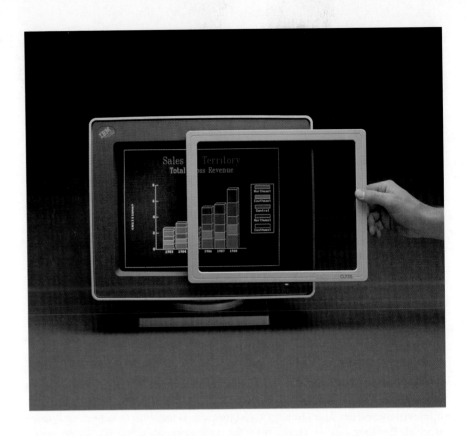

or multiple PCs at work in a relatively small space can result in **noise pollution.** Quite often, workers become unaware of the noise, yet it can still cause problems. It has been shown that long-term noise pollution can affect blood pressure and heart rate or cause unidentified stress in the worker. Stress, in turn, may lead to lower productivity or lost work time. In addition, a condition known as **sonic tinnitus,** which involves loss of hearing or a constant ringing in the ears, may result from long-term exposure to noise. A recent study also showed that the high-pitched tone emitted by some VDTs can cause workers to make mistakes more frequently and make them more prone to headaches and stress-related complaints.

Psychological Problems

Increased use of the personal computer has given rise to a whole new field of study in the behavioral sciences. Initially, computers were used by a very small segment of the population and, as a result, had little or no effect on the general population. However, with business and education using computers for word processing, electronic mail, accounting, and numerous other applications, the emotional effects of confronting the computer have become widespread throughout the general population. Problems include fear of computers, total involvement with computers, and stress-related disorders. **Computerphobia** describes the first case. It is a clinically recognized behavioral condition manifested by fear of the computer. All societal groups have victims of computerphobia, regardless of age, race, sex, education, or economic circumstances. Symptoms of computerphobia include increased blood pressure and pulse rate, headache, and nausea. The symptoms can lead to other somatic complaints or self-medication. Some sufferers turn to drug or alcohol use to cope with their fear and anxiety. Treatment for computerphobia depends on the severity of the condition. For the most severe suffers, a systematic desensitization program is needed, whereas group therapy has been effective for treating individuals who are simply uncomfortable with the machine. The success rate of both these approaches has been high.

Computerphilia is the opposite extreme of computerphobia. Computerphiles are persons who become absorbed in the computer to the exclusion of all other concerns. They become obsessed with the computer, displaying characteristics similar to those of a compulsive gambler. Computerphiles tend to be introverted and detached and usually have fewer communications skills than the average person. They seldom recognize the compulsiveness of their behavior. Researchers have put forth several theories: Some believe that these individuals use the computer as a means of escaping unpleasantries in their lives. Others suggest that, given the computerphile's introverted personality type, these individuals relate better to the computer than to other humans.

Computerphilic behavior may cause legal, social, and psychological problems. As discussed in Chapters 5 and 18, persons who find and implement ways to obtain unauthorized access to computers are breaking the law, and their activities often result in new laws on computer crime. They also tend to alienate themselves from family and friends as their involvement with the computer becomes paramount in their lives. One study of computer club members showed that the average home computer user spend *over* 3 hours per day on his or her computer—not counting computer time at work! The Silicon Syndrome, a type of computerphilia that involves overworking and lack of family contact, has been recognized as a problem in the high-tech areas of our country. It was so named because the behavior pattern was first noticed in the area of northern California termed the Silicon Valley.

The third psychological problem associated with computers involves stress-related problems that occur when workers are pushed to perform at faster rates. This type of problem arises especially when workers are monitored, as discussed earlier in this chapter. Although the problem is stress, the symptoms are often physical. A study at the University of Wisconsin showed significant increase in problems with tension, exhaustion, depression, anxiety, and physical ailments when workers were monitored. Table 19-2 shows the results of this study.

> **Electronic snooping causes fear and stress which leads to illness.**
>
> *Karen Nussbaum, chairperson of 9 to 5, Working Women Education Fund*
>
> Quoted in "Workers' Group Says Computers Used as Whips," *The Atlanta Journal-Constitution,* February 16, 1990, p. A-3.

TABLE 19-2
Effects of Monitoring on Workers

Complaints	Monitored	Nonmonitored
High tension	83%	67%
Exhaustion	79	63
Neck pain	64	41
Sore wrists	51	24

Source: Mitch Betts, "VDT Monitoring Under Stress," *Computerworld,* January 21, 1991, pp. 1, 14.

When not properly programmed or maintained, industrial robots can cause injuries to human workers.

An error in the computer software controlling the USS *Vincennes'* radar protection system led to the mistaken downing of an Iranian civilian airliner.

Health Hazards with Computer-Controlled Machines

The increased use of computer-controlled machines brings increased risk to the workplace. Errors in the software that directs the actions of computer-controlled machines have caused physical injury and death to users of industrial robots and computer-controlled medical devices. At least three deaths and an unknown number of injuries in both the United States and Japan have been directly attributed to the use of robots in factories. In the United States, a misguided robot crushed a worker in an automobile parts factory. Currently, thousands of industrial robots are in use in the United States and more are introduced each year. As the number grows, so do the risks of injury to human workers from improperly programmed robots or from a worker's failure to take precautions when working with or around robots.

Problems can also occur with computer-controlled medical devices if there are errors in the software that controls the machines. There have been at least four accidents involving a linear accelerator used in radiation treatments. In these cases, a software error caused an excessive amount of radiation to be delivered to patients: Two patients died and one patient was badly burned.

In addition to these cases involving robots and linear accelerators, a tragic result of a software error was the destruction of an Iranian airliner in 1988 by the USS *Vincennes*. In this case, the software that operated the ship's Aegis computer system was not designed to update the altitude of an "enemy" aircraft continuously on the computer screens. Confusion over the airliner's altitude led to the decision to shoot it down.

In the *Vincennes* case and the aforementioned cases involving robots and medical machines, injuries and death can be partially attributed to errors in the software that controls the machines. This raises some important practical, legal, and moral issues on the use of computers to control devices that have such a great impact on human life. In fact, some legislators have suggested adopting licensing requirements for computer programmers to minimize these problems. It also points to the need for more testing of software that controls machines. There is no place for software bugs when human life is at stake.

ERGONOMICS

In the previous section, we discussed various health hazards related to the use of computers in an office setting. Finding the means to reduce those health hazards as much as possible falls under a field of science known as ergonomics. **Ergonomics** (also known as **human-factors engineering**) is the *science of designing the workplace in such a way as to keep people healthy while they work, resulting in higher morale and more productivity.* Ergonomics often merges the talents of engineers, architects, physiologists, behavioral scientists, physicians, and furniture designers to determine the best design of tools, tasks, and environments. The goal of the discipline is to create optimum balance between productivity and well-being. An ergonomically designed office will increase worker productivity by allowing him or her to remain comfortable and healthy while pursuing work objectives.

When applied to the VDT workstation, ergonomics includes the positioning of the screen, the height and tilt angle of the keyboard, the distance of the worker from the screen, the chair the worker sits in, and any other environmental factors affecting the worker, such as air quality, temperature, noise, and so on. The detachable keyboard and the tilting, swiveling monitor are examples of ergonomic designs for VDTs. In addition, the chair may be one of the more important, but often the least considered, ergonomic factors of the VDT workstation. The key in selecting a chair is adjustability. Besides allowing for height and back support adjustments, the chair should have a backrest that can be raised or lowered to position the padding; arm rests to reduce upper body fatigue; a seat edge that will not add pressure and constrict blood supply to a user's legs; and a surface that provides good ventilation. Figure 19-2 shows an ergonomically designed work station.

> The cost of improving a computer operator's workstation can range from one-half percent to 10 percent—but typically raises productivity 5-25 percent.
>
> *Julia Lacey, vice president of Workstation Consultants*
>
> Quoted in "Tips, Techniques & Technology for Safe, Stress-Free Computing," *D/FW Computer Currents,* March 1991, p. 24.

Ergonomic Use of the VDT

Not all VDT-related problems can be avoided, but an ergonomic approach can ensure that problems are minimized. First the VDT workstation should be properly designed, as shown in Figure 19-2. Beyond that, it is necessary to deal with the entire environment, including lighting, soundproofing, and ceiling and wall colors. Sitting at a terminal can be as stressful to the body as working on a shop floor. VDT operators must consider, first, the placement of the keyboard, monitor, and material being keyed into the computer. The monitor and copy material should be at equal distances from screen to eliminate excessive focus shifting. (This is especially important for individuals over 40 years of age, because the eyes' focus mechanism becomes less flexible with age.) The screen should be slightly below eye level, with the copy holder near the screen to reduce twisting and turning of the neck and eyes. The keyboard should be located so that the wrist and lower arm are parallel to the floor.

The VDT user's chair must provide proper back support and allow the operator to easily adjust it. The user's feet should be positioned so there is no pressure on the underside of his or her legs. If the chair is the appropriate height,

FIGURE 19-2
Ergonomically Designed Work
Station

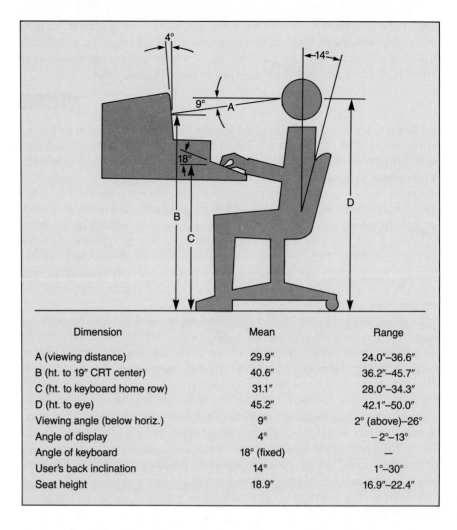

Dimension	Mean	Range
A (viewing distance)	29.9″	24.0″–36.6″
B (ht. to 19″ CRT center)	40.6″	36.2″–45.7″
C (ht. to keyboard home row)	31.1″	28.0″–34.3″
D (ht. to eye)	45.2″	42.1″–50.0″
Viewing angle (below horiz.)	9°	2° (above)–26°
Angle of display	4°	− 2°–13°
Angle of keyboard	18° (fixed)	—
User's back inclination	14°	1°–30°
Seat height	18.9″	16.9″–22.4″

the feet should be placed flat on the floor. However, if the chair is too high, a support for the feet is a necessity.

Workstation lighting should provide room illumination three times brighter than the screen background but not so bright as to cause glare on the screen. The best lighting is directed upward and reflected down to the work area. Screen contrast and resolution have a definite effect on the VDT user. The highest possible resolution monitor should always be used to provide the required sharpness of characters and figures. Working with poor-quality text on a low-resolution monitor, such as a CGA video system, can easily lead to severe eyestrain.

The VDT should be set up so that the screen is not near a window. If the user is working with hard copy and more light is needed, a light may be added to the copy board that holds the hard copy. If the user wears glasses, especially bifocals or trifocals, he or she may want to buy a special set of glasses to handle the distance to the screen and keyboard, since these distances may be different from those for other routine activities. For users working at a VDT on a constant basis, routine eye examinations are recommended for early diagnosis of problems.

When working with a VDT, users should take a short break every two hours. Some users may need a break every hour or a switch to an alternate, non-

AVOIDING VDT PROBLEMS

As noted in the text, VDT problems, such as carpal tunnel syndrome, can be very painful and should not be treated lightly. The best policy is prevention.

The following suggestions may help in avoiding problems from working at a VDT:

- Perform job-specific exercises to strengthen the wrist, fingers, elbows, and shoulders.
- Prior to beginning a job and during breaks, perform finger, hand, and wrist stretching exercises.
- Take frequent rest breaks, or change your work activity.
- Use an ergonomically-designed chair and workstation.

- Ensure that keyboards are at elbow height and use contoured wrist support devices.
- Do not *pound* the keys on the keyboard. Use only the fingers in the typing motion.
- If you use a mouse, place it close to and at the same level as the keyboard.
- If subtle burning pain begins, do not ignore it. Check with your doctor so treatment can begin immediately to avoid serious damage.

VDT task. Moving about enhances circulation in the body and relieves the stress generated by VDT use. At the first sign of the symptoms of cumulative trauma disorder—chronic pain in wrists, arms, neck, or back—the VDT user should consult a physician and request a job reassignment. Ignoring these warning signs can lead to severe pain that may be disabling.

The Future

We have just examined the health hazards associated with the use of VDTs. Some are alarming conditions and are receiving attention. Others are more subtle and will take longer to be resolved. Until recently, government response has been slow in the United States. However, the National Institute for Occupational Safety and Health has responded by monitoring and documenting the problems we have just discussed. Labor advocates have also begun to work for worker protection and education. One group that is actively involved in VDT issues is a national association of office workers called "9 to 5." San Francisco, California, has taken a leading role in requiring ergonomic working conditions for VDT users, and several other states have followed suit with similar legislation. In Europe, governments have moved to issue standards for VDT design and use.

Some employers are opposed to redesigning their working environments ergonomically, but many others recognize the positive results of redesigning their workstations. For example, workers' compensation costs may decrease if employers take steps to avoid employee injuries, absenteeism decreases, and in general, the cost of doing business decreases.

1. Each new technological advance in communications has given rise to new problems involving the invasion of personal privacy. The newest such advance—the computer—enables us to do many things that would be impossible without it, but it can also be used to invade our privacy.

REVIEW OF KEY POINTS

2. A national data bank was proposed in the mid-1960s but was never implemented. Several important laws were enacted in the 1970s to help protect citizens from invasion of their privacy by use of computers.

3. The Electronic Communications Act of 1986 gives electronic communications the same protection as it gives to verbal communications. Government computer security is protected by the Computer Security Act of 1987.

4. Numerous government and private data banks are in use today. These individual data banks can be combined through cross matching of a common attribute to give the effect of a national data bank.

5. A new type of data being collected, which can be used for unethical surveillance, is "transactional data." These data are created when individuals use credit cards; make airline, hotel, or rental car reservations; or place long-distance phone calls. These data are being used to create private data banks.

6. Target marketing is a new process that matches private data banks to develop specific information that is sold to advertisers.

7. Criminal invasion of privacy involves illegal access to computers containing medical, personnel, or financial records.

8. The use of the computer in the workplace creates new problems. Electronic supervision (computer monitoring) uses the computer to monitor the amount of work performed by an employee on a VDT. Other problems in the workplace include misuse of the company's computer or data and reading of others' electronic mail.

9. Telecommuting may allow workers the flexibility of working at home, but it may lead to abuse of the worker.

10. Long-term use of VDTs has led to reports of health problems such as cumulative trauma disorder, eyestrain, radiation problems, and noise-related problems.

11. Psychological problems of computerphobia, computerphilia, and stress due to monitoring are resulting from the impact of the computer on the home and workplace.

12. Computer-controlled machines, such as robots and medical devices, can cause harm to humans when errors exist in the software controlling the machine.

13. Ergonomics is the study of designing the workplace to make it more comfortable and, hence, more productive. Careful attention must be given to the VDT workstation to ensure proper body alignment in relationship to the VDT. Proper environmental factors, such as lighting, monitor resolution, and low noise levels, are also important.

KEY TERMS

carpal tunnel syndrome
cathode ray tube (CRT)
computeritis
computer matching
computer monitoring

computerphilia
computerphobia
Computer Security Act of 1987
credit check
cumulative trauma disorder

data bank
Electronic Communications Privacy
  Act of 1986
electronic supervision
ergonomics
eyestrain
Fair Credit Reporting Act of 1970
Freedom of Information Act of 1970
hacker
human-factors engineering

1974 Privacy Act
noise pollution
repetitive strain disorder
sonic tinnitus
target marketing
telecommuting
terminalitis
transactional data
video display terminal (VDT)

1. Why do we say that technological advances in communications always bring problems with invasion of privacy? Why do we include computers in this category?

2. Discuss past attempts to set up a national data bank. Why are private data banks now of more concern?

3. What laws have been passed to protect personal privacy in a computer age? Discuss one of these laws in detail.

4. List three uses of computer matching of private data banks, other than those mentioned in the chapter, that may create problems.

5. Why has the introduction of the computer increased the fear that data banks are being used to invade personal privacy?

6. Why do we say that individual data banks can be combined to give the effect of a national data bank?

7. Discuss the use of matching to combine data from individual data banks.

8. Describe the criminal invasion of personal privacy by hackers.

9. Why are transactional data different from traditional types of data? Give examples of transactional data other than those listed in the chapter.

10. List some examples of electronic supervision.

11. List the pros and cons of management monitoring of use of terminals and personal computers.

12. What health hazards have been reported from the long-term use of video display terminals? Discuss one of these problems in detail.

13. Discuss the difference between a computerphobe and a computerphile. Why are stress-related problems a concern?

14. Describe problems with computer-controlled machines. Why do we say that these problems are a result of software errors?

15. Discuss the use of ergonomics in the use of computers. Why is this an important concern for management?

Computers at Work in the Arts

1. ModelShop is a CAD program for the Macintosh that helps users do architectural design and city planning. Here, for the cathedral at Amiens, France, ModelShop has reproduced (on the left) a color image of a portion of a wall and also shows (on the right) a three-dimensional wireframe massing model of the next segment of the wall.

2. In her work, *Beyond Picasso*, Lillian Schwartz used Symbolics hardware and software to create her own interpretations of Picasso's work. This screen shows especially well, in the face on the far right, the three-dimensional capabilities of the Symbolics system.

3. To create *Forest Devils' Moon Night*, Kenneth Snelson used a computer to "build" the objects— the sculpture, landscape, and so forth—position them in relation to each other, and then reproduce the sculpture portion from two different viewing angles.

4. Sandra Filipucci creates her "digital monotypes" on Amiga computers. Her pieces are not reproduced from screen images on disk, but rather, they are printed on specialized ink-jet and laser printers.

5. Artist Tyrone Depts used a 3-D modeling and animation program to create the body in this piece, the scanned photos of a woman for the face and and of Jupiter for the backdrop, pulling all together in Photoshop.

6. *Valley of the Kings* was created on a Macintosh by Cheryl Stockton by manipulating a variety of photographs she shot and scanned.

7. Using OASIS™ from Time Arts, Jerry Derry has drawn *Apple Still Life* simulating a charcoal and watercolors effect with pressure input digitizers.

8. At *About Faces,* a science exhibition prepared by San Diego's Reuben H. Fleet Space Theater and Science Center, computers play a large role in making the exhibits work. In "Expression Recognition" (top), using a number of pixels as a measure of distance, visitors can test their ability to discriminate among the universal expressions. Do you recognize "sadness" here? (row 3, third from left) In "Mix and blend" (bottom), visitors can either exchange features or totally blend their faces with other, well-known ones from the exhibit's data base.

9. Five computer graphics teams at Industrial Light and Magic collaborated on creating the special effects seen in *Terminator 2: Judgment Day*, using a Silicon Graphics supercomputer.

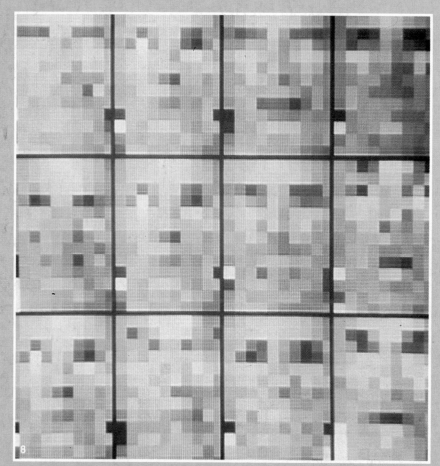

9

10. The IBM PS/2 personal computer can be easily connected to a keyboard to provide additional effects in a music performance.

11. Although George Gershwin has been dead for more than a half-century, his performing style has been saved by using an optical scanner to convert into computer files the holes in player piano scrolls cut by Gershwin. These files are then used either to "play" a specially designed piano or to transcribe piano scores into a book.

12. The computer image behind this dancer was created in real time—moving and changing to follow the dancer during a performance.

20

Computers: The Future and You

As we have discussed throughout this text, smart machines in the form of computers, microprocessor-controlled devices, telecommunications equipment, and so on will be a dominant force in the future of our society. Whereas these devices are often conveniences or work savers today, they very well could be required to complete any job or task in the future. In this chapter, possible careers in the computer field will be considered. Careers in computers are expected to grow dramatically over the next few years. A totally new position—end-user programmer—will become very important in the future. We will also look at some of the changes forecast for computer hardware and software, at information systems, and at the impact of computers and telecommunications on society. Hardware is expected to become smaller, faster, and cheaper, and software must become easier to use to attract new users. Information systems are expected to have an increased impact on organizations, and the impact of computers on society is expected to grow as smart machines become more a part of our everyday lives.

STUDY OBJECTIVES

After reading this chapter, you should be able to

- discuss the movement toward an information society dependent on smart machines;
- describe computer-related careers, the education needed to enter each career, and the potential for growth for professionals in each area;
- understand the growth in demand for end-user programmers;
- list some of the trends in hardware development that will increase speed and decrease the size and cost of computers;
- discuss future changes in software that will make the computer easier to use, including the trend toward graphical interfaces and nonkeyboard means of input;
- describe the changes that information systems are forecast to bring to organizations;
- discuss ways in which computers will affect society in the areas of crime, privacy, and health.

LEARNING MEDICINE WITH VIRTUAL MEMORY

In the not-too-distant future, medical students will don a special set of gloves and headset that are linked to a computer and perform surgery on a simulated patient. Wearing this gear, they will encounter all aspects of a living patient—limitations of muscles and tendons, movement of fluid-filled tendons, and so on—without endangering a life. This approach offers an advantage over the traditional use of cadavers, because dead bodies often lack the resilience of vital fluids necessary to accurately reproduce the effects of surgery on a live patient. Sound farfetched? Well, this approach to medical training may not be as futuristic as you would expect. The Stanford Medical School, in conjunction with NASA, has created a prototype system for doing just this. The software allows for operating on simulated bodies and comes complete with calculations that generate accurate representations of body parts.

This approach to teaching medicine is just one aspect of an exciting new area of research called **virtual reality,** which creates a custom universe within a computer. With this technology, the computer creates imaginary worlds that seem "virtually" real, and it interprets body movements as commands. You can walk through these imaginary worlds, move objects around, and even throw a virtual rock against a virtual wall. The user wears a headset, goggles, and wired gloves that allow the computer to track the user's location in the electronic world.

In another medical application of virtual reality, the Loma Linda Research Center has implemented a special glove to provide extremely accurate measurements of trembling in patients suffering from Parkinson's disease. Accurate measurements enable physicians to better assess a patient's response to various experimental drugs for the disease.

Source: Harvey P. Newquist, "Simulated Surgery," *Computerworld,* March 30, 1992, p. 93.

This virtual environment head-mounted display and dataglove operate with a Macintosh Quadra 950 system.

In considering where the computer field is heading, it is useful to examine what has happened in the last ten years. Just more than ten years ago, IBM introduced its first personal computer, and now the PC is a fixture in almost all offices and in many homes. This amazing growth extends to not just the personal computer but also to the use of mainframes and supercomputers. On an even more personal note, each of us uses many different types of microprocessor-controlled **smart machines** almost daily without even thinking about how they work. Through the use of smart machines, we can carry out many activities not even thought of 10 or 20 years ago. These activities include programming a VCR or microwave oven, accessing our money on a 24-hour basis over worldwide automatic teller networks, and purchasing goods and services using the personal computer. The future holds many exciting possibilities, such as the use of virtual reality to train physicians, as discussed in the box at the beginning of the chapter. Other exciting developments involving smart machines that we cannot imagine will certainly come about in the near future.

The advances made in the last decade are mind-boggling, yet experts predict that we are only on the threshold of even more dramatic advances through computers. In the next five to ten years, computers of all sizes will become smaller, faster, less expensive, and easier to use than those of the last ten years. At the same time, the job market for persons with computer interests and skills will continue to be among the fastest growing of all occupational fields. A severe shortage of programmers in the United States already exists and is predicted to increase during the coming decade.

> **The [computer] industry is over 30 years old, and it's not reached its infancy.**
>
> *John Imlay, chairman,*
> *Management Science America*
>
> Interview with the author.

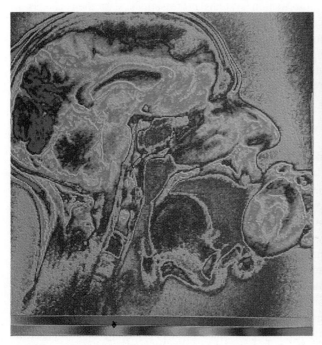 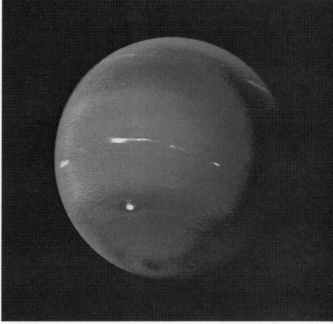

(Left) With nuclear magnetic resonance, it is possible to construct very clear, color-enhanced pictures of internal organs such as the brain. (Right) In its record-setting journey, *Voyager 2* took pictures of the outer planets that were then computer enhanced to reveal previously unseen details.

The Information Society

In Chapter 1, we discussed John Naisbitt's views on the direction of our economy toward one based on information. In fact, he predicted that we will become an **information society** in which smart machines will have a tremendous effect on our personal and professional lives. To prepare you for these changes, this chapter is devoted to two important topics on the future of computers in the information age: career opportunities and advances in the development of computer hardware and software. We begin this discussion by first looking at employment opportunities.

CAREERS IN COMPUTERS

With the United States moving into an information-oriented economy, the job market in the computer and communications industry is growing by leaps and bounds. Employment in computer and computer-related fields is expected to continue to increase in the 1990s. In fact, it is predicted that computer and data processing services will be one of the fastest growing industries through the year 2000, faster even than health services.

In organizations that use computers, there are six major career fields, each requiring different levels of education and experience. These are information systems (IS) management, end-user support, communications, systems/programming, technical services and operations, and data base administration. IS managers manage the information system, and end-user support technicians support PC-based end users. Communications is a rapidly growing area of employment as more and more organizations rely on networks to handle information needs. This reliance requires qualified individuals to keep the networks running. Analysts and programmers design and write the software that is used with the computer system. Many information systems professionals start their careers as programmers and then branch out into other areas as they gain experience and knowledge of the whole IS field. Technical services and operations handle much of the data processing actually performed on the mainframe. Finally, the data base administration group oversees designing and maintaining the organization's data base to ensure its integrity and stability. Table 20-1 shows job titles in each major category along with the salaries listed in a 1991 survey of major corporations. We will now take a more detailed look at each of these categories.

> **Perhaps the most important issue facing information system managers during the 1990s will be the impending shortage of new workers.**
>
> *J. Daniel Couger, distinguished professor of information systems and management science, University of Colorado at Colorado Springs*
>
> Quoted in "Motivating Analysts and Programmers," *Computerworld,* January 15, 1990, p. 73.

Information Systems Management

As with any organization, managers are necessary to ensure that objectives are met and that the operation stays within budget or makes a profit. An entirely new top management position evolved during the 1980s—**chief information officer (CIO).** Many progressive companies have added this position to their top management team because they believe that a CIO will enable them to harness their information to gain a competitive edge in the marketplace. Various companies use various titles, not necessarily CIO, for their chief information officer, but the responsibilities of the job are the same: strategically managing and using the corporate information resources. The CIO is a member of top management and performs much the same role for company data as does the chief financial officer for the company budget, including planning new pro-

TABLE 20-1
IS Job Titles and Compensation

Area	Job Titles	Compensation
IS management	CIO	$79,362
	IS manager/supervisor	62,426
End-user support	Manager, End-user computing	48,359
	PC specialist	33,455
Communications	Network manager	51,519
	Telecommunications manager	50,768
	LAN manager	43,304
	Communications specialist	39,597
Systems/programming	Systems/programming manager	58,455
	Project leader	53,779
	Senior systems analyst	47,214
	Senior programmer/analyst	43,598
	Programmer	29,633
Technical services and operations	Technical services manager	57,825
	Senior operating systems programmer	51,236
	Operations manager	46,443
	Operations shift supervisor	35,552
Data base	Data base manager/administrator	57,819
	Data base analyst	43,862

Source: David A. Ludlum, "Relative Deprivation," *Computerworld,* September 2, 1991, pp. 59, 62, 63.

grams, controlling the use of the data, and educating other members of management on the use of information.

Other executive-level titles in the information management field, in addition to CIO, include programming manager, applications programming manager, and data base manager. In the first two positions, the manager supervises analysts and programmers who do the actual work. This is a very "people-related" position. In the third position, the person oversees the organization's data base operations. Salaries for managers are at the top of those paid to information professionals, with CIOs often making in excess of $100,000 per year.

End-User Support

If you recall from previous chapters, we defined the **end user** as a non-data processing professional who uses the computer to solve problems associated with his or her job. While the end user is not an information systems professional, he or she is often an extremely sophisticated user of computers. This class of computer users has grown tremendously with the increase in availability of personal computers, and as a result, the need for end-user support has also increased. The end-user support category often includes the positions of information center manager and PC specialist. The PC specialist position is fairly new and involves providing technical support to end users in acquiring and using PC hardware and software. It may also include management of the local area network (LAN), although this position is shown under communications in Table 20-1.

Communications

Because communications are so important to the well-being of any organization, this category of positions is crucial. Communications positions can involve managing the organization's local area or wide area networks and overseeing the voice and data communications, including electronic data interchange (EDI). The LAN manager must ensure the security of the local area networks, bring new users online, and install new software in the system. This can be a very exciting position with the many changes occurring almost daily in the world of LANs, but it can also cause a great deal of stress when problems occur in the network and users demand solutions.

Systems/Programming

We have already discussed in some detail the job of systems analyst in Chapters 4 and 15. Recall that these people evaluate and generate solutions to problems. The solutions are then turned into software by the programmer. Ideally, analyst and programmer are separate positions, but in many smaller organizations, the title "programmer/analyst" is used to denote the person responsible for both operations. Job titles in this group include programmer (I, II, etc.), information analyst, systems designer, and systems support specialist.

The demand for well-trained programmers in the United States is at an all-time high, owing to continuous expansion of the software market. The world

The demand for programmers is expected to continue to grow significantly in the near future.

software market, valued at $50 billion in 1988, is expected to grow to $1 trillion by the year 2000. This will result in a need for almost 350,000 more programmers. Although there is an increasing demand for programmers, the number of college students entering this field is dropping from a high of 8 percent in 1982 to less than 3 percent today. The result of this increasing demand for programmers with a decreasing student pool will mean a short supply of qualified programmers during the 1990s. For this reason, if you choose to study programming, you should have no problem finding a desirable programming position upon leaving school.

A fairly new type of programmer is the **end-user programmer,** who creates specific applications using popular software packages. As end users become more familiar with using various PC-based software packages, they demand more ready-made applications developed on such packages as Lotus 1-2-3 or dBASE IV. End-user programmers use the commands and programming language of each package to develop applications. For example, an end user may need a business analysis application on Lotus 1-2-3. Rather than expend time and effort to create the application, the end user interacts with an end-user programmer who is an expert on 1-2-3. The end-user programmer will actually create a spreadsheet template to meet the end user's needs.

Because end users and the application software packages they use did not exist less than ten years ago, the position of end-user programmer did not exist until recently. However, it is expected that the demand for persons with expertise in various popular PC-based software packages will grow dramatically. End-user programmers may have training and experience in creating applications in various software packages, or they may choose to specialize in one, Lotus 1-2-3, for example. Many colleges and universities now offer advanced courses in popular packages, thereby preparing students for jobs in this field.

Technical Services and Operations

Accompanying the ever-increasing demand for mainframe computers is the demand for qualified on-site personnel to actually operate the computer or prepare data to be entered into the computer. Sample job titles in this classification include computer operator, data entry operator or clerk, EDP (electronic data processing) clerk, tape or media librarian, and EDP specialist. While some of these positions (for example, data entry operator) may be open to persons with only a high school education, the increasing sophistication of the equipment often requires at least two years of education beyond high school. Many times, these positions offer flexible work hours that allow a student to obtain valuable practical experience while attending school. This experience in computer operations is very valuable, because it will enable the person to move into and perform the required work of a similar operation.

Operators are expected to know how to initialize (start up) the computer system, monitor its operations, load tapes when requested by users, and take any preventative or remedial actions necessary. Data entry operators and clerks prepare or enter data into the computer, and the tape or media librarian maintains the tapes or written documentation. Operating system programmers are in this group because they must be available to solve any problems that arise in the mainframe operating system.

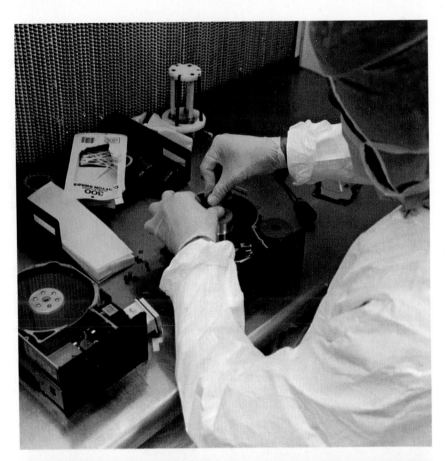

A common maintenance operation on a personal computer is to repair or realign disk drives.

Repairing a given type of mainframe computer requires specific training.

Data Base Administration

Because the data base is the repository of all data and information used by an organization, the administration of the data base is an important position. The **data base administrator** controls the overall operations of the data base and, as such, acts as the custodian of the data base. This involves creating, adding, and deleting records and ensuring security and recovery. He or she ultimately decides on the organization of the physical data and determines the various logical relationships needed to satisfy user requests.

Other Computer Careers

In addition to the positions in organizations discussed already, there are several other categories of computer careers that exist both inside and outside of organizations. These include repair and servicing, sales and marketing, instruction, and consulting.

The area of repair and servicing computers is predicted to grow dramatically over the next few years as the number of computers being sold and used increases. Maintenance personnel for mainframe or minicomputers usually work for a company that provides a maintenance contract to the owner or lessee of the computer. Maintenance people must have training specific to the type of computer used by their company. On the other hand, repair persons for personal computers are often entrepreneurs who devote a business to servicing or repairing small computers. These machines are usually quite sturdy, but occasional problems arise, especially with disk drives and printers. PC repair does not require the same level of specific training as does mainframe repair, but it does require a thorough knowledge of PC hardware.

Individuals who are interested in computers, have some knowledge of how they work, are articulate, and enjoy meeting people may want to consider the

> **People can't fix their computers any more than they can fix their own cars. If you have the knowledge and the know-how to market yourself, there is a lot of business out there.**
>
> *Bernadette Grey, executive editor of* Home Office Computing *magazine*
>
> Quoted in "Computer Tinkerers Can Earn a Living," *The Atlanta Journal-Constitution,* October 8, 1990, p. D-1.

Being able to present a computer in an unintimidating fashion is critical to being a successful computer salesperson.

computer sales and marketing field. A growing need exists for salespeople who can present a computer in a nonintimidating fashion. It is not necessary to be a technical expert on computers but, rather, to have a working knowledge of computers. Marketing involves the presentation of the hardware and software products through written and illustrated material to prospective buyers. It also includes writing the **documentation** buyers use to learn how to use the hardware and software after they buy it. Evidence suggests that individuals with a liberal arts background and some knowledge of computers may be the best-qualified people to write both the sales material and the documentation.

With interest in computers growing at all levels of the educational system, there is a corresponding need for people to provide instruction. Here again, demand is greater than supply, so anyone with knowledge of computers wishing to go into teaching should have little difficulty finding a suitable job. A degree in education with extra coursework in computer science is usually satisfactory for teaching at the elementary and high school level. Teaching at the technical school and college level usually requires at least a master's degree in computer science or a related field. At the university level, where the greatest demand for teachers exists, a Ph.D. is usually required. Many fine professors of computer science are lured from the university by industry, and the supply of new Ph.D.s is not increasing fast enough to take up the slack. Combine this situation with demands for more computer science courses, and it is easy to see why the demand for teachers is increasing.

Computer instruction is a rapidly growing field at all levels of formal education—elementary, high school, college, and university.

EXECUTRAIN

The Leader in Computer Training

Like most successful businesses, ExecuTrain was started to meet a perceived need—in this case, a need for training courses on the use of personal computer software. ExecuTrain was started in 1984 by three University of Georgia business school graduates—David Deutsch, Kim Kienzle-Deutsch, and Mike Addison. They were later joined by Mike Moss. Since its inception, ExecuTrain has grown to be a leader in the computer training field.

In 1992 alone, the company trained over 200,000 people out of over 60 offices nationwide and had system sales of over $37 million.

The success of ExecuTrain is due in large part to the foresight of its founders. Deutsch and Addison both went to work for large corporations when they graduated from college in the early 1980s in the computer support areas. In their positions, both recognized the tremendous and increasing need for training in the then-new field of PC software. At the same time Kienzle-Deutsch was finishing an MBA in business information systems and was available to spearhead the development of courseware and reference materials. Deutsch and Addison worked their regular jobs to

pay the bills, but by the middle of 1984 the first course had been developed and was being taught at a few locations. By early 1985, the threesome had put together a total of 12 courses, and the response was great enough that Deutsch and Addison could quit their jobs and work full time on ExecuTrain.

Why has ExecuTrain been so successful? Possibly because of the company's emphasis on always putting the client first. Over 40 courses are offered in subjects ranging from spreadsheets to word processing to data base management. The courseware can be customized to the client's needs and can be taught at ExecuTrain's facilities or at the client's offices. Classes are kept small and there is a free support line for follow-up questions.

Source: ExecuTrain press release and interview with Mike Addison, March 5, 1992.

Small classes and customized courseware are just two aspects of ExecuTrain's program that have made the company—and its clients—successful.

There is a growing market for instructors of short training courses on specific hardware and software products. These courses are organized to provide hands-on experience with the product. Popular short courses include introduction to the PC; use of commonly used software packages, such as WordPerfect, Lotus 1-2-3, and so on; and advanced or industry-specific courses on various software products. Providing these courses is a rapidly growing industry that includes writing instruction manuals and teaching classes.

At the university level, instruction is often carried out in specialized computer classrooms.

There is also a growing need for consulting services. A consultant studies a prospective user's needs and recommends hardware and software. A consultant typically has extensive experience in the computer industry before entering this field.

THE FUTURE OF COMPUTING

In predicting the future of computing, we will look at the four major topics of this book: hardware, software, ISs, and the impact of computers on society. Of these, the future of hardware is the easiest to predict, but each of the other three areas is equally important. Moreover, combined changes in hardware and software will affect predicted changes in the last two areas.

The Future of Hardware

As computer chip technology continues to evolve and become more sophisticated, computers, simultaneously, will become smaller, faster, and cheaper. From our previous chapters, you know that the beginning of modern computer technology began in 1947 with the invention of the transistor. In the late 1960s, chips contained 1,000 transistors. Over the past 20 years, however, the number of transistors has increased dramatically: Today, chips such as the Intel i486 contain over a million transistors, and chips still on the drawing board will contain upwards of 25 million transistors. Although this is an enormous advance, particularly compared to early chips, experts predict that by the end of this century chips will contain 100 million transistors. The miniaturization of various computer components has revolutionized the computer industry, allowing for the wide availability of laptop computers that weigh significantly less than 5 pounds, but are as powerful as a desktop PC, and special-purpose handheld computers that weigh less than 1 pound.

Some researchers think that current technology may be limited to 100 million transistors on a chip, so they are seeking other ways to increase chip capacity. New chip architectures may be physically larger than today's one-half-centimeter square surface chips or may utilize a three-dimensional design. Research is also ongoing in nanotechnology. **Nanotechnology** uses atom-by-atom precision to build complex objects on a molecular scale. Whereas current microtechnology uses a micrometer scale (one-millionth of a meter), nanotechnology will work on a scale of a nanometer—one-billionth of a meter. One object of nanotechnology would be to create a memory chip one millimeter on a side capable of storing *trillions* of bytes of information.

The speed of computers is measured in mips—millions of instructions per second—and bips—billions of instructions per second. The original IBM PC ran at approximately one-third mips, but this speed has increased: Currently, low-priced PCs run at approximately 1 mips, mainframes run at 100 mips, and supercomputers run between 1 and 10 bips. However, these speeds are predicted to increase significantly over the next 25 years. Figure 20-1 shows an expert's prediction of increases in speed for various types of computers. This prediction, however, may be conservative. For example, consider the Intel i486 chip that was introduced in 1989. It runs at 15 mips and is twice as fast as the widely used Intel 80386 chip. This is just the beginning, for Intel has announced plans to produce a version of the i486 chip using a new type of technology called **emitter-coupled logic (ECL),** which will run at *120* mips.

Today's chips not only contain more transistors and run faster but cost dramatically less. Richard Shaffer, editor of *Technology Computer Letter,* states that computers are decreasing in price at the rate of between 20 and 35 percent per year. Shaffer believes that today's $2 million mainframe may cost $10,000

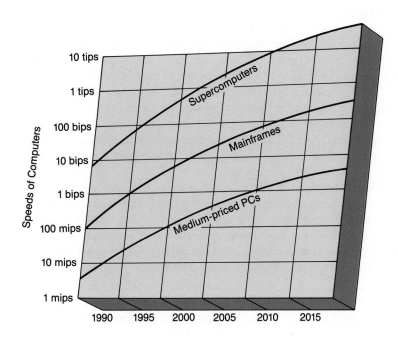

FIGURE 20-1
Prediction of Computer Speeds

Source: James Martin, "Modeling Technology: Trends for the Late 1980's," *PC Week,* October 24, 1988, p. 35. Adapted from original art by David Hannum.

The Intel i486 computer chip is the first personal computer chip to contain more than one million transistors.

in 12 years. It is not difficult to see how Shaffer came to this conclusion, considering that an IBM System 370 mainframe cost over $1 million in 1976 and that, today, a PC can provide the same computing power for less than $5,000.[1]

Experts believe that miniaturization of silicon chips will reach its theoretical limit in five to ten years, and researchers are already working with new substances, superior to silicon, for chips. One substance is a semiconductor called **gallium arsenide.** It transmits electrons three times faster than silicon does, thereby increasing computing speed. IBM announced that it has developed a gallium arsenide chip that uses **optoelectronic technology,** which uses a laser light to transmit data at the rate of 1 billion bits per second. IBM believes this technology could be used to create detailed images of, for example, economic forecasts, hypersonic aircraft simulations, or demographic studies, which require billions or even trillions of data bits.

Recent developments in superconductivity have renewed interest in the Josephson junction, an alternative to the transistor. **Superconductivity** refers to the complete disappearance of electrical resistance in a metal at low temperatures, and a **Josephson junction** is a very fast type of switch that works with superconductors. Until recently, superconductivity was only possible at temperatures near absolute zero. Because of the problems involved in achieving super-

[1]Robert Moskowitz, "A Typical Desktop System in the Year 2001," *Lotus,* December 1988, p. 10.

Both IBM and AT&T have announced breakthroughs in the development of optoelectronic chips, such as the one shown here.

conductivity, IBM terminated its research on the Josephson junction in 1983. In the last few years, however, researchers have found materials that exhibit super-conductivity at higher temperatures, which has revived interest in the Josephson junction. Two Japanese firms, Hitachi and Fujitsu, have announced that they

Shown is a close-up of a superconductor chip using the Josephson junction.

VIEWS OF THE FUTURE

Gordon Bell

Alan Kay

In a series of interviews with *Computerworld* magazine, six computer industry leaders gave their ideas about what is ahead in information technology. The six individuals are Alan Kay, Gordon Bell, Arno Penzias, Bill Gates, Therese Meyers, and Michael Dell.

Alan Kay is a fellow with Apple Computer and is best known for his pioneering work with personal computers. Gordon Bell is the chief scientist at Stardent Computer, Inc., and was previously with Digital Equipment Corp., where he was instrumental in the design of the DEC VAX family of minicomputers. Arno Penzias is vice president of research at AT&T Bell Labs and was co-winner of the 1978 Nobel Prize in physics. Bill Gates is CEO and co-founder of Microsoft Corp., and he co-developed a BASIC language for the first commercial PC. Therese Meyers is president and co-founder of Quarterdeck Office Systems, which markets the Desqview operating environment. Michael Dell founded his PC mail order and manufacturing company when he was 19. Excerpts from these interviews follow.

Alan Kay: The third revolution [in the computing industry] will be from the desktop to what I like to call "intimate computing" [which] will be enabled by portable computers that will probably weigh less than a pound and will act as communications devices.

Gordon Bell: The price of hardware is heading to zero. With more powerful machines on which to run software, this will be a very exciting decade in terms of applications.

Arno Penzias

Therese Meyers

Bill Gates

Michael Dell

Arno Penzias: The real leadership positions [in the computer industry] will go to people who can integrate their own thinking into how the system plays with the world, not just put their noses down into the design and the code.

Bill Gates: The 1990s will be the decade of "information at your fingertips," or IAYF. This term embodies the concept of making computers more personal, making them indispensable, making them something you can reach for naturally whenever you need any kind of information.

Therese Meyers: Software developers will be working on products with the assumption that they will be used on a network rather than as stand-alone applications. Products will be designed with the idea of how a whole group of people relate to the program, not just one person.

Michael Dell: In the future, computers are going to enable a worldwide information democracy in which information is no longer reserved for large companies. We still have a way to go, however. User interfaces are one of the barriers to improved computing.

Source: "What's Ahead," *Computerworld Campus Edition,* October 11, 1991, pp. 26, 27, 37, 45, 52, and 63.

have successfully tested superconducting microprocessor units that use the Josephson junction technology to process over 1 billion instructions per second.

Research is also ongoing in **parallel processing,** which, as discussed in Chapter 6, describes the use of multiple CPUs to execute several instructions simultaneously. Clearly, parallel processing is much faster than serial processing, because it can execute multiple instructions in the same time it takes serial processing to execute a single instruction. However, current programs must be rewritten to take advantage of parallel processing; therefore, this type of computing will not be widely available for commercial use for several years.

The Future of PCs

Ten years ago, there were very few PCs in the home or office. As we noted in Chapter 1, today there are tens of millions of PCs, and this trend toward increased usage of PCs is expected to continue. In fact, it is predicted that, by 1999, each household in the United States will house more PCs than it will house children! The Channel Marketing Corp., a sales and marketing firm, predicts that there will be 2.2 PCs in every home in the United States. It also predicts that notebook computers will be as common in schools as pocket calculators are today.[2]

With the increasing speed of chips, discussed earlier, PCs will become faster and better able to handle computing requirements once reserved for minicomputers and mainframes. Probably the biggest change in the near future (within five years) will be the inclusion of multimedia on all PCs. Recall from Chapter 1 that **multimedia** refers to the combination of the traditional PC with a VCR, optical storage disk, compact disks, and high-fidelity stereo, which will provide interactive full-motion video. Experts also predict that stand-alone PCs in an organization will become a thing of the past as all PCs become linked in local and wide area networks. This would allow users to access data banks of all types and at widely-separated locations and communicate with other users using full-motion video.

Many applications of multimedia are expected in business, education, and the home. In business, where multimedia is already used for sales demonstrations and training, it is predicted to become an important part of the over $4 billion worldwide market for presentations. For example, using multimedia, a person moving to a new city can preview houses and narrow choices without ever leaving his or her hometown. In education, a multimedia system would have many applications, ranging from language study (recall the language system discussed earlier); to conducting geography lessons with a mix of words, maps, video, and sound; to viewing historical films that can be stopped to bring up and view related history videos. In the home, many industry leaders believe that multimedia may be the system that will make the PC as widespread as the television and VCR. However, most analysts believe that this will not happen until multimedia systems cost less than $1,000, which may occur by the mid-1990s.

Trends in PC data storage are toward increased memory capacity for RAM chips in the computer and increased storage on hard, floppy, and microfloppy

---

[2] "And PC Makes Three," *The Atlanta Journal-Constitution,* January 16, 1992, p. B3.

disks. RAM capacity of over one million characters is standard on many personal computers, and memory in the 4 to 8 megabyte range is now very common. RAM will continue to increase in the future. Microfloppy disks that hold almost $1\frac{1}{2}$ million characters are already available, and capacities of over 10 megabytes will soon be on the market. Owing to increased storage and convenience, microfloppies have surpassed the $5\frac{1}{4}$-inch floppy as the standard form of disk storage. Indeed, the larger-sized floppy may follow the 8-inch floppy into disuse. Hard disks will probably shrink from the current $5\frac{1}{4}$-inch and $3\frac{1}{2}$-inch diameters to $2\frac{1}{2}$ inches. Availability of optical disks that store gigabytes (one billion characters) of external memory to the PC user is expected to expand. Use of CD-ROM for disseminating encyclopedic information will increase as more applications are found.

A Caveat on Predicting the Future

Most predictions of the future of computer hardware have been conservative; that is, innovations and developments have usually appeared earlier than predicted. The same is probably true of the predictions made in this text. For example, Alan Kay predicts (see "Views of the Future" box), that "intimate computing" will be enabled by portable computers weighing, probably, less than a pound and acting as communications devices. He does not date his prediction, but other experts have predicted that it will take until the end of the century for the PC to become an "information appliance" more portable and personal than any of today's PCs. However, the prediction has come true sooner than expected, as have other predictions about computers. Apple Computer recently announced its release of a line of computers it calls the "personal digital assistant" (PDA). The PDA fits Kay's prediction, for it will be very light, use pen-based input, and act as an all-in-one appointment calendar, notepad, calculator, and portable phone. So, when you hear *wild* predictions about the future of computers and electronics, watch out! They may come true sooner than you expect.

Multimedia combines text, graphics, animation, video, and sound.

> **Ten or fifteen years down the road, people are going to be controlling computers using throughts . . . [outstripping] every other interface technology.**
>
> *Tim Clifford, owner of Cybertechnics*
>
> Quoted in "PC Mind Control," *PC/Computing,* November 1989, p. 155.

SOFTWARE OF THE FUTURE

That computers are becoming faster every day does not ensure that the general public will use them more. Increased usage depends on ease of use, and ease of use depends on the introduction of truly "user-friendly" operating systems and applications programs, as well as on expanding the applicability of the computer to more problems at home and in business. Even current PC users constantly expect more from their computers. As one person said: "The more we use computers, the more we expect from them."

The future of software is in making easier-to-use packages for a wider range of applications. The use of a **graphical user interface (GUI),** such as those discussed in Chapter 9, is an important move in this direction. Recall that GUIs use icons to represent commands and data. The release of Windows for IBM compatible PCs has accelerated the GUI movement and, as more packages are rewritten for use on Windows, this trend will continue. Similarly, the capability to move data between different software packages or between different types of computers is also crucial to making computers easier to use. Again, operating environments like Windows make this operation much easier.

Windows 3.1 from Microsoft is an operating environment that allows users to shift material easily between applications.

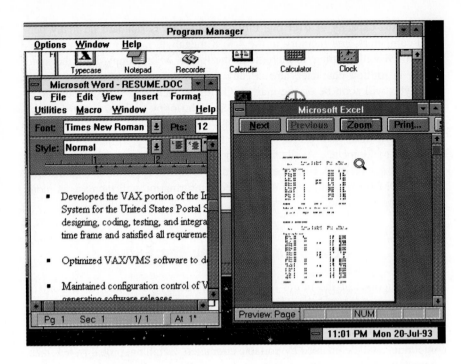

Windows 3.1 from Microsoft is an operating environment that allows users to shift material easily between applications.

The movement toward multimedia, discussed in Chapter 1 and earlier in this chapter, is another key example of the movement toward making computers more friendly. In multimedia, all forms of data—text, graphics, video, sound, and so on—are combined dynamically. As mentioned earlier, it is predicted that soon all computers will be multimedia machines. Another key aspect in making computers easier to use is the movement toward nonkeyboard forms of input,

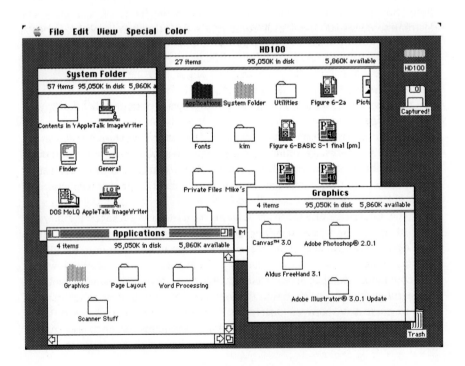

Graphical-based interfaces, such as those on the Apple Macintosh, make the computer easier to use.

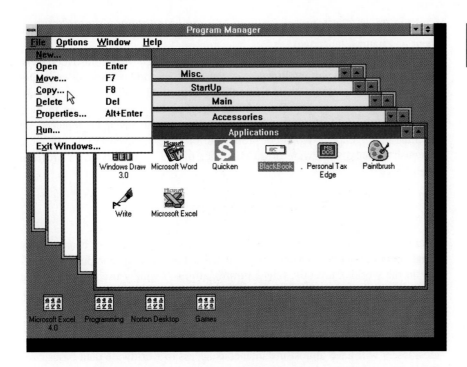

including pen-based input and voice-recognition input, that make communicating with computers easier. For many of these examples, progress depends on improvements in artificial intelligence. Last, progress in telecommunications depends on the availability of appropriate software.

Artificial Intelligence

As we just mentioned, making computers easier to use depends, in many cases, on developments in artificial intelligence. For example, both voice input and handwritten input are applications of artificial intelligence in that they require the computer to display some degree of intelligence to decipher what is input or written. Similarly, natural languages require the computer to convert English, or other human languages, to commands the software package or operating system understands.

Artificial intelligence (AI) has been defined in many ways, but for our purposes, it is any combination of computer hardware and software systems that exhibits some level of human intelligence. Because this is such a broad definition, the term *AI* has been applied to many different types of computer systems, besides those just discussed. These include the robots discussed in Chapter 6, the expert systems discussed in Chapter 14, and the area of research termed artificial reality discussed in the opening box. These are by no means all the applications of artificial intelligence, but they should give you an idea of what AI is all about.

Artificial intelligence is of such importance that it is one of the fastest-growing fields of high-tech. Many companies are spending large amounts of money either to develop AI systems or purchase systems developed by other companies. The computer may never display truly human intelligence, such as HAL displayed in the book *2001* by Arthur C. Clarke; however, it is hoped that

More advanced graphical software, graphical input devices, video, and sound are essential in humanizing the interface.

*Pierluigi Zappacosta,
president, Logitech*

Quoted in "View from the Top,"
Personal Computing, October 1989,
p. 261.

software can be engineered to handle problems involving voice and handwritten input and natural languages.

AI is being applied in many exciting areas, but it is very controversial. To many people, artificial intelligence is the most important area of computer research today. However, others refute the concept of AI, stating that intelligence is a strictly human quality. Dreyfus and Dreyfus, for example, argue in their book *Mind Over Machine* that human intelligence can never be replaced by machine intelligence.[3] We do not propose to become involved in this argument but wish to make you aware of the existence of and controversy over artificial intelligence.

Telecommunications

Data transfer from user to user, from one mainframe to another, or between personal computers is fast becoming one of the hottest areas of computer technology in the world. Currently, **telecommunications** is widely used for electronic mail, accessing data bases and bulletin boards, electronic funds transfer (EFT), and communicating with other users with voice, data, and graphics. The implementation of the **Integrated Service Digital Network (ISDN)** will dramatically transform telecommunications of the future by increasing transmission capabilities. Users will have almost instantaneous access to worldwide data bases over ISDN at speeds beyond current telephone networks and will be able to transfer voice, data, images, and text at high speeds over the same lines. Use of networked PCs and videotex, which allows individuals to order goods and services by computer and telephone without leaving the home or office, will probably also increase. From a technological point of view, the use of glass-fiber cables promises a great stride in transferring information over a telecommunications network. A glass-fiber cable can carry the same volume of information in one second that would take copper cables 21 hours to carry. In LANs, considerable work is ongoing in developing wireless systems that will not require the expensive and often difficult-to-install cable. Many of these developments, however, must await the development of software to match available hardware systems.

INFORMATION SYSTEMS

As with the other areas of information technology, the future holds many exciting developments in the application and development of information systems. Experts predict that information technology will dramatically affect competitive organizations of the twenty-first century. Drucker suggests that information technology will transform the way organizations make decisions, their management structure, and even the way they perform their work.

According to Drucker there are two requirements for the organization of the future to take full advantage of the information technology available to it. First, it must be structured around clearly stated organizational goals that detail what it expects of each element of the organization. Just as an orchestra is composed of many specialists working toward a single goal, so too must the organization of the future be composed of many specialists working toward one goal

> **Businesses, especially large ones, have little choice but to become information-based.**
>
> *Peter Drucker, noted management author*
>
> Quoted in "The Coming of the New Organization," *Harvard Business Review,* January–February 1988, p. 45.

---

[3] H. L. Dreyfus and S. E. Dreyfus, *Mind Over Machine* (New York: The Free Press, 1986), p. xx.

or, at most, a few goals. Second, each individual must take responsibility for the information with which he or she works. In other words, all users should constantly consider which information they need to carry out their responsibilities and which the organization needs to meet its goals.[4]

Two somewhat controversial trends in information systems are downsizing and outsourcing. **Downsizing** is the process of moving processing applications from a mainframe to PCs, replacing a mainframe with a PC network, or both. Organizations downsize for several reasons, including reducing costs, increasing flexibility, and simplifying use. However, problems may occur with downsizing, especially when the wrong application is moved to a PC system. Applications involving many transactions are not usually amenable to running on a PC system. Also, there is the problem of cultural differences between mainframe systems programmers and many PC-based end users; they simply do not speak the same language! This can result in a massive failure in communication or entire mainframe staffs quitting when the downsizing takes place.

Outsourcing is also predicted to grow in the next few years. With outsourcing, the entire responsibility for the information system is turned over to an outside group. Its future appears to brighten as more and more companies determine which factors make them competitive. If they ascertain that they can "buy" the information system more effectively than they can "make" it, outsourcing may be feasible. Andersen Consulting predicts that more than 50 percent of major multinational corporations and government agencies will be using outsourcing to some degree by the mid-1990s.

Developing Information Systems

As discussed in Chapters 16 and 17, computers require explicit instructions from human users to solve problems. This seriously hampers their applicability to some types of problems. It is hoped that research in neural networks will result in increasing the number of areas in which computers can be applied. **Neural networks** use multiple processors that are "trained" to handle a specific task. As with training animals or educating humans, this "learning" process relies on repetition. Assume, for example, that the network of chips—the **neurons** in the network—is being taught to recognize a dog. With a traditional computer system, a human would have to write a program that would give the computer instructions for recognizing a dog. However, with a neural network, the computer would be shown a dog and simultaneously be told that this is a dog. After sufficient repetition, the computer would learn to recognize a dog on its own.

As hardware, software, and information systems change and become more powerful, the impact of computers on society will also change. These changes are expected to affect computer crime and security as well as privacy and health issues. In this section, we will briefly look at changes in these areas.

> The microprocessor revolution is becoming an irresistible force. Ultimately, every business will want to move from their mainframes to microprocessor-based systems.
>
> *Charles E. Exley, Jr., CEO of NCR Corp.*
>
> Quoted in "Rethinking the Computer," *Business Week,* November 26, 1990, p. 117.

IMPACT OF COMPUTERS ON SOCIETY

[4] Peter F. Drucker, "The Coming of the New Organization," *Harvard Business Review,* January/February 1988, pp. 45–53.

FIGHTING CREDIT CARD FRAUD WITH A NEURAL NETWORK

For banks such as Mellon Bank Corp. in Pittsburgh, credit card fraud is a big problem—it cost Mellon $3 million in 1991. Currently, credit card purchases by the bank's MasterCard and Visa cardholders are monitored by a rule-based expert system. This system triggers a request for positive customer identification if card activity is unusually high or if the purchase amount is over a certain amount. The system is often fooled, however, by criminals who continually change their methods.

In the hope of stopping credit card fraud, Mellon is testing the Fraud Detection System (FDS), which uses a neural network. FDS is "taught" to recognize irregularities in credit card use patterns and "decide" if a potential fraud exists. When FDS receives information on a purchase, it calculates the odds of whether the charge is fraudulent and issues one of three instructions: accept, deny, or request additional identification. A model of six months' worth of real credit card transactions will be used to "train" the neural network to discern fraudulent activities.

Source: Kim S. Nash, "Bank Enlists Neural Net to Fight Fraud," *Computerworld,* January 2, 1992, pp. 53, 55.

Changes in Computer Crime and Security

> **There is less business crime because of the use of computers, but at the same time the losses per case are going up dramatically.**
>
> *Donn Parker, SRI International*
>
> Quoted in "New Security Risks Seen for '90s," *PC Week,* December 11, 1989, p. 55.

Computer crime and associated security problems increased tremendously in the 1980s. This trend is expected to continue in the 1990s as the use of computers proliferates. In the 1980s, the top computer crimes were software piracy and computer viruses. However, in the opinion of computer security expert Donn Parker, other types of crime will be more prevalent in the future. Mr. Parker believes that personal computer theft, EDI fraud, phantom network nodes, and voice mail terrorism will become the leading computer offenses.[5] PC theft will increase as criminals realize the value of information stored in computers. Electronic data interchange can be used fraudulently by criminals who avoid automatic background checks on transactions of more than $10,000 by transferring funds of up to $9,000. Criminals can also illegally access a network and strip information from it through so-called "phantom nodes." Finally, voice mail terrorism describes illegally tapping into or bringing down a voice mail system.

---

[5] Jane Morrissey, "New Security Risks Seen for '90s," *PC Week,* December 11, 1989, p. 55.

Future Privacy Issues

As technology makes communication easier, privacy tends to be more at risk. For example, because portable and cellular telephones are but small-scale radio transmitters, an individual with a simple radio system could more readily listen to the telephone conversations of his or her neighbors or business competitors.

Another area of concern involving privacy is the increased use of Social Security numbers as identifiers. Social Security numbers were never intended as a means of identification; therefore, the majority of numbers in use today were assigned without verifying the identity of the applicant. Yet, many government agencies and private companies require an individual's Social Security number before doing business with him or her. Concerns for privacy arise when criminals falsely obtain Social Security numbers and use them to gain personal information about others. The ease with which this can be done was demonstrated by a newspaper reporter who obtained private information about Vice President Quayle by using his Social Security number. A 1991 hearing before the U.S. House of Representatives Subcommittee on Social Security explored this issue in detail and discussed many other related problems.

Future Health Issues

As discussed in Chapter 19, there are health hazards associated with the use of VDTs. Alarming conditions such as repetitive motion syndrome are receiving attention, but other conditions are more subtle. With the proliferation of VDTs in offices, these problems will not disappear in the foreseeable future.

Some employers are opposed to redesigning their work environments ergonomically; whereas, many others are realizing that positive results may be gained from doing so. For example, workers' compensation costs, absenteeism, and the costs of doing business may be reduced.

REVIEW OF KEY POINTS

1. Our society is moving toward an information-based society that will depend on the use of smart machines even more so than it does today, with the information industry becoming one of the largest industries in the world.
2. Careers in computer-related fields have a bright future with an expanding need for workers. The top information manager in a corporation is becoming known as the chief information officer (CIO).
3. Six important types of computer careers in large organizations are information systems management, end-user support, communications, systems/programming, technical services and operations, and data base administration.
4. Other types of computer careers include repair and servicing, sales and marketing, instruction, and consulting.
5. The future of hardware is easier to predict than the future of software, information systems, or the future impact of computers on society.
6. Computers are expected to continue to become smaller, faster, and cheaper. The eventual use of gallium arsenide, optoelectronic

technology, and, possibly, super-conductivity at higher temperatures will further increase computing speed.

7. PCs are predicted to include multimedia in the future. Internal and external storage capacities will also continue to increase. PCs are predicted to become information appliances.

8. Software is expected to become easier to use for a wider range of applications. Artificial intelligence will play an important role in the trend toward easier-to-use software.

9. Telecommunications may be the most rapidly expanding computer-related field in the future with the implementation of the Integrated Service Digital Network (ISDN), which will allow transferring voice, data, images, and text over the same lines simultaneously. Improvements in software hold the key to wider availability of telecommunications.

10. Information systems are predicted to change entirely how organizations make decisions, structure their organization, and perform their work. Two important trends in information systems are downsizing and outsourcing.

11. Neural networks, which are "taught" rather than programmed, are expected to become an alternative method of developing information systems.

12. Changes in technology are expected to bring about dramatic changes in computer crime and security, with future crimes involving theft of PCs, EDI fraud, phantom network nodes, and voice mail terrorism.

13. Privacy and health concerns will continue to be important as technology improves and computers become more widely used in organizations.

KEY TERMS

artificial intelligence (AI)
chief information officer (CIO)
data base administrator
documentation
downsizing
emitter-coupled logic
end user
end-user programmer
gallium arsenide
graphical user interface (GUI)
information society
Integrated Service Digital Network (ISDN)

Josephson junction
multimedia
nanotechnology
neural network
neuron
optoelectronic technology
outsourcing
parallel processing
smart machine
superconductivity
telecommunications
virtual reality

REVIEW QUESTIONS

1. How have the changes in technology over the last ten years affected you? Name two smart machines that you use on a regular basis.

2. What is an information society? Name some jobs in the information industry.

3. What are six important computer career fields in organizations? What are other career fields?

4. What is the role of the CIO in a corporation? How does the CIO's role differ from that of the head of the MIS department?

5. Discuss the difference between mainframe and personal computer repair and service.

6. Why is it easier to predict the future of hardware than it is to predict the future of other computer areas?

7. Why is gallium arsenide being considered as a replacement for silicon in chip manufacturing? What is a Josephson junction?

8. How is multimedia expected to impact PCs in the future? What is an information appliance expected to be?

9. How is future software expected to differ from current software? How is artificial intelligence expected to impact software of the future?

10. What single development in the future will have a dramatic impact on telecommunications?

11. What two changes must organizations make to take full advantage of information technology?

12. Discuss the two trends regarding information systems that are mentioned in the text.

13. What new method is being used to create information systems? How does this method differ from traditional programming methods?

14. Name four areas of crime and security that are predicted to be important in the future.

15. Discuss two areas of future privacy concerns that were mentioned in the text.

APPENDIX A

Using DOS

APPENDIX B

Appendix B: Programming in BASIC is contained in the alternative version of this textbook, entitled *Living with Computers* with BASIC.

APPENDIX C

American Standard Code for Information Interchange (ASCII) Ordering of Symbols

APPENDIX A

Using DOS

INTRODUCTION TO DOS

Recall from the text that the operating system of a personal computer manages all other operations of the computer, including accepting input from the keyboard or mouse, displaying information on the monitor screen, sending information to the printer, managing the data and information stored on the disk drives, and enabling the execution of applications software programs. Currently, the most widely used personal computer operating system is the Microsoft Disk Operating System (MS-DOS). PC-DOS is another operating system that is almost identical to MS-DOS and was developed exclusively for the original IBM PC. They are used on all IBM compatible PCs, including the IBM PS/1 and PS/2 series of computers. Because PC-DOS and MS-DOS are so similar, this tutorial will refer to both as DOS.

DOS has been issued in various releases—the higher the number, the more recent the release. Currently, copies of MS-DOS 3.x, 4.x, and 5.x are in circulation. DOS can be either command driven or, for versions 4.0 and higher, menu driven. In this tutorial, we will discuss the command-driven form of DOS, because the commands we cover here will work with all versions in use today. To use the command-driven form of DOS, you must know some of the over 50 commands that the operating system will accept. Most of these commands can be input from the keyboard *interactively*, but some are **batch commands** that are entered from a program.

Parts of the IBM Compatible PC

Your IBM compatible PC should include at least a system unit with one or more disk drives, a monitor, and a keyboard. A printer and mouse may also be connected to your machine. Three disk-drive configurations are common: (1) two floppy drives, (2) one floppy drive and one hard disk drive, and (3) one or two disk drives (and possibly a hard drive) connected to the central hard disk of a network (called the **file server.**) In all cases, the floppy drives are called drives A and B and the hard drive is drive C. In a configuration with one floppy drive, the drive is referred to as drive A. Two types of floppy drives are currently in use: the older 5¼-inch floppy drives and the newer 3½-inch microfloppy drives. As long as you use the correct size disk, there is essentially no difference in using either type of drive. If your computer is connected to a network, the file server will be denoted with a higher letter, drive F for example.

With any personal computer, the keyboard is essential for inputting data and commands. For that reason, you may want to review the discussion of personal computer keyboards in Chapter 2. The two most widely used keyboards for IBM compatible computers are shown there along with a table showing the operations of important keys.

TRY IT YOURSELF

1. Identify the various elements of your PC. Note the keyboard, monitor, and secondary storage units. Determine whether you have one or two floppy drives. Also determine whether the drives are 5¼ inch or 3½ inch or a combination of the two.
2. Identify the location of the various keys on your keyboard. Point to the Enter key, cursor control keys, and function keys.

A CLOSER LOOK AT DOS

Information in a personal computer is stored in **files** on the computer's disk drives. One of the primary roles of DOS, or any other operating system, is to manage these files: saving files to disk, retrieving files from disk, copying a file from one disk to another, and so on. There are many different types of files, including those that are part of DOS, those that are needed to execute applications software packages, and those that are used or created by applications software packages.

Parts of DOS

DOS can be divided into three parts: DOS system files, internal commands, and external commands. **DOS system files** include two files called IO.SYS and MSDOS.SYS. These system files are read from the disk that contains the DOS operating system—the **system disk**—and are stored in RAM when the system is started or "booted." Because they are *hidden files*, the user never sees them. The system files receive requests for DOS and manage input and output, including controlling the keyboard, the disk drive, the monitor, the printer, and the mouse. **Internal commands,** which are also read into RAM from the system disk during the booting process, are stored in a special DOS file. Finally, the **external commands** are stored not in RAM but on the system disk. The system disk can be either drive A or C, but the DOS external commands must be read from the system disk before they can be used.

All internal and external commands can be entered interactively at the **prompt**, which signals that the computer is awaiting a command. The DOS prompt is displayed as the **active disk drive** (the disk drive from which the operating system is expecting a command) and the greater-than sign (>). For example, if drive A is active, the prompt will be A>; but if a hard disk (drive C) is active, the prompt will be C>. Since it is possible to personalize the prompt to include other information, the prompt you see may differ somewhat from the example, but it will always include the drive letter and the greater-than sign. After you enter the command at the DOS prompt, you must press **Enter** to execute the command.

DOS File Names

For DOS to handle file management, the files must be named. A file name can be made up of letters or numbers and can be up to eight characters long. For example, 456 and TESTFILE are both legitimate file names. It is not valid to have a file name containing a blank. For this reason, GO DOGS is *not* a valid file name. If necessary, you can make a name longer by placing a period (.) after the name and adding a one- to three-character extension. For example, we can extend the names of the two previous examples to become 456.BAT and TEST-FILE.TXT. Some extensions are automatically added by the applications software program creating the file, whereas others are added by the user to help identify the file. An example of the first case is the .WK1 extension that is automatically added to any file created by the Lotus 1-2-3 spreadsheet package. Common examples of the second case include .TXT for text files and .LTR for letters.

Special DOS Files

DOS attaches special extensions to three types of files—batch, command, and executable. The extensions for these files are, respectively, .BAT, .COM, and .EXE. You can execute commands stored in these files by entering only the name of the file, without entering the extension. For example, when the executable file for Lotus 1-2-3, 123.EXE, is stored on a disk in drive A, you can execute it by entering 123 at the A prompt, that is,

A>123

A **batch file** contains a series of DOS commands. Because the commands are incorporated in a single file, you can execute an entire series of commands by entering the file name at the A prompt. The **AUTOEXEC.BAT** file is a special batch file used in many situations. When it is placed on the disk that is used to boot an IBM compatible PC, it is automatically executed when the computer is powered up. An AUTOEXEC.BAT file can be used, for example, to automatically enter time and date from a clock card in the computer or to automatically execute a commonly-used program.

Command files, with a .COM extension, and **executable files,** with an .EXE extension, are two other types of files. They store software programs in a form that the computer can execute when the file name is entered. For example, the executable part of the WordPerfect word processing package is stored in WP.EXE, and you execute it by entering the command WP. Similarly, the executable part of the DOS operating system is stored in COMMAND.COM, which contains the internal operating system commands.

A common approach to program execution is to create a batch file that contains the names of all the command files and executable files that must be executed as part of the software package. The user simply types the name of the batch file, and the command files and executable files are executed.

Another important file is the CONFIG.SYS file, which DOS uses to configure the computer. This file is often used to define special devices, such as the mouse, or to set aside parts of memory for special purposes. Like the AUTO-EXEC.BAT file, it is composed of a series of commands and can be displayed as text on the screen. In general, the AUTOEXEC.BAT and CONFIG.SYS files should not be changed.

TRY IT YOURSELF

1. Determine whether each of the following DOS file names is valid or invalid:

   MYLETTER.TXT   MY PAPER   456.BAT   ALONGNAME

2. Create appropriate file names for the following files:
   a. a letter to a friend
   b. a budget for this month
   c. a list of your friends and their phone numbers
3. Identify the following files as being an executable file, command file, batch file, or none of these:
   a. 456.EXE
   b. GOMOUSE.BAT
   c. MYPROG.BAS
   d. DB.COM

BOOTING AN IBM COMPATIBLE PC

To use your IBM compatible PC, you must go through the startup, or "booting," process using instructions permanently stored in ROM (read-only memory). When you start the computer by turning on the power switch, ROM first provides instructions to the processing unit to perform a power-on self-test (POST), which checks the various components of the computer to ensure that they are working correctly. After the POST, ROM provides instructions to the processing unit, telling it to find the system disk and read the system files and COM-MAND.COM into RAM.

Once, the system disk was always a floppy disk in drive A, but now the system disk is often the hard disk (drive C) or the network file server disk. If your system disk is either a hard disk or a network disk, you may skip some steps in the booting process. If you use a floppy disk as a **boot disk,** follow the process shown below to boot your computer, or follow the specific instructions your instructor gives you for booting your computer.

The booting process for an IBM compatible PC from a floppy disk can be outlined as the following five-step process:

   Step 1: Locate the disk drives on the front of the system unit. If you have only one floppy disk drive, it is drive A. If you have two floppy disk drives, drive A is usually the one on the left or top. If you have a hard disk, or if your machine is set up to boot off the network file server, go to Step 3; otherwise, go to Step 2.

Step 2: If you are booting from a 5¼-inch floppy disk, open drive A by gently pulling up the flap on the drive or by turning the lever up. Insert the DOS system disk with the label *up* and the oblong read/write window of a 5¼-inch disk away from you. Close the disk drive by closing the flap or by turning the lever down. If you are booting with a 3½-inch microfloppy, simply insert the disk with the label up and the metallic shutter away from you.

Step 3: Find the on/off switch, which, depending on the type of computer you are using, may be located on the right front, on the rear of the right panel, or on the rear panel of the computer (your instructor will tell you where to look for it). Turn on the computer. If the monitor has a separate on/off switch, turn it on also. Alternatively, if the machine is already on and the DOS prompt is on the screen, carry out a **warm boot** by holding down the Ctrl and Alt keys and pressing the Del key. (Release all three after you press the Del key.) A warm boot restarts the computer and clears the computer's memory, just as if you had turned it off and then back on again.

Step 4: Your computer will go through a brief power-on self-test (POST) and look for a system disk in drive A. If a DOS disk is found there, the internal commands on the disk will be loaded into RAM. If your computer does not find a disk in drive A, and if you have a hard disk on your computer, the internal commands will automatically be loaded into RAM from either the hard disk (drive C) or from the network file server. During this process, the red drive light for drive A or C will go on. Regardless of which drive configuration you have, it is important to remember that it is impossible to boot the computer with a nonsystem disk in drive A. If you attempt this, you will receive an error message instructing you to insert a system disk in drive A.

Step 5: If your system disk has an AUTOEXEC.BAT file (most do), the DOS prompt will be displayed. On the other hand, if you are using a system disk without an AUTOEXEC.BAT file, the current time and date known to the computer will be displayed and you will be asked to enter the time and date. If your computer has a clock/calendar in it, the time and date will probably be correct and you can simply press **Enter** twice to accept them. If the time and date are incorrect, type the correct time and date and press **Enter** after each entry. For example, if the time is 10 A.M., you would enter 10:00. If the date is December 15, 1992, you would enter 12-15-92. If you do not wish to enter the date and time, press **Enter** twice. We strongly suggest that you enter the date and time when you create files with a software package. Knowing the date and time of creation of a file can help you, for example, determine if you are working with the most recent version of the document.

Next, the computer will display the A prompt:

A>

signifying that the booting process is complete. If you are booting off drive C instead of drive A, the C prompt will appear:

C>

If you are using a network boot disk, your instructor will provide you with further instructions on your system.

The booting process may seem complicated, but it is very simple if you follow the steps outlined above (assuming there is no AUTOEXEC.BAT file on the system disk). A summary of the booting process follows.

Booting Your PC from Drive A

Insert:	A DOS disk in drive A
Turn on:	The computer (and monitor) (or press **Ctrl** + **Alt** + **Del**)
Action:	The POST will take place and the current time is shown
Type:	The time in HH:MM:SS format and press **Enter** (just press **Enter** if the time is correct)
Action:	The current date is shown
Type:	The date in MM-DD-YY format and press **Enter** (just press **Enter** if the date is correct)
Action:	The A> prompt is displayed

If you are booting from a hard disk (drive C), you need only turn on the computer and monitor or press **Ctrl+Alt+Del** to perform a warm boot if the computer is already turned on. The DOS instructions on the hard disk will take care of the rest of the process.

Figure A-1 shows the booting process for a PC on which the system was booted from drive A, and the date and time were entered by the user.

TRY IT YOURSELF

1. Boot your computer and identify the DOS prompt when it appears on the screen.

FORMATTING A DISK

After you boot your computer, you will need to format a disk. Any disk *must* be formatted before you can store data and information on it. Recall from Chapter 8 that when a disk is formatted, it is divided into sectors that determine the

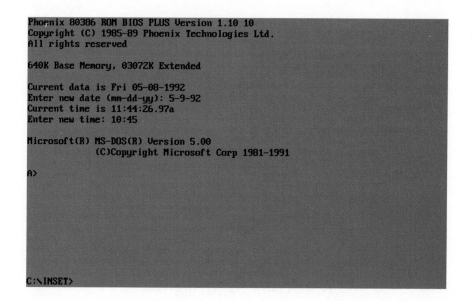

```
Phoenix 80386 ROM BIOS PLUS Version 1.10 10
Copyright (C) 1985-89 Phoenix Technologies Ltd.
All rights reserved

640K Base Memory, 03072K Extended

Current data is Fri 05-08-1992
Enter new date (mm-dd-yy): 5-9-92
Current time is 11:44:26.97a
Enter new time: 10:45

Microsoft(R) MS-DOS(R) Version 5.00
          (C)Copyright Microsoft Corp 1981-1991

A>




C:\INSET>
```

amount of information that can be stored on the disk. For example, a 3½-inch microfloppy disk used on many IBM compatible PCs has 80 tracks and 9 sectors. Each sector has 512 bytes, so the total storage capacity of the diskette on one side is 9 × 80 × 512 bytes = 360 Kbytes. Since this is a double-sided diskette, it can hold a total of 720 Kbytes.

In the formatting process, a list of the diskette's contents is recorded on a specific sector and track in the form of a **file allocation table (FAT)**. The disk controller (part of the personal computer's hardware) and DOS use the FAT to determine where the programs and files are stored so that the read/write head can move to the proper position on the disk.

In DOS, formatting is handled through the FORMAT command. All DOS commands are made up of three parts: the file name, parameters, and switches. Switches are always optional, so they are indicated to DOS by a slash mark (/). Parameters immediately follow the command name and usually give the command further instructions. Because FORMAT is an *external command,* it must be read from the system disk. If you have a two-floppy-drive machine, the system disk must remain in drive A during the formatting command. To format a data disk in drive B, you would type

A>FORMAT B:

and press **Enter.** If you are using a computer with a single floppy drive and a hard disk, you may enter a similar command for drive A, that is,

C>FORMAT A:

and press **Enter.** If you are using a computer with a hard disk or one connected to a network, the FORMAT command will be read automatically.

It is absolutely necessary to type a colon (:) after the name of the drive being formatted. The colon tells DOS that A, for example, is a drive and not a part of a command. This is true of any command that references a disk drive.

NOTE: Do *not* use the FORMAT command with any disk on which you have stored software or data that you want to keep.

Formatting a Disk on a Two-Floppy-Drive System

Insert: A DOS disk in drive A

Insert: The disk to be formatted in drive B

Type: **FORMAT B:** (the colon is an essential part of the drive designation in all DOS commands) and press **Enter**

Action: A message will be displayed instructing you to insert a new diskette in drive B

Insert: The diskette to be formatted in drive B and press **Enter**

Action: The disk is formatted, and you are requested to enter a volume name for the disk or to press **Enter** for none

Type: A name for the disk (your last name is a good volume name) and press **Enter**

Action: The available storage space on the disk is displayed and you will be asked if you want to format another disk

Type: **N** for no and press **Enter**

NOTE: If you are working on a hard disk system, you will insert the disk to be formatted in drive A and replace the FORMAT B: command with FOR-MAT A:. If you are working in a local area network, you may be directed to use a menu option to a disk. Figure A-2 shows the formatting process for a hard disk system.

Because today's disks have various capacities, it is occasionally necessary to ensure that a disk is formatted to the appropriate capacity. For example, if you have a 3½-inch double-density (720K) microfloppy that is being formatted in a high-density (1.44M) disk drive, it is wise to add switches to the FORMAT command to force the drive to format the disk to the appropriate capacity, that is, to 720K rather than 1.44M. If this is not done, the drive will attempt to format

```
C:\-> format a:
Insert new diskette for drive A:
and press ENTER when ready...

Format complete

Volume label (11 characters, ENTER for none)? McKeown

    362496 bytes total disk space
    362496 bytes available on disk

      1024 bytes in each allocation unit
       354 allocation units available on disk

Volume Serial Number is 0A3D-13DA

Format another (Y/N)?n
C:\->
```

FIGURE A-2
Formatting Process

the disk to the higher capacity, with the result that the disk may be readable only on a 1.44M drive. (Or it may not be readable on any drive!) To force the disk to be formatted at 720K, the command is

```
C>FORMAT A:/t:80/n:9
```

which tells DOS to format the disk with 80 tracks and 9 sectors, yielding 720K of storage on the disk.

To reinforce our earlier statement about commands, parameters, and switches, in this example, the command is FORMAT, the parameter is the drive name, B:, and two switches are turned on.

Changing Drives

Once you have a formatted disk in a drive, you can change control to that drive. For example, you can change control from drive A to drive B, from drive C to drive A, or to some other combination of drives. To change active drives, you simply enter the letter for the new drive followed by a colon and press **Enter**. For example, to change from drive A to drive B, you would enter

```
A>B:
```

and press **Enter**. Similarly, to change from drive B to drive C, you would enter

```
B>C:
```

and press **Enter**. A formatted disk must reside in the drive to which you switch control; otherwise, an error message indicating a disk-drive failure will be displayed.

TRY IT YOURSELF

1. Format a disk with a volume label consisting of your last name.
2. If you have a second disk, you may also format it at this time.
3. Change control to drive A if it is not already the active drive.

WORKING WITH DIRECTORIES AND SUBDIRECTORIES

In the early days of IBM compatible PCs and DOS, 360K floppy disks were the primary form of secondary storage, and organizing files on these low-density disks was fairly easy. Today, however, the vast majority of PCs have a hard disk and use high-capacity (720K or more) microfloppy diskettes. To organize the large number of files that can be stored on a hard disk or microfloppy, DOS has the capacity to create and work with directories on the disk. When the disk is formatted to receive software or data using the FORMAT command described above, a root directory is established on the diskette. The **root directory** is the starting point for creating a hierarchical file system and is the **working directory** when a computer is booted. The root directory is indicated by a backslash (\).

Hierarchical file directories are created on all formatted disks; however, they are most useful on hard disks because so many hard disks can store large numbers of files. A hierarchical file system divides the disk space into a series of **subdirectories,** each of which is given a name and is analogous to a separate disk. This makes it easier to organize the mass of files that can be stored on a high-capacity hard disk or microfloppy disk.

You can create subdirectories using the MD (make directory) command followed by a name (which must follow the same rules as file names). Subdirectories created with this command are separate from each other, and most DOS commands will affect only those files within the current subdirectory. For example, to create a subdirectory named WPFILES from the root directory on drive A, the command is

```
A:\>MD WPFILES
```

Note that, in this case, the current (root) directory is shown as a part of the prompt. This was done through the use of the PROMPT command. (The PROMPT command is beyond the scope of this introductory discussion.) If the MD command were also used to create subdirectories called 123FILES and DBFILES, the resulting directory structure would be as that shown in Figure A-3.

You can switch to any subdirectory by using the CD (change directory) command. For example, to switch from the root directory to the WPFILES directory, the command is

```
A:\>CD WPFILES
```

and WPFILES becomes the working directory. (We will be using the disk in drive A for all examples, but you could be working with the B or C drive instead.)

```
A:\>tree
Directory PATH listing for Volume MCKEOWN
Volume Serial Number is 0A3D-13DA
A:.
├───WPFILES
├───123FILES
└───DBFILES

A:\>
```

FIGURE A-3
Relationship of Root Directory to Subdirectories

If you are in the WPFILES subdirectory and want to create a subdirectory called LETTERS and then switch to that subdirectory, enter the following series of commands:

```
A:\WPFILES>MD LETTERS
A:\WPFILES>CD LETTERS
A:\WPFILES\LETTERS>
```

The prompt now shows the full path name of the working subdirectory, \WPFILES\LETTERS. The **path name** is the name of the current subdirectory preceded by a list of all directories "above" it, including the root directory, with each subdirectory name separated by a backslash. To switch to another subdirectory that is *not* immediately above or below the current subdirectory, you must enter the *full* path name of the subdirectory as part of the CD command. For example, to switch from \WPFILES\LETTERS to the 123FILES subdirectory, the command would be

```
A:\WPFILES\LETTERS>CD \123FILES
```

where \123FILES is the path name of that subdirectory.

In switching subdirectories, you should remember the following rules:

1. If you are switching to a subdirectory immediately "below" the current directory, enter the name of that subdirectory, without backslashes.
2. The shorthand name of the directory immediately "above" the current subdirectory is two periods (. .). To switch to the "parent" directory, simply use the CD . . command.
3. To switch to any other subdirectory, use the full path name.
4. Because the backslash by itself represents the root directory, use the CD\ command to leave any subdirectory and return to the root directory.
   When you switch to a different disk drive, the working directory becomes either the root directory or the previous working directory of the disk in the new drive.

TRY IT YOURSELF

1. Using the disk you formatted previously in drive A, switch control to drive A. Create three subdirectories on this disk using the MD command. Call them WPFILES, 123FILES, and DBFILES.
2. Use the CD WPFILES command to switch to the WPFILES subdirectory. From this directory, use the MD LETTERS command to create a subdirectory. Switch to the new subdirectory. Then use the CD \123FILES command to switch to the 123FILES subdirectory. Why did we have to begin the subdirectory name with a backslash in the second case? Finally, use the CD . . command to switch back to the root directory.

IMPORTANT DOS COMMANDS

DOS includes over 70 commands, both internal and external. We have discussed the commands needed to format a disk and to work with the subdirectory system. In this section, we will consider some of the other commonly used DOS commands. Throughout this discussion, we will assume that you have a formatted disk in drive A and that drive A is the active drive.

The DIR Command

The DIR (DIRectory) command is used to determine the files stored on the disk. The command is

A:\>DIR

The DIR command is an internal command, so it can be given with any disk in drive A. An example of the result of the DIR command is shown in Figure A-4.

The files listed in Figure A-4 include each file's full name, including the three-letter file-name extension. The figures in the other columns show the amount of storage space each file uses on the disk and the date and time the file was last stored on the disk. The figures at the bottom show how much storage space is used by the files and is left on the disk.

To determine the files on a disk in drive B from the A prompt, you would enter

A:\>DIR B:

Another way of using the DIR command is to type it as DIR/W. The /W (wide) switch tells the computer to display the directory in wide format. Disks

```
A:\>DIR

 Volume in drive A is ANDREWS
 Directory of A:\

FINWINC1 WK1       3191 12-17-91    3:27p
PROJCF91 WK1       5427 09-23-91   11:05a
PROJBW92 WK1       3749 12-11-91   12:48p
PROJCS91 FIN      13791 04-04-91   10:33a
LOTUSFWB WK1       2947 11-19-91   10:20p
LOTUSFWT WK1       3186 11-19-91   10:23p
LOTUS333 WK1       3191 12-11-91   10:12a
PROJBW91 PIC         21 12-11-91   12:57p
PROJBW92 PIX <DIR>      12-11-91   12:59p
PROJROC  PIX         21 12-11-91    1:05p
NEWPROJB WP5       3003 12-11-91    1:57p
MARWINC           24525 12-18-91    8:57p
MARWINA           49905 12-18-91    5:36p
FINWINB            9080 12-18-91    8:05p
FINWNTXA           8353 12-18-91    3:16p
        15 file(s)      130390 bytes
                        223232 bytes free

A:\>
```

FIGURE A-4
Disk Directory

with long directories require this format for displaying entire directories on the screen at once. Otherwise, some files on long lists may scroll off the top of the screen before the last files appear. In wide format, the disk directory shown in Figure A-4 would look like that shown in Figure A-5.

Another switch for the DIR command is /P (page). When this switch is invoked, one screen of files is shown, along with the message "press any key to continue." When a key is pressed, another screen of files is shown. This process continues until all files are shown, one screen at a time.

If you are using a disk with subdirectories, issuing the DIR command allows you to see only the files of the current directory or subdirectory. If you want to see the files in another subdirectory, you must change subdirectories with the CD command or type the subdirectory's path name as part of the DIR command. For example, if you are in the WPFILES directory and want to list the files in the 123FILES directory *without* switching to that directory, the command would be

```
A:\WPFILES>DIR \123FILES
```

You may use wildcard characters to extend the use of the DIR command. **Wildcard characters** can be used to replace groups of characters or single characters. They are the asterisk (*), which can be used to replace an entire file name or extension, and the question mark (?), which can be used to replace a single character. Wildcards enable you to work with groups of files. For example, if you want to see the names of files having a specific name or extension, you would use a wildcard character with the DIR command. To see only those files with a .WK1 extension, the command would be

```
A:\>DIR *.WK1
```

To see all files with .WKS, .WK1, or .WK3 extensions, you would use ? to replace the last character of the extension in the DIR command, that is,

```
A>DIR *.WK?
```

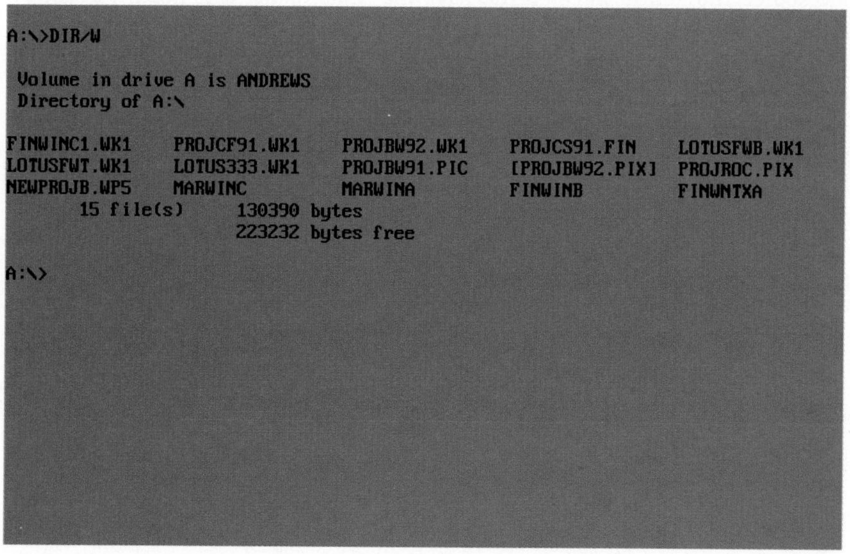

```
A:\>DIR/W

 Volume in drive A is ANDREWS
 Directory of A:\

FINWINC1.WK1    PROJCF91.WK1    PROJBW92.WK1    PROJCS91.FIN    LOTUSFWB.WK1
LOTUSFWT.WK1    LOTUS333.WK1    PROJBW91.PIC    [PROJBW92.PIX]  PROJROC.PIX
NEWPROJB.WP5    MARWINC         MARWINA         FINWINB         FINWNTXA
        15 file(s)       130390 bytes
                         223232 bytes free

A:\>
```

FIGURE A-5
Disk Directory in Wide Format

As we discuss the various DOS commands, we will show you how to use wildcards.

You may also search for a specific file by entering the file name after the DIR command. For example, to look for a file named MYNAME.TXT, you would enter

`A:\>DIR MYNAME.TXT`

If the file is on the disk, the file name will appear in the directory listing. If the file is not on the disk, the message "File not found" will be displayed.

TRY IT YOURSELF

1. Switch to the drive you used to boot the computer (A, C, or the network file-server drive) and list the contents of the system disk. Carry out the same operation in wide format and one screen at a time.
2. List all files with a .COM extension. List all files with a .BAT extension.

The COPY and TYPE Commands

The COPY command is used to copy one or more files from one disk or directory to another. It combines the word COPY with the drive and name of the source file and the drive and name of the destination file, in that order. For example, to copy a file named TEST from the disk in drive A to a disk in drive B with a new name (NEWTEST), the command is

`A:\>COPY A:TEST B:NEWTEST`

The COPY command may be shortened under certain circumstances. If the source file and destination file have the same name, it is *not* necessary to enter the name as part of the destination. It is also unnecessary to give the name of the current (active) disk drive. For example, to copy a file named TEST from drive A to drive B, you would enter

`A:\>COPY TEST B:`

The previous command can be given as

`A:\>COPY TEST B:NEWTEST`

Wildcards can greatly extend the power of the COPY command by allowing you to copy groups of files that have names or extensions in common. For example, to copy all files with a .BAT extension from drive A to drive B, we could use

`A:\>COPY *.BAT B:`

Similarly, because spreadsheet files can have either a .WK1 or a .WKS extension, to copy all spreadsheet files on the disk in drive A to drive B, we would use the command

A:\>COPY *.WK? B:

where * replaces the file name and ? replaces the last character of the extension.

Finally, to copy *all* files from drive A to drive B, we could use

A:\>COPY *.* B:

In this case, we used wildcards for both the file name and the extension to copy all files, regardless of their names or extensions.

The COPY command can be used to copy files between subdirectories, just as it can be used to copy files between drives. The only difference is that you must give the path name, instead of the drive and file name, to copy between subdirectories. For example, if you were in the WPFILES subdirectory on drive A and wanted to copy the file EXERCISE to the 123FILES subdirectory under the name FINAL.S91, the command would be

A:\WPFILES>COPY EXERCISE \123FILES\FINAL.S91

In this case, the complete path name for the new file is \123FILES\FINAL.S91 on drive A.

The COPY command can also be used to create or print the contents of a text file. In the first case, the command

A:\>COPY CON TEST.TXT

will copy from the keyboard (CON) to the file named TEST.TXT. When this command is given, *everything* entered from the keyboard will be saved in the destination file *until* the F6 function key is pressed. For example, if you entered

A:\>COPY CON MYNAME.TXT
SARAH JONES

and pressed **F6**, you would create a file named MYNAME.TXT with a single line containing the name SARAH JONES. DOS does not *seem* to do anything when you enter the COPY CON command, but it *is* waiting for you to enter the information to be copied to the file.

To print the contents of a text file, the destination of the copy command is given as PRN (printer). For example, the command

A:\>COPY MYNAME.TXT PRN

would print the contents of the file named MYNAME.TXT to the printer. (Be sure your printer is turned on and online before invoking this command.)

You can display the contents of a text file on the screen using the TYPE command. For example, to view the contents of the file named MYNAME.TXT on the screen, you would enter the command

```
A:\>TYPE MYNAME.TXT
```

It is also possible to print the contents of the file by *redirecting* the output of this command using the greater-than symbol (>) followed by PRN. For example, to print the contents of the MYNAME.TXT file displayed earlier, be sure your printer is turned on and online. Then give the command

```
A:\>TYPE MYNAME.TXT > PRN
```

CAUTION: If you attempt to use the TYPE command on nontext files, such as .EXE or .COM, you will see "garbage" on the screen, because the binary contents of the file are displayed.

TRY IT YOURSELF

1. With your formatted disk in drive A, switch to that drive. Use the CD\WPFILES command to ensure you are in the WPFILES directory. Then use the COPY CON command to create a file called MYDATA.TXT. This file will contain your name on the first line, your street address on the second line, and your city address on the third line. Remember to save the file by pressing **Enter** after each line and **F6** after the last line.
2. Display the contents of MYDATA.TXT on the screen.
3. If you are connected to a printer, print the contents of MYDATA.TXT in two ways.
4. Copy MYDATA.TXT to a file named YOURDATA.DAT in the LETTERS subdirectory of the WPFILES directory on the same disk. If you have a second disk and B drive, copy MYDATA.TXT to B:YOURDATA.DAT.
5. Use the DIR command to ensure that both MYDATA.TXT and YOURDATA.DAT are on the disk in drive A.

The ERASE and RENAME Commands

To delete a file from your disk, use the ERASE command with the file name you want to delete. (The DEL command has exactly the same effect.) To delete the file named NEWTEST on drive A, enter

```
A:\>ERASE NEWTEST
```

If the file is on a disk in drive B, the command is

```
A:\>ERASE B:NEWTEST
```

If you want to erase *all* the files on a disk, you can use wildcards. For example, to erase all files on the disk in drive B, enter the command

```
A:\>ERASE B:*.*
```

If you enter this command, you will be asked if you want to erase all files on the disk. If you answer Y (for yes), all files will be erased. NOTE: This can be a dangerous command and should be used with caution!

For subdirectories, the ERASE *.* command applies only to the current subdirectory, *not* to the entire disk.

DOS does not actually wipe an erased file from the disk. Instead, it changes the first letter of the file name to a question mark on the file allocation table (FAT), and it makes the disk space occupied by the erased file available for storing new files. Thus, when we erased NEWTEST, its name became ?EWTEST in the FAT. If you use this method to erase files and have an "unerase" utility program, such as the Norton Utilities, you can unerase a file that was erased erroneously.

To rename a file instead of erasing it, use the RENAME (REN) command. This command is invoked by typing the old file name followed by the new file name. For example, to rename the file MYNAME.TXT as YOURNAME.TXT, the command would be

```
A:\>REN MYNAME.TXT YOURNAME.TXT
```

TRY IT YOURSELF

1. Make a copy of MYDATA.TXT called MYDATA.BAK on the disk in drive A. Erase MYDATA.TXT. Now, do a DIR on this drive to verify that MYDATA.TXT is no longer shown in the list of files.
2. Use the RENAME command to change the file name MYDATA.BAK back to MYNAME.TXT. Use the DIR command to verify that the file was renamed.

The REMOVE DIRECTORY Command

To remove a subdirectory, use the REMOVE DIRECTORY (RD) command. DOS will not accept the command, however, until two conditions are met:

1. The subdirectory you want to remove *must* be empty. To accomplish this, switch to the subdirectory and enter the ERASE *.* command.
2. You must be in the "parent" of the subdirectory you want to remove, so after you erase all files in the subdirectory, switch to the parent directory by entering the CD .. command.

Once you have erased all files in the subdirectory you want to remove and have switched to its parent subdirectory, enter the RD command. For example, use the following commands (with comments) to remove the LETTERS subdirectory, whose parent directory is WPFILES.

```
A:\>CD \WPFILES\LETTERS            (switch to desired subdirectory)
A:\WPFILES\LETTERS>ERASE *.*       (erase all files in subdirectory)
A:\WPFILES\LETTERS>CD ..           (switch to parent subdirectory)
A:\WPFILES>RD LETTERS              (remove desired subdirectory)
```

1. Remove the LETTERS subdirectory of the WPFILES directory from your disk in drive A.
2. Remove the DBFILES directory from your disk in drive A.

The CHKDSK and DISKCOPY Commands

CHKDSK and DISKCOPY are useful external DOS commands. Because they are external commands, the DOS system disk must be in drive A to use either command if you are using a two-floppy-drive system without a hard disk or network connection. The CHKDSK command is used to check the status of a disk. When invoked, this command scans the directory of the disk in the designated drive and checks it for consistency. It also provides any error messages and displays a status report on the disk and internal memory. For example, if drive A is a 3½-inch drive, the command

A:\>CHKDSK A:

will display a report similar to that shown below:

```
730112  bytes total disk space
729088  bytes in 23 user files
  1024  bytes available on disk

655360  bytes total memory
167280  bytes free
```

The CHKDSK command alerts you to problems it finds with your file allocation table. You can have CHKDSK fix these problems by using it with the /F switch. For example, if the command CHKDSK A: found problems with the disk in drive A, you could give the command

A:\>CHKDSK A:/F

to have DOS attempt to fix the errors.

To make a backup of a floppy disk, use the DISKCOPY command. When the command

A:\>DISKCOPY A: B:

is given, you will be instructed to insert the source disk in drive A, insert the destination disk in drive B, and press any key. Once this is done, everything on the source disk will be copied to the destination disk. If you have only a single disk drive, the command

A:\>DISKCOPY A: A:

can be used to copy entire disks. When this command is used, you will be instructed to swap disks in the disk drive until all material on the source disk is copied to the destination disk.

In working with the DISKCOPY command, you should be aware of several restrictions. First, this command cannot be used to back up a hard disk to multiple floppy disks. The DOS BACKUP command or any of several commercial backup packages should be used for this operation. Second, if you are using DISKCOPY to copy one floppy to another, the floppies must be *exactly* alike—that is, a 360K 5¼-inch disk to a 360K 5¼-inch disk or a 720K 3½-inch disk to a 720K 3½-inch disk. Any attempt to violate these restrictions will result in an error message.

TRY IT YOURSELF

1. Use the CHKDSK A: command to check the status of the data disk in drive A. How much storage space is available on the disk? How much internal memory is available?
2. If you have a formatted blank disk, use the DISKCOPY A: A: command to make an exact copy of the data disk in drive A.

Miscellaneous DOS Commands

Four other useful DOS commands are DATE, TIME, CLS (CLearScreen), and VER (version). The first two commands allow you to change the date and time from within DOS, the third command clears the screen, and the fourth command displays the version of DOS you are using. When the DATE or TIME command is entered, the current date or time is displayed, and you are requested to enter a new date or time. You can do this, or you can simply press **Enter** to accept the current date or time.

To clear the screen of previous DOS commands or the results of those commands, use the CLS command. When you enter this command, the screen is cleared. Only the DOS prompt remains. To determine the version of DOS installed on your computer, use the VER command. When you enter this command, the version of DOS is displayed, for example, MS-DOS 5.0.

TRY IT YOURSELF

1. Clear the screen.
2. Check the date and time on your machine and, if they are incorrect, change them.
3. Determine the version of DOS you are using.

Appendix B: Programming in BASIC is contained in the alternative version of this textbook, entitled *Living with Computers* with BASIC.

APPENDIX C

American Standard Code for Information Interchange (ASCII) Ordering of Symbols

ASCII Order	HEX Symbol	Control	Character	ASCII Order	HEX Symbol	Character
000	00H	NUL	(null)	032	20H	(space)
001	01H	SOH		033	21H	!
002	02H	STX		034	22H	"
003	03H	ETX	♥	035	23H	#
004	04H	EOT	♦	036	24H	$
005	05H	ENQ	♣	037	25H	%
006	06H	ACK	♠	038	26H	&
007	07H	BEL	(beep)	039	27H	'
008	08H	BS	(backspace)	040	28H	(
009	09H	HT	(tab)	041	29H	)
010	0AH	LF	(line feed)	042	2AH	*
011	0BH	VT	(home)	043	2BH	+
012	0CH	FF	(form feed)	044	2CH	,
013	0DH	CR	(carriage return)	045	2DH	−
014	0EH	SO		046	2EH	.
015	0FH	SI		047	2FH	/
016	10H	DLE	▶	048	30H	0
017	11H	DC1	◀	049	31H	1
018	12H	DC2		050	32H	2
019	13H	DC3	!!	051	33H	3
020	14H	DC4	¶	052	34H	4
021	15H	NAK	§	053	35H	5
022	16H	SYN	■	054	36H	6
023	17H	ETB		055	37H	7
024	18H	CAN		056	38H	8
025	19H	EM		057	39H	9
026	1AH	SUB	→	058	3AH	:
027	1BH	ESC	←	059	3BH	;
028	1CH	FS	(cursor right)	060	3CH	<
029	1DH	GS	(cursor left)	061	3DH	=
030	1EH	RS	(cursor up)	062	2EH	>
031	1FH	US	(cursor down)	063	3FH	?

ASCII Order	HEX Symbol	Character	ASCII Order	HEX Symbol	Character
064	40H	@	096	60H	'
065	41H	A	097	61H	a
066	42H	B	098	62H	b
067	43H	C	099	63H	c
068	44H	D	100	64H	d
069	45H	E	101	65H	e
070	46H	F	102	66H	f
071	47H	G	103	67H	g
072	48H	H	104	68H	h
073	49H	I	105	69H	i
074	4AH	J	106	6AH	j
075	4BH	K	107	6BH	k
076	4CH	L	108	6CH	l
077	4DH	M	109	6DH	m
078	4EH	N	110	6EH	n
079	4FH	O	111	6FH	o
080	50H	P	112	70H	p
081	51H	Q	113	71H	q
082	52H	R	114	72H	r
083	53H	S	115	73H	s
084	54H	T	116	74H	t
085	55H	U	117	75H	u
086	56H	V	118	76H	v
087	57H	W	119	77H	w
088	58H	X	120	78H	x
089	59H	Y	121	79H	y
090	5AH	Z	122	7AH	z
091	5BH	[	123	7BH	{
092	5CH	/	124	7CH	|
093	5DH	]	125	7DH	}
094	5EH	^	126	7EH	~
095	5FH	—	127	7FH	

GLOSSARY

absolute address   The actual location of a record in secondary storage. (Chapter 8)

access speed   The amount of time required for a disk to find and move data. (PC Guide)

accounting   A process that tracks the financial health of a company or an individual. (Chapter 11)

accounting software   Software that is used to handle the accounting function of a business. (Chapter 3)

accounts payable   A module of a business accounting software package that monitors the money the firm owes its suppliers. (Chapter 11)

accounts receivable   A module of a business accounting software package that keeps track of money owed to a firm and when payments are due. (Chapter 11)

acquisition/programming analysis   In the systems analysis and design process, the step in which a new system is acquired or programmed. (Chapter 15)

active drive   On a personal computer, the disk drive from which the operating system is expecting information. (Appendix A)

address   The location of data or instructions in internal memory; the location of a record in direct-access secondary storage. (Chapters 6 and 8)

address bus   The communications line over which the address of the data or instruction is transferred to the control unit. (Chapter 6)

algorithm   A step-by-step procedure used to solve a problem. (Chapters 4 and 16)

analog computer   A machine that uses physical relationships to make its calculations; a measuring machine. (Chapter 1)

analog equivalent   Data converted from serial form to analog form so that the telecommunications link can carry it. (Chapter 13)

analysis   The third step in the systems analysis and design process, in which the analyst fills in the details of the system under study. (Chapter 15)

analysis graphics   A graphics software package that allows analysis of data to determine if patterns exist or to gain a better understanding of the data. (Chapter 10)

Analytical Engine   The computer designed but not built by Charles Babbage in the mid-nineteenth century. (Chapter 1)

androids   Robots that have a built-in microprocessor and can move around. (Chapter 6)

antivirus software   Software that limits or prevents the entry of a virus into a computer system. (Chapter 18)

applications software   Software that constitutes the greatest proportion of software used on computers and performs specialized tasks. (Chapter 3)

applications tools   A fourth-generation language developed to create new applications quickly and easily. Used especially by experts to create custom applications for distribution to other users. (Chapter 17)

archival storage   The storage of infrequently used data and programs to tape. (Chapter 8)

argument   A variable or constant that gives a function the information it needs to perform its operation. (Appendix B)

arithmetic-logic unit (ALU)   The part of the CPU that handles the actual manipulation of the data. (Chapters 2 and 6)

array   A list or table of numbers or strings. (Appendix B)

artificial intelligence (AI)   Hardware and software systems that exhibit the same type of intelligence-related activities as humans—listening, reading, speaking, solving problems, and making inferences. (Chapters 5, 14, 17, and 20)

ASCII   An acronym for American Standard Code for Information Interchange—a code for the binary representation of characters within the computer. (Chapter 2)

ASCII files   Another name for text files on personal computers. (Chapter 8)

assembler   A translation program that converts the mnemonic commands in assembly language into machine language. (Chapter 17)

assembly language   A machine-specific language that uses words and letters for commands. (Chapter 17)

assignment statement   A statement in BASIC that assigns a value to a memory cell. (Appendix B)

asynchronous communication   A form of communication between computers that does not require that the computers be synchronized in the rate at which they process data. (Chapter 13)

authoring languages   A computer package that enables the user to create a sequence of interactive learning activities by using the mouse to select a "hot button" to answer a question or seek additional information. (Chapter 5)

auto-answer modem   A modem that receives outside calls under the direction of the computer. (Chapter 13)

auto-dial modem   A modem that dials a number under the direction of a computer. (Chapter 13)

AUTOEXEC.BAT file   A batch file that is automatically executed when the computer is booted up from the system disk. (Chapter 17 and Appendix A)

automated teller machine (ATM)   A financial transaction terminal used to carry out banking business. (Chapter 7)

automatic pagination   A word processing operation that allows the user to include a page number automatically on each page of text. (Chapter 10)

backlog   In an MIS department, jobs that have been submitted for systems analysis and design but have not been completed. (Chapter 15)

backspace key   Key used to delete text to the left of the cursor. (Chapter 10)

backup   A copy of software or data that is made by the user to guard against accidental loss of software or data. (Chapters 2, 5, 8, and 18)

backup hierarchy   A policy of backing up information on floppy disks and rotating the use of three or four disks. (Chapter 8)

backup tape   Magnetic tape used for storing files from disks. (Chapter 8)

bar codes   Combinations of light and dark bars that are coded to contain information. (Chapter 7)

bar graph   A type of analysis graphics that uses vertical or horizontal bars to show relative differences between categories of data. (Chapter 10)

batch commands   Especially in MS-DOS-based personal computers, commands that cause batch files to execute. (Chapters 9 and 17 and Appendix A)

batch file A file composed of DOS commands that will execute when the file name is entered. (Chapter 17, Appendix A)

batch mode A job entry mode in which the entire job is entered at one time from a disk drive or tape drive. (Chapter 9)

batch processing system Combining data from multiple users or time periods and submitting them to the computer for processing in a batch. (Chapters 4 and 14)

bidirectional printing Achieved by a printer that prints with the printhead moving in either direction. (Chapter 7)

binary files Program files that have been translated into a binary form. (Chapter 8)

binary number system Base 2 number system based on zero and one. (Chapter 2 and Binary Essay)

bit The basic unit of measure in a computer; contraction of BInary and digiT. (Chapters 2, 6, and 13)

bit-mapped graphics A type of graphics in which each pixel on the screen can be controlled individually. (Chapter 10)

bits per second (bps) A measure of the speed at which modems can send and receive information. (Chapter 13)

block-action command In word processing, the definition and subsequent movement, deletion, or other action on a block of text. (Chapter 10)

blocked records Logical records combined into a physical record that is read by the tape drive. (Chapter 8)

blocks On a computer disk, the smallest addressable units by which a user can locate data. (Chapter 8)

body of loop The part of a loop that is being repeated. (Chapter 16)

boiler plate material In word processing, a block of text that has been defined and copied to different points in a document or to different documents. (Chapter 10)

boldface Word processing operation that gives a heavier version of type. (Chapter 10)

boot disk The disk containing operating system commands that is used to start a computer. (Appendix A)

booting process The process of starting up a computer. (Chapters 2, 6, and 9 and Appendix A)

boundary The delineation between the system and its environment. (Chapter 4)

bridge A combination of hardware and software that connects two similar networks. (Chapter 13)

broadband transmissions High-speed transmission requiring media that can transmit large amounts of data. (Chapter 13)

buffer A temporary storage area for input/output that keeps the CPU from being slowed down. (Chapters 7 and 9)

bugs Errors in the execution of a program. (Chapter 16)

bulletin board service A telecommunications service that enables users to interact with each other. (Chapter 13)

bus The main cable in a bus network that links the central computers with all other computers in the network. (Chapter 13)

bus network A computer network in which computers are tied into a main cable, or bus, without a central computer. (Chapter 13)

business accounting package Computer software package designed to handle accounting for businesses. (Chapter 11)

business graphics Analysis graphics. (Chapter 10)

byte A group of eight bits—equivalent to a single character. (Chapters 2 and 6)

bytes per inch (bpi) A measurement of the storage density on magnetic tape. (Chapter 8)

cache memory A very fast temporary memory used for memory transfer and processing. (Chapter 6)

call-back system A type of computer security system that accepts calls and passwords from a user, looks up the phone numbers associated with the user, and calls the user back at that number. An unauthorized user would not be at the correct number, so access would be denied. (Chapter 18)

Carpal Tunnel Syndrome A painful wrist condition that can result from excessive keyboarding. (Chapter 19)

cartridge A form of magnetic tape, stored in a cartridge, that stores data using a magnetic bit pattern. (Chapters 2 and 8)

CASE tools Specific CASE software used in systems development. (Chapter 16)

cathode ray tube (CRT) A vacuum tube "electron gun" from which cathode rays are projected onto the computer screen, causing it to light up. (Chapters 7 and 19)

CD-ROM A form of read-only optical storage using compact disks. (Chapter 8)

cell The intersection of a row and a column. (Chapters 3 and 11)

cell identifier A letter (for the column) and a number (for the row) that together indicate which cell is being referred to in a formula, such as A10 or B2. (Chapter 11)

cell pointer A special cursor used to designate the spreadsheet cell into which the information is being entered. (Chapter 11)

centering The word processing function that centers material between the margins. (Chapter 10)

central processing unit (CPU) The part of the computer that handles the actual processing of data into information. (Chapters 2 and 6)

chain printer A printer using letters and digits attached to a chain that rotates between two pulleys. (Chapter 7)

channel A hardware unit that controls the input/output process without direction from the CPU. (Chapter 9)

character field A data base field that will contain any sequence of letters and numbers. (Chapter 12 and Appendix C)

character generator A function of ROM in which it supplies the appropriate character to be displayed on the screen. (Chapter 6)

character graphics Symbols that result when the dots on a screen can be controlled as a group, not individually. (Chapter 10)

charting package A presentation graphics package that shows the relationship between sets of numerical information. (Chapter 10)

Chief Information Officer (CIO) The top information manager in an organization; ensures that the greatest possible competitive advantage is gained from corporate information. (Chapter 20)

children In a hierarchical data model, the lower-level elements. (Chapter 12)

chip A tiny piece of silicon that can consist of over a million electronic elements. (Chapters 1, 2, and 6)

ciphertext A coded, unreadable form of information. (Chapter 18)

cleartext A readable form of information. (Chapter 18)

client-server configuration A LAN in which the processing burden is on the central computer. (Chapter 13)

clip art Desktop publishing element that imports previously created art images into a document. (Chapter 10)

clock A device in the CPU that sends out electrical pulses at a set rate, which the control unit uses to synchronize its operations. (Chapter 6)

clock speed A machine's top CPU processing speed, measured in megaHertz. (PC Guide)

coaxial cable A type of LAN cable similar to that used to transmit cable television signals into your home. (Chapter 13)

Color Graphics Adapter (CGA) A graphics board that allows an IBM PC or compatible to show four-color graphics as well as text. (Chapter 10)

color monitor A multicolor monitor. (Chapters 2 and 7)

column A series of values placed vertically. (Chapter 11)

command Instruction to the computer to carry out a specified operation; in BASIC, commands input by the user for immediate execution. (Chapter 3, Appendix B)

command driven Requiring the user to know and enter the needed commands and data. (Chapter 3)

command files Files that will execute a program which a file name is entered. (Chapters 12 and 17 and Appendix A)

command interpreter A part of the operating system that interprets the user's keystrokes and sends a message to the appropriate utility or applications program to carry out the command. (Chapter 9)

comment statements In a program, statements that explain the purpose of the statements that are actually carrying out the logic of the program. (Chapter 17)

communications software A type of software package that enables the computer and the modem to communicate with the other computers, including uploading and downloading files. (Chapter 13)

Compact Disk Read-Only Memory *See* CD-ROM.

compiled language A high-level language in which the entire source program is converted to object code before being executed. (Chapter 17)

compilers Translator programs that convert the high-level language into machine language by compilation. (Chapter 17)

completion screen A screen that requests information and data from the user. (Chapter 11 and Appendix C)

compound document A form of telecommunications combining written, voice, and computer communications to express an idea clearly. (Chapter 13)

compound logical condition In BASIC, the use of the AND or OR operator to combine two or more logical conditions. (Appendix B)

computer An electronic, automatic machine that manipulates and stores symbols based on instructions from the user. (Chapter 1)

computer-aided design (CAD) A graphics software package that assists the user in developing engineering and architectural designs. (Chapter 10)

computer-aided software engineering (CASE) The use of software to help in all phases of system development, including analysis and design and writing programs. (Chapter 16)

computer-based information system (CBIS) A system that uses computers to provide information needed by management. (Chapters 4 and 15)

computer chip *See* chip.

computer competence The level of computer knowledge reached by an individual who can use a computer to solve sophisticated problems in his or her field of expertise. (Chapter 1)

computer crime The unauthorized invasion of a computer data file, or theft of money, merchandise, data, or computer time, using a computer. (Chapters 5 and 18)

computer disk *See* disk.

computer error A misnomer—actually a human error. (Chapter 1)

computer language A language used by humans to give instructions to computers. (Chapters 2 and 3)

computer literacy An understanding of what a computer can and cannot do and an ability to make the computer do what is desired. (Chapter 1)

computer mastery The level of knowledge required of an individual who wants to be a success in the computer field. (Chapter 1)

computer matching The process of matching records in two data banks to determine which records exist in both data banks. (Chapter 19)

computer monitoring Management's monitoring of an employee's use of a personal computer or computer terminal. (Chapter 19)

computer network A combination of two or more computers with a communications system that allows exchange of information between the computers. (Chapters 1, 3, and 13)

computer package Commercially available software. (Chapters 1 and 3)

computeritis Painful musculo-skeletal problems associated with day-in/day-out use of the keyboard. (Chapters 5 and 19)

computerphobia A fear of the computer, especially among first-time users. (Chapters 5 and 19)

computerphile A person who is totally involved with the computer to the exclusion of all other concerns. (Chapter 19)

computer program A set of specific instructions for controlling the computer. (Chapter 3)

computer security A wide range of methods used to protect the computer, the data, and the computer user from natural and criminal forces. (Chapter 18)

Computer Security Act of 1987 Law designed to ensure the security of U.S. government computers. (Chapter 19)

computer terminal A keyboard and monitor without a CPU or any secondary storage devices. (Chapter 1)

computer virus A self-replicating, potentially damaging computer program sent over a computer network by mischievous or malicious persons. (Chapter 5)

computer word The number of bits processed by the registers in the ALU at one time. (Chapter 6)

computer worm A stand alone computer program that replicates itself over and over after gaining access to a computer network. (Chapter 5, Chapter 18)

conceptual computer A simplified computer that can demonstrate the major functions of a computer without involving the operational details of the machine. (Chapters 2 and 6)

connector symbol In flowcharting, a circle that is used to show a connection between two parts of a flowchart. (Chapter 16)

constants The data that go into the computer's memory cells. (Appendix, B)

control bus The communications line over which an instruction is transferred to the ALU from the internal memory. (Chapter 6)

control structures In BASIC and in structured programming generally, blocks that control the flow of statement execution within the program. (Appendix B)

control unit Part of the CPU that handles the management of the symbol manipulation process. (Chapters 2 and 6)

conventional memory The first 640 Kbytes of RAM recognized by MS-DOS for executing programs. (Chapter 6)

copy protection The process whereby software manufacturers guard against software piracy by making it impossible to make copies of personal computer software. (Chapter 5)

cost/benefit analysis A comparison of two proposed systems that weighs relative costs against projected benefits. (Chapter 15)

counter In programming, a variable that is used to count the number of repetitions. (Appendix B)

credit An accounting term used in double-entry bookkeeping. (Chapter 11)

credit check Information from a credit bureau on the past credit history of an individual. (Chapter 19)

cumulative trauma disorder Musculo-skeletal problems resulting from extensive use of a VDT. (Chapter 19)

cursor A blinking rectangle of light on the screen that designates the current position. (Chapters 2 and 10)

cursor control keys Keys on a personal computer keyboard that control the movement of the cursor on the screen. (Chapter 10)

cut-and-paste In word processing, a block-action command that defines a block of text and then moves it to another part of the document or to another document. (Chapter 10)

cyberphobia *See* computerphobia.

cylinder On disk packs, a storage scheme in which all tracks with the same track number make up a vertical cylinder. (Chapter 8)

data The raw facts that are fed into the computer for processing. (Chapter 1)

data bank A store of information on people or organizations. (Chapters 5 and 19)

data base A collection of information that is arranged for easy manipulation and retrieval. (Chapters 3, 4, 12, and 14)

data base administrator The person who controls the overall operations of the data base and, as such, acts as the custodian of the data base. (Chapter 20)

data base management software Software that manages an electronic data base in such a way that it is possible to find elements that fit some criteria. (Chapters 3 and 12)

data base management system (DBMS) A data base software system that can work with multiple files. (Chapter 14)

data base structure The data base fields defined in terms of their names, widths, and types. (Chapter 12)

data base vendors Companies that offer subscribers extensive, often full-text, data bases on specialized topics. (Chapter 13)

data bus The communications line over which the data flow to the ALU from internal memory. (Chapter 6)

data communications Any communication between two computers that involves a transfer of data. (Chapter 13)

data dependence The dependency between data and data storage. (Chapter 12)

data dictionary A list of data elements, along with information regarding name, source, description, and use. (Chapters 12 and 15)

Data Encryption Standard (DES) A standard method of coding information into ciphertext. (Chapter 18)

Data encryption system Combinations of software and hardware that convert data coming out of a computer into an unreadable form for transmittal over a network. (Chapter 18)

data entry problem The problem caused by slow and/or incorrect data entry to the computer. (Chapter 7)

data entry screen A set of requests for data, displayed on the screen of a monitor. (Chapter 12 and Appendix C-6)

data file A file containing any type of information, including data, text, or programs. (Chapter 8)

data flow diagram A pictorial representation of the flow of data into and out of the system. (Chapters 4 and 15)

data hierarchy The order in which data or information is organized in the computer. (Chapter 12)

data integrity The correctness of data in a data base. (Chapter 12)

data models One of several models of the way data will be represented in a data base management system. (Chapter 12)

data processing The mechanical process of converting raw data into meaningful information; usually refers to the processing of numeric data. (Chapters 1 and 4)

data redundancy The repetition of data on multiple files. (Chapter 12)

data security The protection of a computer's software and data from unauthorized manipulation, destruction, or theft. (Chapter 18)

date field A numeric field that can store only the date in dd/mm/yy format. (Chapter 12)

debit An accounting term used in double-entry bookkeeping. (Chapter 11)

debugging The process of tracking down and correcting execution errors in a program. (Chapter 16)

decision block One or more statements that handle choosing between alternative program sections based on whether a condition is true or false. (Appendix B-2)

decision support system (DSS) A subsystem of the MIS that combines data with models and graphics to answer a decision maker's questions about the data. (Chapters 4 and 14)

decision symbol In flowcharting, a diamond shape that is used to designate a decision

between two or more alternatives. (Chapter 16)

default answer The answer to a prompt that will be accepted if the user presses the Enter key without changing any information. (Appendix C-1)

delayed conference A form of teleconferencing in which the participant's comments are stored sequentially as they are entered; these comments are read and replied to by other participants over a long period of time. (Chapter 13)

demand reports Reports that are generated by the MIS upon a request by a manager. (Chapter 14)

density A measure of the amount of information that can be stored on a floppy disk. (Chapter 8)

desktop computers *See* personal computers.

desktop metaphor A view of the computer as a desk equipped with a file cabinet, telephone, wastebasket, scratch pad, and so on. (Chapter 7)

desktop publishing Combining word processing, graphics, and special page-definition software to create documents. (Chapters 3, 7, and 10)

destructive replacement The process of replacing the contents of a computer memory location with a new value and consequently losing the old value. (Chapter 6 and Appendix B-1)

diagramming package A presentation graphics package that works with shapes to display a set of facts graphically in the form of organizational charts, flowcharts, schedules, office layouts, and so on. (Chapter 10)

dialog base A part of the decision support system that handles the interaction between the manager and the computer. (Chapter 14)

dial-up computer systems Computer systems that can be reached from a personal telephone. (Chapter 18)

digital computer A machine that uses numbers to make its calculations; a counting machine. (Chapter 1)

digitizer board A piece of computer hardware that will convert a blueprint or photographic image into a digital form. (Chapter 12)

direct-access file organization Files organized so that each record may be accessed directly, regardless of its relative position on the file or the order in which the records were placed on the file. (Chapter 8)

direct-access storage Secondary storage on which information may be accessed in any desired order. (Chapter 2)

direct-access storage device (DASD) A secondary storage device on which information can be accessed in any desired order. (Chapters 2 and 8)

direct conversion A conversion from one system to another in which the old system is discarded at the time that the new system is installed. (Chapters 4 and 15)

direct mode Mode in which program statements are entered into the computer without formal line numbers and are executed immediately as they are entered. (Appendix B-1)

disk A thin, recordlike piece of metal or plastic, covered with iron oxide particles whose magnetic direction can be arranged to represent symbols. (Chapters 2 and 8)

disk directory A list of the files that are stored on a disk. (Chapter 9)

disk drive A device that writes information onto or reads information from magnetic disk. (Chapter 2)

disk operating system (DOS) An operating system for a personal computer that depends on disks for secondary storage. (Chapters 3, 8, and 9)

disk packs Collections of magnetic disks, each about the size of a record album, used on mainframes. (Chapters 2 and 8)

diskette *See* floppy disk.

diskless workstation In a LAN, a personal computer that does not have a disk drive and is dependent on the file server for disk access. (Chapter 13)

distributed data bases Small, specialized data bases that are separate from a primary data base; usually associated with minicomputers in a distributed data processing arrangement. (Chapter 13)

distributed data processing (DDP) A processing system that uses a mainframe computer for storage or data bases and for large-scale processing; combined with minicomputers or personal computers for local processing. (Chapter 13)

division/remainder procedure A hashing procedure that uses the remainder from division as the relative address of a record in secondary storage. (Chapter 8)

document translation A word processor function to convert documents from one word processing package to another. (Chapter 10)

documentation A written description of a software package and the tasks it can perform; in a program, the explanation of the logic and program statements. (Chapters 3, 17, and 20)

DOS A name commonly used to refer to MS-DOS or PC-DOS. (Appendix A)

DOS system files Two hidden files that contain important DOS operations. (Appendix A)

dot matrix printer A personal computer printer that uses a matrix of wires to form symbols on paper. (Chapters 2 and 7)

dot pitch The width of a dot on the monitor screen; the smaller the dot pitch, the sharper the image. (PC Guide)

double-entry bookkeeping An accounting system that enters each transaction as an increase to one account and a decrease to another account. (Chapter 11)

downloading The process of shifting software or data from a central computer to a personal computer and saving it on disk. (Chapter 13)

downsizing The process of replacing a mainframe or a minicomputer system with a LAN. (Chapter 13, Chapter 20)

drawing package A presentation graphics package that allows the user to add lines to library shapes or create onscreen animation, usually using a mouse as an input device. (Chapter 10)

drum printer An impact printer made up of 132 cylinders, each of which contains all of the letters, digits, and symbols needed to print documents. (Chapter 7)

DSS model generator A general-purpose decision support package that contains many models that the user can combine to solve his or her problems. (Chapter 14)

dual in/line package (DIP) A plastic carrier that protects the tiny chip and is the means by which the chip is connected to a circuit board. (Chapter 6)

dumb terminal A computer with no CPU or secondary storage. Its sole purpose is as an input/output device for a mainframe. (Chapters 2 and 13)

dynamic random-access memory (DRAM) RAM chip composed of many capacitors that need constant energy. (Chapter 6)

EBCDIC An acronym for Extended Binary Coded Decimal Interchange Code and a code for the binary representation of characters within the computer. (Chapter 2)

edited to check computer data for reasonableness or discrepancies; also, the process of changing a statement without having to reenter it entirely. (Chapter 7 and Appendices B-1, C-2, C-4, and C-6)

edit line The line above or below a spreadsheet, on which the information being entered actually shows up. (Chapter 11)

Electronic Communications Privacy Act of 1986 A law that extends the previous wiretap law to include communications between computers by giving electronic communications the same constitutional protections afforded telephone conversations. (Chapter 19)

electronic data interchange (EDI) Allows computers to exchange electronic transmissions of data and information thus automating routine business between retail stores, distributors, and manufacturers. (Chapter 13)

electronic filing Storage of a document on some form of secondary storage for later retrieval. (Chapter 14)

electronic forgery Computer crime wherein desktop publishing equipment is used to create phony work orders, receipts, bank checks, and even stock certificates. (Chapter 18)

electronic funds transfer (EFT) The payment of bills and other forms of funds transfer via computer. (Chapters 1 and 7)

electronic mall The process of sending letters, documents, and messages between computers. (Chapters 13 and 14)

electronic spreadsheet On a computer, a spreadsheet that allows for easy recalculation of values based on changes within the spreadsheet. (Chapter 11)

electronic supervision The process of using a computer to monitor the actions of employees. (Chapter 19)

emitter-coupled logic (ECL) A new chip technology that will allow computers to process at incredible speeds. (Chapter 20)

End key A key on the IBM compatible PC keyboard often used with word processing packages to place the cursor. (Chapters 2 and 10)

END statement In BASIC, the statement to indicate normal termination of a program. (Appendix B-1)

end user A non-data processing professional who uses the computer to solve problems associated with his or her job and may be quite sophisticated in the use of the computer. (Chapters 1, 15, and 20)

end user computing (EUC) The work of the end user on the computer (Chapter 15)

end-user programmer A programmer who creates specific applications for a popular software package. (Chapter 20)

end-user tools Nonprocedural packages oriented toward allowing the average computer user to solve problems without having to learn a programming language. (Chapter 17)

Enhanced Graphics Adapter (EGA) A digital computer graphic board that displays 16-color graphics in 640 × 360 resolution as well as displaying high-quality text. (Chapter 10)

environment All elements outside of a system that have some effect on the system. (Chapter 4)

erasable programmable read-only memory (EPROM) A PROM chip that can be erased and reprogrammed. (Chapter 6)

ergonomics The study of the relationship between efficiency and comfort in a worker's use of machines. (Chapters 5 and 19)

error trapping A mechanism in a software package that keeps a user from entering the incorrect type of data. (Chapter 11)

exception report A report that is generated by the MIS only when an abnormal event occurs. (Chapter 14)

executable file A file that, when its file name is entered, will execute a program. (Appendix A)

Execution-time (E-time) In the execution process, the period during which the instruction is carried out by the ALU and the results are sent to internal memory. (Chapter 6)

Executive Information System (EIS) A personalized, easy-to-use system for executives, providing data on the daily operations of an organization. (Chapters 4, 14)

expanded memory Includes conventional memory plus any RAM up to 8 Mbytes that has been modified to work with MS-DOS-based software. (Chapter 6)

expert system A computer system that makes the collective knowledge of various experts in a field available to the user. (Chapters 1, 4, 14, and 17)

expert system shell A software system that contains an expert system inference mechanism but not the knowledge base; the user adds the rules and facts to create an expert system. (Chapter 14)

extended memory All RAM between 1 and 32 Mbytes. MS-DOS-based software programs cannot use extended memory because they were written to another type of memory called **expanded memory.** (Chapter 6)

external commands Operating system commands that require that the system disk be in the active drive to be implemented. (Chapter 9 and Appendix A)

external modem A modem that is outside the computer but is connected to the computer through the serial port. (Chapter 13)

eyestrain A condition of eye discomfort sometimes associated with long-term use of a VDT. (Chapter 19)

facsimile (fax) machine A telecommunications machine used to send a reproduction of any document over phone lines to any place in the world. (Chapter 13)

Fair Credit Reporting Act of 1970 A national law that controls the actions of credit bureaus and allows consumers to view and make additions to their file. (Chapter 19)

feasibility study The second step in the systems design and analysis process, in which the analyst determines whether or not an acceptable solution to the problem exists. (Chapter 15)

feedback A form of output that is sent back to a system's input or processing function, enabling a system to change its operation if necessary. (Chapter 4)

fetch, decode, and execute process A process that fetches an instruction, decodes that instruction, and then executes it. (Chapter 6)

fiber optic cable The newest type of media that consists of thousands of glass fiber strands that transmit information over networks. (Chapter 13)

field A single piece of information—such as a name, a Social Security number, or a profit value. (Chapters 8 and 12)

field name An identifier given to a field in a data base file. (Chapter 12)

field type The type of information—that is, character, numeric, date, or logical—that will be stored in a field. (Chapter 12)

field width The number of positions set aside for data in a particular field. (Chapter 12)

file A collection of records all having the same fields, to which the user can attach a name. (Chapters 3, 7, 8, and 12 and Appendices A and B)

file allocation table (FAT) A list of the diskette's contents, used to locate programs and files. (Chapters 8 and 9)

file manager A part of a data base management package that controls the actual creation of the file and various utility functions associated with the use of the file. (Chapter 12)

file processing system (FPS) Data base management software that can work with only one file at a time. (Chapter 12)

file processor *See* file processing system.

file server A hard disk that provides users of a network access to files. (Chapter 13, Appendix A)

financial analysis software *See* spreadsheet.

financial transaction terminal Terminal used to carry out an individual's financial business—e.g., an **automated teller machine (ATM).** (Chapter 7)

firmware Instructions on a ROM chip. (Chapters 1 and 6)

first-level decision In a nested loop, the independent decision, whose execution does not depend on the other decisions. (Appendix B)

fixed expenses Expenses that do not change from month to month. (Chapter 11)

fixed-length word A word that consists of a specific number of bytes. (Chapter 6)

flash memory Nonvolatile memory chips arranged on a credit-card size circuit board that acts as another disk drive. (Chapter 8)

flat file Another name for a table in a relational data model. (Chapter 12)

flat-screen display Computer displays that use non-CRT technology to display computer output on a flat screen. (Chapter 7)

floppy disk Disk made of Mylar plastic and covered with iron oxide particles for use with the personal computer. (Chapters 2 and 8)

flowchart A pictorial form of an algorithm that can easily be converted into a computer program. (Chapters 4 and 16)

footers A text entry operation that allows the display of special information at the bottom of each page. (Chapter 10)

footnotes A word processing operation that allocates spacing at the bottom of a page for cited references. (Chapter 10)

FOR loop A pre-test loop in BASIC that is controlled by a counter variable. (Appendix B).

forecasting model A process that uses currently available information to predict future occurrences. (Chapter 14)

formal documentation For the systems analysis and design process, the data dictionary and list of data elements; for a software package, the user's manual and other written descriptions. (Chapters 3 and 15)

formatting The process of organizing the sectors and tracks of a floppy disk; in word processing, the process of setting up a document in a particular form. (Chapters 8 and 10 and Appendix A)

formula Values in the spreadsheet combined with other constants to define the relationships among the spreadsheet values. (Chapter 11)

fourth-generation languages (4GLs) Advanced computer languages that make prototyping possible by not requiring the user to develop a complete logical plan before solving a problem on the computer. (Chapters 15 and 17)

frames In desktop publishing packages, holes left in the text for graphics, drawings, and photographs. (Chapter 10)

Freedom of Information Act of 1979 Law that gives individuals the right to inspect information of concern to them held in U.S. government data banks, and requires that certain data about federal agencies be made available to individuals and organizations for inspection. (Chapter 19)

freeware Software packages that can be obtained for free or for a small fee. (Chapter 3)

full-duplex mode A mode of communication between computers in which both computers can send at the same time. (Chapter 13)

function In a spreadsheet, a specific operation; in programming, a short program stored in computer memory that can be accessed by the program as needed. (Chapters 11 and 17 and Appendix B)

function (built-in) A specific numeric or string operation in BASIC that can be accessed by the programmer as needed. (Appendix B)

functional electrical stimulation (FES) A field of research seeking ways to help paralyzed individuals walk again using computers. (Chapter 6)

gallium arsenide A semiconductor material that transmits electrons five times faster than silicon. (Chapter 20)

gateway A combination of hardware and software that connects two dissimilar computer networks. It allows a LAN user to access a mainframe network without leaving his or her PC. (Chapter 13)

general ledger Record that contains all the firm's financial transactions. (Chapter 11)

general-purpose computer A computer that can be used for many purposes. (Chapter 1)

general-purpose DSS A decision support system that can be used to solve various types of problems by the user developing a model and then manipulating variables to simulate results. (Chapter 14)

general-purpose languages Languages used to perform tasks ranging from computing payrolls to computing satellite orbits. (Chapter 7)

generic operating system Personal computer operating system that runs on many different makes of computers. (Chapters 3 and 9)

geographical information system (GIS) A computer system used to work with geographical entities, such as states, counties, or census blocks. (Chapter 4)

gigabyte (GByte) The largest commonly used measure of computer storage, equal to 1 billion (2^{30}) bytes of storage. (Chapter 2)

global change In a spreadsheet, a change made by the user to change all cell widths. (Chapter 11)

GOTO statement A transfer statement that is avoided in structured programming. (Appendix B)

graphical user interface (GUI) A GUI uses icons to represent commands and data. (Chapters 7 and 20)

graphics adapter board Computer hardware that supports color and graphics. (Chapter 10)

graphics digitizing tablet Electronic table capable of transmitting free-hand drawings to the computer. (Chapter 7)

graphics software A group of programs for visual presentation of information or for creation of new and different art forms. (Chapter 3)

hackers Individuals who gain unauthorized access to a computer for fun or challenge. (Chapters 5, 18, and 19)

half-duplex mode Communications between two computers during which both computers can send and receive information but only one computer can send at a time. (Chapter 13)

handheld portable A battery-powered, pocket-sized personal computer. (PC Guide)

hard copy A printed version of what appears on the video screen. (Chapters 2 and 7)

hard disk A scaled-down version of a mainframe disk pack with metal disks that is used for storing information from a personal computer. (Chapters 2 and 8)

hard-disk card The combination of a hard disk and a controller card. (Chapter 8)

hard sectoring A sectoring plan that is defined by the use of additional index holes. (Chapter 8)

hardware The electronic part of the computer that stores and manipulates symbols under the direction of the computer software. (Chapters 1 and 2)

hashing The process of converting the primary key on a record into a relative address. (Chapter 8)

Hayes compatibility Whether a modem uses the same commands as a Hayes modem, which has become the industry standard. (Chapter 13)

head crash The result of the read/write head making contact with the magnetic disk, leading to the destruction of the disk and any data on it. (Chapter 8)

head window The area of a floppy disk that is in contact with the read/write head. (Chapter 8)

headers A text entry operation that allows the display of special information at the top of each page. (Chapter 10)

Hercules Graphics Card The add-in board necessary to display high-resolution (720 × 348) monochrome graphics on the monochrome monitor. (Chapter 10)

hexadecimal (hex) number system A number system that uses the digits 0–9 and the letters A–F to represent the numbers 0–16. (Binary Essay)

hierarchical data model A data model in which each element has only one parent or owner—similar to an organization chart. (Chapter 12)

Hierarchical Input/Process/Output (HIPO) technique A process used in the system design stage to develop the high-level design of the recommended software system. (Top-Down Design Essay)

hierarchical structure Division of long lists of files into subdirectories that are easier to keep track of. Also called a tree structure. (Chapter 9)

hierarchy chart A chart that breaks the software package down into smaller pieces until a program can be written to implement each piece of the package. (Top-Down Design Essay)

hierarchy of operations The order in which arithmetic operations are carried out. (Appendix B)

high-level languages Languages combining English words with a specific grammar to give the computer instructions. (Chapters 11 and 16)

Home key A key on the numeric keypad that is often used in word processing packages. (Chapter 10)

horizontal scrolling In a spreadsheet, the horizontal movement of the columns across the screen. (Chapter 11)

host computer In a star network configuration, the central computer to which all other computers are linked. (Chapter 13)

hub ring The part of a floppy disk where the disk drive clamps onto the disk and rotates it. (Chapter 8)

human-factors engineering *See* ergonomics.

hypertext Information retrieval software that stores information in discrete nodes that can be reached from any other node, allowing users to move about within the data base according to whatever mental connections they make. (Chapter 12)

IBM compatible PC A computer with the ability to run software written for the original IBM PC or one of its successors. (Chapters 2 and 3)

icons Pictures that represent various operations on the computer. (Chapters 3, 7, and 9)

if–then rule Used in an expert system that, together with facts, create the knowledge base. (Chapter 14)

IF–THEN statement In BASIC, a statement that implements a one-alternative decision. (Appendix B-2)

IF–THEN–ELSE statement In BASIC, a statement that implements a two-alternative decision. (Appendix B)

image scanner A device often used in desktop publishing that allows images to be scanned and converted into a digital form that can be included in a document. (Chapter 10)

impact printer A type of printer that uses some form of hammer to press ink onto a page. (Chapter 7)

implementation The process of installing the information system that has been designed and acquired or programmed. (Chapter 15)

index hole A hole in the vinyl cover of a floppy disk that indicates to the computer the current position of the disk in its rotation. (Chapter 8)

indexed sequential access method (ISAM) A method of storing and retrieving records from secondary storage. (Chapter 8)

indexing A system of keeping track of records in a data base using record numbers. (Chapter 12)

inference engine The deductive part of an expert system that uses the information in the knowledge base to make suggestions or ask additional questions. (Chapter 14)

informated factory A workplace where computers perform operations and supply workers with information on the processing operations. (Chapter 5)

information Data that has been processed into a form that is useful to the user. (Chapter 1)

information society A society in which the majority of the workers are involved in the transmittal of information. (Chapters 1 and 20)

information specialist A person who works with a personal computer to perform such wide-ranging tasks as word processing, data base management, and spreadsheet analysis. (Chapter 5)

information system Within an organization, a system that converts raw data into information that is useful to managers and other interested parties. (Chapters 1, 4, and 14)

information technology The use of computers for information and productivity. (Chapter 1)

initialize The process of setting one or more values to some beginning value. (Chapter 16)

ink-jet printer A nonimpact printer that forms symbols by spraying dots of ink on the paper. (Chapters 2 and 7)

input Receiving the data to be manipulated and the instructions for performing that manipulation. (Chapters 2 and 4)

input crime A computer crime in which the user changes, fabricates, or manipulates data when they are entered into the computer. (Chapter 18)

INPUT loop A pre-test loop in BASIC that inputs data as long as valid data are received. (Appendix B)

input/output (I/O) The process of instructing the computer, feeding it data, and receiving processed information from the computer. (Chapter 7)

input/output symbol In flowcharting, a parallelogram that is used to designate the input and output operations. (Chapter 16)

Input/Process/Output (IPO) table A table for each module of a software package, showing the input to the module, the processing that takes place in the module, and the output from the module. (Top–Down Design Essay)

insert mode A word processing mode in which new symbols that are entered are inserted to the left of the existing symbols, pushing the existing material to the right. (Chapter 10)

Instruction-time (I-time) The period in the execution process in which the instruction is fetched and decoded. (Chapter 6)

integer field A data base field that will contain a number without a decimal. (Chapter 12 and Appendix C)

integrated circuit (IC) The combination of transistors and circuits on a chip. (Chapters 2 and 6)

Integrated Service Digital Network (ISDN) Digital network of the future that will dramatically increase telecommunications transmission capabilities. (Chapters 13 and 20).

integrated package Software that contains some or all of the most commonly used packages and a procedure to access the various packages. (Chapters 3 and 11)

interblock gap (IBG) On magnetic tape, the space between blocks—where the tape starts and stops. (Chapter 8)

internal commands Operating system commands that do not require that the system disk be in the active drive. (Chapter 9 and Appendix A)

internal memory The part of the computer used to store instructions and data internally. (Chapters 2 and 6)

internal modem A modem that is located in a slot inside the computer in the back. (Chapter 13)

interpreted language A high-level language that must be converted into machine language as each statement is encountered in the execution process. (Chapter 17)

interpreter A translator program that converts high-level language statements into machine language statements. (Chapter 17)

inventory control A process that keeps track of raw materials, goods in process, finished goods, and other supplies for a company. (Chapter 11)

investment analysis package Packages to keep track of investments and help choose the best way to invest money. (Chapter 11)

invisible backlog A backlog of jobs that have not been submitted to the MIS department for analysis and design. (Chapter 15)

Job Control Language (JCL) An English-like computer language that allows the user to communicate with the operating system. (Chapter 9)

Josephson Junction A super-fast electronic switch that works at temperatures close to absolute zero. (Chapter 20)

Kbit 1 Kbit equals 1,024 bits. (Chapter 6)

Kbyte 1 Kbyte equals 1,024 bytes. (Chapters 2 and 6)

keyboard An input device made up of keys that allow input of alphanumeric and punctuation characters. (Chapters 2 and 7)

keywords Words that are a part of the syntax of a language. (Chapter 17)

knowledge base In an expert system, the facts, judgments, rules, intuition, and experience provided by the group of experts. (Chapter 14)

knowledge engineer A specialist who can convert an expert's knowledge into the rules and facts in an expert system. (Chapter 14)

label For a spreadsheet, a combination of letters and numbers that defines a cell; in programming, a number that allows reference to a statement in the program; in BASIC, any string constant enclosed in quotation marks. (Chapters 11 and 17 and Appendix B)

LAN operating systems Systems that operate at a level above the basic operating system to allow users access to software and files on the file server. (Chapter 9)

laptop computer A portable computer designed to fit on one's lap or some other nonpermanent surface where no AC power is available. (PC Guide)

laser disk A form of optical storage that uses laser technology to read information from the disk. (Chapter 8)

laser printer A nonimpact printer that uses a laser beam to write dots on a drum coated with light-sensitive material that transfers ink to the paper. (Chapters 2 and 7)

last-record check Terminating a loop when a value is found that matches a predetermined termination condition. (Chapter 16)

leased lines Special high-speed telephone lines that are leased from the telephone company for the express purpose of carrying data between computers. (Chapter 13)

letter-quality Printer output that is equal in quality to that produced on a typewriter. (Chapter 7)

library routines Short, preprogrammed standard procedures—e.g., finding a square root—that are stored in the computer, separate from the program being run, and available as needed. (Chapter 17)

light pen An input device that allows the user to select a command by pointing it at a portion of the screen. (Chapters 2 and 7)

line graph A type of analysis graphics that shows relationships by connecting points on the screen. (Chapter 10)

line numbers Numbers between 1 and 99999 that are used to identify the lines in a BASIC program. (Chapters 17 and Appendix B)

link-editor A part of the operating system that links the object code to any necessary library routines. (Chapter 17)

liquid crystal display (LCD) A flat-screen display composed of a thin layer of liquid crystal molecules placed between two sheets of glass and separated into sections. An individual liquid crystal molecule can be made opaque by applying a voltage to it. (Chapter 7)

list A column of numbers or strings of characters. (Appendix B)

local area network (LAN) A network of personal computers within one building. (Chapters 3, 13, and 13)

local change A change made by the user in a spreadsheet to change the width of only a designated group of cells. (Chapter 11)

logic Step-by-step solution in computer programming. (Chapter 16)

logic bomb A computer crime in which a disruptive program executes whenever a certain command is given. (Chapter 18)

logical field A field whose format can only be true or false (yes or no). (Chapter 12)

logical record A piece of information in a block of records stored on tape. (Chapter 8)

loop The repetition of one or more actions. (Chapter 16 and Appendix B)

loop termination decision A decision that determines where a loop will terminate. (Chapter 16)

low-level languages Languages at the computer's level, such as machine and assembly languages. (Chapter 17)

luggable PCs Portable personal computers that weigh over 10 pounds, require AC power, and are portable from desk to desk. (PC Guide)

machine language A computer's binary language, which is a very specific language that details every computer operation as a series of zeroes and ones. (Chapters 4, 16, and 17)

macro A facility in a spreadsheet that allows the user to do an operation once and then to save that series of keystrokes by assigning a name to them. (Chapters 11 and 17)

magnetic disk A metal or plastic disk coated with ferrous oxide particles, on which information can be stored via a magnetic bit pattern. (Chapters 2 and 8)

magnetic link character recognition (MICR) The input procedure, used to process checks, that reads characters printed on the checks that have been printed in magnetic ink. (Chapter 7)

magnetic (mag) tape A form of secondary storage composed on thin Mylar tape coated with ferrous oxide particles, on which information is recorded in binary form by selective magnetization of spots on the tape. (Chapters 2 and 8)

magneto-optical technology A combination of magnetism and optical principles used in erasable optical storage. (Chapter 8)

mail-merge A function of word processing that prepares form letters by combining a letter with different names and addresses. (Chapter 10)

mainframe A very large and fast computer that requires a special support staff and a special physical environment. (Chapter 1)

main memory *See* internal memory.

main program In a top-down designed program, the top-level program that manages the modules that perform the actual work; in BASIC, a list of the general procedures (the GOSUB instructions) to be carried out; followed by subroutines containing the detailed logic. (Top-Down Design Essay and Appendix B)

maintenance For an existing program, the process of fixing bugs, adding features, altering parts of the program, and performing other activities to keep the program current; in the systems analysis and design process, keeping the new system's hardware and software running smoothly and up-to-date after installation. (Chapters 15 and 17)

management information system (MIS) An integrated user-machine system for providing information to support operations, management, and decision-making functions in an organization. (Chapters 4 and 14)

many-to-many relationship In a data model, the situation in which multiple fields are related to one another. (Chapter 12)

massively parallel computers Computers that speed up data processing by performing many different operations at one time. (Chapter 5)

math coprocessor A special chip that supersedes the CPU to handle the various arithmetic operations needed in many mathematical calculations. (Chapter 6)

megabyte (Mbyte) Measure of computer memory equal to 1 million (2^{30}) bytes of storage. (Chapter 2)

megaHertz Unit of measurement or the clock speed of a CPU. (PC Guide)

memory manager A type of utility software that causes the extended memory to emulate expanded memory. (Chapter 6)

menu A list of commands or requests for data. (Chapter 3)

menu driven A software package that uses a menu to allow the user to make selections of commands or to enter data. (Chapter 3)

microchip *See* chip.

microcomputers *See* personal computers.

microfloppy disk A floppy disk that is less than 4 inches in diameter and is usually contained within a hard plastic cartridge. (Chapter 8)

microprocessor A computer chip that is programmed to control a machine's actions; also, a CPU on a chip. (Chapters 1, 2, and 6)

microwaves High-frequency radio transmissions that can be transmitted between two earth stations or between earth stations and communications satellites, which are commonly used to transmit such things as television signals. (Chapter 13)

mind tool Another name for a computer. (Chapter 1)

minicomputer Computer size between a mainframe and a personal computer. (Chapter 1)

model A simplified version of the system that allows the analyst to understand the system's important parts. (Chapters 4 and 15)

model base In a decision support system, a collection of models used as needed to arrive at a solution. (Chapter 14)

modem A communications device that modulates computer signals into outgoing audio signals and demodulates incoming audio signals into computer signals. (Chapters 2 and 13)

module A separate program that performs a specific task and shares data with the other modules to lead to an integrated system. (Chapter 11, Top–Down Design Essay, and Appendix B)

monitor A cathode ray tube output device that shows the output on a video screen. (Chapters 2 and 7)

monochrome monitor A one-color monitor. (Chapters 2 and 7)

mouse An input device—about the size of a mouse and connected to the computer by a long cord—that allows input through movement over a flat surface. (Chapters 2 and 7)

MS-DOS A single-user, single-task generic operating system for use on IBM compatible PCs; currently the most popular disk operating system. (Chapters 3 and 9)

multiple-access network A local area network in which all users can transmit at any time, but collision-detecting software is necessary to control transmissions. (Chapter 13)

multimedia The traditional PC along with a VCR, optical storage disk, compact disks, and high-fidelity stereo that will provide interactive, full-motion video. (Chapters 1 and 20)

multiscanning monitor A computer monitor that can display the output from analog VGA or from any digital graphics adapter. (Chapter 10)

nanotechnology The ability to build complex objects on a molecular scale using atom-by-atom precision. (Chapter 20)

natural languages Languages that use everyday terminology and grammar to communicate with the computer. (Chapters 5, 12, and 17)

near-letter-quality output A quality of dot matrix print, created by a 24-pin printhead, that is close to that created by a daisy wheel printer. (Chapter 7)

nested decisions In BASIC, one decision depending on another decision. (Appendix B)

nested FOR loops In BASIC, an inner FOR loop within an outer FOR loop. (Appendix B)

network A combination of two or more computers with a communications system that allows exchange of information between the computers. (Chapters 1, 3, and 13)

network data model A data model in which each element may have more than one parent or owner. (Chapter 12)

neural network Computer processing using multiple processors that are "trained," through repetition, to handle some task without an extensive, highly specific program. (Chapters 5 and 20)

neuron The many chips in a neutral network. (Chapter 20)

node The location of a computer or terminal in a network or electronic mail system. (Chapter 13)

noise pollution A condition caused by continuous noise in the home or workplace; sometimes associated with continual use of computer printers in a small space. (Chapter 19)

nondestructive fetch A process in which data can be retrieved from any address without destroying the data. (Chapter 6 and Appendix B)

nonimpact printer A printer that uses some device other than a hammer to form symbols with ink on the paper. (Chapter 7)

noninterlaced monitor A monitor that paints each line during each pass, which

results in a sharper screen image. (PC Guide)

nonprocedural language A computer language that does not require the user to develop a logical procedure but only to answer questions or make choices from a menu. (Chapters 12 and 17)

nonvolatile memory Memory that does not disappear when the power is removed from the computer. (Chapter 6)

notebook PCs Portable, full-power personal computers that can run on either AC power or rechargeable batteries and are similar to **laptops** but are generally lighter. (PC Guide)

numeric field A field with the ability to store numeric information and make calculations. (Chapter 12)

numerical constant A positive or negative number that is placed in a memory cell. (Appendix B)

object code A machine language program that is actually executed by the computer. (Chapter 17)

object-oriented language A language based on the concept of sending messages using icons. (Chapter 17)

object-oriented programming systems (OOPS) Systems that use objects (self-contained items that combine data and algorithms) that cooperate in the program by passing strictly defined messages to one another. (Chapter 17)

office automation *See* office information system.

office information system (OIS) A machine or machines combined with a communications system and users to efficiently handle the job of obtaining, organizing, storing, retrieving, and preparing needed information; also called **office automation.** (Chapters 4 and 14)

one-alternative decision A decision for which if the condition is true an action is taken but if the condition is false no special action is taken. (Appendix B)

one-dimensional array A list of numbers or strings. (Appendix B)

one-to-many In a data model, the situation in which one field is related to multiple other fields. (Chapter 12)

one-to-one In a data model, the situation in which one field is related to only one other field. (Chapter 12)

online services Companies that provide a wide range of computerized information to their subscribers. (Chapter 13)

operating environment A program that overlays the operating system to allow a menu-driven operating system, multitasking, or the use of windows. (Chapters 3 and 9)

operating system The primary component of systems software; manages the many tasks that are going on concurrently within a computer. (Chapters 3 and 9)

operator In BASIC, a symbol for one of the five arithmetic operations. (Appendix B)

optical character recognition (OCR) A process that reads characters in a special font into the computer. (Chapters 7 and 14)

optical disk A form of secondary storage that uses lasers and pits in a reflective surface to store information. (Chapter 2)

optical mark reader An optical character recognition system that picks up black pencil marks on a special answer sheet and compares them to the correct answers. (Chapter 7)

optical storage media Secondary storage using laser disks. (Chapter 8)

optimization The use of a mathematical technique to find the best solution to a model. (Chapter 14)

optoelectronic technology Laser light used to transmit data at the rate of 1 billion bits per second. (Chapter 20)

order processing A module that a retail or wholesale operation uses to make sure that customers' orders are filled in a timely manner. (Chapter 11)

OS/2 A single-user, multitasking generic operating system for use on some IBM compatible PCs. (Chapters 3 and 9)

outline processor An operation that aids the user by automatically numbering the various levels of an outline. (Chapter 10)

output The result of the processing as displayed or printed for the user. (Chapters 2 and 4)

output crime The theft of processed information for resale, extortion, or the criminal's personal use. (Chapter 18)

outsourcing A process that involves turning over the entire responsibility for the information system to an outside group. (Chapter 20)

overflow area In ISAM, an area of storage to which new records are added when the original storage area is filled. (Chapter 8)

packet switching In a wide area network, dividing long messages into smaller data units to be transmitted more easily through a network. (Chapter 13)

packets The smaller data units that long messages are divided into for packet switching. (Chapter 13)

page description language (PDL) In a desktop publishing package, the operation that combines the user's text and graphics into a final page format. (Chapter 10)

page printer A laser printer capable of printing an entire page at a time. (Chapters 2 and 7)

paint packages Graphics packages that are used to develop artistic creations on the computer screen. (Chapter 10)

paragraph indention A function of a word processing package that allows an entire paragraph to be indented. (Chapter 10)

parallel conversion The conversion of one system to another in which both systems run in parallel before the conversion is completed. (Chapters 4 and 15)

parallel form The processing of data 8, 16, 32 bits at a time. (Chapter 13)

parallel processing A form of computer processing that allows multiple instructions to be processed simultaneously. (Chapters 6 and 20)

parallel storage device A secondary storage device on which an entire byte is encoded in one operation. (Chapter 8)

parallel-data computers Computers capable of simultaneously performing the same operations on many different data items. (Chapter 6)

parallel-process computers Computers that divide a problem into many smaller parts, each of which is solved by a separate processor. (Chapter 6)

parent In a hierarchical data base, the data element that is linked in a superior fashion to other elements called children. (Chapter 12)

parity bit On magnetic storage devices and in communications, an extra bit that is used for error-checking. (Chapters 8 and 13)

password A secret combination of letters, numbers, and/or symbols that is used to ensure that only the legitimate user can access a computer with the given user number. (Chapter 18)

password policies Specific company policies designed to protect data and software through responsible use of passwords. (Chapter 18)

path name The name of the current subdirectory preceded by all subdirectories "above" it separated by backslashes. (Appendix A)

payroll A list of employees to be paid and the amount each is paid by the organization. (Chapter 11)

peer-to-peer configuration A LAN configuration in smaller networks in which the emphasis is on users sharing files. Each computer can function as both a server and a workstation instead of as a single dedicated file server. (Chapter 13)

pen-based computing A form of input in which the user writes directly to the screen. (Chapters 2 and 7)

personal accounting packages Software designed to help keep track of an individual's or even a small business's finances. (Chapter 11)

personal budgeting package A group of programs that includes checkbook accounting and home budget planning. (Chapters 3 and 11)

personal computer Small, one-user computers that are relatively inexpensive to own and do not require a special environment or special knowledge to use them. (Chapter 1)

personal financial management package Software designed to help the individual monitor his or her finances. (Chapter 11)

personal identification number (PIN) A secret numerical password used to access a bank account from an automatic teller machine. (Chapters 7 and 18)

personal productivity software PC applications software, so-called because it allows individuals to increase their productivity. (Chapter 3)

PgDn key A key on the IBM compatible PC keyboard that facilitates large downward movements of the cursor. (Chapters 2 and 10)

PgUp key A key on the IBM compatible PC keyboard that facilitates large upward movements of the cursor. (Chapters 2 and 10)

phosphor A phosphorescent compound coated on the inside of a computer screen to make it light up. (Chapter 7)

photomask A procedure, similar to the making of a photographic negative, used to imprint an electronic circuit on a chip. (Chapter 6)

physical record The actual amount that is read by a tape drive before it stops at an interblock gap; made up of one or more logical records. (Chapter 8)

physical security The protection of the computer hardware from natural and human damage. (Chapter 18)

pie graph A type of analysis graphics that demonstrates the manner in which some quantity is proportionally divided by showing those divisions as pieces of a pie. (Chapter 10)

piping The ability to send output from one program to another program, where it becomes input. (Chapter 9)

pixel A picture element made up of a dot of light on the screen. (Chapters 7 and 10)

plotter Nonimpact hard-copy output device that uses moving pens to draw charts and graphs on various types of paper, vellum, or transparencies. (Chapter 7)

pocket PCs Portable personal computers are about the size of a large calculator and replace traditional address books, calculators, and appointment calendars. They are battery powered and do not usually include a disk drive. (PC Guide)

pointer system An indexing system in which the value associated with each element in a list points to the next element in the list. (Chapter 12)

port An entry line to the computer. (Chapters 13 and 18)

port protection device An extra level of security, at the entry level to the computer, that requires the user to have an additional password and that can camouflage the computer's answering device. (Chapter 18)

portable computer   A computer that can be transported. (PC Buying Guide)

post/test loop   A loop in which the loop termination decision comes after the body of the loop. (Chapter 16)

pre/test loop   A loop in which the loop termination decision comes before the body of the loop. (Chapter 16)

predefined process symbol   A symbol used to designate a procedure that is part of the flow of control but requires a separate flowchart. (Chapter 16)

preprocessor   A small computer that controls the terminals and RJEs to relieve the CPU from this responsibility. (Chapter 9)

presentation graphics   Graphics software packages that allow the presentation of data and information in a more understandable or dramatic form. (Chapter 10)

Presentation Manager   A graphical interface incorporated into OS/2. (Chapter 9)

primary key   The one field or combination of fields that uniquely identifies a record among all records on a data base. (Chapter 8)

primary storage   *See* internal memory.

primitives   Basic graphic objects such as points, lines, and circles used in designs. (Chapter 10)

print spooler   A word processing function that allows text to be printed while other text is being entered or edited. (Chapter 10)

PRINT zones   In BASIC, zones 14 spaces wide that control the exact spacing between labels and variables. (Appendix B)

printer   An output device that places words and symbols on paper. (Chapters 2 and 7)

printer codes   Instructions that the printer uses to convert the special characters for underlining, boldface, and subscripts. (Chapter 10)

printer driver   In word processing, a software package that handles the conversion of special characters in the document to symbols the printer can use. (Chapter 10)

1974 Privacy Act   Law that applied principles of privacy to the recordkeeping practices of the federal government. (Chapter 19)

problem definition   The first step in the systems analysis and design process; the process of defining the problem to be analyzed and the system to be designed. (Chapter 15)

procedural language   A computer language that requires the programmer to use a logical procedure to perform some task. (Chapters 12 and 17)

processing   The conversion of data into information. (Chapter 4)

processing block   One or more statements that handle the input, output, and calculation functions in a program. (Appendix B)

processing crime   Manipulating software so that it or the data it is processing are used to steal, sabotage, or fudge results. (Chapter 18)

processing/internal memory unit   The part of the computer of the computer where data are stored and manipulated. (Chapter 2)

processing symbol   In flowcharting, a rectangle used to designate any type of processing operation. (Chapter 16)

program   A series of instructions to the computer. (Chapters 1 and 16)

program file   A file made up of a list of program statements. (Chapter 8)

program flowchart   A pictorial form of the logic needed to solve a problem. (Chapter 4)

program generator   A prototyping tool that allows the user to generate computer code in a high-level language without having to actually write the code. (Chapter 15)

program mode   Mode in which program statements are entered into the computer with formal line numbers that indicate their sequence of execution; the program is not processed until the user enters the RUN command. (Appendix B)

program statements   Line-by-line statements in a computer program. (Appendix B)

programmable decisions   Day-to-day operational decisions based on basic rules and policies set at higher management levels. (Chapter 4)

programmable read-only memory (PROM)   A ROM chip that can be programmed by the user. (Chapter 6)

programming   The process of writing a series of instructions for the computer to follow in performing some specific task. (Chapters 1, 3, and 16)

prompt   A signal on the screen, indicating that the computer is waiting for a command or data. (Chapters 3, 9 Appendix A)

proportional spacing   A text print that creates different amounts of space between different letters. (Chapter 10)

proprietary operating system   Personal computer operating systems that run on only one type of computer. (Chapters 3 and 9)

protocol   The set of rules two computers follow when communicating with each other. (Chapter 13)

prototyping   Creating a "quick and dirty" prototype of software to get around the lengthy systems analysis and design process. (Chapter 15)

pseudocode   A written form of an algorithm that can easily be converted into a computer program. (Chapters 4 and 16)

public domain   Noncopyrighted software, which may be copied legally.

puck   A stylus on a digitizer tablet used in computer-aided design. (Chapter 10)

pull-down menu   A menu that uses icons to represent various commands or operations and appears as needed. (Chapter 3)

pushover mode   *See* insert mode.

query language   A computer language associated with the use of data base management packages that allows a user to request information. (Chapter 12)

queue   The use of a waiting line by operating systems to execute jobs according to their level of priority. (Chapter 9)

RAM-resident program   A program that, once run, remains resident in RAM and can be called up during the operation of another program. (Chapter 9)

random-access memory (RAM)   The section of memory that is available for storing the instructions to the computer and the symbols to be manipulated. (Chapters 2 and 6)

range   In a spreadsheet, a part of a row, a part of a column, or a rectangle of cells. (Chapter 11 and Appendix C)

read-only memory (ROM)   The section of memory that is placed in the computer during the manufacturing process and remains there even after the computer is turned off. (Chapters 2 and 6)

read/write head   The part of a disk or tape drive that handles the actual transfer of information to or from the disk or tape. (Chapters 2 and 8)

real field   A data base field that will contain a number containing a decimal. (Chapter 12 and Appendix C)

real-time conference   A form of teleconferencing in which all participants are logged onto the system at the same time. (Chapter 13)

real-time processing   Used when several users are competing for the same resource—e.g., an airline reservation system. (Chapters 4 and 14)

record   A collection of fields with information that usually pertains to only one subject (person, place, event, and so on). (Chapters 8 and 12)

record number   The physical position of a record in a list. (Chapters 8 and 12)

redundant arrays of inexpensive disks (RAID)   Replaces the larger disk packs with a "gang" of 5¼-inch disk drives similar to the ones used in personal computers.

reel-to-reel magnetic tape   A form of magnetic tape that runs between two reels and is used in minicomputer and mainframe applications for secondary storage. (Chapter 8)

reformatted   The realignment of a paragraph's margins after material has been deleted. (Chapter 10)

register   A temporary holding place for a particular instruction, data item, or piece of information. (Chapter 6)

relational data model A data model in which elements are represented as being parts of tables, which are then related through common elements. (Chapter 12)

relational operator In BASIC, one of six arithmetic operators that handle comparisons between constants and variables or between variables. (Appendix B)

relative address The location of a record in secondary storage relative to all other records. (Chapter 8)

relative copy A copy of a formula being moved that retains the original formula structure but changes that formula to match the location of the new cell. (Chapter 11)

remark (REM) In BASIC, a statement that is added to explain a program and its logic to other users. (Appendix B)

remote job entry (RJE) site A batch job entry site that is separate from the CPU. (Chapter 9)

repetition block A block of statements that handles the repetition of one or more actions. (Appendix B)

repetitive strain disorder Musculoskeletal problems resulting from extensive use of a VDT. (Chapter 19)

replace mode The word processing mode in which current symbols are replaced by new symbols. (Chapter 10)

report generator The part of a data base management package that handles the reporting of information in whatever order the user desires. (Chapter 12)

request for proposal (RFP) The process of requesting that vendors submit a proposal on a hardware or software job. (Chapter 15)

reserved word In BASIC, any one of almost 160 words that cannot be used as variable names. (Appendix B-1)

resist A chemical that is used to build up each layer of a chip. (Chapter 6)

resolution The quality of the picture on a monitor as defined by the number of pixels on the screen. (Chapters 7 and 10)

reverse polarity Reversed electrical current; when a computer system with normal polarity is plugged into such an outlet, an explosion and damage will occur. (Chapter 18)

reverse Polish notation (RPN) A method of organizing arithmetic operations that places the operators before the values. (Chapter 17)

reverse video On a computer screen, dark letters appearing on a light background instead of vice versa. (Chapter 1)

RGB monitor A monitor that uses a Red/ Green/Blue technology to show colors. (Chapter 7)

right justification The addition of extra space in a line to make the right margins line up. (Chapter 10)

ring network A computer network that links multiple computers in a circle or ring with no host computer. (Chapter 13)

robotics The use of machines to perform physical tasks in place of humans. (Chapters 6 and 17)

robots Automated machines. (*Also see* robotics). (Chapter 1)

root directory The starting, or main, directory for creation of a hierarchically structured file system. (Appendix A)

rotational delay time The time it takes for the appropriate sector of the disk to come under the read/write head. (Chapter 8)

row A series of values placed horizontally. (Chapter 11)

scanner A device used to translate a page of a document into an electronic form that OCR software can understand. (Chapters 7 and 14)

scatter diagram A type of analysis graphics that uses a symbol such as the asterisk to plot the relationships between values on the horizontal and vertical axes. (Chapter 10)

scheduled report A report generated by the MIS on a regular basis, containing summary reports of the results of the data processing operation. (Chapter 14)

scrolling For word processing, spreadsheets, or telecommunications, the up and down or left and right movements of the text or cells on the screen so that additional material can be seen. (Chapter 10 and Appendix C)

search and replace In word processing, the operation of searching for and replacing a particular character string with another string. (Chapter 10)

second-level decision In a nested loop, the dependent decision, whose execution depends on the other decisions. (Appendix B)

secondary keys Fields or combinations of fields that are not necessarily unique to a record but that can be used to find a group of records. (Chapter 8)

secondary storage Storage area outside of the computer, used to hold an overflow of information or to save information when the computer is turned off. (Chapters 2 and 8)

sector A pie-shaped section of a floppy disk that is used to divide the tracks on a floppy disk. (Chapter 8)

security software packages Software designed to protect a computer system through various methods. (Chapter 18)

seek time The time it takes the read/write head to move to the correct track on a disk. (Chapter 8)

self-documenting language A computer language that does not need comments or other documentation. (Chapter 17)

semiconductor A mineral that conducts electricity only under certain conditions. (Chapter 6)

sentinel value A record value that signals the end of the loop in a last-record check. (Chapter 16)

sequential access A form of access in which the records are accessed in the same order in which they are physically stored. (Chapter 2)

sequential access file A file organization system used for records that need to be accessed in the order in which they were physically stored. (Chapter 8)

sequential storage device A secondary storage device that stores information in such a way that information must be read in the same order that it is written onto the device. (Chapter 8)

serial form The processing of data one bit at a time. (Chapter 13)

serial machine A computer that can process only one instruction at a time. (Chapter 6)

serial port The connection between the computer and the modem cable. (Chapter 13)

serial storage device A secondary storage device on which the data are stored one bit at a time. (Chapter 8)

shareware Software that is made available to users for a nominal fee or donation. (Chapter 3)

shell A software application working with MS-DOS to allow a graphical interface, multitasking, and the use of windows. (Chapter 9)

simplex mode Communications between computers, in which the communication can be in only one direction. (Chapter 13)

simulation The process of exercising a model using multiple values to determine the outcome under different circumstances. (Chapter 14)

smart machine Computer-based machine that can make decisions and provide information. (Chapters 1 and 20)

soft sectoring A sectoring plan that depends on the personal computer in use and on the disk operating system. (Chapter 8)

software The programs that direct the activity of the computer. (Chapters 1 and 3)

software package A combination of one or more computer programs and documentation describing the programs and their use. (Chapter 3)

software piracy The unauthorized copying of software for either personal use or financial gain. (Chapters 5 and 18)

sonic tinnitus A condition involving loss of hearing and/or a constant ringing in the ears, resulting from long-term exposure to noise. (Chapter 19)

sorting The process of arranging records in ascending or descending order. (Chapters 3 and 12 and Appendices B-3 and C-6)

source program The original high-level language program written by the computer user. (Chapter 17)

special-purpose computer A computer designed for only one purpose. (Chapter 1)

special-purpose languages A language developed to handle a specific task. (Chapter 17)

specific DSS A decision support system that has been developed to solve a specific problem; it is usually written in a high-level language. (Chapter 14)

speller A function of a word processor that checks the spelling of words in a document. (Chapter 10)

spike A voltage surge, such as lightning or some other electrical disturbance, that causes a sudden increase in the electrical supply. Delicate chips and other electrical parts can be destroyed. (Chapter 18)

spreadsheet A table having rows and columns of values, labels, and formulas that can be used to make calculations, plan budgets, make forecasts, and ask "What if?" questions about the data. (Chapters 3 and 11)

spreadsheet linking The capacity to link data and formulas in multiple spreadsheets so that a change in one spreadsheet is transferred to other spreadsheets using the same value or formula. (Chapter 11)

spreadsheet macro A sequential series of Lotus 1-2-3 commands that the user determines and thereafter can put into play by pressing the few keys that represent the particular macro. (Chapter 17)

stacked bar graphs A type of analysis graphics that places multiple quantities on the same bar. (Chapter 10)

star network A computer network with one host computer, to which many smaller computers or terminals are linked. (Chapter 13)

start bit A bit at the beginning of a character in asynchronous communication that signals the computer that a character is beginning to be sent. (Chapter 13)

static electricity Electricity created in dry climates that can cause significant damage to data or electrical parts. (Chapter 18)

static random access memory (RAM) A special RAM chip using electronic switches that allow very fast temporary memory called **cache memory.** (Chapter 6)

status line A line at the top or bottom of the screen that provides information regarding the current status of the screen. (Chapter 10)

stepwise refinement In top-down design, the process of adding more detail to a program design. (Top-Down Design Essay)

stop bit A bit at the end of a character in asynchronous communication that signals the computer that the transmission of a character is ended. (Chapter 13)

STOP statement In BASIC, the statement to indicate that a program has been abnormally terminated. (Appendix B)

storage crime Stealing stored information by stealing a disk or tape. (Chapter 18)

strategic decisions Top-level decisions that are not easily programmable. (Chapter 4)

strategic information system (SIS) An information system used to support or develop a company's competitive strategy. (Chapters 4 and 14)

streaming tape A special high-density recording tape that streams by the tape head at high speeds to back up a hard disk. (Chapter 8)

string constant In BASIC, a string of ASCII symbols or characters that are enclosed in quotation marks. (Appendix B)

strongly typed language A computer language that requires that all variables be declared as to their type. (Chapter 17)

structured approach The movement from a logical design to a physical design following a set pattern of steps. Also called **top-down approach.** (Chapter 4)

structured decisions Decisions that can be programmed in advance. (Chapter 14)

structured program A program using the processing block, the repetition block, and the decision block with no transfers into, out of, or between blocks. (Chapter 16)

structured walkthrough A part of the systems analysis and design process in which the analyst presents the current status of the process to his or her peers. (Chapter 15)

stylesheet An operation of the desktop publishing package that specifies the format of a document. (Chapter 10)

subdirectories Subgroups of files, each of which is assigned a name. (Chapter 9, Appendix A)

subprograms In top-down design, smaller, manageable sections of a program that can be written separately and then reunited. (Appendix B)

subroutine A section of a program that carries out a specific operation; another name for a module in a top-down-designed program. (Appendix B)

supercomputer The biggest, fastest computers used today. (Chapters 1 and 6)

superconductivity The ability of certain materials at low temperatures to conduct electricity without resistance. (Chapters 5 and 20)

supervisor program The major unit of the operating system that resides in internal memory at all times to manage the loading of other parts of the operating system and the applications programs. (Chapter 9)

surge protector A device that protects the computer's hardware and memory from a voltage surge. (Chapter 18)

symbol processor A computer that can manipulate symbols as well as numbers; another name for a computer. (Chapter 10)

synchronous communications A form of communication between computers that does not require the computers to be synchronized and allows large numbers of characters to be sent as a block. (Chapter 13)

syntactical (grammatical) form In programming, the syntax that must be followed in the writing of the programs. (Chapter 16)

syntax error In a computer program, an error in the syntax or vocabulary of the program. (Appendix B)

system A group of elements organized for the purpose of achieving a particular goal. (Chapters 2 and 4)

system bus A communications system that allows the transfer of instructions, data, and control commands among the control unit, the arithmetic-logic unit, and the internal memory unit. (Chapter 6)

system command In BASIC, a command that results in some action by a program. (Appendix B)

system design The fourth step in the systems analysis and design process, in which the analyst develops a high-level design of the new system that includes its actual parts. (Chapter 15)

system disk The disk that contains the operating system. (Appendix A)

system interrupt A command from the operating system for the current job to be temporarily interrupted so another job can be executed. (Chapter 9)

systems analysis and design process The process of developing a system design to meet a new need or to solve a problem in an existing system. (Chapters 4 and 15)

systems analyst The person who carries out the systems analysis and design process. (Chapters 4 and 15)

systems audit software Security software that keeps track of all attempts, especially unsuccessful ones, to log on to the company's computer system. (Chapter 18)

systems development life cycle *See* systems analysis and design.

systems flowchart A special type of flowchart that demonstrates the flows of information and control in the existing system. (Chapters 4 and 15)

systems life cycle *See* systems analysis and design.

systems programmers Programmers that maintain mainframe operating systems. (Chapter 9)

systems software The programming that controls the operations of utility software and applications software. (Chapter 3)

table A group of numbers or strings organized into rows and columns. (Appendix B)

tactical decisions Decisions made by middle-level managers using summary reports. These are not easily programmable. (Chapter 4)

tape *See* magnetic tape.

tape cartridge Storage medium used by personal or mainframe computers to back up hard disks. (Chapter 2)

tape drive An electronic device that uses a read/write head to transfer information to and from magnetic tape. (Chapters 2 and 8)

target marketing The process by which advertisers use data banks to select a group of individuals who are most likely to buy their products, thereby allowing advertisers to spend more time and money on fewer prospects. (Chapter 19)

tax planning and preparation package A package used to keep track of tax records throughout the year and to determine the effects of financial decisions. (Chapter 11)

telecommunications The combining of a computer with a communications link, a modem, and appropriate communications software to become a communications tool. (Chapters 13 and 20)

telecommunications software A group of programs allowing a personal computer user to communicate with other people, computers, and data bases. (Chapters 3 and 13)

telecommuting The process of working at home using either a personal computer or a terminal tied into a mainframe. (Chapters 13 and 19)

template A skeleton spreadsheet that matches a particular application but does not include the data. (Chapter 11)

temporary variable A variable that is used to store a value temporarily. (Appendix B)

terminal A keyboard and a monitor connected to a computer. (*Also see* computer terminal) (Chapters 1 and 2)

terminal emulation A hardware/software combination that allows a personal computer to work like a dedicated mainframe terminal. (Chapter 13)

terminal symbol In flowcharting, an oval shape that is used to start and end all flowcharts. (Chapter 16)

terminalitis Musculo-skeletal problems resulting from extensive use of a VDT. (Chapter 19)

test data Data that are used in hand calculations to determine in advance the results expected from the program. (Chapter 16)

text editing The word processing function that allows material to be changed, inserted, or deleted from existing text. (Chapter 10)

text files Materials stored on files in the form of readable text, as opposed to binary. (Chapter 8)

thermal printer A nonimpact printer that uses a matrix of heated wires to form symbols on special paper. (Chapter 7)

thesaurus An editing tool that provides synonyms and antonyms for specified words. (Chapter 10)

time bomb A computer crime in which a disruptive program is timed to execute itself on a certain date. (Chapter 18)

time slice A small fraction of the total execution time that is allocated to a terminal in a time-sharing system. (Chapter 9)

token A special bit pattern used in a token-sharing local area network to determine which user can transmit information. (Chapter 13)

token/sharing network A local area network in which a bit pattern called a token is used to determine which user on the network can send information. (Chapter 13)

top-down approach *See* structured approach.

top–down design An approach to writing structured programs that breaks the program up into blocks or modules to be written individually and then combined into the final program. (Top–Down Design Essay and Appendix B)

touchscreen An input device wherein the user simply touches a part of the screen to enter information. (Chapters 2 and 7)

trackball A device to move a cursor. The user rolls a plastic ball with his/her fingertip or wrist. (Chapter 7)

track Parallel magnetic lines, running the length of magnetic tape, on which information is stored; also, concentric regions on a magnetic disk. (Chapter 8)

trailer record A special data record that signals the end of data to an INPUT loop. (Appendix B)

transaction log tape A tape that contains a copy of each transaction that is processed on disk storage. (Chapter 8)

transaction processing system (TPS) Converting raw data into a usable, electronic form. (Chapters 4 and 14)

transaction screen A screen on which the user enters actual income and expenses. (Chapter 11)

transactional data Data that are created when a transaction takes place that requires the customer to reveal his or her identity. (Chapter 19)

transactional processing Data are processed as they occur at the time of entry—e.g., grocery checkout systems. (Chapters 4 and 14)

transfer The return to the beginning of a loop that starts the repetition again. (Chapter 16)

transistors Solid-state elements on a chip that carry out the control and logic operations. (Chapter 2)

transmission time The actual time needed to transfer data to or from a disk. (Chapter 8)

trapdoor A part of the operating system that will allow knowledgeable users unauthorized access. (Chapter 18)

tree structure *See* hierarchical structure.

Trojan horse A computer program that sabotages the original program or modifies it to perform illegal activities. (Chapter 18)

turtle A graphics character used in the LOGO computer language. (Chapter 17)

two-alternative decision A decision in which one set of actions is taken if the condition is true and another set of actions is taken if the condition is false. (Appendix B)

two-dimensional array A table of numbers or strings. (Appendix B)

type-ahead buffer A keyboard's ability to store data typed by the user that the computer is not ready to accept. (Chapter 7)

typeover mode *See* replace mode.

unblocked record A physical record that corresponds to one logical record. (Chapter 8)

uninterruptible power supplies (UPS) A device that continues power to a personal computer if the electrical current is disrupted. (Chapter 18)

UNIX Originally developed for use on minicomputers, a multiple-machine, multitasking generic operating system converted to work on PCs. (Chapter 9)

unstructured decisions Decisions that cannot be programmed in advance. (Chapter 14)

uploaded The process of shifting software or data from a personal computer to a central computer. (Chapter 13)

upper memory The 384 bytes above conventional memory up to 1 Mbyte. Upper memory is normally reserved for software that is required for hardware devices, such as monitors or network linkages. (Chapter 6)

user friendly A software package that is easy to use. (Chapter 3)

user interface Allows the software user to enter data and commands. The three most common are menu driven, command driven, and graphical. (Chapter 3)

user prompt In BASIC, a string constant that is included in the INPUT statement to prompt the user to enter the needed data. (Appendix B)

user-defined function A specific numerical or string operation in BASIC that is defined by the user. (Appendix B)

user's manual A set of directions for the use of software packages. (Chapter 3)

utility software Software that controls the computer's day-to-day housekeeping operations. (Chapter 3)

value A number, either positive or negative, with or without a decimal. (Chapter 11)

value-added network (VAN) Public networks available by subscription to provide clients with data communications facilities. (Chapter 13)

variable The name for a memory cell used in writing a program. (Chapter 17 and Appendix B-1)

variable expense Expense that tend to fluctuate from month to month. (Chapter 11)

variable-length word A word that combines as many bytes as necessary to represent a symbol. (Chapter 6)

verification The process of comparing correct information to the information on punched cards, tape, or disk. (Chapter 7)

video disk A read-only form of secondary storage using a laser or an optical disk. (Chapter 2)

video display terminal (VDT) Any personal computer or terminal tied into a mainframe that uses a cathode ray tube (CRT) to echo input and display output. (Chapters 2, 5, 7, and 19)

Video Graphics Array (VGA) An analog graphics adaptor that will display 256 colors in 640 × 480 resolution as well as displaying high-quality text. (Chapter 10)

video page The amount of word processing text that can actually be seen on the screen. (Chapter 10)

videotex The process of shopping, banking, or managing stocks and bonds from the home using a computer and a communications link. (Chapter 13)

virtual memory The use of disk drives to give the appearance of increased internal memory. (Chapter 9)

virtual reality Input devices dependent on artificial intelligence that seek to make computer and human interaction transparent in order to create a custom universe within a computer. (Chapters 5 and 20)

virus A computer program whose purpose is to replicate itself, with mischievous or malicious intent, within the computer's memory. (Chapter 18)

voice-grade transmissions A slow type of information transmission that generally uses twisted pairs as a media device. (Chapter 13)

voice mail Allows the user to send, receive, store, and relay spoken messages. (Chapter 14)

voice recognition systems A form of input to computers that uses the spoken word to enter data and instructions; also called **voice input.** (Chapters 2 and 7)

volatile Computer memory that exists only while there is power to the computer or while the user is connected to a mainframe. (Chapters 2 and 6)

voltage surge A surge of electricity that can destroy a computer's hardware or memory. (Chapter 18)

wand An input device that reads bar codes. (Chapter 7)

warm boot "Booting," or starting up, the software when the machine is already turned on. (Appendix A)

weakly typed language A computer language that does not require that variables be declared as to their type. (Chapter 17)

WHILE loop A pre-test loop in BASIC that continues as long as (while) some condition is true. (Appendix B)

wide area network (WAN) A network covering more than a single building. (Chapters 3 and 13)

wildcard character In an MS-DOS command, a character such as an asterisk or a question mark that replaces an unknown character in a file name. (Appendix A)

wildcard search In word processing, a search for a word when only part of the word is known. (Chapter 10)

window A section of the monitor screen that is set aside by the software package to display a specific portion of output. (Chapters 3 and 11)

wireless LANs Local area networks that use radio waves rather than wires for transmission of data. (Chapter 13)

word processing software Software designed to manipulate letters, digits, and punctuation marks to compose letters, papers, and documents. (Chapters 3, 10)

word wrap The word processing function that causes words that fall outside the right margin to be moved to the next line. (Chapter 10 and Appendix C)

working directory The current directory or subdirectory in a hierarchical file system. (Appendix A)

worksheet A computer spreadsheet. (Chapter 11)

workstation A terminal tied into a mainframe or minicomputer or a personal computer that allows a worker to process information. (Chapter 1)

worm A disruptive program that travels through the computer's memory, wiping out information in the process. (Chapter 18)

Write Once, Read Mostly (WORM) disk A type of optical storage that allows a user to write information onto the disk once and then read it as many times as needed. (Chapter 8)

write-protect notch A notch in the vinyl cover of the floppy disk that, when covered, keeps the disk from being written on. (Chapter 8)

WYSIWYG (What You See Is What You Get) A function of word processing that allows the user to see on the screen exactly what will be printed. (Chapter 10)

x-terminal A special type of workstation which uses high-resolution graphics to display subscripts and special symbols on the screen. (Chapter 3)

2 Stephen Marks/The Image Bank. 4 Steven Hunt/The Image Bank. 6 Joel Gordon. 7 Weinberg-Clark/The Image Bank. 8 Gupton/Stock, Boston. 10 Reprinted with permission of Compaq Computer Corporation. 12 Horace Heafner, Video Imaging Laboratory, The National Center for Missing and Exploited Children, Arlington, Virginia. 13 Brett Froomer/The Image Bank. 14 Lou Jones/The Image Bank. 15 *bottom:* Dan McCoy/Rainbow; *top left:* University of Georgia, Office of Public Information; *top right:* Control Data Corporation. 16 Digital Equipment Corporation. 17 Courtesy of International Business Machines Corporation. 20 Courtesy Philips Consumer Electronics. 21 National Medical Enterprises, Inc. 22 John Coletti/Stock, Boston. 23 *bottom:* Ken Kaminsky/Lightwave. 24 Apple Computer. 25 NASA. *top:* Joseph Nettis/Stock, Boston. 26 Hank Morgan/Rainbow. 27 *bottom:* Ventura Educational Systems; *top:* Bob Daemmrich/The Image Works. 29 Courtesy of International Business Machines Corporation. 30 *bottom:* Spectrum Holobyte Sphere, Inc.; *top:* John Sterman. 31 AT&T Archives; *top:* Links 386 courtesy Access Software. 32 Courtesy of International Business Machines Corporation. 36 Eric Meola/The Image Bank. 38 Courtesy of Campbell Scientific. 41 *bottom:* © Joel Gordon 1989; *top left:* Jon Feingersh/Stock, Boston; *top right:* John Coletti/Stock, Boston. 42 *bottom:* Richard Palsey/Stock, Boston; *top:* © Joel Gordon 1982. 44 Ernest H. Robl. 45 *bottom:* Dan McCoy/Rainbow; *top:* Jon Feingersh/Stock, Boston. 46 Georgia Bureau of Investigation, Division of Forensic Sciences. 47 Courtesy NEC. 48 Dion Ogust/The Image Works. 49 *bottom:* Reprinted by permission of Texas Instruments Incorporated. 50 *bottom:* Dan McCoy/Rainbow; *top:* Richard Palsey/Stock, Boston. 51 Stan Wolenski. 56 Courtesy International Business Machines Corporation; Courtesy International Business Machines Corporation; *left:* Courtesy Iowa State University. 57 Courtesy International Business Machines Corporation; Courtesy of International Business Machines Corporation; *top left:* Courtesy of Unisys Corporation. 62 Michel Tcherevkoff/The Image Bank. 64 Bill Gallery/Stock, Boston. 65 Courtesy Quarterdeck Office Systems. 67 Courtesy of International Business Machines Corporation. 68 Courtesy of International Business Machines Corporation. 71 National Science Center Foundation. 72 *left:* Dan Bryant; *right:* © Joel Gordon 1989. 73 Donald Dietzl/Stock, Boston; *bottom:* Macintosh System 7. 75 Dion Ogust/The Image Works. 76 *left:* Courtesy Apple Computer, Inc.; *right:* Courtesy Microsoft Corporation. 77 Microsoft Corporation. 79 Courtesy Auto Map. 80 Dan McCoy/Rainbow; *top:* Photographs of Harvard Graphics are used with permission of Software Publishing Corporation, which owns the copyright to such products. Harvard Graphics℠ is a trademark of Software Publishing Corporation. 81 *bottom:* Courtesy of Borland International; *top:* Lotus Development Corporation. 83 *bottom:* Courtesy Fox Software; *top:* dBase IV from Borland International. 84 *left:* ProComm Plus; *right:* Courtesy Prodigy. 86 Microsoft Corporation. 87 Courtesy of Aldus Corporation. 92 Michel Tcherevkoff/The Image Bank. 94 Bob Daemmrich/The Image Works. 97 Dan McCoy/Rainbow. 98 *bottom:* Courtesy International Business Machines; *top:* Courtesy NCR Corporation. 100 *center:* NCR Corporation; *left:* Photo used by permission of the REI/Lundy Systems Division of Recognition Equipment Incorporated; *right:* American Airlines. 101 Courtesy of International Business Machines Corporation. 102 Courtesy International Business Machines Corporation. 106 U.S. Department of Commerce, Bureau of Census. 107 Courtesy of International Business Machines Corporation. 110 Courtesy Merck and Company. 111 Courtesy Merck and Company. 113 Northrop Corporation. 116 Courtesy of International Business Machines Corporation. 117 Courtesy of Hewlett-Packard. 118 B. Ullman/Taurus Photos. 124 Michel Tcherevkoff/The Image Bank. 126 Courtesy International Business Machines Corporation. 127 NYT Pictures.

128 Susan Holtz. 129 Courtesy of International Business Machines Corporation. 130 Frank Micelotta/Time Magazine. 131 Eye Denify, Inc. 132 William Geiger. 134 Jon Feingersh/Stock, Boston. 136 AP/Wide World Photos. 137 Jon Feingersh/Stock, Boston. 138 Courtesy Barbara Clements. 139 Comdex, produced by the Interface Group. 141 Courtesy Apple Computer. 142 Charles Moore/Black Star; Courtesy National Language Inc. 146 Francesco Ruggeri/The Image Bank. 148 Michel Tcherevkoff/The Image Bank. 150 Courtesy Sigmedics, Inc., Northfield, IL and Drs. Daniel Graupe and Kate H. Kohn, University of Illinois, Chicago, IL. 152 Courtesy of Hewlett-Packard Company. 156 Courtesy of International Business Machines Corporation. 157 Courtesy Intel Corporation. 161 Mark Leet Photography. 162 Courtesy STB Systems, Inc. 164 Reprinted with permission of Texas Instruments Incorporated. 166 *bottom left:* © Paul Hollerbach 1990/Design Conceptions; *bottom right:* Pentax Corporation; *top:* Courtesy of National Semiconductor Corporation. 168 Reprinted with permission of Texas Instruments Corporation. 169 Courtesy Transitions Research, Inc. 170 Courtesy of Intel Corporation; *left:* AP/Wide World. 171 Courtesy of Intel Corporation. 172 Ellis Herwig/Stock, Boston. 176 Courtesy of Motorola, Inc. 177 *bottom left:* Courtesy of Motorola, Inc.; *bottom right:* Courtesy of Motorola, Inc.; *top:* Erich Hartman/Magnum. 178 Courtesy of Hewlett-Packard Company. 179 *bottom:* Courtesy of Motorola, Inc.; *top:* Roger Ressmeyer/Starlight. 180 *bottom left:* Courtesy of Motorola, Inc. *bottom right:* Courtesy of Hewlett-Packard Company; *top:* Courtesy of Motorola, Inc. 181 Courtesy of Hewlett-Packard Company. 182 *bottom:* Courtesy of Hewlett-Packard Company; *center:* Courtesy of Hewlett-Packard Company; *top:* Courtesy of Motorola, Inc. 183 Courtesy of Hewlett-Packard Company. 188 Steven Hunt/The Image Bank. 191 Ralph Barrera Photo/TexaStock. 193 Courtesy of International Business Machines Corporation. 194 *bottom:* Courtesy Apple Computer, Inc.; *top left:* © Joel Gordon 1990; *top right:* Oscar Palmquist/Lightwave. 195 *bottom:* Oscar Palmquist/Lightwave; *top:* Courtesy of Apple Computer, Inc. 196 Dan McCoy/Rainbow. 197 John Coletti/Stock, Boston. 198 Richard Palsey/Stock, Boston. 199 © 1991 Carolco Pictures. 200 Hank Morgan/Science Source/Photo Researchers. 202 Courtesy GRiD Computer. 203 *left:* Stacy Pick/Stock, Boston; *right:* Courtesy of Patrick G. McKeown. 204 Courtesy U.S. Postal Service. 205 Leonard Lessin/Peter Arnold. 207 Courtesy NCR Corporation. 208 Aldo Mastrocola/Lightwave. 209 Oscar Palmquist/Lightwave. 210 Courtesy of Apple Computer, Inc. 211 *bottom:* Courtesy Unisys Corporation; *top:* Courtesy Dell Computer Corporation. 214 Courtesy Hewlett-Packard Company. 215 Courtesy of International Business Machines Corporation. 216 McDonnell Douglas Information Systems Group. 217 Printed on a QMS ColorScript℠ 100 printer, the First Color Adobe PostScript Printer. © 1988 Adobe Systems, Inc. All rights reserved. 220 Steven Hunt/The Image Bank. 222 Courtesy of Federal Express. 223 Courtesy of Hewlett-Packard Company. 224 Hank Morgan/Rainbow. 227 Courtesy of International Business Machines Corporation. 228 Courtesy of Seagate Technology. 232 Courtesy EMC Corporation. 235 *bottom left:* Courtesy of International Business Machines Corporation; *bottom right:* Courtesy of International Business Machines Corporation; *top:* Oscar Palmquist/Lightwave. 236 Courtesy of Toshiba America Information Systems, Inc. Computer Systems Division. 237 Courtesy of International Business Machines Corporation. 238 Ben Mitchell/The Image Bank. 239 Courtesy of Seagate Technology, Inc. 241 John Colleti/Stock, Boston. 242 Courtesy of International Business Machines Corporation. 243 Courtesy of FileNet Corporation. 244 *left:* Seth Resnick/Stock, Boston; *right:* Dan McCoy/Rainbow. 245 Courtesy of NeXT, Inc. 250 Steven Hunt/The Image Bank. 252 Steven Hunt/The Image Bank. 254 James Aronovsky/Picture Group. 255 Courtesy of

International Business Machines Corporation. 256 Aldo Mastrocola/Lightwave. 257 Stacy Pick/Stock, Boston. 258 University of Georgia, Office of Public Information, Photo by Rick O'Quinn. 265 *bottom:* Courtesy of International Business Machines Corporation; *center:* Courtesy of Hewlett-Packard Company; *top:* Courtesy of International Business Machines Corporation. 269 Courtesy of International Business Machines Corporation. 270 *left:* Courtesy Lotus Development Corporation; *right:* Kirkland/Sygma. 271 Courtesy NeXT, Inc. 273 Novell Netware. 274 DESQview by Quarterdeck Office Systems, courtesy of Pollare/Fischer Communications. 276 *bottom:* Courtesy of TechSoft Systems, Inc.; Courtesy of Microsoft Corporation. 277 Courtesy Borland International. 278 Courtesy of Unisys Corporation. 279 *left:* Courtesy of Digital Research Corporation; *right:* Courtesy of General Magic, Inc. 282 Steven Hunt/The Image Bank. 284 Courtesy Buddy Woods. 285 Courtesy of Microsoft Corporation; Courtesy of WordPerfect Corporation. 286 Courtesy of WordPerfect Corporation. 288 Charles Feil/Stock, Boston. 290 Courtesy TCI Software Research, Inc. 291 Courtesy of WordPerfect Corporation. 292 Courtesy Lotus Development Corporation. 294 Courtesy of WordPerfect Corporation. 295 Courtesy Apple Computer, Inc. 296 *left:* Courtesy of International Business Machines Corporation; *right:* Dan McCoy/Rainbow. 297 Courtesy ADAM Software. 299 *bottom left:* Stacy Pick/Stock, Boston; *bottom right:* Courtesy of Aldus Corporation; *top left:* Courtesy of International Business Machines Corporation; *top right:* Courtesy of International Business Machines Corporation. 300 Will Mosgrove/Apple Computer. 301 Dan McCoy/Rainbow. 302 *bottom left:* © 1986 RIX Software; *right:* Courtesy of International Business Machines Corporation; *bottom:* Courtesy of International Business Machines Corporation; *top left:* Courtesy of International Business Machines Corporation; *top right:* Courtesy of ATI Technologies, Inc. 303 Courtesy of Matrox Electronic Systems, Ltd. 304 Courtesy of Lotus Development Corporation. 305 Courtesy of Microsoft Corporation. 306 Courtesy Micrografx. 307 *bottom:* Courtesy of Houston Instrument; *left:* Courtesy of International Business Machines Corporation; *right:* Courtesy of Computer Associates, design by Software Superior. 308 Gregory Heisler/The Image Bank. 309 VersaCAD Graphics courtesy of Computer Vision, A Prime Company. 310 *bottom left:* Courtesy of Digital Research Corporation; *bottom right:* Chris Springfield/Clark Central Graphics; *top left:* Courtesy Apple Computer, Inc.; *top right:* Created in PC Paintbrush IV Plus℠. Used by permission of ZSoft Corporation. PC Paintbrush IV Plus is a trademark of ZSoft Corporation. 311 *bottom:* Jeff Persons/Stock, Boston; *top:* Courtesy Aboud Group. 314 Courtesy Aldus Corporation; *top:* Ted Kawalerski/The Image Bank. 315 *bottom:* Courtesy of Hewlett-Packard Company; *top:* Courtesy of International Business Machines Corporation. 318 Michel Tcherevkoff/The Image Bank. 320 Steve Liss/Time Magazine. 321 Courtesy Lotus Development Corporation. 322 Courtesy Lotus Development Corporation; *top:* © Joel Gordon 1988. 326 Courtesy Lotus Development Corporation. 330 Courtesy Microsoft Corporation. 334 Microsoft Excel. 337 *bottom:* Courtesy of Borland International; *top left:* Courtesy Microsoft Corporation; *top right:* PFS: First Choice by Spinnaker Software. 339 Courtesy ChipSoft. 340 W. Mark Bernshaw/The Image Works. 342 Courtesy of DacEasy, Inc. 343 *bottom:* Courtesy of Microsoft Corporation; *top:* Courtesy of DacEasy, Inc. 344 Courtesy of Lotus Development Corporation. 348 Michel Tcherevkoff/The Image Bank. 351 Courtesy Apple Computer. 352 Courtesy of Microsoft Corporation. 354 Dan Bryant; *top left:* Jack Deutsch/Innervisions; *top right:* Courtesy of International Business Machines Corporation. **355** Screen capture from Professional File® version 2.0, including text material, is used with the permission of Software Publishing Corporation, which owns the copyright to such product. Professional File (®) is a registered trademark of Software Publishing Corporation. **363** Stacy Pick/Stock, Boston. **367** © Joel Gordon 1984. **368** Bloodstock Research Information Services. **370** National Medical Enterprises. **371** Charles Paley/Stock, Boston. **373** Courtesy Natural Language, Inc. **376** Courtesy Borland International. **380** Steven Hunt/The Image Bank. **382** Copyright 1990, Los Angeles Times. Reprinted by permission. **383** Courtesy of AT&T Archives. **384** *left:* T. J. Florian/Rainbow; *right:* Jon Feingersh/Stock, Boston. **385** Courtesy CompuServe. **387** *left:* Oscar Palmquist/Lightwave; *right:* Courtesy of Microsoft Corporation. **394** University of Georgia, Office of Public Information. Photo by Rick O'Quinn. **395** TYMNET, McDonnell Douglas Information Systems Group. **398** Courtesy of Prodigy Services. **399** Courtesy of Hayes Microcomputer Products, Inc. **402** Courtesy TOPS Division, Sun Microsystems. **403** *bottom:* Jack Deutsch/Innervisions; *top:* Courtesy of CompuServe Incorporated. **404** Drew University/Peter Howard. **405** Courtesy Video Telecom. **407** Courtesy Prodigy Services. **413** *bottom:* Courtesy of International Business Machines Corporation; *top left:* Courtesy of International Business Machines Corporation; *top right:* James Wilson/Woodfin Camp. **415** Courtesy of Egghead Discount Software. **418** *left:* Courtesy of Toshiba America Information Systems, Inc., Computer Systems Division; *right:* Courtesy of Apple Computer, Inc. **420** *left:* Courtesy Dell Computer; *right:* Courtesy of International Business Machines Corporation. **421** *bottom:* Courtesy of International Business Machines Corporation; *top left:* Jay Fries/The Image Bank; *top right:* Courtesy of International Business Machines Corporation. **422** *bottom:* James D. Wilson/Woodfin Camp; *top left:* John Greenleigh/Apple Computer; *top right:* Courtesy of Apple Computer, Inc. **425** Courtesy of Egghead Discount Software. **428** Courtesy of International Business Machines Corporation. **430** Michel Tcherevkoff/The Image Bank. **432** Michel Tcherevkoff/The Image Bank. **436** *left:* © Joel Gordon 1990; *right:* Dan McCoy/Rainbow. **437** *left:* Reprinted with permission of Compaq Computer Corporation. All rights reserved; *right:* Courtesy of Unisys Corporation. **438** Courtesy of International Business Machines Corporation. **443** Courtesy of Exe-

cucom Systems Corporation. **444** Courtesy of Execucom Systems Corporation. **445** Charles Feil/Stock, Boston. **449** W. Marc Bernshaw/The Image Works. **450** *left:* © Joel Gordon 1990; *right:* Courtesy of International Business Machines Corporation. **452** Courtesy of International Business Machines Corporation. **453** Jim Cambon/TSW-Click, Chicago. **458** *bottom:* Courtesy of Toshiba America Information Systems, Inc. Computer Systems Division; *top:* Courtesy of Stone & Webster Corporation, Boston. **462** Michel Tcherevkoff/The Image Bank. **470** Frank Siteman/Rainbow. **478** Kevin Vandivier/TexaStock. **483** Courtesy of International Business Machines Corporation. **486** Charles Gupton/Stock, Boston. **489** Courtesy of International Business Machines Corporation. **490** Herb Snitzer/Stock, Boston. **492** Richard Palsey/Stock, Boston. **498** *bottom:* Courtesy of International Business Machines Corporation; *top:* Will and Deni McIntyre/Science Source/Photo Researchers. **502** Steven Hunt/The Image Bank. **506** *bottom left:* Kolvoord/TexaStock; *bottom right:* Hank Morgan/Science Source/Photo Researchers; *top left:* John Colletti/Stock, Boston; *top right:* © Joel Gordon 1990. **518** © WINS/Blue Thunder. **524** Aldo Mastrocola/Lightwave. **534** Steven Hunt/The Image Bank. **543** Courtesy of ARCO. **545** Courtesy of International Business Machines Corporation. **547** Courtesy of Dartmouth College Library, Special Collections. **548** Courtesy of Microsoft Corporation. **553** Courtesy of Microsoft Corporation. **554** Courtesy of Borland International. **556** Bob Bickford/MIT. **558** General Instrument Corporation. **562** Courtesy National Language Inc. **566** *bottom left:* Courtesy of Rochester Robotics, Inc., Photo by Matt Matteo & Associates, Inc.; *top left:* Hank Morgan/Rainbow. **567** Courtesy of Carnegie-Mellon University. **568** *bottom:* Honeywell Marine Systems Division; *top:* Courtesy of ABB Robotics, Inc.; *top:* James Wilson/Woodfin Camp. **570** *bottom left:* Courtesy of U.C. Davis, School of Medicine Photo; *bottom right:* Bill Gallery/Stock, Boston. *top:* Courtesy of Lucasfilm Ltd.Ⓡ. **571** *bottom:* Courtesy of United Airlines; *top:* James L. Varon/Detroit News. **572** Courtesy of Deneb Robotics, Inc. **573** *bottom right:* Dan McCoy/Rainbow; *bottom left:* Courtesy of Bell & Howell Mailmobile Company; *top right:* Courtesy of Cybermotion, Roanoke, VA. Photographer, William Nelms. **574** Michel Tcherevkoff/The Image Bank. **576** Steven Hunt/The Image Bank. **578** Fort Worth Star Telegram/Dale Blackwell. **580** AP/Wide World. **581** Courtesy of Flagler Grey-

hound Track. **585** Courtesy McAfee Associates. **588** AP/Wide World. **591** *left:* Liane Enkelis/Stock, Boston; *right:* Courtesy of Bellcore, Photographer, Patricia Kocornik. **593** Courtesy of Inmac Corporation, Santa Clara, CA. **597** Courtesy Inmac Corporation, Santa Clara, CA. **598** Photo by Chris Springfield/Clark Central Graphic Arts. **599** Courtesy of Novell, Inc. **602** Steven Hunt/The Image Bank. **606** Peter Arnold. **610** Susan Holtz. **611** *left:* Susan Holtz; *right:* NCR Corporation. **614** Frederick D. Bodin/Stock, Boston. **615** Bob Daemmrich/The Image Works. **616** Courtesy of the Los Angeles Times. **618** Courtesy of Curtis Manufacturing. **620** *bottom:* AP/Wide World; *top:* Kevin Vandivier/TexaStock. **626** *bottom:* Image AI-2 from video "Beyond Picasso" by Lillian Schwartz. Discussed in *The Computer Artist's Handbook*, W. W. Norton. Copyright 1989 Computer Creations Corporation. All rights reserved. This image may not be reproduced without written authorization; *top:* Courtesy of Paracomp, Inc. **627** Kenneth Snelson, artist. Hardware, Silicon Graphics Computer Systems, Wavefront Technologies. **628** *bottom:* Tyrone Depts/Pratt Manhattan; *top:* Sandra Filippucci. **629** *bottom:* John Derry/Wacom Technologies; *top:* Cheryl Stockton/Pratt Manhattan. **630** Courtesy of the Reuben H. Fleet Space Theater and Science Center. **631** © 1991 Carolco Pictures. **632** *bottom:* Armen Kachaturian/Time Magazine; *top:* Courtesy of International Business Machines Corporation. **633** Courtesy of the University of Michigan, Center for Performing Arts and Technology, Michael Knight, Videographer/Photographer. **634** Eric Meola/The Image Bank. **636** Courtesy of VPL Research, Inc. © 1992. **637** *left:* Alexander Tsiaras/Stock, Boston; *right:* NASA. **640** Frank Siteman/Rainbow. **642** *bottom:* Bill Gallery/Stock, Boston; *top:* Serviceland and Computer Services. **643** S. E. Byrne/Lightwave. **644** Courtesy of International Business Machines Corporation. **645** Courtesy of ExecuTrain. **646** Courtesy of John F. McIntosh, Arch. D., Director, Systems Support, College of Architecture and Environmental Design, Arizona State University. **648** Courtesy Intel Corporation. **649** *bottom:* Bill Pierce/Rainbow; *top:* Courtesy of International Business Machines Corporation. **650** Alan Levenson; Inset photo courtesy of Alan Key. **651** *center bottom:* Andrew Popper/Picture Group; *center top:* Courtesy Quarterdeck Office Systems; *left:* AT&T; *right:* Bob Daemmrich/The Image Works. **653** Courtesy International Business Machines Corporation.

INDEX

Numbers in italics indicate boxed inserts.

NOTES

NOTES

NOTES